Mystery Women:
An Encyclopedia of
Leading Women Characters
in Mystery Fiction

Vol. 1 (1860-1979)
Revised

Also by Colleen Barnett

Mystery Women: An Encyclopedia
of Leading Women Characters in Mystery Fiction,
Vol.1 (1860-1979)

Mystery Women: An Encyclopedia
of Leading Women Characters in Mystery Fiction
Volume II (1980-1989)

Mystery Women: An Encyclopedia
of Leading Women Characters in Mystery Fiction
Volume III (1990-1999)

Mystery Women:
An Encyclopedia of
Leading Women Characters
in Mystery Fiction

Vol. 1 (1860-1979)
Revised

Colleen Barnett

Poisoned Pen Press

Library of Congress Catalog Card Number: 2006929253

ISBN-10: 1-59058-225-X / ISBN-13: 978-1-59058-225-1

Poisoned Pen Press
6962 E. First Ave. Ste. 103
Scottsdale, AZ 85251
www.poisonedpenpress.com
info@poisonedpenpress.com

Printed in the United States of America

To those who sustained me during the lengthy
gestation period of this book by their affection,
encouragement and active support:

John (1922-2004)
Patricia, my sister and dearest friend
Jerry and Susan
Andrew and Laura
Cathie and Steve
James
Maggie
Tom and Vonne
Ted and Cathy
The "Collins girls"
The grandchildren
and
My new great-grandson

Contents

**Women at War; Then, a Return to Domesticity—
Women Sleuths of 1940-1959** **123**

Out of Turbulence, Equality (Or at Least, a Start)—
Women Sleuths of 1960-1979 229

Introduction

Growing up in the 1930's and 1940's in a household where books were important, I moved beyond the Nancy Drews and Judy Boltons to search for more mature female characters, most frequently in the mystery novel. The rare specimens available included Harriet Vane (too sophisticated for my tastes then), Jane Marple (too old, then); but I delighted in Agatha Christie's minor heroines: Tuppence Beresford and Eileen "Bundle" Brent.

My interest in mystery stories was a resource to me as I moved through college, marriage, and parenthood. It was an antidote for cabin fever. Through mystery stories I toured distant lands when personal travel was impossible. Mystery stories created tensions, but provided solutions, and involved exciting characters. I particularly enjoyed female series investigators who showed enterprise and independence.

My decision to collect novels containing female series investigators was triggered by Maggie, my younger daughter, who requested a book with a strong heroine. She had read Elizabeth Peters' first Amanda Peabody and enjoyed it. My interest in the evolution of the female series sleuth came even earlier, combining my own early values with my professional awareness of the need for positive role models for young women and girls. I had worked in a social services agency, and as a family practice attorney, and a mediator in custody battles.

Since this project began in 1975, I have read thousands of mysteries. I am indebted to Michelle Slung's *Crime on Her Mind* and Patricia Craig and Mary Cadogan's *The Lady Investigates* for initial coverage. Allen J. Hubin's *Crime Fiction, 1749-1980* and subsequent editions provided a plethora of names, supplemented by the several editions of *Twentieth Century Crime and Mystery Writers* and the magazine *The Armchair Detective*. More recently I have benefited from new names and titles found in Willetta L. Heising's editions of *Detecting Men* and *Detecting Women*.

Wisconsin's excellent inter-library system provided books not locally available. The librarians at the Boscobel Library and Southwestern Wisconsin Library System filled long lists of needed items. The University of Wisconsin—Madison's Inter-Library Loan Department initially helped me obtain rare books from the Library of Congress. Used book dealers and staff at mystery bookstores were unfailingly helpful. Mary Helen Becker, then owner of *Booked for Murder* in Madison, Wisconsin, and her successors shared knowledge and enthusiasm. Jeff Hatfield of Uncle Edgar's in Minneapolis provided insights and encouragement.

Not everything came easy. Some of the books were unpleasant or difficult reading. Justifiably, some books could not be removed from their library settings. I traveled to academic and public libraries across the United States, Canada, and England for access to rare books.

My children, their spouses, and my nieces utilized card catalogs and computers in the communities in which they lived to direct me to obscure mysteries. Family members waited patiently as I dawdled in libraries and used bookstores. My son Andrew, a public librarian and computer guru, not only initiated me into the wonders of the library's reference section, but also supplemented my basic knowledge of the computer to turn out a presentable manuscript.

The most generous support came from my husband, John, who subsidized the thousands of dollars I spent each year on book purchases. He endured countless overcooked meals while I read "just a few more pages." Doing a revision now keeps me busy at a time when I am dealing with widowhood.

I am grateful to Peg Eagan and Larry Names of Ravenstone/E.B. Houchin Publishing for their initial support. They had faith in my work at a time when I wondered if my research would ever get into print. When Ravenstone went out of business, I was deeply discouraged as to prospects for the future. Fortunately, while attending the 1999 Bouchercon at Milwaukee, I picked up a pamphlet called *Imprints* that listed specialized publishers. Poisoned Pen Press was identified for its dedication to the genre and interest in preserving the historical aspects of the mystery novel. My subsequent contacts with Robert Rosenwald and his wife, Barbara Peters, verified the commitment of Poisoned Pen Press. Our joint goal was to publish a reference series that would be useful to librarians and booksellers; add to awareness of how women have fared in the mystery genre over the years; and direct mystery lovers to books they might enjoy. I am further convinced that it will preserve information about early mysteries as I see them disappearing from library shelves. My editor, Joe Liddy, and his wife, Lisa, of The Printed Page proved to be a great help in this and subsequent volumes.

Enid and Tom Schantz of Rue Morgue Press have not only alerted me to female sleuths deserving of inclusion but have reprinted the work of many early mystery authors, making it available to current readers. They are probably the best-informed mystery couple in the business.

As I have spent over thirty years on the research, I wanted to pass it on to others who enjoy mysteries as I do, and as an expression of gratitude to the genre itself for the pleasure it has provided me. I am particularly grateful to authors who widened my horizons, challenged my assumptions, and explored issues of concern to women.

Each book utilized in this research was reviewed in a written format. From the accumulated books on a character, a biography was prepared. Some books were boring; others, personally distasteful and therefore merely skimmed for basic information.

My criteria for inclusion included: the number of significant appearances; emphasis on the novel and only rarely a collection of short stories; the exclusion of books of interest primarily to juveniles or young adults, but the inclusion of negative characters, women who were anti-heroes. The most difficult factor to evaluate was whether the character (sometimes a spouse, lover, or assistant) played a significant role. My decisions were inevitably subjective. Defining the mystery itself was a personal task as there were crossovers with science fiction, romance, westerns, Gothics, and horror series. Other far more noteworthy researchers have defined mystery series differently than I did. For the errors, omissions, and failure to properly evaluate an author's material, I accept full responsibility. I will welcome corrections and additions, hopefully of a kindly nature.

In order to make the work meaningful, I increased my knowledge of the social, legal, political and economic status of women over the past 140 years. That lent itself to a chronological approach that had both defects and advantages. It made it possible to document observable trends, but more difficult for readers to locate sleuth biographies in the appropriate era. Hopefully the appendix will solve that problem.

This volume covers the female sleuths from 1860 to 1979. It was followed by *Volume II, 1980-1989* and by *Volume III, 1990-1999*. The increase in female sleuths was so great that *Volume III* had to be printed in two separate covers.

Remarks as to the Current Revision

There had been omissions in the prior edition that have been corrected. Mystery enthusiasts and Allen J. Hubin's latest bibliography, *Crime Fiction III*, set me on the trail of new authors and sleuths unknown when Volume I was printed in 1997. Thanks to Rue Morgue Press I was able to include Lady Lupin Hastings (author: Joan Coggin) and several other sleuths recommended by Tom and Enid Schantz of Rue Morgue Press in this revision. Judy Ashbane (author: Mairi O'Nair) still proved to be elusive.

It was possible, thanks to the Internet (Bookfinder.com, Amazon.com, and Barnes & Noble.com) to locate and read books by included authors that had been unavailable for prior editions. There was a sense of completion in finding books previously not accessible for review as to Mavis Seidlitz (Carter Brown), Daphne Wrayne (Mark Cross/Valentine), Honey West (G. G. Fickling), Charlotte Eliot (Macartney Filgate), Madame Rosika Storey (Hulbert Footner), Kate Marsh (Gret Lane), April Dancer (Simon Latter), Norma "Nicky" Lee (Norma Lee), Ann McIntosh (Evalina Mack), Angel Brown (Graham Montrose), Palmyra Pym (Nigel Morland), Maria Black (John Slate), Kitty Telefair (Florence Stevenson), and Daye Smith (Frank Usher). Some books were obtained only to learn that the female sleuth did not appear in that narrative.

My initial goal was to fill in the gaps by adding new sleuths and recently located books featuring sleuths already included. However, my searches for rare books made me aware that books that were accessible twenty years ago have disappeared. Where? Into private collections? Removed from libraries because of condition or lack of space? Hard to say, but I had in my filing cabinets thousands of book reports which will at some time become rubbish. So when I reread each biography and its included reviews, I often returned to my original book report and redid the review with greater detail, hoping to keep alive a memory of what these antiquated books were about. Not many people will care, I suppose, but it was worth the extra effort to me.

Are there still gaps in coverage? Unfortunately, yes. Some books were nowhere to be found. They were often paperbacks that had disappeared from view. Others were available, but at prohibitive price. A Mabie Otis (Ben Sarto) book surfaced on the Internet, but priced at $154! Although I returned to London's British Library twice since the prior edition, there simply was not time to read all of the Mark Cross, Nigel Morland, or Graham Montrose books to be found there. Devotees are directed to the appendix for their availability.

Enjoy.

Section 1:
Women Sleuths of the Victorian Era—
1860-1899

*"Not only do...women suffer...ever-recurring indignities in
daily life, but the literature of the world proclaims their
inferiority and divinely decreed subjection in all history,
sacred and profane, in science, philosophy, poetry and song."*

Elizabeth Cady Stanton, Susan B. Anthony, and M.J. Cage, Eds.,
History of Women Suffrage II 1882, from *Feminist Quotations,
Voices of Rebels, Reformers, and Visionaries,* compiled by
Carol McPhee and Anne Fitzgerald, Thomas Y. Crowell, 1979

During the period when American women were struggling to achieve the
right to hold property, make valid wills and contracts, retain the wages they
earned outside of the home, and gain custody of their children at divorce, it is
not surprising that few sought employment as investigators or used their leisure time to detect. Predictably, there would be few fictional women sleuths.
Male authors had strong markets for heroic adventures, where women were
portrayed as victims or villains. Women rarely played a significant role in
determining outcomes. Female authors who wrote in the mystery genre often
hid their gender under androgynous names or initials. They lacked Virginia
Woolf's "room of their own" which would enable them to experiment,
develop, and produce narratives to meet the needs of women readers.

Changes came slowly in the literary world, reflecting the social, political, and economic shifts in society. When a woman was featured as an
investigator during this period, she was usually single, widowed, or in a few

instances the sole support of a family. Female investigators were even less likely to appear in a series (defined as at least two). The happy solution for a heroine was to achieve marriage and a family, which could be accomplished in a single book. Once married, she was expected to conform to the role of wife and mother, eschewing work outside of her home.

Upper and middle class women were not encouraged to appear in public without an escort, certainly not in the evening. Single women lived under the protection of male relatives; wives, under the control of their husbands. Only with increased leisure and educational opportunities for women in the privileged classes did a readership develop for intrepid and adventurous females.

It is generally conceded that Edgar Allan Poe's short stories published in the 1840's initiated the mystery genre. Amelia Butterworth, the first woman to appear in a mystery series, was developed by an American in 1897. Amelia's predecessors had been a mixed lot, often depending upon intuition, special psychic gifts, or such skills as lip reading to solve problems.

Amelia was a wealthy spinster, allied with a New York City police inspector. She narrated the books in which she appeared and had a significant role in solving the mysteries.

Loveday Brooke

Author: C. L. (Catherine Louisa) Pirkis

Loveday Brooke, an austere woman of thirty who worked as a private detective for the Lynch Court Detective Agency in London, appeared in seven short stories, collected as *The Experiences of Loveday Brooke, Lady Detective* (Hutchinson, 1894, reprinted in 1986 by Dover).

She set an excellent example, often solving cases when the authorities failed, unafraid of physical risks and painstaking in her work. Except for dressing in black and a habit of squinting when she concentrated, she appeared average in all aspects. This made it possible for her to go undercover to investigate instances of robbery, disappearance, and murder. Loveday indicated that she became a detective because of financial reverses, finding it one of the few jobs for which she had a talent. She preferred to work alone, calling on her employer only when it was time to contact the police. Even on vacation, she found herself intrigued by rumors of ghosts in homes, connecting them with disappearing checks.

Pirkis presumably used the initials to hide her gender, because few women wrote novels, much less mysteries, under their own names in this period.

Amelia Butterworth

Author: Anna Katharine Green aka A. K. Green

Amelia (christened Araminta) Butterworth, a member of upper class New York society, fit the acceptable pattern of a female sleuth at the turn of the century. Although a "stately" spinster, Amelia was one by choice, having rejected two suitors as possible fortune hunters. Even though she appeared as a secondary character in three Ebenezer Gryce books, she narrated and played significant roles in each. She was acerbic but compassionate; staid, but displayed a sense of humor.

In *That Affair Next Door* (Putnam, 1897), when Amelia noticed a young man bringing a woman to a supposedly empty house, she contacted the police. After the young woman was found dead, Amelia offered shelter to the two daughters of the house, who had just returned from Europe and were understandably reluctant to stay in their own home. Gryce, assigned to the case, recognized Amelia's value as an observer, but allowed her to expand beyond that role, which she did by locating a valuable witness.

By *Lost Man's Lane* (Putnam, 1898), Gryce, now a close friend, consulted Amelia when four men disappeared from a small New York village. Amelia made an extended visit to personal friends in the area, noting the behavior of younger members of the family. Her information led first to the discovery of a corpse, then to the killer.

During *The Circular Study* (McClure, 1900, reprint by Garland in 1976), Gryce found a parasol belonging to Amelia at a crime scene. She had entered the house after she noticed suspicious behavior, and was again a witness to potential suspects. After identifying the young woman involved, Amelia learned that she was the victim of a family quarrel dating back to the Civil War. Although Gryce and Amelia discovered the killer, they agreed that she would never come to trial.

Lois Cayley

Author: Grant Allen

Lois Cayley, at 21, had crisp black hair, large dark eyes, and a swarthy complexion. A graduate of Girton, Cambridge, she behaved scandalously for a young woman of her class and time; i.e., serving as a maid for an elderly woman, riding an American-designed bicycle in a contest in which all other entrants were men, rescuing a suitor when he fell over a cliff.

During *Miss Cayley's Adventures* (Putnam, 1899), she traveled through Europe; into Egypt, where she rode a camel and rescued a young Englishwoman from Arabs; and to India, where she hunted tigers from the back of an elephant. On her return to England, she and her fiancé, Harold, were accused of tampering with a will under which Harold inherited. They married in Scotland, with Harold returning to surrender to the authorities while Lois proved their innocence.

The novel was typical for the times, in that a fictional young woman was allowed considerable freedom before her marriage, particularly if her underlying purpose was noble.

Dorcas Dene

Author: George R. Sims

Dorcas Dene entered private investigation only when she was sure that "it would not involve any sacrifice of her womanly instincts." In her late twenties, she was described as having soft brown wavy hair and a light complexion. Her motives were financial. Her artist husband, Paul, had lost his sight, so she supported the London household, which also included her mother, and bulldog Toddleking. She had been an actress, which served her in good stead when she entered households undercover to gain information. At various times she disguised herself as a nurse, as an American tourist, and as an elderly German frau. Her next-door neighbor, a retired policeman, hired Dorcas to help in his investigations. When he retired, she took over the agency, working conscientiously to verify her conclusions by researching official records.

Dorcas Dene, Detective (White, 1897) was narrated by dramatist Mr. Saxon, who had known Dorcas when she was on stage, and admired her ability to use disguise and drama in her investigations. A second collection, *Dorcas Dene, Detective, Second Series* (White, 1898) followed, but was not available for review.

Mrs. G.

Author: Andrew W. Forrester, Jr.

Such formidable genre theorists as Ellery Queen and E. F. Bleiler identified Mrs. G. as the first fictional female investigator in *The Female Detective* (Ward, 1864). Her author, Andrew W. Forrester, Jr., gave few insights into her character or motives, but she presumably worked for the money. In *The Lady Investigates* by Patricia Craig and Mary Cadogan, it was reported that Mrs. G. did not disclose her work to her friends, but led them to believe she was a dressmaker. Nor did Forrester ever make it clear whether Mrs. G. was widowed or married, or did or did not have children. As a matter of fact, since the title "Mrs." during that period was given to older women indiscriminately, she might have been single. Michelle Slung, in her preface to *Crime on Her Mind*, referred to Mrs. G. as likely to be single and working to support herself. In her first person narrative, Mrs. G. commented that she believed that women criminals were worse than men.

In 1978, Dover Publications included *The Unknown Weapon* by Forrester in *Three Victorian Detective Novels*, edited by E. F. Bleiler. In the narrative, Mrs. G. investigated the death of young Graham Petleigh at his father's country estate. Although she determined how, why, and by whom the murder had been committed, she lacked proof for a conviction. She interviewed witnesses, had a woman assistant who went undercover at the estate, and searched the premises. She described her approach as believing "every man, a rogue till...we can only discover that he is an honest man."

Madame Katherine Koluchy

Author: L. T. (Lillie Thomas) Meade (Smith) and Robert Eustace

Madame Katherine Koluchy was the Italian leader of The Brotherhood, who used her London business as a beauty specialist as a front for robbery, blackmail, kidnapping, and murder. She was described as having dark hair and eyes, erect posture, and considerable intelligence.

In *The Brotherhood of the Seven Kings* (Ward, 1899), narrator Norman Head challenged Madame Koluchy in a series of adventures, determined to bring her and her associates to justice. She had been accepted into society, praised for her high skills as a musician and composer, but finally destroyed herself by a trap she set for others.

Caroline "Cad" Mettie

Author: Harlan Halsey, writing as "The Old Sleuth"

Cad Mettie (birth name Caroline), an impulsive young woman, detected not for economic reasons but because she enjoyed the excitement.

In *Dudie Dunne or the Exquisite Detective* (Ogilvie, 1895), Dudie met young Cad but was suspicious of her until she saved him from a trap. He realized that she was still not to be trusted so left her in the charge of a former prison matron until he captured the crooks.

By *Cad Mettie, the Female Detective Strategist* (an Old Sleuth Dime Novel by Ogilvie, 1895) she was a girl of the streets usually working with Dudie, who was tougher than he looked. Cad, whom Dudie loved, was beautiful, could sing and dance, "fence or wrestle like a man," and disguise herself as a male. She planned to become a famous female detective. As a pair, Cad and Dudie were so successful that the government hired them to investigate Italian gangs who were robbing banks and counterfeiting money.

Ogilvie published other dime novels featuring colorful women sleuths, but they were few compared to hundreds of dime novels with youthful or adult male heroes.

Mrs. Paschal

Author: Anonyma

Little is known of the widowed Mrs. Paschal who worked with the Metropolitan Police in London in the 1860's. She had few, if any, real life counterparts. Lower class women acted as matrons in prisons, but not, as author "Anonyma" proposed, as a member of a special unit composed of female detectives. Amnon Kabatchnik (*The Armchair Detective*, Vol. 7-2, p. 131) related that in *The Revelations of a Lady Detective* (George Vickers, 1864), Mrs. Paschal was described as just short of forty, "vigorous and subtle." *Revelations* included ten short stories featuring Mrs. Paschal's exploits.

Kabatchnik believed that *The Experiences of a Lady Detective* (Charles H. Clarke), published in 1861, was a separate book, and therefore that Mrs. Paschal was the first female sleuth. E. F. Bleiler refuted this contention in a subsequent article in *The Armchair Detective*, Vol. 8-3, p. 202. Bleiler examined the tables of contents of the two books, found them to be the same, and identified William Stephens Hayward as the probable author. If so, then *The Female Detective* by Andrew J. Forrester, Jr., was the first female sleuth.

Madeline Payne

Author: Lawrence L. Lynch, pseudonym for Emma Van Deventer

Madeline Payne's mother died, leaving her with a cruel and lecherous stepfather. Her father, whom she never knew, had been a detective. An attractive young woman with golden hair and brown eyes, she had been educated in a convent school.

In *Madeline Payne, the Detective's Daughter* (Loyd, 1884), Madeline, desperate to be free of her stepfather, left town with a charming but faithless young man. After Lucian Davlin betrayed her, she assumed another identity until she could claim her inheritance.

Needing to support herself, Madeline became a detective in *Moina, A Detective Story* (Ward, 1891). While a guest at the home of a wealthy industrialist, Madeline learned that her host had been threatened. After his injury from a bomb, she involved herself with Russian imperialists, Socialist conspirators, and the historic Haymarket riot. When she found romance with friend Dr. Vaughn, she withdrew from her career.

Author Van Deventer, like others in the period, felt she would be more successful under a male pseudonym.

Hagar Stanley

Author: Fergus Hume

Hagar Stanley was a young gypsy who left her tribe to avoid an unwanted marriage. Described as having dark hair and dark eyes in *Hagar of the Pawn Shop* (Buckles, 1898), she worked for pawnbroker Jacob Dix who bequeathed the shop to her. In the course of her work, Hagar cleared a falsely accused black woman of murdering her employer. Most cases arose from items pawned in the shop. Although she enjoyed her work, Hagar longed for the open road. Eventually, she and the man she loved set up a bookseller's caravan and returned to the highway.

Valeria Woodville

Author: Wilkie Collins

Valeria Woodville, a tall slender woman with black hair and dark blue eyes, searched for proof that her husband, Eustace, did not kill his first wife in *The Law and the Lady* (Harper, 1875).

While living with her aunt and uncle, Valeria had married a young man of whom she knew little. Concerned by her mother-in-law's opposition to the marriage, she learned that Eustace had a prior wife under the name Macallan. Furthermore, he had been tried and received a Scottish verdict when accused of Sara's death. Finding herself pregnant, she was more determined than ever to clear the name of her child's father. The narrative included fifty pages of trial transcript, which Valeria read in the course of her investigation.

Collins, a prominent Victorian, had several other interesting women characters in his books.

Section 2:

Seeds of Discontent—Women Sleuths of 1900-1919

"It is still felt that woman's life, in its civil, economic, and social bearing, is essentially and normally a vicarious life, the merit or demerit of which is, in the nature of things, to be imputed to some other individual who stands in some relation of ownership or tutelage to the woman."

Thorstein Veblen's "Theory of the Leisure Class" (1899),
quoted in *Up from the Pedestal*, by Aileen Kraditor (1965)

Women, although still held closely to hearth and home, were offered more freedom in their social life after the turn of the century. Their clothing became less cumbersome and restrictive. American girls were more likely than their brothers to graduate from high school. New occupations—usually extensions of female nurturing skills—were opened to them in nursing, teaching, and libraries. The typewriter made secretarial work a low paying job, no longer appealing to men. As more goods were mass-produced and sold in stores, female factory workers and clerks were needed. Such occupations were considered acceptable for those who could not or did not choose to marry, or as temporary bridges between school and marriage. Private investigators and police officers continued to be males, capable of handling violent criminals.

Women had improved their property and legal rights, but were still denied the vote, although both American and British suffragettes campaigned for recognition. Individual American states had already granted their female residents the right to vote when Congress finally passed the Nineteenth Amendment, which was then ratified by the required number of states. Congress had been influenced by women's contributions during World War I in the service and in civilian life.

More women were writing novels, including mysteries. The mystery format was changing from short stories to novels. Surprisingly, while mystery heroes might be philosophic (Father Brown) or scientific (Dr. Thorndyke), mystery series heroines such as Dora Myrl, Mercedes Quero, and Millicent Newberry were professional investigators. These fictional heroines were unrealistic and not reflective of the positions occupied by women of the period. In contrast, several women featured in mystery novels or collections of short stories of the period were villainesses.

Frances Baird

Author: Reginald Kauffman

Frances Baird, a small woman with brown eyes and black hair, lived in a Philadelphia apartment with her maid, Betty. In *Miss Frances Baird, Detective* (Page, 1906), she and fellow investigator Ambrose Kemp guarded jewels displayed prior to a wedding. Frances suffered personal heartbreak and loss of her job, but persisted to find a thief and a killer, and to reunite young lovers.

She had her own agency and an international clientele by *My Heart and Stephanie* (Page, 1910), narrated by reporter Sam Burton. Frances and Sam journeyed across the ocean and through Europe to find an espionage agent and save the reputation of a lovely young countess. Of historical interest only.

Mary J. "Polly" Burton

Author: Baroness Emmuska Orczy

Although she did little detecting of her own, Polly Burton, a young reporter, had a vicarious investigative career through her contacts with the "Old Man in the Corner," an elderly string-twisting savant with whom she exchanged ideas in London teashops. The pair appeared in three collections of short stories: *The Case of Miss Elliott* (Unwin, 1905), *Old Man in the Corner* (Greening, 1909; Dodd Mead; 1909, reprinted in 1977 as part of the Classic Short Stories series), and *Unravelled Knots* (Hutchinson, 1925; Doran, 1926).

The "Old Man" was the prototype for such armchair detectives as Nero Wolfe, but he viewed the cases as intellectual challenges unrelated to the justice system.

Letitia "Tish" Carberry

Author: Mary Roberts Rinehart

Tish Carberry, a lighthearted and lightheaded spinster, careened around the countryside with two "girlfriends," involving themselves in other peoples' business, which occasionally included crimes. At one time or another, she and/or her friends (1) were abducted by rum runners; (2) checked out a missing corpse at the hospital, and took a ride on top of an elevator;

(3) were conned into subsidizing a crooked race; (4) captured real robbers, thinking they were part of a movie scene; and (5) sheltered a criminal and captured the lawmen who pursued him.

During World War I, Tish modified her behavior to drive a Red Cross ambulance across France and, on her return, concerned herself with possible "communists" in the United States.

See *The Amazing Adventures of Letitia Carberry* (Bobbs, 1911), *Tish* (Houghton, 1916), *More Tish* (Doran, 1921), *Tish Plays the Game* (Doran, 1926), *The Book of Tish* (Farrar, 1926), and *Tish Marches On* (Farrar, 1937). These are collections of short stories, which appeared first in popular magazines of the period.

Constance Dunlap

Author: Arthur R. Reeve

Constance Dunlap was a complacent housewife whose life changed when she schemed to prove her husband innocent of embezzlement in *Constance Dunlap, Woman Detective* (Harper, 1913). After he killed himself, she became an adventuress. She was an attractive young woman, with big brown eyes and dark hair, who relished excitement and wealth. Her talents included not only art, but also forgery; not only bookkeeping, but also embezzlement; not only eavesdropping, but also gunrunning. Tiring of her life of crime, she became a detective, defending the weak and helpless.

Ruth Fielding

Author: Alice B. Emerson, through the Stratemeyer Syndicate

Ruth Fielding was an innovation to girl readers accustomed to passive, well-behaved heroines when introduced in 1913. She appeared in 30 books over the next 21 years. Ruth was an orphan, unrestricted by parental protection. She attended a boarding school (*Ruth Fielding at Briarwood Hall*) and worked as a nurse with the Red Cross in World War I. She became an actress, writer (*Ruth Fielding in Moving Pictures*), and director (*Ruth Fielding at Cameron Hall*), then settled down, married, and had children (*Ruth Fielding and Baby June*).

According to Carol Bellman (*The Secret of the Stratemeyer Syndicate*, Unger, 1986, from which the above information was garnered), Emerson's publishers learned from the decreased market never to allow their heroines to mature, marry, and have children. This was evidenced in the lack of maturation in later publications, like the Nancy Drew series.

Judith Lee

Author: Richard Marsh

Judith Lee, a teacher of the deaf, used her lip reading skills to solve mysteries by "overhearing" conversations. Miss Lee was bilingual in lip reading, as she spoke and understood French. She had studied jujitsu, an unusual skill for the time. Judith had dark skin, hair and eyes, and a "gypsy-like" appearance. Deafness was a significant factor in Judith's family. Her mother had been deaf, and both her father and grandfather had taught the deaf.

Judith was dedicated to her work, which included the development of training for deaf children in foreign countries. Although she received at least one proposal, she rejected the idea of marriage, preferring her career.

Judith Lee (Methuen, 1912) and *The Adventures of Judith Lee* (Methuen, 1916) were collections of short stories. As a teenager she had used lip reading to learn where robbers planned to hide out. As her reputation increased, she used her skills to protect herself from personal attack and efforts to damage her reputation. She helped a socially prominent thief return stolen goods and retrieved blackmail letters; was sent a bomb; posed as a maid to spy on crooks; and foiled German efforts to get plans of a new plane.

Madelyn Mack

Author: Hugh C. Weir

Madelyn Mack modeled herself on Sherlock Holmes, although she chewed cola berries instead of injecting cocaine, and played the piano, not the violin. She had no acknowledged medical training while at college, but observed the dissection of corpses. Like Holmes, she asked seemingly irrelevant questions that solved her cases.

Madelyn was described as a slight woman with dull gold hair and gray-blue eyes, always attired in either all white or all black. She shared her Hudson River chalet with housekeeper Susan Bolton and a longhaired dog, Peter the Great. Her agency was located on Fifth Avenue, but work as a consultant involved considerable travel. Madelyn had originally planned to be a store detective but was refused work so she set up her own business.

Madelyn's exploits were narrated in short stories by female reporter Nora Noraker in *Miss Madelyn Mack, Detective* (Page, 1914). The stories included her experiences with a runaway bridegroom and two locked room mysteries. Although Nora found romance, Madelyn showed no interest in marriage.

Madame X

Author: J. W. McConaughy, based upon a play by Alexandre Bisson

Although she abandoned her husband, attorney Louis Floriot, and their tiny son, Raymond, in *Madame X* (Grosset & Dunlap, 1910c), Jacqueline Floriot was a victim rather than a villainess. Louis was cold and inattentive to his younger wife once they were married. He encouraged his friend, Albert Lescelles, to escort Jacqueline to social events while he devoted his time to advancing his career. Upon learning of her infidelity, Louis drove her away without any concern for her welfare. When she returned two years later, having learned that Raymond was ill, he would not even let her see their son. Penniless, she was eventually forced into prostitution and drug addiction. On her return to France after many years, she killed a man who threatened to expose her current condition to Louis and Raymond. Unaware that Louis had heeded the advice of his friend Noel, accepted some responsibility for the family tragedy, and hired detectives to find his wife, she hated him. Still she loved Raymond too much to speak in her own defense. He was now a court advocate and had been assigned to her case. This was a tearjerker, but it exposed the dire straits of women who lost the protection of the men in their families.

Two silent movies and three sound movies were based on the book and play.

Molly Morganthau

Author: Geraldine Bonner

Molly Morganthau was the first blue-collar worker who, while not a paid investigator, was a female detective. A slim, dark, young high school graduate, she worked first in a department store, then became a telephone operator. She listened to the conversations of persons in whom she had an interest.

Molly encountered murder in *The Girl at Central* (Appleton, 1915), when, believing that an innocent man was suspected of murder, she and reporter "Soapy" Babbitts cleared his name, partly by matching voices of suspects with those she heard on the phone.

By *The Black Eagle Mystery* (Appleton, 1916), Molly had married Soapy, and no longer worked out of the home. Still, when a top corporate attorney, Hollings Harland, jumped, or was pushed, from the 18th floor of the Black Eagle Building, Molly took a job at the switchboard to monitor calls, risking Soapy's wrath when she over-involved herself in the case. There were several unpleasant racial epithets in the book.

Molly did not appear early in *Miss Maitland, Private Secretary* (Appleton, 1919). Still, her intervention came in time to save a young woman from a false accusation of theft, and to assist the family in recovering a kidnapped child. Mission accomplished, Molly was happy to return home to "Soapy."

Dora Myrl

Author: M. McDonnell Bodkin

Dora Myrl was a slim, athletic young woman with brown hair and blue eyes, who claimed a degree from Cambridge, where her father had been a don. Her mother had died when she was born; her father died when she was 18. After working first as a telephone girl, then a journalist, Dora became a private investigator, carrying a gun for protection.

She appeared first in a collection of short stories, *Dora Myrl, the Lady Detective* (Chatto, 1900), during which she contended with gamblers, robbers, bank theft, blackmail, and murder, while playing cupid among her clients.

Dora found romance for herself when she competed with detective Paul Beck in *The Capture of Paul Beck* (Unwin, 1909). The two began as rivals with Dora seeking to help a friend whose sweetheart had been accused of a crime. Beck initially worked for an older suitor of the young woman, but later cooperated with Dora.

Dora and Paul appeared in a parental role in *Young Beck* (Unwin, 1911), another collection of short stories, featuring their son, also Paul. When he and his sweetheart visited his parents in Kent, Dora was about 50 years old. She and her husband had retired, now competing only at golf. The older couple helped young Paul solve the murder of Colonel Maddox. Alone or with help, young Paul unmasked a man posing as a politician, caught an aristocratic jewel thief, saved a young man from poison, foiled a hypnotist who sought to commit murder second handed, and proved a young woman to be a legitimate offspring appropriate for a good marriage.

It should be noted that male authors also wrote series with independent female sleuths.

Millicent Newberry

Author: Jennette Lee

Millicent Newberry was different—and different not just for the period from 1917 to 1925, when the series was written. Millicent would be different today because of the conditions under which she undertook her cases. She was a tiny woman, appearing in monotone, with gray hair and eyes, gray dresses with accents of green. Originally a seamstress, she knit while talking to a prospective client, stitching coded memos into her handiwork in lieu of taking notes.

Millicent became a detective after she contacted Tom Corbin's agency with a clue that led to the solution of a crime. She accepted a job with Corbin but eventually established her own agency. Before Millicent accepted an assignment, she reserved to herself the decision as to whether or not to involve the police, even if a crime had been committed. On occasion she exercised that right to give the perpetrator a second chance. She lived simply with her invalid mother and a former female "probationer" who cared for Mrs. Newberry.

In *The Green Jacket* (Scribner, 1917), Millicent's former employer and suitor brought her an "unsolvable case," involving the theft of emeralds. Millicent went undercover as a seamstress, detected the "thief," and cleared up serious misunderstandings within the family.

In *The Mysterious Office* (Scribner, 1922), a businessman whose office had been robbed consulted Millicent when other agencies failed to solve the thefts. When Millicent joined his business as an efficiency expert, she uncovered a hidden romance, then explained how the money disappeared.

In *Dead Right* (Scribner, 1925), Millicent sought a missing will under peculiar circumstances. If she failed, she agreed she would marry Tom Corbin, her former employer.

The books had charm, but lacked narrative tension.

Mercedes Quero

Author: G. E. (Gladys Edson) Locke

Mercedes Quero was an early London private investigator, who worked primarily in rural areas. She was a tall, slim woman with brown hair and eyes, capable of assuming identities at different social levels. She was physically adept and carried a revolver when necessary, but relied upon logic and the process of deduction to find a culprit.

In *That Affair at Portstead Manor* (Sherman, 1914), when a valuable necklace belonging to a guest at the Manor was stolen, the Earl was unaware that Mercedes was already on the scene as Mary Grey, a lady's companion. She not only restored stolen items, but also identified the Earl's murderer.

Mercedes made a late appearance in *The Red Cavalier* (Page, 1922). Murder and a jewel theft at Twin Turrets appeared to be one of a series of local robberies by a masked cavalier. The family hired Mercedes, who came in disguise. Although working with Inspector Burton on the case, Mercedes allowed the killer to relocate in Australia.

In *The Scarlet Macaw* (Page, 1923), Burton and Mercedes worked together again on the murder of playwright Genevra Tressady, which took place in a locked room.

Mercedes was already on scene as a parlor maid in *The House on the Downs* (Page, 1925), when novelist Mark Brandon discovered a corpse on the premises. The victim was the husband of Lady Eve Rotherdene, his hostess. When Lady Eve was murdered, Mercedes—who had been hired to protect her—set a trap for the killer.

The Locke books were lengthy for this period, running 250 to 300 plus pages.

Lady Molly Robertson-Kirk

Author: Baroness Emmuska Orczy

Lady Molly Robertson-Kirk accepted employment at Scotland Yard only until she could achieve a personal goal, but she began at the top as head of a mythical "Female Department" in *Lady Molly of Scotland Yard* (Cassell, 1910). During the narration by Mary Granard, her doting assistant, the reason for Molly's interest in crime was disclosed gradually as she solved a series of cases. Molly had married Captain Hubert de Mazareen, just before he was accused and convicted of having killed his grandfather's attorney. Molly never lost faith in his innocence, eventually cleared his name, and retired.

Madame Sara

Authors: L. T. (Lillie Thomas) Meade (Smith) and Robert Eustace

Madame Sara was an Italian-Indian blonde murderess of considerable intelligence. Her adventures were described in *The Sorceress of the Strand* (Ward, 1903) by Dixon Druce, the manager of an inquiry agency. Dixon saved several young women who were preyed upon, blackmailed, or framed by the devious Madame Sara, who was never brought to justice, but met her death when attacked by a Siberian wolf.

Violet Strange

Author: Anna Katharine Green

Violet Strange has been considered by some (including Michelle Slung in *Twentieth Century Crime and Mystery Writers*) to be the prototype for Nancy Drew. However, she was an older, more mature woman and only appeared in a single book of short stories, *The Golden Slipper and Other Problems for Violet Strange* (Putnam, 1915).

Violet, a member of upper class society, concealed her activities from her father, who would have been horrified to discover her occupation. She needed money so that her disinherited sister, Theresa, could take singing lessons.

Violet dealt primarily in society cases, in the course of which she met young widower Roger Upjohn, a former gambler and wastrel, suspected of his wife's murder. After Violet cleared Roger, they fell in love.

Evelyn Temple

Author: Ronald Gorell Barnes aka Lord Gorell

Evelyn Temple appeared first as a woman in her early twenties during *In the Night* (Longmans, 1917). She was a guest at the home of Sir Roger Penterton, whose male secretary was her sweetheart. Sir Roger was murdered while a Scotland Yard inspector was nearby. However, neither he nor Evelyn would have solved the case had the guilty party not confessed to the accident that caused Sir Roger's death.

Then, in her mid-thirties, Evelyn returned in *Red Lilac* (Murray, 1935), a guest at the home of her cousin Caroline, who was bullied by here husband, Theophilus. When he was murdered, no cooperation could be expected from the local police official, who had his own reasons for not actively seeking the killer.

Henrietta Van Raffles

Author: John Kendrick Bangs

Not all villainesses were morbid, sinister women. Henrietta Van Raffles was a figure of fun, a parody of the Raffles series by E. W. Hornung. "Bunny," Raffles' best friend and chronicler, teamed with his widow, Henrietta, in *Mrs. Raffles* (Harper, 1905). They had met again after Raffles' death, both broke. Together they defrauded wealthy Americans until they had amassed a fortune. Bunny, who had posed as Henrietta's butler during their criminal period, married her and gave up crime to become a minister.

Olga von Kopf

Author: Henri de Halsalle

At the height of World War I, female spies were big news. Mata Hari, a German spy, and Nurse Edith Cavell, sentenced as a British spy, were well known. De Halsalle's narratives of Olga von Kopf, the daughter of an English mother and a German father, were topical.

A Secret Service Woman (Laurie, 1917) reported the author's personal contact with Olga, who described herself as an innocent journalist, but later sent him her experiences in the German Secret Service. According to her material she had trained as a singer and artist, but she lost her basic source of income when her parents died, so began work for the German government. Olga described incidents in which she spied and related stories of the work done by other spies. She was anti-Semitic, and eventually turned against Germany and returned to England.

In *A Woman Spy* (Skeffington, 1918), further adventures of "Germany's principal Secret Service Woman" were described, including episodes in which she assisted in an escape from a Russian prison, met Rasputin, masqueraded as an Englishwoman, and traveled through the Balkans and the Netherlands.

Hilda Wade

Author: Grant Allen

Hilda Wade was an attractive young nurse who traveled around the globe, marrying only after she had cleared her father's name. Her adventures were narrated by Dr. Hubert Cumberledge, who loved her. He described her as a dusky blonde with brown eyes. Hilda was physically active, riding and playing tennis. She had total recall and intuitive powers, enabling her to read faces and handwriting.

As she traveled in *Hilda Wade* (Richards, 1900), she solved cases but worked ceaselessly to exonerate her father, who died of a heart attack while awaiting trial for poisoning a patient.

Prudence Whitby

Author: Phoebe Atwood Taylor

Prudence Whitby was a spinster in her fifties who was called "Snoodles" by her niece, Betsy. They shared a small cabin during Cape Cod summers, and became friends with Asey Mayo, a local handyman and sailor. Asey Mayo appeared in two dozen mystery novels; Prudence Whitby appeared as narrator in two.

In *The Cape Cod Mystery* (Bobbs Merrill, 1931), Prudence became involved when one of Betsy's suitors was murdered, and her preferred beau, Bill Porter, was arrested for the crime. She and Asey uncovered multiple other suspects. During their investigation, Prudence saved Asey when he was attacked.

By *Death Lights a Candle* (Bobbs Merrill, 1932), Asey had achieved status as the sheriff. He was contacted with regard to a disappearance and two subsequent murders by means of poisoned candlewicks. Prudence and Asey became victims themselves. Prudence proved her long time beau innocent and then married him, thus removing herself from the series.

Section 3:
Years of Plenty, Years of Famine—
Women Sleuths of 1920-1939

*"An examination of the standard histories of the
United States and of the history textbooks in use in
our schools raises the pertinent question, whether
women have ever made a contribution to American
National progress that is worthy of record."*

New Viewpoints in American History, by Arthur M. Schlesinger,
(1922), quoted in Mary Beard's *Woman as a Force in History*,
Macmillan, 1946, p. 68.

The Nineteenth Amendment vastly expanded the number of women
allowed to vote, but it did not produce the changes the suffragettes had
anticipated. Many women failed to use the privilege; those who did, scattered their votes so as to make little impact.

The Twenties were turbulent, marked by postwar euphoria, the
excesses of a society denied legal alcohol—but willing to pay for smuggled
booze—and unbridled speculation in the stock market. Women's behaviors
changed markedly. They joined the men in drinking and smoking. Their
hems and hair were shorter. The automobile and expanded public transportation made it possible for women to travel independently by day or night.
Young women in jobs no longer felt it necessary to abide by family house
rules. They rented apartments. Female students may have had to conform
to college curfews, but they had expanded personal freedom.

The financial bubble burst in 1929, sending women home so that men could continue to work. Female teachers who married were expected to resign. Federal employment did not allow both parties in a marriage to work. Since the husband's salary was usually higher, the women had no choice. The women who needed to work to support their families were shunted to low paying, arduous physical labor. Women at home raised vegetables, canned meat, mended clothes, and did without. Only when the war in Europe sent American factories back to full time capacity did the specter of the Depression lift. For those who experienced unemployment or the loss of their bank deposits, life was never the same.

The Twenties and Thirties were termed the "Golden Years" in the mystery genre. Exceptional authors, many of them women, wrote books that are still in print. The English "cozy" or puzzle mystery dominated the Twenties. The American hard-boiled mystery emerged in the Thirties, as Chandler said, "returning murder to those who really commit it." Many private investigators were misogynists, suspicious of women, who, as in the Victorian period, were portrayed as victims or villainesses.

However, within the hard-boiled sub-genre were the seeds of a new type of mystery, the "couples" formula. Nick and Nora Charles, through Hammett's book *The Thin Man* but even more through the successful William Powell/Myrna Loy movies, lifted the spirits of depressed moviegoers. Fans enjoyed the witty dialogue, the romance and fellowship between Nick and Nora. Dozens of clones appeared in books, movies, and on radio.

Lippincott, Dutton, Houghton, Simon & Schuster, Random, Farrar and Rinehart, and Doubleday were major publishers of mystery books in the United States. Jenkins, Joseph, Collins, Cassell, Hutchinson, Hodder & Stoughton, and Hale were prominent English publishers of mysteries.

America was learning style, language, and morals from the media. If Jean Harlow dyed her hair, so did her female fans. If she wore blood-red fingernail polish, then it appeared at Woolworth's. The homogenization of America began with mass media. Divorce increased. Families were small because money was tight, but no one talked about birth control. Americans remained remarkably quiescent during a depression that might have toppled less stable governments.

Adelaide Adams

Author: Anita Blackmon (Smith)

Adelaide Adams was financially secure during the Depression when few were so fortunate. A spinster who had spent her eligible years caring for her father, she now lived in the Richelieu Hotel of a small Southern town. In her fifties, she had iron gray hair, glasses, and a "florid complexion." Nothing in life had prepared Adelaide for a private detective hanging from her chandelier in *Murder à la Richelieu* (Doubleday, 1937). Adelaide visited a mountain inn to help an old friend in *There Is No Return* (Doubleday, 1938), a narrative overloaded with seances, hypnosis, and possession by the dead.

Limited appeal, except for historical interest.

Hilda Adams

Author: Mary Roberts Rinehart

Hilda Adams, a registered nurse, worked with police inspectors who needed a discreet ally where murder had occurred or was suspected. Nicknamed "Miss Pinkerton" for her detecting, Hilda was tiny but sturdy with graying hair and blue eyes. Although she rented an apartment shared with a canary called "Dick," she often lived in a nurse's dorm or stayed in the homes of her wealthy patients.

In *Miss Pinkerton* (Farrar, 1932), Hilda's patient, Miss Juliet Mitchell, had suffered a heart attack upon the discovery of the apparent suicide of her nephew. Nevertheless, she became a suspect because she inherited under his will. When switched medication caused Miss Juliet's death, Hilda had a professional interest in discovering the killer.

By *Haunted Lady* (Farrar, 1942), Hilda was ten years older, more assertive in her detection, but still without a personal life. She nursed matriarch Eliza Fairbanks, who, after being terrorized by bats and rodents, was murdered.

Hilda's subsequent appearances were in novelettes, published in magazines, then collected in the *Mary Roberts Rinehart's Crime Book* (Farrar, 1933). The stories detailed her early contacts with the police department, her unsuccessful efforts to serve overseas during World War II, and a battle against bubonic plague.

Episode of the Wandering Knife (Rinehart, 1950) included a novella, *The Secret*, during which Hilda went undercover in the home of spinster

Alice Rowland. Guests included a niece who might have been trying to kill her mother. Hilda had a ruthless streak, and on more than one occasion when she identified a killer, urged suicide as an alternative to the justice system. Her position in the homes of prosperous patients made her aware of the family stresses that led to murder.

A solid effort by a pioneer in female sleuths.

Janet "Janie" Allen

Author: Ruth Darby

See: Janet "Janie" Allen Barron, Section 3, page 25.

Agatha Troy Alleyn aka Troy Alleyn

Author: Ngaio Marsh

Agatha Troy was an established artist, described as "attractive" with short dark hair and gray-green eyes. She wore "trousers" and traveled in unconventional circles. Troy was unimpressed by Inspector Roderick Alleyn's noble connections and official status when they met on board ship. She had to deal with him later when murder was committed at her home in *Artists in Crime* (Furman, 1938).

She continued to use her maiden name professionally after their marriage, but, disliking the name "Agatha," she used Troy as a first name in her personal life. Roderick wanted Troy kept out of his investigations, but she provided him with access into the artistic, sometimes Bohemian, circles where on occasion murders were committed.

In several books, Troy carried a major part of the early narrative, meeting the suspects for an impending murder and then sharing her insights with Roderick when he investigated, as in *Final Curtain* (Little, 1947), *Tied Up in Tinsel* (Little, 1972), *Clutch of Constables* (Little, 1969), and to a lesser extent in *Photo-Finish* (Little, 1980). She often pointed Roderick in the correct direction, but was rarely involved in the action.

The couple had a son, Ricky, kidnapped during *Spinsters in Jeopardy* (Little, 1953), who became a novelist and did some detecting of his own. Marsh concentrated on Roderick but provided him with an interesting spouse.

Hilea Bailey

Author: Hilea Bailey, pseudonym for Ruth Lenore Marting

Hilea Bailey, a fair-haired, blue-eyed woman in her late twenties, lived at home with her disabled father. Hilary Dunsany Bailey III, a widowed private investigator, had hoped for a son, but accepted Hilea's assistance to remain in his profession.

In *What Night Will Bring* (Doubleday, 1939), when an unknown man was found dead in the offices of an advertising company, Hilea went undercover. Working with Hilea was her "boyfriend," Jake Jones, a flip, fast-talking newspaperman. Mr. Bailey researched records and charted the probabilities that different suspects might be guilty.

In *Give Thanks to Death* (Doubleday, 1940), Kathryn Pelham believed that she might be the granddaughter of the deceased Cabot Pelham, whose expanded family lived in an isolated house. Hilea insinuated herself into the household to gather information for Mr. Bailey.

During *The Smiling Corpse* (Doubleday, 1941), mortician Harvey Smith not only had problems with his adult children, but someone was damaging his business. Hilea joined the family as a visiting niece from Oregon, but narrowly averted cremation.

As *Breathe No More, My Lady* (Doubleday, 1946) opened, Jake, who had been demobilized from the service, convinced Hilea to move into a rooming house adjacent to a defense plant. Although she gathered information for Jake, Hilea spent much of her time helping to run the boarding house.

Like many Doubleday heroines of the period, Hilea was narrator and assistant, rather than an independent investigator.

Janet "Janie" Allen Barron

Author: Ruth Darby

Janet Allen, a 32-year-old secretary, accompanied investment broker Peter Barron on a Caribbean cruise to provide clerical services. Before *Death Boards the Lazy Lady* (Doubleday, 1939) ended, she had proved him innocent of two murders with the help of police chief Kurt Christiansen, and accepted his proposal of marriage.

During *Death Conducts a Tour* (Doubleday, 1940), Janie and Peter were on their honeymoon. When an elderly passenger was murdered in a bolted room, Peter, Kurt Christiansen, and Janie worked together to probe deaths among cruise passengers.

The trio combined vacation and detection in Mexico in *If This Be Murder* (Doubleday, 1941), as guests of Janie's cousin, Geraldine. By the time Geraldine's husband was murdered, Peter, Kurt, and Janie had worn out their welcome, but remained in Mexico until they trapped the killer.

By *Beauty Sleep* (Doubleday, 1941), Janie was listed as a partner in Peter and Christiansen's detective agency, but spent most of her time as a bored housewife in a small Long Island village. When a woman died in the local beauty parlor, Janie was present, but Peter did the detecting.

Murder with Orange Blossoms (Doubleday, 1943) began with a wedding during which the bride collapsed and died. Almost everyone in the wedding party had a motive for her death.

Janie was bright and adoring in a traditional role. When she risked danger, Peter rescued her. Her early potential never developed into meaningful participation, and her character and background were never explored.

Prudence "Tuppence" Beresford
Author: Agatha Christie

Tuppence Beresford was the rare representative of the young female detective in the 1930's when other sleuths were spinsters, male dilettantes, or hard-edged private eyes. To those who had outgrown Nancy Drew and Judy Bolton, she was a joy. Christie was indulgent with Tuppence, allowing her to marry, raise a family, grow old, and yet remain curious and vibrant.

The fifth daughter of a poor rural archdeacon, it was too late for Prudence, so she became known as Tuppence. A small woman with bobbed black hair and gray eyes, she married Tommy Beresford when he returned from service in World War I. From then on, they were inseparable in their private and professional lives. When they worked on parallel tracks, it was as equals. Tommy was more cautious and pragmatic while Tuppence was intuitive and, at times, restless.

In *The Secret Adversary* (Dodd, 1922), they used a newspaper advertisement to solicit clients for their "Young Adventurers, Ltd.," eliciting a response from an American millionaire, which pitted them against "Bolsheviks."

Partners in Crime (Dodd, 1929) was a collection of short cases, each of which parodied a currently popular fictional detective. The stories revealed an unsuspected sense of humor in Christie, but have less meaning to readers unfamiliar with the fictional investigators of the period.

During *N or M?* (Dodd, 1941), set in World War II, the adult Beresford children were in military service. British Intelligence recruited Tommy for espionage work. Not to be left out, Tuppence investigated on her own.

By the Pricking of My Thumbs (Dodd, 1968) took the Beresfords to a nursing home where Tuppence became aware of missing jewels and a long-lost child. A painting which had seemed vaguely familiar to Tuppence led her into danger as she returned to the setting on which the painting had been based.

In *Postern of Fate* (Dodd, 1973), the Beresfords were ready to retire, and perhaps it was time. The narrative, in which a child's book sent the couple on the trail of British fascists, had too much talk, too little action.

Theolinda "Dol" Bonner
Author: Rex Stout

Theolinda "Dol" Bonner was about 30, with amber eyes, coal black hair and eyelashes, and a tiny mole near her right ear. Her father had been a wealthy man who lost his fortune in the stock market crash, then committed suicide. The subsequent disgrace caused Dol's fiancé to abandon her. Embittered by his betrayal, she never married.

Her first big assignment, in *The Hand in the Glove* (Farrar & Rinehart, 1937), was for a man concerned about a religious leader to whom his wife had been making substantial contributions. On reaching the family estate, Dol found her client hanging from a tree.

She appeared next in a novella, *Too Many Detectives,* published in *Collier's* magazine, then in *Three for the Chair* (Viking Press, 1957). Dol was one of seven detectives in a wire-tapping investigation that ended in murder. She worked with Nero Wolfe to pinpoint the murderer, but her role was supportive. Later sightings of Dol were as a minor character in Nero Wolfe and Tecumseh Fox mysteries.

Dame Adela Beatrice Lestrange Bradley
Author: Gladys Mitchell

Dame Beatrice appeared in 66 books, some fascinating, some bizarre, and some virtually unreadable because of the regional dialects. Her physical appearance was mentioned frequently, although the aging process was held in abeyance during the 50 years the series was published. She was described as small, with dark hair and dark beady eyes, yellowed skin, and beak-like features, and was often compared to crocodiles or macaws, or referred to as "saurian." Surely she looked nothing like actress Diana Riggs who portrayed her in the British television series 30 years after the last book was published. Although her laugh was unpleasant, Mrs. Bradley's speaking voice was described as beautiful. She had a gift for eliciting information from suspects and witnesses, particularly children. Mrs. Bradley had skills but did not waste them on those she considered to be fools. She was a frequent guest at dinners and weekends, played excellent bridge and chess, was skilled at pool and snooker, threw darts and knives, and on occasion carried a gun, which she was obviously capable of using.

Although she declared herself uninterested in children, Mrs. Bradley spent much of her leisure time with her extended family, which included not only sons and grandchildren, but also nieces and nephews, grandnieces and grandnephews of the Bradley and Lestrange family, plus an assortment of godchildren.

Mrs. Bradley, later honored as "Dame British Empire," had been married first to Charles Lestrange, by whom she had one son, Ferdinand, later a distinguished barrister. After Charles' death, Beatrice married Bradley and had a second son, who had a medical specialty in topical diseases and lived in India (*St. Peter's Finger,* Joseph, 1938). The third marriage received even less attention, but she was referred to in *The Croaking Raven* (Joseph, 1966) as three times widowed. Particularly in the earlier books, Mrs. Bradley was physically active, and, according to *The Dancing Druids* (Joseph, 1948), she swam the Hellespont.

Bradley was "nothing like a Dame" when she was introduced to the British reading public in *Speedy Death* (Gollancz, 1929). A guest at the country estate where a transsexual explorer was murdered, she used her talents and knowledge of George Joseph Smith's methods of drowning to discover the murderer. When the suspect was killed, Bradley was accused and tried for the crime but found not guilty. The reader knew otherwise.

The books became annual events, and included:

The Longer Bodies (Gollancz, 1930), in which a family bequest to subsidize athletes led to murderous competition, and *The Saltmarsh Murders* (Gollancz, 1932), wherein she stated that anyone was capable of murder and that she considered a painless death penalty to be preferable to a confinement in an insane asylum.

Bradley's professional qualifications were never made clear. She was, at times, referred to as a psychoanalyst (*Saltmarsh*), a psychologist (*When Last I Died*, Joseph, 1941), and a psychiatrist (*The Rising of the Moon,*

Joseph, 1945). The last would be the most compatible with her skills as a medical doctor in *Faintley Speaking* (Joseph, 1954). Her connection to Scotland Yard was equally tenuous. She referred to her position as consulting psychiatrist to the Home Office, but in later books her access was through Scotland Yard Inspector Robert Gavin, husband of Dame Beatrice's secretary, Laura Menzies. Although her specialty was psychological evaluation of the suspects, she did not disdain alibis or physical clues, such as the staples, that attached a body to the bottom of a boat in *The Echoing Strangers* (Joseph, 1952), during which a pair of brothers hampered the police investigation of murder.

She had a variety of assistants, including Curate Wells, who narrated *The Saltmarsh Murders,* and then came to her assistance in *Death in the Wet* (MacRae-Smith, 1934), and George, her chauffeur, who picked up valuable information in the local pubs and garages. Somewhat unscrupulous, George, in *Brazen Tongue* (Joseph, 1940), siphoned gas out of the village ambulance during wartime to make it possible for his employer to go on long trips.

But her closest companion and assistant was Scotswoman Laura Menzies (later Gavin), described as "Amazonian" in *The Devil's Elbow* (Joseph, 1951)—a fine swimmer, horsewoman, and hiker. Laura was introduced as a student in *Laurels Are Poison* (Joseph, 1942) when Mrs. Bradley assumed the role of "Warden" (housemother) to investigate serious pranks and the disappearance of her predecessor. This mystery was solved, as were *Printer's Error* (Joseph, 1939) and *Here Comes a Chopper* (Joseph, 1946), when a person presumed dead turned out to be alive.

Later, Laura became the active party in investigations, sending data to her mentor, who provided the solution: *Skeleton Island* (Joseph, 1967), *Three Quick and Five Dead* (Joseph, 1968). At her employer's suggestion, Laura took her infant son, Hamish, to a vacation island in her investigations in *The Twenty-Third Man* (Joseph, 1957). Hamish, when a young adult, became a teacher at a Borstal type coeducational school (*A Javelin for Jonah*, Joseph, 1974), and Laura's daughter, Eiladh, took part in a deadly ghost hunt (*Wraiths and Changelings*, Joseph, 1978).

Also involved were the members of Dame Beatrice's extended family. Relatives were presented in such large numbers in *My Father Sleeps* (Joseph, 1944) that they kept meeting one another in the woods as in Shakespeare's *A Midsummer Night's Dream*. Grandson John appeared in *Watson's Choice* (Joseph, 1955), where guests at a party dressed as characters from the Sherlock Holmes stories. Ferdinand's daughter, Sally, sought help in *Brazen Tongue* (Joseph, 1940), when a co-worker at an Air Raid Report Centre was killed. Then, as in other instances, Dame Beatrice had her own standards of justice. When proof was unavailable for a killer in *Brazen Tongue* (Joseph, 1940), her response is to "let her go." She also permitted killers to leave the country in *The Mystery of a Butcher's Shop* (Gollancz, 1929), in *St. Peter's Finger* (Joseph, 1938), and in *Nest of Vipers* (Joseph, 1979).

Children made frequent and sympathetic appearances in Gladys Mitchell's books. *The Rising of the Moon* (Joseph, 1945) centered on two young orphaned brothers. Author Mitchell, a teacher herself, took aim at progressive parenting when her heroine civilized an 11-year-old boy in *The Twenty-Third Man* (Joseph, 1957). In a rare burst of humor in *Printer's Error* (Joseph, 1939), Dame Beatrice entered a nudist colony, taking a reluctant nephew, Carey, and a young solicitor along to "uncover" a missing man.

As was common in this period, a considerable number of the Bradley stories were concerned with inheritances and extended families: *Merlin's Furlong* (Joseph, 1953), *My Bones Will Keep* (Joseph, 1962), and *Death of a Delft Blue* (Joseph, 1964), and with impostors in the family: *The Croaking Raven* (Joseph, 1966) and *Dance to Your Daddy* (Joseph, 1969).

Other subjects included: illegitimacy, *Twelve Horses and the Hangman's Noose* (Joseph, 1956) and *The Man Who Grew Tomatoes* (Joseph, 1959); competing half-brothers, *My Father Sleeps* (Joseph, 1944); buried treasure, *Death of a Burrowing Mole* (Joseph, 1982); and infants switched at birth, *The Devil at Saxon Wall* (Grayson, 1935). On the unfortunate side, there were occasional anti-Semitic comments or patronizing treatment of darker skinned foreigners in the books.

Readers should be aware of:

- Heavy dialect: *Dead Men's Morris* (Joseph, 1936), *My Bones Will Keep* (Joseph, 1962), and *Gory Dew* (Joseph, 1970)

- Rural customs of a pagan or medieval derivation: *A Hearse on May-Day* (Josuces and Re   *The Death-Cap Dancers* (Joseph, 1981)

- Greek mythology: *Lament for Leto* (Joseph, 1971) and *Come Away, Death* (Joseph, 1937), one of the most unreadable books encountered

- Archeology with mythical overtones: *The Whispering Knights* (Joseph, 1980) and *The Greenstone Griffins* (Joseph, 1983)

- Water nymphs: *Death and the Maiden* (Joseph, 1947)

- Witchcraft: *The Devil at Saxon Wall* (Grayson, 1935) and *Tom Brown's Body* (Joseph, 1949)

- Pig farming and/or Morris Dancing: *Dead Men's Morris* (Joseph, 1936), *Spotted Hemlock* (Joseph, 1958); and

■ Mayering: *A Hearse in May-Day* (Joseph, 1972).

It can be assumed that those books recently reprinted in England and the United States were among the better narratives.

Others, all published by Joseph, included:

■ *Hangmen's Curfew* (1941), wherein Dame Beatrice came to the aid of a young woman, Gillian, who, while hiking, had connected with a man who was the potential heir to buried treasure.

■ *The Worsted Viper* (1943), in which Laura Menzies played a significant role as Dame Beatrice followed a trail of multiple bodies to a Satanist ritual.

■ *Sunset Over Soho* (1943), during the Blitz in London, where Dame Beatrice worked in a shelter connected to a Baptist church. In a confusing narrative she traced a recently recovered body, mixed with heroic nuns who rescued men at Dunkirk, and took part in a story of rescue at sea.

■ *Groaning Spinney* (1950): Dame Beatrice retained a fond feeling for the relatives of her deceased Bradley husband, including his nephew Jonathan, who was having problems with a parson's ghost who appeared near a spinney gate on his property. The corpse found later on the gate was no ghost.

■ *Say It With Flowers* (1960): Skeletons dug up by students along the old Roman Wall turned out to be recent. Dame Beatrice shared her investigation with Laura and Robert Gavin, even babysitting Hamish, while they deducted on their own.

■ *The Nodding Canaries* (1961): A former classmate of Laura's from her days at Athelston Hall, Alice Boorman needed help when she was suspected of murder. Laura and Dame Beatrice arrived to investigate other members of the local Archeological Society.

■ *Adders on the Heath* (1963): Rival members of running clubs were highly competitive, but surely not willing to murder. Tom Richardson of the Hen Harriers was a friend of Denis, Dame Beatrice's great-nephew. She was called in when Tom found a corpse in his tent, but not the one he had seen shortly before.

■ *Pageant of Murder* (1965): It was Laura who became involved in the Brayne Festival, which included a parade, a performance of *The Merry Wives of Windsor,* and eventually two murders. She called on Dame Beatrice for assistance.

- *The Murder of Busy Lizzie* (1973): "Lizzie" Chayleigh inherited an island with the proviso that she must live on the premises. She was not lonely. Several possible heirs came to visit, just in time. "Lizzie" was no longer busy. She had been murdered. Dame Beatrice, a tenant on the island, was called in as a doctor to check the body.

- *Winking at the Brim* (1974): Sally Lestrange, Dame Beatrice's granddaughter, expected to be bored while visiting her grandmother. Not likely when she joined an expedition to find a monster in a nearby lake. When Sally found the body of a fellow camper, she rejected the local authorities decision to call it a suicide. Dame Beatrice and Laura took over. There was a monster, after all.

- *Convent on Styx,* (1975): Dame Beatrice was described as being somewhere in her seventies, but that didn't stop her from getting involved when residents at a nunnery were threatened and one was murdered. She had serious and unexpected adversaries, members of the I.R.A.

- *Late, Late in the Evening* (1976): Buried treasure and a possible inheritance figured in the motivations when a young girl was killed and a remittance man disappeared. Dame Beatrice came on the scene in a medical capacity, to treat the missing family member, so she had an interest in finding him. She did—dead in a hole in an abandoned cottage.

- *Noonday and Night* (1977): Dame Beatrice had a long-time interest in antique kitchen and dining ware. Her expertise came in handy when she was hired by County Bus Tours to investigate the disappearances of three of their drivers while on duty.

- *Fault in the Structure* (1977): There was also fault in the structure of this disjointed narrative. Alfrist Swinburne (who changed his name to T. E. Lawrence) had been a rotter since childhood. Sir Ferdinand Lestrange, Dame Beatrice's son, was called in because of his legal expertise. However, more than legal expertise was needed when Lawrence's second (bigamous) wife's body was unearthed. Lawrence avoided blame because of a strong alibi. Dame Beatrice remembered the family years later when Lawrence himself was murdered.

- *Mingled With Venom* (1978): Romula, a 70-year-old-widow, must have known she was setting herself up when she invited possible heirs and heiresses to be her guests at a family dinner. It had been expected that she would make an announcement, but she delayed, preferring to dangle her wealth in front of potential aspirants. When she was poisoned, the family called Dame Beatrice in to investigate.

■ *The Mudflats of the Dead* (1979): Colin Palgrave, seeking a breakthrough on his writer's block, set off on a holiday. Because of a booking error, he found himself sharing a cottage with five others. One was the fiancée he had dumped; another, her husband. A third drowned under suspicious circumstances. The other couple contacted Dame Beatrice, who had time on her hands.

■ *Uncoffin'd Clay* (1980): Michael, a widowed writer, narrated the incidents, which occurred when a sheik purchased property in a rural English area, including the disappearance and murder of a shady real estate dealer. He sought Dame Beatrice out and acted as her assistant. There were signs of Gladys Mitchell's declining narrative powers.

■ *Lovers, Make Moan* (1981): A local production of *A Midsummer Nights'es and* was the background for murder. Laura and Dame Beatrice were in the audience when the cast member playing Bottom stabbed himself with a real dagger exchanged for a prop. Had he been the target of the killer, or was it the man whose part he had taken over at the last minute?

■ *Here Lies Gloria Mundy* (1982): Dame Beatrice was a house guest of Anthony Wotton, who possessed a portrait resembling Gloria Mundy, a woman who had figured in the lives of Wotton and two college classmates. Then Gloria appeared in person and was killed——or was she?

■ *Cold, Lone and Still* (1983): Alan, a literary agent, had a second sight experience as a child, so when he and his fiancée, Hera, tripped over a corpse while hiking on the moor, and later found the victim alive, he went to Dame Beatrice as a psychiatrist.

■ *No Winding Sheet* (1984) detailed the disappearance of a schoolmaster who had a briefcase full of money. After his body was located, two students disappeared. Dame Beatrice was consulted, but her role was minimal. Laura and a detective inspector did most of the work.

■ *The Crozier Pharaohs* (1984): This was the last of the Mitchell crime novels, and along with the two prior ones was published after her death. Dame Beatrice and Laura resided at her country home, where they worked on her memoirs. The Rout sisters, who raised Pharaoh Hounds, called on Dame Beatrice when their kennel maid, Susan, found a partly clad corpse while searching for a missing dog. A second corpse was found in an area where Susan had been walking the dogs. Dame Beatrice believed there had been an earlier murder, that of the Rout sisters' father, a local doctor. An exhumation led to the killer.

Helene Brand
Author: Craig Rice, pseudonym for Georgiana Ann Randolph

See: Helene Brand Justus, Section 3, page 56.

Angela Bredon
Author: Ronald Knox

Although insurance investigator Miles Bredon occasionally had wife Angela accompany him on cases as he traveled through rural England, her contributions were not professional. It was not for lack of intelligence or interest. During World War I, Angela had chauffeured military brass around London, and she was a bright young woman.

The couple was introduced in *The Three Taps* (Methuen, 1927), when technicalities as to euthanasia in an insurance policy written by Miles' employer, the Indescribable Company, made it important to determine whether or not a man committed suicide. Although the narrator described Angela as more clever than her husband, she had little opportunity to prove him right. Her involvement was limited to seeking information from potential heirs and guests at the inn where the death took place.

Angela paddled up an English river as Miles pulled a towrope to trace a missing policyholder whose creditors could collect only if he were proven dead in *The Footsteps at the Lock* (Methuen, 1928). She had a high tolerance for "bores," and was willing to listen to rambling conversations in an effort to find information that she could relay to her husband.

While Miles protected his company's interest in a policy on a wayward son during *Still Dead* (Hodder & Stoughton, 1934), Angela listened to the local gossip by mixing with the townspeople, talked with those suspects and witnesses with whom Miles lacked rapport, reported on events that took place when he was absent, and served as a sounding board for his theories.

In *The Body in the Silo* (Dutton, 1934) aka *Settled Out of Court*, the Bredons accepted a weekend invitation to a country estate from casual acquaintances, only to find a fellow guest in the farm silo. A high spirited game of "elopement" had established the alibis for most of the suspects, but Bredon saw past the initial murder to the one yet to be committed.

When Miles and Angela occupied a gardener's cottage in *Double Cross Purposes* (Hodder & Stoughton, 1937) to watch over a treasure hunt on a Scottish estate, Angela found a key to the outcome and penetrated a disguise.

Very little physical description or background information on Angela was provided.

Carey Brent

Author: M. W. Glidden

Authenticity did not have a high value in this series. Carey Brent was identified as working for the Federal Secret Service under the supervision of Captain Ramsey. She had control over a group of agents, but operated primarily through her lover/partner George McFarland. McFarland, nicknamed "The Automaton" because of his stiff composure, lack of expression, and diligence, was known to be a private investigator. Carey, nicknamed the "Butterfly," was a socialite, noted for her lack of intelligence. She was stated to have attended college. Admission standards may have been lower at this time.

All public matters went through McFarland to protect Carey's secret role in the investigations.

Carey's approach to investigation was modern for the period. She used a camera to photograph documents and measured footprints. Although she and McFarland met at a secret house, she owned a penthouse and a country estate for public appearances and was driven by a chauffeur. Frequently she proclaimed her need for action, excitement, and even danger—a habit that McFarland hoped to temper when, and if, they married.

Murder occurred at her country estate, Shadow Hill, in *Death Strikes Home* (Phoenix, 1937). A man whom Carey did not recognize was the victim. Claire Fontane, a personal friend, was obviously withholding information as to his identity. While McFarland monitored Claire's effort to escape from a blackmailer, Carey went undercover in a state prison, knowing her life was at risk, but determined to find the inmate/mastermind.

Carey's ties to a federal agency were no better explained in *The Long Island Murders* (Phoenix, 1937). Both she and McFarland were present at an elaborate party during which a notorious womanizer was killed. While Carey continued her role as a flighty young socialite, their hostess asked McFarland to investigate. Several of the guests had motives to kill the victim, and the hostess had connections to a group smuggling Chinese aliens into the United States. Carey's determination to do more than work behind the scenes led to her capture by the smugglers. She managed her own escape. In the conclusion, she and McFarland let the killer go unpunished.

Phoenix Press was a frequent supplier of lending libraries.

Eileen "Bundle" Brent

Author: Agatha Christie

Bundle Brent, the radical young daughter of a noble English family, was one of Agatha Christie's minor creations. She appeared in two novels in the Twenties, but never achieved the fame or tenure of Tuppence Beresford.

Bundle appeared mid-narrative in *The Secret of Chimneys* (Dodd, 1925) as a guest at Chimneys, a country estate where assorted killers, secret agents, and victims were spending the weekend looking for crown jewels and injudicious letters. Among the victims was the heir to the throne of Herzoslovakia, so British Intelligence and Scotland Yard became involved. During the investigation Bundle met Bill Eversleigh, a Foreign Office bureaucrat who fell in love with her.

Four years later Bundle and her father returned to Chimneys in *The Seven Dials Mystery* (Dodd, 1929). After a practical joke gone awry, a young Foreign Office employee died of an overdose, but Bundle was certain this was no accident. Her further investigation convinced her that foreign agents, known as the "Seven Dials," were the culprits. Fortunately Inspector Battle of Scotland Yard intervened to prove otherwise.

The narratives seem simplistic when re-read, but at the time they were written, blended the humor of Wodehouse with the thrills of Oppenheim.

Rosie Bright

Author: Judge Ruegg, K.C.

Rosie Bright was a small but well proportioned lower class Londoner, who had little education but was cheerful and warm hearted. She had been a dancer and the mistress of a stingy nobleman.

In *John Clutterbuck* (Daniel, 1923), Attorney Clutterbuck met Rosie when he sought to clear a young friend, Roger Cheveley, of the murder of his older brother Edward, the Earl of Elvington. The motive was there. Now Roger became the Earl and could care for the woman he had secretly married two years before. Clutterbuck discovered letters from Rosie to Edward. She had been his mistress, but was not his killer. Clutterbuck's collapse into epilepsy revealed his secrets.

By *David Betterton* (Daniel, 1931), Rosie had become a contented rural housewife and stepmother in what was less a mystery than a second-rate novel. Betterton, a man with a past, had been helped by Rosie to begin a new and successful life as an actor. Even then, he was a victim of black-mail, relieved only by events occurring during his service in World War I.

Avis Bryden

Author: Eden Phillpotts

Avis Bryden was neither a heroine nor an investigator, but a villainess. Nor was she likely to arouse much sympathy as a young widow, because she caused her husband's suicide. She was amoral, killing without compunction to advance her personal or economic goals.

In *Bred in the Bone* (Macmillan, 1933), Avis wanted financial security. She had been poor, but she didn't intend to stay that way. Her marriage to Peter Bryden was facilitated when she became pregnant. His brother Lawrence, who had title to the family estate, was killed. When Peter seemed about to confess his guilt in Lawrence's murder, she wanted him dead.

By *Witch's Cauldron* (Macmillan, 1933), Avis, then 45 and widowed, devoted herself to son Peter and the further expansion of the family farms. Her determination that Peter marry into additional wealth, although he was deeply in love with a farmhand's daughter, drove her to two murders. She lost Peter's love when he became aware of her depravity, but escaped conviction for her crimes.

In her most sympathetic showing, *A Shadow Passes* (Macmillan, 1934), Avis resisted the blandishments of a rascally young man that they conspire to kill his wealthy aunt. Instead she nursed the elderly woman tenderly and killed the nephew. Habits were hard to break.

Avis fit a pattern that interested Phillpotts, an amateur rural sociologist. Her father, a fisherman, had killed her uncle in order to inherit. Avis was uneducated but shrewd, and had no belief in any religion or moral standards. She was stronger than the men she loved, a rural Lady Macbeth without remorse.

Amanda Fitton Campion
Author: Marjorie Allingham

Amanda Fitton, a tiny redhead who became an airplane designer, was in her teens when she met effete British sleuth Albert Campion. During *The Fear Sign* aka *The Kingdom of Death* (Doubleday, 1933), Campion and his friends restored the Fitton family to their rightful heritage, membership in a foreign nobility, convincing Amanda that he was the man she intended to marry. She did not contact Albert for seven years; instead, she finished her education and went into business.

When they met in *The Fashion in Shrouds* (Doubleday, 1938), the age differential did not seem as important. Peter's subterfuge in a murder investigation was that he and Amanda were engaged. Amanda rescued him from a killer and earned a genuine proposal.

Albert dallied about until Amanda became interested in a powerful and dangerous entrepreneur in *Traitor's Purse* (Doubleday, 1941). A bout of amnesia prompted him to re-evaluate his life and win Amanda back.

She used her electrical skills and her insights in *The Beckoning Lady* (Doubleday, 1955), but gradually faded out of the action in the series. What a shame! Amanda was an enchanting heroine, spirited, intelligent, and independent. The couple had a son, Rupert, who made minor appearances.

Mary Carner
Author: Zelda Popkin

Mary Carner was a matter-of-fact young woman whose involvement in crime was based on her job as a department store detective. Slim, "pretty and well groomed," with brown hair and eyes, Mary blended easily into the crowded store aisles. She held strong opinions, smoked, swore, and was active in a professional woman's group.

Death Wears a White Gardenia (Lippincott, 1938) began when a veteran shoplifter found a corpse in the delivery area of the Blankfort store during the 50th anniversary sale. The victim, Andrew J. McAndrew, was probably involved in blackmailing. Mary, helped by a tip from a flower seller, traced an illicit liaison to find the killer.

By *Time Off for Murder* (Lippincott, 1940), Mary and her supervisor Chris Whittaker were dating. She was interested in the disappearance and subsequent death of young attorney Phyllis Knight, who had been assisting the police in a criminal investigation. Mary networked successfully with other women professionals (including a judge, a prison psychologist, a theatrical producer, and a former prostitute) to find the killer.

Murder in the Mist (Lippincott, 1940) took the couple on their honeymoon at a New England seaside hotel. When Nola Spain, resident in an adjacent room, was murdered, her tiny daughter attracted Mary's attention. First Mary had to prove that neither she nor Chris was the killer. They provided care for the child, "Baby Doll," whom they eventually adopted, then Mary convinced the local authorities that she could help in the investigation. Having a child did not cause Mary to retire from her job.

Dead Man's Gift (Lippincott, 1941) was based on an extended family in an isolated location scenario. Mary accompanied her co-worker, Veronica Carmichael, to Pitt Haven. Veronica had been notified that she was the heiress of Michael Carmichael, a man of whom she knew nothing. Mary, Veronica, and others who might have inherited were stranded at the family estate when the Susquehanna River overflowed. After the corpse of Michael's sister was found, Mary took charge and reopened the question as to whether or not Michael's death had been a natural one. Once the waters receded, the local authorities wanted Mary to mind her own business. Not likely.

By *No Crime for a Lady* (Lippincott, 1942), Mary and Chris had settled down, but she could not ignore the explosion that killed the local political boss Harry Martz. While Chris stayed home babysitting, Mary and a friendly police officer discovered the intended victim. This was not a "couples" series. Chris was happy to leave his profession at the store.

Although advanced as to Mary's role, the books were dated by their dialogue.

Georgia Cavendish

Author: Nicholas Blake, pseudonym for Cecil Day-Lewis

See: Georgia Cavendish Strangeways, Section 3, page 97.

Nora Charles

Author: Dashiell Hammett

Although best remembered for his tough private investigators, Dashiell Hammett was responsible for the popularity of the "couples" mystery. Hammett established the characters of Nick and Nora Charles in *The Thin Man* (Knopf, 1934), stating later that he patterned them on his relationship with playwright Lillian Hellman. Fortunately for mystery fans, the movie version starring actress Myrna Loy turned Nora into a much more winsome character than the acerbic Miss Hellman. The film relationship between Nick (played by William Powell) and Nora was warm and sophisticated. Their popularity cloned similar series in books, and radio and television shows.

Clarice Claremont

Author: Claudia Cranston

Clarice Claremont, who narrated, neither described herself physically nor gave any background material, except that she was a Texan who now lived in a New York hotel. Although she worked as a copywriter for a New York City department store, she was convinced that she had special investigative skills and "a fever to detect which came upon her at the scene of a crime."

With the assistance of her docile beau, Dick Kent, Clarice put these talents to work in *Murder on Fifth Avenue* (Lippincott, 1934) when pressures at the department store ended in the murder of Miss Carteret, a new employee who had responsibility for making changes. She did not initiate the changes. Mr. Reiser did so, but Miss Carteret was given the task of bringing them about, thereby alienating long-time employees. Clarice found the corpse and was targeted by the police as the killer. She had returned to the store to get Miss Carteret's approval of an ad. The paper, which had been moved, could have the killer's fingerprints on it, a matter Clarice withheld from the police for some time.

During *Murder Maritime* (Lippincott, 1935), Clarice was on a transatlantic ship with a demonstration car in which she was to tour Europe. Her credibility with the captain was damaged when she saw what she considered attempted murder and the participants denied it. The intended victim later turned up dead in Clarice's car. A confusing and badly written book.

Lizzie Collins

Author: E. Laurie Long aka Ernest Long

Lizzie Collins was a plucky lower class English sleuth during the Thirties. While working as a waitress, she was recruited for a job as stewardess for the Molson ship line.

In *Port of Destination* (Eldon, 1933), penniless orphan Lizzie was to watch over spoiled young Dorothy Wharton, daughter of the ship-owner, who had quarreled with her naval officer husband. The voyage provided Dorothy with a chance to grow up and Lizzie with a mystery and a handsome Secret Service agent, who had disguised himself as a seaman. He proposed, but Lizzie felt the difference in their social standing made marriage impossible.

In *Foul Hawsers* (Ward, 1935), Lizzie was promoted to Chief Stewardess on a slack ship. Pieters Patterson, her suitor, was also on board. Lizzie saved Joan, Dorothy Wharton's infant, from Chinese warlords, earning a second proposal, which she accepted.

Lizzie convinced her husband to retire from the service, but in *A Cumshaw Cruise* (Ward, 1937), they returned to rescue a young heiress and foil an Italian plot to hobble the British navy.

By *Unhappy Ship* (Ward, 1951), Lizzie was the widowed and childless Lady Patterson. Recruited again by the Molson Line, she and her old pals kept a sinking ship afloat and solved the personal problems of staff and passengers before the voyage ended. Although identified elsewhere as a Lizzie Collins mystery, *Purser's Mate* (Ward, 1938) was not.

The series was remarkable for its time in England, when sleuths of either sex tended to be rich, educated, and socially prominent.

Bertha Cool

Author: A. A. Fair, pseudonym for Erle Stanley Gardner

The 29-book series subtitled *Bertha Cool/Donald Lam* failed to make it clear how small a part Bertha played. She was described by disbarred attorney/ narrator Donald Lam as unattractive, with small gray eyes and gray hair that turned white. She had poor clothes sense and wore too much jewelry, but must have had some charm because she received gestures of affection from Sgt. Frank Sellers, Lam's nemesis. Bertha cursed, complained, and was tightfisted about Donald's expenses. Donald, a cocky little man with many of the required characteristics of the "private eye" genre, was a woman chaser who never had a successful long-term relationship. Bertha was a widow, whose husband had been unfaithful. She began overeating during the un-happy marriage, and weight was always a problem for her (varying from 160 to well over 200 pounds).

According to *Traps Need Fresh Bait* (Morrow, 1967), she indulged herself away from the office. In her luxurious apartment, she changed into pajamas and a silk robe, and listened to classical music! Although Bertha showed no compassion for indigent clients, she went to great lengths for those who paid, and when the chips were down, she rescued Donald from assorted police and sheriff departments.

The series followed a pattern. The first book, *The Bigger They Come* (Morrow, 1939), found Donald applying for a job at the B. L. Cool Agency, not realizing he would be working for a woman. Donald and Bertha worked together, but it wasn't easy. From then on, the plots usually began with Donald entering the office to find Bertha interviewing a prospective client. Whatever story the client told about his or her plight was only half-true. There was always a hidden agenda and a surprise ending. Bertha, after working out the financial details, would send Donald out on the case, and often not reappear until the concluding chapter.

Turn on the Heat (Morrow, 1940) was the second in the series, during which Bertha still had some authority over Donald's behavior. They worked together on locating a wife who had disappeared during divorce proceedings, unaware that their client was the husband, now practicing medicine under a different name and married (bigamously?) to his nurse. It didn't help that a woman who claimed to be the wife turned out to be an imposter, and then a corpse. Donald and Bertha both resorted to chicanery.

Repeatedly, as in *Fools Die on Friday* (Morrow, 1947), Bertha was depicted as a mercenary woman without any personal interest in the clients or in justice. Even less appealing was the frequency with which Donald and Sellers expected Bertha to bully, threaten, or muscle female suspects: *Beware the Curves* (Morrow, 1956), *Some Slips Don't Show* (Morrow, 1957), *Bachelors Get Lonely* (Morrow, 1961), *Try Anything Once* (Morrow, 1962), *Fish or Cut Bait* (Morrow, 1963), *Cut Thin to Win* (Morrow, 1965), *Widows Wear Weeds* (Morrow, 1966), *Traps Need Fresh Bait* (Morrow, 1967). Meanwhile Donald was the primary who solved the crimes.

In *Some Women Won't Wait* (Morrow, 1953), Bertha was not only ineffective at solving the murders in the case, but was duped into being a witness for the killer.

She saved Sgt. Frank Seller's life in *Bedrooms Have Windows* (Morrow, 1949), although he preferred to believe it was an accidental move on her part. Donald had been working a possible murder-suicide, but became a suspect in a third death. Bertha's fall over a suspect's wheelchair solved the case.

Her best chances came during World War II when Donald served in the U.S. Navy.

During *Spill the Jackpot* (Morrow, 1941), Bertha had been ill and her weight was down to 160. A client helped her diet by complimenting her on her appearance, but when he was cheap about the fee for finding his son's missing fiancée, she dumped him and her appetite returned.

In that weakened condition, she agreed in *Double or Quits* (Morrow, 1941) to Donald's demand for a partnership. They had worked together on a theft investigation that changed focus when their client died under suspicious circumstances. The goal then became to prove it had not been suicide in order to get an insurance payout. Donald's maneuvering almost got him killed.

When Donald went in the service, Bertha, then in her fifties, did her own fieldwork. In *Bats Fly at Dusk* (Morrow, 1942), she sought the missing victim in a car accident, and the cause of wealthy Harlow Milbers' death. It was during this case that Bertha met Sgt. Frank Sellers. Totally confused, Bertha wrote the details to Donald. He solved the case on a 36-hour pass. All Bertha got out of the experience was a kiss from Sellers.

Cats Prowl at Night (Morrow, 1943), the only book in which Bertha dominated, which was not narrated by Lam. Although Bertha was ready to go back to her more limited practice while Donald was in service, she could not resist a client who looked wealthy. When a murder occurred in her client's home, Bertha and Frank Sellers worked together, but not without problems. Bertha was knocked unconscious and sued for defamation of character. Gardner just wasn't fair when it came to giving Bertha a break.

The following other titles were all published by Morrow:

Gold Comes in Bricks (1940): Donald had a chance to use his recently acquired jiu jitsu lessons when he and Bertha were hired to learn what Henry Ashbury's daughter Alta was doing with her money. The case brought them into gambling and stock fraud. Since Bertha had purchased some of the bogus stock, she couldn't complain when Donald tricked the manipulator into buying it back. The narrative revealed more of Bertha's background—why she had become so mercenary and demanding.

Owls Don't Blink (1942) featured a new title for the firm, Cool and Lam. Donald narrated his adventures in New Orleans, seeking Roberta Fenn for an attorney who needed her to close an estate. Roberta was located, only to disappear after a murder was committed in her apartment. A second party was also looking for Roberta. At one point Cool and Lam weren't sure that their client wasn't the killer. Bertha had been busy setting up a construction company in the hope that it would keep Donald from being drafted. He volunteered, joining the navy.

Give 'Em the Ax (1944): Bertha was lean and mean, stressed by trying to keep the agency going, when Donald returned from his wartime service. Not one of Gardner/Fair's better efforts, as the duo dealt with lying clients and suspects. Bertha used her feminine lures, such as they were, to keep Sellers from jailing Donald.

Crows Can't Count (1946) found Bertha and Donald working for Harry Sharples, who was concerned about his young ward Shirley's behavior with regard to income from a trust set up by Cora Hendricks. They found the corpse of Sharples' co-trustee, Robert Cameron, when they went to question him. The title referred to the scattered emeralds found near the victim's body and in the cage of a talking crow. Donald and Bertha eventually traveled to Columbia, where Cora, Sharples, and Cameron had been involved with emeralds. After Bertha and Donald were evicted from Columbia by the local police, he figured it out.

Top of the Heap (1952): Donald got all the action in this one, looking for a pair of young women who had been picked up at a "nitery" by John Carver Billings II. This led him into financial shenanigans by brokers and mobsters. Smart tips enabled Donald to come out of it with major profits. When he returned to the office, Bertha was scratching his name off the door. His threat to open up his own agency convinced her to welcome him back.

In *You Can Die Laughing* (1957), another search for a recent heiress kept Donald busy. Yvonne Wells was either still alive or someone was impersonating her. If she was dead, someone else would inherit the property, which may have uranium resources. Instead of working with Bertha, Donald teamed with Frank Sellers on this one.

The Count of Nine (1958): Bertha was in charge when the firm was hired to screen guests at an exclusive party held by Dean Crockett II. It did her reputation no good when antique items (a blowgun and a jade piece) were stolen during the event. Donald took over and located both missing items. He insisted on handing them over to Crockett himself, but it was too late. Crockett was found dead in his private apartment, having been shot with a blowgun. Crockett's wife then hired Donald to find the killer so that she would not be charged with the murder. Again Donald and Sellers had the action. Bertha's appearance was limited to her initial screw-up.

In *Pass the Gravy* (1959) Bertha was representing Daphne Beckley in a search for her missing husband when 15-year-old Sandra Eden tried to hire her to find her missing uncle, Amos Gage. Bertha turned Sandra down, but Donald saw a connection between the two cases and eventually convinced Bertha to coordinate. If Amos were to be convicted of a crime, i.e., the murder of Daphne's husband, he could not inherit from a family trust. They eventually sort it out, but too late for justice

During *Kept Women Can't Quit* (1960), Bertha (who designated herself as B. Cool on the agency sign) came to Sgt. Frank Seller's assistance when he was accused of skimming $50,000 off recovered funds from an armored car robbery. Donald was tracing Standley Downer, who purportedly left town with $60,000 of his wife's money. Donald's plan was to keep the money safe by mailing it to himself. That didn't work out when he became the prime suspect in Standley's death and someone intercepted the mail. Only when Donald was in serious trouble did Bertha show up. She had the $50,000. It was not the armored truck money, but Hazel Downer's. Whatever—they earned a reward and Bertha got credit for straightening things out.

By *Shills Can't Cash Chips* (1961) Donald had his own secretary, Elsie, who also assisted on his cases. It was she who came up with a significant clue that explained the connections between two hit-and-run accidents and a bank robbery. That, along with some rough stuff by Bertha, produced a confession to bank robbery and murder.

In *Up for Grabs* (1964) Donald did the fieldwork while Bertha played "Nero Wolfe" at the office. Between them they worked a case involving fraud to insurance companies.

During *All Grass Isn't Green* (1970), not telling the truth about why they wanted to find a missing person seems endemic among the Cool/Lam clientele. Donald had a chance to use his legal training when he coached a client to represent himself in court.

It can be noted that Erle Stanley Gardner did not give Della Street much attention either.

Patricia "Pat" Preston Cordry

Author: James O'Hanlon

Patricia Preston, a trim young redhead from Wyoming, married one of the worst dolts in mystery fiction, Jason Cordry. The Cordrys lived in the Los Angeles area while working as movie extras. When Jason involved himself in other people's business, including murder, Pat was drawn in against her better judgment.

In *Murder at Malibu* (Phoenix, 1937), after actress Lilyan Layton, a movie star with whom they had minimal contact, was killed, Jason investigated her "accidental" death, receiving a reward when he was successful.

Jason had a winning bet at the racetrack in *Murder at 300 to 1* (Phoenix, 1938). When a nearby gambler was murdered, Jason fled to avoid suspicion.

The Cordrys moved to the East Coast for *Murder at Coney Island* (Phoenix, 1939), a narrative featuring midgets, sword swallowers, and snake charmers as characters.

While Pat supported Jason and his racehorse in *As Good As Murdered* (Random, 1940), he worked on a screenplay featuring a "Mysterious Stranger" who was paid to confess to a crime he did not commit in order to protect the real conspirators. When this actually happened in his life, Jason failed to involve Pat.

While out West in *Murder at Horsethief* (Phoenix, 1941), the Cordrys' car ran out of gas near a drunken lynching party. Pat worked as a dancing girl in a local revue to gather evidence that Jason used to avoid his own hanging. The series ran out of gas much earlier.

O'Hanlon's writing was inept and intolerant. There were unpleasant references to "the mingling of the races." Phoenix Press, which published the series, churned out third-rate mysteries for lending library consumption.

Kay Cornish

Author: Virginia Hanson

Kay Cornish, a blue-eyed redhead from Chicago and the daughter of a widowed college professor, was a magazine writer.

In *Death Walks the Post* (Doubleday, 1938), she visited her fiancé, Charlie, at a Midwestern Army post. When a young woman was shot at a party attended by Kay, Major Adam Drew, who headed the investigation, asked her to take notes. However, she concealed clues because of her loyalty to Charlie.

During *Casual Slaughter* (Doubleday, 1939), Adam was preoccupied with attacks on servicemen and civilian personnel by a masked robber who disrobed his victims. When a young lieutenant was implicated in the crimes, Kay challenged the Army authorities to prove his innocence. Adam's amnesia left him unwilling to make a commitment to Kay.

Mystery for Mary (Doubleday, 1942) was written as a journal by a retired general to his deceased wife, exploring the relationships of two extended households living near an Army base. Using the journal as a resource, Kay and Adam solved a mystery. The general, in turn, helped Adam to put his past behind him and plan to marry.

Although the focus of the mystery genre had moved from puzzles and cozies to hard-boiled investigators, Doubleday, aware that the women's market for light mystery fiction still existed, continued to publish for it, not necessarily at a high quality.

Susan Dare

Author: Mignon Eberhart

Susan Dare, who appeared in a collection of short stories, *The Cases of Susan Dare* (Doubleday, 1934), was a tiny woman with fair hair. After gaining experience in crime while writing short stories, Susan became a consultant to the Chicago Police Department. She actively participated in investigations, posing as a nurse, substituting herself for a victim, and risking attack. Although she worked with newspaperman Jim Byrne, she used her own deductive skills to solve crimes.

Anne "Davvie" Davenport

Author: Margaret (Evelyn Tayler) Yates

See: Anne "Davvie" Davenport McLean, Section 3, page 70.

Fidelity Dove

Author: David Durham aka Roy Vickers

Fidelity Dove appeared in a collection of short stories, *The Exploits of Fidelity Dove* (Hodder, 1924). Her role as an altruistic avenger was similar to those of Daphne Wrayne and Angel Brown, who had extended careers in later years.

Fidelity, an ash blonde with violet eyes, had the face of an angel. This helped her gather a coterie of actors, scientists, electricians, and artists who worked with her to solve crimes which baffled the authorities. More principled than Daphne or Angel, she was also duller.

Nancy Drew
Author: Carolyn Keene, house name for the Stratemeyer Syndicate

The perennially 16-year-old blonde Nancy Drew had a profound effect on girls growing up in the Thirties and Forties. The daughter of a widowed criminal defense attorney, she lived a charmed life, enjoying luxuries her readers never even considered—a roadster, a horse, and access to an airplane. Motherless, she was free to take risks, move about without restrictions, and avoid the drudgeries of helping around the house.

Nancy shared her adventures with sweet Bess Marvin, tomboy "George" Frayne, and All-American boy Ned Nickerson. She became modernized in updated versions, but never grew up. The Stratemeyer syndicate had learned with Ruth Fielding that young readers fell by the wayside when the heroine matured.

Nancy has lasted through millions of books and a hundred titles without ever casting a vote, paying taxes, or making a total commitment. Readers interested in Nancy are directed to:

- Bobby Ann Mason's *The Girl Sleuth*, which covers Nancy and her contemporaries Judy Bolton and the Dana Sisters;
- Betsy Caprio's *The Mystery of Nancy Drew*; and
- Carol Billman's *The Secret of the Stratemeyer Syndicate*.
- Mabel Maney ridiculed Nancy and her imitators in a Nancy Clue series that will not please Nancy's fans. See Volume III.
- The outstanding book on the authors of the Nancy Drew Series, Melanie Rehak's *Girl Sleuth: Nancy Drew and the Women Who Created Her*.

Iris Pattison Duluth
Author: Patrick Quentin, pseudonym for Hugh Wheeler and Richard Webb

Iris Pattison, a brunette with "sad" eyes, had problems with "melancholia," (clinical depression).

Her father had committed suicide as a result of his financial problems during the Depression.

During treatment in a private sanitarium in *Puzzle for Fools* (Simon, 1936), she met alcoholic Broadway producer Peter Duluth. As he returned to sobriety, Peter investigated the murders of a staff member and a patient for which Iris was a suspect.

Iris and Peter rebuilt their lives together around the theater. In *Puzzle for Players* (Simon, 1938), she made her debut in a play produced by Peter in a theatre with a history of violent death. The cast included almost as many disturbed personalities as had been found in the sanitarium. A theatre fire that recalled his wife's death sent Peter off on a binge, during which he married Iris.

By *Puzzle for Puppets* (Simon, 1944), Peter was on leave from the Navy, while Iris worked in Hollywood movies. On their second honeymoon, the Duluths proved that Peter, whose uniform had been stolen in a Turkish bath, did not kill Eulalia, Iris' look-alike cousin.

Iris had the spotlight in *A Puzzle for Wantons* aka *Slay the Loose Ladies* (Simon, 1945). Peter was on leave but Iris had become a star. While visiting at a Nevada estate, Iris set a trap for a murderer.

Iris had virtually no role in *Puzzle for Fiends* (Simon, 1946) or *Run to Death* (Simon, 1948). The Duluth marriage was in trouble in *Puzzle for Pilgrims* (Simon, 1947). They reconciled only after a tragic death and mutual disappointments in love affairs.

Earlier in their marriage, Iris had left Peter for another man. Peter had no such plans when he befriended Nanny Ordway in *Black Widow* (Simon, 1952) during Iris' vacation. Nanny's schemes led to her murder, but also to Peter's selection by the police as her killer.

Peter and Iris were on the sidelines in *My Son, the Murderer* (Simon, 1954), narrated by Jake Duluth, Peter's brother. Jake, already despondent over the suicide of his wife, took another blow when his partner, Ronnie Sheldon, was murdered, purportedly by Jake's son. Although initially Jake had assumed Bill's guilt, as evidence piled up against the young man, Jake came to believe in him. He rallied Peter and Iris to prove he was right. So, which of the men and women whom Ronnie had abused had killed him?

Iris and Peter were among the least happy couples in mystery fiction. Both Peter and Iris seemed drawn to troubled individuals and unable to live with or without one another. Although there was some humor in the series during the wartime books, most were gloomy and brooding.

Valerie Dundas

Author: Virginia Rath

Rath selected an unusual occupation for her amateur detective Michael Dundas—couturier. Michael was a new tenant in a San Francisco apartment house when he met his future wife, Valerie. She was then an unhappy young woman lacking self-confidence, who lived with her neurotic mother and a rich stepsister. Rath patterned her couple on the "Nick and Nora" series, and reference was made to them in the introduction.

In *The Dark Cavalier* (Doubleday, 1938), Michael and Valerie worked together to solve two separate murders before she learned that he was "Gisele," designer of women's clothes and the owner of a well-known specialty shop.

As *Murder with a Theme Song* (Doubleday, 1939) began, Michael and Valerie encountered a former acquaintance, Edith Parnell, once a nurse in the home where a famous kidnapping had taken place. In a story reminiscent of the Lindbergh kidnapping, Michael, with very little involvement by Valerie and an assist from sheriff Rocky Allan, solved the nurse's murder and a series of other crimes.

Death of a Lucky Lady (Doubleday, 1940) barely mentioned Valerie's name, but Michael ended up in the hospital while working to solve a mystery with roots in California history.

The Dundases accepted an invitation to stay at Summit House, an inn partly financed by San Francisco businessman Barney Gould, in *Death Breaks the Ring* (Doubleday, 1941). During their visit, they became aware of the romantic entanglements within Barney's family that led to murder. Even after the weekend, the Dundases kept in touch with their new friends, and eventually Michael unraveled the mystery.

Epitaph for Lydia (Doubleday, 1942) had little to do with Valerie. She was available to Michael on social occasions but it was he who followed up on the death of a young woman who had been on her way to visit him when killed.

In *Posted for Murder* (Doubleday, 1942), Michael's cousin, Ian Maclean, and his rigid wife, Adela, visited San Francisco. Ian's romantic indiscretion with former girlfriend Toni had enraged Adela, leading to an unpleasant scene. Ian left the home they were visiting to cool off, but on his return found Adela dead. Knowing that he would be the obvious suspect, Ian contacted Michael for help. Michael's response was to knock him unconscious and place him in a sanitarium so that he could not turn himself in, until the murderer had been found.

In *A Dirge for Her* (Ziff-Davis, 1947), Valerie never even appeared. She was visiting her mother in New York City. Michael, suspected of murdering a former employee, had to clear himself to protect his business interests.

Wealthy Rowena Talcott had left her home seven years ago. In *A Shroud for Rowena* (Ziff-Davis, 1947), her potential heirs were eagerly anticipating the end of the seven-year period before she could be declared legally dead, but there was some evidence that she might have returned. Her brother Chris sought Michael for help, but he was on his way back from overseas. Valerie took charge temporarily, but faded into the background as soon as Michael returned.

Valerie perceived herself as uninhibited and independent, à la Nora Charles, but her participation was limited to questioning female suspects and eavesdropping. She did offer some "feminine" insights as to the character of other women. Valerie had no children, and no employment or career goals. A maid did her housework. She was patronizing when referring to "colored" servants. Michael and Valerie enjoyed square dancing and had an active social life, but she seemed to have no independent interests. She was rarely described physically, but referred to as "girlish."

Jane Amanda Edwards

Author: Charlotte Murray Russell

Jane Amanda Edwards was a middle-aged spinster, who bullied her sister Annie and emasculated her brother Arthur. As a young girl she had been an active "tomboy"; in adulthood, she was a heavyset woman weighing close to 200 pounds. She used her strength in several incidents (once knocking a killer down a flight of stairs).

The Edwards family lived in a northern Illinois city called Rockport (Rockford?) but the narratives were occasionally set elsewhere: Chicago (*The Tiny Diamond*, Doubleday, 1937), Wisconsin (*I Heard the Death Bell*, Doubleday, 1940), and Mexico (*Ill Met in Mexico*, Doubleday, 1948).

The middle class Edwards family was comfortable for their period, employing a servant, able to forgo working out of the home except as a wartime service (*No Time for Crime*, Doubleday, 1945).

When the war ended (*The Bad Neighbor Murder*, Doubleday, 1946), Jane reverted to a more leisurely life, available to assist Police Chief George Hammond. He earned his home cooked meals at the Edwards house by sharing the details of his cases.

In *Murder at the Old Stone House* (Doubleday, 1935), Hammond had asked Jane to take notes during a murder investigation. He was often Jane's ticket into the investigation, and she envisioned her role as prodding him into action. He seemed tolerant of her aggressive, rude behavior.

She removed mail from mailboxes, opened, and read it (*Death of an Eloquent Man*, Doubleday, 1936), and not surprisingly irritated someone enough to take a shot at her.

Annie was the target of humor when she showed an interest in spiritualism (*Hand Me a Crime*, Doubleday, 1949), but the focus was more frequently on Arthur's misbehavior. He got drunk. He fell in love with unsuitable women (*The Clue of the Naked Eye*, Doubleday, 1939). He involved himself in politics, or financial deals, and ended up a suspect in a murder. During *The Message of the Mute Dog* (Doubleday, 1942), when Arthur worked as a factory security guard, he was suspected of industrial sabotage. Jane had to rescue him over and over again, returning him humiliated to the family home and her dominance. Arthur was supposed to be comic relief, but he was pitiable.

Jane threatened to write a cookbook in *Cook Up a Crime* (Doubleday, 1951), but her pursuit of recipes was diverted when Arthur found a corpse and came under suspicion.

Jane's persistence was not always a negative. Her sifting through a vacuum cleaner bag (*The Tiny Diamond*, Doubleday, 1937) provided a clue to a murderer.

Jane was hard working and sensible but unappealing, and the books were relatively boring.

Fah Lo Suee
Author: Sax Rohmer, pseudonym for Arthur Henry Sarsfield Ward

Fah Lo Suee, tall and slim, with emerald eyes and dark hair, was the daughter of Rohmer's most famous villain, Fu Manchu, and a Russian mother. A talented woman, who spoke several languages, she assisted her father in his evil schemes but had her own interests.

Fah Lo Suee became a leader of the rejuvenated Si Fan organization, rivaling her father (*Daughter of Fu Manchu*, Doubleday, 1931), and released her father's prisoner, Shan Greville, because she loved him (*The Mask of Fu Manchu*, Doubleday, 1932).

She resented her father's dynastic plans and sabotaged Fu Manchu's intended marriage to a young and unwilling bride in the hopes of a male heir (*Fu Manchu's Bride*, Doubleday, 1933).

Her rebellious nature led to her death (*The Trail of Fu Manchu*, Doubleday, 1934). Rohmer resurrected her under the name Koreani, "reincarnated, with no memory of the past," to do her father's will (*The Drums of Fu Manchu*, Doubleday, 1939).

Her characters fit into the popular notion of Oriental women as scheming beauties—"Dragon Ladies" (as illustrated in Milton Caniff's comic strip *Terry and the Pirates*).

Peggy Fairfield

Author: E. S. Liddon

Peggy Fairfield, as described by her college chum Millie, was determinedly feminine, small, and slightly plump, sporting a Southern drawl, blonde "ringlets," frills, and ruffles even at age 30.

In *The Riddle of the Russian Princess* (Doubleday, 1934), Peggy investigated the disappearance of a Russian brooch and the death of its owner, forcing a suicide by her suspicions.

By *The Riddle of the Florentine Folio* (Doubleday, 1935), Peggy, a student of criminology, used scientific methods to investigate the death of wealthy Ophelia Clifford and the destruction of her will. The series was promoted by Doubleday for female readers.

Amanda Fitton

Author: Marjorie Allingham

See: Amanda Fitton Campion, Section 3, page 38.

Solange Fontaine

Author: F. Tennyson Jesse

Solange Fontaine was a Parisienne, the daughter of an Englishwoman and a French scientist. After her mother's death, Solange became the assistant in her father's police laboratory. She had short fair hair, olive-gray eyes, and a boyish physique. Even though expert at chemical analysis, metric photography, and fingerprints, Solange depended upon her instincts. She could "smell" evil. *The Solange Stories* (Macmillan, 1931) detailed her use of visions and dreams in a series of short stories.

Four Square Jane

Author: Edgar Wallace

Jane was not a detective—although she posed as one on occasion—but a thief who donated robbery proceeds to charity or stole property to which she had a claim. In *Four Square Jane* (Readers Library, 1929) she was matched against Scotland Yard Inspector Peter Dawes. Dawes sought out Jane's potential victims, whose valuable treasures were ill gotten. Her real identity was revealed only when she and her husband had left England for South America taking considerable wealth with them.

Meg Garret

Author: Collin Brooks

Margaret Evelyn Garret was small, slightly plump, fair-haired, the daughter of a solid landowning family. She was athletic, swam, rode, hunted, and could handle a revolver. At the time they met, Raeburn Steel was looking for a woman partner, not an assistant, for his Confidential Agency.

Although Steel had impressive credentials—a bachelor's degree in medicine, a law degree, and service in British Intelligence during World War I—Meg could match them. After serving in the Women's Auxiliary Army Corps, she earned a Ph.D. from a minor English university (Ladyport) and was referred to as "Doctor Dimples" by her contemporaries. Steel was impressed to learn that she was the author of *Kantian Categories in Relation to Behaviorism*. Who wouldn't be! When he offered Meg the partnership, it was on the condition that she not marry. She participated fully in interviews at the insistence of Steel, who would not allow her contribution to be minimized.

The couple's first assignment was to discover the identity of *Mister X* (Hutchinson, 1927), mastermind of a Communist inspired plot to derail negotiations among the British government, Eire (Ireland), and the United States. The Irish representatives were suspected of the death of an American detective, but Meg believed them to be innocent. When Meg was kidnapped on a yacht, Steel, now in love with her, pursued them in a British destroyer commanded by his brother.

In *The Body Snatchers* (Hutchinson, 1927) their marital and professional partnership had been established in a combined home/office in London. A reporter, concerned that his editor had disappeared, approached them. Not only did Scotland Yard Inspector Forray join the investigation, but so did his twin daughters (Josephine and Jacqueline). Meg and Raeburn uncovered a plot to obtain secret information about a new oil extraction process.

During *The Ghost Hunters* (Hutchinson, 1928) a bet at a house party at Marly Grange ended in the death of one woman and serious mental disturbance in another. Meg and Steel visited the Grange accompanied by the Inspector and his daughters, posing as servants. Meg occupied the "haunted" room while Steel pretended to return to the city, exposing a plot to gain control of valuable resources.

Ellen Gilchrist

Author: Margaret Behrens

See: Ellen Gilchrist Soames, Section 3, page 94.

Coco Hastings

Author: Lenore Offord

Coco Hastings, a petite redhead, worked in an antique store, selling silver and glassware. She and her husband, Bill, had two small children and lived in San Francisco, where he worked for an electrical equipment company.

As *Murder on Russian Hill* (Macrae-Smith, 1938) began, Coco thought she would enjoy a murder. When her boss was killed, she became a suspect, and then an endangered amateur investigator. Not always enjoyable.

In *Clues to Burn* (Duell, Sloan & Pearce, 1942) the Hastings visited a college friend at her island home. During the visit Sally's stepson Joel disappeared, and a mentally ill woman was found dead after a fall from a seaside bluff. Coco lost her composure when Bill was injured, and used a gun to force her fellow guests to cooperate in her investigation.

Anne Holt

Author: Theodora DuBois

See: Anne Holt McNeill, Section 3, page 71.

Juliet Jackson

Author: Margaret Turnbull

"Female Ferret" was the nickname given to petite young widow Juliet Jackson, because of her relentless search for inside information. She had bobbed red-brown hair and cat-green eyes. Because Juliet had ghostwritten the stories assigned to her handsome but alcoholic newspaperman husband, she was hired as a reporter after his death. Their only child, Julian, was placed with friends of the family on the West Coast. For all of these problems, Juliet was not portrayed as tragic or single minded. She was good-humored, liked to dance and tease. She had a small New York City apartment and when possible, visited her son.

In *Madame Judas* (Lippincott, 1926), Eve, a schoolmate of Juliet's, was convinced that the man accused of killing a popular doctor was innocent. Juliet played an active role in gaining valuable information for his defense.

During *Rogues March* (Lippincott, 1928), while Juliet traveled by transcontinental train, she met a young woman who was being returned for a murder trial. In the belief that she was being "railroaded," Juliet canceled her vacation to cover the trial. Although ambitious, Juliet concealed the real killer.

Juliet's assignment in *The Return of Jenny Weaver* (Lippincott, 1932) allowed her to be near Julian, then living with a friend of his father. Architect Bill Davis, who loved Juliet, helped her trace a skeleton believed to be that of a young woman who had disappeared several years before. When Julian was almost kidnapped, Bill questioned Juliet's care of her son.

He turned his attention to another young woman in *The Coast Road Murder* (Lippincott, 1934). When an uninvited guest was murdered at a party attended by Juliet and Bill, the local police chief sought her help because the investigation required "new methods—psychology, analysis, or woman's instinct, or whatever your specialty is." Juliet agreed as long as she could "scoop" the other papers. Her increased awareness of a child's need for a home helped her make the decision to marry Bill.

The books were notable for better than average courtroom scenes for the period.

Helene Brand Justus

Author: Craig Rice, pseudonym for Georgiana Ann Randolph

Helene Brand Justus represented a type, popular 60-plus years ago, but anachronistic today, the "madcap heroine." She added warmth and class to her co-sleuths: public relations expert Jake Justus and seedy criminal attorney John J. Malone. Helene was a tall, slim blue-eyed blonde, who was deeply affected by her parents' divorce and her mother's multiple marriages. Even in the Depression, the Brand family was wealthy and socially prominent, but there was a dangerous, risk-taking edge to Helene, which showed in her drinking and driving. Helene needed someone who offered her stability.

Jake Justus might not have been considered a likely prospect, but the chemistry was there. Malone, who later came to dominate the series, was tiresome, unable to sustain a long-term relationship with a woman, frequently drunk, and chronically behind on his bills. Still, Craig Rice managed to make the relationships among the trio believable.

In *8 Faces at 3* (Simon, 1939), Jake accompanied friend Dick Dayton to pick up Dayton's new bride, Holly, only to find her under arrest for the murder of her wealthy Aunt Alexandria. Helene, a friend of Holly's, made her appearance dressed in a fur coat, overshoes, and satin pajamas. She, Jake, and Malone arranged Holly's escape, hiding her in a brothel until the real killer was identified.

In *The Corpse Steps Out* (Simon, 1940), Jake discovered the corpse of a blackmailer, but did not contact the police and learned later that the body was missing. Helene rented an apartment in the victim's building to reclaim missing letters, and aided the others when they shifted corpses in her car.

Helene and Jake's plans to marry were delayed in both *The Wrong Murder* (Simon, 1940) and *The Right Murder* (Simon, 1941) by a bet Jake made with adventuress Mona McClane. Mona bet her nightclub that she could commit a murder in public and get away with it. Helene had an active role, proving Jake's innocence when he was jailed for murder.

Jake and Helene ventured into rural Wisconsin in *Trial by Fury* (Simon, 1941), only to learn that the natives were not all friendly. As Illinois residents, they were prime suspects when a local politician was murdered. Malone, who came to their rescue, barely escaped a lynch mob.

During *The Big Midget Murder* (Simon, 1942) Jake owed a loan shark money borrowed to remodel his casino. When the trio found a midget comedian dead in a dressing room, they stuffed him in a bull fiddle case to remove him from the premises.

Jake and Malone got into trouble when they traveled to New York City in *Having a Wonderful Crime* (Simon, 1943). Helene hired a gigolo, set herself up to be robbed, and, in a risky incident, recovered missing jewels. From then on, they worked together to find the killer.

Malone, who had few intimates besides Helene and Jake, fell in love with an accused murderess in *The Lucky Stiff* (Simon, 1945) and needed his friends.

The most intriguing plot in the series was in *The Fourth Postman* (Simon, 1948), when Malone discovered why three mailmen had been murdered on the same route. Helene played only a minor role, as she did in *Knocked for a Loop* (Simon, 1957). Malone looked for the killer, who left a corpse in his office while the Justuses spent most of their time looking for one another. The emphasis had shifted and Malone dominated the series. The Justuses had minor roles in *My Kingdom for a Hearse* (Simon, 1957).

But the Doctor Died (Lancer, 1967) was based on a manuscript found after Craig Rice's death. Helene was hypnotized by conspirators seeking to take control of a company where she worked. Malone, who had always loved Helene, cleared her name when she became a murder suspect. It was an injustice to Craig Rice to publish this inferior material.

Drunkenness, disregard for speed limits, moving corpses, and breaking out of jail are not so funny anymore. Today Helene might be seen as deeply troubled, in need of psychological counseling, rather than a "madcap heiress." The setting and the dialogue represent a place and time that no longer exist, at least not in Helene's age group.

Sarah Keate

Author: Mignon Eberhart

Sarah Keate was a no-nonsense registered nurse who frequently worked with the police. She was a plump middle-aged woman with long red hair. After service as an Army nurse in World War I, Sarah did private duty work in hospitals and homes. She had accepted a spinster role for herself, although she showed some interest in police detective Lance O'Leary.

Sarah was the supervising night nurse at St. Ann's Hospital in *The Patient in Room 18* (Doubleday, 1929) when she discovered a patient murdered, the radium with which he was being treated stolen, and the body of the hospital chief of staff stuffed in a closet.

In *The Mystery of Hunting's End* (Doubleday, 1930) Sarah accepted assignment to a private residence where O'Leary was a houseguest, available to investigate a death that had occurred five years before.

A lonely mansion provided the setting for *While the Patient Slept* (Doubleday, 1930). When a family member was shot the first night that Sarah was on duty, she called on O'Leary for assistance.

From This Dark Stairway (Doubleday, 1931) brought Sarah back to a hospital setting. Without hesitation she stole and hid clues to a murder to protect a young nurse suspected of killing a surgeon.

In *Murder by an Aristocrat* (Doubleday, 1932), her patient was a young man believed to have injured himself. Attempted suicide seemed less likely after several attempts were made to enter the patient's room, the last ending in his death. Eventually Sarah accepted a confession from the killer with the understanding that it could be revealed if an innocent person were accused.

The Wolf in Man's Clothing (Random, 1942) was a wartime story about Nazi spies. With O'Leary gone, Sarah depended upon the assistance of local police and her injured patient to prove the innocence of a young nurse.

In *Man Missing* (Random, 1954) Sarah served as a civilian employee at a U.S. Navy hospital. During her watch, Sarah found a young Navy lieutenant with his throat cut. A more assertive, self-reliant Sarah protected Sally, a widowed young WAVE ensign, from suspicion.

Eberhart went heavy on atmosphere (ghostly music, dimly lit rooms, mysterious footsteps), but her later books had more action.

Gwynn Leith Keats

Author: Viola Brothers Shore

Gwynn Leith, a college graduate and writer whose inquisitiveness caused her to become an amateur detective, was married twice. Gwynn's first husband, a young pilot, disappeared behind enemy lines during World War I. Her second husband, Colin Keats, chronicled her adventures in two books. They met when he visited an old friend, who happened to be Gwynn's brother.

He was attracted to the tall, brown-haired widow during *The Beauty Mask Murder* (Smith, 1930) when he was a suspect in the violent death of a female blackmailer. The convoluted narrative posed a number of red herrings before Gwynn uncovered the killer, who was conveniently allowed to kill herself.

The couple had married by *Murder on the Glass Floor* (Smith, 1932) and were working on a play in Paris when a group of friends convinced them to return to New York for the holidays. During the voyage, a sinister young woman who was connected with many of Gwynn's friends, including her former brother-in-law, was murdered. Although Gwynn and Colin discovered the killer, they did not disclose his identity to the police.

Gwynn made another appearance in a short story printed in Ellery Queen's *101 Years' Entertainment* (Modern Library, 1941).

Olga Knaresbrook

Author: Hazel Campbell

In *Olga Knaresbrook, Detective* (Long, 1933) Olga was described as "callous and unsexed." She and her demure cousin Molly Kingsley joined together in an investigation agency. Molly was to take notes while Olga did real detection, but author Hazel Campbell surprised her readers.

Sophie Lang

Author: Frederick Irving Anderson

What was to be expected of a woman appearing in a book entitled *The Notorious Sophie Lang* (Heinemann, 1925)? During short stories, Sophie Lang, a demure-appearing female, assumed multiple identities, always one step ahead of the police. She posed as a French maid, a Spanish-Irish art curator, and a fashion model, always eluding her nemesis, Deputy Parr.

Grace Latham

Author: Leslie Ford, pseudonym for Zenith Jones Brown

Grace Latham, an attractive 38-year-old blonde widow of independent means, appeared in 15 murder mysteries during the 1930's and 1940's. She was rarely the primary in the case. Her frequent rescuer and admirer, Colonel John Primrose, made the deductions. She kept busy loyally defending her friends, reuniting young couples, and concealing valuable information.

Grace, the widow of an attorney who was killed in a plane crash, was wealthy enough to live in a gracious Georgetown home, employ an African-American servant, and educate two sons in fashionable prep schools. She was above average in height (5' 7"), trim but not slim, with light hair and brown eyes. A gracious woman with social skills, young enough to be attractive to men, she never remarried. Primrose was ten years older and considered a confirmed bachelor. When he finally did propose, it was too late in the relationship and Grace refused him. Anyway, Sergeant Phineas Buck, Primrose's aide and houseman, would have made for a difficult ménage à trois.

Grace often participated in investigations as the person who discovered the body, as a witness to events leading to the murder, or as a loyal friend of a suspect.

In *Ill Met by Moonlight* (Farrar, 1937), Grace housed a friend's overflow guests, Colonel Primrose and Sergeant Buck, at her summer place in April Harbor Colony. When a young wife was murdered, Grace furnished Primrose with inside information as to the relationships among the suspects.

In *The Simple Way of Poison* (Farrar, 1937), the nearly simultaneous deaths of Grace's friend Randall Nash and his first wife could determine who would inherit. Primrose used Grace's excellent memory to reconstruct the events of the evening.

In *Three Bright Pebbles* (Farrar, 1938), when Dan Winthrop returned from Paris, he learned that his sweetheart had married his brother, Rick. Rick was sufficiently unpopular so that there were several suspects when he was shot with an arrow. Primrose was not available to help on this one.

During *Reno Rendezvous* (Farrar, 1939) Grace's niece spent the time prior to her divorce with a debonair playboy, who was murdered. Primrose proved her innocence and rescued Grace from an anxious killer.

False to Any Man (Scribners, 1939) used the by now familiar pattern wherein young lovers were separated by a quarrel or family interference. When the lovers met again, one of the pair was involved in murder.

Old Lover's Ghost (Scribners, 1940) took place in Yellowstone Park, where a young woman learned that her "dead" fiancé was employed as a park ranger.

As wartime came to the United States, domestic murder was replaced by espionage. *The Murder of a Fifth Columnist* (Scribners, 1941) related the death of a newspaperman who had threatened to expose the publisher of a fascist newsletter.

In *Murder in the O.P.M.* (Scribners, 1942) the director of the Office of Price Management was found dead along the Georgetown Canal. Grace and Primrose thwarted a conspiracy to seize a new process for extraction of valuable minerals.

While Grace was in San Francisco in *Siren in the Night* (Scribners, 1943) an air raid warden discovered a corpse when he entered a home to extinguish a light. At Primrose's request, Grace became acquainted with the neighbors, learning the character of the victim and the reason for his death.

When, in *All for the Love of a Lady* (Scribners, 1944), a returning soldier visited a married woman just before her older husband was murdered, Grace and Primrose reluctantly confronted a killer and notified the authorities.

During *The Philadelphia Murder Story* (Scribners, 1945) an ambitious writer used Grace to meet the family of a judge whom he was profiling. When the author was murdered, the manuscript disappeared and the family was under suspicion.

While Primrose was investigating the death of a young sentry on Oahu in *Honolulu Story* (Scribners, 1946), Grace visited friends and gained insights, that helped Primrose in his assignment. The narrative was marred by its treatment of interracial marriage, although the attitude probably was consistent with the times.

In *The Woman in Black* (Scribners, 1947), an indiscreet young woman who feared that she had compromised her husband's government work consulted Grace for advice. With Primrose suffering from the measles, Grace had to depend on Sergeant Buck in a subsequent murder investigation.

The Colonel scolded Grace in *The Devil's Stronghold* (Scribners, 1948) for "reckless excursions," concealing evidence, and unrealistic trust in people. These negative characteristics were all displayed by Grace when son Bill and a friend encountered murder while helping a young actress.

Washington Whispers Murder (Scribners, 1953) was set at the time of the McCarthy hearings. An unscrupulous congressman was exposed and the killer of a reporter arrested through the connivance of Grace, Primrose, and Buck.

Anne Layton

Author: Marion Roberts

The "couples" series was never as popular in England as in the United States. Anne Layton and her husband, David, were secretly allied with Scotland Yard, investigating cases where an official presence would stifle information. Anne, the daughter of a Scottish Earl, had "dark plaited hair with deep blue eyes," lived in Chelsea, and partied within a powerful and wealthy level of society.

During *Red Greed* (Eldon, 1934) Anne was kidnapped by Chamorin, a Red spymaster who was infatuated with her, even though she refused to join in his activities.

The Laytons were in the East in *A Mask for Crime* (Eldon, 1935) when Anne met Chamorin again, still determined to win her over. He eventually died, while saving Anne's life. She was more a pawn or victim, than an investigator.

Gwynn Leith

Author: Viola Brothers Shore

See: Gwynn Leith Keats, Section 3, page 59.

Baroness Clara Linz

Author: E. Phillips Oppenheim

The Baroness, who was English by birth but married an Austrian, belonged to an international secret service agency in *Advice, Ltd.* (Little, 1936). She was a sophisticated woman, who smoked using a cigarette holder and lived in a fashionable London home. In a series of adventures, the Baroness shared assignments with other members of the group, solving problems and mending romances along the way.

Lynn MacDonald

Author: Kay Cleaver Strahan

Lynn MacDonald's physical appearance stressed her need for anonymity. She was above average height, and was well built but not overweight, had "carroty" red-gold bobbed hair and gray eyes, and was well dressed. Her dominant characteristic was competence, rather than flair. Other characters in the series were better developed, partly because Lynn often entered the story after the plot was well advanced.

In *The Meriweather Mystery* (Doubleday, 1932) Lynn was called to the scene of the crime because a wealthy young man who was a suspect in a murder did not believe the local police were capable. Her arrival by plane was delayed, but within 24 hours she had identified the killer, although she needed time to determine the motive.

Lynn was a professional investigator with a $10,000 contingency fee in *The Desert Moon Mystery* (Doubleday, 1928). She solved a mystery primarily through reading letters in *Footprints* (Doubleday, 1929), and she came incognito as a nurse into a household in *Death Traps* (Doubleday, 1930).

The plots were intricate, with bizarre aspects, including characters assuming other identities, a man masquerading as a woman in *October House* (Gollancz, 1931), and a 24-year-old midget posing as a child in *The Hobgoblin Murder* (Bobbs, 1934).

During *The Desert Lake Mystery* (Bobbs, 1936), an isolated party vacationing in the wilderness was decimated by murder and disappearances, while their powerful and dominating host dictated policy to the sheriff/narrator. Lynn arrived, late in the narrative, to sort things out. Strahan situated many of the stories in a Western locale, peopled with tangled family groups. There were multiple deaths, often ending when the murderer committed suicide or died accidentally. Strahan generally provided a surprise ending.

Sue MacVeigh

Author: Sue MacVeigh, pseudonym for Elizabeth Custer Nearing

Except for the fact that she was physically small, there was almost no personal information about Sue MacVeigh. She and her husband, Captain Andrew MacVeigh, a railroad detective, had no children or pets. Their lives were bounded by Andy's job and the people with whom he worked.

In *Murder Under Construction* (Houghton, 1939) Sue and Andy went undercover when a railroad official was threatened. Sue ingratiated herself with the wives of the suspects, sharing with Andy the hostilities and jealousy within the group.

She had a smaller role in the next two books, *Grand Central Murder* (Houghton, 1939), where Andy scanned the railroad yards for a killer, and *Streamlined Murder* (Houghton, 1940), where the couple traveled on the maiden voyage of a new streamlined train.

Sue emerged on her own in the wartime *The Corpse and the Three Ex-Husbands* (Houghton, 1941) when she visited her cousin Henry in Michigan. Two suspicious deaths occurred when the extended family was isolated by road and weather conditions. Sue used unmailed letters to Andy to relate her suspicions and deductions to the reader. Eventually she, Cousin Henry, and a local police officer solved the murders.

Although the books were not highly regarded as suspense literature, they provided mildly interesting insights into the fraternity of railroad families.

Jane Marple

Author: Agatha Christie

A tall spare woman with erect carriage, Jane Marple was described as white-haired with pale blue eyes. The reader was allowed to assume a modest but secure income based upon inherited money.

Jane enjoyed interests common to those in her social position: gardening, sketching, and knitting. She showed an unexpected gift of mimicry (*A Murder Is Announced,* 1950) and on rare occasions became very angry (*A Pocket Full of Rye,* 1954). All books in the series were published by Dodd in the United States and by Collins in England except where noted.

Jane's father had been able to provide her with some foreign education (*Murder With Mirrors,* 1952), but she was essentially a rural English character, most at home in the village of St. Mary Mead. Further evidence of Miss Marple's adequate income would be her occasional trips to London—to stay, of course, *At Bertram's Hotel* (1966); the succession of maids who received their training in her household (*A Pocket Full of Rye,* 1954); and her comfortable relationships with the local gentry (*The Tuesday Club Murders,* 1933).

The characteristic of Jane Marple that pervaded the series was her sense of evil. She was aware of evil as a constant presence within the human character. The village of St. Mary Mead was her textbook for crime. Frequently as she puzzled over new relationships, she remembered parallel situations, such as the local dentist who wanted to divert business to his father, the maid who would believe anything a handsome young man told her, or the solicitor's son who couldn't settle down.

As a laboratory technician could recognize the tuberculosis bacilli from a prior pictorial representation, so Jane Marple could call upon her recollections to recognize the presence of evil in new and different surroundings. There were extensive periods of time between the early books, but Jane took on a life of her own. She was allowed to grow older, even somewhat forgetful, but continued to be attentive to those around her and to make new friends, including among younger people.

When Jane was introduced in *The Murder at the Vicarage* (1930), she appeared in her garden with her "bird watching binoculars" and might have been dismissed as an old busybody. She worked with the local vicar and a police official, piecing together bits of information and baiting a trap for the conspirators to murder.

As *The Body in the Library* (1942) opened, Dolly Bantry called upon Jane when her husband was suspected in the death of a flashily dressed young woman found on his library floor.

In *The Moving Finger* (1942), a young man, sent off to recuperate in the country, and his sister were disturbed by vicious anonymous letters. Although Jane appeared late in the book, she saw the flaw in the profile of the poison pen writer built up by the police.

The "murder game" became an overworked gimmick but in *A Murder Is Announced* (1950) it still had freshness. An advertisement in the local weekly paper announced that a murder would take place at 6:30 p.m. on October 29th at Little Paddock.

The reader glimpsed a younger Jane Marple when she was reunited with old school friends in *Murder With Mirrors* aka *They Do It With Mirrors* (1952). In order to safeguard her friend Carrie Louise, whose idealistic husband ran a residence for juvenile delinquents, Jane visited and became a confidante to staff and students.

A Pocket Full of Rye (1954) seemed contrived because of the effort to fit the deaths of a businessman, his second wife, and an adenoidal maid, once employed by Jane, into the nursery rhyme.

What Mrs. McGillicuddy Saw aka *4:50 from Paddington* (1957) focused on an unhappy family when Jane's friend, Elspeth, saw a murder committed while riding a train. Jane recruited a younger woman to go undercover as a maid.

During *The Mirror Crack'd* (1963) aka *The Mirror Crack'd from Side to Side,* the visit of a film company to the St. Mary Mead community highlighted the changes from the isolated village of the earlier books and the new community of supermarkets and housing developments. There was, of course, still murder, and old friend Dolly Bantry brought Jane on scene to solve it.

Jane took her skills on tour in *A Caribbean Mystery* (1965) when she vacationed in the West Indies, becoming embroiled in the death of a man who had been about to say something very important. Jane acquired an ally in the prickly invalid Mr. Rafiel, who helped prevent another murder.

Jane noticed that something was not quite right *At Bertram's Hotel* (1966), where she regularly stayed when she visited London.

Mr. Rafiel, impressed by Jane's sense of evil when they met in the West Indies, challenged her in *Nemesis* (1971) to right a wrong.

Sleeping Murder (1976) had been written during World War II and set aside for later publication. The home purchased by Gwenda and Giles Reed seemed oddly familiar, giving Gwenda a flashback of a murder she may have witnessed as a child. Jane warned Gwenda and Giles that it might be wise to "let sleeping murders lie."

The most common criticism of Christie has been that she concentrated on plot to the detriment of characterization, but she had memorable characters in her books, many of whom were women. Her books can be reread over a period of years with fresh enjoyment.

Those who knew Miss Marple through the books would have been horrified by the boisterous portrayal given by actress Margaret Rutherford in early movies adapted from the Christie narratives. Television producers were more respectful of the Jane Marple character, employing women of quiet dignity and intelligence, such as Helen Hayes and other less well known but equally appropriate actresses to play the part.

Emma Marsh

Author: Elizabeth Dean

Emma Marsh, although not the narrator, received very little description: 26 years old, a smoker, with "large" feet (whatever that was in 1939) and black hair. She was the secretary and assistant to Jeff Graham in his Boston antique business, and showed considerable knowledge of the field. Emma eventually earned a proposal from her long-time "boyfriend," Hank Fairbanks, an investigator who served in U.S. Navy Intelligence during the wartime portion of the series. Hank was an inconsiderate suitor, but suited Emma.

Murder Is a Collector's Item (Doubleday, 1939) placed Emma in a difficult position. She returned to the antique shop one night to find a corpse on the floor and her employer missing. The police, who were unsympathetic to Emma's sense of loyalty to her boss, sent her to jail for concealing information.

In *Murder Is a Serious Business* (Doubleday, 1940) Emma and Jeff's visit to a prospective client set her up as a suspect for murder, when she was identified as the heiress to one of the victims.

Although Hank played a dominant role in the first two books, in *Murder a Mile High* (Doubleday, 1944) Emma had an opportunity to work on her own. What began as the murder of an operatic tenor eventually included espionage and hidden treasure. Even though Hank joined in, Emma solved the murder, and found the treasure.

Kate Marsh

Author: Gret Lane

Kate Marsh had been born in England, moved to the United States as an infant, and returned to England as an adult. Because her mother died when she was 10, she had traveled the Orient with her father, learning several languages. She married fellow reporter Tony Marsh. The Marshes had no children, but owned a Pekingese, Cocoa, and a parrot, named Blaster

Murphy. Although she still managed an occasional magazine article, Kate's primary interest was in detecting with her friend John Barrin, a retired Scotland Yard inspector. Redheaded Kate was eager to get involved, while Tony was laid back, uninterested in detection, but willing to go along on the adventures to keep Kate happy.

In *The Curlew Coombe Mystery* (Jenkins, 1930) a client approached Barrin about his unattractive but wealthy sister's fiancé. The Marshes, posing as friends of the family, were present when the bride-to-be was murdered. Kate's knowledge of the Chinese language and Canadian accents and her attention to physical features led to the solution.

During *The Lantern House Affair* (Jenkins, 1931), Aldo Castro was concerned that his cousin, Ramon, intended to drive his wife, Louisa, mad to gain control of her inheritance. Kate and John Barrin arranged a fishing holiday for Tony in the area without making him aware of their hidden agenda.

As *The Hotel Cremona Mystery* (Jenkins, 1932) began, John Barrin and the Marshes needed temporary quarters and moved into a hotel. They shared their accommodations with a cruel mother, a jewel thief, and a compassionate killer.

In *The Unknown Enemy* (Jenkins, 1933) Barrin and the Marshes intervened when their friend Min Ling needed help to discover by whom potential heirs to a fortune were being murdered.

The Marshes and Barrins vacationed during *Death Visits the Summer-House* (Jenkins, 1939). Kate, who did not care to fish, spent her time listening to gossip about an elderly woman whose life was endangered by her husband's will.

The couples responded immediately in *Death in Mermaid Lane* (Jenkins, 1940) when Jennie Barrin's childhood friend needed help. Jennie and Kate became emotionally involved in the plight of a "mixed blood" child who might be related to a prominent family. The child's nurse, critically ill, was determined to survive until her mission was accomplished, but she died of cyanide poisoning.

By *Death Prowls the Cove* (Jenkins, 1942), Kate had built up an ensemble of helpers, including an American thug, a Chinese merchant, and a French crook. She needed them all when her neighbors turned out to be smugglers.

Tony's World War II service in the Navy during *The Guest with the Scythe* (Jenkins, 1943) ended when injuries caused him to be released. A trip to a rural spa was ostensibly to help Tony recover his health, but Kate had an agenda of her own, finding a blackmailer among the tenants of a rooming house. Thanks to her blackjack (named Bedelia) and her new dog, Taffy, Kate avoided becoming the victim of a killer.

The Cancelled Score Mystery (Jenkins, 1929) was still unavailable in 2005.

Dr. Joan Marvin

Author: Leonora Eyles

Dr. Joan Marvin was an unusual sleuth for the 1930's in that she was a short, stocky English psychologist who operated a free clinic for poor women. Although she was on occasion referred to as a psychologist, the work she did would indicate that she might have had a medical doctor's training.

In *Death of a Dog* (Hutchinson, 1936), Joan came to the rescue of columnist Lesley Fane, whose drunken husband, Jake, had taken their two children to Paris. Jake threatened to expose Joan, who may have broken the law by advocating birth control, but she encouraged Lesley to divorce him nonetheless. After someone killed Jake, Joan proved that Lesley was not responsible, discovered who the real killer was, and obtained a confession. There was more than a hint that she might have assisted the murderer to commit suicide.

In *They Wanted Him Dead* (Hutchinson, 1936), Inspector Jack Johnson was not sure that Greta, who had been imprisoned for the murder of her husband, was guilty. Johnson worked with Joan to solve the murder, and then he proposed to her.

Leslie Maughan

Author: Edgar Wallace

Leslie Maughan was the 22-year-old daughter of a deceased Assistant Commissioner at Scotland Yard. As with so many mystery heroines, her mother had died when she was young. Leslie's investigations as related in *The Girl From Scotland Yard* (Doubleday, 1927) were dependent upon coincidences. Independently wealthy, she was offered a position as assistant to a Chief Inspector. Although she worked on a variety of cases, the most important to her was proving that the man she came to love had been framed for forgery.

Gail McGurk

Author: Dwight Marfield

Missouri native Gail McGurk worked as a crime reporter in Chicago after graduating from college. When she moved to New York City, she carried with her a letter of introduction to Dudley Brent, the New York City District Attorney. Gail and Dudley spent both personal and professional time together. He referred to her as the "Little Woman from the West," and used her as an unofficial advisor. She carried a magnifying glass in her purse, which she used to examine evidence. Gail, a dainty woman with dark curly hair, lived in a hotel suite, but it was unclear how she supported herself.

In *Mystery of the East Wind* (Dutton, 1930), Brent and Gail were out for the evening when he was called to the East Wind Apartment complex, where a murder and a disappearance had taken place. Gail, who accompanied him, convinced Brent and Inspector Skane to recreate the crime.

As *The Man with a Paper Skull* (Dutton, 1932) opened, masked men invaded a wild party. When the police arrived, the lights dimmed and the host was murdered. Gail joined Brent at the murder scene and helped him locate a secret room where a suspect had hidden. Gail's accusation drove the murderer into a suicidal act, exposing his guilt.

In *The Sword in the Pool* (Dutton, 1932) a bank official, worried when a young heiress made a large withdrawal from her account, contacted the police. After the young woman's dead body was discovered in her pool, Gail unmasked the killer in a classic meeting of all the suspects.

Marfield had a few ingenious twists to his plots, but the books were confusing to read. There was evidence of bigotry, particularly by Inspector Skane.

Anne "Davvie" Davenport McLean

Author: Margaret (Evelyn Tayler) Yates

Anne "Davvie" Davenport, a tiny U.S. Navy nurse, married Dr. Hugh McLean, U.S.N., but this was not a "couples" series.

In *The Hush-Hush Murders* (Macmillan, 1937), Hugh was confined to quarters as a suspect after the death of Captain David Holmes' wife, Tamara. The action took place on a U.S. Navy vessel in the harbor at Shanghai. Davvie operated under authority as a member of a group investigating the disappearance of Bob Harvey, U.S. vice-consul for Shanghai. Harvey and Tamara were suspected of having a relationship. A typhoon in the area caused the ship to leave the harbor. A personal attack on Davvie led to her identification of a killer as her memory gradually returned. One positive result was the acknowledgement by Hugh and Anne that they were in love. When they married, naval regulations required her to resign her commission.

Death Sends a Cable (Macmillan, 1938) took place at the naval base at Guantanamo, Cuba. While Hugh was assigned to Tom Patterson's death officially, Davvie challenged the decision that he had killed himself. Her concern led her into a major espionage case.

Midway to Murder (Macmillan, 1941) returned the couple to the Pacific. Davvie went to Midway on assignment for Naval Intelligence, posing as a mystery writer. Somehow the locals decided she was author Leslie Ford under an assumed name, an unexpected bit of personal humor. She ordered fingerprints, measured footprints, and asked questions at a meeting of the residents called by Hugh.

The most interesting book in the series, *Murder by the Yard* (Macmillan, 1942), was set at Pearl Harbor during the December 7, 1941 weekend. Yates provided insights into the tension felt at that time by loyal Japanese-Americans, who were suspected of espionage. Chiyoko, Davvie's maid, and her husband tipped off Naval Intelligence when Davvie was abducted by Japanese spies.

Anne Holt McNeill

Author: Theodora DuBois

Initially Anne Holt was a single woman, who supported her hospitalized younger brother by working as caretaker for a motherless 9-year-old girl. She was described as more than usually beautiful, 5' 7", 125 pounds, with butter-colored hair and brown eyes. Over the years she aged from the mid-twenties to the later thirties. There were effusive comments about how irresistible she was to male characters in the stories. She enjoyed the compliments without encouraging the attentions.

In *Armed with a New Terror* (Houghton, 1936), Anne and a child were part of an extended household dependent upon the largesse of a dominating grandfather. Jeff McNeill, a neighbor and distant relative, intervened when Anne was accused of the murder of a cousin from whom she inherited. Anne loved Jeffrey, but he did not share his feelings for her until he had unmasked the surprise killer. This shy, at least temporarily indigent Anne became the glamorous, self-assured Mrs. McNeill of the later stories. She and Jeff had three sons, but they were significant to the plots only when their safety was threatened.

The McNeills were drawn into investigations not only through Jeffrey's work as a medical researcher and clinician, but through their relationships with other faculty members, as in *Death Wears a White Coat* (Houghton, 1938). Artist Alice Cramer was insistent that her husband Burton abandon his research career and move to Paris. Her subsequent death after being injected with medication for her thyroid condition by Burton was identified as murder. Burton and his nurse, Peggy, were the obvious suspects. Jeff focused on the physical evidence while Anne was more aware of other motives.

They also became involved through their interest in sailing, as in *Death Sails in a High Wind* (Doubleday, 1945), when their response to a call for help from Peter Shand led to the discovery of a dying female reporter. Nona Esmond was known to be investigating two stories: corruption of a public official and sewage leaking into oyster beds. Attacks were made on the McNeills, and the welfare of their son, Michael, was threatened. As additional murders occurred, the McNeills persisted, eventually physically overpowering the killer.

They encountered murder during visits to the homes of friends in *The Devil and Destiny,* (Doubleday, 1948). The body of Miles Sparkman's alcoholic wife was found in the swimming pool during a party attended by the McNeills. Jeff was called to check the body. Anne was more interested in the family skeletons revealed by the two Sparkman children as to a possible prior murder and multiple infidelities. The ending stretched credibility.

While visiting Ireland in *The Cavalier's Corpse* (Doubleday, 1952) they were asked to investigate the death of a young woman purportedly killed by a man dead 300 years. This would be a stretch even for the Irish.

Anne shared Jeff's official status during World War II. In *The Wild Duck Murders* (Doubleday, 1943), the couple worked together at the request of the FBI, investigating the murder of an informant about to expose a pro-Nazi group operating on the medical school campus.

In *The Case of the Perfumed Mouse* (Doubleday, 1944) residents of the Ivory Tower complex owned by a friend of Anne were bitten by rats. Anne solved the mystery when she learned of an obscure disease spread by rats attracted to perfume.

During *Murder Strikes an Atomic Unit* (Doubleday, 1946), Anne was included in the unit working on nuclear energy. Some of the young scientists had moral scruples about their work. When she and Jeff discovered a murderer and a spy, the murderer went unpunished.

Some later books hinged upon medical experimentation, such as in *The Footsteps* (Doubleday, 1947), wherein the family of Judge Joseph Role was troubled by fears of inherited insanity. Jeff, a surgeon, was asked to intervene in what was a psychiatric matter because of the McNeills' reputation as crime solvers. They were badly needed because a peripheral family member was setting Role's daughter Joan up for madness.

Another dysfunctional family appeared in *Money, Murder and the McNeills* aka *It's Raining Violence* (Doubleday, 1949). Former college professor Griswold Herbert subsidized a household that included his elderly wife and five of his six sons. His income was no longer sufficient to manage. Anne was contacted by a granddaughter who had been bilked of a substantial sum. Jeff was called in when a dying man was discovered on the family estate. During their investigation Anne was shot at and arrested. The discovery of the sixth son solved the case, but it was unrealistic.

Even on a much needed vacation in *Death Tears a Comic Strip* (Houghton, 1939), the McNeills could not avoid murder. Jeff's medical skills were needed when a neighbor of their hosts suffered from what was diagnosed as appendicitis. After Bigelow Dowd's death, Jeff realized that he had been ingesting morphine in his food and died from shock caused by its withdrawal. Only those who had access to the Dowd household could have planted the drug, but which one? A family member or a more casual visitor? Recent thefts of morphine from drug stores were tied in.

The McNeills rented a summer place during *Death Dines Out* (Houghton, 1939), but at a dinner party a wealthy man died of poison in the punch. Although Jeff did the scientific testing, it was Anne who tied motive and access together to identify the killer.

Jeff was out of town when, during *Death Comes to Tea* (Houghton, 1940), one of his associates died in the presence of five women. Anne was involved, but only until Jeff returned, when she was relieved to have him take charge. The murder was accomplished by the substitution of a poisonous substance for the cleaning fluid used on the victim's clothing. One killer was jailed, but another was allowed to leave the country due to lack of evidence.

By *The McNeills Chase a Ghost* (Houghton, 1941), Jeff was teaching at the medical school. They had a son, Michael, and a cat named Cornflakes. Thanks to household help, Anne was free to investigate a murder, that arose from the ghostwriting of academic material. The student who had discovered the fraud had been murdered.

Medical knowledge was often a factor in the solution of crimes, as in *The Body Goes Round and Round* (Houghton, 1942), when digitalis was added to party food, but only one person, already on medication, died. Someone should hire a food taster for the McNeills' meals.

The McNeills had a second son by *The Face of Hate* (Doubleday, 1948), but left the boys behind as they traveled down the Inland Waterway with a fleet of murder suspects. Unlike other narratives, this was written in third person, which diminished Anne's involvement.

When Anne and Jeff moved to a new home in *Fowl Play* (Doubleday, 1951), they had some unusual neighbors, including a mynah bird who inherited a fortune and relatives of the deceased testator who wished it an early death. Anne and Jeff took custody of the bird, which had the information to solve his owner's death.

Seeing Red (Doubleday, 1954) took place during the McCarthy era. Anne and Jeff, now parents of a third son, came under suspicion from events relating back to their work at Dr. Julian's Atomic Unit at the University. (See *Murder Strikes an Atomic Unit*, above.) They were threatened that Anne would be exposed as a Communist spy and that their sons would be harmed. Her connection was based on an unexplained gift of money and jewels. When she realized they were not from Jeff, Anne turned them over to an FBI agent, but unfortunately he was dead and could not testify on her behalf. Other members of the atomic unit urged Jeff not to investigate.

Anne was a sympathetic listener, causing suspects to share information that they would not have divulged to the authorities. She sometimes went "undercover" to build up such relationships, as in *Death Is Late to Lunch* (Houghton, 1941), when she saved a woman who was contemplating suicide, and *It's Raining Violence* (Doubleday, 1949), when she shot a suspect in the foot.

Anne's involvement was substantial early in the series, peaked during the war years, and then diminished. She narrated most of the early books, published by Houghton Mifflin. The later books, published by Doubleday through the Crime Club series, had no narrator, lessening her role.

Penny Mercer

Author: Henrietta Clandon,
pseudonym for John George Vahey, aka Vernon Loder

Penny Mercer and her husband, Vincent, were both authors. She wrote "sleuth stories" under the pseudonym Henrietta Clandon. The Mercers worked in tandem with Mr. Powers, an attorney who dabbled in detective work.

In *Fog Off Weymouth* (Bles, 1938), the Mercers encountered international espionage, but never clearly understood, nor did the reader, which characters were Special Branch or Scotland Yard, or who might be Nazi or Russian agents. Penny was captured but escaped by "coshing" one of the gang and sending a coded message to Vince.

In *Rope by Arrangement* (Bles, 1935), Penny helped author Montgomery Brace write a true crime book. He had testified at the trial of James Ponter for the death of his wife, Cecelia. Ponter had been unfaithful and had been found in possession of the murder weapon and was convicted. Brace's motivation in writing the book was to clear his name. Not only had there been rumors that he and Cecelia had an affair, but he was the residual heir of her estate, an honor he declined in favor of James' sister, Daphne. The book, published under a pseudonym, was a great success, but only increased suspicion that James may have been innocent. A strange narrative in which Penny played a minor role.

During *This Delicate Murder* (Bles, 1936), Vince and Penny joined a group of authors invited by an unpopular novelist to a shooting weekend. Not surprisingly, the host was the first thing shot. Much ado about the cartridge and shotgun bores, but Attorney Powers came on scene to help the Mercers solve the case.

Attorney Powers dominated *Power on the Scent* (Bles, 1937), but included Penny and Vincent in his investigation of two deaths blamed on a rose and a Great Dane, but tied to the cocaine trade. The ending was inconclusive.

The books were difficult to locate and dull to read (except for *Rope by Arrangement*), in part because the dialogue was dated. Vahey/Clandon tried to write light, humorous stories, but failed.

Daisy Jane Mott
Author: Jennifer Jones, pseudonym for Margaret Lane and Enid Johnson

Daisy Jane Mott, a plump spinster selling real estate in Reuterskill, New York, enjoyed her involvement in local theatre. *Murder-on-Hudson* (Crowell, 1937) opened with Daisy cruising the countryside to check for houses to sell. When she entered the vacant Thompkins place, she found the corpse of the local banker. The disappearance of the body did nothing to bolster Daisy's credibility with the police.

When Daisy took temporary residence in a summer cottage in *Murder al Fresco* (Doubleday, 1939), she was recruited by her new landlord to serve as prompter for a local theatre production. The very amateur star of the play was killed when a real knife was substituted for the stage prop. Evidence that Lotus, the victim, was a gossip gatherer who enjoyed disclosing negative information and may have been a blackmailer provided multiple suspects, but young Donna Wright's fingerprints were on the knife and a suicide note. Daisy finally talked the detective into letting her set a trap for the killer.

In *Dirge for a Dog* (Doubleday, 1939) Daisy's client Hannah had severe health problems, severe enough to cause her death after a series of accidents. Daisy was suspicious that Hannah's unconventional servants might be responsible or that her death was connected to the discovery of body parts scattered in various localities. Run of the mill.

Lucy Mott
Author: E. P. Oppenheim

Lucy Mott, a newspaper columnist who advised the lovelorn, seemed an unlikely heroine for *Ask Miss Mott* (Little, 1937). Still, she was as proficient with a gun as she was with a pen, and eager to enter the world of crime. She was assisted by her uncle, a Scotland Yard official, and by a handsome gentleman crook, Violet Joe, determined to become worthy of her love. With their help, Lucy rescued letters from a blackmailer, exposed titled criminals, and battled the Big Five of the criminal world.

Rachel and Jennifer Murdock
Author: D. B. Olsen, pseudonym for Dolores Hitchens

Septuagenarian spinster Rachel Murdock lived, and sometimes detected, with her even older sister, Jennifer. Rachel was petite and delicate with white hair, ready to rush in where the sturdier Jennifer feared to tread. The sisters, graduates of Miss Burton's School, were independently wealthy. Father had been a banker, and theirs had been a conservative Methodist upbringing. Rachel's wild streak was attributed to their mother, whose parents had been "in the theater." Rachel and Jennifer had a deceased brother, Philip, and a sister, Agatha. Both women were devoted to cats, and coal black Samantha featured in several of the narratives, which often had the word "cat" in the title. Rachel liked mystery books and movies, enjoyed an occasional drink, and did not scruple at lying to the police. She had no hesitation about entering other people's houses at night, misrepresenting herself, opening locked file drawers, or listening to conversations. She was socially conscious, as shown by her reactions to racial discrimination or intellectual arrogance. Over the series, she developed a reputation as an investigator, annoying the Los Angeles Police Department. Nevertheless, Lt. Steve Mayhew and his wife became her friends.

Rachel's first venture into crime detection came in *The Cat Saw Murder* (Doubleday, 1939), when she and Samantha visited Philip's adopted daughter, Lily. Lily was murdered, Rachel heavily drugged, and an attempt made to poison the cat.

The death of a child's pet frog aroused Rachel's interest in *The Alarm of the Black Cat* (Doubleday, 1942). Rachel had temporarily rented the house next door to young Claudia's family. Claudia lived with her widowed father, but only two houses away were her maternal grandparents. Rachel took personal risks because she believed that the child, who would inherit money from a trust left by her mother, was in danger.

In *Cat's Claw* (Doubleday, 1943), Rachel noticed a bandy-legged man watching a nearby house. Later he was struck by a car. The residents of the house he had been watching disappeared. After conferring with Mayhew, Rachel and Jennifer followed a lead to San Cayetano. They rented property on the estate of the Aldershot family, whose car had been involved in the accident. Jennifer discovered the body of a member of the Aldershot family who had been brutally murdered. She was ready to go home, but was convinced by Rachel to stay on one more night. A decision Rachel may have regretted when she was locked into a spider house.

During *Catspaw for Murder* (Doubleday, 1943), Prudence Milk sent Jennifer a drawing of a hand that had been slipped under her door and asked Rachel to advise her. Poor Prudence, already suffering from a nasty facial scar due to an attack, needed help. A young woman who resembled Prudence was killed. While investigating, Rachel fell and was injured sufficiently so that she had to move in with the major suspects. The local police mistrusted Rachel, but Mayhew was called in to help. Rachel disappeared, creating alarm, but turned up helping out in a local bar! Rather a poor trick on the reader was the exposure of a least likely suspect.

As *The Cat Wears a Noose* (Doubleday, 1944) began, Jennifer witnessed a murder while out for a walk, but was so traumatized that initially she did not share her experience with Rachel. The house where the death took place contained multiple suspects, but the family conspired to cast suspicion on young Shirley Grant. To get more information, Rachel hired on when the family cook quit. Lt. Mayhew was well aware of her motivation. Jennifer had a short stay in the local jail but handled it well.

In *Cats Don't Smile* (Doubleday, 1945), the sisters, while "house-sitting" for a cousin, were drawn into the murder of one of the boarders. Rachel was even more interested in the goings-on at the next door neighbor's. When an elderly invalid living there needed nursing care because his attendant had been murdered, Rachel volunteered to help. Her presence did not end the killing. The plotting was weak and unrealistic.

In *Cats Don't Need Coffins* (Doubleday, 1946) Rachel and Jennifer worked together when their hostess was found dead in bed, but she had not died there. Her body had been crushed elsewhere and then placed in the bed. A subsequent murder was equally bizarre. Incredulity piled upon incredulity.

The sisters traveled to Oregon in *The Cats Have Tall Shadows* (Doubleday, 1948), stopping at a beachside hotel with strange fellow guests. Away from Mayhew's influence, Rachel learned that the local police had limited tolerance for her interference. They determined two deaths to be murder-suicide, but Rachel refused to settle for that.

Rachel visited Reno in *The Cat Wears a Mask* (Doubleday, 1949) because Gail Dickson, her goddaughter, had been receiving poison-pen letters. Gail invited those she suspected of authoring the letters to stay at her home. Rachel, bold as always, planned to search their rooms. One of the guests was bitten by a rattlesnake, subsequent to a performance of the Hopi Snake Dance for entertainment. The Snake Dance achieved its purpose: rain, lots of rain, enough to isolate the group from the authorities. A second guest was strangled. One death never seemed to be enough for this series. When Rachel identified the killer, she was saved by a police captain.

Rachel needed to prove Jim Bayliss was not a murderer in *Death Wears Cat's Eyes* (Doubleday, 1950) because he was a witness in her own traffic accident. A convoluted and unrealistic plot.

The sisters' cousin Rod Bruell was one of Priscilla Beckett's four husbands in *The Cat and Capricorn* (Doubleday, 1951). All four had serious accidents, which they blamed on Priscilla. When she was murdered, the police had obvious suspects. No need for a trial. The killer crumbled when confronted.

There had to be a reason why an heir would not step forward and claim his share of an inheritance in *The Cat Walk* (Doubleday, 1953), so the executor of Aunt Gertrude's estate asked Rachel and Jennifer to check Paul Postelwait out. None of the other four heirs could get their portion until he showed up. He did, but only as a corpse. Rachel solved the crime in time to find a treasure.

Rachel and Jennifer were witnesses in *Death Walks on Cat Feet* (Doubleday, 1956) when a woman was tossed through a pet store window, but all bets were off in this one because the victims and villains were gamblers. The big winner was Jennifer.

Olsen's writing was intended to provide light entertainment, and did so. She explored the personalities of the two sisters—reckless Rachel and cautious Jennifer.

Ariadne Oliver

Author: Agatha Christie

Biographers of Agatha Christie have suggested that she imbued Ariadne Oliver with several of her personal characteristics. Like Christie, Ariadne wrote detective stories with a foreign-born hero, Finnish Sven Hjerson, whom she came to detest. She shared Christie's fondness for apples, and exceeded her mild feminism, arguing that more cases would be solved if a woman headed Scotland Yard. Ariadne rarely wore hats; suffered with her false teeth, but enjoyed her food; was modest about her writing skills; and disliked politics. She was a widow (but the former husband was never alluded to), heavy set with gray hair, a deep voice, and fine eyes.

Ariadne was disorganized in her personal habits and thinking patterns, and likely to jump to conclusions. She drove her detective friend and frequent collaborator, Hercule Poirot, to distraction. Although her character was treated with humor, Ariadne retained her dignity as an intelligent and sensitive woman, respected as an equal by Poirot, Colonel Race, and Superintendent Battle.

Ariadne first appeared in a short story in *Parker Pyne, Detective* (Dodd, 1934), using her dramatic skills to create a scenario in "The Case of the Discontented Soldier."

In *Cards on the Table* (Dodd, 1937), Mr. Shaitana invited four detectives, including Ariadne and Poirot, and four possible murderers into his home. When Shaitana was murdered, the four investigators combined their skills as their host may have intended. Inspector Battle used official resources to check out the pasts of the suspects, while Colonel Race and Ariadne each focused on a single person. Poirot was most interested in the personal temperaments each displayed as they played cards. Each of the four detectives added to the sum total of information that pointed to the killer.

During *Mrs. McGinty's Dead* (Dodd, 1952), a police official concerned that he might have convicted an innocent man sought help from

Poirot, who involved Ariadne. Poirot was feeling his age, but agreed to help because it was important to exonerate James Bentley, who had been sentenced to death. Mrs. McGinty, the victim, was a cleaning woman, not a common target for a murderer, but she may have witnessed a crime. Ariadne had her own theory, but missed the solution by a mile.

She invited Poirot to a "murder hunt" held as part of the village fete in *Dead Man's Folly* (Dodd, 1956). When a real murder occurred she provided him with important insights about the victim and suspects. Poirot paid tribute to her as a "shrewd judge of character."

Mark Easterbrook, a friend of Ariadne's, came upon a list of potential murder victims, which included his grandmother, in *The Pale Horse* (Dodd, 1962). Mark had heard that murders could be purchased so posed as a man who wanted to get rid of his estranged wife. His girlfriend, Ginger, posed as the potential victim. Ariadne provided an important clue pointing to thallium poisoning.

Poirot was annoyed when Norma, a potential client referred by Ariadne, considered him too old in *Third Girl* (Dodd, 1967). After Norma disappeared, Ariadne did some sleuthing on her own. She found Norma confused and uncertain as to whether or not she might be a poisoner. Ariadne was attacked subsequently and ended up unconscious in a hospital. Based partly on Ariadne's remarks as to how easily a woman can disguise herself, she and Poirot found the killer who had been framing Norma.

In *Hallowe'en Party* (Dodd, 1969) a teenage guest, who had boasted that she "had seen murder," was drowned. While the aging Poirot and a retired police official investigated past murders, Ariadne was assigned to guard a real witness to murder. Unfortunately 11-year-old Miranda was abducted, but Poirot had assigned two men to watch over the girl.

In *Elephants Can Remember* (Dodd, 1972), Ariadne and Poirot sought persons with extensive memories to relieve the anxiety of a young woman about to be married. Celia Ravenscroft was Ariadne's goddaughter, who had survived when her parents had been killed in what was written off as a possible murder-suicide. A prior death in the Ravenscroft family was suspect, partly because the victim was suspected of injuring children. Celia's prospective mother-in-law was leery of having her join their family. Poirot and Ariadne sought out "elephants," elderly persons who held minor positions in the Ravenscroft family and might remember significant facts.

Ariadne was the least well known of the Christie sleuths, but is an interesting reflection of how Christie perceived herself and therefore has a value of her own.

Jane Ollerby

Author: Edgar Wallace

Jane Ollerby, the short dumpy widow of a police sergeant, freelanced for Scotland Yard. She solved cases together with her son, Hector, calling the authorities only when she needed their assistance. Jane kept scrapbooks of crimes, had an astounding memory for faces, and used her gun when necessary.

She kept turning up in *The Traitor's Gate* (Doubleday, 1927) when a wealthy young orphan tried to discover her parents. Ollerby was suggested as the prototype for Nigel Morland's Palmyra Pym by Craig and Cadogan in *The Lady Investigates*.

Iris Pattison

Author: Patrick Quentin, pseudonym for Hugh Wheeler and Richard Webb

See: Iris Pattison Duluth, Section 3, page 48.

Alice Penny

Author: Adam Bliss, pseudonym for Robert and Eve Burkhardt

Mrs. Alice Penny, left deeply in debt when her husband died, survived by renting out rooms. She was a stocky 5' 5" at 160 pounds with gray-blonde hair and dark eyes, and narrated her own adventures.

When one of her roomers was stabbed to death in *Murder Upstairs* (Macrae, 1934), Alice had to eliminate herself as a suspect, because she inherited $200,000 in Darien's will! She ended up with a broken leg and a fractured skull when she used herself as bait in a trap.

A tough lady, she returned in *Four Times a Widower* (Macrae, 1936), when Lt. Kirk Larrabee asked her to move into the Jerrold family home as a housekeeper. Four of Jerome Jerrold's wives had died, and the fifth Mrs. Jerrold was not feeling well.

Matilda Perks

Author: Ralph Woodthorpe

A former teacher, Matilda Perks must have had other sources of income because she lived in a large Sussex home and employed two servants. She was a plump little woman with a hooked nose, who usually dressed in black. Miss Perks, who collected china, enjoyed a garden, and had a parrot named Ramsay MacDonald, had other less admirable characteristics. She was intolerant of religion, contemptuous of the villagers, bragged about having an unpleasant mind, and admired Adolf Hitler. In 1937, that would not have been a popular viewpoint in England.

In *The Shadow on the Downs* (Doubleday, 1935), Miss Perks became embroiled in a local argument about whether or not to build a racetrack in the area. When the chief sponsor of the track was discovered dead in the church, authorities pronounced it a natural death, but Matilda was not fooled.

During *Death in a Little Town* (Doubleday, 1935), rich newcomer Douglas Bonar, who had blocked off a walkway commonly used by his neighbors, was found dead. Although Miss Perks witnessed the killing, which took place under the influence of alcohol, she told no one, allowing the perpetrator to leave the country. He left behind a letter admitting his guilt to be opened when he died.

Polack Annie

Author: Jack Lait

Fancy anyone writing a book today with a heroine named "Polack Annie," but ethnic sensitivities were not as great in the Thirties. Annie was a tough redhead, what used to be called a "gun moll," and the Edgewater Kid was her man.

As *Put on the Spot* (Grosset, 1930) began, the Kid had been machine-gunned. Annie would not rest until she avenged his death by Kinky King, head of the West Siders, and everyone knew it. Kinky's death ignited street warfare between two gangs. The mayor and chief of police sought to defuse the matter by arresting Annie for the murder. That didn't help the local authorities. A gang broke into the police department and rescued Annie. She was housed at the country estate of Goldie Gorio of the Northside gang, but did not repay his hospitality. The police brought no charges against Annie.

Annie got a one-way ticket out of town in *Gangster Girl* (Grosset, 1930). She left Chicago for New York City, finding shelter with the unsuspecting friend of a man she had murdered. While organizing beauty parlor operators for the New York mob, Annie was charmed by Tommy, a handsome Yale graduate whom she was supposed to vamp. Instead she fell in love. Tommy's father, a powerful politician and contractor, would not settle for a daughter-in-law who barely spoke English.

These were incredible stories, and were provided with a glossary of gangster terminology.

Patricia "Pat" Preston

Author: James O'Hanlon

See: Patricia "Pat" Preston Cordry, Section 3, page 46.

Palmyra Pym

Author: Nigel Morland

The daughter of a rural doctor, Palmyra Pym worked as a reporter and served in the WRNS (Women's Royal Naval Service) during World War I. She and her deceased husband, Richard Pym, a retired ironmonger, did not have children during their short marriage. After his death she was employed by the Shanghai Municipal Police; she then became the only female Scotland Yard inspector.

Mrs. Pym was, by then, in her fifties, a solid figure with gray hair and gray-blue eyes, but few endearing characteristics. She was assisted by Chief Inspector Shott, who sometimes wondered what it would be like to be married to her, and by reporter Dick Loddon, to whom she provided inside information. Mrs. Pym enjoyed notoriety and rejected the authority of her superior officers. She drove flashy cars without regard to traffic regulations and carried a gun that she was not reluctant to use.

She seemed asexual, disliking both men and women. There was an international aspect to Mrs. Pym, the result of her work and travel abroad. Her servants were blacks or Orientals. Often sarcastic and vindictive, she was nevertheless popular with "the ranks" and street people. Her professional standards were flawed, although she was conversant with modern criminology. She ignored human rights, threatening and brutalizing prisoners to get information or confessions.

Sing a Song of Cyanide (Cassell, 1953), during which she mentored Larry Baker, a Canadian reporter who narrated, harkened back to Pym's employment by the Shanghai Municipal Police. She and young Larry Baker investigated the disappearance of a beautiful young Russian dancer and the death of a Chinese bookkeeper for Cathay Oil. Their probe brought the wrath of a tong (the Hop-Ley Dancers), a local politician, and the Cyanide Man. When they kidnapped Baker, Palmyra charged in to rescue him. killing four men. Her flair for publicity was exploited by Baker's lurid stories.

The Concrete Maze (Cassell, 1960) was another retrospective featuring Baker and Pym in Shanghai. This time their adversaries included the Little Tall Rabbit tong, active in a turf war, and members of the Japanese diplomatic service and its sympathizers. Palmyra had already developed a disdain for human rights and human life.

The Moon Murders (Cassell, 1935) introduced Mrs. Pym to Scotland Yard at a time when the police were trying to solve a series of deaths connected to the Orient. The officers, awaiting the new Assistant Commissioner, P. Pym, were shocked to learn that the "P" stood for Palmyra. From the start Palmyra was destined to create controversy. She enjoyed physical combat, brandishing her gun at a time when British policemen were unarmed.

Unimpressed by the British government's diplomatic obligations, Mrs. Pym assisted young reporter Dick Loddon in rescuing Maraday, the woman of his dreams, from a Japanese commercial conspiracy and a vengeful husband in *The Street of the Leopard* (Cassell, 1936).

Loddon, then married to Maraday, was sure that Mrs. Pym could make sense out of the midnight gambols of a supposedly paralyzed woman in *The Clue of the Bricklayer's Aunt* (Farrar, 1937), and so she did, defeating the plans of a British financier to bilk his creditors.

Palmyra avenged a young boy who photographed a corpse in a supposedly empty warehouse in *The Clue in the Mirror* (Farrar, 1938). By the time his father arrived, the body had disappeared and Alfred's picture was the only proof that the murder had occurred. Young Alfred's death enraged Palmyra, encouraging her in behaviors unacceptable to the Scotland Yard hierarchy.

Although educated at Oxford and a linguist, she frequently used gang slang, as in *The Case Without a Clue* (Farrar, 1938), that required translation by footnotes. Admiral Sir Edward Tolespone's memoirs must have been too hot to handle, because publication was suspended and all copies destroyed. However, the edited galley proofs were entrusted to Donald Laidlaw, a classmate of Dick Loddon. Donald died, but no one could find the proofs...until Loddon did. Fanciful narrative in which a killer's behavior was traced to mercury fillings in her teeth and Palmyra joined the British Navy in a battle to rescue Loddon at sea.

The plots were equally fantastic in *Murder at Radio City* (Farrar, 1939) aka *A Knife for the Killer*, when a man dressed in evening clothes parachuted from the Rockefeller building. When Mrs. Pym visited New York, she took advantage of a fashion update from a female police officer to become a more attractive, well-dressed woman.

Returning to England for *A Rope for the Hanging* (Farrar, 1939), Palmyra was told by her superiors to drop a case involving an American expatriate who had government contracts. He incited a mob to attack Palmyra by telling them that she was a slum landlord.

After being threatened in *Murder in Wardour Street* (Farrar, 1940) aka *A Gun for a God*, Palmyra shot two men, participated in an effort to control a race riot, and had to be rescued.

In *The Corpse on the Flying Trapeze* (Farrar, 1941), murder occurred during a vaudeville act. When informed that the next death would be that of the U.S. President, she flew to Washington to intervene. Morland dedicated this narrative to J. Edgar Hoover, then head of the FBI.

Mrs. Pym did not always escape unscathed. During *The Clue of the Careless Hangman* (Farrar & Rinehart, 1941) aka *The Careless Hangman*, she was injured by gunmen, leaving her assistant Shott to sort out a skeleton hidden in a dummy. The case began when a headless corpse was found wearing the clothing of a prominent businessman, Sir Rudolph Hackett. Palmyra tied the first corpse to a prison hanging and Sir Rudolph to chicanery.

In *A Coffin for the Body* (Cassell, 1943), Palmyra accompanied a beat officer on his rounds; she then inadvertently triggered a set gun, which killed a man tied in a chair. London had been taken over by U.S.-style gunmen. Loddon was showing some signs of maturity now that he was a father, but he still followed Palmyra's plan, which placed both Maraday and the baby in danger.

By *Dressed to Kill* (Cassell, 1947), Palmyra had seen further signs of U.S. influence in England when the child of a movie executive was kidnapped and his nurse murdered. After the child's body was found, all restraints were off. She took over a case assigned to another officer and trapped a crooked policeman and a faithless father. Palmyra's top assistant, C. I. Shott, was so seriously injured in the case that he would never walk again.

Mrs. Pym made provision for Shott to have transportation, a fine office, and a desk job in *The Lady Had a Gun* (Cassell, 1951), so she had a heart. She also had a gun and she used it frequently in this narrative, going into battle against criminals, striking them with the butt of the gun, and on occasion shooting them. A strange incident was the death of a corset sales-man in Piccadilly Square during which the murder weapon was discovered on the lap of a mummy in a car. The vehicle started without a live person aboard and drove off. Loddon and his boss agreed this was a Pym case. The theft of a large quantity of nutmegs at the same time in the same area might have been written off as a coincidence by anyone but Mrs. Pym. She discov-ered a sinister use for nutmegs, which had gangs fighting one another for control of the drug market. Still, who killed the corset salesman? She fig-ured that out, too.

American gangsters who had moved to London tangled with Mrs. Pym in *Call Him Early for the Murder* (Cassell, 1952). The first evidence of the intrusion came when the naked body of an Italian-American gangster was found in the river. The parents of the three Truetooth children (who found the corpse) disappeared. The boys rounded up their pals and began a search on their own. When Palmyra deduced that gangsters were hiding out at Camber Camp, she organized an attack force. The leader escaped. She hunted him down and shot him.

By 1957, when *Look in Any Doorway* (Cassell) was written, Mrs. Pym was in disrepute at Scotland Yard, relegated to paperwork. Still, when Loddon brought news of a headless corpse, the old warhorse could not resist the temptation.

Official disapproval had kept Mrs. Pym in her tiny office even when, in *A Bullet for Midas* (Cassell, 1958), a police constable was murdered on station. When toughs physically attacked Maraday Loddon, Palmyra sallied forth, and was needed when Loddon was arrested as a murder suspect.

Death and the Golden Boy (Cassell, 1958) may be Morland's most inventive book. Loddon was assigned to the murder of Pops Golden, the father and manager of music sensation Johnny Golden. He sought Johnny out, told him about his dad's death, and took him to Palmyra as the most likely person to find the killer. Although Palmyra carried on with her usual law-breaking tactics, the plot featured unusual aspects of blackmail. Loddon handled them adroitly.

There seemed to be no reasonable motive for a series of kidnappings in *So Quiet a Death* (Cassell, 1960). News of the incidents came first to Loddon, small children of prominent women abducted, then returned without any payment of ransom. Palmyra did not get interested until one of the children mentioned seeing an artwork by painter Hieronymus Clagg during his captivity. Clagg's model, Lillian Cellini, was murdered and he disappeared. Only when Loddon and Palmyra distinguished between the murder and the kidnappings did they find solutions. There had been ran-soms paid.

In *The Dear Dead Girls* (Cassell, 1961), Pym and Loddon took an interest in the murders of an elderly drunk and the unarmed police constable who had chased his killer. The constable's death raised public ire, and the first victim was the uncle of two prominent movie starlets and could not be ignored. The disappearance of the Fairlight twins ended with the discovery of a bloody but alive Dilly and a murdered Milly. Dilly kept disappearing until Palmyra discovered more about the births in the Fairlight family.

Mrs. Pym was included with other Morland sleuths in *Mrs. Pym and Other Stories* (Ellis, 1976). Her appearances (1) took her back to China in her thirties when she solved the murder of the wife of an oil executive; (2) showcased her discovery of how an artist had been killed; (3) related a case in which she helped an old lady prove that her friend had been murdered by a greedy relative; and (4) covered her intervention in the police investigation in rural New York State.

Reading the books requires a suspension of disbelief and a willingness to put up with a heroine who is difficult to like or respect. Others available at the British Library were *The Phantom Gunman* (Cassell, 1935) and *The Hatchet Murders* (Martin, 1947).

Blue Jean Billy Race

Author: Charles W. Tyler

Charlie Race had been an honest fisherman in the Massachusetts Bay area until a vicious police officer abused him during an interrogation. Charlie had been released because he was not guilty of the crime being investigated, but the experience changed his life. From that day on, he was not only a criminal, but inculcated his daughter in the belief that the police could not be trusted.

Her father raised Blue Jean Billy Race because her mother died very young. She had a proper education that enabled her to fit into upper class circles, but her roots were with common people. She had no respect for the idle rich. When Charlie died, he had second thoughts, wishing he could have raised Billy to be the woman her mother would have been proud to bear. He entrusted several of his henchmen to guard Blue Jean, by now a grown woman of striking beauty.

After Charlie's death, Blue Jean began her own criminal career. She disdained the lowlife criminals as she did the idle rich, and worked only with the men she trusted as Charlie's friends.

The graces that she had learned in school stood Blue Jean in good stead in *Quality Bill's Girl* (Chelsea House, 1925). She planned and carried out two successful group robberies at social gatherings. However, she was besieged on one side by the police and on the other by criminals who envied and resented her. Even with her acquired fortune gone and two of her allies dead, there was a happy ending for Blue Jean in the arms of Detective Robert Wood.

Robert and Blue Jean married and spent a happy two years together among simple fisherfolk. As *Blue Jean Billy* (Chelsea House, 1926) began, their idyll ended. Tenacious detective J. V. Brinall located Blue Jean as she was trying to resuscitate Robert, a victim of a terrible storm while lobstering. His intervention may have caused Robert's death. At any rate it returned Blue Jean to a life of crime. Although her integrity and Robin Hood approach to robbery earned Blue Jean the respect of Brinall and his chief, she was eventually captured and mistreated. Her last adventure was to expose the dishonest detective who had treated her cruelly.

Anne Seymour

Author: Frank Presnell

See: Anne Seymour Webb, Section 3, page 105.

Sylvia Shale

Author: Mrs. Sidney Groom

Sylvia Shale, whose mother died when she was young, was determined to follow in her father's footsteps as a detective at Scotland Yard. She was small and innocent looking, with a soft voice. Nevertheless, she was "brave and resolute."

In *Detective Sylvia Shale* (Hurst, 1923) James Penberthy, head of a New York detective agency, gave Sylvia a job, hunting down Notorious Nick, who had baffled police with three years of robberies. While en route to Europe on the Karnak, Sylvia fell in love, only to suspect that the man might be either Nick or a confederate. The Karnak, with its load of gold bullion, was sunk, leaving Sylvia as one of the few survivors. When she saw the man she loved still alive, she could not rest until she found him guilty or innocent.

Miss Maud Silver

Author: Patricia Wentworth

Maud Silver was a constant in a series of mysteries in which she often appeared after the characters and plot were well established. She never aged and had little or no character development of her own. Maud was devoted to her nieces and nephews and passed her leisure time knitting for them and their offspring. A tiny woman, her physical appearance (and that of her home) did not change over the decades—netted mouse colored hair with an Alexandra fringe (probably what a later generation would call Mamie Eisenhower bangs). She had been a teacher and governess to wealthy children, which provided her with the tones of authority that worked so well when she encountered men who had been privately educated.

Maud rejoiced in her work as a home based private investigator. She did not advertise, but her successes were well known to those whom she had helped, and they often referred new clients. There was a pattern. A young man or young woman got into trouble; then, they called upon Miss Silver, who reunited couples, established inheritances, and kept innocent parties out of prison. Over the years, Miss Silver appeared in 32 such narratives.

In *Grey Mask* (Lippincott, 1929), wealthy Charles Moray returned to England to learn that the woman who had rejected him had never married, and that his home was being used as a meeting place for conspirators headed by a man in a gray mask.

During *The Case Is Closed* (Lippincott, 1937) the innocence of a young man imprisoned for the murder of his uncle was at stake. Geoffrey Grey had a motive for the crime. He had been disinherited. His wife, Marion, and her cousin Hilary Carew believed him to be innocent. A chance encounter sent Hilary on the trail of a woman who might have lied in the trial. Much of the investigation had been carried out by the time Maud was consulted, but she made the connections.

Maud did not always remain in her comfortable apartment, as in *Lonesome Road* (Lippincott, 1939), when Rachel Treherne feared someone intended to kill her. Maud went undercover as a resident of a home for indigent elderly.

During *Danger Point* aka *In the Balance* (Lippincott, 1941), Maud made an early appearance, offering her services to a young woman whom she believed to be in danger. Another chance meeting on a train had alerted her to the problems in Lisle Jermingham's marriage. Lisle did not follow up on Maud's offer, even after a friend wearing her coat was killed.

The Chinese Shawl (Lippincott, 1943) was one of Wentworth's best. Miss Silver had been the guest of housekeeper Lucy Adams when a party ended in murder. Although physical evidence implicated the traditional ingenue, Maud thwarted the unexpected killer. Chief Inspector Lamb and the patrician detective Frank Abbott worked with Miss Silver. Abbott, who began as a sergeant, became an unofficial "nephew" to Maud.

By *Miss Silver Deals in Death* aka *Miss Silver Intervenes* (Lippincott, 1943), Lamb and Abbott saw Maud as having special gifts. They had been baffled by a case with multiple suspects for the death of sadistic Carola Roland. Amidst romances among the characters, Maud set a trap and caught a nasty blackmailer/killer.

In *The Key* (Lippincott, 1944), scientist Michael Harsch was shot before he could reveal the results of his research. The inquest brought a verdict of suicide, which satisfied no one. Crucial to the outcome was the possession of keys to the church in which the death took place. Maud suspected the murderer but was not the determining factor in uncovering an espionage network.

As *The Clock Strikes Twelve* (Lippincott, 1944) began, industrialist James Paradine suspected that the thief who stole important blueprints from his study was a member of the household. He made them aware that he would be available one evening to accept the return of unnamed items. He was murdered. The efforts of the family to smooth things over were no longer acceptable. Maud uncovered several family secrets before she identified the killer.

She Came Back aka *The Traveller Returns* (Lippincott, 1945) focused on the reappearance of Anne Jocelyn, who was believed to have died in France after the German invasion. Not everyone welcomed her. Her husband, Philip, claimed that the woman who returned was really Annie Joyce, an illegitimate cousin. Lyn, the woman Philip planned to marry, shared her concerns with Maud, whom she met on a train. Maud seems to spend a lot of time on trains! Anne may be more than a fraud. She may be a German spy.

Frank Abbott was concerned about Judy Elliot's plan to work at the home of the Pilgrim family in *Pilgrim's Rest* (Lippincott, 1946). He was aware that there had been attempts to kill his friend Roger Pilgrim, owner of the property. On Frank's advice, Roger consulted Maud, revealing his plan to sell the house and a superstition that any heir who tried to do so would die. Although she was unable to save Roger's life, Maud identified his killer. Frank, who had hoped for a future with Judy, was rejected.

The familiar pattern of an extended household with jealousies and anger against a dominating second wife (Lois Latter) formed the plot in *Latter End* (Lippincott, 1947). The stresses and a possible poisoning caused

Jimmy, Lois' docile husband, to seek Miss Silver's advice. When Lois died of poison, Miss Silver moved in and explained how a simple error had saved Jimmy's life.

Maud's quiet observance in *The Wicked Uncle* (Lippincott, 1947) saved Dorinda Brown from an accusation of shoplifting. She had seen another woman planting the items in Dorinda's pocket. Long before Maud became more heavily involved, the reader was aware that Dorinda's "wicked uncle," Gregory Porlock, was a blackmailer. When Dorinda's employer, Linnet Oakley, insisted that she accompany her to Gregory's home, he made a second attempt to frame Dorinda for theft. Later, during a game of charades, the lights went out and Porlock was murdered. The shock was that he had left his estate to Dorinda. Dorinda insisted on Maud Silver's presence during the investigation.

Coincidences abounded in *The Case of William Smith* (Lippincott, 1948), a story reminiscent of James Hilton's *Random Harvest*. William Smith, found in a German POW camp, lost his identity. When Katherine Eversley entered the toy store where Smith's wooden figurines were sold, she recognized him. They fell in love and married, only she knew that it was for the second time. When accidents threatened William, Katherine sought help from Maud.

Frank Abbott brought Miss Silver on scene in *Eternity Ring* (Lippincott, 1948) when Mary Stokes told the authorities that she had seen a corpse, which resembled Louise, a missing woman. Both women had worn "eternity" earrings. After Mary's death, Miss Silver took a hand, knowing that the murderer had served in France during the War, but there were several suspects who qualified.

It was Chief Constable Randal March, for whom Miss Silver had special feelings, who sought her help in *Miss Silver Comes to Stay* (Lippincott, 1949). Reitta Cray, the woman he loved, became a suspect in the murder of James Lessiter. Later in the series, Randal and Rietta married and had a family.

By *The Catherine Wheel* (Lippincott, 1949), Maud was so well established that the police asked her to check an historic inn, the Catherine Wheel, which they suspected was being used by smugglers. A reunion at the inn brought together a covey of cousins, descendants of the original owners of the property. There were hints that Jacob Taverner, who hosted the reunion, was seeking information about a secret tunnel from the house to the seashore.

In *The Brading Collection* (Lippincott, 1950), Maud had been approached by Lewis Brading, who collected jewelry connected with crimes and thought he was being robbed. She made no contact with his household until after Brading was murdered. At that time suspicion focused on Charles Forrest, who was Brading's heir, but would be replaced if he married. Maud looked further.

In *Through the Wall* (Lippincott, 1950), recent heiress Marian moved into a family home occupied by her disinherited relatives. The disappointed family members all stood to gain financially if Marian died. They lived in half of a "double house"; the occupant of the adjoining house, Helen Adrian, was the murder victim instead, but she had been wearing Marian's coat. Author Richard Cunningham convinced Maud to move in to protect Marian. Her arrival was in time to save another woman's life.

Anna, Where Are You? (Lippincott, 1951) aka *Death at Deep End* showed Maud at her most active, when she went undercover as a lady's companion to solve the disappearance of her predecessor, and brought discipline to the children of the house. The "invisibility" of an elderly woman like Miss Silver made it possible for her to move among the suspects and gain their confidence.

In *The Ivory Dagger* (Lippincott, 1951), Frank Abbott, even though just a sergeant of police, was accepted by members of the upper class because of his family connections and social position. He was comfortable when he interviewed suspects in the death of Herbert Whitall. Herbert's fiancée, Lila Dryden, had awakened while sleepwalking to find herself standing over his corpse, so that was the place to start. Both he and Maud developed cases against other members of the household.

Maud was not always a passive figure. In *The Watersplash* (Lippincott, 1951), another story based on inheritance and the return of a man who had been believed to be dead, she not only set a trap for the killer but also used herself as bait. Again, in *Poison in the Pen* (Lippincott, 1955), Maud went undercover to investigate poison-pen letters, thereby putting herself in danger.

During *Ladies' Bane* (Lippincott, 1952), Ione Muir, a young woman who had recently returned to England, overheard a contract killer in the fog negotiating the terms of his fee. She proceeded to the home of her married sister, Allegra, but was concerned about her physical and emotional condition. Explorer Josepha Bowden, Allegra's godmother, shared those concerns and hired Maud to move into the area and observe the household. It was young Margot Trent, ward of Allegra's profligate husband, who was murdered. Geoffrey seemed the obvious suspect, but Maud looked further with Frank Abbott's and Ione's help.

Even a vacation with her ailing niece, Ethel Burkett, did not give Miss Silver any peace. In *Out of the Past* (Lippincott, 1953), she helped

Frank sort out the suspects in the death of a blackmailer. Blackmailers were frequent characters in the series.

Inspector Lamb and Frank Abbott were the cause of Miss Silver's involvement in *Vanishing Point* (Lippincott, 1953). Her special skills in extracting information from the servant hotline prevented them from making an error and led to the arrest of a jewel robber.

The most common setting for the series was the extended household with a disputed inheritance, as in *The Benevent Treasure* (Lippincott, 1954). Here Miss Silver convinced the police to take action to save the life of a young heiress.

In *The Silent Pool* (Lippincott, 1954), Maud counseled a retired actress who believed someone was trying to kill her, but Adriana Ford ignored the advice. In a repetitious ploy, a visitor wearing Adriana's clothes was murdered. This convinced Adriana to hire Maud to visit her home. Adriana's home included several relatives and servants, and she frequently entertained guests. The police were involved, but their easy solution, a womanizing cousin who was unemployed, did not meet Maud's standards.

In *The Listening Eye* (Lippincott, 1955), gentle Paulina Paine, a deaf woman, learned about a robbery by reading lips while at an art gallery. She went at once to share her concern with Maud Silver. Paulina was killed on the way home. Lucius Bellingham hired Maud on another case involving the theft of a valuable necklace as it was being transferred from the bank to his home. It had to be an inside job, and as always an extended family provided multiple suspects in the robbery and an attempted murder.

Criminals rarely went to trial in the series. More frequently they committed suicide or died accidentally. The quality of the plotting deteriorated over the years.

In *The Gazebo* (Lippincott, 1956), a domineering mother urged her daughter to sell the family home and use the money for a cruise. There were people very interested in the property. Winifred, the mother, resented the romance between her daughter, Althea, and Nicholas Carey. When she went out to the gazebo in the evening, it was because she thought they might be together. Whoever was there killed her. Frank Abbott leaned toward Nicholas as the killer, but Maud was certain that some treasure was hidden in or near the gazebo and that Winifred had surprised an intruder.

The Fingerprint (Lippincott, 1956) got its title from the fact that Jonathan Field insisted on fingerprinting all of his guests. This became significant when he was murdered. Frank Abbott was the investigator, but Maud was visiting in the area. Her hostess entreated her to prove that young Georgina Grey was innocent, even though she was now an heiress. So naturally...she did so.

In *The Alington Inheritance* (Lippincott, 1958) the repetitions were everywhere. Another woman was killed by mistake instead of Jenny Hill, now known to be an heiress to an estate. Her marriage to Richard Forbes during the war had been kept a secret. His death in the service left her unaware of her claim. The father of the man accused of the murder hired Maud to investigate. When Jenny realized the identity of the killer, she warned him that he would be arrested. As in so many of the novels, there was no arrest, no trial. He killed himself.

The Girl in the Cellar (Hodder, 1961) was Anne Fancourt, who suffered from amnesia. Miss Silver met her on the bus and made a tentative identification based on information in her purse. Based on this she went to the home of the man believed to be her husband, where his mother, Lilian, resided. Anne had fled a cellar where she believed someone was lying dead. That was all she could remember. Jim Fancourt returned, but he let "Anne" know that she was not his wife, although he found her very attractive. Jim turned the matter over to Maud Silver, who already had met "Anne," but before Maud could get involved Anne ran away terrified of an attack. She found a refuge, but her pursuers located her. So did Maud, of course.

Like Agatha Christie, Wentworth is never completely out of print. Maud sits on the bookshelves with the hard-boiled feminist detectives, the medical examiners and scientists, the smart young women attorneys, the actresses and TV stars.

Ellen Gilchrist Soames

Author: Margaret Behrens

Ellen Gilchrist, a tiny young Scotswoman, brought her independence and shrewdness with her dowry when she married recently rich Percival Soames. Percival, on the other hand, perceived himself as cosmopolitan, claiming knowledge and background which Ellen knew he did not possess. She loved him anyway. They eventually purchased a yacht, which Ellen hoped would take her across the ocean to America. Percival settled for Monte Carlo.

By the second book in the series, *Puck in Petticoats* (Jenkins, London, 1931), the Soames family included a daughter, Isabel, aged two, and a three-year-old adopted son, Nicko. Although Nicko's parentage was well known to them both, Percival frequently hinted that the boy was of aristocratic stock. At a time when a young heir to a foreign throne had disappeared, this led to the boy's abduction. Percival, with his disregard for the truth, further complicated the situation. He was perceived as a possible suicide risk because the police in Monte Carlo did not understand English. Later, he risked a duel because of his attentions to a married woman. Ellen, although tempted by the attentions of a handsome Spaniard, located Nicko, chased off a predatory female, and extracted Percival from his difficulties.

The prior book, *In Masquerade* (Jenkins, 1930), was still unavailable for review in 2005.

Madame Rosika Storey

Author: Hulbert Footner

The sophisticated Madame Storey never married, although she was an attractive, tall, dark, and slim woman who declared that she "longed for a man who can master her soul." Her household off Gramercy Park in New York City included female servants such as her obsequiously loyal secretary, Bella Brickley. A monkey, Giannino, was the only male regularly on the premises. Rosika Storey was a cosmopolitan woman as comfortable in the notorious Cobra Club as in Newport society.

Her approach to crime solving was a combination of reason and intuition. She did not present herself as a private investigator, rather as a "practical psychologist specializing in the feminine." During the period 1925-1937, Rosika provided an alternative to bright young women and elderly spinsters. At times both Rosika and Bella wore disguises, assumed other identities, and took risks, often on behalf of young women whom Rosika felt had been mistreated by the system.

In *The Under Dogs* (Doran, 1925), Bella, who attended the trial in which Melanie Soupert was convicted of stealing pearls, was surprised at the weak defense put up by her attorney. Melanie escaped thanks to members of her gang after refusing help from Rosika. Rosika was determined to talk to Melanie, even allowing herself to be sent to a prison, from which she escaped to contact the gang now holding Melanie hostage.

Madame Storey (Doran, 1926) was a collection of four novelettes in each of which Rosika used her skills to uncover criminals. One of these was an old and trusted friend, and another was a former district attorney. She also proved the innocence of an unhappily married man whose virago of a wife had been murdered.

The Velvet Hand (Doubleday, 1928) collected four short stories all occurring on an extended trip, which began on an ocean liner. (1) While in Paris Rosika checked up on the former secretary of a deceased man. His wife believed he was murdered. Rosika found clues on the suspect's library card. (2) On board ship, Rosika was asked by the captain to investigate a married couple who traveled back and forth constantly from the United States to England or France, then back again. Rosika verified that the wife had a record as a con woman. Bella followed a woman, who was a prospective victim of the pair. She committed suicide—why? (3) While traveling incognito, Bella and Rosika were drugged during a murder committed on a continental train. Scotland Yard suspected them of being the killers. The victim was a research scientist on the brink of a discovery. (4) An attorney offered Rosika a substantial fee for just three hours' work investigating prospective heirs of his client, Genevieve Brager. Attorney Riordan was trying to convince Genevieve to place her money in trust and live off the income. When she died, Rosika directed the police to an alternate suspect. They had assumed the housekeeper who inherited must be responsible.

In *The Doctor Who Held Hands* (Doubleday, 1929), Rosika gathered evidence against Dr. Touchon, an unscrupulous "psychosynthetist" who blackmailed the women patients who had confided their innermost secrets to him. Rosika convinced Touchon that she might consider marrying him, but intended only to gather evidence.

In *Easy to Kill* (Harper, 1931), an elderly rich man hired Rosika because he received threatening letters. After he died of a heart attack caused by fright, Rosika persisted against the widow's wishes. The man she suspected was determined to ruin Rosika's reputation in society, but working with the local district attorney, Rosika set a trap that would lead to a conviction.

During *Dangerous Cargo* (Harper, 1934) Rosika accompanied a rich but fearful stockbroker on a six-month yacht cruise. Horace Laghet had been warned that he would not survive the trip, but he ignored Rosika's advice to cancel. Among his guests were those who might harbor ill will toward Horace. The ill-fated voyage included kidnapping, desertion, murder, and a possible mutiny.

The Almost Perfect Murder (Lippincott, 1937) was another collection of short stories. (1) Rosika saved a young friend from an unwise marriage to a man whose prior wife had committed suicide. (2) She and Bella attended a servants' ball to gain information about a gang of thieves. A murder took place during the event causing panic. The fire department rescued Rosika and Bella before their identity could be exposed. (3) Footner broke one of the classic rules of the elite English writers when Rosika identified the murderer who killed an attendee at a seance. (4) They were hired by a distinguished scientist to prove him innocent of a colleague's death. In disguise they roamed a tough neighborhood. (5) When a leader of society was killed and his only son was accused of the crime, Rosika and Bella trapped the killer.

Six cases of Rosika were narrated in *The Casual Murderer* (Lippincott, 1937). They took place in a variety of locations: New York City, Monte Carlo, Georgia, and China. Rosika foiled the plans of murderers, kidnappers, gigolos, and art thieves. She was fearless. Each short story exposed her to a risk: kidnapping, arrest, and assault. She and Bella traveled incognito, but her fame preceded her. This book consisted of more short stories, narrated by Bella. (1) Rosika came to the aid of a young librarian whose fiancée had disappeared. She exposed a powerful man who had a history of murder. (2) Rosika used disguises to unmask a mastermind behind a group of dangerous Monte Carlo gigolos. (3) She solved the murder of the daughter of one of her clients, finding the killer whom he had not suspected. (4) While in disguise Rosika and Bella mixed with members of the underworld to prove that a victim can be a villain. (5) A professional kidnapper abducted Rosika and Bella to convince them to act as a "go-betweens" in his crimes. (6) While in China, they searched for friends lost amid battles between opposing warlords.

The series was marred by dated slang and turgid and melodramatic prose and is not known to have been reprinted or issued in paperbacks.

Georgia Cavendish Strangeways/Clare Massinger
Author: Nicholas Blake, pseudonym for Cecil Day-Lewis

Georgia Cavendish was an intrepid explorer when she met Nigel Strangeways, the low-key British investigator in *Shell of Death* (Harper, 1936). When her lover, Fergus O'Brien, a World War I air hero, was murdered, Georgia, who had killed before in self-defense, was a suspect. Nigel and Georgia married, but there was a lack of romance in his unpleasant descriptions of his tiny wife; he referred to her as "monkey-faced." Georgia's other significant role was in *The Smiler with a Knife* (Harper, 1939), when she infiltrated a Fascist organization at the request of Scotland Yard.

Georgia died during World War II. Nigel Strangeways did not remarry, but had a long-term relationship with sculptress Clare Massinger, who preferred to devote her life to her career. Clare accompanied Nigel on his holidays, but they maintained separate apartments. She made some significant contributions, noting a similarity of bone structure in *The Widow's Cruise* (Harper, 1959), defending Nigel's unconscious body in *The Whisper in the Gloom* (Harper, 1954), lassoing a killer in *The Worm of Death*

(Harper, 1961), and manipulating her Citroen across country fields in *The Sad Variety* (Harper, 1964).

Both of the Strangeways women were independent, career oriented, and, when given an opportunity to do so, capable of rising to the occasion with physical violence. They did not have children, seemingly by choice, but were conventional in their faithfulness to Nigel. It was not unusual for male authors to endow their heroes with exceptional wives during the Golden Age of Mystery.

Della Street

Author: Erle Stanley Gardner

Although Della Street has become synonymous with the long-suffering "office wife" secretary, she had very little to do in the Perry Mason series. Perry was wedded to the law. Della was available when needed as a witness, to search an apartment, to watch over a client or suspect. She was convenient when Mason desired a dinner companion, a dancing partner, or a personal confidante. She:

- hid a witness from the police and was arrested for obstruction by Lt. Tragg in *The Case of the Careless Kitten* (Morrow, 1942),
- disappeared so she would not have to testify against Perry or one of his clients in *The Case of the Substitute Face* (Morrow, 1938), and
- was taken prisoner by criminals in *The Case of the Hesitant Hostess* (Morrow, 1953).

The big mystery was why she failed to get herself a life. Her role was expanded in the television series.

Ethel Thomas

Author: Cortland Fitzsimmons

Ethel Thomas was a chain smoking, highly opinionated spinster, aggrieved because she had been considered to be the least attractive of seven sisters. Although she had independent means, she was an author. A vain woman, Ethel sometimes wore a blonde wig over her thinning gray blonde hair, and was partial to younger men. One such young man, who appeared in several books, was Inspector Peter Conklin of the New York Police Department.

During *The Whispering Window* (Stokes, 1936), Ethel's financial interest in a department store motivated her to get involved when a murder occurred on the premises. The victim, a Mrs. Briggs, was assumed to have died of fright, probably while being choked. She was an employee of the Doane's Store and had been rumored to have a child by the father of the current owner. After subsequent deaths, Ethel stayed overnight in the store to trap the killer, who returned to remove another body.

In *The Moving Finger* (Stokes, 1937), Ethel convinced her author/friend Terry Lassimon not to publish the diaries of blackmailer Mortimer Van Wyck. They would expose the secrets of the men and women whom Mortimer had blackmailed. When they were stolen, Ethel bought them back. After Mortimer had been murdered, Ethel and Terry brought the suspects together exposed some secrets, but the killer was allowed to leave and take his own life.

During *Mystery at Hidden Harbor* (Stokes, 1938), Ethel worked with young Albie Abernaty, a divorcee, while vacationing on an island. The summer residents had welcomed the Albatross, Jerry Carter's ship, back from an extended voyage. Jerry hoped to talk to Mary Carter, his former fiancée, who had married older, richer Henry Baldwin. When Baldwin was murdered, the personal relationships among the suspects were the focus of local gossip. The island was temporarily cut off from the mainland. Ethel and Albie had hoped to solve the case before the police arrived, but they needed help to uncover a completely different motive for Henry's death.

After gaining some prestige as an author, Ethel journeyed to Hollywood in *The Evil Men Do* (Stokes, 1941) to supervise the filming of one of her books. Her grandniece Stella was being blackmailed, not for money, but to become the mistress of a powerful gambler. The inducement was that he would destroy films that showed Peter Bradley on the scene of a possible murder. Ethel became an "ear witness" when she overheard a murder while hiding in a closet. She had no hesitation about hiding clues or withholding information from the police. A less likely killer than Peter or Stella was eventually located.

The books were expanded by Ethel's views on herself, society, morals, and handsome young men.

Matilda Townsend

Author: Arthur M. Chase

Matilda Townsend was similar to Amelia Butterworth in that she was an elderly upper class spinster without financial concerns even during the Depression, who lived in New York City and worked with a police professional. A tiny woman, she had traveled all over Europe, Asia, and Africa. Her interest in murder investigations lay in curiosity about the motivations of killers.

Matilda's curiosity was aroused in *Murder of a Missing Man* (Dodd, 1934), when she noted two similar-looking men talking to one another in Central Park. When one of the two men was killed on a westbound train on which she was a passenger, Matilda assisted the police in determining the identity of the victim. Was he Barclay Leland, who was suspected of murdering his brother in New York City, or the man Barclay hired to impersonate him?

Although she was squeamish, Matilda did not hesitate to investigate the murder of wealthy and arrogant Edward Tilden in *Twenty Minutes to Kill* (Dodd, 1936). Matilda was one of ten guests for dinner at the Tilden home when a jewel robbery was followed by Tilden's murder. His widow, Laura, a close friend of Matilda's, and her son Merritt were considered the most likely suspects by Lt. Durkin. Matilda, who had worked with Durkin in the past, used her credibility and the help of a maid to gather evidence to prove him wrong.

An accident on a South Carolina highway as Matilda and her nephew Dick traveled from Florida to New York City caused them to take refuge at Felicity Hall in *No Outlet* (Dodd, 1940). A fellow guest, former opera star Joanna Searles, was murdered. Her estranged husband, Jimmy, was arrested for the crime. Convinced that he was innocent, Matilda cooperated with an undercover private investigator in unmasking an unlikely killer.

The books were from the Dodd, Mead Red Badge series.

Angeline Tredennick

Author: Ruth Burr Sanborn

Angeline Tredennick was a small, friendly woman whose gray curls belied her stated age of "39." She and close friend Marilla Holinshed shared a house, which they financed with paying guests.

She was inquisitive, which was an asset in *Murder by Jury* (Little, 1932) when she served as a juror in a murder trial. Had it not been for Angeline, domineering Mrs. Vanguard might have pressured the other jurors into a "guilty" verdict. However, someone poisoned Mrs. Vanguard. Among the jurors were many who had suffered from Mrs. Vanguard's power in the community. Even more serious was the fact that several jurors had inside information about the murder case on which the trial was based. Angeline not only identified Mrs. Vanguard's killer, but uncovered information that proved defendant Karen Garetti was innocent.

After this promising start, it was a disappointment that in *Murder on the Aphrodite* (Macmillan, 1935), Angeline, while a domestic on board ship, provided information to insurance investigator Bill Galleon, but had no other impact.

Carole Trevor
Author: Judson Philips aka Hugh Pentecost

Red-blonde Carole Trevor was determined to make it on her own after her divorce from playboy Maxwell Blythe. His property settlement enabled Carole to purchase a partnership interest in the Old Town detective agency and build a staff of assistants. What she needed was clients. So Blythe, still very interested in his ex-wife, provided them too.

Fritz Helwig came to Carole in *The Death Syndicate* (Washburn, 1938) only because other agencies had turned him down. Very powerful interests were making it difficult for Fritz to find help and for Carole to work the case. Max helped her discover who was bilking American-Jewish families hoping to get their loved ones out of Germany.

Max brought Carole another case in *Death Delivers a Postcard* (Washburn, 1939) when his friend John Lawrence admitted that he knew the man found dead on his estate. John had hosted a party to celebrate his daughter Janet's engagement to marry a handsome young stage actor. The victim had known that John was an ex-convict, information that could damage the business he had built up after he was released from prison. He was being blackmailed, so Carole set a trap to identify the extortionist, but was kidnapped. Carole's chances of making it on her own ended then, because it took Max and the members of her staff to rescue her.

There were hints that Max had a new case for Carole, but the series ended.

Agatha Troy

Author: Ngaio Marsh

See: Agatha Troy Alleyn, Section 3, page 24.

Tamara Valeshoff

Author: Eric Ambler

Tamara Valeshoff, a rawboned woman who was nevertheless seductive, came into two of the Ambler suspense thrillers through her brother, Andreas. Ochrana, the Russian secret police of the monarchy era, had killed their father. Although their mother escaped to the United States, they felt no allegiance to America. Instead, Andreas was the unofficial representative of the Russian communist government in Switzerland. Although Tamara was a tempering influence on Andreas, he dominated her life and used her in his espionage activities.

Documents carried through customs by impecunious reporter Desmond Kenton were the focus of *Background to Danger* (Knopf, 1937) aka *Uncommon Danger* (Hodder & Stoughton, 1937). By the time Kenton realized that he was carrying not currency but military information, he needed help. Tamara and Valeshoff provided that help. They agreed to give him an inside scoop on an oil company's plan to create mistrust between Russia and Rumania. In exchange, Kenton had to recover the envelope that he had hidden in a café and turn it over to Valeshoff. After considerable risk, Kenton avoided a murder charge and gave up the gambling that had kept him so poor.

During *Cause for Alarm* (Hodder, 1938), Nicky Marlow, another innocent bystander (common in the Ambler thrillers), finally found a job in the Milan office of a munitions supplier. He was appalled to discover that he would need to pay bribes to obtain new business for his employer and to pass information along to a general with Nazi affiliations. Although Valeshoff, who had an office in the same building, was of considerable help to Marlow in aiding the Allied forces, Tamara's role was minimal.

Harriet Vane

Author: Dorothy L. Sayers

Lord Peter Wimsey was the fictional hero of erudite author Dorothy L. Sayers. Some biographers speculated that Sayers fell in love with Wimsey and created in Harriet Vane a character representing herself. Harriet, the 29-year-old daughter of a country doctor, entered Lord Peter's life in *Strong Poison* (Brewer, 1930) as a woman accused of poisoning her lover. She had ended the relationship because he wanted marriage. When the murder trial ended in a hung jury, Peter was determined to prove Harriet innocent. Once acquitted, Harriet rejected Peter's proposal out of fear that she would damage his reputation.

Harriet's hiking tour in *Have His Carcase* (Brewer, 1932) was interrupted when she found a corpse on a rocky beach. Peter solved the crime, but she contributed to the solution by taking photographs of a victim about to disappear and uncovering a second identity for a suspect.

Harriet is best remembered for her appearance in *Gaudy Night* (Harcourt, 1936), set in an Oxford University college for women to which Harriet had returned to find release from personal pressures, but also to investigate vandalism and poison-pen letters. Manuscripts and reputations were being damaged. The culprit had to be someone within the small circle of women on staff. When Peter returned from Europe, he joined Harriet and exposed the culprit.

It might be difficult for a modern woman to understand the impact of Harriet. She was an exception to the rule that "bad" women should come to bad ends. She succumbed to Peter's frequent proposals once assured that marriage would not end her independence.

In *Busman's Honeymoon* (Harcourt, 1937), Harriet and Peter spent their honeymoon in a cottage, which had poignant memories for her. Peter had purchased the country retreat as a wedding gift. Inevitably, a body turned up on the premises. The victim was Mr. Noakes, who had sold them the property. Peter discovered the death trap by which the murder had been committed. His usual post-solution depression caused him to hire an attorney to defend the killer.

In *Lord Peter* (Harper, 1972), a collection of short stories, it was revealed that the couple had three sons, Bredon, Roger, and Paul. Miss Sayers had indicated earlier that romance had no place in mystery stories, but when she changed her mind, she created a memorable heroine.

Over 25 years later, established mystery writer Jill Paton Walsh utilized an outline developed by Dorothy L. Sayers for *Thrones, Dominations*

(St. Martin, 1998), an extension of the series. Peter and Harriet, returning from their honeymoon, stopped off in Paris. While dining, they were introduced to a devoted couple, Laurence and Rosamund Harwell, whose total absorption in one another was contrasted with Peter and Harriet's marriage. Although the Wimseys were committed to one another, each respected the individual needs of the other party. When Rosamund was brutally murdered at the couple's country cottage, Harriet, who had encouraged her to recuperate there, felt some responsibility. Peter was retained on a more official basis by his brother-in-law, a Scotland Yard inspector, but Harriet put aside work on her book in progress to share in the investigation. She successfully negotiated the social scene, provided an unusual bonus to the faithful valet, Bunter, and eased the family's concerns about heirs to the title.

A Presumption of Death (Hodder & Stoughton, 2002), another collaborative effort by Jill Paton Walsh based on the characters, was set in 1939-1940 when Prime Minister Chamberlain held to his policy of appeasement. The Nazis were expanding their conquered territories and the British would soon be retreating from Dunkirk. Harriet and the boys resided at Tallboys while awaiting the return of Peter and Bunter from a secret overseas mission. The local residents were dealing with food rationing, the possibility of air raids, and the absorption of refugee children from English industrial areas and Polish refugees of all ages. The murder of a "land girl" who had toyed with the affections of several men seemed a domestic case; still, the local inspector asked Harriet to assist him in his investigation. Only after a second murder did they realize that they harbored a dangerous stranger in their midst. Peter returned in time to help solve the case.

The two last books were a joy to read; not Sayers, but very good.

Mrs. Elizabeth Warrender
Authors: G. D. H. and Margaret Cole

Elizabeth Warrender, a widow in her sixties, did not depend upon any technical skill or intelligence to help her detective son, James, solve mysteries, but on her knowledge of human nature. She appeared first in a short story in *A Lesson in Crime* (Collins, 1933) in which she quickly deduced that the family maid was implicated in a robbery.

The title *Mrs. Warrender's Profession* (Macmillan, 1939) seemed suggestive of disreputable employment. However, it was instead a collection of short stories in which Elizabeth:

- convinced James that a purported suicide was murder,
- solved a locked room mystery but declined to identify the killer,
- unmasked the vengeful ex-employee who killed Elizabeth's former classmate, and
- involved herself in a case when James was hired to help a guilty party.

In *Knife in the Dark* (Macmillan, 1942), when their flirtatious hostess Kitty Lake was murdered, Elizabeth became convinced that the authorities had arrested an innocent party. Peter Orville had been Kitty's lover, but was planning to leave the area. His knife was the murder weapon. Kitty's husband, Gordon, a professor at Stamford University, was currently very involved in settling refugees, some of whom were foreigners, into the college town. Madame Zyboski, the mother of a young man who was recently released from a refugee camp, became the focus of the police investigation because Kitty was responsible for his incarceration. Neither James nor Elizabeth had an official role in the case, but when Madame Zyboski was arrested, Elizabeth contacted the party whom she believed to be the killer, hoping he would do the right thing.

Anne Seymour Webb

Author: Frank Presnell

Anne Seymour was a stripper before she married attorney Jack Webb. Jack had enjoyed the company of other women much younger than himself before he met Anne, but became a faithful husband. Anne, who had only an eighth grade education, underwent an "Eliza Doolittle" transformation, the result of Jack's training combined with her natural intelligence.

Although listed as a co-protagonist, she had no significant role in either *Send Another Coffin* (Morrow, 1939) or *No Mourners Present* (Morrow, 1940). Her name was probably used to capitalize on the current interest in "couples" mysteries. Her potential was ignored in favor of a routine tough guy investigation.

Mrs. Caywood "Julia" Weston

Author: Eugene Thomas

Julia Weston was a strikingly beautiful older woman—small and slim with white hair and dark eyebrows.

In *Death Rides the Dragon* (Sears, 1932) she and friend Luther Marshall took an active role when her niece Damaris searched for a jade piece used to rally Asian Buddhists against the tyranny of the Japanese. The piece had to be shown publicly every ten years, and that date was approaching. Damaris' father once had the piece and left knowledge as to its whereabouts with a friend, Elleston Carter. Damaris pretended to be a patient to get into a sanitarium where the jade might be located. Julia and Luther came to the rescue.

Julia and Luther reappeared in *The Dancing Dead* (Sears, 1933), but in diminished roles when State Department official Allan Foster sought their help. He had rescued young Elsa Sheridan, whose father, an Orientalist who collected Chinese artifacts, had been robbed and left in a state of suspended animation. A second intrusion into the Sheridan household prompted Allan to seek help. Le Chu-Sheng, a descendent of a sorceress whose brain had been preserved, took Elsa prisoner. She was to marry him and become the reincarnation of his sorceress ancestor. Luther Marshall was involved, as was Prince Lai, head of the Yellow Hats, in aiding Allan, but Julia was kept on the sidelines.

Julia was an effort to present an amateur involved in espionage, something done more successfully by Dorothy Gilman in her Mrs. Pollifax series 40 years later. Very amateurish, indeed.

Lace White

Author: Jeannette Covert Nolan

Lace White initially based her credibility as a detective on an honorary appointment to the Indiana State police by a former pupil, Governor Frank Mathews. She had been a grade school teacher, but retired to write fiction. Lace described herself as short and plump, but provided little other personal information. Her frequent companion in investigations was her nephew Scott, an attorney. She shared her home with her cousin, Effie Wilson.

In *Where Secrecy Begins* (Long, 1938), Lace found a corpse while dining with friends. At their suggestion, she asserted her new authority until the police arrived. The victim was revealed to be King Soames, a blackmailer and ex-convict. The suspects, all of whom had been contacted by Soames, were friends of Lace. She monitored the case, intervened to convince one friend that her attempt to kill Soames was a miss and therefore she was not guilty and then confronted the killer with a pistol.

In *Murder Will Out* aka *Profile in Guilt* (Detective Novel Classics, 1942), Dr. Ultimus Gregory, dean of Redding College, Lace's alma mater, recruited her to investigate the theft of official papers. Among the missing papers was an exam, which strangely all students passed with A's, and a letter questioning the parentage of a young woman in whom the Gregory family had an interest. While Lace was checking out the theft, Susan Bristol, who had written the letter was murdered. The coroner gave Lace 24 hours to solve the murder, at which point he would call in the real police. She contacted Scott for help.

It was Lace's literary skills that were sought in *Final Appearance* (Duell, 1943) to collaborate with author Eric Vigo on the history of an Indiana town built by a communal religious group. After many years, the enterprise was to be sold to the public, but not all descendants of the founding families agreed that was a good idea. Jonathan Ingle, grandson of the founder of Felicity, and current head of the defunct religious group, had promoted the sale to Albert Macbeth, who had indicated he would turn the property over to the state of Indiana. Ingle was murdered. Eve Ropier, another descendant of the founder, may have had a claim to one-half of the sale price. A signed statement from an eyewitness to the murder solved the case.

By *I Can't Die Here* (Messner, 1945) Lace and Effie had moved from their rural home to Capital City with Scott's encouragement. She was contacted by businessman Lionel Mottley to investigate the murder of his brother-in-law, Dudley Shane. Shane had a relationship with Helen Ladd, a young secretary who subsequently died of an overdose of sleeping pills. Lionel wrote the investigation off at this point, declaring that Helen had killed Dudley, and then committed suicide. Lace rejected his convenient solution, going undercover as a bag lady to trap the killer.

During *Sudden Squall* (Washburn, 1955), Lace secluded herself at a lakeside cottage in War Cry, Kentucky. Her neighbors included Eva Sterling, an imperious crippled woman whose husband had drowned in a sudden storm twenty years before. When the corpse of an unidentified man was found in a nearby cabin, Lace made it her business to identify the body, the presumed dead Jack Sterling. The case went up in a blaze of fire in which Jack's killer and the woman who had loved Jack both perished.

In *A Fearful Way to Die* (Washburn, 1956), Lace joined the Board of Directors of Fairhaven Home for Boys. Her first meeting was canceled when Chairman Charles Clarence was hospitalized after a hit and run accident. Lace believed that his subsequent death in the hospital had been caused by fright, perhaps because he was visited by Father Jessup, a young priest who had appeared in his dreams. Who had called Jessup to come to the hospital? The police blamed Ada, Charles' estranged wife, who will now inherit, for the hit and run. She may well have been involved, but there was another layer to the puzzle which Lace uncovered.

Mary Carner Whittaker

Author: Zelda Popkin

See: Mary Carner, Section 3, page 38.

Harriet Vane Wimsey

Author: Dorothy L. Sayers

See: Harriet Vane, Section 3, page 103.

Miss Hildegarde Withers

Author: Stuart Palmer

Hildegarde Withers' father, who had been a Unitarian minister, was stated to have moved his family from Boston to Iowa before she was born. By the time she became a New York City elementary school teacher, she was a tall, angular, acerbic woman in her forties who developed a friendly partnership with Police Inspector Oscar Piper. Hildegarde was a good teacher, able to handle crisis in the classroom, and was an enthusiastic pet owner having, at different times, tropical fish, a wirehaired terrier, and a standard size French poodle.

In *The Penguin Pool Murder* (Brentanos, 1931), Hildegarde discovered a body on a school excursion to the New York Aquarium. Fascinated by the investigative process, she was unwilling to leave it to Inspector Piper. He could hardly ignore her because Hildegarde was not only a witness, but her hatpin had been the murder weapon. At the end Hildegarde and Oscar headed off to City Hall for a marriage license but, like Nancy Drew, she never married.

Even their dates ended up in murder, as in *Murder on Wheels* (Brentanos, 1932) when dinner was interrupted by a man lassoed out of his convertible. Hildegarde bet Oscar that she could find the solution before he did, and won. Was it a coincidence that a rodeo was in town? Probably; a well-used gimmick of mixed-up twins was part of the solution.

Murder came to school in *Murder on the Blackboard* (Brentanos, 1932) when Anise, a young teacher, was killed on the premises. The corpse disappeared and in the search, Piper was seriously injured. Hildegarde took over and located the badly charred corpse in the school furnace. Her search of Anise's apartment produced a clue that later led Oscar and Hildegarde to the killer.

Hildegarde flew to Catalina Island in *The Puzzle of the Pepper Tree* (Doubleday, 1933). When one of her fellow passengers died en route, Hildegarde rejected the diagnosis of heart attack. Learning that the victim may have been dodging an investigation, she contacted Oscar. The corpse was stolen before it could be autopsied, and the identification of the body may have been faked. Hildegarde pressured the local police but took most action on her own. When Oscar arrived, he located her taped up in a closet.

A reward earned in the Catalina mystery made it possible for Hildegarde to take a sabbatical and travel. While she was on an ocean voyage in *The Puzzle of the Silver Persian* (Doubleday, 1934), a haughty young beauty disappeared from the ship. Hildegarde's efforts to prove the young woman had been murdered were ignored by the ship captain, but a Scotland Yard detective welcomed her assistance. The suicide of a passenger was taken as an admission of guilt and the case was closed. On arrival in London, many of the passengers stayed at the same hotel. One was found dead after a fall down an elevator shaft. By the time the body of the missing young woman washed ashore, Hildegarde believed she could identify the killer, but was reluctant to do so. The last two murderers she caught had been hanged. One more death was one too many, so Hildegarde took her information to the authorities.

In *The Puzzle of the Red Stallion* (Doubleday, 1936), Withers was in Central Park when she learned that Violet Feverel, owner and rider of a red Irish thoroughbred horse, had been killed on the bridle path. Hildegarde and her wirehaired terrier, Dempsey, traced the horse back to Thwaites stable. She proved that the horse had been shot by a pellet gun. There was a definite connection to the racetrack, made more clear when Patrick Gregg, who had information to share with her after a race, was killed. Motives for the murder of Violet became less important; it was the horse that had been targeted.

In *The Puzzle of the Blue Banderilla* (Doubleday, 1937), Oscar, who accompanied local politicians on a Mexican junket, was suspected of murdering a customs official. Hildegarde dropped everything to go to his rescue. Among the other suspects was Dulcie Prothero, one of Hildegarde's former students, now maid to Adele, the wife of a Manhattan alderman. Hildegarde came to believe that Adele was the intended target of the attack, but this time she was fooled.

In *The Puzzle of the Happy Hooligan* (Doubleday, 1941), Hildegarde was hired by Mammoth Studio as an advisor on a Lizzie Borden movie. Writer Saul Stafford, a cruel practical joker who occupied the room next to Hildegarde's, was murdered. A contact with Oscar connected the modus operandi with a previous crime. The suspect in that case, Derek Laval, was in Hollywood but could be using a false name. The revelation that "Derek Laval" was a humorous name used à la George Spelvin meant that the killer could be any one of several studio writers.

In *Miss Withers Regrets* (Doubleday, 1947), Hildegarde, who had retired from teaching, was recruited to help a World War II veteran falsely accused of murder. Pat Montague had never forgotten Helen Abbott, but she was now Mrs. Huntley Cairns. He walked to the Cairns estate to see her, only to find Huntley dead in the pool. Even though Pat was able to get away, he had been recognized and became one of several suspects. Hildegarde was led up the garden path by a sweet young woman.

Both Hildegarde and Oscar were aging in *Four Lost Ladies* (Mill, 1949). The New York Police Department wanted to exile Oscar to a desk job. Instead, Hildegarde enlisted him to find a corpse and justify her concern about missing older women and one who had died of a fall. The criminal, nicknamed "Mr. Nemo," contacted the women through newspaper ads. Hildegarde set herself up as a target. Hildegarde and Oscar's effort to find the missing women through nationwide ads got them both in trouble when it was claimed that they were alive and well, but did not wish to be contacted. That didn't fool Hildegarde; she found the killer's hideaway. Her reward included Talleyrand, a standard poodle that had belonged to one of the victims.

Even Oscar had limits to his tolerance. In *The Green Ace* (Mill, 1950), Hildegarde found those limits when she set out to prove that Oscar helped to send an innocent man to Death Row. She took a lot of convincing.

Hildegarde returned East during *Nipped in the Bud* (Mill, 1951). She was so depressed that Oscar, thinking that a good murder would cheer her up, took her to view a trial in progress. The disappearance of an important witness caused a postponement. Hildegarde made good use of the time.

In *Cold Poison* (Mill, 1954), Hildegarde was on a movie set as the owner of French Poodle Talleyrand, who was to be the model for a new cartoon series, but she had a hidden agenda. The studio wanted her to identify the author of poison-pen letters that contained drawings of the cartoon character Peter Penguin. She found her first suspect poisoned. Her next tactic was to find the connection among the four persons who had received the vicious letters. Then to have each suspect draw a Peter Penguin cartoon and have a handwriting expert examine the drawings. Not bad for a little old lady.

Later Hildegarde Withers books were collections of short stories: *People vs. Withers & Malone* (Simon & Schuster, 1963), co-authored by Palmer and Craig Rice, and *The Riddles of Hildegarde Withers* (Jonathan Press, 1947).

A novel, *Hildegarde Withers Makes the Scene* (Random House, 1969) was begun by Palmer and finished by Fletcher Flora. Hildegarde, then in her seventies, needed help when Oscar Piper forwarded an assignment. Lenore Gregory, a young hippie, has disappeared and her father wanted reassurance that she was all right. Feeling her age, Hildegarde enlisted a young neighbor, Al Fister, who not only assisted in the search but fell in love with Lenore.

Hildegarde changed very little over the series. Her relationship with Oscar became a friendship peppered with witty repartee and based on affection. Respected comic actress Edna Mae Oliver played Hildegarde in at least one movie (*Penguin Pool Murder*, 1932).

Louisa Woolfe

Author: Winifred Graham

Louisa Woolfe was a progenitor of the Eighties' Susan Melville. Although "Lou" worked as a thief, not a hit woman, she did not hesitate to kill when it suited her sense of justice. Louisa was tall, slim, and unattractive but with a "compelling" appearance. She was very athletic—important for a cat burglar. Her craft had been learned at a school for housebreakers. Unusual for the time, but practical, she wore men's clothing when at work.

Although she smoked small cigars, she was an excellent swimmer, even a lifesaver in *Wolf-Net* (Hutchinson, 1931). Her father had been a championship boxer, but she claimed that her Russian mother, raised in proximity to the howling wolves of the steppes, accounted for her untamed personality.

In *The Last Laugh* (Hutchinson, 1930), "Gussie," Louisa's cousin and her fence, contracted with her to steal art works. When Lou realized that Gussie's crooked schemes resulted from his connection with a gangster, she killed the gangster. When someone else was accused of the murder, she proved the suspect innocent without taking responsibility for the death.

During *A Wolf of the Evenings* (Hutchinson, 1930) Louisa was temporarily diverted from her plans for future thefts by her affection for young Lady Prudence Price. They initially met when the Vicar of St. Stephens asked Lou to serve on a planning committee for the bazaar. It seemed an opportunity to get access to the homes of wealthy women. When Lou learned that Lady Prudence had been deceived by her unfaithful husband, she determined to make him and his paramour pay. The result was unexpected. Lou returned to her earlier plan to steal St. Stephen's gold communion service. Even, then, fate took a hand.

The local bishop, with whom Lou had developed a close relationship, proposed marriage, but she declined. Instead, Louisa found love and marriage in *Wolf-Net* (Hutchinson, 1931) when she agreed to steal a painting for attractive art critic Maurice Twyford. Because of the disastrous impact of the theft on others, Lou and Maurice returned the painting, resolved to reform and marry.

Daphne Wrayne
Author: Mark Cross aka Valentine, pseudonyms of A. C. Pechey

Daphne Wrayne was in her late twenties when the series began, slim with golden brown curly hair. She had been educated at Roedean and studied to become a barrister. She was an excellent horsewoman, knew jujitsu, was an expert at deciphering coded messages, and shot to kill. Embittered by the ineptitude of British justice, she formed a group called the Adjusters.

Beginning with several men from her father's old regiment, Daphne recruited titled explorer Sir Hugh Williamson, actor-manager Alan Sylvester, criminal attorney Martin Everest, and a young titled playboy, Jimmy Trevitter, whom she planned to marry. Trevitter obviously did not realize what a long engagement he had ahead of him. He was still waiting in book #46. Although Daphne admitted longing for a man, babies, and a home, she said she had been raised more as a boy than a girl, and had become addicted to the excitement. She had independent wealth, a country estate, and an office in London. Joan Braxley ran the laboratory. Other men acted as investigators (Saunders and Masterson), Daphne's chauffeur (Maynard), doorkeeper (Carlton), or her bodyguard (Rayte). They must have had first names, but being servants, they were never used. All were devoted to Daphne.

Daphne was well known to Scotland Yard, the criminal element, and the English public, but the four "Adjusters" remained anonymous. They assisted by shadowing suspects, breaking and entering, searching without warrants, taking prisoners, and occasionally abusing them. On one occasion, the Adjusters shaved the heads of their adversaries, tattooed them, and cuffed them to a public fence to be picked up by the police. The Adjusters' secret weapon was that they felt no necessity to obey the law. This may explain the popularity of the series, appealing to readers who had lost faith in the justice system and were willing to accept vigilante justice.

Although the first book was mildly original, the later ones were increasingly humdrum. The plots were so obvious as to be clear to the reader early in the narrative, but the "brilliant" Daphne required an extra one hundred pages. The simplicity must not have bothered the readers because the series continued to be popular. The Adjusters did not ignore modern technology. They learned to recognize persons in disguise by their ears, to take tire and finger prints, and to use a miniature camera. Scotland Yard provided Daphne and her Adjusters with special badges, access to resources, and gun permits. Each of the Adjusters had opportunities to take the spotlight, but Daphne was always the heart of the group. On occasion, she worked with Scotland Yard, which ignored the breaches of the law committed by the Adjusters because they were overwhelmed by the criminal element. Daphne was referred to as "Her Who Must Be Obeyed," a phrase borrowed from H. Rider Haggard, but popularized more recently by Rumpole (more grammatically referred to as "She Who Must Be Obeyed"). Over the series, definite patterns emerged. Daphne became more self-assured, even arrogant. She worried that each case might be her "first failure," but it never was. The Four treated her with great warmth, although individual members disagreed with her tactics on occasion; e.g., when it was appropriate to involve Scotland Yard. There seemed to be a tendency to select Jewish names for criminals, and too many anti-Semitic sentiments were expressed.

In *The Shadow of the Four* (Ward, 1934), Daphne called the group together after her brother Derek committed suicide because of gambling debts, and her father Colonel Wrayne died of heart failure. When the men who cheated her brother kidnapped Daphne, her friends took revenge and brought them to justice.

Daphne had already received a letter from Joan Westwood before her brother Barry appeared at the Conduit Street office in *The Grip of the Four* (Ward, 1934). Then she learned that not only had Joan disappeared but that hers was one of an extended series of disappearances attributed to a monstrous ape-like creature. Daphne did the initial investigation, but Hugh and Jimmy made the discoveries that led to a monster and a man who was a monster.

Daphne and the Adjusters were building credibility by *The Hand of the Four* (Ward, 1935). Even so, only when his wife insisted did Col. Henry Grayson call upon Daphne for help. The Graysons had purchased a long-vacant home where they planned to spend his retirement years. What Professor Loganton diagnosed as evil spirits haunted the house. Daphne was unsure that this was an appropriate case for her services until she heard that a housemaid had been attacked and a watchdog killed.

John Armstrong and his wife, Nora, rented Redmayne Hall in *The Way of the Four* (Ward, 1936). When Nora's uninsured jewels were removed from the safe in their bedroom, Daphne, who was visiting nearby, boldly announced that she already knew how the theft had been accomplished. Not surprisingly, she had to be rescued from an "accident" by Jimmy and Hugh, after which she disappeared from the area until she was ready to pounce.

Jane Marlow, a classmate of Daphne's, disappeared from a weekend visit at the estate of wealthy Dmitri Aristide in *The Mark of the Four* (Ward, 1936). Her father and her fiancé came to Daphne for help. They were loath to believe that a member of the house party was complicit in the kidnapping. A reconnaissance of the cellar of a country home owned by a reclusive hunchback convinced Daphne and the Four that a gang was involved in cocaine smuggling. The Four did not hesitate to threaten torture (cutting strips of skin off a captive) to get information.

A visit from a bereaved young fiancée made Daphne aware in *The Four Strike Home* (Ward, 1937) that a vicious blackmailer was preying upon members of upper class British society. Efforts by the Adjusters to protect a potential victim failed when the blackmailer was murdered. Daphne's special talents helped her trap the killer and locate the blackmail material. One of the better early narratives.

Elderly George Waring was found stabbed to death in *Surprise for the Four* (Ward, 1937) just before he was to sign a new will. Although the coroner's jury returned a verdict of murder by persons unknown, young nurse Vivienne Charteris was a serious suspect. After her initial interview, Daphne was convinced that the young woman was innocent. Unfortunately she shared her opinion with the wrong person.

Daphne happened upon a murder in *The Four Make Holiday* (Ward, 1938) while visiting Chief Constable Major Jeff Morless and his wife, Eileen. Henry Barton, a neighbor, had been beaten to death, ostensibly by a family pet, a chimpanzee who had escaped from his cage. From the start Daphne was skeptical of the evidence offered by the victim's wife. Even more so when she learned there was a large insurance policy on Henry's life. However, she and the Four came to a surprising conclusion.

When bank manager Arthur George Braxton approached Daphne in *The Four Get Going* (Ward, 1938), he was more interested in clearing the bank's reputation than in prosecuting the man who had posed as a depositor. Within a short time Daphne was convinced that James Davenish had posed as himself and sought to defraud the Northwest & Midland Bank. James had what seemed to be an airtight alibi, but Daphne let the air out of it.

In *Find the Professor* (Ward, 1940), Chief Inspector Montarthur of Scotland Yard was unable to solve the disappearance of Prof. Arthur Maglan. He suggested that Maglan's daughter ask for Daphne's help. Both Sheila and her stepmother, Mary, insisted that Arthur would never leave their home voluntarily. The killer struck back at the Adjusters, searching the Conduit Street office and kidnapping Daphne. A rather hokey ending.

It Couldn't Be Murder (Ward, 1940) can best be described as incredible. William Deverill returned to Britain from Mexico after the death of his father, Sir Henry. After settling in, he received a note informing him that Sir Henry had been murdered and that he was in danger! After an attack, William consulted Daphne. Besides offering him protection, she and the Adjusters checked the death of George Deverill, who reputedly had died, but, if alive, would be the next heir.

In *How Was It Done?* (Ward, 1941), Daphne believed that Frederick Harriman had been killed as an act of revenge, perhaps against moneylender Edward Jannaway, who was accused of his murder. She and Hugh Williamson were the chief investigators as to which of Jannaway's staff set him up. The reader will figure it out long before Daphne did.

In *The Mystery of Gruden's Gap* (Ward, 1942) while picnicking, Daphne and friends discovered a skeleton and a cave used by drug smugglers. The first task was to identify the victim, a young woman. Daphne was not fooled when the prime suspect faked his death.

As *The Green Circle* (Ward, 1942), began, Hugh Williamson and Martin Everett came into possession of a notebook left in a restaurant by a man later found dead. The Green Circle was an organization headed by a master criminal. The Adjusters carried a large part of the action watching over known criminals who were probably part of the gang, building up clues as to who was #1.

Even on a country vacation, Daphne, who had grown tired of her work, could not avoid murder. As *Murder in the Air* (Ward, 1943) began, two young women were killed even though no one had come near them. Both Scotland Yard and Daphne were baffled by the circumstances. She concentrated on motive rather than method, and only when that was clear, on proof.

In *Murder As Arranged* (Ward, 1943), Henry Abernathy, an elderly businessman, believed that someone intended to kill him. He sought protection from the Adjusters. They learned that he was a vengeful man who was more likely to do harm to his neighbor, Martin Bester, than to be in danger himself. Henry disappeared, leaving evidence that Martin might be responsible. Henry's heir, his brother George, arrived to take over the estate. Daphne was ready for him.

During *Murder in Black* (Ward, 1944), Scotland Yard came to the Adjusters for help when Maria Westover, a rich elderly woman, disappeared during a train transfer. Personal items were found along the train track, but no body. Daphne and her dog, Patch, searched Maria's cottage on the theory that the woman on the train was someone else impersonating her. Patch located her body under a pile of coal. The logical suspects were her two nephews who inherited, but which one?

In *The Mystery of Joan Marryat* (Ward, 1945), a lock tender brought Daphne a bottle containing a note, written by Joan Marryat, a young Australian who had been abducted when she arrived in England to claim her inheritance. Yet the estate attorney says Joan was at a local hotel. Was she being impersonated? Fingerprints helped Daphne distinguish between two similar young women.

Nineteen-year-old Deirdre Vavaspur captured Daphne's sympathy in *The Secret of the Grange* (Ward, 1946). Her missing fiancé, Alan Fairfold, had been secretary to Deirdre's guardian, James Seaton. Seaton had delayed their marriage on two occasions. Daphne had her own suspicions as to why Alan had taken the job. Was he a fortune hunter? Once convinced of his good character, she and the Adjusters set out to find Alan and discover the secrets behind his disappearance.

During *The Strange Affair at Greylands* (Ward, 1948), Rosemary, the young ward of Vernon Herapath, a rich elderly gentleman, sought help when her guardian was disturbed by phone calls and visits. The visitor who caused him the most anxiety was Alfred Winters, who left a sealed iron box in the room he had occupied. Responding to a panicky call from Rosemary, Daphne went to the Herapath home only to learn that Rosemary had been kidnapped and her guardian killed. Arthur Herapath, Vernon's younger brother, appeared on the scene. He would inherit if something happened to Rosemary, but she may be his daughter. A resemblance based on ears helped Daphne solve the case. While she dealt with the box (full of stolen jewels), the Adjusters went to Rosemary's aid.

In *Missing from His Home* (Ward, 1949), Julian Carstairs, a prominent inventor for the War Office, was abducted, leaving his plans hidden. Jane Withers, a family friend, had been given a package by Julian to be returned only to him in person, with orders not to contact the War Office. After a consultation with Pamela, Julian's daughter, Jane took her story and the box to Daphne. Even though protection had been provided for Pamela and Jane, Pamela was abducted. Suspicion fell on Major Gerald Stantonley, an official at the War Office. Only when Daphne was able to get information from the owner of the house in which Stantonley was currently living could Julian and Pamela be found.

An elderly man who believed his nephew was involved with a gang of robbers was killed before he could reach Daphne in *Other Than Natural Causes* (Ward, 1949). A letter delivered subsequently indicated that he wanted the Adjusters to identify "The Boss" of the gang, but hoped that his nephew could be exonerated. The case was difficult for Daphne because she needed to work with Scotland Yard, and was known to withhold information from the authorities until the last minute.

On the Night of the 14th (Ward, 1950) had several interesting aspects. Julius Lefferstein had accused Daphne and two of her men of stealing his wife's jewelry. Lefferstein had an alibi for the subsequent death of his butler. Cooperation between the Adjusters and Scotland Yard built a case against Lefferstein. The method of the murder (voice operated equipment) was ahead of its time. The coverage of the trial in which Adjuster Martin Everest served as prosecutor was well handled.

Daphne's long-time friend Rosemary Matthews called on her for help in *Who Killed Henry Wickenstrom* (Ward, 1951). By the time Daphne reached the Matthews home, intruders had tied Rosemary up, left a note for her stepfather Wickenstrom, and departed. Daphne theorized that he was associated with criminals who were now out of prison. His disappearance and apparent death might have ended the case, but Daphne wasn't satisfied.

It was unfortunate for a clever killer that Daphne happened to be a guest of the local Chief Constable as *The Jaws of Darkness* (Ward, 1952) began. The deaths of Hedley Chase and his brother Charles, at different times but at the same place and by the same method, might never have been solved otherwise.

An ingenious form of kidnapping was brought to Daphne's attention in *The Black Spider* (Ward, 1953). The victims were family members of rich and powerful men, with one notable exception. As each victim was abducted, the wealthy parent or spouse was asked for a 5,000-pound ransom and given the name of a prior payee to verify that the victim would be returned unharmed. All were warned not to go to the authorities, but Daphne was contacted. She contacted all victims, but concentrated on the first one and the least wealthy family. Fingerprints proved to be effective in identifying the Black Spider. Daphne, a heavy smoker, often obtained the prints by offering her cigarette case to suspects.

In succession, two young women sought Daphne's help while she was recuperating in *The Circle of Freedom* (Ward, 1953). Jeanne Rutherford had overheard plotting by members of the Circle of Freedom, including her stepfather. Susan Lawrence would not accept the official version of her brother Gerald's disappearance. The authorities claimed he had defected to the Russians. The shape of a person's ears was again a clue, a feature that is difficult to change.

Murder Will Speak (Ward, 1954) had similarities to a prior book (*The Mystery of Joan Marryat*) in that impersonation was the basis for the plot. Terry Westbrook had returned from three years in the East in order to marry his wealthy fiancée, only to be kidnapped. Terry's younger brother Brian, the "black sheep" of the family, had connived to obtain money from Sheila under false pretenses, so he was a logical suspect when Sheila sought help.

During *In the Dead of Night* (Ward, 1955), a series of daring robberies left Scotland Yard holding an empty bag. On occasion, the thieves were caught, but the loot was never recovered. Sheila Marstone, a young heiress, purchased and resided at a cottage where the criminals had hidden the proceeds of a bank robbery. After several strange incidents, she came to Daphne's office. Working with Scotland Yard, the Adjusters set a trap for the thieves.

The Best Laid Schemes (Ward, 1955) concerned Sheila Branscombe, who came to Daphne because her younger sister Pat was not only missing but was suspected of a jewel robbery. The estate of her temporary employer, Sir Reginald Frant, had been robbed at the time when she disappeared. After Joan Braxley, a member of Daphne's staff, moved into Pat's apartment with Sheila, (1) a tenant in the building, Diane, sought to cultivate the two girls' acquaintance; (2) Diane was followed to the home of a man known to Scotland Yard; (3) when Diane's apartment was searched, clothes belonging to Pat were found. Daphne pressured the thieves until they made an offensive move; then, Scotland Yard was waiting for them. This was the third book in a row that had a major character named Sheila!

When Thieves Fall Out (Ward, 1956) began as a young housekeeper, concerned because her employer, James Fothergill, had disappeared after a series of mysterious phone calls, sought help from the Adjusters. The calls concerned Jimmy Jackson, convicted jewel thief, who blamed Fothergill (then under another name) for his imprisonment. However, Fothergill returned and Jackson's corpse was found!

Daphne's game playing with the authorities at Scotland Yard was getting old by *The Mystery of the Corded Box* (Ward, 1956). That did not stop Daphne from responding to Dawn Winstanley, who had been brushed off by Scotland Yard when she argued that her fiancé, Raymond Deverell, had not committed suicide. The coroner's jury had returned a verdict of suicide, but messages written shortly before Raymond's death indicated his concern about a major jewel theft. Daphne's plan was to keep Scotland Yard out of the case until she had it fully developed. She had to change her mind when Dawn was abducted.

Desperate Steps (Ward, 1957) was unworthy of even this series. Major elements of the plot had been used repeatedly. In a minor change, this time the blackmail victim who contacted Daphne was Angela Anstruther, daughter of the Assistant Commissioner at Scotland Yard. Angela's wedding to Jimmy Trefusis was already scheduled, but before she could face the ceremony she had to retrieve amorous letters she had sent to a former lover. Daphne's plan to handle the matter boomeranged when the blackmailer, not her lover, was murdered. There were other victims, and Daphne needed to find the man or men who sold love letters to be used for blackmail.

In *When Danger Threatens* (Ward, 1957), Joan Braxley, Daphne's lab assistant, introduced a friend, Hilary, whose scientist brother James was in danger from foreign espionage agents. The Four captured several men and threatened torture to get information. Daphne and Jimmy Trevitter found the papers and locked them in the office safe, when James was kidnapped. Then the Four and Daphne found and rescued him.

During *Over Thin Ice* (Ward, 1958) Marjorie Featherstone, a terrified young woman, disappeared before Daphne could interview her. A cursory check indicated that Marjorie was engaged to Wyndham Verdonley, whom Scotland Yard suspected of being involved in robberies. Although Marjorie had taken refuge with her old nurse, she was abducted, leaving behind a box, which the nurse turned over to Daphne. The Adjusters followed the suspects and eventually located the place where Marjorie was hidden.

During *Foul Deeds Will Arise* (Ward, 1958), Desmond Winterton, an earnest young man, sought Daphne's help when his fiancée, Diane, ended their engagement. First Desmond and then Daphne were denied access to Diane by her guardian, Elias Bartholomew. Daphne and the Adjusters saved Diane from a watery death, learned of a bank lockbox she was to open on her 21st birthday, and foiled a plot to insert an imposter in Diane's place.

Not Long to Live (Ward, 1959) was the first poison-pen case taken on by the Adjusters. Lester Wylton killed himself, leaving behind a letter attributing the act to the fact that young Jennifer Maxwell had ended their relationship. Given that no such relationship had ever existed, the coroner's jury returned a verdict of suicide without mentioning Jennifer's name.

Nevertheless, Jennifer began receiving threatening letters that alluded to the suicide. Daphne quickly identified the sender, but wanted to apprehend him at the right time and place.

Third Time Unlucky (Ward, 1959) began when they investigated a company, which had experienced three disastrous fires over the past six years, all covered by insurance. This was an unusual case for the Adjusters. Daphne took it because Henry Ditchworth, manager of the fire insurance company had been denied help by Scotland Yard. At best, this might make a good short story.

In *Wanted for Questioning* (Ward, 1960), the disappearance of Rosemary Winstone, a young woman suspected in a jewel robbery, was brought to Daphne's attention by her brother, Charles. The familiar plot had the disappearance linked to a jewel robbery at the home of Rosemary's employer. The Adjusters used their regular techniques: following another employee who had been rejected by Rosemary, threatening torture to abducted criminals, breaking and entering residences to search, then returning with a legitimate search warrant and Scotland Yard help.

The title of *Once Too Often* (Ward, 1960) may refer to the hackneyed plot, which again used impersonation as a narrative gimmick. Another disappearance, another brother of the victim, more kidnappings, suspects tailed by the Four, use of fingerprint clues, and another solution that the reader will anticipate.

As *Once Upon a Crime* (Ward, 1961) began, Deirdre Manning was convinced that her fiancé, Dudley Mortimer, had been framed on a charge of theft at the tennis club. He was placed into a First Offender program after the conviction but the wedding was postponed. The most obvious suspect was Gilbert Jasperly, an older suitor of Deirdre's. The Adjusters agreed that Dudley was set up, but they needed proof, so they set a trap with Dudley as bait.

In *Perilous Hazard* (Ward, 1961), British scientist Sir James Barton had adopted an American niece, sight unseen. He and his wife were disturbed when the young woman fell in love with Vincent Mellerby, an unsuitable older man whom she had met on shipboard. Hugh not only participated in trailing him but read his lips at a restaurant where he met a confederate. No reader will be surprised to learn of another impersonation.

There were four additional titles: *Challenge to the Four* (1939), *The Four at Bay* (1939), *Murder in the Pool* (1941), and *The Strange Case of Pamela Wilson* (1954), all of which were available in the British Library as of 2004. A few are also on the used book market or at other major universities (Oxford; Trinity College in Dublin). The used books sell at high prices, very high considering the quality of the material.

Susan Yates

Author: Emma Lou Fetta

Susan Yates was sparingly described, even though other women characters were given full descriptions. She had brown eyes and was "healthy but fashionable," a businesswoman who had become successful after her socially prominent family lost its money during the Depression. Using her talents as a fashion designer, she developed an international reputation for her New York-based salon.

In *Murder in Style* (Doubleday, 1939), Susan was suspected of murdering an ambitious rival. Lyle Curtis, the assistant District Attorney assigned to the case, conducted a serious investigation. Susan was a member of the Tomorrow Club, which was planning a fashion show. During a committee meeting while the group was watching a display in a darkened room, Nancy Pierce passed out and died. It was proven that her death came as the result of poison inserted into a capsule by a hypodermic needle. Not only did Susan and Lyle work together on the case, but they began a decorous relationship expected to lead to marriage. Susan and Lyle formed that combination that became common in the 1980's of an established female professional in another field romantically tied to a male whose profession dealt with crime.

During *Murder on the Face of It* (Doubleday, 1940), Susan was traveling on a transatlantic ship returning from France when fellow passenger Alma Peters seemingly committed suicide. Many of the passengers were wealthy individuals returning to the United States due to the Nazi blitzkrieg. Lyle boarded the ship when it reached New York Harbor to arrest Peters, unaware that it was no longer possible. Passengers who had shared the experience met informally afterwards. A further complication arose when one member of the group died of a cocaine overdose and another was her supplier. The denouement included the exposé of an assumed identity.

In *Dressed to Kill* (Doubleday, 1941), Lyle included Susan in an investigation because of her expertise in fashion. Prunella Parton had died on the train taking a group back from a skiing holiday. Her unusual attire included long ski underwear covered by a red velvet evening gown. After Susan reached home, she continued to be involved. She belonged to the social set in which the suspects circulated and could pick up clues, which might have otherwise gone unnoticed.

The books, although lacking in tension, were better written than many other American series featuring female sleuths during this period.

Section 4:

Women at War; Then, a Return to Domesticity—Women Sleuths of 1940-1959

Female investigators were no longer a novelty during the period from 1940 to 1959, even though many came in through the back door as the wives or sweethearts of the hero. The "couples" mystery dominated the genre at first, but gradually individual heroines, such as Margot Blair, Dr. Mary Finney, Eve Gill, and Flora Hogg, were introduced. Even when the female was part of a couple, she more frequently carried a strong share in the investigation, as did Pamela North. Several women were villainesses including, Sumuru, the Sinister Widow, and Mabie Otis, all in series written by males. Fewer new sleuths and writers appeared in English fiction, probably due to involvement in the war. The old faithfuls—Christie, Sayers, and Allingham—continued to write excellent mystery fiction.

The mystery heroines changed in character. They were more likely to have attended college, to be employed before their marriages, and/or to do so afterwards. Fewer had children to limit their mobility. There was a mixture of spinsters, bright young women, and wives, but only a small number of professionals. They were professionals in lines of work other than criminal justice. Not all marriages were happy, even in this make-believe world. Several series heroines divorced or were separated from their husbands.

World War II had changed the lives of fictional male detectives. Unless essential to police forces or deferred because of physical impairments, males were expected to put detecting aside until the national crisis ended. This gave women opportunities to take the spotlight, solving crimes while their marital or business partners were overseas.

In the real world, male authors went to war, opening publishers' doors to added women writers. Similar new opportunities existed in education and employment. Many such advantages were temporary and disappeared when veterans returned to claim their jobs and their places in college classrooms. Nevertheless, women had learned that they were capable of more than had been expected of them. Publishers who promoted books with women sleuths included Doubleday, Simon, Random, and Lippincott in the United States. New publishing names were surfacing, including Fawcett, Mystery House, and Pyramid, with many of their products being paperback originals. In England, the traditionals—Hammond, Hutchinson, Hale, Long, Hodder & Stoughton, and Jenkins—dominated in publishing women's series.

Ethel Abbott

Author: James P. Langham

Ethel Abbott and her husband, Samuel (Sammy), were among those who rode the coattails of Nick and Nora Charles.

In *Sing a Song of Homicide* (Simon, 1940), Sammy was a special investigator for the district attorney and Ethel was his bride of nine months. As a teenager, Ethel had written embarrassing letters, which Sammy tried to recover from a potential blackmailer. When the blackmailer was killed, Sammy planted false clues, faked his own alibi, and helped to find the killer, while Ethel looked on adoringly.

Sammy found a decapitated man on a park bench in *A Pocketful of Clues* (Simon, 1941). Rather than work on that case, the mayor wanted Sammy to handle a personal matter involving his daughter. Sammy's professional conflicts with the mayor made him a suspect when "His Honor" was killed. Ethel's only contribution to the narrative was a false pregnancy. She didn't even get that right.

A humdrum series.

Jean Holly Abbott

Author: Frances Crane

After her parents were killed in a car accident, Jean Holly left Elm Hill, Illinois. She was tall, with the Holly family topaz eyes and black hair. Her interest in art prompted her move to New Mexico, where she hoped to make her living as a painter. Dissatisfied with her own work, she eventually set up an art supply store and gallery for local artists.

In *The Turquoise Shop* (Lippincott, 1941), San Francisco private investigator Patrick Abbott joined the group that frequented the shop. Several local deaths were connected to a counterfeiting ring that Abbott was investigating, and Jean became his assistant.

When Jean returned to Illinois in *The Golden Box* (Lippincott, 1942), she learned of the death of local matriarch, Claribel Fabian Lake. The subsequent death of an African-American woman associated with the prominent family was considered suicide until Pat Abbott came to town.

Jean and Patrick married during *The Yellow Violet* (Lippincott, 1942), although they postponed the wedding once due to a murder. The Abbotts eventually acquired a dachshund named Pancho, a home in San

Francisco, an Irish maid, and two children, who were rarely seen or heard from.

Unlike other spouses of the period, Jean did not take over the series during the war. She accompanied Patrick, then a Marine, to England, but before they could leave they visited friends in New York City during *The Pink Umbrella* (Lippincott, 1943). Ellen Bland and Pat went back a long way, so when she was suspected of two murders, he rallied to her defense. Louis, Ellen's ex-husband, seemed determine to cast suspicion on her. That suited the investigating officer just fine. It didn't help matters when Louis was found dead in Ellen's home as she slept nearby.

While in England during *The Applegreen Cat* (Lippincott, 1943), Jean took employment in the Lend-Lease program. While the Abbotts were visiting the Heywoods, who had an art collection, Kip, the son of the household, went for a row on the Thames and found a woman's corpse in the punt. Elsie, the housemaid, had been strangled, but there was a dart in her back decorated with an apple-green cat. Jean was the target of a shooter, but it was Pat who solved the murders, earning two Renoirs as a reward.

The couple returned to New Mexico while Patrick recuperated from a war-connected illness in *The Amethyst Spectacles* (Random, 1944). A former Marine, rancher Ray Thayer died in what might have been an accident, but that became less likely when his wife, Dorrie, was killed under similar conditions (she had been shot first). Karen Thayer had been Ray's sweetheart before he went overseas where he met Dorrie. The ambitious state's attorney had focused on her. The dénouement did not stand up under close inspection.

Pat was still in the Marine Corps and stationed in New Orleans during *The Indigo Necklace* (Random, 1945). Major Dr. Roger Clary, a friend of Pat's, helped them find lodging in a family home that contained separate quarters. Roger's wife, Helen, rarely appeared, and indications were that she was seriously ill. Jean found her body in the courtyard. Victorine, the servant who watched over Helen, had disappeared. Roger, who had fallen in love with another woman, was close to being arrested when Patrick exposed an unlikely killer. The mysteries were solved by Patrick, but narrated by Jean, who shared her insights and on occasion found significant clues.

In *The Cinnamon Murder* (Random, 1946), Pat and Jean assisted Brenda Davison, a single mother whose daughter, Katy, would someday inherit a fortune and whose in-laws sought her custody. They were about to leave New York City after a vacation made possible when oil was discovered on land owned by Pat's family. The Abbotts remained in New York because Brenda disappeared about the time another woman was battered to death and Katy's doctor was shot. Despite all of the emotional entanglements, Pat identified a killer who had a financial motive.

During *The Shocking Pink Hat* (Random, 1946), Pat was on inactive duty from the Marine Corps recovering from wounds. While he and Jean were dining in a restaurant, they noted an older man who was being harangued by a younger woman. Ernest Leland was murdered later. Inspector Sam Bradish of the San Francisco Police Department asked Pat for help, but the suspects were concealing information to protect one another.

The Abbotts traveled to Florida in *Murder on the Purple Water* (Random, 1947) along with their New Orleans detective friend Bill Jonas. They, along with a group of friends, went fishing on Captain Cy Martingale's "Margaret." There were multiple romantic entanglements among the group on the boat. Alcoholic Gerald Deane was assumed to have passed out, but after the others left the boat, Cy realized he had been stabbed to death. The local police wanted help from Bill Jonas, who brought Pat and Jean along for interviews.

Black Cypress (Random, 1948) was disappointing. Pat and Jean became involved in the murder of an heiress to please a shirttail relative. The killer, after several murders, took his own life.

The Flying Red Horse (Random, 1949) took the Abbotts to Dallas, where Pat was doing business with a newly rich oilman. He had married into a family of competitive sisters, one of whom was murdered during their visit. Pat and Jean investigated on different tracks. Jean must have been getting close, because she was attacked and kidnapped. The death of a second sister finally led Patrick to the killer. Weak plotting.

Daffodil Blonde (Random, 1950) took place in Kentucky, where Rob Murray ran a horse breeding farm. The death of Sam Casey, the head horseman at the farm, was not the only shock to the Murray family. Daughter Alex planned to marry Guy Adriance, whom her father did not like. Guy's mother brought Pat and Jean into the investigation when Guy was murdered. Steve, Alex's former fiancé, was targeted by the police, but a ditzy "daffodil blonde" (Guy's unacknowledged wife) was Pat's choice for the killer. While he worked on the physical evidence, Jean probed the personal relationships. There were many of them.

The Abbotts returned to New Mexico to visit old friends in *The Polkadot Murder* (Random, 1951). Unfortunately, the old friends were entangled in marriages, divorces, second marriages, suitors, and murder. The ending is a warning to authors who get too involved with their fictional characters.

Murder in Blue Street (Random, 1951) found the Abbotts in Paris, enjoying that time of October evenings referred to as "blue." Madame Clarisse Latour, an American expatriate whose secretary, Linda Grant, had been murdered, was eager to minimize bad publicity, so she hired Patrick to investigate. Not everyone made them welcome. Someone kept shooting at them as they cooperated with a French detective.

Murder in Bright Red (Random, 1953) was marred by changes in narrators. Jean and Pat were back in her hometown staying with friends. Charley, one of the three Pryor grandsons, inheritors of the Pryor Glassworks, was murdered. At one time he had been engaged to airline hostess Sally Carroll. Phil Williams, a Korean war veteran who worked for the glassworks, called Pat because he worried that Sally would be suspected. Pat's intervention was not welcomed by the Pryor family. When a second Pryor grandson was killed, Hank, the remaining heir, was arrested. Pat investigated the financial affairs of the business, finding clues to the killer. He had told Jean to stay out of it, but she wielded a tire iron with gusto when things got wild.

13 White Tulips (Random, 1953) found the Abbotts at home in San Francisco. The two children were on vacation with Lulu, Pat's secretary. Pat's refusal to take on a murder case wherein artist Jack Ivers had been killed brought down the ire of a prominent but malicious socialite. It was another member of the Abbott family who was at risk in the narrative—Pancho, the dachshund. There was no way Pat could stay out of the case.

The Coral Princess (Random, 1954) took place in Tangiers. Pat was contacted by a local police official because he and Jean were among the last to see drug dealer Hugo Poole, who was believed to be dead because his crippled hand was discovered on the seashore. His death convinced the police that the murder was connected to local drug production. Likely suspect was Nicolas Gannaway, believed to have Mafia ties.

In *Death in Lilac Time* (Random, 1955), Pat and Jean flew to Kentucky for the Derby. On the plane they met Jane Mallory, who had agreed under pressure from her mother-in-law to visit her abusive husband, Richard. He died shortly after Jane assisted him in taking medicine, leaving her as heiress to his estate. Pat investigated but shared little of what he learned with Jean. In an unlikely ending, Pat exposed the killer just as the police were about to arrest Jane.

In *The Ultraviolet Widow* (Random, 1956), Pat and Jean were off again, this time to Alamos, Mexico. It was supposed to be a vacation, but Pat had his own agenda. They met the van Gilder family through a San Francisco neighbor whose daughter Marta had married Rex, a cold, older man. After a dinner at van Gilder's, Pat escorted Audrey, a drunken guest, to her home. She was later found dead at the bottom of a well, murdered. Jean was conscripted by Montoya, the Mexican detective, to take notes, so she and Pat were privy to police interviews. The well was part of a tunnel system connecting assorted buildings. The tunnel could contain gold and jewels, and incidentally more corpses.

In *Horror on the Ruby X* (Random, 1956), Alan Mackenzie did not believe his wife, Ruby's, car wreck was an accident nor the subsequent death of a family servant under similar circumstances. He hired Pat to investigate. A winter storm isolated Pat and Jean, along with all the suspects plus the sheriff and deputies. Under stress, accusations and revelations were made. Alan's Aunt Ada was murdered before she could reveal a secret. In a fiery finish, Jean was in serious danger and another family member was killed.

In *The Man in Gray* (Random, 1958), by which time the Abbots had two children, Pat needed Jean as his secretary as he investigated the death of D.V. Willoz, a winegrower whose business retained the Abbott firm. Finding a babysitter proved to be an even greater problem when one was found murdered!

The Buttercup Case (Random, 1958) found the Abbotts occupying a guesthouse on a Louisiana estate. During a dinner held by their host, Captain Bill Jonas, guest Suzanne Lamont was poisoned. Jean used a poker to protect herself from an irate suspect.

In *Death Wish Green* (Random, 1960), Jean and Pat sought a young woman believed to have dived off a San Francisco bridge. On a foggy evening Katie Spinner had started across the Golden Gate Bridge. Later her abandoned car was located, with no clue as to what had happened to Katie. Liz Brown, Katie's aunt, contacted the Abbotts. Katie was known to be a rebellious hippie, tight with the art community, rejecting the beau selected by her father, Ira. Pat and Jean were successful in locating Katie and returning her to Aunt Liz. While Pat and police Lt. Sam Bradish were off investigating, the killer menaced Jean. Big rescue scene, uncommon in the series.

In *The Amber Eyes* (Random, 1962), the Abbotts rejected accident as the cause of the death of Lisa, the retarded daughter of Dr. Alby. A substantial inheritance from their deceased mother was therefore divided between her two surviving sisters, Caroline and Audrey. Caroline hired Pat to prove that someone had smothered Lisa. Audrey was almost the next victim. At least they kept murder in the family.

The Body Beneath a Mandarin Tree (Hammond, 1965) took place when they vacationed in Arizona. This was not available for review.

The plots were passable, but offered few challenges. Jean was very impressed by her older, self-assured husband, while he tolerated her feminine foibles. Her interest in a career had ended when she married. What made the series attractive was the variety of settings and the fine descriptions.

Kit Marsden Acton

Author: Marion Bramhall

Kit Marsden Acton was one of the series heroines featured by the Doubleday Crime Club in the 1940's. At the beginning, she was a 19-year-old living in a New England college town with her widowed father, a doctor. An only child, whose mother had died when she was young, Kit had grown to be a 5' 2" blonde with blue eyes.

As *Murder Solves a Problem* (1944) began, the Marsdens' next door neighbors were attorney Orrin Winter and his beautiful younger wife, Marta. When Marta was murdered, Kit and her father took an interest because their friend Richard Acton was a suspect. Orrin had pursued the beautiful Marta, but once they were married, he became jealous, cruel, and unfaithful. Ricky, Marta's brother, was incensed at her treatment and wanted to take her back to Cuba. Richard, Dr. Marsden, and Kit, who had a crush on Richard, studied the other suspects as to motive, means, and opportunities. Orrin rated high on the suspect scale until he too was murdered. Only after the killer had died was the case closed.

After Richard and Kit married in *Button, Button* (1944), they moved to Lyford, Massachusetts, while he served in the Navy. In pursuing her new hobby, collecting buttons, Kit and friend Sally Winsted found the corpse of Jake Slezak, an antique dealer who had a valuable button for sale. Sally deliberately confused the scene of the crime because she wanted to protect her former husband, Dr. Bill Barnes, whom she still loved. Kit and Sally scoured the pawnshops for the missing button. One dealer provided a description of a man who tried to sell it. Under pressure, the killer attacked the two women, but Kit fought him off until help arrived.

Later, Kit began work as a nurse's aide in a Boston hospital in *Tragedy in Blue* (1945), where Sally, now remarried to Bill Barnes, was on staff. After Peter Bradford Stone, a wealthy alcoholic patient, was poisoned, Kit moved into his family mansion and worked with his sister to find the killer. There was one there, because someone went in for wholesale poisoning. Once the mercenary member of the family was disclosed, the rest shaped up.

After the war ended, Richard and Kit were summertime boarders at a Cape Cod home in *Murder Is an Evil Business* (1948). When Tina, the daughter of their domineering landlady, was found hanging from the rafters, Richard insisted that the death was murder. Information that Tina was pregnant, had a miscarriage, but intended to leave the family home and move to Boston put a different light on the matter. The ending was a surprise. Kit described her role as "gathering the facts while Dick sifted through them and made the deductions." This was the pattern that they followed in detection.

In *Murder Is Contagious* (1949), Richard taught at a small Michigan college, where returned veterans and their families lived in temporary housing. He had become pompous and impatient with his younger and less educated wife. Ken Kimberley was allowed to live in Quonset Village because he provided care for his paraplegic roommate, Jim Van Smythe. The deaths of Van Smythe and Ken's former fiancée drew Kit into the relationships among the residents. She dominated the books issued during the war, but resumed a supportive role in the last two books of the series, mirroring the experience of women in the post World War II period.

A run-of-the-mill series for its time.

Christine Andersen
Author: Merlda Mace, pseudonym for Madeleine McCoy

Christine Andersen, a blonde Scandinavian from rural Minnesota, had problems adjusting to the big city.

In *Headlong for Murder* (Messner, 1943), she lied to the police when her friend Lila Leeds was murdered. She had no intention of having her vacation trip spoiled. She had agreed to take a package from Lila to Gwen LaMar, who, together with her husband, Nick, ran the vacation inn. Anson Reed and his wife were also guests at the inn. Chris realized that he was the man who had been visiting Lila. The motivation for Lila's death and that of another guest at the inn was tied to a secret formula. Finally Christine cooperated and, for her reward, was used as bait.

When her steady beau went off to war in *Blondes Don't Cry* (Messner, 1945), Christine moved to a secretarial job in Washington, D.C. Her new residence came equipped with an unknown dead blonde in the dumbwaiter. Christine was clever enough to realize the police had arrested the wrong suspect, but dumb enough to rely on a killer for help.

Nothing special.

Soeur Angele

Author: Henri Catalan, pseudonym for Henri Dupuy-Mazuel

Soeur Angele was a French nun, a member of the Sisters of Charity. Before joining the order, Angele, the daughter of the Marquis Persent d'Ericy, had trained as a medical doctor. Given that she was clothed as a nun with her hair covered, she was described as slim with freckles and laughing eyes. Angele had worked under atheist Professor Robin while earning her degree in forensic medicine. Robin and his servant Claudius, a former criminal, often assisted Soeur Angele in her investigations. Many of the Catalan books were never translated into English.

Soeur Angele first appeared in a U. S. publication in *Soeur Angele and the Embarrassed Ladies* (Sheed, 1955). She had been serving in a Bethlehem orphanage, but had returned to France to raise funds, when she learned of the death of her cousin, Baron d'Orchais. Because she was certain that the police were mistaken when they arrested two of his servants, she intervened.

Soeur Angele did not believe in ghosts, but her next adventure was *Soeur Angele and the Ghosts of Chambord* (Sheed, 1956). She and another nun visited the Castle of Chambord as chaperones for a group of school-children, while a film company was on location. When a man was killed, she had only a vocal clue to the identity of the murderer, but it proved to be enough.

Soeur Angele shared her medical skills with the residents of a small village in *Soeur Angele and the Bell Ringer's Niece* (Sheed, 1957). The bell-ringer of the local church was murdered shortly after Angele spoke to him. Monique, a teenager, had an emotional episode at the funeral, announcing that she had seen the Blessed Virgin Mary. Although the villagers saw the economic benefits of such an apparition, Soeur Angele persisted in her opposition to the claimed miracles and unmasked the conspirators.

Soeur Angele's technical skills and deep faith were balanced against Professor Robin's cynical and worldly attitudes.

Nell Bartlett

Author: David Elias

Nell Bartlett was a redheaded, green-eyed secretary, who had worked with the San Francisco police for four years. Purportedly she was fired because her fellow police officers' wives complained.

She was in New York City, acting as secretary/researcher for absent-minded professor Ernest Hamilton as *The Cause of the Screaming* (Hammond, 1953) began. He had walked out of the Prince Albert Hotel minus his pants and had never been seen alive again. His naked body was discovered on the floor of his shower. Hamilton's murder set Nell on the trail of a killer, who had been beside her most of the time. This seemed to have been planned as a "madcap" mystery like the Craig Rice tales, but it didn't come off that well.

In *The Gory Details* (Hammond, 1954), Nell monitored the presentation of new Gory Electrics products after she was upgraded to advertising executive. She was on the scene when CEO Fred Gory was murdered. Police Lt. O'Mara, smitten by Nell's beauty, included her in his interviews of suspects. She asked probing questions, picking up on relationships, and correctly identifying the killer. She was unpleasant. The puns were distasteful and the premise unbelievable.

The books, although set in the United States, were published by Hammond in London for an English audience, and lacked credibility.

Amanda and Lutie Beagle

Author: Marjorie Torrey Chanslor

Amanda and Lutie Beagle operated a detective agency bequeathed to them by their brother Ezekiel. The sisters left their rural home to come to New York, bringing along Martha Meecham, a younger (52) cousin who narrated. At that time Amanda was 65 and Lutie, 52. Lutie was the more adventurous of the pair.

In *Our First Murder* (Stokes, 1940), John Bynum, their first client, found a decapitated man in Hester Gale's bed. She was a nightclub singer whom the sisters took under their wing when she became a suspect. Both Hester and the victim, Vincent Smyth, lived in a theatrical boarding house. Only later did Hester admit that Vincent was her husband, an ex-convict. Lutie had in her possession a suitcase she obtained using a key dropped by an intruder. The suitcase was filled with money. They joined the world of vaudeville and theatre to find the killer, an unexpected person.

During *Our Second Murder* (Stokes, 1941) the agency was hired to protect valuable jewelry to be worn by models in a fashion show. There were romantic connections between Ted Green, the bandleader, and two of the models when he announced his engagement to a third woman. One of the models, Hero Lynn, was strangled by a valuable necklace. A note implied suicide, but that seemed physically unlikely. Inspector Moore, a friend of the deceased Ezekiel, cooperated with Amanda and Lutie, even letting them stay for the interviews. They learned that Hero was wealthy and that her death passed a considerable amount of money to Kate, her widowed sister, and Elinor, her stepmother. When Elinor was found dead, the sisters followed on Kate's trail, found the killer, and overpowered him.

No third murder.

Petunia Best

Author: Bridget Chetwynd

Petunia Best, a redheaded ex-WAAF in World War II, might be considered a British equivalent to Honey West (See Section 4, page 223), although she could be taken more seriously. She worked with former British Intelligence officer Max Frend in a private investigation agency. They did a motive/opportunity chart on suspects in their cases.

In *Death Has Ten Thousand Doors* (Hutchinson, 1951), the agency had no clients. Their first case arose out of a personal visit to a family where murder came as no surprise. They spent an afternoon at the Desert home, ruled by Ailsa, a domineering mother. She failed to arise from her afternoon nap and was found dead. The guests at the house party had moved about considerably, but Petunia had a clear recollection of their whereabouts so was a help to the Scotland Yard investigators. Chetwynd's plot had elements of the murder trade-off in Patricia Highsmith's *Strangers on a Train.*

In *Rubies, Emeralds, and Diamonds* (Hutchinson, 1952), Max and Petunia were sent on the trail of "Red" Carter, who was missing along with valuable jewels given her by her rich fiancé, Edward Swayne. They were hired by the insurance company that covered the loss of the jewels. When Red's body was located in a cave, the jewels were there, too. Swayne was found dead later, poisoned with the same substance as had killed "Red." Mrs. Carter, Red's mother, demanded the jewels. Petunia had no intention of turning them over.

Miriam Birdseye

Author: Nancy Spain

Miriam Birdseye was a free spirit, at least free of marriage after three divorces, able to work as an entertainer or an unorthodox investigator. Natasha Nevkorina (see Section 4, page 179), a former ballet dancer, was

Miriam's off-again, on-again partner in detection. Natasha also married several times, but tired of her husbands quickly. Miriam, who was tall and thin with blonde hair and blue eyes, worked primarily in musical comedy revues. She had no gift for solitude, needing to be surrounded by people, preferably of an artistic nature. When traveling, she was often accompanied by Natasha (with or without her current husband) or by barrister/poet Frederick Pyke, who loved Miriam until he fell in love with Natasha.

Even when not working, Miriam kept theatre hours, up late at night and sleeping until late morning. Although loyal to friends, she had a wicked tongue, disliked children, and was not fond of her own mother. At times, she showed prejudice against both Jews and blacks. As a sideline, she and Natasha opened an "investigation service" called Birdseye et Cie.

When Miriam, Natasha, and her then husband, Johnny Du Vivien, an ex-wrestler, visited a ski resort in the aptly named country of Schizo-Phrenia in *Death Goes on Skis* (Hutchinson, 1949), they made friends with the erratic Barny Flaherte family. Both Barny's wealthy wife, Regan, and his current mistress, Fanny, died mysteriously. Johnny and Barny detected the killer of Mrs. Flaherte. It was Miriam's photographic memory that trapped the murderer of the mistress.

In *Poison for the Teacher* (Hutchinson, 1949), Natasha's marriage was in trouble, so she joined Miriam in seeking a job. Janet Lipscoomb of the Radcliff Hall School for Girls (sounded like trouble) hired the pair to discover who was ruining her school. As might be expected, there were undercurrents of emotional relationships among staff and pupils. Miriam and Natasha tried to work with the local police when two staff members were murdered.

By the time Natasha's divorce was final in *Cinderella Goes to the Morgue* (Hutchinson, 1950), she had selected her next husband. Meanwhile she accepted a part in a Christmas pantomime. Miriam joined the show to replace Vivienne Gresham, who had died in a fall, in the role of Prince Charming. A second death made it likely that Vivienne, heavily insured, had been murdered. A third death clinched it.

Miriam was accompanied by Frederick Pyke in *"R" in the Month* (Hutchinson, 1950) when she visited a resort area, staying at the local inn run by the profligate Tony Robinson and his weary wife. When Eithne Bognor, a domineering widow, was murdered, the police included Miriam in the investigation, but it was Pyke who actually solved the mystery.

Miriam and Pyke traveled together on a cruise in *Not Wanted on Voyage* (Hutchinson, 1951). She had been hired by Douglass Comett, director of the shipping line, to discover how, and by whom, heroin was being smuggled. Mrs. Speak, Comett's mother-in-law, was pushed under a train when she hurried to give her daughter, Hero, a warning. One shipmate, C. B. Bunyip, was an author working on an historical account of a Marlene Speak, a bordello madam and an ancestor of Hero. Hero might well be embarrassed. Instead, Hero was drowned.

Out, Damned Tot! (Hutchinson, 1952) continued the trip as Miriam, Natasha, and Pyke visited the South Atlantic island of Manya, a colony of Schizo-Phrenia. Pyke arranged for a dinner invitation to the house of resident author Evelyn St. Leonard. The police, summoned by a report that Natasha had smuggled currency, found St. Leonard dead. Natasha was not only jailed for smuggling but also considered a murder suspect. When released, Natasha ended up in a factory that employed child labor just as a fire broke out. Nothing funny there.

These were farces, replete with witty but dated dialogue, improbable situations, and memorable characters, but disjointed and undisciplined. Author Nancy Spain indicated that she based Miriam on British actress Hermione Gingold.

Maria Black

Author: John Fearn, writing as John Slate

Unlike the women portrayed in Fearn's science fiction, Maria Black was unimaginative and colorless. She was a heavyset woman in her late fifties with blue eyes and black hair worn in a bun, employed as the headmistress of Roseway, a British women's college. Her two "Watsons" were Eunice Tanby, a fellow staff member, and "Pulp" Martin, a slangy American.

Maria met Pulp during *Black Maria, M.A.* (Rich, 1944), when she solved her brother's murder while in the United States. Ralph Black had left a considerable amount of money to Maria to be used in the investigation. She quickly figured out how the murder had been done in a locked room. The more difficult task was to identify the killer. Suspects included his widow and his three children. Maria came to realize that Ralph had been ruthless in both his domestic and business affairs.

In *Maria Marches On* (Rich, 1945), Maria enrolled a "teenager" whose widowed father was going abroad. She used methodical reasoning when the young woman was murdered to uncover a Nazi plot to steal a chemical formula. The Scotland Yard superintendent involved in the case offered Maria both a marital and professional partnership, which she declined.

One of Maria's special interests was crime movies. In *One Remained Seated* (Rich, 1946), she was present when a fellow movie patron was murdered. Nancy, the usherette, feared that her fiancé, Fred Allerton, the projectionist, might be suspected and asked Maria for help. The victim, "Douglas Farrington," had seen the film three times, and Maria suspected that he was related to Lydia Fane, the lead actress. That might be true, but he was also a financier who had been sent to prison for murder. Lydia, when interviewed, gave Maria information that led her to the killer.

A young Roseway alumna, Betty Shapely, had three suitors, one of whom, Herbert, was killed, perhaps by another in *Thy Arm Alone* (Rich, 1947). Understandably interested in the character of the remaining suitors, Betty asked Miss Black to investigate. She may not have found a killer, but she identified the cause of death and helped Betty know which suitor she could trust.

The engagement of Patricia Taylor to unstable Keith Robinson in *Death in Silhouette* (Rich, 1950) was considered a mistake by both of their families. Patricia, a former student at Roseway, invited Maria to the engagement party. She arrived after Keith had been discovered hanging in the cellar. The use of a silhouette obscured the time of death temporarily and prompted a premature finding of suicide.

Run of the mill.

Nora Hughes Blaine

Author: Lavinia Davis

Eleanor (Nora) Hughes had been a young debutante until the Depression wiped out the family fortune. Undaunted, she went into the antique business and became successful.

During *Evidence Unseen* (Doubleday, 1945) Nora visited Atlantic City, leaving Maisie, her partner, to manage the business. While Nora enjoyed supper, someone deposited the body of Daniel Scott, an American intelligence agent, in her hotel room. Captain Larry Blaine, an old friend, currently assigned in the United States, became involved with the case, and with Nora. Concerned with her safety, he arranged for her to leave the hotel and move into the home of Eudora Singleton. Heedless of her own vulnerability, Nora gathered information on possible espionage.

Nell and Larry married and moved to Connecticut, where she concentrated on decorating their home. In *Taste of Vengeance* (Doubleday, 1947), Nora discovered the body of handyman Abel Patterson on the premises, when she, her husband, and his Uncle Tip moved into a new house. Two other deaths followed: Dr. Jon Scott, a friendly physician, and Clara Pritchard, a self-appointed guardian of local morality. Tip had been active in intelligence work during World War II and had made enemies who did not forget. The killer died in an accident.

Author Davis was competent. The two-book series was better than many Doubleday book series with longer runs.

Margot Blair

Author: Kathleen Moore Knight

Margot Blair was described by partner Felix Norman as having a "steel trap" mind. She needed it because Felix, his family, and their clients in a public relations agency were often in trouble.

Rendezvous with the Past (Doubleday, 1940) found Margot "mothering" Sherry, Felix's 19-year-old daughter. The divorce settlement between Felix and his former wife, Irene, had denied him visitation. Sherry had already married and had an annulment, and was a "jet setter." When Sherry's trustee/stepfather, Dabney Grandon, was murdered, Margot took on the added task of proving not only Sherry, but Felix, innocent. The motive was there. Grandon had "wasted" assets in the trust.

The Norman-Blair agency assigned the "woman's angle" of the business to Margot. In *Exit a Star* (Doubleday, 1941), that role included nurturing the career of aspiring actress Susan Holland. Broadway star Lucia Drocott went out of her way to scuttle Susan, who had a small role in her new play. Somehow the two women kept appearing in identical gowns. Not funny! Even less funny when Lucia and her couturier were murdered. None of the obvious suspects panned out, but Margot found a surprise killer.

In *Terror by Twilight* (Doubleday, 1942), Benjamin Embrie selected Margot as trustee for his granddaughter Deborah's inheritance, but died before a new will could be executed. He had taken full control of Deborah's life because her mother had a history of depression. In an upbeat story with improved action, Margot rescued Deborah and reunited the young woman with her mother.

During *Design in Diamonds* (Doubleday, 1944), Felix and Margo held smuggled diamonds for refugee Adrien ter Broek, until they could be turned over to his family. Nazi sympathizers were determined to intercept the diamonds. With Felix, now in the military, about to be sent overseas, Margot handled the delivery when "Katrien ter Broek" in Mexico City claimed the jewels.

Although they were less than spine tingling and featured dated dialogue, the Blair books provided some excitement. Margot was physically active, took risks, and gave a good account of herself for a 38-year-old professional woman.

Arabella "Arab" Blake

Author: Richard Powell

In most couple series, when a narrator was used, the wife obliged. Not only did Powell utilize Andy Blake as his narrator, he did so with humor and warmth. Andy described his wife, Arabella, as petite (5' 7" in heels!), slim and trim, with long black hair and blue eyes. She was more aggressive and athletic than Andy—an excellent shot, angler, and competitive field hockey player. Her technical skills or inclinations did not extend to such household items as vacuum cleaners and toasters.

Fortunately the Blakes, both of whom were from prominent Philadelphia families, usually had household help. Arabella was a former debutante, who selected Andy over more dynamic suitors and became jealous when he was attentive to other women. She was intuitive and foolhardy while Andy, against his natural instinct, was brave and resourceful.

In *Don't Catch Me* (Simon, 1943), Andy impulsively bought a second-hand chair. When it was stolen, Arab wanted to know why. Andy was disinterested, but had to join in the investigation when he realized that Arab was in danger. Was the chair he bought for five dollars, a real antique or one of the replicas made by dishonest dealers? H. P. Meredith, owner of the collection currently on loan to a museum, was behaving strangely. When Andy figured out that Meredith's daughter was a hostage, he called in the volunteer fire department.

Now a first lieutenant, Andy Blake was assigned to a Washington, D.C., desk job in *All Over But the Shooting* (Simon, 1944). The city was overcrowded. Arab posed as a single woman to get a place at Renee Fielding's boarding house. Trying to keep Arab out of trouble, Andy found himself committing a variety of criminal offenses. He believed that something was going on at the Fielding house, but his superiors would take no action until he had proof. He got it the hard way.

By *Lay That Pistol Down* (Simon, 1945) the Blakes had moved to the Virginia countryside. As in the first book, Arab made an intriguing purchase, an antique pistol that was subsequently stolen. At Andy's insistence, Arab agreed to a 36-hour time limit during which she had to discover what was unique about the pistol. At least two other buyers were more than willing to purchase it…or steal it.

At the time of *Shoot If You Must* (Simon, 1946), Andy had left the Army to return to his Philadelphia antique business. While the Blakes were out for a neighborhood stroll, they overheard voices discussing what might have been a jewel robbery, making themselves vulnerable to attack.

Finally, in *And Hope to Die* (Simon, 1947), while on vacation in Florida, the Blakes rescued Sherry, a 12-year-old girl whose sore wrists would indicate that she had been a prisoner. Their efforts to return her to her proper home were finally successful, but they had to tangle with Nazis again.

Thanks to Powell's light touch, the Blakes were an enjoyable pair.

Louise "Liz" Boykin

Author: Manning Long

See: Louise "Liz" Boykin Parrott, Section 4, page 189.

Amy Brewster

Author: Sam Merwin, Jr.

Amy Brewster was a caricature of a woman. One can only speculate that she was designed to have a novelty value in the mystery story field. Merwin had featured attractive and intelligent women in his science fiction; to Amy, he was generous only as to her intellect. She graduated from Radcliffe at age 16 with a Phi Beta Kappa key, earned a law degree and was admitted to the Bar in both Massachusetts and New York, but did not practice. Nor did she use her full name, Amelia Winslow Brewster.

Amy did not approve of inherited wealth, but her financial acumen had not only enhanced her income, but made it possible for her to have a distinguished career in international finance. She was middle-aged, short, grossly fat, with gray-black hair worn in a bob, and black eyes. She took no interest in her clothes, which were "stained and shapeless." Her personal tastes included drinking straight gin, gambling, and smoking cigars. She had minimal social skills, or used them minimally, belching loudly on occasion. The narratives introduced a hero or heroine in trouble, with Amy appearing later as a friend of the family.

In *Message From a Corpse* (Mystery House, 1945), elderly attorney Brian O'Connell was killed in the waiting room of Breck Barnum, a press agent and former athlete. Only when he was knocked unconscious and his manuscript stolen did Breck realize that this death might be connected to his biography of deceased industrialist Tom Flanders. Amy lent a hand by checking Breck's original biographical material for clues as to where a valuable jewel collection had been hidden.

When *Knife in My Back* (Mystery House, 1945) began, Christopher Horton, in the mistaken belief that he was going to die, had turned over control of his bank. After a voluptuous secretary was found dead in the family home, younger brother Joe Horton called on his racing buddy, Amy Brewster, for help.

In *A Matter of Policy* (Mystery House, 1946), Joe Leavitt was surprised to learn that a $500,000 life insurance policy had been purchased on his life with an unknown woman as beneficiary. When Leavitt's bodyguard was killed, his boss at Stuyvesant Trust called Amy. The named beneficiary denied any knowledge of the policy, but who believed her? Someone at Stuyvesant must be involved.

Amy had no feminine characteristics and, if her name had been Amos, no alterations would have been necessary.

Jane Hamish Brown

Author: Delano Ames

What was maddening about Jane Hamish Brown was her husband, Dagobert. She was an attractive, well-educated, self-supporting young Englishwoman, swept into marriage by a divorced, upper class Cambridge graduate. Dagobert was self-centered, financially irresponsible, and willing to let Jane support him. She measured 35-22-35, had blue eyes and blue-black hair. A law office clerk when she met Dagobert, Jane became a novelist, basing her books on their adventures, which she narrated in the series. As Dagobert changed from one preoccupation to another, Jane followed, moving frequently to indulge his interests.

In *She Shall Have Murder* (Rinehart, 1949), the law firm foisted complaining client Mrs. Robjohn on Jane. When Mrs. Robjohn was found dead of gas poisoning, Jane, working with Dagobert, investigated the circumstances. Dagobert saw the investigation as a challenge, the pursuit of a new hobby or interest, while Jane wanted to avenge a woman who had become her friend.

While touring the American Southwest in *Murder Begins at Home* (Rinehart, 1950), the Browns visited Miranda Ross, a former WAC who had served overseas with Dagobert. When they attended a "murder game" at her house party, she was the first victim; her six-year-old son, the second. Dagobert found proof that Miranda, no paragon of virtue, might have planned her own death because she was ill, but someone beat her to it. Easy out, killer committed suicide.

In *Corpse Diplomatique* (Rinehart, 1951) Dagobert's study of Bertran de Born, an obscure 12th century troubadour-poet, took them into an expatriate Riviera colony terrorized by a "gentle" blackmailer, Major Hugh Arkwright. Arkwright's death was initially thought to have been an error, a bullet intended for another man. Then, they found out the kind of man he was.

When the Browns visited a Welsh coastal community in *Nobody Wore Black* aka *Death of a Fellow Traveller* (Rinehart, 1950), Dagobert had spies on his mind, and wanted Jane's next book to be a spy novel. Maybe that's why he was certain that fellow guest Captain Patrick Blythe had been murdered because of his espionage activities. He had fallen or been pushed off a cliff late at night. Information indicated that Patrick was more of a crook than a spy. Dagobert took a terrible beating, so for a while Jane carried the investigation. Another convenient suicide by the killer.

The Body on Page One (Rinehart, 1951) was a clever spoof of literary mystery conventions. Dagobert decided that Jane should write a mystery, using their current neighbors as characters. Jane had caught Jack Nicholson in their rental apartment. Was he searching for something left behind by the former tenant, Harold Quinn? After a party, there was a murder-suicide (Hilda and Tom Todd) in the building, but Dagobert was convinced it was murder. It didn't help that the killer used a knife similar to one owned by the Browns.

The Browns cycled through the Pyrenees in *Murder, Maestro, Please* (Rinehart, 1952), en route to a music festival where Jane hoped to meet former schoolmates. They had agreed to watch over Dagobert's 19-year-old cousin, Perdita, who was attending the festival with famous test pilot John Corcoran. This time, there really were spies involved, but also a family tragedy.

When dying English matador Denis St. John murmured "Madrecita," in *No Mourning for the Matador* (Washburn, 1953), Dagobert was convinced that the words had a non-familial meaning. Nevertheless, the Browns examined relationships in the St. John family and the members of his fiancée's family to uncover that meaning. When they knew the answer, the killer took the easy way out again.

On returning to London, the Browns rented an apartment formerly used as a "private enquiry" office by Charley Crabb, in *A Coffin for Christopher* (Washburn, 1954). Christopher Piper left few mourners when he died. Not his wife, anyway. Probably only his 11-year-old twin children. Dagobert wondered if it was a coincidence that Crabb disappeared the same day Piper died? Or that Crabb was found dead? Or that this is another one of those mysteries where one brother substitutes for another?

The footloose Browns had to reckon with Andalusian religious enthusiasm in *Landscape with Corpse* (Washburn, 1955). The community of Paradiso de Mar did not want its tourist industry disturbed by murder, so an investigation into the death of Norman Bloomfield, promoter of the festival of Santa Serafina, was quashed. Lt. Pepe Benavente, who had worked with Dagobert and Jane, was demoted for his enthusiastic probe. There had been not one murder, but two. Someone had been reading Patricia Highsmith.

Dagobert became absorbed in psychoanalysis in *Crime Out of Mind* (Washburn, 1956). When the heartless wife of Baron Dietrich von Jenbach, a titled German innkeeper, was killed, her husband asked the Browns to investigate. Jane and Dagobert were only on site to keep an eye on his wayward young cousin Peregrine but couldn't say no because he was one of the suspects. The roots to the crime were in the past, a time when mysterious Lee Smith was in a Hungarian POW camp where the Baron had succeeded his brother as commandant. The Browns reluctantly confronted a vulnerable murderess who never went to trial.

After Dagobert accepted employment and the Browns used inherited money to rent a suburban home in *She Wouldn't Say Who* (Washburn, 1958), he chafed under the pressures of stability. While Jane completed her current book on housekeeping and its dangers, he played truant with a femme fatale named Zizi, according to Beryl Simmons. Zizi was rehearsing a play based on Jane's book, subsidized by Dagobert. There were attacks on Zizi, the murder of Beryl's husband, the drugging of Dagobert. The worse things got, the happier Dagobert was.

In *For Old Crime's Sake* (Lippincott, 1959) aka *Lucky Jane,* Jane was selected by tabloid *Home Truth* for a two-week trip to the Isle of Tabarca. As the fortunate winners progressed on their trip, followed by Dagobert and Albert, a millionaire hitchhiker on a motor scooter, disaster struck repeatedly. There was something not quite right about *Home Truth,* although the publisher had no idea what it was.

Current readers, accustomed to Social Security numbers, computer checks, background investigations, and broader tolerance for sexual indiscretions, might find the motivations and plots in the Ames books unrealistic, even though valid at the time.

Emily Murdoch Bryce

Author: Margaret Scherf

Unusual for a Forties sleuth, Emily Bryce was a divorced businesswoman. She married her easy-going employee Henry Bryce during the series. Her business, Lentament Studio, specialized in furniture refinishing but also built theatrical sets. Emily's first husband had been a railroad engineer, allergic to paint, so was incompatible with her lifestyle. Emily was slightly overweight, a disaster in the kitchen, dangerous at the wheel of a car, and regrettably light-fingered in stores and restaurants. Although expert in her field, she accepted more work than she could handle, then made time to solve mysteries. Their neighbor, Link Simpson, owned an antique store.

Emily, then still Murdoch, in *The Gun in Daniel Webster's Bust* (Doubleday, 1949; Rue Morgue Press, 2004), was interested in Cleo Delphine's murder because Delphine had hired her to do renovations. That didn't explain why she rehid the weapon she found in the bust that she was renovating. Her decision was costly because Henry was knocked unconscious and the gun stolen. When Henry's heroics saved Emily's life, he proposed. Emily accepted Henry, a fine employee who was not allergic to paint.

In *The Corpse with One Shoe* aka *The Green Plaid Pants* (Doubleday, 1951; Rue Morgue Press, 2004), the Bryces had just returned from London when a quartet of British friends visited New York City. The Bryces suspected that their luggage had been used to smuggle items into the United States. When the Brits ran short of money, Link agreed to have them visit his country home. Roy Palling, the least likeable of the group, was murdered there. Henry methodically and Emily haphazardly followed up on the clues.

Link Simpson, whose gun and antique business was located below the Bryce studio, found the corpse of Madge Carver in *Glass on the Stairs* (Doubleday, 1954). She had come to Link's shop to buy a gun. She was also known to Link and the Bryces, because they were doing the sets for a television production in which she was to appear. Henry was the one who figured it out.

During *The Diplomat and the Gold Piano* (Doubleday, 1963), the Bryces worked on projects for Pierre Cloche, a diplomat stationed at the United Nations. When Camilla Lorenz, the decorator who brokered the renovations, was murdered, Henry discovered the body and Emily inadvertently captured the killer.

These were lighthearted narratives in which the action was divided between the spouses. Rue Morgue Press has republished two in its Vintage Series, with perhaps more to come.

Eileen Burke

Author: Ed McBain, pseudonym for Evan Hunter

Although McBain created a multi-ethnic 87th Precinct, Eileen Burke, the only female police officer in the ensemble, received limited coverage.

Detective Second Grade Eileen Burke, 5' 9" tall with Irish red hair and green eyes, was the daughter of a police officer who had been killed by an escaped convict. She wanted full acceptance as a detective, but was usually assigned to act as bait (*The Mugger*, Simon & Schuster, 1956), as part of a lovemaking duo on stakeout for a ransom pickup (*Fuzz*, Doubleday, 1968), or as a decoy for rapists (*Lightning*, Arbor House, 1984).

During *Lightning*, Eileen and fellow officer Bert Kling had become lovers, but their relationship deteriorated when Eileen was raped. She had been located in the apartment of a woman who had been raped several times by a man who said he would return. The rapist's motivation was connected with his pro-choice convictions.

Eileen's emotional scars did not rule out an assignment as a "hooker" to trap a serial killer in *Tricks* (Arbor House, 1987). Kling's interference with the stakeout caused a failure in her backup, resulting in the use of excessive force by Eileen in handling an attacker.

Eileen was featured in one of three story lines in *Lullaby* (Morrow, 1989). She received counseling from Karen Lefkowitz, a police department psychologist, to cope with the frigidity that followed her rape, her overuse of a gun against the serial killer, and the connection between the two incidents. Eileen played no significant part in other books in the series. McBain edited a collection, *McBain Ladies* (Mysterious Press, 1988), that featured Eileen as one of five "women of the 87th precinct."

Eleanora Burke

Author: Virginia Perdue

Widowed Eleanora Burke was a redheaded, 200-pound, almost six-foot tall investigator for the Los Angeles district attorney's office, who could outfight, outshoot, and outrun the criminals. A graduate of Stanford University, she was not all brawn. Her father had been in the diplomatic service; her husband, James Burke, a famous criminologist, and she was their equal.

As *The Case of the Grieving Monkey* (Doubleday, 1941) opened, Eleanora investigated the death of a pet monkey, whose wealthy owner,

Marian Gartley, believed the poison had been meant for her. However, it was Julian, her unfaithful husband, who was found dead in the lab where monkeys were used for tests. Like many mysteries in this time period, Nazis were part of the problem.

Eleanora made only one more appearance, in *The Case of the Foster Father* (Doubleday, 1942). The kidnapping of Johnny, one of a pair of twins, focused the District Attorney's attention on scientist Amadeus Wyatt, who adopted children to use them in environmental experiments. When the child disappeared, Wyatt threatened to disinherit all of the children if he were not returned. Instead someone killed Wyatt.

Perdue showed considerable ability in the Burke stories, but the series never went any further.

Janice Cameron
Author: Juanita Sheridan/Wolfe

Although she shared the detection with Lily Wu (see Section 4, page 227) narrator Janice Cameron was the primary character in their Doubleday series. The daughter of a widowed college professor in Hawaii, Janice left the islands after an unhappy romance. She was a recently slimmed-down, 5' 4" blonde with brown eyes, who had worked as a secretary at a Honolulu women's residence hall. Lily, a college student, had the dark hair and eyes of her racial background.

Both were physically active and reckless in their detection, swimming in underwater caves, searching without any warrant, but were chaste and innocent for young women in their mid-twenties. They had no ties to the authorities and did not share information with them until it was necessary.

When *The Chinese Chop* (Doubleday, 1949) opened, Janice was in New York City. She and Lily came together after Janice placed a newspaper ad for lodgings. When Lily responded to the advertisement, the young women recalled that they had met in Hawaii. Janice agreed that they should rent a single room on Washington Square, unaware of the importance of this location to Lily and the adventure it would bring. Charles Chadwick, another tenant in the building, was murdered. Janice, aware that Lily was lying to her, wondered if she had killed him. Once Lily explained her interest in Chadwick, Janice accepted her innocence and they worked together. They did not tell the police what they were doing or what they had learned, even after they rescued another tenant from danger. When Jarvis Lloyd, also a tenant, was killed, the police decided that he was the murderer and had committed suicide. Very convenient, but all wrong.

Because Janice's novel had sold as a movie plot, she returned to Hawaii in *The Kahuna Killer* (Doubleday, 1951). Her choice for the set was located on land owned by longtime friends, the Avery family. When Janice discovered the corpse of Malia, an attractive hula dancer, on the property, the body disappeared before she could get help. Lily, calm and efficient, came to the rescue, using her Chinese network to investigate.

Newspaperwoman "Steve" Dugan joined Lily and Janice in detection during *The Mano Murders* (Doubleday, 1952). Steve interested Janice and Lily in the problems of young bride Leslie Farnham, whose husband, Dan, had disappeared. Dan's cousin Howard, now in charge of the ranch, not only denied Leslie a place to stay but talked about turning the property into a dude ranch, leased to a hotel chain. All changed when Leslie declared her pregnancy, if she could survive long enough to give birth.

When *The Waikiki Widow* (Doubleday, 1953) began, Lily had just returned from Hong Kong. She seemed disinterested in resuming her close relationship with Janice, and was preoccupied with Madame Li, an ailing relative to whom she was indebted. Madame Li was upset that smugglers might be using her family tea business as a conduit. Lily had tremendous family resources, which she put into play on the mainland and in Hawaii. The tea company manager was bewitched by an evil woman, but when he realized what was going on, he cooperated with Lily. Janice played a subsidiary role in this one.

Sheridan used her extensive knowledge of the physical settings, the racial mixtures, and the history of the islands to good advantage.

Jane Carberry
Author: Beryl Symons, pseudonym for Mary Elizabeth Taubman

Jane Carberry was one of the eccentric upper class heroines so popular with the English. Her connections with the criminal justice system came through her brother Sir Richard, a Deputy Commissioner at Scotland Yard. She was an attractive woman in her fifties, slim with silver-black hair and blue eyes.

In her own way, she was a victim of the First World War. Her plan to marry Duncan Brooks ended with his death in Flanders. She took no solace in religion, was neither scholarly nor intellectually brilliant, but had verve and vitality. Jane was often guided by dreams or prophetic visions rather than deduction.

In *Jane Carberry, Detective* (Jenkins, 1940), as Jane began a plane flight from London to Brussels, she dreamed of jewels and jewel thieves.

The fellow passenger she selected to be the thief of her dreams turned out to be Gregoire, chief of the Belgian Police. When stolen pearls were discovered in her handbag, Jane was arrested but reluctantly released. Using information gained from a dream, she uncovered the identity of a businessman who was responsible for jewel thefts and murder. The Belgian police finally were convinced.

Jane's compassion for others involved her with troubled young persons. When, in *Jane Carberry Investigates* (Jenkins, 1940), heiress Astra Leigh felt threatened, she contacted Jane. In response, Jane kidnapped Astra when she saw her in a theater looking drugged in the presence of an older man. Aware that Astra needed help, her dying guardian, Sir Frederick Vance, passed her care over to Jane.

In *Magnet for Murder* (Jenkins, 1941), Jane took temporary shelter in an abandoned Devonshire cottage, where she found a jeweled earring. The skeleton of a young woman was found later in the same cottage, once the property of the unfortunate Moffat family. Jane traced the earring to learn the identity of the corpse because a friend, Guy Perceval, was suspected of the murder.

Jane was en route from Argentina in *Jane Carberry and the Laughing Fountain* (Jenkins, 1941) when her purse was exchanged with that of another woman who had reportedly died. Jane's life was already complicated by her promise to deliver a secret message entrusted to her by a British diplomat in Argentina. She needed to find someone who would accept the message. After a harrowing adventure, Jane learned that she had been used by British Intelligence to bait a trap. At this point she thought seriously of accepting the marriage proposal of longtime friend Trevor Cardwell.

The marriage proposal was shelved during *Jane Carberry's Weekend* (Jenkins, 1947) when Jane helped Alison, a rich young American heiress. Jane appeared as a guest at Alison's country home, but was made to feel unwelcome by Lord Partyn, Alison's husband. When Partyn was murdered, Jane's behavior made her a prime suspect, but her social position protected her. She became aware that the family butler and housekeeper were sinister influences on Alison, using medicines to control her. The Scotland Yard inspector assigned to the case was skeptical of Jane's "second sight." At the coroner's hearing, further evidence of hypnotism and Lord Partyn's murderous plans for Alison were brought into the open.

As a heroine, Jane relied on psychic abilities rather than deductive processes. She considered herself to be above the law, and had no hesitation about flaunting it, to the embarrassment of her brother.

A period piece, reflecting the interests of a specific class at a specific period in time.

Hortense Clinton

Author: Miriam-Ann Hagen

Hortense Clinton, a single woman in her fifties, was "slim," and very concerned about her "youthful" appearance. Her wealth made it possible for her to travel extensively, often with a paid companion.

Plant Me Now (Doubleday, 1947) (the titles are slangy and possibly derived from a song in *Pal Joey*, a musical of the time) found Hortense and young Janie Chase on a westbound transcontinental train. Among their fellow passengers were two admirers of Hortense, plus an assortment of hard drinkers and members of the Fraternal Order of Ancient Wisdom. The partying was over when Hortense found one of her "beaus" dead in her berth.

Hortense was on her own in *Dig Me Later* (Doubleday, 1949). While putting out her empty milk bottles, she was knocked unconscious by the exiting murderer of her well-to-do neighbor. The notoriety caused her to leave her New York City apartment for a Nova Scotian lodge, but the killer followed.

The peripatetic Hortense was on an ocean liner returning from London in *Murder—But Natch* (Doubleday, 1951). Hortense, wary of bores, avoided Mrs. Booth, who had accused another passenger of being a spy. Later when Mrs. Booth disappeared, Hortense was a suspect. This time her instincts failed her. She befriended villains and avoided those who rescued her later.

The repeated attacks and the laborious red herrings became monotonous. The writing was contrived and the slangy dialogue dated.

Liane "Lee" Craufurd

Author: Susan Gilruth

Liane "Lee" Crauford was curious and determined, but had little focus in her life. Her unhappy marriage had been childless. Although she served for five years in the War Office during World War II, she had no postwar career interests. Her partner in crime detection was Hugh Gordon of Scotland Yard.

In *Sweet Revenge* (Hale, 1951), Lee and Hugh were attracted to one another even though husband Bill had recently returned from his overseas service. While the Craufurds were on vacation, the disappearance and murder of Sandra Cazalet caused Lee and Hugh to spend time together while Bill golfed, fished, and drank beer. After Hugh obtained a confession to the murder, he left rather than cause problems in the Craufurd marriage.

Bill was attending Army Staff College during *Death in Ambush* (Hale, 1952) while Lee attended a party where an unpopular retired judge, Sir Henry Metcalfe, was poisoned. Hugh Gordon intervened when the killer turned to Sonia, the woman whom Metcalfe's son hoped to marry. Liane had missed a clue that would have solved the case earlier.

In *Postscript to Penelope* (Hale, 1954), Penelope Russell-Moore, owner of the building where the Craufurds lived, was believed to be in South America until she was found dead, shot in the heart. A short time before the discovery, ailing businessman Boyd Marshall died what was presumed to be a natural death. An exhumation of Boyd's body was ordered, but the death still seemed to be natural. The death of Alf Biddle, a small time blackmailer, might be connected. Penelope had been very concerned about Boyd's health, and investigation showed that she had a right to be.

In *A Corpse for Charybdis* (Hodder & Stoughton, 1956), Bill's poor health sent the Craufurds on a leisurely but tense cruise on a Yugoslavian tramp steamer. When Gail, an obnoxious young woman, disappeared, presumably overboard, Hugh Gordon appeared, but this was Lee's story during a time in the marriage when she and Bill were getting along. Although Gail had not been the intended victim, Lee made sure that the killer knew she was responsible and that Lee could prove it. Suicide was the solution.

Hugh's role had become that of family friend by *To This Favour* (Hodder & Stoughton, 1957), and the Craufurd marriage seemed secure when Hugh investigated the murder of their hostess, Caroline Openshaw. Caroline had asked Lee to visit on a matter of life or death. Although Lee shared only a portion of what she knew with Hugh, it was he who solved the case.

Lee, off on her own again in *Drown Her Remembrance* (Hodder & Stoughton, 1961), vacationed in Majorca's British society. When Helen Britton, a well-insured second wife, disappeared, no legal decision was made as to whether the death was murder or suicide. After the widower died later in London, Lee investigated. Hugh, assigned to the case, seemed disinterested, but was setting a trap for the killers.

The Craufurds had separated by *The Snake Is Living Yet* (Hodder & Stoughon, 1963), not because of Lee and Hugh, but due to Bill's attentions to a younger woman. Lee went to Tangier, where due to her loneliness, she was drawn into a group of tourists and expatriates. When Mulligan, an undercover FBI operative active in the group, was murdered, Hugh, now working for Interpol, came to Tangier to investigate.

Readers never do learn whether Lee and Hugh became seriously involved with one another. Her role was usually supportive, although her narration provided the background and described the relationships among the characters.

Sally Dean

Authors: Leonard Gribble and Geraldine Laws

Sally Dean parlayed her "good education" and a stint as a regular police-woman into an assignment with the Ghost Squad at Scotland Yard in *Sally of Scotland Yard* (Allen, 1954). When sent undercover to keep an eye on television star Tony Marino, she tinted her hair red, because Tony liked red-heads. This did not sit well with Ward, Sally's fiancé, who encountered her with Tony in a nightclub. Tony was deeply involved with blackmailers and South American politicians, causing Sally and Ward to endure abuse before Scotland Yard rescued them.

Marka de Lancey

Author: Barbara Frost (Shivley)

Women attorneys were series heroines long before the 1980's. Marka de Lancey, the daughter of a widowed attorney, was one of the first practicing women attorneys in a mystery series. Others had law degrees but did not use them.

Marka's characterization was not unrealistic. Women were entering law schools in increasing numbers in the Forties. She was a redhead with dark, gold-flecked eyes, slim and attractive. During a period when opportunities as legal interns while in law school did not exist for women, she had worked as a waitress and store clerk. A native New Yorker, she found her first legal employment with a large firm, but moved on to independent practice.

In *The Corpse Said No* (Coward, 1949), although Marka preferred insurance law, she did not turn away Evangeline Kearns Mortby, who wanted a woman to draw up her will. Mortby was ripe for murder because she intended to disinherit her dependent relatives in favor of a museum. Marka combined her efforts with those of New York Police Department Lt. Jeff MacRae to uncover the murderer.

The Corpse Died Twice (Coward, 1951) strained credulity. Artist Jerome Carrigan sought out Marka for legal advice because his obituary had been published. When he was found poisoned in his steam bath, Marka arranged to have MacRae assigned to the case. Efforts to check up on a major insurance policy obtained by Carrigan failed as both the salesman and the beneficiary were murdered. The killer took Marka and the others on a dangerous ride.

Innocent Bystander (Coward, 1955) was not relevant to Marka's profession except that she was choreographer for the local Bar Association musical review. Gregory Trafani, an Italian composer with a distinguished World War II record, contacted Marka when he found the corpse of Trixie Maxon in his bedroom. Marka's life was in danger, because of a trust fund drawn up by her father. Although MacRae rescued her, Marka looked elsewhere for the romance in her life.

Marka was an innocent, even virginal heroine, considering her age and occupation. The series was interesting, if only for the portrayal of an early woman detective-attorney.

Sarah De Long

Author: Melba Marlett

See: Sarah De Long O'Brien, Section 4, page 187.

Elizabeth "Liz" Doane

Author: Frances Shelley Wees

A tiny young woman from Western Canada, Liz Doane moved to Toronto after a disastrous marriage. Her confidence shaken, she moved in with her cousin, Phyllis Cole. Liz found a job and eventually distinguished herself as an investigative reporter.

Liz's skepticism stood her in good stead during *Where Is Jenny Now?* (Doubleday, 1958) when Jenny Barnet disappeared. The police had dropped the case, believing the young woman had run off with a married man. Liz's more thorough investigation developed connections between Jenny's disappearance and a series of robberies. Inspector Bill Blake had been of considerable help, but she kept him at a distance. Her cousin Phyllis found happiness with a wealthy businessman who had been one of the suspects.

Because of her success with finding "lost girls," Liz was asked to locate and bring home 17-year-old Elly Ruttle in *The Country of the Strangers* (Doubleday, 1960). When she located Elly in Vancouver, the girl was no longer interested in returning to her family. In fact, Liz suspected that she was not only addicted, but was being used in a major drug distribution scheme. Aware that she might have been recognized by one of the conspirators and unable to reach her friend, Inspector Bill Blake, Liz impetuously signed up for a tour of the U.S.S.R. She became aware that she was being followed, but was unable to distinguish which of her fellow travelers were there to harm her and which to protect. The narrative showed considerable sensitivity (for that period when McCarthyism was rampant in the United States) for the courage and tolerance of hardships of the average Russian citizen. Blake turned up in time to take official action based on Liz's investigation. He knew that she had been traumatized by her unhappy marriage, but hoped she was ready for a new relationship.

Lorna Donahue

Author: Katharine Hill

Ex-actress Lorna made a career out of marriage, having been four times a widow. She drove a flashy cherry colored car and had a police dog for companionship and a maid to do the housework. Her red hair may have been artificial, but her money was genuine. She worked in a real estate business in Ridgemont, Connecticut, that she had inherited from her fourth husband.

In *Dear, Dead Mother-in-Law* (Dutton, 1944), it was not difficult to figure out why someone would kill Ada Mullins, who had irritated scores of people. The police could not get beyond the stereotypical mother-in-law jokes, so they arrested her daughter's husband. Fortunately for his pregnant young wife, Lorna worked with Police Chief Jim Starkey to find the killer.

Lorna's credibility took a hit in *Case for Equity* (reissued as *The Case of the Absent Corpse,* Dutton, 1945), when she discovered a corpse while wandering around in a mist. The body was missing when she returned with the police. After being rescued by her chief suspect when dumped in a well, she reassessed the situation in time to save another victim from murder.

Elizabeth

Author: Florence Kilpatrick

Elizabeth, a young Cockney who worked at various low-level domestic jobs in England, appeared in a half-dozen books of a humorous tenor. Like the books in which "Tish" Carberry appeared, only a few could be considered mysteries.

Elizabeth was a hall porter in an apartment facility during *Elizabeth the Sleuth* (Jenkins, 1946). Like a Parisienne concierge, she made it her business to know what was going on among the tenants: that lonely and mysterious Miss Fortescue in #27 had a cousin visiting her, that Jonas

Sterne in #49 was stingy, that friendless Mr. Norbury in #46 was working on inventions. So she was in a position to know that the cousin frightened Miss Fortescue to death and that Sterne was an accomplice to a fraud against an insurance company, and to play Cupid among the tenants. The episodes had O. Henry-like twists to their conclusions.

Elizabeth was hired by Mabel Lennox to set up a recently inherited country estate in *Elizabeth Finds a Body* (Jenkins, 1949). Country wasn't her style but this was a short-term assignment. Mabel's husband had become reclusive, spending most of his time in a locked studio at the guesthouse. Not even Mabel was allowed to enter. Rosalie, a frail young woman, was dominated by her avaricious mother. During her short tenure, Elizabeth not only played Cupid again, but cooperated with an undercover government agent to foil a counterfeiting scheme and bring a murderer to justice.

Bernarda "Bunty" Felse

Author: Ellis Peters

Bunty Felse was the wife of Midshire Detective Inspector George Felse, and mother of their son, Dominic, who grew up to solve his own mysteries. Author Peters' sensitivity to vulnerability in an adolescent, a neglected wife, or an unhappily married man were often expressed through Bunty. Bunty, of Welsh descent, had given up a promising career as a classical singer to marry George. She was attractive with chestnut hair going gray, freckles, and hazel eyes.

She was contacted by a private investigator in *The House of Green Turf* (Morrow, 1969) for information about concert singer Maggie Tolliver, who had never recovered emotionally from an accident. George connected a traumatic experience Bunty and Maggie had on a youthful tour of Europe to recent disappearances in the Scheidenau area.

Bunty's major appearance was in *The Grass Widow's Tale* (Morrow, 1968), a poignant story. Husband George was in London and Dominic at Oxford on Bunty's 41st birthday, leaving her vulnerable. She "picked up" Luke Tennant in a nearby roadhouse, and accepted a ride home. When she saw a corpse in the vehicle, Luke kept her prisoner, but was incapable of killing her. During their search for the truth, Bunty and Luke developed a special relationship that restored her sense of worth.

Her connection with the Comerbourne Musical Association provided access and insights for husband George's investigation in *Rainbow's End* (Morrow, 1979). Other Felse narratives that gave George or son Dominic major roles used Bunty as a sympathetic listener and counselor.

Dr. Mary Finney

Author: Matthew Head, pseudonym for John Canaday

Medical missionary Mary Finney from Fort Scott, Kansas, was a competent, matter-of-fact, and dedicated physician. A sturdy woman with red hair and freckles, Mary had served as a doctor in Africa for about 25 years when she met Hooper Taliaferro, the narrator of *The Devil in the Bush* (Simon, 1945). Taliaferro arrived in Congo-Ruiz just as Andre de l'Andreneau, an alcoholic station operator, was dying of amoebic dysentery. When Mary Finney learned of his death, she was convinced that he had been murdered. Andre's brother, whose wife had been unfaithful, was killed soon afterwards. His death was blamed on angry natives. Although their relationship had ended long ago, Andre had been Mary's lover.

Mary developed a friendship with Hooper, but her working companion was Emily Collins, a frail but dedicated New England missionary. During *The Cabinda Affair* (Simon, 1949), Hooper described a suspicious death in Cabinda, involving relationships among other expatriates. Although Mary and Emily had been planning to visit the United States, they detoured to Cabinda posing as tourists. Emily, the timid and devout companion, resorted to violence to save her friends when the killer attacked.

The Congo Venus (Simon, 1950) introduced Liliane, a lush blonde second wife who died mysteriously. Her vindictive sister-in-law accused the attending physician of incompetence, a claim that Dr. Finney refuted after a careful reading of the records. Dr. Gollmer was barely tolerated by his compatriots because he was more interested in the native culture than in the health of the white population.

The African setting was left behind for Paris in *Murder at the Flea Club* (Simon, 1955). Hooper belonged to the Flea Club, a bistro patronized by seamier elements of the city. He detailed the relationships surrounding the murder of Nicole, the manageress of the Flea Club, to Dr. Finney, who was attending a Paris medical convention. Finney used his material as background but chose to meet the suspects personally, then called upon her knowledge of human behavior to identify the killer.

Canaday's Africa centered on the small colony of white foreigners who lived within the African-American population. Hooper, as narrator, portrayed the characters through his vision. Another narrative style might have expanded the reader's understanding of Mary Finney.

Katherine Forrester

Author: Madeleine L'Engle

See: Katherine Forrester Vigneras, Section 4, page 222.

Arabella Frant

Author: Diana Fearon

Arabella Frant was five feet tall, in her late fifties or early sixties, and considered an eccentric by the villagers in Merdley-on-Thames. She courted that distinction with her bright clothes, sometimes living in a tent, painting local scenery, and minding everyone else's business.

In *Death Before Breakfast* (Hale, 1959), Arabella stayed at a pub/hotel while painting the Whintonham Downs. When fellow guest Dr. Gerald Olim, a bullying research scientist, was discovered dead in bed, the police had an obvious suspect, gentle Dr. Ted Tenacem. Tenacem no longer used the title "doctor" or practiced because he had been accused of malpractice in Burma. Although he was cleared of the charge, his spirit had been broken. Olim had taken credit for significant research done by Tenacem, who never complained. Arabella pushed the authorities to find someone with a more recent motive, spoiling what looked like a perfect crime.

When Walter Evans entered the village tea garden, Arabella noticed that someone caused him to react with terror in *Murder-on-Thames* (Hale, 1960). Arabella had taken note of the six people who were in the garden when Evans arrived. After he was found stabbed in the chest, the local policeman would have preferred a verdict of suicide. Evans' daughter, Rachel, was convinced he had been murdered by someone from his past. He had been a witness to a bank robbery shortly after the war ended. Rachel's car was sabotaged as she headed to Scotland Yard to consult on this matter. Arabella saw the accident and verified that the brake line had been cut. She had an inside track at Scotland Yard to Inspector Runfold, who remembered the bank robbery. He and his assistant queried the six as to their whereabouts at that time. A second death brought the number down to five. Arabella gradually cut the number down to one, and alerted the police to prevent another murder.

Average.

Vicky Gaines

Author: Frank Diamond

Vicky Gaines had the potential for an exciting heroine. She grew up in Texas playing hardball with the boys, riding, shooting, and throwing knives with the best of them. After gaining experience in a circus, beauty contests, and on the stage (the Follies), she became an advertising executive successful enough to live in Park Towers and wear a chinchilla wrap. Her statuesque beauty and copper colored hair attracted attention wherever she went.

While trying to locate Bruce McNorton, an errant boyfriend, in *Murder in Five Columns* (Mystery House, 1944), she came upon evidence linking him to espionage. She also met Ransome V. Dragoon, who boasted seven bullet holes, sixteen languages, and three ex-wives. Unsure of whether or not Dragoon was to be trusted, Vicky confided in radio commentator Ralph Livingston. The death of Hugh Wainwright, investment broker tied to the Fascist party, figured into the equation. As she continued to work with both McNorton and Dragoon, Vicky changed her allegiance. Dragoon was very impressed by her investigative skills and more.

In *Murder Rides a Rocket* (Mystery House, 1946), Ransome, after a six-month absence, returned to recruit Vicky. She was so impressed by him that she followed his orders. She was to cultivate Russian intelligence officer Boris Sarodin, exposing her to more than ridicule when she appeared semi-naked to explain Sarodin's death in her apartment. This series had some innovative touches, but went no further.

Gale Gallagher

Authors: Will Oursler and Margaret Scott writing as Gale Gallagher

The fictional Gale Gallagher operated the Ace Investigating Bureau, which concentrated on tracing lost persons. She was programmed for a life of detection. Her father, Patrolman James Patrick Gallagher, had wanted a son; her mother died when Gale was born. Gale finished parochial school, high school, and the police academy, but preferred to work independently, taking her time.

In *I Found Him Dead* (Coward, 1947), television actress Dawn Ferris hired Gale to find the daughter she had given up for adoption 14 years earlier. Ferris feared that kidnapped heiress Bette Alexander might be that child, and that her ex-husband might be involved in the abduction. Gale researched records and came up with enough information to make it possible that Bette was Dawn's child. The father, Eddie Wells, then married to Dawn, had left her when she became pregnant. His murder had to be more than a coincidence. Gale found Bette but barely escaped thanks to Hank Deery, old buddy of Jim Gallagher, who had been following her.

During *Chord in Crimson* (Coward, 1949), Gale monitored Rik, nephew-by-marriage of wealthy blind woman Elizabeth Verheide. He had left town ten days before en route to Florida but never arrived. His wife, Lisa's, body was discovered while Gale was at the Verheide home discussing the case with Elizabeth. Gale had planned to decline the case, but now that was impossible. Convinced that he was innocent, Gale found and concealed Rik until she solved the murder.

Eve Gill

Author: Selwyn Jepson

Eve Gill was destined to be independent. Her mother died at her birth; her father, Commodore Rupert Gill, was a cantankerous one-legged ex-soldier of fortune and sometime smuggler who stayed just a few nautical miles ahead of the authorities. At 24, Eve was responsible for the family estate and her father's welfare. To avoid death taxes, family members had by-passed the prodigal Rupert and directed their fortunes to Eve. Father and daughter lived at Marsh House, Suffolk, where the Gills had resided for ten generations, close enough to the beach for the Commodore's excursions for untaxed French brandy. Although educated abroad, Eve was content at Marsh House, cooking, baking, sailing, and helping to manage the extensive estate farms. There was little physical description of Eve, but she was athletic and knowledgeable in the use of boats and weapons as a result of her father's training.

Charlie Barrington, Rupert's resident accomplice; Detective Inspector Christopher Smith; and local Inspector Billy Bull all sought a romantic commitment from Eve, but she made none. Eve seemed attracted to one, then another. Charlie had the excitement and roguishness, Smith, respectability and security, while Bull was available and persistent.

In *Outrun the Constable* (Doubleday, 1948) aka *Man Running*, architect Jonathan Penrose, a suspect in the murder of his mistress' husband, was saved from arrest by Eve. While awaiting an opportunity to smuggle Jonathan to Holland, where she hoped to fence a stolen portrait, she went undercover as maid for Jonathan's lover, Charlotte Inwood. She and Jonathan had decided there was a better solution than running away.

During *The Golden Dart* (Doubleday, 1949), Eve and "Boy," her 11-year-old cousin, came upon a three-year-old child carrying a suicide note from her mother. James Belsin, Eve's current suitor, was a guest on the cabin cruiser from which the child and her mother had exited. The police had been notified that Louise Frampton had drowned herself and were already searching for her body. Given her suspicions of Belsin, it was surprising that Eve became engaged to him. When the corpse of Jonathan Penrose, formerly Eve's lover, was dumped in her bedroom, it was a wake-up call for Eve.

The Hungry Spider (Doubleday, 1950) began with Eve in jail and flashed back through her day. While trying to deliver smuggled brandy, she had an accident that left her in a dazed condition. The Forsyth family, which offered her refuge, had problems of their own. There was a possibility that a member of the household had killed Col. Forsyth. Inspector Christopher "Ordinary" Smith was involved in the smuggling investigation, so Eve waited a long time to share what she knew.

The Black Italian (Doubleday, 1954) made it possible for Eve to save Inspector Chris Smith's reputation. A letter from Angela Sawyer made Eve worry about Angela's safety, but she arrived in Italy too late. Angela was the illegitimate child of a powerful member of the English aristocracy. He enlisted Eve to find her killer. When she did so, she lured the man back to England so Chris Smith could get credit for the arrest, which mended the breach in their relationship.

In *The Verdict in Question* (Doubleday, 1960) aka *The Laughing Fish,* Eve took an interest in David Fortis, an amnesiac patient whose wife, Catherin,e had disappeared. Eve spirited him out of the hospital, where he was under police surveillance. After the wife reappeared, David was found dead, an apparent suicide. Determined to make a fuss, Eve planted rumors that David had been murdered, then visited the unfaithful Catherine to offer condolences about the "terrible rumors." Meanwhile Christopher Smith was recuperating at the Gill home from injuries incurred in the Black Italian case.

Commodore Gill, then 65, was intrigued by mysterious widow Gertrude in *Fear in the Wind* (Allen, 1964). Eve investigated Gertrude and her friends, whom she suspected of using her father in a gold-mining scam, or smuggling, or dealing in stolen bank funds. Whatever, she did not intend that her father be drawn into Gertrude's schemes. He got into enough trouble on his own.

Eavesdropping made Eve aware that her beloved uncle, Baron Portargy, Minister of Economic Affairs in Her Majesty's Government, had been compromised by his relationship with a call girl in *The Third Possibility* (Allen, 1965). As usual, she hoped to avoid involving the police in general, and Inspector Christopher Smith in particular. Not only was that impossible, but Smith inadvertently teamed her with John Addis Hammond, whose ambitions to be a police officer were thwarted by his height (or lack of it). Together they undermined an attempt to embarrass the government.

Although she frequently had help from the assorted men in her life, Eve was a competent heroine.

Jenny Gillette
Author: Elizabeth Gresham under her own name and as Robin Grey

See: Jenny Gillette Lewis, Section 4, page 173.

Jane Hamish
Author: Delano Ames

See: Jane Hamish Brown, Section 4, page 141.

Shirley Leighton Harper
Author: Paul Ernst aka Kenneth Robeson

Shirley Leighton Harper tagged along behind her big brother Brooke and his pal Bill Harper for years, unable to get Bill's attention. A petite brunette tomboy, she and Brooke had been raised by their widowed father. By the time, Shirley was 20, Bill was 31, divorced, and working for Brooke's advertising agency, where Shirley could keep an eye on him.

In *Hangman's Hat* (Mill, 1951), Shirley and Bill were concerned because Brooke had been missing since the death of nightclub entertainer Anita Phelps. This was a shock because Brooke had been seeing his ex-wife Cecelia, now Mrs. Harold Kamp. Cecelia was the next murder victim. Bill, who had worked for Brooke for years, spent considerable time keeping him out of trouble, or at least keeping Brooke's father unaware of the trouble. It was too late this time. Bill solved the mystery, but Shirley got her man.

Even when Shirley and Bill vacationed in Florida in *Lady, Get Your Gun* (Mill, 1955), they could not avoid murder. A motorboat with a dead handyman at the wheel crashed into their boat dock. This was the second recent murder. Kevin Bauer, a marginal member of their social circle, had been shot, and Betty Norton, a longtime friend of Bill's, was suspected, as was her husband, Harry. Bill solved the case, but, as frequently occurred in cozies those days, the killer committed suicide when exposed.

The books were run-of-the-mill. Shirley was immature, awed by her older husband, and still tagging along.

Abbie Harris

Author: Amber Dean (Getzin)

When she inherited sufficient money to retire from teaching, widowed Alberta "Abbie" Harris returned to her maiden name and the family home on Ogg Lake in upper New York State. As an amateur, Abbie shared her investigations with Max Johnson, a neighbor with professional credentials, and on occasions with his wife, "Mommie."

Abbie, a stocky blonde going gray in her forties, had an admirer, Dr. Fitzgerald Custom, a diminutive medical examiner, but she gave him short shrift. A kind woman, she allowed her curiosity to involve her in other people's problems, sometimes beyond her depth.

Dead Man's Float (Doubleday, 1944) introduced Abbie and her sisters, Lily and Maggie. Bill Hunt, son of deceased sister Carrie, was welcomed when he visited, but the death of Bethine Cort, a young married woman, created problems. Max Johnson almost shared her fate during a boat race. Max, suspicious of Bethine's purpose in coming to the area, arranged for Abbie to search the Cort home. She found what she was looking for, and more: another corpse and clues to a tragic misunderstanding.

On a bus trip in *Chanticleer's Muffled Crow* (Doubleday, 1945), a fellow passenger slipped an important letter into Abbie's purse shortly before being killed in an accident. Max, now an Army captain, seemed changed. He had become very interested in cockfighting and acted more like a suspect than an investigator when two men were found dead after an evening of cockfights. Abbie still trusted him enough to give him the mysterious letter.

Call Me Pandora aka *The Blonde Is Dead* (Doubleday, 1946) found Maggie and Abbie in the big city, where Maggie found work in a munitions factory. The sisters had recently come into money, which they invested in an apartment building that included a beauty parlor—with a resident corpse. The corpse was Rose Norton, the prior owner, and there was a question as to where the cash payment had gone. Max and his friend, police Lt. York, did most of the detecting in this one. When Abbie went out on her own, they had to rescue her.

A different Bill Hunt visited in *Wrap It Up* (Doubleday, 1946) while recovering from a head injury. When his friend painter Johnny Rutland was killed up in the hills, the amnesiac Bill was taken into custody as a possible murderer. Early on, Abbie and Max realized that the paints Bill had in his car were connected to the killing. A former student of Abbie's provided warning that Max, who now had the paint tubes, was in danger. Fortunately, Max had a careful wife.

In *No Traveller Returns* (1948), Abbie's role was diminished. Coralbelle Britton, who had inherited the White Horse Tavern, left its management to Gus Ferdelance and his hard-working wife, Bertha. The death of Bob Wing, local car dealer, was investigated by his brother, Cris, working with Max and a former FBI agent. Abbie was close to Coralbelle, but not to the action.

In *Snipe Hunt* (1949) Max's services were co-opted by Treasury agents on the trail of counterfeiters. Abbie was present only as neighbor to the Johnsons.

Driving on a foggy evening to visit Orville Smith, a Treasury agent, during *August Incident* (Doubleday, 1951), Abbie had not one, but two accidents. She struck a tree on the way to the hospital where Smitty was recovering from injuries. When she assisted him to leave the hospital prematurely, she ran into a car on the way home. A photo left in the other car cued Abbie, Smitty, and Max in to a child kidnapping scam.

Max Johnson, now a U.S. Customs agent, was seen hurrying away from a murder site in *The Devil Threw Dice* (Doubleday, 1954). He shared attention as the #1 suspect with Bill Burch, a bridegroom who financed his honeymoon with a forged check. Abbie sorted it out, found a third suspect, but needed to be rescued.

The series would grade out as mildly humorous, fair in plot, weak in characterization, but enjoyable. It was one of many in which an amateur teamed with a professional.

Lady Lupin Lorrimer Hastings

Author: Joan Coggin

Somewhat frivolous Lady Lupin surprised everyone by marrying Rev. Andrew Hastings, Vicar of St. Mark's Church in Glanville, Sussex. She was the daughter of an Earl, raised in wealth and social position, so had an adjustment to make as the pastor's wife.

It was not surprising that there was considerable cultural shock for Lady Lupin when she took on her new tasks in *Who Killed the Curate?* (Hurst, 1944; Rue Morgue Press, 2001). As the Vicar's wife she was expected to show an interest in Girl Guides, Mothers' Club, and Sunday School. What was unexpected was her involvement in the murder of Curate Charles Young. Lupin may not have been the smartest kid on the block, but she was sensitive to the reactions of others and intuitive.

An invitation for Rev. Andrew Hastings to be the guest preacher in rural Much Lancing exposed Lady Lupin to the travails of the Stevenson family in *Penelope Passes or Why Did She Die?* (Hurst, 1947; Rue Morgue, 2003). Penelope, the unmarried daughter, was revered for her devotion to her widowed father and her younger brother, Dick. Closer acquaintance with the family, particularly after Dick and his wife, Betty, became parents, made Lupin aware of the stresses caused by Penelope's self-sacrifice. Her death was perceived as murder. Lupin was shocked at the number of eligible suspects. This was a surprisingly perceptive portrait of a woman whose neediness destroyed her.

Fatigued by a bout of flu, Lady Lupin was sent off by her husband and doctor for a rest as *The Mystery at Orchard House* (Hurst, 1947; Rue Morgue, 2003) began. The Hastings' friend Diana Turner had inherited lovely Orchard House, but had no funds to maintain it. She considered turning it into a country hotel. Her cousin Paul, who had received liquid assets from the same testator, helped Diane to hire servants and acquire guests. Lupin was among them, but found her fellow guests to be quarrelsome and tiring. There were thefts and two car accidents. Again her insightful questions solved a mystery.

Lady Lupin was summoned to the farmhouse where her dearest friends, Tommy and Duds Lethbridge, were living in *Dancing With Death* (Hurst, 1949; Rue Morgue, 2003). The narrative switched back to explore the dynamics of Duds' tragic houseparty: her cousins, a pair of twins whom she remembered fondly from the past, but who were estranged; the men who had loved Flo and Jo; and the ensuing murder. Lady Lupin entered the story when it was well advanced but used her special insights to sort things out. The twin gimmick is old stuff now. The seasoned reader will spot its use early on, but it wasn't so in 1949.

The Lady Lupin series had disappeared from view and was not covered in the earlier printings of *Mystery Women, Volume 1*. Tom and Enid

Schantz of Rue Morgue Press deserve credit for re-issuing the series, and for the many other reprints of excellent mysteries.

Sally Merton Heldar

Author: Henrietta Hamilton

Sally was Miss Merton, a russet-haired young Englishwoman working in the Heldar family 's antiquarian bookshop, when she met Johnny Heldar, partner and grandson of the founder of the firm.

The Two Hundred Ghost (Hodder, 1956) explained that the bookshop was located in premises formerly occupied by a disreputable inn. The staff was distracted by what seemed to be ghosts, but also by the actual murder of Victor Butcher, an unpopular employee. His unwelcome attentions to Sally had caused a quarrel between Butcher and Fred, a shell-shocked veteran who worked at the store. Fred became a serious suspect, but not one acceptable to Sally. While she and Johnny worked together on the investigation, they became romantically involved.

The Heldars were newlyweds in *Death at One Blow* (Hodder, 1957) when they cataloged two recently merged private libraries on the Thaxton estate. When offensive Sir Mark Mercator, a relative of the Thaxton family by marriage, was murdered, followed by the suspicious death of the land agent, Johnny and Sally investigated at the request of Richard, the black sheep heir and obvious suspect. Richard had been believed dead, but returned to disagree seriously with Mercator. Johnny and Sally had the skills to realize that valuable books had been removed from the joined libraries or replaced by forgeries.

At Night to Die (Hodder, 1959) began when Johnny, but not Sally, was recruited as a crime investigator by a young couple. Innkeepers Colin and Sheila Kennedy became caretakers for 17-year-old Malcolm after the local laird, his grandfather, died in an "accident." Sally and Johnny knew Malcolm's step-father and did not approve of him. A check of historical resources indicated the possibility of Jacobite treasure in the decaying family home.

In *Answer in the Negative* (Hodder, 1959), the Heldars posed as researchers at the National Press Archives in London to investigate a series of obscene letters, practical jokes, and acts of vandalism. When Morningside, the worker most cruelly affected by the jokes, was murdered, the Heldars uncovered the past crime that led to his killer.

The books were comparatively short, intelligently written but lacking in dramatic tension and without well-developed characters. Again, as in other mysteries of the period, a Jewish name was used for a villain.

Miss Flora Hogg

Author: Austin Lee

Flora Hogg was described as having red hair, which in those times would indicate that she was still no more than middle-aged. She was a woman of some education. Although her degree was from Bristol, not Oxford or Cambridge, Flora taught French at the secondary school level and read herself to sleep with Proust. She always wanted to be a detective like her father, who had been the local superintendent of police.

Flora's personal appearance was not of great importance to her. She wore shapeless tweedy clothes, and sensible shoes, and had worn a dental plate since she knocked out two front teeth playing field hockey. She had accepted the single life and lived in her own home, sometimes shared with an old schoolmate, Millicent Brown, who also served as narrator on occasion.

A friendly woman, Miss Hogg smoked, enjoyed an occasional drink, and took great interest in her former pupils. Her father's reputation was an asset when Flora worked with the local constabulary of South Green, Surrey. Determined though she might be, Flora was a creature of her times with no formal training, no microscope, camera, or physical equipment. She operated on a psychological level, probing for motivation.

In *Sheep's Clothing* (Cape, 1955), Flora was contacted by Miss Emily Dewdney, literary executor of the papers for her father, a biblical researcher. Miss Dewdney was disturbed because the family home had been burglarized. When an "American bishop" was found dead in the family library, Flora probed deeper into the secular aspects of the murder.

When, in *Call In Miss Hogg* (1956), Flora and Millie attended a party, Hazel, a young orphaned actress, consulted Flora about an attempted poisoning and her concern that she was being followed. She was absolutely right. She was being followed by an American private investigator, but he was murdered. Someone else had it in for Hazel, who might well inherit a fortune.

During *Miss Hogg and the Bronte Murders* (Cape, 1956), the mysterious murder of American tourist Ellis Gubbenheim seemed to be tied to the literary Bronte sisters, once resident in the area. The disappearance of Bronte expert Dr. Andrew Appleby and the death of a Shakespearean expert sent Flora after a literary killer. That decision seemed logical.

In *Miss Hogg and the Squash Club Murder* (Cape, 1957), Flora assisted Vanda Fitzgerald, a former pupil whose jealous husband was a suspect in the murder of Norman Potter. Potter played regularly at the local squash club, as did several officials of the nearby Atomic Research Station. Information indicated that Potter may have been a spy. To learn more about other suspects, Flora went undercover as a filing clerk at the Atomic Research Station.

In *Miss Hogg and the Dead Dean* (Cape, 1958), when Rev. Samuel Sheepshanks, the Dean of Warchester Cathedral, was murdered, there were too many suspects. Young Rev. John Parker, chaplain of the local college, concerned that he might be among them, contacted his former neighbor, Miss Hogg.

In *Miss Hogg Flies High* (Cape, 1958), school friend Beryl Cunningham was social secretary to Lady Anne, a member of the minor nobility. Lady Anne was irritated that she had to hostess a weekend, which would be a secret conference on weapons at her unfaithful husband Charles' country estate. Unsure that security would be adequate, she called on Flora to monitor behavior. The death by poisoning of Tony Frant, Charles' secretary and heir to a peerage, posed two possible motives: espionage and envy at Tony's inheritance.

Society woman Mrs. Haliburton-West made her living sponsoring and indoctrinating newcomers to upper class London Society. In that capacity she came upon the naked body of a woman at dawn in Covent Garden in *Miss Hogg and the Covent Garden Murders* (Cape, 1960). Mrs. Haliburton-West would have been inclined to pass along without reporting the discovery, but there were others present, including a reporter. A newspaper editor hired Flora to solve the mystery, which moved along when the victim's identity was known. The location of her car pointed to a possible scene of the crime, and a list of suspects was built up. Identifying the killer was not enough, but that was the way the narrative ended.

During *Miss Hogg and the Missing Sisters* (Cape, 1961), elderly Miss Gertrude Hooley consulted a neighbor about libel laws, pertaining to memoirs she was completing. When Gertrude, her sister, and the manuscript disappeared, Flora and Milly flew to Ireland to trace the de Ferrers family described in the memoirs. It was appropriate timing because the descendant who had inherited the money was about to marry the one who inherited the land. There just might be a flaw in the plan.

Miss Hogg decided she had enough of being a detective in *Miss Hogg's Last Case* (Cape, 1963). She had been called in by a former classmate Peg Houghton, whose husband, Rev. Arthur, was the rector at Ludby-in-the Marsh. Arthur had found the bloody body of a Polish émigré who had consulted him "under the seal of the confessional." After an evening with the local gentry, Miss Hogg was convinced that many of her fellow guests were using narcotics. After she identified the killer, Miss Hogg decided to return to teaching, even though or, perhaps because, she had just uncovered drug dealing, blackmail, and murder.

The Miss Hogg books were short, unpretentious, simplistic, and lighthearted, like Flora herself.

Jean Holly

Author: Frances Crane

See: Jean Holly Abbott, Section 4, page 125.

Nora Hughes

Author: Lavinia Davis

See: Nora Hughes Blaine, Section 4, page 137.

Elsie Mae Hunt

Author: Aaron Marc Stein

Archaeologists have frequently been mystery sleuths, enjoying the unraveling of current mysteries along with those of the ancient past. Elsie Mae Hunt was no pompous academic, although she graduated from Bryn Mawr and spoke a half-dozen languages. She enjoyed the tabloids, the pulps, trashy magazines, and the comic strips as well as the classics. Her hair, held up by hairpins in an attempt at a bun, was constantly falling down. Although she was not unattractive, there was no romantic interest between Elsie Mae and her younger partner in detection and archaeology, Tim Mulligan, or with any other character in the series.

Tim and Elsie Mae were seen only in their professional aspects, and displayed few ties to any university, community, or persons. They were an engaging pair who took their readers to exotic locations with considerable authenticity. Generally, they showed respect for the countries they visited and the inhabitants.

A few of the narratives were set in the United States; others, in foreign countries. But their primary location was in Mexico, and the books provided charming descriptions of the local population, the physical setting, and regional customs.

The Sun Is a Witness (Doubleday, 1940) centered on Tim, only mentioning Elsie Mae as his assistant. While they were digging in the Western U.S. deserts, they were criticized for opening a grave, which might have released Indian spirits. Tim felt certain that this was a setup to close down the digging. After a terrific flood and rockslide, they found the body of Matt Casey, secretary to James Dillon, who owned the property. Dillon died of a wrong medication. The heir to the property had an alibi, but not one good enough for Tim.

During *Up to No Good* (Doubleday, 1941) Tim and Elsie Mae's Peruvian expedition involved them with a group headed by archaeologist Dr. Gregg Howard, some of whom were more interested in finding gold than antiquities. There were too many blondes and too many murders. Local authorities were under pressure to avoid unpleasant situations, so Tim and Elsie did their own investigation. There was Inca gold in the cave, but it had been removed by the killer through a secret exit.

While in Colombia for *Only the Guilty* (Doubleday, 1942), attacks on the estate of their host, Simon Fonte, were attributed to a tribe that used poisoned arrows. Elsie and Tim, aware that the Mitilones tribe was not found in the area, looked for deeper motives to the murders: the existence of spies near the Panama Canal.

Elsie's role in *The Case of the Absent Minded Professor* (Doubleday, 1943) was minimal. She and Tim believed that midwestern Professor Alf Chambers was being framed, either because he had flunked the star football player or inquired too deeply into the handling of college funds.

They were investigating Mississippi Mound Builders in *...And High Water* (Doubleday, 1946) when bridges and telephone lines were damaged by floods. While Elsie recuperated from an injury caused when their car window was shot out, Tim was suspected of murder. He had tangled with local bullies, some of whom were connected to the Ku Klux Klan. Tim challenged them, but had to be rescued when the killer's wife, encouraged by Elsie, proved Tim's innocence.

We Saw Him Die (Doubleday, 1947) pitted Tim and Elsie Mae against a murderer who used the cloak of a religious cult, the "Little White Lambs of the Lord," for concealment. They had gone to a strange old California mansion at the request of friend Stephen Ames, who was appraising an art collection there. Inheritance was significant along with the pseudo-religious group. Tim did the detecting.

Elsie Mae stayed in an ancestral Southern home during *Death Takes a Paying Guest* (Doubleday, 1947). She discovered Mr. Haas, a fellow lodger, dying of stab wounds, only to have his corpse disappear while she sought help. Her landlady evicted her. The police considered her unstable until they found a body, which met her description. Two more murders absolutely convinced them that Elsie Mae was on the right track.

Tim and Elsie Mae visited archaeology professor Tommy Milton, mentor for a volatile group of former Marines, in *The Cradle and the Grave* (Doubleday, 1948). The finding of the corpse of Curtis Howard, questions as to the paternity of the child of Slug Pavlevic, one of the former marines, and the child's disappearance, were followed by the discovery of the mother's dead body. Elsie Mae and Tim saved the kidnapped infant but had a difficult time convincing the police that they were the rescuers. The suicide of the killer made a trial unnecessary.

They were in Oaxaca for *The Second Burial* (Doubleday, 1949), where they were arrested as thieves while visiting an archaeological site in Santiago de los Borrachoes (St. James of the Drunkards). A tomb site had been pirated. Two other visitors to the area were murdered. Complex plotting that didn't quite come off.

The Yucatan was the location in *Days of Misfortune* (Doubleday, 1949), where Elsie, for whom loyalty was of prime importance, could not stand by when their pilot, Pablo Pablo, disappeared, leaving a corpse behind. Avoiding police participation, Else Mae and Tim tried to identify the dead man. The young woman whom Pablo had been seeing, "Miss Smith," was in danger…from her husband. That became less of a problem when the husband was found dead. The police were involved now, looking for Pablo and "Miss Smith." A rush was on to find them before they left the country.

Tim and Elsie Mae were in Jalisco, Mexico, in *Three—with Blood* (Doubleday, 1950), where they traced rumors of a "golden cockerel." They made friends among the locals and learned of the tensions among them, exacerbated by the heavy consumption of alcohol and competition for the attentions of a beautiful blonde. Tim and Elsie Mae proved the innocence of a cuckolded young bartender accused of murdering a prominent citizen.

In *The Frightened Amazon* (Doubleday, 1950), they were in Tehuana, where the women were big, beautiful, and in control of their own lives, but where virginity at marriage was essential. Their original goal had been to establish connections between this area and other Mayan sites. Tim and Elsie Mae protected young Josefina from a plot to defame her purity.

Whatever tolerance Elsie Mae may have had for foreigners, she had none for the bureaucracy of the New York City police in *Pistols for Two* (Doubleday, 1951). She found a corpse in the reconstructed tenth century cloister that wealthy art collector Harrison Gillette had transported to the United States. Once the corpse has been identified as that of an art expert, Lt. Gregory announced that Ferruccio Manfredi, a young scientist friend of Elsie Mae and Tim, was the prime suspect. As a foreigner who had participated in a duel, he was vulnerable.

While Elsie Mae and Mulligan were in Dublin for *Shoot Me Dacent* (Doubleday, 1951), they were drawn into the Irish revolutionary movement by new friends whom they met on the ship crossing the Irish Sea. Kevin Larrity's alibi after the murder of an Irish-American, believed to be hostile to the rebels, was evasive because he did not want to disclose where he had been. Money smuggled into the Irish Republic to subsidize the rebels was the source of the problem.

Back to the Yucatan in *Mask for Murder* (Doubleday, 1952). Wealthy Caroline Hammersmith, who had taken up archaeology, arrived in the small town of Tizimin about the same time as Elsie Mae and Tim. They were on the trail of a 16th century mask. All three were on a train when the body of money lender Jaime Ortega was found on board. Tizimin was crowded for the celebration of the Fiesta of the Three Kings. Everyone bought tickets for the big lottery. Two more corpses, including Caroline's, disrupted the festivities. The motive was new money, not ancient relics.

A suburb of Mexico City was the location in *The Dead Thing in the Pool* (Doubleday, 1952), where American movie actress Dolores Conway had a corpse in her spring-fed pool. When it vanished, the police settled for arresting a servant, Eulogios, who had been knocked unconscious during the disappearance. The rock used to weight the body down was of volcanic origin and indicated the possibility of a tunnel or cave. The body of El Maestro, a jai alai star, was found in the cave, which was probably a storage place for drugs.

It was on to Acapulco for another catchy title, *Death Meets 400 Rabbits* (Doubleday, 1953), a reference to an all-out alcoholic binge. Tim and Elsie were introduced to Juanito, a bullfighter who found danger outside of the ring and was murdered at a beach party. Helen, the wealthy woman with whom Juanito shared a house, was killed that same evening. A third death, that of Helen's sister Flo, only made the case more complicated.

Moonmilk and Murder (Doubleday, 1955) took Tim and Elsie Mae to France to explore the Vezere Caves, where they discovered the corpse of a man due to be lynched anyway for collaboration during World War II. There was definite hostility against "foreigners" at the site, but Elsie Mae and Tim stayed on to protect the recently discovered prehistoric wall paintings and rock sculptures. The villain was another collaborator who feared disclosure, a man who had become a local leader since the war ended.

The series lacked the ingredients currently popular in mystery stories—explicit sex and/or violence—but provided low-key reading with colorful descriptions of the settings.

Marion Kerrison

Author: Edward Grierson

Marion Kerrison, a 30-year-old Oxford graduate, was featured in a fascinating courtroom drama, *The Second Man* (Knopf, 1956). When she was assigned to defend John Maudsley for the murder of his wealthy aunt, the British judicial system had not adjusted to the female of the legal species. Even though her client did not have confidence in Marion, she believed him to be innocent. Women readers will enjoy the discomfiture of those who were unwilling to accept her qualifications.

Gypsy Rose Lee

Author: Gypsy Rose Lee, ghostwritten by Craig Rice

Gypsy Rose Lee was described as tall with dark hair and eyes, and obviously with a figure that attracted attention.

In *The G-String Murders* (Simon, 1941), Gypsy was working in a top New York City burlesque theatre when she found Lolita La Verne, a rival stripper, strangled in the dressing room toilet. When the police killed Louie Grindero, a saloonkeeper brandishing a gun, they assumed he was the murderer. Gypsy worked with comedian Biff Brannigan to prove otherwise. (Made into the movie *Lady of Burlesque*, 1943.)

Mother Finds a Body (Simon, 1942) focused on Evangie, Gypsy's mother who shared Biff and Gypsy's honeymoon trailer. This time Evangie found the corpse and then buried it, managing to set the forest on fire. By the time the sheriff arrived, a second body was found in the woods.

The prose was bawdy and funny, the plots improbable, but with realistic touches about life in burlesque and on the road. Rose Louise Hovick, professionally known as Gypsy Rose Lee, was a memorable character, whose mother pushed her and her sister into the theatre business. Her personal story was made into the stage musical and movie *Gypsy*.

Norma "Nicky" Lee

Author: Norma Lee, probably a pseudonym

Norma "Nicky" Lee was a highly successful New York City actress working in a radio series, *The Beautiful Gunner*. Her fictional radio character was a detective who championed the underdog, so Nicky tried to do the same with the help of her patient fiancé, FBI agent Gil Harris. Nicky claimed to work undercover for the FBI, unlikely considering J. Edgar Hoover's attitude toward women agents. She was a reader, a good shot, and an excellent swimmer; a blonde with hazel eyes and a beautiful figure. All the males in the narratives, criminals or policemen, fell in love with Nicky. While living in Paris she had an affair with Mel, an Army deserter and gangster.

In *The Beautiful Gunner* (Laurie, 1953), Nicky dyed her hair red to pose as Tex Beguine (a take-off on Texas Guinan of the 1920's?) to get compromising material from blackmailers to pass along to the FBI. The real Tex Beguine came on the scene, kidnapped Nicky, but indicated she had information she was willing to sell. In a second, non-related case, Nicky, who solved problems on her radio show, was contacted by Pauline Kellaway. Her sister, Red had disappeared, leaving a packet with Pauline. When Nicky returned with FBI agent Harris, Pauline was dead. "The Coyote," a major criminal, let Nicky know that Red was dead and she would be too if she didn't back off.

As *Lover—Say It With Mink* (Laurie, 1953) began, Nicky and Gil Harris were ready to marry when she was kidnapped by former lover Mel Crawshay. She escaped, but the wedding was postponed again when the FBI sent her on a drug smuggling assignment. A third try was foiled when Mel kidnapped her again. Monotonous.

During *The Broadway Jungle* (Laurie, 1954), Nicky planned a Broadway show based on her radio series, but had problems with Dudley Nelson, a disappearing writer, and nervous financial supporters. Before the opening in New York City, Nicky attended a party, during which out-of-work actress Anne Casey was murdered—or was she? Nicky's ongoing contacts with major criminals made her vulnerable to blackmail and violence. The play was a success, but at what a cost.

Another Woman's Man (Laurie, 1954) abounded with proof that the author knew little of U.S. law, government, or politics. Major Larrabee of the FBI was difficult for Nicky to turn down, so she agreed to entice Senator Earl Cromwell away from his current woman "friend," Anne Savitsky. Why not? Nicky and Gil's romance was on hold after Mel Crawshay interrupted the wedding with another abduction. Nicky had been rescued, but Gil was not appeased. They all loved Nicky: Mel, Gil, gambler Bitsy Riordan, gangster Chip Ryan, reporter Joe Cleary, and now the senator. She was starring in a television version of the "Beautiful Gunner" show while trying to locate a missing female FBI agent. The editing was terrible. Names changed. Two totally different backgrounds were provided for the senator.

The plots were unbelievable, partly because of the English author's ignorance or naiveté about the FBI, organized crime, and the entertainment industry in the United States. They may have passed muster to an English reader in the 1950's, but are ridiculous now.

Shirley Leighton

Author: Paul Ernst aka Kenneth Robeson

See: Shirley Leighton Harper, Section 4, page 160.

Jenny Gillette Lewis

Author: Elizabeth Gresham under her own name and as Robin Grey

Jenny Gillette Lewis, who narrated, described herself as having cinnamon-colored hair, but gave little other physical information. She had attended both college and secretarial school, but had no ambitions beyond working with Hunter Lewis.

Hunter, an inventor and craftsman, was consulted by his rich and powerful new neighbor, Pottle, in *Puzzle in Porcelain* (Duell, 1945 by Grey; Curtis reprinted as by Gresham in 1973). Pottle, while walking home alone after a dinner party, died from a rattlesnake bite. Hunter agreed to help interview suspects, with young Jenny Gillette to take notes. Jenny, then in her late teens, had known Hunter for years but had never been able to get his attention.

In *Puzzle in Pewter* (Duell, 1947 as Grey; Curtis reprinted as Gresham in 1973), widower Blair Cameron, obsessed with his chess collection, believed someone was trying to drive him mad. A major inheritance depended upon Cameron's sanity, so there was motivation for unsettling him, even more for killing him. As Hunter and Jenny investigated, he became aware of his romantic feelings for her.

Jenny took a more active role in *Puzzle in Paisley* (Curtis, 1972), posing as Jenny Jones, a deaf-mute orphaned servant, to watch over a fragile elderly woman. Linda Parkinson and her brother Ted had leased a home in Nantucket. William Rowan, the owner of the house, now in the Coast Guard, was concerned about the welfare of his grandmother, who had remained there. The solution had been to send Jenny in undercover. By the time she had enough information to bring in the police, Ted made her a prisoner. She was able to get a coded message out to Hunter, who arrived to save all three women (Jenny, Linda, and grandma).

By *Puzzle in Parquet* (Curtis, 1973), Jenny and Hunter were newly-weds, invited to meet with the Magpies, a club of collectors (coin, stamp, pulps, marbles, etc.). Jenny's discovery of a leather bag full of old coins led the couple into theft, disappearances, and murder.

Hunter had always blamed femme fatale Phillipa for the death of his best friend, Hap, while both were in the service. When, in *Puzzle in Patch-work* (Curtis, 1973), she was accused of murdering her husband, Gilbert, a U.S. congressman, her father hired Hunter to clear his daughter's name. The domineering father had been part of Phillipa's problem. The story veered off as Hunter and Jenny sought others who might have motives to kill Gilbert, including Steve Currier, another former beau of Phillipa, who disappeared and was found dead. Not well organized.

During *Puzzle in Parchment* (Curtis, 1973), Hunter was to authenticate an ancient missal found by Dr. Sara Quarles, a historian at a New Hampshire college. After Sara was strangled, he and Jenny discovered how the document was being used to convey secret information.

These are among the duller mystery books in paperback form.

Eve MacWilliams

Author: Marie Blizard

Eve, a young, blonde newlywed, was lamentably superstitious, believing that "things happen in threes," and for her they did. Originally raised by a grandmother in Wisconsin, she was married to FBI agent Tom Mac-Williams, an FBI agent, and lived in Connecticut.

As *The Late Lamented Lady* (Mystery House, 1946) began, recently injured Eve stayed with Rosemary while Tom was absent on assignment. Sneaking downstairs for a midnight snack, she tripped over her hostess' corpse. Although Rosemary's husband, Jim, had recently returned from hospitalization for war injuries, Eve decided to take their baby, Ginny, home with her. With friend Mac Bronson, Eve checked into Rosemary's past and her connection with others in the community.

Tom left the agency to work in a law firm in *The Men in Her Death* (Mystery House, 1947). When they entered their Maine vacation cottage, they found the corpse of landlady Hester Bruce, a Hollywood writer. Because the police insisted that the MacWilliamses stay temporarily in the Bruce family house, Eve and Tom became acquainted with Hester's house-guests, one of whom inherited under her will. Tom broke an "unbreakable" alibi to solve the case, releasing the heir, movie actor Tucker Ames, from suspicion.

Madame Maigret

Author: Georges Simenon

Inspector Jules Maigret of the Police Judicaire appeared in countless novels and movies. His wife was in the background in all but one of the narratives. She prepared his meals, cared for their home, and accompanied him on social occasions, but never played a role in his investigations until *Madame Maigret's Own Case* (Doubleday, 1959), during which the newspapers noted that a small child had been left in her care. En route to a dental appointment, Madame Maigret had encountered a mother and child, whom she agreed to watch for a few minutes while the mother tended to some business. When the woman reappeared, Madame Maigret was too late for her appointment, but the investment of time was worthwhile. It was her recollection of the hat worn by a servant woman that led the police to her mistress' corpse and a connection to the case on which Maigret had been working.

Kit Marsden

Author: Marion Bramhall

See: Kit Marsden Acton, Section 4, page 130.

Suzanne "Suzy" Willett Marshall

Author: James M. Fox, pseudonym for Johannes Knipscheer

Russet-haired Suzanne Willett Marshall's involvement in detection was narrated by her private investigator husband, Johnny. His references to Suzy were not so much sexual as high calorie—"Honey Bun," "Cherry Pie," and "Sugar Lamb." Once married, Suzy refused to remain in the kitchen, and whenever possible involved herself in Johnny's cases.

In *The Lady Regrets* (Coward, 1947), Johnny, just demobilized, accepted an invitation to visit the California home of a prominent business-man, only to learn that he was not the Johnny Marshall for whom the invitation had been intended. The Marshalls weren't sure they wanted to be guests of the dysfunctional Havers family. They stayed just long enough for Johnny to be a suspect when the daughter of the house was kidnapped. The cops were after the Marshalls as the Marshalls probed the kidnapping that might initially have been a fake but was now real.

Death Commits Bigamy (Coward, 1948) set the police on the Marshalls' trail when they were suspected of involvement in the deaths of two officers. Even when they proved their innocence to Lt. Dave Hogan, who knew them from the prior case, they fell prey to killers who tried to drown them at sea. Fortunately the Coast Guard arrived in time and the killers died in their escape.

Although he was made unwelcome by the local police, Johnny used Suzy and their Great Dane, Khan, in *The Inconvenient Bride* (Coward, 1948) when Barbara Taylor, a British war bride, was rejected by her husband's family. The police in San Benito protected the wealthy inhabitants from outsiders. Johnny had been hired by a British enquiry agent to check out Stacy Taylor, who married Barbara when he was stationed in London. Stacy, who had been injured in France, returned home and never contacted his wife again. Now Stacy seemed drugged or disturbed but definitely under the influence of his mother and her second husband.

John was hired to trace Helen Algood, a radio show contestant who left with a valuable diamond, in *The Gentle Hangman* (Little, 1950). He found her hanging in a motel room. Then, Johnny was hired by screenwriter Luanna Bouquette to trace Eileen Price, a secretary who left her employment with a valuable briefcase, but he continued to work on Helen's murder. She definitely had the diamond and had been trying to peddle it. The police arrested Ernie Jordan, a smalltime pickpocket who had the ring in his possession. That wasn't good enough for Johnny, who believed that Helen's murder was connected to Luanna's case. There were two cases, and maybe there were two Helen Algoods.

In *Fatal in Furs* aka *The Aleutian Blue Mink* (Little, 1951), while on the trail of a mink coat, Johnny discovered the body of Clifford Bush, a dead police officer, putting him on the hit list of local cops. The mink coat, which had been given to Leila de Jong by her fiancé Keith McElroy and then taken back, was worth $20,000. The cops were working to break up a prostitution ring, and in desperation Lt. Hogan deputized Johnny in the search for McElroy and the coat. Suzy redirected Johnny's attention to the real culprit, based on evidence in the mink coat.

During *The Iron Virgin* (Little, 1951) and *A Shroud for Mr. Bundy* (Little, 1952), Johnny had all the action while Suzy tended house.

For a change, in *The Scarlet Slippers* (Little, 1952), Suzy investigated on her own when Joe Hedley, Jr., an ex-convict who had turned his life around, was accused of perjury in a murder trial. The victim in the case had been Sam Walker, Joe's girlfriend's father; the accused, Bill Brown, was a man Joe had known from prison and had already been executed. What never came out at the trial was that Brown had an alibi, a night spent with a police lieutenant's wife. A stoolie tipped Johnny off to the two killers, who were active in drug dealing. One closely resembled Bill Brown. Suzy was contacted by Wilma, the police lieutenant's wife. She sounded drunk on the phone, but by the time Suzy got to her house, she was dead. Suzy could have been dead, too, had it not been for Johnny.

In *Bright Serpent* (Little, 1953), wealthy Bob McAlistair claimed that he was confined in a mental institution by his wife, Eleanor, and Dr. Raymond Arness, administrator of the sanitarium. *Was* held, because he escaped. Johnny was hired to find him and bring him back, but he and Suzy had their doubts, and sought a second opinion. They also costumed themselves and infiltrated the sanitarium to gain evidence, but needed help to get out again.

Suzy was very decorative, occasionally useful in a series that provided fast action but is outdated. There are several other books identified in Hubin but unavailable for review: *Cheese from a Mousetrap* (Davies, 1944), which took place in Germany, *Don't Try Anything Funny* (Davies, 1943), and *Journey into Danger* (Cherry Tree, 1943). However, there are serious questions as to whether or not Suzy appeared in any of these earlier books.

Ann McIntosh aka "Mrs. Mac"
Author: Evalina Mack, pseudonym of Lena B. McNamara

In an early series that featured the charm of the South, Ann McIntosh was a middle-aged widow who had raised two children to adulthood after her husband, Tom, died. Ann taught art classes in a school system and painted portraits to supplement her income.

State Senator Stuart Randolph had been waiting in Ann's studio while she went next door to take a phone call as *Death of a Portrait* (Arcadia House, 1952) began. By the time Ann returned, he had died in an accident so bizarre that murder had to be considered. Several attacks and a subsequent death made it likely that this killer was connected to the discovery of a valuable painting. Ann was smart enough to identify the killer, but foolish enough to confront him alone.

During *Corpse in the Cove* (Arcadia House, 1955), Ann taught summer art school at a mountain resort run by her elderly friend Emily Fontaine. Among Emily's neighbors was Mr. Hardy, who pressured her to sell her property to be used for a development project. His death cast suspicion on Emily's nephew. Young Bill was popular among the art students, even earning a place in Violet Hart's will. When Violet died of snakebite,

Ann checked among the other student guests to prove that Bill was not the guilty party. Her discovery almost came too late as the killer struck again to protect himself.

Two murders took place in *Death Among the Sands* (Arcadia House, 1957) before the question was even raised. With her 19-year-old daughter Patricia considering marriage to a well-to-do young man, and son Tom, Jr., an attorney, Ann was free to meet her own needs. Ann agreed to paint the domineering widow Barbara Sands, even staying at her estate for the sittings. While there she became acquainted with other members of the Sands family—Richard, the bookish son, and Madge, the shy granddaughter, who was deeply in love with Lon, an unacceptable suitor. When Richard was murdered, shortly after learning that Barbara had suppressed a will in which he inherited, Ann used her influence with the authorities to blame Lon for the crime. To serious mystery fans, the past death of a twin always invokes the "which one died question." In 1957, it was more of a novelty.

These were simplistic novels that created multiple conflicts but then glossed over the details of the actions that led to their resolution.

Georgine Wyeth McKinnon

Author: Lenore Glen Offord

Georgine Wyeth was a young widow of 27, living in Berkeley with her seven-year-old daughter, Barbara (Barbie).

During *Skeleton Key* (Duell, 1943), Georgine did clerical work for Prof. Paev, a scientist who wanted a typist without any science background. She became suspicious of her employer, and noted that her house had been searched. Working late one night during an air raid alert, she discovered the body of civil defense warden Roy Hollister, the victim of a hit and run. As a single mother, Georgine had no interest in taking risks, but someone was concerned that she knew too much. Todd McKinnon, a true crime writer who also worked as a warden, rescued Georgine and solved the mystery. He had appeared without Georgine in at least one other book.

In *The Glass Mask* (Duell, 1944), Georgine and Todd were consulted about the death of an elderly cousin. Georgine understood that Todd, very sensitive about his 4F draft status, wanted to clear a younger cousin, Gilbert, of any complicity. Their intervention brought Georgine great pain when Barbie was taken hostage, but the couple married at the conclusion.

In *The Smiling Tiger* (Duell, 1949), Hugh Hartlein, currently doing an exposé of a spiritual cult, shared his information with Todd and

Georgine. Todd showed no interest, but Georgine checked out the isolated house where members of the cult lived. Hartlein was killed, leaving Todd and Georgine certain that his exposé was responsible. Georgine's interest was complicated by false rumors that her first husband was alive and in need of help.

Ten years later, Offord centered *Walking Shadow* (Simon & Schuster, 1959) around Barbara Wyeth, Georgine's daughter then working at an Oregon Shakespeare festival. She was independent, but needed help when she was accused of theft. Georgine was unavailable, but Todd came at once.

The books were competent, workmanlike books, easy to read.

Kitty McLeod

Author: David Dodge

See: Kitty McLeod Whitney, Section 4, page 226.

Sally Merton

Author: Henrietta Hamilton

See: Sally Merton Heldar, Section 4, page 164.

Emily Murdoch

Author: Margaret Scherf

See: Emily Murdoch Bryce, Section 4, page 144.

Natasha Nevkorina

Author: Nancy Spain

Natasha Nevkorina, a former ballet dancer, was Miriam Birdseye's off-again, on-again partner in detection. Like Miriam, Natasha also married several times, but tired of her husbands quickly. See also Miriam Birdseye, Section 4, page 134.

Toni Ney

Author: Lucy Cores

Russian-born Toni Ney built her life around the ballet. She had been educated at the Daillart School of Dance, performed professionally, but retired. As the two-book series began, she ran the fitness/exercise program at a salon, eventually becoming a dance critic for a newspaper. Rue Morgue Press brought the series back to the attention of serious mystery readers. Their introduction included information about author Lucy Cores and female sleuths in general. Rue Morgue regularly rescues interesting early mysteries from oblivion

The House of Lais, a haven for rich, self-centered women, was ruled over by a tyrant, Lais Karaides, who demanded loyalty and hard work from her employees. In *Painted for the Kill* (Duell, 1943; Rue Morgue Press, 2004), there were serious repercussions. Eric Sheets, the public relations director, had the bright idea of luring French actress Lili Michaud to the salon for massage, a coiffure, and the special Winogradow facial. Lili was one too many high-strung pampered females for the facility. Someone eliminated her. Captain Anthony Torrent availed himself of Eric and Toni's knowledge of the suspects and the setting. Another "client" was murdered before Torrent picked up on Toni's intuitive remarks. The victims were not the only ones wearing a mask.

Dancer/choreographer Vova Izlomin asked Toni in *Corpse de Ballet* (Duell, 1944; Rue Morgue, 2004) to connect him with a detective because he had received threatening messages. He had retired from the stage years before because of chronic mental illness, but was making a comeback. Toni, based on her backstage access as a dance critic, was aware of the high level of tension among company members. Natalie, Vova's wife, who had nursed him back to sanity, sought to protect him from pressure. Vova made trouble for himself, engaging in romances with a young dancer and the prominent female owner of the American Ballet Drama. Other male dancers resented the favoritism shown Vova. Mike Gorin, longtime friend of Toni and of Captain Torrent, whom she invited to the opening, was a primary suspect when Vova's body was discovered hanging from the rigging after a remarkable performance. Again, Torrent brought Toni into the investigation, which made it possible for her to score with her news articles. The powerful publisher of Natalia's proposed book captured Toni's time and attention, leaving newly trained Army Lt. Eric Skeets out in the cold.

Mrs. Annie Norris

Author: Dorothy Salisbury Davis

Mrs. Norris teamed with detective Jasper Tully in several mysteries. Annie, who described herself as short and "dumpy," had been compared to Queen Victoria in her younger days. Her brief marriage to a young sailor left her childless, so she devoted 40 years of her life to the Jarvis family. It was "Young Jimmie" to whom Annie Norris had given her allegiance when, as a 20-year-old widow, she came from Scotland to be a nursemaid and then stayed on as housekeeper. Jimmie became a 42-year-old bachelor with political ambitions and a ladyfriend, Helen.

Although Annie and Jasper did the detecting in *Death of an Old Sinner* (Scribner, 1957), the focus was on cantankerous General Ransom Jarvis. The 72-year-old General, frustrated by the inability of his retirement income to maintain his roistering lifestyle, decided to write his memoirs. He thought that "spicing" them up with an altered diary of a former president would increase their sale value. Jarvis' scheme coincided with a struggle between gangster factions that left the General dead of a heart attack and a gambler murdered.

Annie's relationship with Tully became personal when she moved to New York City. *A Gentleman Called* (Scribner, 1958) joined Tully's investigation of the murder of landlady Arabella Sperling together with Jimmie's and Mrs. Norris' involvement in a paternity case. Unknown to Annie, a rotund charmer had selected her as his next ladylove victim.

Annie and Jasper's relationship ended there, because *Old Sinners Never Die* (Scribner, 1959) returned to Washington, D.C., and the earlier days of General Jarvis, Jimmie, and Mrs. Norris, when Joe McCarthy relentlessly searched for Communists and Jimmie was a congressman. In a narrative that frequently switched focus, the trio encountered murder, vicious politics, and international intrigue.

Tales for a Stormy Night (Avon, 1985) was a collection of short stories by Dorothy S. Davis, most of which had previously appeared in *Ellery Queen's Mystery Magazine*. Mrs. Norris appeared in only one, however.

Pamela "Pam" North

Authors: Richard and Frances Lockridge

Pam and Jerry North were childless urban dwellers, sharing their apartment with cats to which they were deeply attached. They enjoyed alcohol and parties, theater, and the world of publishing, where Jerry made his living. Pam, who relied upon her instincts and curiosity rather than any technical skills, worked with Lieutenant Bill Weigand of the New York City Police Department. She was sensitive to relationships. Her emotional antennae picked up on undercurrents in conversation and demeanor.

Jerry and, after some experience, Bill Weigand and his wife, Dorian, respected Pam's gifts, and learned to follow her seemingly disorganized thought processes. It was not so much that she changed the subject as that she did not articulate the connections as she processed information.

Pam never held herself out as a detective; she and Jerry just "happened to be there" when murder occurred. Weigand, who became a social friend, indiscreetly shared new cases and continuing details in the Norths' apartment or over martinis in one of their favorite drinking places.

In *The Norths Meet Murder* (Stokes, 1940), Pam, while using a vacant apartment in their building for a party site, discovered the nude body of Stanley Brent in the bathtub. Weigand, whom they met for the first time here, valued the Norths' insights as to the suspects. Later, when Pam threw another party to include the suspects, she allowed herself to be isolated by the murderer.

Bill had become a part of the Norths' social circle by *Murder Out of Turn* (Stokes, 1941). Pam and Jerry rented a cabin within a compound in New England that featured a lot of socializing. When Bill stopped by for a visit he met Dorian Hunt, a fashion artist. She detested him on sight because her father had been charged with embezzlement. Two young women, one of whom was Dorian's hostess, were murdered in the vacation colony. Bill set up a working relationship with state police officer Merton Heimrich. Heimrich was to work with the locals, while Bill returned to New York City to get background on the suspects. Dorian witnessed a murder attempt; now she was vulnerable. (There was a second series begun later that featured Heimrich.)

Bill was spending a social evening at the Norths' in *A Pinch of Poison* (Stokes, 1941) when he was called to work. Socialite volunteer Lois Winston had been poisoned. Pam knew Lois so was able to fill Bill in on her relationship with Dave McIntosh and the problems with her younger half-brother, Buddy, but was unaware of her problems at the office of the

Placement Foundation, where Lois had replaced a paid social worker. Pamela and Dorian learned about a couple who had "adopted" a child to protect an inheritance. Little Michael's real father was unknown until a connection was made as to a medical problem. The women figured it out and located the boy and his mother.

Pam and Jerry were in the darkened theatre during a play rehearsal in *Death on the Aisle* (Lippincott, 1942) when Dr. Dorsey Bolton, a financial backer of the production, was killed. Much of the narrative centered on Bill and Dorian, and their wedding plans. Pam did involve herself in the case and was confronted by the killer, who believed she had solved it. Pam hadn't, but by the time the killer had exposed herself it was too late to reconsider.

Although the close relationship between Pam and Jerry was not emphasized, it surfaced through their letters in *Hanged for a Sheep* (Lippincott, 1942). While Jerry was in Texas, Pam was recruited by her four-time married Aunt Flora to detect a poisoner. Her potential heirs and heiresses were logical suspects, and they were shirttail relatives of Pam. When she made her selection, she fought off the killer with a vase.

World War II had less personal impact in the North series than on many of its contemporaries. Bill's police work was an essential occupation, and Jerry, well into his thirties, had eye problems.

In *Death Takes a Bow* (Lippincott, 1943), Pam and Dorian were in the audience at the Today's Topics Club when author Victor Leeds Sproul died as Jerry was about to introduce him. Sproul, who had languished as a second rate author, received attention with a new book about the last days of Paris. He had been poisoned. It was noted that before the program he had met with other expatriates from his Paris days. The impression that Sproul might have intended an exposé was strengthened when his notes were left at Bill's burgled apartment. They included negative comments about potential suspects. All that was put aside when Pamela connected a remark by one of her Midwestern nieces to Sproul's origins.

In *Killing the Goose* (Lippincott, 1944), propinquity brought Pamela and Jerry into a case again when Bill and Dorian were socializing at the North home. They were frequently interrupted when Bill received updates on the murder of Ann Laurence. Her beau, Frank Martinelli, had left earlier that evening after a quarrel and was not to be found. A parallel case involved Frances McColley and her hot-tempered boyfriend. Pamela tracked down a killer and broadcast his confession.

By *Payoff for the Banker* (Lippincott, 1945), Pamela and Mary Hunter had met at a party. When Mary entered her new apartment to find banker George Merle's dead body, her first call was to Pam. This did not sit well with Bill Weigand. Merle had succeeded in separating Mary from his son, Josh, recently discharged from the service due to medical problems. In her enthusiasm, Pam was injured and only vaguely remembered by whom. The motive for Merle's death was somewhat difficult to accept.

In *Death of a Tall Man* (Lippincott, 1946), Weigand's tolerance of Pam's interference in the murder of optometrist Dr. Andrew Gordon was incredible. It was even less appropriate for Bill to encourage Jerry, Pam, and Dorian to follow the police car to the Gordon home and enter. They all piled in, probed the relationships between Gordon and his second wife, his war veteran stepson, and his comely nurse. On her own, Pamela interviewed each of the patients whom Gordon treated that morning, providing her with a clue, but the motive was personal, not medical.

Author Amelia Gipson was poisoned in the library while researching a book on unsolved murders in *Murder Within Murder* (Lippincott, 1946). She was a judgmental person who interfered in the lives of family members and colleagues at Ward College. While the police focused on personal relationships, Pam traced the individuals who were involved in the unsolved murders. Good work by Pam in this one.

Untidy Murder (Lippincott, 1947) was really an adventure story featuring Dorian Hunt, now Weigand. On a visit to a business office, she became a witness to murder and was kidnapped.

Based upon her answers to a test, John Leonard, the teacher of a night school psychology course, pinpointed Peggy Mott as potentially homicidal in *Murder Is Served* (Lippincott, 1948). He contacted Jerry even before Peggy's husband, Tony Mott, was killed at his office. Mott owned a controlling interest in a popular restaurant. Peggy had been seen entering the building and admitted her presence, but no complicity in her husband's death. Whoever framed Peggy by calling her and asking her to come to the office was someone intimately connected. Bill Weigand figured that if he didn't arrest Peggy, the real killer would take an aggressive step. It happened.

By now the series had developed a pattern. Crime occurred. Bill and Pam investigated on parallel tracks. He used conventional police procedural systems; she operated by instinct. Often she identified the killer first, but had to be rescued.

Young war widow "Freddie" Haven was the focus of *The Dishonest Murderer* (Lippincott, 1949). Her fiancé had been found dead from a "Mickey Finn" on lower Broadway, while dressed like a vagrant. Freddie thought she had seen him, but didn't worry until he failed to appear for the New Year's Eve party in their honor. The Norths were among the guests. Pamela intervened to save her from a "Mickey Finn" of her own. At least Pam had learned to leave messages for Jerry and Bill so they knew where she was.

Artist Liza O'Brien, who used the North cats as models, found J.K. Halder's body stuffed into a pet shop kennel in *Murder in a Hurry* (Lippincott, 1950). There were connections. Liza was engaged to Brian, Halder's son. Halder, a very wealthy man, had become eccentric and gave up his business interests to run the pet shop in which he was murdered. Pamela, suspecting that Liza might be at risk, decided to protect her, but Weigand's electronic surveillance did it more competently.

The Misses Whitsett, Pamela's maiden aunts, were having tea with old friend Grace Logan when she was poisoned in *Murder Comes First* (Lippincott, 1951). Pamela, with whom they were visiting, intervened because Aunt Thelma, who had never forgotten that Grace stole her beau, was a suspect. Captain Artemus O'Malley, who detested the Norths and resented Weigand's successes, took Bill off the case. This time there were three parallel tracks: Bill acting unofficially; Pam and Dorian investigating; and dainty little Aunt Lucinda, who had ideas of her own.

Dr. Orpheus Preson of the Bradley Institute was at work on a Pleistocene history when he was disturbed by practical jokes in *Dead As a Dinosaur* (Lippincott, 1952). He contacted the police department for help. Preson lost some credibility when his fingerprints were found on a bottle of milk that caused his sister to become ill. After his death from the same poison, a will contest put Jerry's publication of Preson's treatise on hold. Pam's discovery as to how the poison had been administered facilitated the solution.

In *Death Has a Small Voice* (Lippincott, 1953), attention focused on Harry Eaton, a petty thief who intended to use stolen information for blackmail, until he was murdered. However, the information was on a record sent to Jerry North, who was out of town. Pam took it to Jerry's office to listen and hid it, but was kidnapped by Harry's killer. The record contained autobiographical material by poetess Hilda Godwin. It took a while for Jerry and Bill to figure out what had happened. Hilda was dead by now. Meanwhile, Pam, knowing that if she told him where the record was, there would be no reason to keep her alive, escaped...at least for the time being.

In *Curtain for a Jester* (Lippincott, 1953), the Norths attended a party hosted by Byron Wilmot, a notorious practical joker and neighbor, who was funny once too often. He was stabbed later that evening. Logistics were important. Who could have returned to take vengeance on Byron, because so many of the guests had motives?

Jerry and Pam took a personal interest when their attorney was killed in *A Key to Death* (Lippincott, 1954), even postponing their Florida vacation. Forbes Ingraham also represented many prominent authors, including Phoebe James, with whom he was in love. It was Phoebe who convinced

Pam to investigate. The circle of suspects included Ingraham's partner, Reginald Webb, and Nan Schaeffer, widow of a former partner, both of whom would benefit from insurance; a labor leader backed by the Mafia; and staff members with romantic interests. The result was a surprise.

(Now Captain) Bill Weigand took the lead in *Death of an Angel* (Lippincott, 1955), when Brad Fitch, fiancé of Broadway actress Naomi Shaw, was murdered. Naomi, who was currently starring in a successful play, had made it known that she would retire to marry. Her decision would end the run of the play. Pamela had an active role in the investigation, but this was a police department success story.

The Norths and Weigands took a Caribbean cruise, along with one hundred plus members of the "Ancient and Respectable Riflemen" in *Voyage Into Violence* (Lippincott, 1956). J. Orville Marsh, an investigator who specialized in missing persons, was killed with an ARR ceremonial sword. Bill had agreed to the trip because he was burned out and needed the rest. A case with a potential list of so many suspects would hardly fit the bill. The assumption was that Marsh had noticed someone among the passengers who had disappeared at one time and built a new identity. Bill used his resources to get background on the suspects and on two cases on which Marsh was currently working. When the passengers went ashore in Cuba, things unraveled. Pam fiddled with red herrings, but it was police procedure that solved the case.

In *The Long Skeleton* (Lippincott, 1958), the Norths found the corpse of Amanda Towne, a television celebrity, in the hotel room they occupied while their apartment was being painted. Jerry encouraged Pam to "sit this one out," and she could have because the killer was obvious to the readers.

Professor Jameson Elwell, a friend of the Norths, was murdered in his own home at a study/laboratory on the third floor that could be entered either from Elwell's or from the house next door, in *Murder Is Suggested* (Lippincott, 1959). Bill was the publisher of Elwell's last book. Elwell, unlike so many other victims, had few obvious enemies. About the only person who seemed to dislike him was Hope Oldham, the mother of Faith, one of his students. She thought Elwell achieved success by stealing ideas from her deceased husband. Weigand even toyed with the idea that Elwell, who had cancer, might have planned his own death. Pam read Elwell's book and knew better.

It became more difficult to justify the Norths' involvement in Bill Weigand's cases in *The Judge Is Reversed* (Lippincott, 1960). After John Blanchard was murdered, Weigand had suspects brought to the North apartment to be questioned. This was clearly a conflict of interest. Bill, a tennis enthusiast, knew Blanchard in his role as a tennis official. Pam, who was looking to purchase a replacement for their Siamese, Martini, was familiar with him as a judge at cat shows. Actually, Pam was so busy checking out cats that she had little time to detect.

In *Murder Has Its Points* (Lippincott, 1961), Pam and Jerry were hosting a cocktail party for vindictive but popular author Anthony Payne. Many of the guests and several members of the hotel staff had good reason to detest Payne. When Bobby, a young busboy who was Payne's unacknowledged son, went missing, his mother, Pam, and Faith Constable, another of Payne's wives went looking for him at Payne's Connecticut home. Lauren, Payne's most recent wife, was there and in danger because she might have seen the killer.

The last North mystery, *Murder by the Book* (Lippincott, 1963), found Pam and Jerry vacationing in Florida. Although the Weigands stayed home, Bill had to vouch for Pamela when she discovered the body of Dr. Edmund Piersal, recently vindicated in a malpractice suit. Pam didn't solve the case alone. Chief Deputy Sheriff Ronald Jefferson finally learned to understand her methodology and used her information to solve the crime.

The series had become less relevant. By 1960, heroines were harder edged, and more technically skilled. But, for a reader tired of the cynical, crusading private investigator, Pamela was and remains a pleasant read. She never grew up, but then neither did Nancy Drew.

Sarah De Long O'Brien

Author: Melba Marlett

After years of caring for an invalid mother, redheaded Sarah De Long, an urban high school teacher, was, at age 35, single and without prospects. A minister's daughter, she was from a prominent Philadelphia family and had a Vassar education.

In *Death Has a Thousand Doors* (Doubleday, 1941), the murder of Arlette Hendricks, a married student, brought Police Inspector Jim O'Brien to school. Arlette was pregnant, so special attention was paid to male students, coaches, and teachers. Due to two more murders, the school was forced to close. After a testy beginning, Sarah and O'Brien found romance and a youthful killer.

Sarah experienced her first pregnancy at age 38 in *Another Day Toward Dying* (Doubleday, 1943) and had a son, Brian. When she declared that wealthy Hetty Willoughby's death was an intentional hit-and-run accident, everyone believed that she was suffering from emotional problems. Battling nausea and a possible miscarriage, Sarah trapped a killer.

Miss Mabie Otis

Author: Ben Sarto, a house name, but many books are attributed to
Frank Duprez Fawcett

"Miss Otis Regrets (She's Unable to Lunch Today)" was a sophisticated Cole Porter song of the 1930's, which created the illusion of a world-weary but gallant woman, who could not keep an appointment because she had murdered the man who betrayed her and been lynched. Any hope that the Miss Otis of the Ben Sarto books was patterned on this image was dashed with a peremptory reading. Murderous, yes! Gallant, unlikely!

Mabie was a tall peroxide blonde with blue-gray eyes and two dimples in her chin. She may have received some education, but it was not apparent in her grammar or vocabulary. Mabie was a cruel, mendacious woman without loyalty, who committed crimes rather than solving them. Although the books were published in England, the series was set in the United States. The dialogue read like American slang written by an Englishman who had never crossed the Atlantic.

Miss Otis Throws a Comeback (Modern Fiction, 1947) began with Mabie married to former FBI agent Granger Girton, who managed the business affairs of their restaurant bar. Bored with Girton and the business, Mabie philandered with Dacosta, a Mexican arsonist, in a notably unhealthy relationship, driving her husband to commit murder.

Girton was found not guilty by reason of self-defense in *Miss Otis Goes Up* (Modern Fiction, 1947), but he was murdered. Mabie left the nightclub business, attached herself to ruthless businessman Carter Schooling. When attorney Sigmund Kneiffer tried blackmail, Schooling shot him in Mabie's presence. By helping to dispose of the body, she became an accessory to murder. Although Mabie was not sentenced to jail for her part in the murder, she was left penniless. Resourceful as ever, she took a new name and found employment as a cashier in a restaurant, eventually becoming a co-owner.

One of Mabie's problems grew up in *Miss Otis Has a Daughter* (Modern Fiction, 1948), when she had a visitor, the daughter she had given up for adoption. At this point Mabie was still part-owner of the Paradise restaurant. Frank Taufelt was a decent man who had married her even after she told him of her past. Frank was under pressure not to testify in a case, so they had moved to Florida, but he was subpoenaed and had to return to New York. It was something of a shock for Ruthie to learn who her real mother was. The genetics were there. If possible, daughter Ruthie made Mabie look good.

This 18-book series must have achieved some level of popularity in England, but copies are extremely difficult to find. Others identified in Hubin: *Miss Otis Comes to Piccadilly* (Modern Fiction, 1946), *Jaws Pellegrini* (Modern Fiction, 1940), *Miss Otis Blows Town* (Milestone, 1953), *Miss Otis Goes French* (Milestone, 1953), *Miss Otis Hits Back* (Milestone, 1953), *Miss Otis Makes a Date* (Milestone, 1953), *Miss Otis Makes Hay* (Milestone, 1954), *Miss Otis Moves In* (Milestone, 1953), *Miss Otis Plays Eve* (Milestone, 1953), *Miss Otis Says Yes* (Milestone, 1953), *Miss Otis Takes the Rap* (Modern Fiction 1953), *Miss Otis Desires* (Milestone 1954), *Miss Otis Gets Fresh* (Milestone, 1954), *Miss Otis Plays Ball* (Milestone, 1954), and *Miss Otis Relents* (Milestone, 1954) are almost impossible to find. *Miss Otis Comes to Piccadilly* was listed as being held by the British Library, but when requested was described as "mislaid." A used copy of *Miss Otis Blows Town* was advertised for sale in 2005 at $158.00.

After a brief popularity in the Forties, the series stopped and then was resumed with heavy publication in 1953 and 1954.

Louise "Liz" Boykin Parrott

Author: Manning Long

Liz Parrott had been an Arkansas schoolteacher before she came to New York City. She was a beautiful redhead with amber-gray eyes whose career as a model lasted four years. Her husband, Gordon, was an investigator for the District Attorney's office, who served in Intelligence during World War II. The Parrotts eventually purchased the bookstore where Liz worked part-time during the war years. Although they were expecting a child in the final book, Liz's only responsibility until then had been a cat named "I Am."

The relationship between Liz and Gordon began with murder. An early affair that had ended in tragedy was not something that Liz had shared with her then fiancé, wealthy and conservative Husted Breamer. The death of a blackmailer at a party attended by Liz in *Here's Blood in Your Eye* (Duell, 1941) provided multiple suspects. Gordon, already an investigator for the district attorney's office, was aware that the police suspected Liz. He was so smitten with her that he remained glued to her side until she was proven innocent. Although she had disdained his attentions initially, she changed her mind and married him.

In *Vicious Circle* (Duell, 1942), Gordon's cousin Clifford and his friend Quentin Alexander had been arrested and mistreated while in Russia. Quentin died as a result of their experiences, which Clifford used as the basis for a successful book. When Clifford's ex-wife, a foreign correspondent, was killed, it was Liz who uncovered the motive for the murder.

During *False Alarm* (Duell, 1943), while Gordon was in service, Liz worked at Post C-21, an air raid center and shared an apartment with Mollie O'Sullivan, co-owner of the bookstore. Sandra Colling, wife of the Zone commander, transferred to C-21, where she manged to irritate the other volunteers within a short time. Mollie was suspected when first Sandra and then another volunteer were poisoned. Liz put herself in danger when, having failed to reach Detective Marvin Langmede to share her information, she went on rooftop duty alone.

In *Bury the Hatchet* (Duell, 1944), while Gordon was on leave, he and Liz vacationed at a island cabin. Gordon was preoccupied by checking out the possibility that Hale Harrison, son of a friend, had been murdered. The Harrisons' daughter Ann had died two years earlier after a botched abortion. Liz, on the other hand, was concerned that Gordon was paying too much attention to Vera Ingram, the man-hunting occupant of a nearby cabin. Jo Gibbs, who had shared the cabin with Vera, was found after a heavy storm with her head scalped. It got worse, but Gordon and Liz settled their personal problems, and Pearline, an African-American maid, captured the killer.

In *Short Shrift* (Duell, 1945), Liz accompanied her friend Kathy Floyd on a trip to Virginia, where she co-owned land that her former husband's family coveted. Kathy's intent was to visit her sick Cousin Nannie. She was, however, brought into contact with Monroe Floyd, the ex-husband whom she still loved, Julia, his new wife, and their child. Miss Muriel, head of the family, had been instrumental in causing the divorce. Nannie's death, that of her visitor William Combes, and finally Julia's set Liz to work detecting.

In *Dull Thud* (Duell, 1947), while Gordon traveled for Army Intelligence, Liz's free time was enlivened by her membership in W.W.W. (Wistful War Wives). The connection turned sour when several members of the group, including Liz, received blackmail letters. The janitor who was suspected of sending the letters was murdered, as was a member of the W.W.W. Gordon returned in time to work with Liz setting a trap for the killer.

During *Savage Breast* (Duell, 1948), Gordon and the pregnant Liz sublet an apartment from her gynecologist, Dr. Howard Fawcett. They made the move because gangster Teaball Bishop had threatened Gordon. The penthouse was luxurious, but Liz discovered the corpse of Dr. Tom

Culley, Fawcett's partner, in the woodpile. Not only had Fawcett and Culley quarreled about research they were doing on a new anesthesia, but there was discord in Culley's family. Teaball, who had come to admire Liz, captured the killer as Liz was giving birth to a son.

Although the effort was for a light and humorous series, it was not always successful.

Mother Paul

Author: June Wright

Neither Wright nor her protagonist, a Catholic nun living in Australia, will be familiar to many readers in the United States. Her books are extremely difficult to find. Little background was given as to Mother Paul (which anyone familiar with religious orders during that period of time will not find surprising). Parochial school students of that period might accept with equal gullibility the fact reported by Patricia Craig and Mary Cadogan in *The Lady Investigates* that Mother Paul had the ability to "see things in people's eyes." She was an older woman of considerable authority, denoted by the title "Mother" as contrasted with "Sister." The character was underdeveloped in at least the first two books, where young women who resided in facilities directed by Mother Paul were the viewpoint characters.

Reservation for Murder (Long, 1958) was narrated by Mary Allen, a resident of the hostel for working women and students run by Mother Paul's order of nuns. Mary developed an unfortunate habit of discovering corpses, first a recently released convict who had been in jail for attempting to rob the hostel, and twice more, the bodies of fellow residents. Mary, a legal secretary, enjoyed excitement, but had not intended to be used by Mother Paul and handsome detective Steve O'Mara as bait to capture a killer and uncover a drug ring.

Mother Paul emerged in a different role in her second appearance, *Faculty of Murder* (Long, 1961), as "warden" (director) of a women's private dormitory at Melbourne University. Assisting her at Brigid Moore Hall were two tutors, one of whom, Elizabeth Drew, was drawn into the action. An entering freshman, Judith Mornane, had shocked her fellow students by announcing that she was there to discover her sister's murderer. Maureen Mornane had disappeared within days of moving into Brigid Moore Hall. Unlike others who ridiculed Judith, Mother Paul and eventually both Elizabeth and the local police came to believe that Maureen's disappearance was connected to at least one other murder. An implausible explanation for Maureen's involvement marred the dénouement.

The final mystery in the Mother Paul series, *Make-Up for Murder* (Long, 1966), was flawed. Had Mother Paul made a stronger case that she needed to confer with Inspector Robert Savage, a second murder might not have occurred. Among those attending a reunion at Maryhill were singer Rianne May, her assistant Sue Berry, and other members of the Past Student's Association. When an officer of the group was poisoned, an assumption was made that Rianne had been the intended victim. Mother Paul saw the difference between illusion and reality, but was dilatory in sharing her information with Savage. He shared in the responsibility because he had ignored several messages indicating her need to speak to him.

Bessie Petty and Beulah Pond

Author: Hilda Lawrence

Bessie Petty and Beulah Pond were small-town New Englanders who worked with big-city investigator Mark East. Little old lady sleuths were more acceptable when packaged with a hard-edged private investigator. They were designed for contrast: Bessie, a short, chubby, scatterbrained retired schoolteacher, and her more assertive friend Beulah, tall and gaunt, who ran a lending library out of her home.

In *Blood Upon the Snow* (Simon, 1944), shortly after East went undercover as a private secretary to protect Joe Stoneman, someone burned down the servants quarters, killing the cook. Jim Morey, his wealthy wife, Laura, and their children were guests in the main house. The maid Florrie, who had cared for the children, disappeared, then was found dead. Beulah and Bessie were drafted to take over her responsibilities. There continued to be violent incidents; finally, Stoneman disappeared. While Mark and Sheriff Perley Wilcox checked outside sources in Europe and Florida, Bertha and Bessie took action on their own.

On a personal visit to Beulah and Bessie in *A Time to Die* (Simon, 1945), Mark joined them and 13-year-old Floyd Wilson, son of the sheriff, in searching for Mary Cassidy, a young governess for the Beacham family, who were staying at a summer hotel. After Mary's corpse was found in a well, Mark returned to New York to check on her background. She was a registered nurse who had worked with mentally ill patients. Had she recognized one of them at the hotel? Floyd saved an abducted child.

When salesclerk Ruth Miller, who lived at a New York City residence for women, died in an apparent suicide in *Death of a Doll* (Simon, 1947), Roberta Beacham Sutton called on Beulah and Bessie to look into the matter. Roberta, a member of the Beacham family from the prior book, remembered their skills. She knew Ruth well enough to dismiss the possibility of suicide. While Mark worked the case in an official capacity, Beulah and Bessie checked out the neighborhood merchants and the other residents, enabling him to uncover a thief who killed to protect her identity.

Pleasant series.

Katherine "Peter" Piper

Author: Amelia Reynolds Long

Hidden under the masculine name, the close-cropped hair, and the trousers (still unusual in the Forties), Katherine "Peter" Piper was an overachieving young woman waiting to melt into the arms of a dashing Southern gentleman—just the heroine of which lending libraries (which catered to women readers) approved.

While still a graduate student in Philadelphia, Peter was a mystery author and a member of a group of women writers, the Quill Society. When Marguerite English, one of the writers, who was suspected of sending scurrilous letters to other members, was killed in *The Corpse at the Quill Club* (Phoenix, 1940), Peter worked with criminal psychologist Ted Trelawney. Their initial suspect was attorney Warren Dane, whose close friend Tim Kent killed himself two years ago because of false information supplied by Marguerite, but they looked further.

The Quill Club planned a weekend party to take place at Helen Blake's rental home in Philadelphia in *Four Feet in the Grave* (Phoenix, 1941). Kate Hutton was an unexpected addition to the group, convincing Peter to allow her to impersonate another woman. Once on site, they learned that a murder had been committed in the house. Not surprisingly, Kate was connected to the victim, at least one of them, as a second murder occurred.

Peter metamorphosed into a gothic heroine in *Murder Goes South* (Phoenix, 1942) when she visited Louisiana for her friend Lavinia Dumont's wedding. Lavinia, whose motives for the marriage were suspect, disappeared. Gaston Dupres, the prospective father-in-law, died. The secret that haunted the Dupres family was exposed, but only after another death. Ted Trelawney came on scene to detect while Peter succumbed to romance with Amadee, the groom's half-brother.

Still in the south in *Murder by Scripture* (Phoenix, 1942), Peter visited Amedee, now her fiancé, during an investigation into voodoo practices. Dr. Gabriel Devereux headed a group called "The Cult of Gabriel." Several members had died recently, leaving their estates to the organization. Peter ignored alibis and physical clues, focusing on motive, thereby avoiding the need for careful plotting.

Death Looks Down (Ziff-Davis, 1944) returned Peter and Trelawney to Pennsylvania, where she attended an American Literature course on Edgar Allan Poe taught by Prof. Patrick Rourke. Archie Schultz, an expert engraver, was murdered in the library stacks. Controversy surrounded the discovery of a handwritten copy of Poe's *Ulalume*. Rourke had authenticated it, but a colleague said it was a fake. Trelawney arranged for a second opinion, but in the meantime two more students in the class were murdered. Using the procedures of the fictional C. Auguste Dupin, Trelawney forced the killer to disclose his identity.

In *It's Death, My Darling!* (Mystery House, 1948), Peter revisited New Orleans to meet Amadee's family, and bask in such clichés as Confederate swords, baying hounds, and werewolves. While there she attended the funeral of the head of the family Colonel Etienne Dumont. The disposal of Etienne's property among family members led to disputes. One of the heirs was eliminated the next morning, stabbed posthumously by a Confederate sword. Eventually Peter figured it out, but not until she was at the mercy of the killer and needed to be rescued.

Peter was aware that individuals who became characters in her novels often ended up in trouble in real life. That did not stop her from writing a mystery play for the local theater group in *The Lady Saw Red* (Phoenix, 1951). Moreover, she modeled her plot on an infidelity within the theater group which would perform her play. Although the plot never thickened, it reflected Peter's script so closely that she had to solve the crime. She did not, however, share her findings.

These were run-of-the-mill mysteries.

There was evidence in the series that Peter reflected the patronizing attitudes of her author about African-Americans.

Grace Pomeroy

Author: Anna Mary Wells

Grace Pomeroy had initially been a teacher, but went on to study nursing and became the assistant to a young psychiatrist, Dr. Hillis Owen.

During *A Talent for Murder* (Knopf, 1942), Owen was so convinced that his patient Doris Meredith was not only innocent of killing her husband, but needed protection that he set out to find the real murderer with

Grace's help. She checked out his clues initially, but when he was attacked and hospitalized, she played a more active role and brought Doris and Hillis together romantically.

Murderer's Choice (Knopf, 1943) took place during World War II. While Hillis was serving in the Armed Forces, Grace took employment in the Keene Detective Agency. Charles, a disgruntled writer, had threatened to kill himself in such a manner that his cousin Frank would be convicted of murder. His death almost achieved that result, although Frank needed mercy rather than justice from Grace.

She had no role of any importance in the final Hillis Owens book, *Sin of Angels* (Simon and Schuster, 1948).

Beulah Pond

Author: Hilda Lawrence

Beulah Pond and Bessie Petty were small-town New Englanders who worked with big-city investigator Mark East. Little old lady sleuths were more acceptable when packaged with a hard-edged private investigator. They were designed for contrast: Bessie, a short, chubby, scatterbrained retired schoolteacher, and her more assertive friend Beulah, tall and gaunt; who ran a lending library out of her home. For more information, see Bessie Petty, Section 4, page 192.

Julia Probyn

Author: Ann Bridge, pseudonym for Lady Mary O'Malley

Julia Probyn was tall with a "full, if graceful" figure, tawny hair, and gray-blue eyes. Her aristocratic carriage mirrored her loyalty to British upper class attitudes in politics and economics. Her widowed father, an Army officer, had remarried, virtually ending their ties. Personally kind and understanding, Julia was a prisoner of her class, unable to comprehend nationalistic sentiments within the British Empire. She spoke Gaelic, but couldn't understand the Irish need for change. Although she initially camouflaged her intelligence, she was enterprising, financially independent, and physically daring. Julia became a dedicated professional agent, turning the care of her only child over to others.

In *The Light-Hearted Quest* (Macmillan, 1956), Julia, then a freelance journalist, was recruited by family members to trace her cousin, Colin

Monro, who had disappeared while yachting in the Mediterranean. She used her official and commercial contacts and must have aroused some concern, because she was being followed. Julia was unaware of Colin's connection with British Intelligence until she was deeply involved and had been injured by a bomb.

In *The Portuguese Escape* (Macmillan, 1958), Julia sought Hetta, a young refugee, who was the daughter of a Hungarian countess. Hetta, who had worked in a convent kitchen, was familiar with the appearance of Father Antal Horvath, a distinguished Hungarian cleric smuggled from behind the Iron Curtain. Initially safe in Lisbon, Hetta was kidnapped but rescued by Mrs. Hathaway, a friend of Julia's. Julia had been in Lisbon to report upon a royal wedding.

During *The Numbered Account* (McGraw, 1960), Julia agreed to withdraw Aglaia Armitage's inheritance and an important secret document from a Swiss bank, as a favor to Colin, who was engaged to Aglaia. Unfortunately, an imposter had already withdrawn the account. Julia worked with agent John Antrobus in preventing the stolen money and documents from leaving Switzerland. Although she was very much in love with Antrobus, he did not return her interest.

In *The Dangerous Islands* (McGraw, 1963), Julia, Colin, his sister Edina, and her husband discovered Russian satellite stations on outlying islands. A message to the authorities resulted in the appearance of Philip Jamieson of British Intelligence. When the probe spread to Ireland, Julia's ability to speak Gaelic and her friendships with the Anglo-Irish were critical. Again, Julia suffered a serious injury while investigating. Julia and Philip, now a widower, became engaged.

Julia's marriage to Jamieson and her subsequent pregnancy limited her activities in *Emergency in the Pyrenees* (McGraw, 1965), so she spent the "waiting months" at a French mountain home, near the Spanish border. Colin took advantage of her location for activities involving borderline smuggling. Twins Nick and Dick Heriot, sons of neighbors, were eager to help. Julia needed all the help she could get when she went into premature labor and required caesarian surgery. Colin needed help to smuggle a former British Intelligence agent out of France. He may have been involved in smuggling, but he had served the Allies well.

Julia's role as wife and mother was more pronounced in *The Episode at Toledo* (McGraw, 1966), which centered on Hetta, the Hungarian refugee whom Julia had befriended in an earlier narrative. Hetta, now the wife of Richard Atherley, a British diplomat, and expecting her second child, was in danger when she recognized Hungarian espionage agents in Spain.

By *The Malady in Madeira* (McGraw, 1969), Philip had died mysteriously. In her grief and to get more information about his death, Julia worked with Colin. She made a commitment to British Intelligence work, leaving her son with cousins in Scotland. Colin, too, was in grief, blaming himself for a failed mission and affected by the death of an expected child. They both met their needs as they followed up on a Russian trawler off the Portuguese coast that might have transported a nerve gas.

Julia in Ireland (McGraw, 1973) introduced her new fiancé, Gerald O'Brien, an Irish solicitor whom she hoped would be a father for her son. She opposed the efforts of real estate developers to buy Irish land for a hotel and casino in the belief that Ireland should be kept in its "natural" condition, uncorrupted by money. Very little tension generated here.

Lucy Pym

Author: Josephine Tey, pseudonym for Elizabeth MacKintosh

Lucy Pym was an elementary teacher thrust into prominence by a successful novel. When her lecture tour ended at Leys Physical Training College in *Miss Pym Disposes* (Macmillan, 1948), Lucy was burned out. She remained on campus, forming relationships with the students that facilitated her investigation into murder.

Tey was a sensitive, intelligent writer. Pym is of interest because she was Tey's only female sleuth.

Andrea Reid Ramsay

Author: Cecile Matschat

Andrea Reid, the daughter of a rural medical practitioner, considered medical school but was diverted into research. Auburn-haired Andy was employed by a New England sanitarium for mental diseases. She had been engaged to architect David Ramsay until she met actor Peter Ravenel.

As *Murder in Okefenokee* (Farrar, 1941) opened, Andy visited Florida, where Ravenel had purchased a plantation home surrounded by dismal swamps. David Ramsey's presence made her uncomfortable. The home was cold and dark. There were snakes and quicksand. The second day, Andy found Aunt Hortie, sister to Dr. Stone, for whom Andy worked, dead in the barn. There were sinister references to a "little black book." Andy's knowledge of genetics helped her through a series of mysterious deaths.

In *Murder at the Black Crook* (Farrar, 1943), Andy and David were honeymooning in New Orleans. Oil tycoon Robert Brooks found it difficult to believe that one of his guests was diverting oil to Nazi submarines. Army Intelligence had asked Andy and David to visit Brooks and learn more about the diversion. Brooks' daughter, Judith, who had been trapped in the Philippines when the Japanese invaded, surprised everyone with her appearance. Tensions arose as to the sale and inheritance of oil stocks, culminating in murder.

Second rate, maybe third rate.

Andrea Reid

Author: Cecile Matschat

See: Andrea Reid Ramsay, Section 4, page 197.

Clare Liddicotte Ringwood

Author: Katharine Farrar

Clare was engaged to Det. Insp. Richard Ringwood of Scotland Yard as *The Missing Link* (Collins, 1952; Rue Morgue Press, 2004) began. They had a good working relationship in that Clare did research on cases at the Oxford Library and was allowed to be present during interviews. Perdita, infant daughter of Oxford Don John Link and his wife Perpetua, was being raised with due attention to all scientific information as to parenthood. Unfortunately, that was of no avail when Perdita was kidnapped from an unattended baby carriage in their yard. Possible connections were made with the disappearance of Gladys Turner, nursemaid for the Luke family next door, or gypsies, based upon a prediction that "two will be returned." A chance remark by Clare clued Richard in to tracing the child and retrieving her from an unlikely mother.

Archaeologist Sir Alban Worrell had refused to be tested for ulcers, so his death after eating at Ninos, a Greek style restaurant, came as no surprise in *The Cretan Counterfeit* (Collins, 1954; Rue Morgue Press, 2004). However, an attack on his dedicated colleague Janet Coltman brought Richard into the picture. When Janet recovered, she remembered little except that she had returned to Ninos to retrieve a briefcase. Clare, concerned about Janet's vulnerability, invited her to recover at the Ringwood home. Her future contribution, taking her to a beauty parlor, had more impact on

Janet's romance than on the case. Richard focused on sales of false antiquities and the fact that Worrell's death was probably murder.

A series of fires at Oxford University was brought to the attention of Scotland Yard in *Groomsman's Gallows* (Hodder, 1957; Rue Morgue Press, 2005). They preferred to have Ringwood assigned to the case because of Clare's connection. However, her pregnancy kept Clare from taking any active role in the case. Using a bloodhound, which he had trained, Richard located the burned corpse of Jean Despuys, a missing Frenchman. As reluctant as he was to leave England at this time, Richard traveled to France to make connections between Despuys and suspects in Oxford. Clare produced a son.

Clare was another of the intelligent, challenging women who were married to and participated with professional investigators and police officials during this period. Unfortunately, she was not given as much opportunity to take part in cases as were some of her contemporaries. Rue Morgue Press has included all three of the Ringwood cases in its Vintage Series.

Haila Rogers
Author: Kelley Roos, pseudonym for William and Audrey Kelley Roos

See: Haila Rogers Troy, Section 4, page 215.

Laura Scudamore
Author: Raymond Armstrong, pseudonym for Norman Lee

Laura Scudamore, aka "The Sinister Widow," the great-grandchild of a western outlaw, had no respect for authority. She grew up on the wrong side of the tracks in New Haven, Connecticut. After her father was killed by a policeman, 18-year-old Laura left home to join a burlesque show. Criminal friends taught her safe cracking and bank robbery, and eventually she headed a gang. Reputedly, her right arm had been amputated after a gun battle with American State Troopers, forcing her to wear a prosthetic device, which should have simplified identification.

Her nickname, "Sinister Widow," referred to her reputation (like the black widow spider) for killing ex-lovers and husbands, six of whom she was suspected of strangling. Not easy with an amputated arm.

Laura never softened or reformed, rarely was proven guilty of a kindly act, and failed to develop loyalty for her associates. To her credit, she never dealt in narcotics, blackmail or prostitution. One unsubstantiated report claimed that she gave 25 percent of her profits to charity. By age 28, Laura was a ruthless gang leader operating primarily in England, where she owned several homes. Her personal appearance changed as she changed identities and settings. At one time she was described as a blonde with gray eyes and medium height, but later as having lustrous black hair. When one of her gang was arrested, Laura made no effort to help, merely cut off the connection.

In the initial book of the series, *The Sinister Widow* (Long, 1951), Scotland Yard set up a commando unit to thwart the Sinister Widow's plans for a major robbery. Potential informants were found dead. Continued pressure by the authorities forced the Widow to leave London disguised as an effeminate male columnist. Although a member of the commando unit had an opportunity to shoot Laura, he declined to do so.

During *The Sinister Widow Again* (Long, 1952), Laura, after a sojourn in Africa, returned to England, where she took control of a gang headed by the Anaconda until she killed him. In a confusing narrative marred by frequent changes of narrator, she assumed different identities, including that of a Canadian police officer, in order to confound both Scotland Yard and rival gangsters, but in the end had to leave England hurriedly.

The Sinister Widow Returns (Long, 1953) began with Laura playing a minor stage role on Broadway. She moved on to marry the elderly but wealthy Count Gregori in Brazil, then to Italy, where she wooed and wed Sir Elben Fitzhardinge, who was well connected in British official circles. Although initially successful, the widow was always foiled in the end.

In *The Widow and the Cavalier* (Long, 1956), adventurer Rocky Stone, while trying to help a young couple, convinced Scotland Yard that Laura was the Comtesse de Futrelle, but she was one step ahead of them, posing as a flighty blonde actress.

In *The Sinister Widow Comes Back* (Long, 1957), Laura had to combat Scotland Yard, the members of a rival gang, and weaknesses in her own organization. She escaped only by substituting her double, an American film actress, and fleeing England.

Efforts to trap Laura extended to Australia, where Laura had relocated in *The Sinister Widow Down Under* (Long, 1958). One of her lieutenants, who now had his own territory to protect, made her unwelcome. Laura moved again, using the daughter of the Police Commissioner as a hostage.

The Sinister Widow at Sea (Long, 1959) concentrated less on the Widow than on those who sought her or wanted to steal or prevent the theft of valuable jewels. These included a Chinese private detective, a newspaperman, ship officials, police officers, and a variety of thieves. The Widow was ready to give up her life of crime and to pursue a new identity. It must have worked, because this was the last Sinister Widow book.

Mavis Seidlitz

Author: Carter Brown, pseudonym for Alan Yates

Although Mavis Seidlitz was a caricature of a blonde bimbo, she provided occasional flashes of humor that even a feminist might enjoy. She evoked instant admiration and lust in all the men she encountered, but was easily seduced by any man who treated her decently. Long on pulchritude, she was short on brains. She traded her original job as secretary for Johnny Rios' detective agency to work for him as a private investigator at a lower salary.

A Bullet for My Baby (Horowitz, 1955) was published with the author identified as Peter Carter-Brown. Johnny Rios narrated this book. He was tired of Mavis making him look like a fool. Recent widow Fiona Van Bruton hired Johnny to attend a two-week party on an isolated island off the Florida coast. A fellow guest, Dr. Kestler, was the director of the mental sanitarium where Johnny had been confined to keep him from going on the trip. When, after he escaped, Mavis saved him from a return to the sanitarium, he could hardly leave her behind. Two murders later, Johnny was perceived as a killer, not a private investigator. Even when he narrated, he came off as incompetent.

There came about a gradual deterioration in the series, an increase in sadism, less humor and more brutality. Mavis was on a Mexican vacation in *Murder Wears a Mantilla* (Horowitz, 1957, as Peter Carter-Brown; reissued by Signet, 1962), but agreed to deliver a suitcase full of money for a dying bullfighter. When her luggage was inspected at the airport, it contained not money but a corpse. Mavis' idea of close cooperation with Mexican police chief Vega was unusually close.

The Fabulous (Horowitz, 1959) aka *None But the Lethal Heart* was more of the same. Mexican police official Rafael Vega came to Mavis for help in disposing of a corpse. He had come to Los Angeles as a bodyguard for Arturo Santerres aka "The Fabulous," son of the president of his country. Arturo's mission was to arrange a loan from financier Jonathan B. Stern. Unfortunately, he was the man Rafael shot and whose body he had hidden in his car trunk. More sexual sadism, more violence, even Mavis got tired of it.

In *The Loving and the Dead* (Signet, 1959), Mavis posed as the third wife of Donald Ebhart, whose sadistic father, Randolph, required his heirs to be married and to spend 72 hours at the family home after his death. Mavis allowed Rios to use her as bait for possible murderers among the prospective heirs. A second will placed even more stress upon the rival heirs.

When Mavis' professional relationship with Rios ended, she worked as a single in *Tomorrow Is Murder* (Signet, 1960). She failed in her assignment to protect Raymond Romayne, whose imminent murder had been announced. Romayne wanted to hire Johnny but settled for her. She didn't have it easy, either, but survived betrayal and torture to catch the killer, with help from a handsome police lieutenant.

Mavis teamed with Los Angeles police deputy Al Wheeler in *Lament for a Lousy Lover* (Signet, 1960). She was hired to keep guest star Amber Lace away from series hero Lee Benning. After Benning's death, her task was to keep Amber away from a gambler and ex-gangster. Wheeler manipulated the suspects into a crisis situation, saving Mavis just in time.

Mavis and Johnny Rios worked together in *The Bump and Grind Murders* (Signet, 1964). She went undercover (not much cover, however) to guard exotic dancer Irma der Bosen. Mavis' unintentionally funny strip act was a great success, leading to a job at $250 a week. Even though she was knocked unconscious twice, there was no discernable brain damage.

Mavis turned to international intrigue in *Seidlitz and the Super Spy* (Signet, 1967). Her trip to Rome and Capri had been planned as a vacation, until handsome Frank Jordan in the next hotel room was shot. Under pressure, Mavis agreed to become a guest of a Contessa, to spy on other guests, and to lure Prince "Harry" (Haroun el-Zamen) away from his bodyguard so he could be assassinated. Sadly, in his mad passionate moves on Mavis, Harry learned that she was wired for sound. Mavis aligned herself with the Contessa, even resorting to torture.

In *Murder Is So Nostalgic!* (Signet, 1972), Nina Farr, an ex-musical comedy star, sought protection for her daughter, Celestine Manning. The young woman had money and was prey to aging film stars who needed a bankroll. Mavis appeared as a prospective participant in the movie they hoped would restore their faded careers. A tinge of Satan worship led to the obligatory naked scene, in which Mavis found Celestine on an altar preparatory to death. Celestine was no innocent herself, as Mavis eventually learned. Fortunately Boy Scouts were available to bring help.

And the Undead Sing (Signet, 1974) gave Mavis another chance to "act out." She posed as a great blues singer known only through her records. Criminals who had counterfeited her records, threatened her (or Mavis, as it turned out). She was kidnapped, tattooed, and stored in a whorehouse, but survived. The series didn't.

Mavis was listed in Hubin as having made a number of other appearances (all by Horowitz or Horowitz-Transport): *Honey, Here's Your Hearse* (1955), *The Killer Is Kissable* (1955), and *Good Mourning, Mavis* (1957), none of which were available for review in 2005.

"The Sinister Widow"
Author: Raymond Armstrong, pseudonym for Norman Lee

See: Laura Scudamore, Section 4, page 199.

Maggie Slone
Author: Elizabet M. Stone

Maggie Slone was an early Southern sleuth, a redheaded, abrasive, New Orleans newspaper reporter, constantly feuding with her city editor—like Hildy Johnson in *His Girl Friday*, a popular movie of the period. More conventional in her personal life, Maggie lived with her widowed mother, her brother Brett, and here sisters, Vangie and Marian. Although the family was barely surviving financially, they employed servants.

In *Poison, Poker, and Pistols* (Sheridan, 1946), Maggie knew Dr. Ned McGowan too well to believe that he committed suicide. It was she who pinpointed curare as the cause of his death and posited that it had been administered to him on his toothbrush. Ned was a womanizer who had left a trail of broken hearts behind him. Realizing that her sister Vangie might be involved, she sabotaged the police investigation by stealing evidence, lying, encouraging Vangie to do the same, and using a stolen key to enter the apartment/laboratory where Ned carried out experiments. She was too smart to challenge the killer without backup.

In *Murder at the Mardi Gras* (Sheridan, 1947), while partying at a fashionable restaurant, Maggie noticed two argumentative couples who created a disturbance. Two of the foursome, small-time singer Don Barnett and seductive Nita Jeans, were later found dead. The police initially wrote them off as murder-suicide. She and Johnny Morrow, a rival reporter, had a bet as to her finding the real killer. The police arrived at the solution as quickly as did Maggie. She handled it, because losing to Johnny wasn't that bad. She was in love.

Daye Smith

Author: Frank Usher aka Charles Franklin

Daye Smith, a professional artist, had been raised by her father, Nevill, a hard-drinking author and news correspondent. Her mother deserted the family shortly after Daye's birth. This may explain why, in her mid-twenties, she still shared a home with her father. There was little description of Daye except that she had brown eyes and dark hair. Her other relationships were connected to her father. Her best friend and sometimes roommate, Stevie Phillips, was in love with Nevill. Samuel Kingsley Polecraft, a middle-aged magazine editor and television personality, who occasionally employed Nevill, wanted to marry Daye. She drove a white two-seater sports car named "Peewee."

Ghost of a Chance (Long, 1956) began with the death of Leslie Thornton, manager of a record company, who needed money and was willing to blackmail his married lover, Bea, to get it. Daye offered to paint the victim from photos and therefore needed to "know him"; thereby, she learned of several persons who wanted Leslie dead, but balked at a 150-year-old ghost. She had the clout to invite the suspects and Detective Inspector Michael Sefton to her home to view her completed painting of Leslie. A possible killer emerged, but there was a post-climactic revelation.

In *The Lonely Cage* (Long, 1956), when Daye agreed to paint a portrait of Leonard Charlesworth, a retired publisher, she did not expect his proposal. Laborers found an unidentified body in the Charlesworth well, later identified as John Hardy, Leonard's former partner, who disappeared two years before. When Leonard died of an overdose, the assumption was made that he had murdered Hardy and killed himself rather than be exposed. Daye had become fond of the old man and wouldn't accept that solution.

Daye's excursion into Central American politics in *Portrait of Fear* (Long, 1957) was ill advised. Lt. Raimundo Mariscol offered her an enticing fee to visit Estacoda and paint the reclusive dictator, Dr. Francisco Garcia. She soon realized that Garcia was fading and had become heavily influenced by El Commandante Filipe Marquand. When Garcia died, Marquand took over as president. Nevill and Stevie came to help because Daye had virtually become a prisoner. Only a rebellion made it possible for Daye and her friends to leave the country.

The Price of Death (Long, 1957) fell into the pattern of prior books, but there were some interesting touches as to the role of women in the East. Nevill, who was enjoying France, arranged for Daye to paint the portrait of

Rashid bin Said, heir to the throne of Qadim. Nevill came into possession of a map drawn in blood, which pinpointed the location of potential Qadim oilfields. Dagmar, the woman who had provided Nevill with the map, was murdered under conditions that made Nevill suspect. At that point Daye's top priority was to protect her father.

In *Death Is Waiting* (Long, 1958), Daye traveled to meet Stevie on the French Riviera. Stevie was not at the station to meet Daye. Stevie had gone off in a car that was later found burned out with a corpse inside, but not Stevie's. The remainder of the narrative covered Daye's search first for Stevie, then for underwater treasure.

In *First to Kill* (Long, 1959), Daye visited the mother of Alec Vesey, a freelance photographer and film producer who had been presumed drowned. She offered to paint his portrait from photographs. Part of her technique in portrait painting was to understand the character of the subject, so she investigated the young man, whose mother believed he was alive. When she found Alec, she still had a problem: how to get him out of the country safely.

Another trip to Paris in *Death in Error* (Hale, 1959) was designed to introduce Daye to the European art world through an exhibition underwritten by Samuel Kingsley Polecraft. The exhibition was successful; especially a nude painting of her friend, Stevie, but Daye was distracted by the murder of a reporter, ostensibly by mistake for an atomic scientist. Polecraft not only sponsored Daye, but also saved her life in this narrative.

In *Die, My Darling* (Hale, 1960), Daye was hired by businessman Richard Godfrey to paint a portrait of his estranged wife, Ursula. When Daye called on Ursula, she found her dead. Daye uncovered Ursula's relationships with a police official and the owner of an unsavory nightclub. Daye's attempt to learn who killed Ursula were thwarted by the police department, which was rife with corruption. Things changed when Scotland Yard entered the case.

Shot in the Dark (Hale, 1961) placed Daye at the Surrey home of the Falklands family, engaged in painting Anne Melville, the family's beautiful but cold daughter. There she met Mary Baker, a "poor relative" presented as mentally ill, but who told Daye that her unstable episodes were caused by medical treatments. Mary was arrested when her doctor, Guy Stevenson, was murdered. Daye was clever in her assessment but reckless in the way she handled the information.

Daye returned to international intrigue in *The Faceless Stranger* (Hale, 1961). At a party hosted by concert pianist Miranda King, Daye witnessed the abduction of refugee Vlado Zeman. Aware that he was removed from Britain by a Russian ship, Daye accompanied Miranda on an Eastern European concert tour. They did not realize that their plan to contact resistance hero Paul Fleckhart with a musical clue was designed to lure Fleckhart so he could be taken prisoner. Daye was shocked to learn who had betrayed her.

In *Who Killed Rosa Grey?* (Hale, 1962) Daye was hired by a couturier to paint several of her models, one of whom, Jackie Lewis, became a friend. When Jackie's wealthy aunt and the housekeeper were murdered, Jackie disappeared. Daye, who was caring for Jackie's young brother, Robin, had to decide whether or not Jackie was a murderer and learn who was Rosa Grey?

In *Fall into My Grave* (Hale, 1962), Daye made a strange bargain with art dealer Alberto Pavlo. She would paint the notorious Baroness Sezanne, a Fascist collaborator during World War II. In exchange Pavlo would give Daye a Renaissance painting she had admired. During the process the Baroness was found dead. Daye's association with questionable figures caused British Intelligence to take a hard look at her. It was not the painting of the Baroness that attracted danger, but the "Julia" painting, which she had received as a fee.

Businessman Gregory Dekker was so concerned that his daughter might be kidnapped in *Stairway to Murder* (Hale, 1964) that he isolated her from the world. Daye was allowed on the premises only to paint Adele's portrait. She learned that Adele did not cooperate with her father, but left the house surreptitiously to meet a lover, Emile. After Emile was murdered and Adele kidnapped, Daye worked with reporter Lambert Reid to uncover the truth.

The books were repetitious. The settings changed, but Daye never developed as a person. The mystery connection was through her painting, which required her to delve into the personality of the subject. Each book had a personable young man who fell desperately in love with Daye, but death, duty, or rejection prevented any lasting relationship.

Kate Starte

Author: Eric Williams

Kate Starte was described by her husband, Roger, as having golden brown hair and dark amber eyes. After Roger retired from the British Air Force, they traveled extensively. Although Kate had studied history at the University, she never mentioned employment. She had many of the characteristics of espionage heroines: a good shot, skilled driver of cars and boats, a risk taker, willing to kill in self-defense. Roger and Kate were committed anti-Communists, but they set out in a Land Rover to travel through Rumania, Hungary, and Bulgaria to the USSR.

In *Dragoman Pass* (Coward, 1959), they encountered hostile peasants, skeptical officials, and an English-speaking Rumanian who wanted them to meet a mysterious Englishman. Archaeologist Burt Carter was unwilling to seek help from the British legation in order to leave the country. His plan was to get Roger and Kate to smuggle him out.

In *The Borders of Barbarism* (Coward, 1962), the Startes visited Yugoslavia, hoping to locate gold, diamonds, and incriminating documents left behind in a Serbian cave by Major Edmund Hampton during World War II. British Intelligence would prefer that they destroy the documents, but wanted them to photograph rocket platforms on the Rumanian border. Roger, who was very interested in the gold and diamonds, consistently placed himself in danger, forcing Kate to kill to save his life.

Second rate.

Sally Strang

Author: Henry Brinton

John Strang, a Socialist Member of Parliament, included his tiny brunette daughter in his investigations, whether he wanted to or not. He had a high tolerance for her precocious behavior, and she just happened to be with him when murders occurred. Sally's mother had died, and Sally had once been referred to as Strang's elder daughter.

Sally made only a token appearance in *Death to Windward* (Hutchinson, 1954), when at age ten she was awakened by a trespasser and, after being locked in, thumped until she roused the household. Her mother was still alive at that time.

By *One Down, Two to Slay* (Hutchinson, 1954), time had elapsed. Her mother and a younger sister, Ann, had disappeared from the narratives. John thereafter included Sally in many of his adventures. Sally was about 12 when, while sailing, the Strangs rescued an unhappy couple. After visiting the Farrens at their home, Strang took an interest when the wife was murdered and the husband arrested. Sally stayed in the background until an effort was made to kidnap her.

While her father was busy during *Coppers and Gold* (Macmillan, 1958), Sally, then 14, set out to prove the innocence of her refugee governess, Gretel, who, along with her unfaithful lover, was suspected in a bullion robbery. On Strang's return, he and Sally worked together, but it was Sally, armed with a catapult, who disarmed the culprit, saving her father's life.

Sally's friend, Jessica Grant, had not been welcomed in her grandfather's home during *Ill Wind* (Hutchinson, 1957). She thought her grandfather, uncle, aunt by marriage, and cousin lived in the past. After her grandfather's death, Jessica was ridiculed when she insisted that he had been murdered, and the police did not take her seriously. Sally believed Jessica and visited to help. The murder was connected to the rights of various individuals to inherit from the estate. Sally's well-meant assistance was targeted against the wrong person.

John Strang had become a television personality by *Apprentice to Fear* (Macmillan, 1961) aka *An Ordinary Day*, a narrative presented from the viewpoint of George Cole, an unhappily married banker who faced a terrible choice when his only daughter, Tipsy, disappeared. He was ordered to help rob the bank in exchange for the girl's return. When everything bad happened that could happen to poor George, the Strangs took a hand. They provided a resource when he too was abducted, overcame his captors, and rescued him from the guilt and depression that had overwhelmed him.

John Strang appeared without Sally in other books by Brinton. After all, a man had to have some time to himself. Even he admitted that Sally could be a bit too much.

Sumuru

Author: Sax Rohmer, pseudonym for Arthur Henry Sarsfield Ward

Sumuru was ageless and indescribable, an Eastern superwoman. Her physical characteristics, except for references to her great beauty, were never made clear, except that she had no earlobes and wore a tattoo on her ankle. Over the years, she had married at least five times: a Japanese Marquis, a Swedish Baron, an English Lord, a French Duke, and a South American millionaire.

Nude in Mink (Fawcett, 1950) began when Dr. Steel Maitland and his newspaper friend, Mark Donavan, noticed that prominent young women were disappearing. The women became prisoners of Sumuru, who won them over to her theory that women, not warmongering men, should rule the world. Sumuru used the beautiful women in her organization, called OOL (Order of Our Lady), to enslave powerful men.

Mark Donavan married Claudette, a dropout from OOL. in *Sumuru* (Fawcett, 1951), but Sumuru tried to kidnap their child, also named Claudette. Sumuru used her charms and drugs on Drake Roscoe, a former U.S. intelligence officer, to enlist him in her plans. An associate, Sister Viola, was assigned to apply the same techniques on Tony McVeigh, a

British intelligence officer. but Viola fell in love with him. All this was to further Sumuru's plan to extend her empire to the United States.

In *The Fire Goddess* (Fawcett, 1952), Drake Roscoe still had a love-hate relationship with Sumuru, then working out of Jamaican headquarters, but her evil empire was endangered by a voodoo priestess, Momma Melisande. When Chief Inspector Gilligan of Scotland Yard developed a case against Sumuru, Drake warned her and she escaped again.

During *Sand and Satin* aka *The Return of Sumuru* (Jenkins, 1955), Drake Roscoe joined in the efforts to save a young woman who had defected from OOL. Sumuru was currently located in Egypt and facing competition from white slavers. When Dolores d'Este, whom Roscoe loved, and Carol, the other young woman, were on the slave block, Rick Carteret and Roscoe rescued them. Rick and Carol escaped, but Dolores remained faithful to Sumuru, and Roscoe to Dolores.

Drake, no longer a slave of Sumuru, but still in love with Dolores d'Este, secretary to Sumuru, surfaced in an English hospital in *Sinister Madonna* (Fawcett, 1956). Sumuru was seeking a jeweled dagger with Solomon's Seal. Dr. "Curly" Bowden had possession of the weapon and had discovered the secret compartment which held the Seal. Inspector Gilligan, who had thwarted Sumuru before arrived to checkmate her again. Sumuru not only failed to get the Seal, but her plans for a perfect child to be raised as her successor failed.

These were melodramatic stories more likely to appeal to male readers than to women. The women were either villains or victims, but not heroines.

Martha "Ma" Tellford

Author: Douglas Fisher

About the only one who ever called Mrs. Tellford "Martha" was Miss Blanche, the restored mistress of Pyford Hall, whom she had served as an "unofficial nanny."

After her husband died, Jeff, their son, was hired to work at Middleways Farm, then owned by wealthy brewer Robert "Baldy" Baldwin, and located adjacent to the Pyford Estate. A comfortable home on the farm property was part of Jeff's employment. It was his mother, as housekeeper, who made it comfortable. The rapport between Jeff and his mother, with Miss Blanche currently living in the dower house at Pyford Hall, was unusual.

A series of nasty incidents (the destruction of machinery, murder of a prize bull, and a fire) seemed to be aimed at Baldy, whose innovations did not set well with all of the locals, including Miss Blanche. In *What's Wrong at Pyford* (Hodder & Stoughton, 1950), Baldy assigned Jeff to investigate. He was a common laborer with limited education, whose primary interests were beer, women, and machinery (not necessarily in that order). Jeff asked questions but relied heavily on his mother's advice as to what to ask and where to look. Two disappearances added to the confusion. Although Jeff solved the barn fire, it took Ma's wisdom to assign the responsibilities for the other problems. Four romances blossomed as a result, not the least of which was between Miss Blanche and Baldy, who decided to purchase Pyford Hall.

Again, no police were involved in the investigation during *Poison-Pen at Pyford* (Hodder & Stoughton, London, 1951). Baldy and Blanche, who had received a total of six taunting letters, turned instead to the Tellfords. The Baldwins were not the only victims, and the mounting total included Jeff and Ma. Even more seriously, later missives were threatening, and the threats were fulfilled. Still, no official intervention occurred. Although Jeff did much of the questioning, particularly where females were involved or with local residents who spent time in the inn, Ma sought the patterns in the letters. Did they match the envelopes? Where were they mailed? What time of day? Hand delivered or through the mail? There were too many clues, and too many suspects, not one of whom could have sent all of the letters. Was there one poison-pen writer, or two, or were there more?

Jeff and Ma occupied Pyford Hall as caretakers when *Death at Pyford Hall* (Hodder, 1952) began. Then the Baldwins, off on an extended trip, rented it out to Julian Comstock; his psychiatrist, Edgar Radley; and Belle, Radley's daughter. Ostensibly, Comstock and Radley were researching the concept of racial memory. They wanted isolation, but Jeff and Ma (now providing for the guests) noted that they attracted attention like a magnet. Photographer Lena Peck was determined to take pictures of the Hall and its gardens. Local reporter Tim Tustain sought an interview. Ronnie Frensham, who had met the Radleys and Comstock on the Queen Elizabeth voyage to Britain, stopped by for a visit. A mysterious intruder was killed on site. Colonel North encouraged the local Inspector to use Jeff and Ma as resources.

Unlike most cozies, these featured basically lower class working people as the sleuths. Ma was an enthusiastic student of history, however, often finding parallels to current situations. Neither of the first two books had murder as the focus—even the bull was killed in self-defense.

Terry Terence

Author: Gordon Brandon

Theresa "Terry" Terence was a slender platinum blonde with gray-green eyes and "an erect carriage." The daughter of a steel industrialist, she worked as a reporter under an assumed name, so her husband, Mike, never realized she was an heiress when they married. The knowledge that she had deceived him contributed to their divorce. So did the accusation that he had fathered an illegitimate child before he met her. Unlike his socialite wife, Mike had risen from poverty to become a private investigator, then a crime novelist. When they met again in London, both were dating but unattached.

In *A Swell Night for Murder!* (Wright, 1947), the murder of Andre Durand, a French couturier, who was a friend of Terry's, brought them together. Durand had been poisoned by nicotine while enjoying the evening with a group of mutual friends. The possibility that Durand was involved in blackmail was strengthened when attempts were made to search his apartment. Mike went underground as an American criminal but had to be rescued by the police and his wife. After the reconciliation, Mike accepted that whatever he earned, his wife would be even wealthier. They lived well in England, had an expensive apartment and cars, partied with upper class Englishmen, and seemed to have no professional responsibilities. They developed connections with Scotland Yard Inspector Daniel "Sunny" Johnston and several young men, seemingly left over from a P. G. Wodehouse book (Lawrence Benson, the Honorable Bill Beverly, and Lord Anthony Dilworth).

When Beverly and Dilworth found themselves with the dead body of recently married Kitty Manton, in *Here Comes the Corpse* (Wright, 1949), they contacted Mike. Someone else had contacted Scotland Yard. It became more serious when someone returned to cut off Kitty's hand. After Mike and Terry came to the rescue, there was some confusion as to whether or not this was Kitty's corpse. Beverly, Benson, and Dilworth assisted in the investigation, but it was Mike who was kidnapped. Terry, in the presence of the police, shot a prisoner in the kneecap to learn where Mike had been hidden. Reunited, they exposed a plot to capture an inheritance.

Terry was abroad when Mike, Beverly, and Dilworth went "on the town" in *Murder in Maytime* (Wright, 1950). Mike was so intoxicated that he ignored the plight of young heiress Celia Rosen, who was killed later that evening. On Terry's return, the Terences were caught up in a gang war, and she was taken hostage. On her release, she threatened a man with a blowtorch in order to get information.

A Mild Case of Murder (Wright, 1951) blended Wodehousian humor with arrogant violence. Beverly and Benson helped a young woman who had a corpse in her car to escape from pursuing gangsters. The Terences found this interesting because they were searching for missing "crooner" Tony Hind, who could be the unidentified corpse. Hind would be ruined if he did not return in time to fulfill his contractual obligations. His corpse was found in his apartment. At least it seemed to be Hill. The face was so damaged as to make recognition difficult. Mike insisted on sharing what they had learned with friendly Scotland Yard detective Sunny Johnston, but Bill Beverly proceeded on his own, convinced that drugs were behind the killing. He feared that his friends might be involved.

Mike was recovering from injuries from the prior case when the Terences visited a rundown resort area in *Homicidal Holiday* (Wright, 1954). While at an amusement park, they observed events leading to the murder of American con man Perry Transey. The ensemble was called in to help protect young Hilary Clive, who had been with Transey earlier. Terry carried a major role in the investigation, setting up a séance to trap the murderer.

The books used pseudo-American slang, as so often happened when Americans were depicted by English authors. The unpleasant references to Jews and Italians, plus the callous attitudes displayed by Terry, flawed mildly entertaining stories.

Ginger Tintagel

Author: Julia Davis, writing as F. Draco

Redheaded Ginger (Virginia) Tintagel from Dubois, Wyoming, had married Robert, Ninth Baron Tintagel, during her service as an American WAC stationed in London during World War II.

In *The Devil's Church* (Rinehart, 1951), she needed all her American brashness to determine who was murdering their houseguests and to overcome an ancient curse on the Tintagel family, which would affect Robert and their unborn child. The tradition had been that no Tintagel man would survive to see his heir. There was some history in the family also of trafficking with the devil. Major (ret.) Mark Buxton was attacked and his wife, Natasha, killed after an uncomfortable dinner with assorted guests. The knife used to attack Mark belonged to Robert. Valuable family goblets had been stolen. Ginger might not believe in devil worship, but she had to deal with others who did. When their son, Bobs, was born, Robert was alive, ending the curse.

In *Cruise with Death* (Rinehart, 1952), Darius Opdyke, the Tintagels' host on a yacht trip, encouraged ill feeling among his guests. When he disappeared, there were bloodstains on the deck and instructions that the yacht was to remain at sea until his killer was identified. The crew was composed of criminals on the verge of mutiny. Robert took charge after two more deaths, solving the mystery so the ship could end its voyage.

These were barely average for mystery/horror crossovers.

Doris "Dodo" Trent

Author: Anne Nash

Dodo Trent, who narrated, and Nell Witter (see Section 4, page 227) were middle-aged women who shared a home and co-owned a flower shop in a small California town, Pinecrest. They were intelligent women who frequently displayed their education by quoting from the classics, including the Bible. Dodo was more interested in gardening as a hobby; Nell, in sketching. Both spent long hours in the shop, particularly during holiday seasons.

They were in the midst of a Christmas rush as *Said with Flowers* (Doubleday, 1943) began, coping with an injury to their handyman. Replacement young Barney Miller seemed too good to be true. He was experienced with flowers, energetic, and copcetic with the customers. Skeptical Dodo wondered if he might be Karp, a serial murderer who attacked young women, leaving behind a fish sketch. Even worse, could it have been Barney, who killed their friend Rosalind while secretly romancing her younger sister, Sheila? The women were naïve as to the source of Sheila's fear.

Over a period of several days in *Death by Design* (Doubleday, 1944), Dodo and Nell made the acquaintance of members of the prestigious Trask family. When artist Stephen Trask, who lived in Pinecrest, was charged with the murder of a lascivious broker, his sister Mary asked Nell and Dodo to involve private investigator Mark Tudor. Tudor, his dog Sven, and the two women solved the crime, but the dog deserved top billing.

After a busy and prosperous Easter season, Nell and Dodo needed a vacation. En route to Death Valley, they stopped to visit Dodo's cousin, Andy, in *Cabbages and Crime* (Doubleday, 1945). Andy's wife was about to deliver their first child, so the women offered to stay overnight and supervise Andy's kennel and dog training business. The overnight stay became a two-week nightmare when the corpse of a local family despot was deposited on the property. Although Dodo and Nell involved themselves as witnesses and friends to the bereaved, the local sheriff deserved credit for solving the murder. However, he credited Dodo with having "planted the first seeds of suspicion in his mind."

Very ordinary.

Marla Trent

Author: Henry Kane

Marla possessed bountiful dimensions, blonde hair and blue eyes, inherited wealth, a Phi Beta Kappa key from Vassar, a Ph.D. from Columbia, and a divorce. She was a private investigator who worked out of her own Madison Avenue agency in New York City. Her former husband, Inspector Andrew King, did not make any meaningful appearances in the cases. Her primary assistant was William Winkle, known as Wee Willie, an ex-jock with a Ph.D. who was raising two children since his wife's death.

In *Private Eyeful* (Pyramid, 1959), Marla's agency was hired to obtain the release of Tony Jurillo, imprisoned in the murder of Mary Salvatore. When his sister Katrina Jurillo came to Marla for help, another prisoner, Tom Randall, had not only confessed to the killing but denied that Tony had been involved on any level. However, at a hearing on the Salvatore murder, Randall pulled a gun and killed prosecuting attorney David Harrison. Tony's defense attorney, Simon Duncan, was accused of providing the weapon. Marla's method of investigation was to seek dates with two attorneys, both possible suspects; fortunately, she had a legitimate romance lined up with plastic surgeon Harvey Britt. Wee Willie was more conventional in his efforts.

Kisses of Death (Belmont, 1962) was just that for Marla. Although private investigator Peter Chambers respected her professionally and lusted after her personally, he handled the blackmail/murder/bank robbery alone. (Chambers had his own series written by Kane.)

Marla's report that she enjoyed the experience of being raped by her former husband in his police department office will not be viewed favorably by most women.

Hilda Trenton

Author: Dana Lyon

Hilda loved Roger, and after a short courtship and elopement went with him to visit his parents in California.

She had no idea that he was the child of a domineering mother and a manipulative father, but learned it quickly in *The Tentacles* (Ace, 1950), which ended after her mother-in-law's death and an attempt to murder Hilda. Here the male was more deadly than the female.

The succeeding narrative, *Spin the Web Tight* (Ace, 1963), picked up on the relationships. Roger had aligned himself with his father, treating Hilda as though she were a replacement for his cold, tyrannical mother. Even the birth of their child, Gerry, did not heal their marriage; only death ended Roger's plan to take their son away from his mother.

Dismal.

Haila Rogers Troy
Author: Kelley Roos, pseudonym for William and Audrey Kelley Roos

Brunette beauty Haila Rogers had been a model and a Broadway actress before her marriage. There was almost no description of her. Jeff carried the action, but Haila earned a lot of bruises along the way. She also narrated.

When *Made Up to Kill* (Dodd, 1940; Rue Morgue Press, 2005) began, Haila was sharing a New York City apartment with actress Carol Blanton. Carol was on stage opening night when an attempt was made to poison her. Jeff, an advertising executive on vacation, and the police were present the second night to keep an eye on Carol. Eve North, an aging actress who was having difficulty with her role, was murdered while wearing Carol's cape. Jeff learned more about Carol when he researched her stage history. The clue that closed the case was in Eve's history.

Jeff and Haila were married by *If the Shroud Fits* (Dodd, 1941), when Julie Taylor of Photo Arts Studio sought Jeff's help because she expected a murder. She had been attacked, but no harm came to her. Her conclusion was that she was not the intended victim. So who was? In Jeff's absence, Haila responded, substituting for missing model Madge Laurence. She was on site when socialite Isabelle Fleming was murdered. Photographer Mac MacCormick's fingerprints were on the weapon; his former wife, Erika, was Fleming's heir. At this point, Jeff, who was currently unemployed, took over as detective.

In *The Frightened Stiff* (Dodd, 1942; Rue Morgue Press, 2005), the Troys moved to a decrepit Greenwich Village basement apartment, not realizing that their bathtub would be used to drown Mike Kaufman. Except for the fact that she felt someone was watching them, Haila seemed content in the small apartment. She had abandoned her career, even though Jeff's employment in a photographic studio was not very productive. His investigation was. He learned that Kaufman was a blackmailer, that the tenants whom he blackmailed had banded together, but that the killer was now using Kaufman's material to blackmail them again.

They had no children, but in *Sailor, Take Warning!* (Dodd, 1944) took an interest in Chuckie, the son of their cleaning woman. While the Troys were in Central Park with Chuckie, Austin Marshall, who sailed model ships in the pond, was found dead on a park bench. Jeff took an interest when someone left a $1,000 fee, which was stolen when an intruder entered while they were sleeping. Jeff developed information that changed the time of Marshall's death and therefore the validity of alibis. Haila rescued Jeff from a murderous attack by the killer. In order to make the narrative timely, an elaborate scheme of passing military information to the Nazis was inserted.

Although Jeff did not serve in the military during World War II, in *There Was a Crooked Man* (Dodd, 1945) he had war related assignments that kept him out of town. Shortly after Haila moved into a boarding house, the landlady's husband, Fred Girard, returned after a seven-year absence. He was a disturbing presence among his wife, Lucille's, tenants. Otis Block, the 300-pound handicapped man who occupied the penthouse, was found dead in his room. When Jeff returned, they investigated together, but it was Haila who identified the killer.

Roos' light touch was well displayed in *Ghost of a Chance* (Wyn, 1947), when Haila's Aunt Ellie visited. Frank Lorimer, an elderly hansom cab driver, who suspected that a woman would be murdered, sent a note to that effect to Jeff. Before Haila and Jeff could get any more information Lorimer had been murdered. After extensive activity in which they were captured and escaped, Haila saved Jeff's life (again?) and Aunt Ellie helped solve the case. Ladies' Day.

During *Murder in Any Language* (Wyn, 1948), Haila resumed her education, taking Spanish at the Randall School of Languages. When Gerald Stewart, her Spanish teacher, was murdered, the school proprietor hired Jeff to investigate, and the police obliged by allowing him to be present during the search of Stewart's rooms. A mysterious Mary Collins made phone calls and rented a room, but disappeared. Haila was knocked unconscious while detecting on her own. There were an alarming number of incidents in which Haila was knocked unconscious during the series.

Triple Threat (Wyn, 1949) was a combination of two novelettes (and a short story)—*She'd Make a Lovely Corpse*, during which the Troys solved a murder tied to the destruction of a portrait, and *Beauty Marks the Spot*, wherein Haila enrolled as a student in a beauty school to investigate the death of a co-owner.

As *One False Move* (Dodd, 1966) opened, Haila and Jeff were divorcing. While visiting Aunt Ellie in Texas, Haila attended a centennial pageant, which, among other events, recreated a 50-year-old murder. Shortly before he was murdered, Haila had heard historical researcher Ross Anders blackmailing someone. Retired Admiral Dan McKevin was the next victim. He had left the area 50 years before. When Jeff came to town, they both worked on the subsequent murder and their marriage. Haila acknowledged that her need for excitement had contributed to their rift.

The series followed a common pattern: Haila narrating, using her intuition, unearthing clues, and showing a deeper understanding of relationships; Jeff operating more cautiously, placing a higher value on physical evidence, and often saving his wife from her indiscretions.

Julia Tyler

Author: Louisa Revell, pseudonym for Ellen Hart Smith

Miss Tyler was the daughter of an Episcopalian priest and an intellectual mother. A slim, gray-haired woman of average height, she taught Latin for 40 years in an upper class community, while raising her orphaned grandniece, Anne. Julia maintained a lovely home in Rossville, Virginia, but did most of her detecting elsewhere. Anne and her husband, Dick, provided Julia with access to several murder settings. Although she was a conservative Southerner in many aspects, Julia enjoyed unconventional people. Her approach to crime detection blended understanding of the suspects and the "psychology of the crime."

In *The Bus Station Murders* (Macmillan, 1947), Julia was riding a bus to visit Anne and Dick in Annapolis, when she noticed passenger Eleanor Barnes was dead. Julia's connection with the case was facilitated by the personal information provided by Anne and Dick about some of the suspects and her friendship with police investigator Ben Kramer, a former pupil. The killer was a person with a long memory and a taste for vengeance.

In *No Pockets in Shrouds* (Macmillan, 1948), Julia went to visit her old friend Charlotte Buckner in Louisville. Charlotte's home was currently untenable, so they moved in next door at the Helm house. Elderly patriarch Breckenridge Helm was poisoned before he could sign his new will. Emily Craig, a beneficiary, had been a suspect in the death of Gus, the Helms family butler, and was secretly married. Julia worried about her on all three counts.

At 68, Julia was still an active teacher. When she agreed to tutor Latin at a Maine summer camp in *A Silver Spade* (Macmillan, 1950), she did not realize that there would be more problems with fellow staff members than with her pupils. Anonymous letters had caused the previous Latin teacher to resign. Then there were stray bullets of which only Julia and young Sally Tilden were aware, but they felt Mrs. Turner, camp director, should be told. Finally, at an evening ceremony, a shot rang out. Captain Willi Benesch, the riding instructor, was killed. Julia was assigned to take notes by the deputy in charge. Mrs. Turner was the next to die. They were running out of suspects, so someone had to confess.

In *The Kindest Use a Knife* (Macmillan, 1952), Emily Morris, abandoned 20 years before by her husband, lived in the Episcopalian parish house with her multiply handicapped son, Jack, and her caretaker daughter, Cary. Julia was back home now in Rossville, Virginia. Given the state of Jack's health, the last thing anyone expected was that Emily would die, and that she had been murdered. Julia's discovery of the body inadvertently cast suspicion on her best friend, Adelaide Bliss. Commonwealth Attorney Lewis Wyeth worked with Julia and was primarily responsible for solving the case.

During *The Men with Three Eyes* (Macmillan, 1955), Julia traveled to Washington, D.C., to visit Ruth Gibbons, a settlement house worker. While most neighbors attended a party, Vic Caprio, a notorious drug dealer, was shot in the forehead (third eye) sitting in his parked car. Vic had a terrible reputation and his engagement to sweet Eileen Byrne was frowned upon. Julia, who was suspected of drug dealing, used a room wired for social work observation to overhear police interviews. One murder was not enough, so there were two more before the killer was identified.

As a Latin teacher, Miss Julia had always wanted to visit Rome. In *See Rome and Die* (Macmillan, 1957), her contacts in Virginia society provided her with introductions to Italians, expatriates, and government officials. Several of the Italian nobility were married to wealthy American women. Harvey Meecham, an American businessman, was in the process of adopting a 10-year-old boy, Eduardo. Meecham, who was a clothing manufacturer, had pirated designs, which may explain the threatening letters he received before he was stabbed to death. Later, a bishop was murdered. Julia gathered information about different members of the social group and learned how they were viewed by the average citizens of the area, but she was not responsible for the outcome.

When Julia and Anne went to England in *A Party for the Shooting* (Macmillan, 1960), their connections in Virginia "hunt country" earned an invitation to the Colburn-Fane family estate. Their hosts were Sir Robert and his daughter, Diana. After Turnour, the family butler, was found dead in the burial crypt, Julia and Anne were less welcome but remained in the area, housed at Colburn Hall, and continued to sift through local gossip for a killer. Inheritance, as usual, was a factor. A tourist, Mr. Cooper, was shot. There seemed to be no connection to the family, but he may have shared the pro-Fascist leanings of Sir Robert. Next, Mark Colburn, the heir apparent, was shot at but emerged unharmed, and a visiting professor of English literature was killed. It seemed to be open season. Given all of the possible motives, the actual one seemed trivial.

Julia served as narrator, provided background, and identified relationships, but it was the commonwealth attorney, the camp cook, or the police sergeant who unraveled the mysteries.

Sister Ursula

Author: H. H. Holmes, pseudonym for
William Anthony Parker White aka Anthony Boucher

The convent was a second choice for Ursula, who had planned to follow in her father's footsteps and become a police officer, but poor health made that impossible. Nevertheless, Sister Ursula, as a member of the Order of Martha of Bethany, kept her interest in crime and mystery.

In *Nine Times Nine* (Duell, 1940), intellectual curiosity about a locked-room murder was the focus rather than emotional involvement. A cult debunker, Wolfe Harrigan, who had been formally cursed, was found dead. Sister Ursula and Police Inspector Terence Marshall used John Dickson Carr's "locked room" theories to solve the case.

Ursula's religious knowledge explained a seven-decade-old rosary found in the possession of a murdered vagrant in *Rocket to the Morgue* (Duell, 1942) and helped to identify the victim. Holmes parlayed the rosary, a convention of science fiction writers, and another locked room into a narrative that puzzlers may enjoy. There was none of the character development to be found in later nun sleuths, such as Sir Mary Helen O'Connor or Sister M. T. Dempsey, who appeared in the 1980's.

Sister Ursula failed to develop beyond the gimmick level.

Hannah Van Doren

Author: Dwight Babcock

Hannah Van Doren was a freelance true crime writer, who used a camera to illustrate her magazine articles. She had little or no sympathy for victims or suspects. Her interest was in getting the inside story and selling it. Hannah's father had been killed while a captain in the Los Angeles Police Department. Although Hannah was tiny and slim with blue eyes and long gold hair, appealing to the "protective instinct in man," she was a barracuda. The man in Hannah's life was Joe Kirby, a rude, crude, heavy-drinking car salesman and detective.

During *A Homicide for Hannah* (Knopf, 1941), Joe, currently unemployed, befriended an injured naked woman. He brought her into his apartment, then went out looking for Steve Wurtzel, who owed him money. When he returned, the young woman was gone. Wurtzel was lying there dead. Later elements in the crime included an American fascist group, a secret formula for anti-chlorine gas, and a murder in Wurtzel's past. Hannah, although she did not hesitate to knee Joe in the groin when he became passionate, proved his innocence and saved his life.

In *The Gorgeous Ghoul* (Knopf, 1941), "Homicide" Hannah and Joe coveted a $10,000 reward offered by powerful Sybil Peabody for the return of her missing nephew, Ted Logan. Their success was short-lived. While Hannah went to collect, Joe was enticed away, and Logan was gone again. They traced the enticing young woman, Delphine Moore, only to discover her dead. Hannah's first reaction was to get pictures of the nude body to sell her article; fortunately, she made better use of her camera later in the narrative.

During *Hannah Says Foul Play* (Avon, 1946), Hannah was investigating the death of detested Hollywood columnist Floyd Spicer. Russ Henderson, a buddy of Joe's, asked him to get her off the case. Fat chance! Hannah probed relationships, with a surprising conclusion. The best of the three books.

She was tough, quick witted, good humored, and able to take care of herself.

Sarah Vanessa

Author: Joan Storm

Actress Sarah Vanessa was slender, with red-gold hair and slanting green eyed. Her widowed mother, a poetess, had married a distinguished research scientist. Sarah's closest family relationship was with her brother Rupert, a war correspondent. Her first love, Jonathan, had died in a German prison camp. Charles Meredith, whom she married on the rebound, was a difficult man.

As *Dark Emerald* (Hammond, 1951) opened, Sarah had put her career on hold to salvage her marriage to Charles, who was then serving as a civilian with the Military Occupation Forces in Germany. Because Sarah, who did not speak German and remembered Jonathan's death too well, was hesitant about making friends with Germans, her social life was restricted to residents of the British government enclave. The Meredith home served both as a hostel for important guests from England and a gathering place for staff and families. To Sarah's dismay, Meredith had close ties with German officials of whom she did not approve. After she discovered the corpse of Charles' secretary during a late evening walk, Sarah felt obligated to remain with her husband, even though she was attracted to Nick Cavan, the investigating officer.

While her divorce was pending in *Bitter Rubies* (Hammond, 1952) Sarah worked as an actress and manager of a British theatre group entertaining troops in Austria. Sarah anticipated that she might not be accepted by the existing performers. She did not realize that Captain Gerald Morne, the arrogant British officer in charge of the theatrical unit, had earned the hatred of many members of the group. As they traveled to Vienna for their next performance, Sarah found his dead body, but told no one. Even when it was revealed, she kept back information from Nick. Several cast members confessed, but they couldn't all be guilty. By the last night in town, Sarah had identified the killer, but hesitated too long. Her divorce from Charles was finalized, opening the way for Nick and Sarah to marry.

During their Swiss honeymoon in *Deadly Diamond* (Hammond, 1953), the Cavans joined friends of Sarah on a bus journey to Milan. Their movement across the Italian border was complicated when Sarah found the body of Xanthia, a beautiful and mysterious fellow passenger. They returned to the villa where Xanthia; her husband, painter Kit Mason; and other members of the group had been living. Nicky coordinated with the Swiss police. They discovered that the roots of the problem lay not only in the political backgrounds of the suspects but also in the tangled personal relationships.

The stories were well organized and had adequate plotting and some interesting characters.

Tessie Venable

Author: Helen Holley

Tessie was more interested in reuniting lovers than in solving mysteries, but, when detection was necessary, she could do that, too. Her granddaughter Joy loved Nicky Hammond, the "spitting image" of his great uncle Nick, the man whom Tessie had never forgotten.

When Ida Lou Brown, the woman who had enticed Nicky away from Joy, was murdered, Tessie found her body in *Blood on the Beach* (Mystery House, 1946). At a party that evening, things had seemed to be going better. Nicky had ended his relationship with Ida Lou under considerable family pressure. Tessie had mixed feelings about the investigation by detective Tim Maloney because of her close feelings for members of the Hammond family. A second murder made it impossible for her to hold back.

In *Dead Run* (Mystery House, 1947), Tessie's old friend Matilda served as housekeeper for Emmy Colfax, her wealthy niece. The family lived on a plantation where Uncle Marcus Redding ran a stable and horse farm. Matilda contacted Tessie, concerned about voodoo being practiced by staff. Tessie knew enough about horses to prove that greed, not voodoo, was behind the accident in which Emmy was injured.

Although minor mysteries, the books read easily and Tessie was an agreeable heroine.

Katherine Forrester Vigneras

Author: Madeleine L'Engle

Readers of *A Severed Wasp* (Farrar, 1982), featuring Katherine Forrester, may be surprised to learn that the elderly concert pianist appeared in an earlier non-mystery novel, *The Small Rain* (Vanguard, 1945). Ten-year-old Katherine, already a skilled pianist, lived with her musician mother, who had been seriously injured in an accident. After her mother's death, Katherine's Aunt Manya married her father and put Katherine in a Swiss boarding school. Her stay was made endurable by her affection for music teacher Justin Vigneras. After graduation Katherine moved to Paris to study privately with Justin, who loved her but was cautious because of the difference in their ages and his professional role.

Author L'Engle brought Katherine back in *A Severed Wasp*, set in the Cathedral Close of St. John the Divine, Morningside Heights, New York. Katherine, now Justin's widow, mother of his children, and a grandmother, had retired from a distinguished career as a concert pianist. Her friend Bishop Felix Bodway convinced her to give a concert for the Cathedral's building fund. Flashbacks depicted the cruel treatment Justin endured during Nazi occupancy of France, the birth and death of a son, the birth of a daughter, and Katherine's complex relationship with Cardinal von Stromberg.

Agatha Welch

Author: Veronica Johns

Agatha, a New England spinster in her fifties, had devoted much of her life to raising a much younger sister, Clotilda.

When *Hush, Gabriel!* (Duell, 1940) began, Clotilda, now married to Malcolm Allen and pregnant, invited Agatha to visit on Westover, an isolated Caribbean island. There were other guests present when Beatrice, a servant, announced at breakfast that Dr. Harry Estey was dead in his bed. Even more shocking was Clotilda's confession that she had killed him. Judge Jack Prentiss, a neighbor whose only claim to the title was judging a flower show, offered to help Agatha prove otherwise. Agatha proved that the victim was already dead when Clotilda fired her gun, but it was Prentiss who brought the case to an end in what many will consider an unacceptable manner.

After Jack Prentiss, who helped solve the case, proposed marriage, Agatha returned to Connecticut to sell her home in *Shady Doings* (Duell, 1941). A welcome-home party was disrupted when hostess May Ingoldsby's dog appeared with a human bone. It was thought to have been left behind by one of the nine young people who occupied May's boarding house the week before. In search of the former boarders, Jack and Agatha traveled to New York City, where Frank Langwell, one of the group, was murdered. The action centered on model Penelope Post, with whom Frank had been obsessed. There remained questions as to whom the bone belonged. Although Jack did the planning, Agatha was more adept at identifying the participants in murder.

Honey West

Authors: Forrest and Gloria Fickling, writing as G. G. Fickling

Honey West's mother died when she was born. Her father, Hank, a private investigator, was killed on the job. Honey, who earned a master's degree at USC, also studied judo and wore a .22 garter holster. She enjoyed rare steaks, martinis, and fast cars. Her ongoing beau was LAPD Lt. Mark Storm, who transferred over to the CIA when Honey switched from private investigator to espionage agent.

In *This Girl for Hire* (Pyramid, 1957), Honey was hired by aging movie hero Herb Nelson to discover who was trying to kill him. He wasn't far wrong: Mark and Honey stopped by to check on him and found him dead. Although the suspects were isolated on an island, the narrative was a variant on the *And Then There Were None* theme. Suspects died off one after another, saving Honey a lot of effort.

Margo Stevens, a college friend, called Honey from the maternity ward of a hospital in *Girl on the Loose* (Pyramid, 1958). Then it got weird. Honey was abducted and forced to wear a Marine Corps uniform. En route to the Marine Corps base at El Toro, the car was stopped and her abductor was murdered. Honey had identification as Sylvia Verse and was arrested for the murder. Margo had died in the hospital. Concurrently, the infant son of millionaire Phillip Sharkey was kidnapped by a woman resembling Honey. Honey set out to find the child, accompanied by Web Stevens, supposedly a bereaved husband. They were diverted to Las Vegas, where Honey encountered Sylvia Verse, who may have had a personal connection to Phillip Sharkey. Totally confusing.

It was easy for Honey again in *A Gun for Honey* (Pyramid, 1958), the case of the "kissing killer." Honey had been hired by movie director Rote Collier to protect his second wife, Helena, and Fawn, the adult daughter of his first marriage. Multiple motives based on blackmail, cross-dressing, and bi-sexual encounters dragged out the process. Suspects in the death of Rote and the purportedly pregnant Helena were gradually eliminated by murders. That's one way to solve a case.

In *Honey in the Flesh* (Pyramid, 1959), a scarred, drowned corpse found in the harbor was identified as Josephine Keller. Josephine Keller was also the winner of the Miss 20th Century Pageant produced by Mawson Lawrence. The pageant could be a front for Bodies Incorporated, which provided women for brothels. Honey became a murder suspect and was mugged and drugged in a convoluted plot. Poor Lt. Mark Storm wanted to marry Honey, but she kept poaching on his jurisdiction as a homicide detective.

Kirk Tempest, one of a pair of kinky twins who shared the same first name although they spelled it differently, was harpooned while manhandling Honey in his swimming pool as *Girl on the Prowl* (Pyramid, 1959) opened. His sister Jewel wore a mask as a result of serious burns years before and did very well as a strip-teaser. At one point Honey filled in for her on a television show. At least two other people may have filled in for her in the past. Plot was confusing.

Lest the reader not take Honey West seriously, *Kiss for a Killer* (Pyramid, 1960) began when she learned that her 6' 6" beau had been run over by a steamroller. By page 10, she had been attacked by tarantulas. By page 17, she had a naked ex-football player sharing the front seat of her car. Honey was so unconventional that she kept her clothes on when she entered a nudist health camp...at least until she was hypnotized.

In *Dig a Dead Doll* (Pyramid, 1960), Honey traveled to Mexico to see an American bullfighter, only to watch him die in the ring. As she methodically investigated his death, she was arrested for possession of narcotics, strafed by an airplane, and had to use judo to get out of a Mexican police station. As usual, the suspects remaining alive in the last chapter were all guilty of something.

Blood and Honey (Pyramid, 1961) took Honey to New York City, where old friend Vic Kendall was producing a musical about a female detective. Honey was obviously the model for the main character, but someone didn't want the show to go on. There were the usual ludicrous situations in which Honey was forced into the open while scantily clad. Vic's wife, Tina, was found dead in Honey's hotel bathtub. Honey was the obvious suspect, or was it look-alike Pepper Parker, who was playing the Honey West role in the play?

Obviously the Ficklings read the headlines and noted the popularity of James Bond. In *Bombshell* (Pyramid, 1964), Honey was lured to Florida by old family friend, Raven McCormick. Once there, she learned of a resurgent Nazi-Fascist group in Florida, eager to force the United States into a Cuban War. Getting no response from the locals when Raven disappeared, she contacted Mark Storm. Working meantime with bounty hunter Johnny "Boom Boom" Doom, she discovered an atomic submarine hidden under an oil rig. Between a hurricane and the U.S. Navy, things worked out.

In *Honey on Her Tail* (Pyramid, 1971), Honey had just returned from Europe, where she had been on unofficial assignment for both the CIA and FBI. An incident caused the CIA to wonder if Honey had changed sides. Her adventures took her back to Paris, where she had to be rescued from the top of the Eiffel Tower. Readers who want to learn more about secret formulas for invisibility and anti-invisibility, with undersea cities thrown in, should read this one.

It was hard to believe that the series could get any worse, but in *Stiff as a Broad* (Pyramid, 1972) it did. The routines were repetitious. How many times has Honey been abducted and stripped. (She rarely had much on in the first place.) She and several handsome men took on an aging Dragon lady, a Pulitzer Prize-winning traitor, and a self-proclaimed messiah to save the western United States from disaster.

The plotting in the series was gimmick ridden. Honey's technique was to press on until the culprit or conspirators revealed themselves, or were the only survivors. The titles of the books and the paperback covers were demeaning to women. A television series featuring Anne Francis as Honey ran for 30 episodes during the 1965-66 season.

Kitty McLeod Whitney

Author: David Dodge

Hard-drinking accountant hero James "Whit" Whitney met Kitty when she was suspected in the death of her husband. A tall, brunette ex-showgirl, she had a mind of her own.

In *Death and Taxes* (Macmillan, 1941), George McLeod, Whit's partner, uncovered a tax scam shortly before he was murdered. The police suspected Kitty, George's wife, and Whit, rather than focusing on the tax files. Whit reviewed the paperwork, focusing on the Woolf file. He had been a brewer who kept going during Prohibition, but was now dead. Wolff's daughter Marion may be entitled to a major refund on an IRS payment, a matter which George and Whit had been pursuing. Time was of the essence. The rebate had to be applied for by a certain date. Whit would get $50,000 if the rebate went through. After they solved the case, he celebrated by inviting Kitty on a Mexican vacation.

In *Shear the Black Sheep* (Macmillan, 1942), Whit used his skills as an accountant and a detective to help woolgrower John Clayton, who suspected his son Robert had embezzled money from the business. Robert had been writing large checks, which may have been going to finance redheaded Gwen Storey. Kitty was not supposed to be around, but arrived in time to save Whit from pursuing the wrong criminal.

Whit was about to be drafted as *Bullets for the Bridegroom* (Macmillan, 1944) opened. En route for a wedding and honeymoon, Whit and Kitty visited old family friend Pop Foster, who was murdered during their stay. Whit was suspicious of some of the individuals that Pop had been hanging around with. Another close friend, Casey Jones, turned up in town, claiming to be AWOL from army service and wanted for murder. Whit helped Casey expose a Nazi radio network that alerted Nazi ships to the location of U.S. shipping. A side-effect was the postponement of Whit's military service because both he and Kitty were injured in the outcome.

In *It Ain't Hay* (Simon & Schuster, 1946), Kitty left Whit when he refused to abandon his vendetta against shady businessman Barney Steele.

Barney had urged Whit to help him avoid paying taxes by means of an illegal scheme. However, she reserved the right to change her mind in spite of his infidelity. Whit solved the murder of Elmo Powell, a CPA who wouldn't hesitate to fudge his figures, and put drug dealers into police custody.

Dodge's taut, hard-nosed mysteries gave Kitty a chance to show her abilities.

Nell Witter

Author: Anne Nash

Nell Witter and Dodo Trent (see Section 4, page 213), who narrated, were middle-aged women who shared a home and co-owned a flower shop in Pinecrest, a small California town. They were intelligent women who frequently displayed their education by quoting from the classics, including the Bible. Dodo was more interested in gardening as a hobby; Nell, in sketching. Both spent long hours in the shop, particularly during holiday seasons.

Lily Wu

Author: Juanita Sheridan/Wolfe

Although she shared the detection with narrator Janice Cameron (see Section 4, page 146), Lily Wu was not the primary character in their Doubleday series. Lily, a college student, had the dark hair and eyes of her racial background.

Both Lily and Janice were physically active and reckless in their detection, swimming in underwater caves, searching without any warrant, but were chaste and innocent for young women in their mid-twenties. They had no ties to the authorities and did not share information with them until it was necessary.

Georgine Wyeth

Author: Lenore Glen Offord

See: Georgine Wyeth McKinnon, Section 4, page 178.

Section 5:
Out of Turbulence, Equality (Or at Least, a Start)— Women Sleuths of 1960-1979

The Forties had provided women with increased opportunities to seek paid employment. The end of World War II sent many of them to suburbs, big families, and volunteer work. Some went joyously; for others, the lost access to education and employment meant economic deprivation, frustration, and festering resentment. Evidence of this dissatisfaction was revealed by Kate Millett, Germaine Greer, and most notably by Betty Friedan.

The Sixties encompassed a triad of protests: (1) opposition to U.S. military intervention in Vietnam, (2) civil rights activity focused on racial minority groups, and (3) the beginnings of a women's movement, which adopted tactics used successfully by African-Americans. The Equal Employment Opportunity portion of the Civil Rights Act of 1964 and successive amendments enabled women to break down barriers that prevented them from working in higher-paid job categories.

An expansion in mystery fiction, embodying the concerns of women, was on the horizon. During most of the Sixties, bookstore shelves featured espionage and hard-boiled investigator novels in which females played subsidiary roles (Len Deighton, Ian Fleming, John D. MacDonald). The Cold War focused national concerns on internal subversion and foreign enemies. There were some female mystery series written by males in which women were demeaned or portrayed as superwomen (Modesty Blaise, Shauna Bishop, Anna Zordan, and Angela Harpe)

Mystery heroines were more likely to be single or divorced, to be employed outside the home, to have college educations, and to be neither youthful nor elderly, but mature. Because job opportunities had opened up for women, fiction portrayed realistic policewomen, female investigators, doctors, and attorneys. Women, particularly American women, were writing a higher percentage of mystery novels. Sexuality, including homosexuality, became more explicit in fiction generally and in mystery fiction. Series heroines appeared in novelizations of television programs, such as "The Girl from U.N.C.L.E.," "Policewoman," "Mod Squad," "The Avengers," and in inexpensive paperbacks targeted to young adults, such as the Zebra Puzzlers.

There were crossovers from the western (Charity Ross and Molly Owens), science fiction (Hildy Pace, Effie Schlupe, Sibyl Sue Blue, and Claudine St. Cyr), and the occult (Kitty Telefair and Molly Fountain).

Among the turgid and the trivial were two dozen or more exceptional series featuring:

- Professional policewomen like Charmian Daniels, Christie Opara, and Norah Mulcahaney;
- Private investigators who would rival their male counterparts such as Sharon McCone, Cody, and Anna Peters;
- The Victorian team of Charlotte and Thomas Pitt;
- Academic mysteries featuring Kate Fansler;
- Amazing and amusing heroines such as Amelia Peabody Emerson;
- Attorney-investigator Rosa Epton;
- Investigative reporter Jemima Shore;
- Endearing con-woman Lucilla Teatime;
- The best "significant other" since Patricia Holm in Leslie Charteris' Saint series, Susan Silverman; and
- Charming amateurs, including Julie Hayes, Melinda Pink, Maggie Rome, Emily Pollifax, Lucy Ramsdale, and Persis Willum.

Catherine Alexander

Author: Sidney Sheldon

See: Catherine Alexander Douglas, Section 5, page 293.

Telzey Amberdon

Author: James Schmitz

Telzey, the daughter of Giles and Jessamine Amberdon, a Federation councilwoman, was born in the future. She lived in Orado City in the Galactic Federation, studied law at Pehanron College, and was a "psi" (having the ability not just to read, but to invade another person's mind). On occasion Telzey used her talents for Kyth Instellar, a detective agency.

In *The Universe Against Her* (Ace, 1964), when Telzey visited her unpleasant Aunt Halet on the planet Jontarou, she realized that she could thought-communicate with other life forms. She used this power first to help an endangered creature and then to reprogram her aunt. When the Federation Security agency became aware that Telzey had psi to the third degree, she had to safeguard herself from absorption into the Agency.

During *The Lion Game* (DAW, 1973) Telzey pitted her psi against that of the Lion people. She had gone on vacation with college friends, when she encountered Robane, a pseudo psi. He made her aware of a malign influence, but later she realized that he was part of a plan to lure her into the hands of others who wanted to catch a psi. The dog Chomir, whom she was watching for a friend, rescued her. This book was close to unreadable.

The Telzey Toy and Other Stories (DAW, 1973) contained novelettes in which Telzey:

- Resisted a puppeteer who wanted to create a Telzey puppet,
- Drew information from another mind to save a man encased in an undersea bubble,
- Contacted the Sirens, another life form, and
- Investigated a cosmetology resort where the female relatives of prominent officials were subverted into enemy agents.

These narratives would have primary appeal to science fiction fans.

Marilyn Ambers

Author: Elizabeth St. Clair, pseudonym for Susan Cohen

Marilyn Ambers was an actress who lived in a small apartment on the Upper West Side of New York City but did summer theater in Pennsylvania. Between plays she worked at whatever she could find: waitress, receptionist, typist, or saleswoman.

In *Murder in the Act* (Zebra, 1978), she found herself part of a contentious cast in a play backed by Silas Bishop. Bishop was rude to cast and crew, and jealous of attention paid to his wife by a handsome actor. He displayed the same qualities to townspeople when he appeared at a tavern where the cast was relaxing. When Bishop was murdered, Sheriff Ed Simpson convinced Marilyn to provide information on fellow performers. However, her real contribution was the discovery of a photograph, that pinpointed the killer.

Marilyn and her friend Serena Austin vacationed on Nantucket Island during *The Sandcastle Murders* (Zebra, 1979). There was early evidence of tension between jet-setter Peggy de Beers and her husband, Jack, fellow guests at the hotel. Marilyn noticed a strong reaction when Peggy encountered Dr. Wayne Matthews. When Peggy was found drowned along the beach, Marilyn assumed that Jack was responsible. She had no compunction about searching the rooms and belongings of the victim and suspects, many of whom had had connections with Peggy in her early years.

Trek or Treat (Zebra, 1980) found Marilyn working in a *Star Trek*-like television program. During a Chicago science fiction convention, a character named "Smock" was murdered. Hokey, not advised for anyone unfamiliar with the staff of the Enterprise.

Typical Zebra series in the Seventies.

Pepper Anderson

Author: Leslie Trevor's novelized episodes of the television program "Policewoman"

Pepper Anderson was a tall, slim ash-blonde who attended the UCLA drama school until the murder of her parents motivated her to join the police force. Her younger sister Cheryl had been institutionalized since the attack on their parents. Pepper's dramatic skills were used when she went undercover to trap killers.

In #1 *The Rape* (Award, 1975), a series of rapes developed a pattern. The victims were women who were visiting their husbands in a hospital. A trap was set at Bryan Memorial Hospital with Pepper as the wife visiting her husband (Lt. Bill Crowley) and Officer Joe Styles as a male nurse. Although staff members were considered the obvious suspects, there was a surprise, followed by the conventional encounter on the hospital rooftop.

#2 *Code 1013: Assassin* (Award, 1975) began with the murder of Anna Lomax, a successful politician, and her pilot by a man who boarded their private plane at Los Angeles airport. After a period of four years, Elida Quinn, who was featured in a "crusader type" television show, was injured in a hit-and-run accident. She had been a witness to Anna Lomax's death. A short time later reporter Charles Betz, also a witness, was killed by a drugged stallion. The entire unit was assigned tasks. Pepper's was to guard Elida, made more difficult when Elida didn't cooperate.

#3 *Death of a Call Girl* (Award, 1975) described Pepper's infiltration of the Classic Modeling School, an agency that lured teenage girls into prostitution through ads in throwaway magazines. Debbie Sweet, grand-daughter of Lt. Crowley, who had just graduated from the Police Academy, looked young enough to go undercover as an applicant. Pepper presented herself as trying to trace her runaway younger sister. The undercover plan had its casualties. The book had more than its share of explicit sex and violence. It was hard to believe that the material was presented on national television at this time. There may have been adaptations to the book to make it spicier.

Although the episodes dealt with themes interesting to women, the presentations were superficial.

Mici Anhalt

Author: Lillian O'Donnell

Mici (pronounced Mitzi) Anhalt was an ex-ballet dancer and former political activist. After the deaths of the Kennedy brothers, she channeled her idealism into a New York City Victim/Witness Assistance Program. Her responsibilities were a blend of social work and claims investigation. Mici, christened Maria Ilona, was the daughter of a naturalized American citizen from Hungary. She was tall, still slim and athletic in her thirties, with red-gold shoulder length hair and blue eyes.

As *Aftershock* (Putnam, 1977) began, Faith Tully came into the agency, angry because the police showed no interest in the death of her husband, a hairdresser who had intervened in a fight between two female gangs. The case was assigned to Mici, who was already working on the problems of Simon Creedy, a retarded man whose injuries deprived him of his part-time work, and aging tennis star Ramon Lara, who had been seriously injured in a subway robbery by teenagers. Mici's personal interest in her clients put her at odds with the bureaucracy and its hobbling regulations. Her dance training made it possible for her to overcome a killer.

During *Falling Star* (Putnam, 1979) Mici was juggling her caseload and dealing with an angry co-worker. For Mici, investigating the death of alcoholic actress Julia Schuyler may have posed a conflict of interests. Both Julia, daughter of famed star John Malcolm Schuyler, and Julia's estranged husband, Alfred Cassel, were friends from Mici's days in the theatre. Julia had kept occupied writing her father's memoirs. Alfred, whose star potential had risen as Julia's had declined due to her drinking, was the primary suspect.

In *Wicked Designs* (Putnam, 1980), Norman Landry, an acquaintance of Mici's grandfather, sought help when his wealthy Aunt Blanche disappeared. Finding Aunt Blanche in the morgue had been easy enough, but finding her killer took longer. Blanche had significant connections. Her former pupil Vanessa Walsh was currently married to a gubernatorial candidate, but had been rumored to have been involved in drugs. Needle marks had been found on Blanche's body when it was discovered at the bottom of subway steps. The killer was close to home.

The unusual aspects of Mici's character—the Hungarian connection, the ballet, and her involvement in liberal politics—were under-explored. O'Donnell had turned to her Norah Mulcahaney series (see Section 5, page 350).

Clare Reynolds Atwell
Author: Michael Underwood, pseudonym for John Michael Evelyn

Fair-haired Clare Reynolds' status changed over the duration of the series.

A WDC (woman detective constable) as *The Juror* (St. Martin's, 1975) began, Clare assisted fiancé Police Sgt. Nick Atwell in his investigation of the death of juror Lawrence Pewley, a man with an unusual memory and a collection of clippings. The case of alleged pornographer Bernie Mostyn was declared a mistrial due to the murder. Relegated to checking out the newspaper clippings, Clare found a lead to the killer. This narrative contained little or no background information on either Nick or Clare.

By *Menaces, Menaces* (St. Martin's, 1976), Clare was married and pregnant, so her role diminished even further. However, her theory that a habitual criminal had solicited an arrest to provide an alibi for a more serious crime solved the case.

Clare was a stay-at-home mother during *Murder With Malice* (St. Martin's, 1977), when Nick was accused of soliciting a bribe. Because Nick was in no position to protect himself from the charge and was placed on suspension, there was a change of roles. He cared for the baby while Clare investigated the family affairs of Sir Guy Frensham, who had brought the charges against Nick. Sir Guy's 17-year-old son had been accused in the murder/robbery of widowed Florence Isaacs. Nick had been the investigating officer. With help from the Deputy Chief Inspector, Clare found the real criminal. It took more effort to clear Nick's reputation.

In *The Fatal Trip* (St. Martin's, 1977), Clare took an unofficial assignment when Nick feared he might have helped to convict an innocent man, Stephen Burley, of burglary at the Rickard Motor Company. At Nick's request Clare had attended both the verdict and sentencing and agreed with him that Burley might be innocent. The death by poison of Eva Sharman, the primary witness against Burley, and the asphyxiation death of her employer, Miles Rickard, added credibility to Nick's concern.

Crooked Wood (St. Martin's, 1978) focused on a jury-tampering charge. Clare provided support, but this was Nick's story and led to his promotion.

The narratives were well constructed but low-keyed. Underwood's character development was less effective than his plotting.

Madame Dominique Aubry

Author: Hugh Travers (Mills)

Widowed Dominique Aubry had studied for the French Bar and then worked in the office of her psychoanalyst father. She had a full life, writing an advice column for the weekly magazine *Madame*, under the pseudonym "Femina" and enjoying a relationship with Michel Vallin, a prosperous winegrower.

Madame was enjoying dinner with Leon Chantal, the prefect of police, in *Madame Aubry and the Police* (Harper, 1967), when he was called to investigate the death of Suzanne Greville, the fifth wife of Julian, an aging dramatist and novelist. A servant, the only witness to the crime, was also killed. Julian requested that Madame investigate. Her theory was that the two deaths were unconnected: that Suzanne had been killed by a jealous lover, while the servant had interrupted the theft of a Goya. Both premises proved to be correct.

In *Madame Aubry Dines with Death* (Harper, 1967), her hostess at dinner, Jennifer de Nolay, was found dead of cyanide poisoning. Jennifer was the heiress to a meat-canning factory. Her husband, Nicolas, was the head of a venerable winery family. Jennifer had pressured Nicolas against joining the family business with a larger combine. Unhappily, Madame Aubry's lover, Henri, was the heir to the vineyard as Nicolas' son. Her investigation jeopardized their relationship to the point where he struck her. After she had solved the case, he forgave her. Hopefully he also apologized.

Competent for its time period.

Jannine Austin
Author: Elizabeth Welles, possibly a house name used by Lyle Kenyon Engel

Jannine Austin had inherited Grandview Incorporated, a real estate agency, from her widowed father. A petite woman with chestnut hair and green eyes, she had her early education abroad and then graduated from Sarah Lawrence College. Although single and without close relationships, she was portrayed as very attractive and flirtatious. Several men fell in love with her in each book. Her selling technique often included having the prospective purchaser move into the otherwise empty house to check it out or moving in with them to help them settle in after the purchase.

In *Fahnsworth Manor* (Pocket Books, 1976), Jannine joined C. Compton Matthews, an American author, and his artist son, Chris, at the historic Irish manor he had purchased. Attacks on Jannine, Compton, and Chris, followed by the murder of a stranger, were given little attention by the local constable. Jannine had hallucinations during which she thought she saw the family ghost. Sean O'Riordan, a Dublin police inspector, was sent in to check things out. The resolution was faulty. Jannine's role was more victim than detective.

During *Waterview Manor* (Pocket Books, 1976), Jannine settled Hal Cranshaw, a potential home purchaser, into a Maryland estate. His wife, Yvonne, was terrified by rumors that the place was haunted by a Black Monk and insisted that the deal was off if anything eerie happened before the papers were signed. That would not suit Jannine, who was aware that other real estate dealers had the property on their listings. She blundered into the solution, listened to the killer explain his motivation while she was taped to a chair, and was rescued.

In *Spaniard's Gift* (Pocket Books, 1977), Jannine investigated rumors about the air/boat traffic near the waterside estate she was proposing to sell to Ernest and Valerie Sorenson, fearing that there were drugs involved. The house had been cared for by Bernardo Carrera and his wife, Lydia, while the sale was in process. Jannine seemed to have no support staff and cried on the shoulder of the nearest male when upset. Frank Mason, the maintenance man, had his skull crushed, so the police became involved. Jannine shared little information with them until the case was solved.

Seagull Crag (Pocket Books, 1977) involved Jannine with Lucy Fairly, an elderly widow who wanted her family home sold to someone who would restore the property. Jannine had come to care for the old woman and tried to meet her needs. Her family was more interested in getting a good price and sharing in the profits. After several accidents to family and staff, Gloria (Lucille's step-granddaughter) was murdered. Jannine concealed Juan, a servant whom the family insisted was responsible, but he too was murdered. Although the killer made his guilt obvious, at least Jannine worked out a solution to protect Lucy from her grasping family.

Captain's Walk (Pocket Books, 1976) was the name of the extensive estate that Grandview sold to Amanda Winton. Amanda, her two children, and her cook-companion Nora Lewis and son moved in before the transaction was complete. The house had a bad name based on rumors of ghosts, and had been vacant for the prior six plus years. To help Amanda and finish the sale, Jannine joined them. Both Nora and Amanda had recently become widows and they were pleased to acquire artist Albie Portman as a chauffeur. He seemed an educated man for the job but explained he would only stay for the summer while painting part-time. There were moans and groans in the night, but after two murders occurred, Jannine did some investigating. She spent a considerable period of time checking out innocent people, but finally blundered into the killer's hands.

These are, at best, weak gothic/mysteries.

Julie Barnes

Author: Richard Deming, novelized segments of television program, "Mod Squad"

Julie Barnes, a former juvenile delinquent, was recruited by the Los Angeles Police Department to work with Pete Cochran, a WASP, and Linc Hayes, an African-American male, in situations where traditional police methods were unsuccessful. Pete had been disowned by his parents and found guilty of car theft. Linc had been arrested during the Watts rioting. Julie was a slim, trim, brown-eyed blonde in her early twenties, the daughter of an alcoholic mother and an unknown father. They were supervised by Captain Adam Greer.

The stories were patterned with the trio going undercover in dangerous circumstances:

- *Mod Squad #1: The Greek God Affair* (Pyramid, 1968) introduced the trio and explained the decision of the police department. They attended the Police Academy. Their first case involved the "Sanctuary" of the "Temple of Olympus," a religious cult run by Reverend Zeus, which offered sanctuary to runaway juveniles. The Temple catered to wealthy people interested in the "hedonistic" practices to be enjoyed there. All three got jobs at the Sanctuary or Temple. Several of the girls who sought Sanctuary were missing. One, Elizabeth Turner, shot Zeus purportedly because she was pregnant by him. The cult was taken over by Zeus' wife and her brother, who used hypnotism to control the runaways.

- *Mod Squad #2: A Groovy Way to Die* (Pyramid, 1968) centered on a right wing organization that received a large donation from a Mafia leader; the trio infiltrated PUSPE (Patriot's Union to Support Private Enterprises). After an evening spent in the home of Big Jake Casale, the major supporter of PUSPE, they awakened to learn he was dead. Each of the trio took an assignment, Julie was to check out Norman Shill, executive of a suspect agency. Their cover was blown when Julie dropped her purse, exposing her official credentials.

- *Mod Squad #3: The Sock-It-To-'Em Murders* (Pyramid, 1968) was set at Boyer Fabrications, which had a concern about industrial spies. Linc and Pete went on the floor doing a factory time study while Julie took a job as a filing clerk. All seemed to be going well until the confidential file clerk was killed in an accident on the factory floor. Suspicion focused on a business rival that seemed to know what bid Boyer was going to make on projects and then slightly underbid. The "spy" was identified and admitted his crime, but denied any involvement with the murder and a subsequent attack. The killer took Julie hostage but was foiled by Linc and Pete.

- *Mod Squad #4: Spy-In* (Pyramid, 1969) was set on the Baldwin Hills College campus, where Linc and Pete posed as student athletes while Julie took an administrative staff position. Their mission was to check whether or not student athletes were taking bribes to shave points in games. Their technique: move in with the athletes and staff and date them. The campus was already stirred up by anti-Vietnam protests. After Pete and Linc were made aware that their police connection was known, Scooter Miller, with whom they shared an apartment, was murdered. The killer was a surprise.

■ *Mod Squad #5: The Hit* (Pyramid, 1970) placed the trio in the midst of racial conflict between white supremacist and black terrorist groups. Businessman Everett Peterson came to Captain Greer after he overheard a conversation concerning an attempt to kill Julian Ward, a local African-American leader. The trio split up with Linc joining the Black Vigilantes and Pete and Julie, the Downtown Vigilantes. Special efforts were made to guard Ward when he came to town for a speech; however, it was Councilman Frank Gardner who was killed. Late in the game they learned that they had been set up to attribute the death to racial animosity.

Although there was some merit in a television program that gave a female equal status with two males, the books were third rate.

Kay Barth

Author: Norma Schier

A divorcee with an eight-year-old daughter (Jodi), Kay Barth's connection with crime was more realistic than most heroines in books published by Zebra. She was an assistant District Attorney in Aspen, Colorado.

In *Death on the Slopes* (Zebra, 1978), Kay became attracted to Jason Ryder, who was suspected in the death of Valerie Mayne. Valerie had attached herself to Jason after his wife died, and had become a problem. She had been killed with a ski pole on the slopes. It didn't help that the autopsy showed she was three months pregnant. There was no DNA at this time to exonerate Jason. Eager to believe that he was innocent, Kay did some checking around about his past and Valerie's. Her probing brought danger to Jodi.

In *Murder by the Book* (Zebra, 1979), Kay was now the elected District Attorney and still seeing Jason Ryder. Brad, who had given up his job as a stockbroker to open a mystery bookstore in Aspen, was found dead at his desk. His wife, Adele, whom he had deserted, was in town. Their daughter, Ronnie, had chosen to live with her father. On Brad's desk was a strange list (names in one column; mystery book titles in the other). Brad had told people that someone in town had a secret and he was going to have some fun with it. During Jason and Kay's joint investigation, they realized that they were in love and planned to marry.

Death Goes Skiing (Zebra, 1979) revolved around the death of an unknown man, shot while on the ski slopes. His assailant, who had skied off pretending to go for help, was described as wearing a green jacket. Eventually the man was identified as Eric Mulligan, who had been looking for his wife. It took longer to learn that Kay knew the wife and their child very well. She used the color spectrum to solve the case.

Kay visited Santa Fe, New Mexico, during *Demon of the Opera* (Zebra, 1980) to help Denise, an old friend whose husband had been accused of creating "havoc" at the opera house. Denise's new husband was Harrison King, assistant stage manager of the Sante Fe Opera House. The charges against King were based on several incidents: a musical score burned up in a waste basket, a false letter telling King's boss that he had to go to a meeting in Albuquerque, and an accident on stage. Ray, King's boss, blamed him for all these incidents and the subsequent damage to a singer's costume and the musical conductor's car. Kay downplayed the evidence against King, believing that he had been set up. Why? She figured that out, too.

These were above average…but only for Zebras.

Tory Baxter

Author: Marcia Blair, pseudonym for Marc Baker

Tory Baxter, a registered nurse, accepted only those assignments that appealed to her. Since the death of her widowed father, the chief criminologist for the San Francisco Police Department, Tory lived with her Aunt Tildy, a popular mystery writer. Tory had a semi-romantic relationship with Police Lt. Jay Thorpe. She was taller than average, slim, with ash-brown hair and hazel eyes. There were extensive descriptions of her off-duty clothing, presumably intended to appeal to a clothes-conscious young reader. Tory encountered murder investigations when:

- In *The Final Lie* (Zebra, 1978), the hit-and-run death of her cousin Ann left Kate Jeffers enraged. Ann had purportedly had a "secret love" whom she subsidized. Given that background, it was hard for her friend Tory to accept that Kate too had a "secret love" and was subsequently found dead. She tried to interest Jay Thorpe in the case, but she and Aunt Tildy had the killer roped and tied by the time Thorpe figured it out.

■ En route to the home of the Blaine family in Spain, during *The Final Pose* (Zebra, 1978), Tory was accosted by Tom Rennel. He gave her a newspaper clipping and a "garbled message" and then died of a heart attack. She proceeded to the home of the "Badluck Blaines." Rennel was a newspaper reporter who had persisted in trying to talk to Ann Blaine Milton. A pathological killer who had nurtured hatred for decades was finally stopped.

■ In *The Final Guest* (Zebra, 1979), elderly Mrs. Vestry, who supposedly had a mild heart problem, died the first night that Tory took over her care. Mrs. Vestry lived in an upscale boarding house run by Miss Lucinda Prescott. Even though she had no patient to care for, Tory decided to stay on to help Lucinda adjust and to learn more about Mrs. Vestry's death. Anonymous calls were made to two of the other boarders and to the police, stating that she had been murdered. Jay Thorpe passed them off as crank calls. The group transferred to Lucinda's home at Lake Tahoe, where another boarder, wearing Tory's cape, was murdered. That, along with an attempt to murder a precocious child, finally brought Thorpe into the case. The motivation of the killer was not credible.

■ As *The Final Appointment* (Zebra, 1979) began, Tory was approached by three young women for help in a mystery. Within days two of them were dead. The survivor, Dina Severson, had known her friends since childhood. Their fathers were members of a brokerage firm. After Dina's parents died, she had spent most of her time with the families of the two victims, both of whom were wealthy. Dina did not believe she was in danger. This was the best plotted of the series.

■ In *The Final Fair* (Zebra, 1979), Tory and her friend Dr. Sandy Brochman went to a Renaissance Fair in costumes. When a call went out that a doctor was needed, they responded to the death of Dr. Michael Peters. His death had been caused by a knife, that was part of the costume worn by his fiancée, Leanne Davis. Leanne confided in Tory that the engagement was a cover-up. She had been paying Peters blackmail money to keep quiet about her affair with a married man. When Leanne was found, an apparent suicide, Tory would not accept that result.

■ Jay Thorpe was injured by a bullet shot into Aunt Tildy's house during *The Final Target* (Zebra, 1979) when he, Tory, and Aunt Tildy were in the living room. The obvious suspect was a man who had accused Tildy of plagiarizing his book. Tory and Aunt Tildy went to Mazatlan to be safe, but there was an attempt to poison Tildy there. Allan Masterson, a new man about town who was very interested in Tory, had joined them in Mazatlan. All returned home as soon as Tildy recovered. Big ending. Jay Thorpe finally kissed Tory. Compare this virginal approach to the paperback thrillers of the 21st century.

■ Tory was convinced that a hit-and-run accident during *The Final Ring* (Zebra, 1978) was murder. Peg Morse, a diabetic nurse who was a close friend of Tory died mysteriously. Tory agreed to fill in for Peg at the Harrington home, where wealthy Eve Harrington was recovering from a broken leg, the result of the hit and run. There had been other accidents in the home. Ethel, one of the maids, was killed in a fall down the stairs. It was noted later that there was wax on her heels. Cassidy, the chauffeur, had an accident driving Eve's car. Tory remembered Peg's last remark about a "mailman…two rings" before she died. The plot of the book, by James M. Cain, clued Tory in to the killers' identity.

■ Tory and Aunt Tildy were kidnapped by jewel thieves while attending a séance in *Finale* (Zebra, 1980). After her chauffeur, Henry Phillips, had been shot, Sadie Solomon needed tender loving care from a nurse. Sadie decided to solve the mystery herself by having a séance in which she could ask Henry who killed him. Aunt Tildy and Tory were among the invited guests. Three masked figures intruded. One shot John Masterson, a neighbor of Sadie's. They panicked, taking Tory and Tildy as hostages. Tildy arranged a chance for Tory to escape, but she remained a prisoner. Big clue to the ransom demand was Tildy's reference to *Citizen Kane*.

Time-passers for light reading.

June Beattie

Author: John Norman Harris

See: June Beattie Grant, Section 5, page 314.

Lucy Beck
Author: Peter Conway, pseudonym for Peter Claudius Gautier-Smith

Lucy Beck, a senior registrar in anesthetics at a major English hospital, was a small, blue-eyed, freckled blonde. Lest this description conjure up images of an angelic girl-next-door, Lucy proved to be a randy thrill seeker. A tomboy in her youth, she led an active outdoor life, parachuting, gliding, mountain climbing, and skiing; and she had an even more active personal life.

During *Motive for Revenge* (Hale, 1972), Lucy was involved with neurologist Paul Manning when he was accused of assaulting Valerie Telford, a female patient. Lucy used her three-week vacation to refute the charge. Valerie earned her living as a stripper and was a drug addict under the power of her dealer. Lucy saved Paul's life from the vengeful man who set him up using Valerie. In the process she helped Paul overcome his psychiatric problems, but she wasn't sure she wanted to marry him. She had enjoyed the excitement and welcomed the suggestion of Inspector Ramsden that she carry out future assignments for the police drug squad.

Professor Sir Francis Charlton was leery of Succour, an anti-drug group to which his daughter Rosemary had made substantial donations in *The Padded Cell* (Hale, 1973). After touching base with Inspector Ramsden, Lucy accepted a nursing position at Brantley Manor, a mental hospital run by Succour. She worked with Richard, Charlton's son, who also got a job there. Rosemary was a patient at Brantley Manor. Once discovered, Lucy was placed in a padded cell, drugged with LSD, and flogged while naked.

Escape to Danger (Hale, 1974) found Lucy en route by car to a medical conference in Poland. Felicity, her companion, was so terrified when they were assaulted that she returned home, leaving Lucy to make the trip alone. Prof. Piotrowski, a pharmacologist at St. Gregory's Hospital, had asked Lucy to take a message to his mother and his son Jan in Poland. She refused. At the conclusion of the conference, Lucy had no choice. After escaping from sadistic Jan, she headed home with a stowaway in the back of her car who planned to smuggle heroin across the border.

Lucy enjoyed opera and classical music, but her adventures exposed her to sexual brutality, perversion, and violence. She was not adverse to voluntary sex with anyone who pleased her. Conway was one of the authors who used female protagonists as sex objects.

Margaret Binton

Author: Richard Barth

Margaret Binton, a New York City widow in her seventies, recruited allies from among the elderly poor to oppose societal crime. Her husband, Oscar, had died after a 46-year marriage, leaving her childless and bored. Margaret battled absentee slum landlords, nursing home abuses, and the problems of bag ladies. She smoked, watched classic movies, worked crossword puzzles, and played bingo, but preferred to spend her time with the friends she made through volunteer work at the Flora K. Bliss Center. Margaret developed a working relationship with Sgt. David Schaeffer, who believed in her from the start, and Lt. Sam Morley, who had to be convinced. It helped that she baked cookies to earn their goodwill. Her ensemble eventually included: Rose Gaffery, a real ragbag lady; Sid Rossman, who played the ponies; Jerry Stein, a pool hall habitué; Bertie, the lady who brought crumbs for the birds; Roosa, who drank too much; and Pancher Reese.

Margaret recruited her "gang" beginning with Rose and Bertie in *The Rag Bag Clan* (Dial, 1978). When bag lady Sarah Feiner was murdered, the police found $1,000 among her possessions. Margaret noted that Rose Gaffery ducked out of the Center when the police came to enquire about Sarah. Rose admitted that she, too, had found money wrapped in a new-looking man's shirt in the trash. Rose wouldn't tell the police. Margaret did. They indicated that drug money was being passed, and that they would send "one of their own" undercover. They disdained Margaret's offer to play the role, so she did it on her own, seeking to be recruited as a drug courier.

In *A Ragged Plot* (Dial, 1981), Margaret helped Luis Valdez and five teenagers develop a community vegetable garden on a gated vacant lot. Luis' murder reminded her that he'd been worried about the lack of growth in his cucumbers. Digging under them, Margaret and Bertie discovered a box of diamonds. Luis' murder had taken place outside of the 81st precinct, so Schaeffer and Morley were not involved, but the diamonds were different. Morley recognized them as the proceeds from the Rosenblatt robbery. Margaret didn't want to believe that one of the teenagers was involved, but she wanted Luis' killer arrested.

In *One Dollar Death* (Dial, 1982), Margaret took a Russian teapot to the Annual Sotheby Park Bernet Appraisal Day. Her friend Hannah Jansen was there with an 1804 U.S. coin left by her deceased husband. Later Hannah was found dead. Lt. Evans, who was in charge of the case had no history with Margaret. When she shared her theory that Hannah had been killed for the coin, he not only ignored Margaret's theory, but suspected her.

She consulted with the author of a magazine column on coin collecting, who provided her with a list of local dealers who might recognize such a coin. She had an old coin of her husband's that she could use to entice the probable killer.

Margaret's police allies could not join her crusade against a vicious landlord in *The Condo Kill* (Scribners, 1985). They were homicide, not rent control. The attack Margaret had witnessed on her friend Thelma was written off as not worthy of their attention because they were short staffed. Mantex Management hired thugs to systematically terrorize tenants of an apartment building until they moved out. Thelma, a regular at the Center, and Angelo Varonetti were the only two left in the building. It had to be empty before Mantex could raze it. Things changed when Angelo was murdered.

After Margaret's raffle ticket won a Winnebago motor home in *Deadly Climate* (St. Martin's, 1988), she and her friends pooled resources for a trip to Florida, where they were amazed at the lethargy of group home residents. When the Forstman Rest Home seemed particularly apathetic, Sid, her gambler pal, entered the home as a new resident, and Margaret posed as a patient to the referring physician.

Concerned about children awaiting adoption in *Blood Doesn't Tell* (St. Martin's, 1989), Margaret became a short-term foster parent for a little boy. Beyond her frustration with the bureaucracy of the Youth Benevolent Association, she suspected that YBA was more interested in the financial status of prospective parents than in their emotional stability.

Deathics (St. Martin's, 1993) was disappointing. Margaret was busy. She attended Smoke Stoppers to deal with her habit, kept an eye on young Peter Frangepani after school on Tuesdays, attended a Law and Ethics class at night school, and continued her involvement at the Center. She was sensitive to the fact that something was bothering young author Adrian Lavin. After he was stabbed, she sought help from Lt. Morley. However, she bypassed the police, entered Adrian's apartment, and stole his computer before the detectives could arrive. The computer held Adrian's unfinished history of St. Martin's Parish. It was fine that she enlisted the Gang to help in the case, but it was unprincipled of her to place Peter in danger. The Law and Ethics class material should have influenced her behavior.

There were Damon Runyan-like touches in the motley crew Margaret assembled.

The Bionic Woman

Author: Eileen Lottman

See: Jaime Sommers, Section 5, page 409.

Adrienne Bishop

Author: Jan Ellery, pseudonym for Jan Ewing

Adrienne Bishop, a tall blonde in her early twenties, had an enviable occupation, as recreational director at Sealpoint Racquet Club, a southern tennis resort. Her responsibilities gave her access to the rich, beautiful, and famous.

In *The Last Set* (Zebra, 1979), a tournament was on the verge of cancellation for lack of prize money. That was averted, but Farley Gibbs, president of the company sponsoring the tournament, was murdered just as action began. Adrienne, ignoring the fact that he was discovered standing over the body and that he had been dropped from the tennis circuit for throwing a match, was convinced that club pro Mike Feld was not guilty. Her theory gained credence when an attempt was made to strangle another tennis pro at a time when Mike was in jail. Lt. Breyer gave Adrienne considerable leeway in investigating the matter.

Bart Jackson, the manager of the resort and Adrienne's beau, had transferred to Greentree, a more opulent resort in North Carolina, by *High Strung* (Zebra, 1980). Adrienne followed. They worked together on an exhibition match with Ichabod Star, an ex-tournament level player, and Marcie Adams, a promising young player, but the relationship between Bart and Adrienne had lost its zest. Eleanor Waltham, depressed since her father's death in a car accident, was found hanged in what the police wrote off as a suicide. When Harriet, Eleanor's mother, was also injured, the incident was seen as attempted murder. Harriet's need for a blood transfusion provided Adrienne with the information she needed to solve the case.

Shauna Bishop

Author: J. J. Montague, pseudonym for James Keenan

Shauna Bishop, code name Black Swan, was an agent for the Central Intelligence Agency, receiving $4,000 per month for dubious "undercover" activities. The bare facts about Shauna were that she was 5' 3", weighed 110 pounds, and had dark hair and eyes. The illegitimate child of a Las Vegas call girl and a Mexican gardener, she utilized sex rather than any skill or intelligence in her work. *The Chinese Kiss* (Canyon, 1974), *The Cong Kiss* (Canyon, 1974), *The French Kiss* (Canyon, 1974), and *The Judas Kiss* (Canyon, 1975) had little to offer a mystery reader.

Modesty Blaise

Author: Peter O'Donnell

Modesty Blaise, who has been referred to as the female equivalent of James Bond, shared his hedonism, use of sex and violence, ties to British Intelligence, and major adversaries, i.e., criminal conspiracies and international intrigues. They shared expensive tastes, a drive for physical fitness, and the enjoyment of lethal gadgets.

However, there were also significant differences. Modesty began as an orphaned refugee in a displaced person camp, where an elderly professor educated her. Although the books frequently referred to Modesty's financially rewarding criminal career in the Network and her recruitment of Willie Garvin as her alter ego, the series began when 26-year-old Modesty retired from organized crime. She had a short marriage to an Englishman, entered to gain British citizenship.

Modesty was 5' 6" tall, with black hair usually worn in a chignon, dark skin, and midnight blue eyes. She exercised regularly with Willie, developing new survival techniques, was fluent in several languages, and expert with weapons. Modesty had learned about gems, art, and gambling while in the Network. Willie and Modesty had no sexual relationship; neither showed jealousy when the other was romantically involved.

Modesty Blaise (Doubleday, 1965) made the reader aware that modesty had little to do with it. Miss Blaise was as natural and comfortable when nude as when dressed in a designer gown. Modesty came to Willie's rescue when he was in prison. They owed Sir Gerald Tarrant of British Intelligence big time, so decided to bring down the gang that planned to intercept a payment in diamonds from the British government to elderly Sheik Abu-Tahir. A short-term relationship with intelligence agent Paul Hagan was not meant to last.

The stories followed a pattern. Modesty and/or Willie would be bored until contacted by an old friend in danger or by Tarrant. Although well aware of her past, Tarrant knew that Modesty had never dealt in drugs, vice, or the sale of British secrets. The pair would take on an assignment, prepare their equipment, and initially be successful, then something would go wrong. The climax would be a scene in which the imprisoned Willie, Modesty, or both, faced with torture and/or death, made their escape or rescued one another by superhuman means, leaving corpses all over the scenery. John Dall, a Native-American industrialist, often intervened to help Modesty.

The narratives were set in exotic locales with flagrant villains:

■ Mongolian mercenary Karz wanted to take over Kuwait in *Sabre Tooth* (Doubleday, 1966). Tarrant had been made aware that a large number of hired killers had disappeared. At his suggestion, Willie and Modesty set themselves up to be recruited. Modesty showed her kinder side when she took risks to save Lucille, a young pickpocket.

■ Handsome young Lucifer could predict death, especially when he ordered it. He extorted money from the rich and powerful in *I, Lucifer* (Doubleday, 1967). Rene Vaubois, a French intelligence official, made Modesty aware of the Lucifer Gang. Their interference caused a potential bomb attack on Rene and the abduction of Willie and psychologist Steve Collier.

■ Gabriel, an old enemy who had been foiled in *Sabre Tooth,* teamed with Simon Delicata, one of the few men whom Willie Garvin feared, in *A Taste for Death* (Doubleday, 1969; reprint of Souvenir edition). They kidnapped Diana Pilgrim, a Canadian who had divining skills enabling her to locate water, pipes, and valuable metals, to help them find lost treasure. In seeking to find Diana, Willie and Modesty were captured and made to help with the digging. They convinced a member of the gang to assist them in an escape. Diana paired up with Steve Collier.

■ *The Impossible Virgin* (Doubleday, 1971) began when Modesty made an emergency landing in Africa. Her intention was to assist Dr. Giles Pennyfeather, a young healer, but they were both deported from Kalimba. Next, Willie and Modesty were distracted into finding tiny Brunel. Brunel used his albino daughter, Lisa, to decoy Willie, Modesty, and Pennyfeather into his hands. Lots of radioactive gimmicks.

■ Colonel James Straik and Mr. Sexton kidnapped Tarrant in *The Silver Mistress* (Archival, 1981), planning to torture him for information that they could use for blackmail. One blackmail victim, Fiona Langford, was brought to Modesty's attention by her sister,

Janet. Modesty's plan to invade Strait's chateau through a cave was betrayed, and she and Willie were captured. They stayed around only long enough to rescue their friends and kill Sexton and Strait.

- Paxero had been raised to hate rich white landowners, so in *Last Day in Limbo* (Mysterious Press, 1985), he targeted Modesty's friend John Dall. His victims were taken to a slave camp in Guatemala, so that's where Willie and Modesty went to save Dinah Collier, Steve's wife, and eventually to release the prisoners.

- Australian tycoon Sam Solon used his evil organization in *Dragon's Claw* (Mysterious Press, 1985) to gather an art collection, which he displayed to captive art experts. The experts were brainwashed so they could not remember the experience. While sailing a boat through the Tasman Sea, Modesty rescued Luke Fletcher, one of the experts who had escaped. Solon posed as a benefactor to keep track of Modesty. Only after she and Willie were tricked into stealing art did Modesty recognize her enemy.

- The sexually confused brothers Jeremy and Dominic Silk served as the disciplinarians for El Mico, a North African cabal that rivaled Modesty's former organization, the Network, in *The Xanadu Talisman* (Mysterious Press, 1984). When Modesty and Louis Gautier, a courier for El Mico, were trapped in the basement garage of a Casablanca hotel due to an earthquake, Gautier gave Modesty a wrist wallet. The brothers and Nannie Prendergast, who kept them under control, wanted to cash it all in and retire, but needed to retrieve the wallet and a silver Talisman coin first.

- Hugh Oberon never forgave Willie and Modesty for his rejection by the Network and sought revenge in *The Night of Morningstar* (Mysterious Press, 1987). Stung by the fact that she had disclosed the identity of CIA agent Ben Christie, resulting in his death, Modesty probed the existence of a new group of assassins, the Watchmen. After the usual capture by her enemies, Modesty used her special muscle control skill to escape.

- Brainwasher Dr. Janos Tyl, who turned Willie Garvin against Modesty in *Dead Man's Handle* (Mysterious Press, 1986), worked for Thaddeus Pilgrim, a former missionary who lost faith when his family was killed by terrorists. Willie was kidnapped when he investigated attacks against an old girlfriend, Molly Chen. He was brainwashed so that when Modesty arrived to rescue him, he would attack her. However, the bonds between Modesty and Willie were too strong for that to work. Plan B involved putting a contract out on Steve and Diana Collier, which would be activated if Willie and Modesty didn't cooperate.

Modesty often used sex as recuperative therapy for the men she befriended (except Willie). Doctors, sculptors, artists, and scientists returned refreshed to their work after an affair with Modesty. She had few female friends who reappeared in the series, but then the narratives were not designed to appeal to women, or to promote feminine equality.

O'Donnell brought out a series of short stories featuring Modesty in *Pieces of Modesty* (Pan, 1972) and *Cobra Trap* (Souvenir, 1996). The series had begun as comic strips, which O'Donnell developed into conventional novels. The comic strips were still running in the *Evening Standard* in England in 1991. Characters, both allies and enemies, come and go throughout the series.

A more recent use of the comic strip technique, aka "graphic novels," of which I know nothing but what I have learned from my grandchildren, Emily and Kevin, has produced new offerings featuring Modesty ("Modesty Blaise: The Gallows Bird" and "Modesty Blaise: The Puppet Master"). "Graphic" as used here refers not to "explicit" but to "pictorial representation," as explained to me in *The American Heritage College Dictionary*. They are available, but I did not consider them appropriate for inclusion.

Jana Blake

Author: Jim C. Conaway aka Jake Quinn

Jana Blake, a slim blonde, was a New York City investigator who shared her combination office/apartment with her cat, Good Ol' Boy. She limited her practice to cases that involved women. Jana shared a physical relationship with fruit seller Gianni Grompone, whose contacts with her were minutely described.

In *Deadlier Than the Male* (Belmont, 1977), Jana was pitted against an unidentified female killer, seeking revenge for her rape by five college students. Although she preferred to use her talents to assist women in trouble, Jana also reached out to the wife of one of the Firehouse Five. The initially unnamed woman, who had been abused by her father, killed her victims with an ax and then beheaded them. All victims belonged to the same fraternity. One, still alive, a Bowery drunk, was given protection by the police. A café owner told Jana about a waitress named Sunny who attended a Beta dance, then never returned to work.

During *They Do It With Mirrors* (Belmont, 1977), Justin Svanire, an illusionist, caused Risa, the eight-year-old daughter of Chiara, an Italian movie star, to disappear. He was part of a plot by "Stash" Tompkins, a pimp and drug dealer, to hold the child for ransom. After seeing Jana's ad in the paper, Chiara hired her to find her daughter, although the police were also involved. Part of the plan had been to substitute a lookalike for Chiara when she went to deliver the ransom. Jana had focused on a large trunk that might have been used to transport the child.

Poor fare.

Dulcie Bligh

Author: Gail Clark

Dulcie Bligh was a voluptuous redhead married to world traveler Baron Maximilian "Bat" Bligh in the early 19th century. Although Bat enjoyed a vigorous social life when abroad, Dulcie always welcomed him home. In his absence she kept busy, interfering in the lives of her household, Bat's extended family, and her friends.

In *Dulcie Bligh* (Putnam, 1978), nephew Benedict was suspected in the death of Lady Arabella, a young and injudicious wife, but not his own. Determined to protect the young man, whose former wife, Gwyneth, was seeking custody of their son, Dulcie arranged for a false alibi; then, she entered the underworld to connive with its Gypsy Queen.

In *The Baroness of Bow Street* (Putnam, 1979), Dulcie kept impetuous female editor Leda Langtry out of jail when she was accused first of libel and then of murder. To safeguard her naive niece, Mignon, who was attracted to mountebanks, Dulcie marshaled her allies, including the Bow Street Runners and her butler Gibbon. She solved these problems before Bat returned and took total possession of her time and attention.

Dulcie was ahead of her time. Historical female sleuths did not become popular until later. Lots of fun and colorful characters, activity and confusion, intrigue and skullduggery.

Vicky Bliss

Author: Elizabeth Peters, aka Barbara Michaels,
pseudonyms for Barbara Mertz

Vicky Bliss was tall (six feet), with a "sexy" build, long blonde hair, and dark blue eyes. Although her Ph.D. was in medieval European history with a minor in art history and a command of German and Italian, she had her lighter side. Vicky could pick a lock or write a soft porn novel. She claimed a heritage of Swiss German, Norwegian/Swedish, and Native American ancestors, and had been raised and educated in the Midwest. Her Doberman, Caesar, never took part in the action.

In *Borrower of the Night* (Dodd, 1973), while working as a history instructor in a small midwestern college, Vicky and co-worker Tony Lawrence discovered a clue to the location of a German religious woodcarving. Being highly competitive, each sought the historic artifact, which was to be found in an area near Castle Drachenstein, now a hotel. Arriving at the Castle, they were surprised to learn that amateur art collector George Nolan was already a guest and probably on the same quest.

Vicky accepted a position in the National Museum in Germany, but was in Rome in *Street of the Five Moons* (Dodd, 1978), assigned to trace possible forgeries of gold pieces. The only clue to the origin of the copies was an address on Street of the Five Moons where an antique shop was located. Her plan to burgle the facility failed; instead, she was kidnapped and warned to leave town. Her adversary was the mysterious Sir John Smythe. They met again at the villa of Pietro Caravaggio at Tivoli. This time Pietro, Sir John, and Vicky were all kidnapped. The narrative grew tiring, but at the end Vicky bargained with the head of the forgers because the police were involved. Sir John left quietly, but she never forgot him.

When, in *Silhouette in Scarlet* (Congdon, 1983), Vicky received a red rose and airfare to Stockholm from Munich, she hoped they were a message from Smythe. There was an invitation from a nebulous cousin, Gustaf Jonsson, to visit, and a handsome Swede, Leif Andersen, who kept turning up and might be a police officer. Gustaf was the owner of a valuable collection of gold archaeological pieces. Vicky was aware that Sir John, who turned up at Jonsson's also claiming to be related, was an art thief who might rob her Swedish relatives. Instead he proved himself a hero.

During *Trojan Gold* (Atheneum, 1987), Vicky was still employed by the National Museum, but Smythe had disappeared. In a search for jewels missing from Schliemann's expedition to Troy, the narrative became a farce with Schmidt, Vicky's employer, following her and Vicky looking for Smythe, while other searchers appeared and reappeared.

Smythe remained the motivating factor in Vicky's life in *Night Train to Memphis* (Warner, 1994). She was offered a position on a cruise of the Nile, during which someone "who knew her" would surface as part of a plot to rob the Cairo Museum. Not only did Sir John appear, along with a new bride, but so also did several prior adversaries and Schmidt, who proved himself a true friend. Vicky was willing to take whatever Smythe offered.

For those who enjoy humor in their mysteries. Elizabeth Peters did much better with Amelia Peabody Emerson.

Sibyl Sue Blue

Author: Rosel George Brown

Sergeant Blue, a tough and sexy woman in her late thirties, drank gin, smoked cigars, and shared her sexual favors generously. After her husband disappeared, leaving her to support their teenaged daughter, Missy, she became a detective, enjoying both the money and the excitement.

In *Sibyl Sue Blue* (Doubleday, 1966), while investigating a foreign virus, that caused suicides, Sibyl fought off the advances (personal and cultural) of Centaurians, who had been migrating to Terra Earth.

In *The Waters of Centaurus* (Doubleday, 1970), Missy, Sibyl's 16-year-old daughter, accompanied her to the uncharted island of Seia. Missy disappeared beneath the sea, stricken with a malady that caused gills to grow on land creatures. Making herself aquarian, Sibyl went undersea to rescue her daughter and thwart a plan to melt the glaciers.

The series, written in the 1960's, was set in the 1990's and was optimistic about what space travel could achieve. Mystery fans may pass these by as science fiction.

Helen Blye

Author: David Delman

See: Helen Blye Horowitz, Section 5, page 321.

Jane Boardman

Author: Joseph Harrington

Jane Boardman, an early entry in the ranks of female police officers, was a secondary character to Lt. Frank Kerrigan of the New York Police Department. She had been provided with impressive credentials: graduate of Hunter College, scored second highest in her class at the New York Police Academy, but had few opportunities once in the system. Single, with black hair and blue eyes, artistic and well read, she was the daughter of a wire chief at the phone company.

When *The Last Known Address* (Lippincott, 1965) began, Kerrigan's career had been seriously damaged by political pressure after he arrested the drunken son of a politician. He had been demoted to sergeant in Special Services and paired with Jane, a young probationary officer. After some minor successes, they were reassigned to a seemingly hopeless search for a witness, an accountant who had worked for the Reddy brothers' financial empire. The Reddys had begun as small-time crooks. Now they were big-time crooks. In the course of the search, Kerrigan taught Jane a lot about patience, process, and persistence.

Blind Spot (Lippincott, 1966) made only passing reference to Jane, focusing on Kerrigan's solo investigation of murder.

Jane and Kerrigan were reunited in *The Last Doorbell* (Lippincott, 1969). Now detective second grade, she called on the vacationing Kerrigan when assigned an 11-year-old file relating to kidnapping. It was Kerrigan who solved the case, going over the facts again and again. One woman died after he questioned her. When Jane and Kerrigan saw their suspect in the park with two children, they arrested him and returned the children to their mother. Their personal relationship never went beyond a chaste goodnight kiss.

Harrington's style was realistic. He used Jane to illuminate Kerrigan's experience and thoroughness, allowing her to provide occasional insights. Low-level tension, however.

Hilary Brand

Author: Hilary Brand, possibly a house name used by James Moffatt

Hilary Brand appeared in at least eight books under the Brand authorship, and in two others co-featuring her with Hank Janson, authored by Hank Janson. Although the series was published in England, the setting was

Chicago. Hilary, a woman in her twenties, was the daughter of a wealthy Texas oilman. She may have overstated her appeal, assuming that every man she encountered desired her. She came to Chicago to make her own way as a news reporter for the Chicago *Chronicle*. Her early assignments from "the Chief" did not satisfy her need for excitement, but she loved Chicago.

In *News Girl* (Compact, 1963), she went beyond her assignment to ferret out political malfeasance (not unusual in Chicago).

During *Brand T* (Compact, 1964) she put herself at risk to catch a serial killer. This information was gathered by references in other books.

Peak of Frenzy (Compact, 1964) took Hilary to Baja California in search of Ray Jennings, the man she had loved but left because of his addiction to alcohol. Unfortunately, he was in no condition to enjoy her visit. Hilary's host was Billy Huntington, who bragged that he was the grandson of Billy the Kid. Ramon and Rafael were the brothers of Antonia, a young woman who was carrying "young Billy's" child. The whole crew ended up in Indian Territory after Ray disappeared. All sacrificed their lives to save Hilary and the pregnant young woman from marauding bandits.

Lest the reader think that Hilary, born in Texas, lacked social concerns, *Black Summer Day* (Compact, 1965) took her to Mississippi to rescue her cousin Caroline, a civil rights worker. Hilary used sexually provocative behavior to attract not only plantation owner Seth Watson but also Bob Ackroyd, a civil rights worker. She sashayed around in skin tight, diaphanous outfits in a deliberate effort to get Watson to admit he had some responsibility for Caroline, now known to be dead. Readers will assume that the author "Hilary Brand" is not only male, but had limited information about Mississippi in the 1960's. Too late, Hilary identified Caroline's killer. The African-American characters were cruelly depicted.

In *All—or Something* (Compact, 1965), Hilary was appalled at the sexism and deceit in the world of wrestling and sports reporting in general. She set herself to disclose the impact of the Cosa Nostra on wrestling. The triggering event was the death of Dare Blade, a big-time wrestler in the ring. Aided by her rival and lover Marty Moffitt, she conducted a two-pronged attack: first, find the killer, then, expose the criminals who controlled the wrestling game.

In *A Flair for Affairs* (Compact, 1966), Hilary was determined to rescue her longtime friend Jason Baxter from making a disastrous decision. Jason, an exceeding wealthy man, had been like an older brother to Hilary in her early years. She seriously mistrusted Olivia Metcalfe, Jason's fiancée. On vacation from her job at the *Chronicle*, Hilary joined Jason's transitory party, which moved from New York City to Paris to San Francisco, where his friend Brad had a yacht. Brad worked with Hilary to get background information on Olivia. He was very interested in Hilary, but her job came first.

Running Scared (Compact, 1966) may not be the worst in the series, but it has to come close. Sent by her editor to find Spencer Kepler, a missing Chicago politician, Hilary came upon a clue missed by everyone else on the case. She located Kepler at the Gila Lodge in Arizona, where he revealed that he was a killer and had provided information to communist agents. Hilary promised to protect his secret, but that was made unnecessary when he was murdered. She returned to Chicago to investigate Kepler's contact, Edward Malory. In her efforts to cozy up to Malory, she encountered his sadistic female companion, Vera Stowe, and allied herself with an FBI agent and a treasury agent. The only excuse for Hilary's stupidity is the number of times she was knocked unconscious.

No Snow White herself, Hilary was horrified to learn in *Strictly Wild* (Compact, 1966) that U.S. swimmer Ginny Staines was carousing in a Bristol teenage bar. Hilary had reported earlier on Ginny's rescue of four persons from Lake Michigan, so was deeply disappointed in the 17-year-old's behavior. Hilary was sent to Bristol to cover Ginny's attempt to swim the English Channel round trip. A casual encounter with Steve Bolman, who managed the Down Beat Club, which catered to teenagers, made Hilary aware of the drug traffic and sexual encounters that took place there. Her subsequent articles went beyond Ginny's swim to cover Bristol's teenage scandal. The good news was that Ginny valiantly made it across the Channel; the bad news, she was unable to make a return trip.

News Girl, Brand T, and the two books by Hank Janson published by Roberts in 1963, *Brand Image* and *Second String*, were either unavailable or prohibitively expensive.

Janna Brill

Author: Lee Killough

This was a science fiction crossover set in the future (late 21st century). Although based in Wichita and Kansas City, Kansas, Janna Brill was a college-educated police officer, methodical in her approach to solving cases. She began her career partnered with Wim Kriest, and they worked their way up the ladder to the rank of investigator. At that point, Wim and his wife decided that he would resign from the Crimes Against Persons Squad and journey to a star as colonists. This involved a long trip during which the passengers slept, sustained by special technology, while a small crew managed the vehicle. Wim wanted Janna to resign too and accompany his family on the adventure.

Wim's injury while on duty in *The Doppelganger Gambit* (Ballantine, 1979) left him blind and Janna in need of a partner. The selection of erratic Mahlon "Mama" Maxwell to fill the gap gave Janna cause to consider becoming a colonist. The first investigation, however, focused on the death of a contract broker for the colonization flights. Mama's flashes of intuition clashed with Janna's conservative approach, but they melded into an effective team and broke the alibi of a Doppelganger.

By *Dragon's Teeth* (Questar, 1990), Mama and Janna were a pair. Although they were not involved romantically, they shared a dwelling. Robberies at a political fundraiser and then a charity function where a man was murdered meant a high-profile case. Mama and Janna were assigned but had to cope with criminals who had better technology than the police department. Thanks to a key observation by Arianna, Mama's girlfriend, they managed to identify the killers but not necessarily apprehend them all.

Spider Play (Questar, 1986) opened with both Mama and Janna uncomfortable in their personal lives. Perhaps that was why they became so obsessed about solving a case that began with a stolen hearse. Even when the incident expanded to include mutilation, perhaps murder, and possibly interspace smuggling, they were reluctant to turn it over to the federal authorities. They followed the trail to a space platform, where they were at a great disadvantage. Not only were the suspects cooperating to deceive them, they couldn't get their bodies accustomed to the lack of gravity.

Angel Brown
Author: Graham Montrose, pseudonym for Charles Roy Mackinnon

Angel Brown, whose mother died when she was young, lost her respect for legal authority when her father, an FBI agent, was killed in action. Angered by the ineffectiveness of the police, Angel sought her father's murderer and killed him. When warned to leave the country, Angel moved to England, using her father's insurance to establish a secretarial business. It prospered, allowing Angel, then only 22, to sell out at a great profit and dedicate herself to fighting crime. She worked with her "Band of Angels," including former stunt man Iain MacKinnon, Angel's lover and second in command; Jack Ironside, a Jamaican; David Crosby, equally devoted to Angel; and Martin Foster, an American. As the original Band of Angels was diminished by deaths, there were new recruits: Tony Gratz, a travel writer from Australia, and Greg Mac Gregor, a Canadian financial consultant. Angel lived the good life, with an expensive car and apartment in London and a home in Oxford. She wore designer clothes and jewelry on her 35-23-36 torso, and had dark hair with violet eyes. Like several other lawless heroines, Angel had a physical imperfection: the lobe on her left ear was missing.

In *Angel of Death* (Hale, 1968), the Band of Angels challenged a sinister organization, "The Club," five powerful men in politics, the media, industry, Scotland Yard, and MI5, who used crime to their own advantage. The group was headed by Arthur Roberts of Scotland Yard, who was in a position to divert any suspicion from his confederates. This was important because Detective Derek Ashmole was checking out names that might lead to industrialist Sir Thomas Clark. Angel followed Ashmole off an airplane just as he was shot by a silenced rifle. Clues led the Band to investigate entertainers, probably hooked on drugs, who were being used to gather blackmail information. From that time on the lines were drawn: the Band of Angels versus The Club.

Angel of No Mercy (Hale, 1968) pitted the Angels against a protection racket, the "Club and Restaurant Society," which took payoffs from nightclubs. There was little doubt in Angel's mind or that of her followers that their old adversaries were at the top level in this scheme. The Band took an aggressive stance: intercepting payments, breaking and entering offices, beating up lower-level thugs. Naturally there was a backlash. Members of The Club had tremendous resources for gathering information about the Band. David Crosby was the first victim of their revenge, but there were more to follow. At the end, Angel and Iain went off on a holiday to recuperate.

Sir Thomas Clark's evil empire extended to Darala in East Africa in *Angel Abroad* (Hale, 1969). Darala, the capital city of Tagenda, had become known as the "Platinum Playground," a tourist area that attracted wealthy Europeans. Until now it had remained relatively untouched. The death of an Australian reporter caused hotelier Nick Zante to contact Martin Foster, one of the Band of Angels. Martin, his wife, Fiona Merry, Angel, and Iain provided the needed help but not without a personal loss.

The lines of battle were drawn when, in *Angel of Vengeance* (Hale, 1970), Iain and Angel returned to England under false identities. Within a short time, former adversary Chief Inspector Keith Hill made a contact through Greg MacGregor. Three major financiers had been savagely murdered. Their family members had been raped and killed. All primary victims had major investments in Sir Thomas Clark's Industrial Group. Hill, currently on vacation from Scotland Yard, enlisted Angel in his unofficial investigation of the murders, possible connections to the Syndicate, and

Clark's personal project involving valuable mineral rights in South America. Their first goal was to identify members of "The Club," the inner circle of the Syndicate. Martin Foster wanted to avenge his wife's death. Angel wanted more—the destruction of the Syndicate—so she took aggressive and risky measures.

The vacuum created in England when Sir Thomas Clark's syndicate was destroyed attracted a new criminal association in *Angel in Paradise* (Hale, 1970): the Mafia. Mafia leaders in Italy were aware of the role played by Angel and her Band. The Band was depleted by the deaths of David Crosby, Martin Foster, and Fiona Merry. Iain and Angel were currently guests at the home of Iain's cousin, the Duke of Santa Alaro. Tony Gratz, a new recruit to the Band, alerted Angel to possible danger. Her friend Mafioso Don Raffaela Giannola provided the Band with protection.

In *Ask an Angel* (Hale, 1970), Rumanian takeover king Tetau Porno used threats and blackmail to infiltrate English businesses. Greg MacGregor called a meeting of the Band of Angels after the suspicious death of industrialist Trevor Bailey. Iain, Greg, Angel, and Tony Gratz assumed new personas to attract Porno's attention. Crucifixion cruelties by Porno's men were gratuitous. Montrose had a predilection for such excesses.

The British government recruited Angel and the Band in *Send for Angel* (Hale, 1970). The Secretary of State for Defense was one of the British Neo-Fascists who planned to assassinate the Royal Family and seize control of the government in the name of White Supremacy. An official deterrent was unlikely. Sir Philip Castle, secretary of the Integrated Security Committee, asked Angel to delve into a conspiracy that included high government personages. She presented herself as Olwyn Bron, a Welsh-American reporter. Because Iain was ill with dysentery, he was not privy to her plans. Her contacts with Colonel Rhys Morgan of the Welsh Republican Army seemed to be going very well, but eventually he realized that she was a spy. By the time Iain learned that Angel was off on her own, she had been taken prisoner. Her escape happened in time for her to reach London and forestall the revolution. The Queen gave Angel a secret decoration!

During *Angel and the Nero* (Hale, 1971), the Mafia, newly reorganized in England, decided to annihilate the Band. Don Raffaele, who had provided the Bank with protection in the past, was dying. He advised Angel that she and the Band were now vulnerable. Don Raffaele had selected Leonardo Mincora as his replacement for Capo, a man who would carry on his policies. Leonardo might not be acceptable to the other powerful leaders. One, Renzo Saragat aka Ronnie Sergeant, was related to a man killed by the Band. He wanted the leadership role and vengeance. Internecine war within the Mafia followed. Keith Hill and Sir Philip Castle went to work with the Band of Angels. Angel's behavior was a surprise. She seemed willing to negotiate with the Mafia and set up a meeting with Sergeant. The critical moment was a rapier fight between the two of them. Shades of Modesty Blaise! The Band of Angels took a bribe from the Mafia not to interfere. Iain and Angel were tired of violence, ready to retire and marry.

Fanfare for Angel (Hale, 1971) owed a lot to *The Prisoner of Zenda.* Angel, a little bored by retirement, agreed to substitute for Chantal Riprande, who became regnant of Montetauro when her aunt, uncle, and cousins were all killed. The multiple deaths should have been a tip-off that there was trouble ahead. Iain became tense after an attempt was made on Angel/Chantal's life, so he posed as Irish communist Mulvaney and went to Montetauro. He joined the local communists, and even suggested a way to set off a bomb in the palace, but his cover was blown and he was taken prisoner. In order to rescue Iain, Angel pretended to tell the communists where they could find the real Chantal. It all worked out.

The Band had disintegrated by *Angel and the Red Admiral* (Hale, 1972), when the MacKinnons visited Malta. Peter Moore, a former British secret agent who had been underground in Russia, was murdered before he could forward his information on the USSR plans for the Mediterranean area. Sir Philip Castle visited to convince Angel of the need to identify the "Admiral," head of the communist movement on Malta, who had ordered Moore's death. Angel and Iain proceeded by making themselves conspicuous to draw the Admiral out. It worked too well. Iain and a young friend, Maxine, were taken prisoner. Angel, who had barely recovered from dysentery, marshaled her resources, including making the media aware of the possible identity of the Admiral. Young Maxine had fallen deeply in love with Iain. She lay dying in his arms when Angel came to the rescue, but she understood.

The series was never published in the United States. *Where Angel Treads* (Hale, 1969) and *Angel at Arms* (Hale, 1971) were either unavailable or prohibitively expensive in 2005.

Forsythia Brown

Author: Rachel Payes

Forsythia Brown was a naive young novelist living in Greenwich Village. Her beau, Tubby Alexander, was a man in his thirties still dominated by his mother.

In *Forsythia Finds Murder* (Avalon, 1960), she was on vacation in the Poconos when she overheard an altercation between an unidentified man and woman. The woman had threatened to contact the man's wife. Barbara, Mark Thorne's wife, had had one accident already. Mark's first wife indicated that she feared Mark would kill Barbara to inherit her money. Genevieve, a prior wealthy wife, had died in what was determined to be a suicide. With all that background, it might be expected that Barbara would be murdered, but it was Stan Fenton, who had been very attentive to Barbara, who was found dead. Mark was arrested. Forsythia and Tubby proved that the authorities had arrested an innocent person.

As *Shadow of Fear* (Avalon, 1961) began, Forsythia, using binoculars to spy into the dressing room of nightclub singer Estelle Kane, saw the hands of the person who pushed Estelle out of the window to her death. Unwilling to share with the police what she saw, Forsythia settled for an anonymous call insisting that Estelle did not commit suicide. The only ones who didn't figure out that Forsythia had important information were the police and Tubby.

In *Memoirs of Murder* (Avalon, 1964), shortly after thrice-married Addie Montgomery hired Forsythia to ghost write her memoirs, Addie was murdered. Addie had made it clear that she intended to use the memoirs to strike back at people who shared her past. On the assumption that Forsythia had Addie's notes, she was mugged and her apartment burglarized. Forsythia showed little common sense, but there was someone new to rescue her.

The series was bland and simplistic, most suitable for young adult reading.

Helen Bullock

Author: Barbara Ninde Byfield

Helen Bullock, a Pulitzer Prize-winning photojournalist, shared her personal life and her investigations with Rev. Simon Bede, an aide to the Archbishop of Canterbury. A woman with "mousy" brown hair, dark skin, and brown eyes, she was an upper middle class Midwestern liberal with inherited wealth. As her career developed, she maintained a Greenwich Village apartment from which she traveled around the world.

In *Solemn High Murder* (Doubleday, 1975, co-written with Frank Tedeschi), widower Simon Bede visited New York City to interview Rev. Dunstan Owsley for a position in the Church of England. When Owsley was found dead, Simon and Helen learned more about his rigid but highly principled character. At this time there was considerable controversy about who might be the author of *The Black Mass,* a scandalous book. A church much like St. Jude's was described in the narrative. Helen's connections with the publishing industry helped her to identify the author, but Simon looked elsewhere for the killer. In the process, Helen and Simon became a couple.

Byfield continued the series alone with *Forever Wilt Thou Die* (Doubleday, 1976), in which Helen returned to the Midwest to settle the estate of her Uncle Murray, including property in a summer colony. Ambitious plans to develop the area clashed with deeply held feelings that the cottage colony should be preserved. Helen put her own life at risk, but the vicious killers were identified through the efforts of others.

Simon and Helen visited a semi-retirement community designed for creative persons in the Berkshires in *A Harder Thing Than Triumph* (Doubleday, 1977). Their stay was expected to be a short one until Helen broke her leg. Then she became privy to the secrets within the community. Channing Adaams was killed by a fall from a sundeck, possibly as a result of a prank. They delayed his funeral because his wife, Louisa, had disappeared. Belatedly they learned that she too was dead, and the tragic cause of her death. That information explained how Channing died.

Although the couple lived together in England as *A Parcel of Their Fortunes* (Doubleday, 1979) opened, Helen traveled to Morocco to help an old friend who was suffering from hepatitis. Arthur didn't want a nurse. He wanted Helen's help in securing a commission to build a villa and perhaps hotels. Lord Stanley Overton was spending a considerable amount of money in the area on projects that included movies. Coincidentally, Simon's son Fergus was in charge of the movie project. Helen and eventually Simon were drawn into the problems of a rehabilitation center funded by Overton. The death of an elderly man, also suffering from hepatitis, led to the first hint of murder in the narrative. The motive was in the past, events occurring in a Spanish Moroccan prison camp.

Byfield provided excellent physical descriptions of her settings and interesting characters with complex motivations, usually involving events in the past.

Sue Carstairs
Author: Elizabeth Linington aka Lesley Egan and Dell Shannon

See: Sue Carstairs Maddox, Section 5, page 336.

Vera Castang

Author: Nicolas Freeling

French police officer Henri Castang married Vera, a Czechoslovakian gymnast, who defected to be with him. Later, an accident at the exercise bar left her seriously disabled. Vera's struggle to regain mobility, her desire to have children, her political ties to her homeland, and her work as a graphic artist all figured in the Castang series. She was not a classic beauty, but before her accident had been graceful. It was her athletic ability that brought her from a peasant home to international gymnastic competitions. The defection ended her relationship with her father, a dedicated communist.

Vera's insights as to the peasant mentality helped Castang in *A Dressing of Diamond* (Harper, 1974). Both Henri and Vera had been shocked at the disappearance of eight-year-old Rachel, daughter of their friends Bernard and Collette Delavigne. Collette served as a Children's Judge, and the possibility existed that the abduction was connected to her work. A telephone call from the kidnappers was recorded, Collette's court records were checked, and a tentative identification made.

Vera served as a volunteer visitor in the prison system during *The Bugles Blowing* (Harper, 1976). She was assigned to Gilbert La Touche, formerly a senior government official, accused of killing six persons including his wife. They became close, so close that eventually she made certain that she told him of a possible conflict of interest and discontinued her visits. La Touche would not defend himself against the charges. Vera respected his wish to die and kept his confidences even from Henri.

Her artistic ability contributed in *The Night Lords* (Pantheon, 1978). A young woman's corpse had been found in the trunk of a car belonging to a distinguished English jurist, Sir James Armitage. Powerful forces pushed the idea that no one could seriously consider Armitage or members of his family to be involved. A casual meeting in the park between Vera and the Armitages convinced Vera otherwise. She confronted Sir James with his guilt and insisted that he confess his responsibility to Henri.

Vera's participation in *Castang's City* (Pantheon, 1980) had nothing to do with Henri's investigation. While he focused on the murder of businessman Etienne Marcel, Vera gave birth to their daughter, Lydia.

During *Wolfnight* (Pantheon, 1982) Henri's relentless pursuit of those who kidnapped and killed Viviane Kranitz had unexpected consequences. A Polish-French-American organization seeking to free Poland from Communist domination struck back. The Comtesse de Rubempre, a member of the group, had been arrested. After Vera was kidnapped, Henri resigned his position and set out to exchange the Comtesse for Vera. She remained calm throughout the experience.

The Back of the North Wind (Heinemann, 1983) contained no role for Vera in Henri's official investigations, but it explored her friendship with Judith Richards, wife of Henri's superior officer at the time. They shared a semi-feminist view as to the role of a policeman's wife. They neither sanctioned equality nor competition with men, but acknowledged what a woman can bring to a relationship or a community.

No Part in Your Death (Heinemann, 1984) narrated a series of three incidents in Henri's professional and personal life. Vera had the greatest impact in the first episode, during which she accompanied Henri to a conference in Germany. While she and daughter Lydia roamed the city, they met Birgit, a young woman whose in-laws had the authorities searching for her as mentally ill. Vera took Brigit back to Henri, who counseled her to return to her husband's family, even accompanied her there. He felt some responsibility for a resulting murder. So, probably did Vera.

Three strands of narration entwined in *Not As Far As Velma* (Mysterious Press, 1989). Vera played no role until the final act. Vera and Judith, Adrian Richards' wife, warned Robert MacLeod, an erratic news correspondent, and Ada Sergent, proprietor of a popular hotel, to leave the country because they were in danger from local right-wing groups. The couple escaped to South America, but were killed there.

In *Those in Peril* (Mysterious Press, 1990), Henri betrayed both his wife and his daughter Lydia. His punishment for balking the political police had been reassignment to the Art Fraud Unit in Paris. He betrayed Vera by an affair with his female superior officer even as Vera was fighting off a rapist. Her defense ended in the man's death. In an effort to get evidence against an aristocratic pederast, Henri used Lydia as bait for a trap. Once again he was reprimanded, then promoted and reassigned to Brussels in an administrative capacity. Their marriage had suffered from Vera's illness and the long wait for children, but his infidelity did the most serious damage. He had resisted a temptation earlier in *Cold Iron* (Viking, 1986)

Henri's lateral transfer to Brussels added espionage cases to his duties in *Flander's Sky* (Mysterious Press, 1992) aka *The Pretty Howtown.* Uprooted by the move, Vera planned a trip to Slovakia to see her mother. Her estranged father had died without forgiving her "desertion." The trip did not live up to Vera's expectations. On her return, both she and Henri were shocked at the rape/murder of Iris, Irish wife of Henri's superior officer and friend, Harold Claverhouse. The chapters alternated between Vera and Henri.

The Seacoast of Bohemia (Mysterious Press, 1995) brought Madame Rogier, the mother of a missing child, to Henri because the police had failed. Although Vera actually found the boy, made arrangements for his transfer, and escorted him home, Henri used the information gained during his investigation to thwart a white slavery ring operating in Europe.

Vera was deeply affected in *A Dwarf Kingdom* (Little Brown, London, 1996) when her first grandchild was kidnapped. Her independent efforts to trade a major inheritance for the infant only complicated Henri's search. Freeling indicated in the conclusion that Henri and Vera would not return. It was time. Each narrative had become more introspective, more difficult to read.

Vera played no significant role in *You Who Know* (Mysterious Press, 1994), or *Sabine* aka *Lake Isle* (Random House, 1980).

Darby Castle

Author: Jan Michaels, pseudonym for Jan Milella

Darby Castle's career as a country music singer would not usually lead to solving mysteries. She was a casually dressed Southerner who spent most of her personal time with her manager/lover Jimmy McShane as they traveled via a personal bus between appearances.

Nashville promoter Max Kingston may have been skimming off Darby's profits in *Sing a Song of Murder* (Zebra, 1978), but it was not she who strangled him. Joe Green, her New York accountant, had checked Max's books and demanded that he repay the money. Jimmy wanted to punch Max out, so after the murder he was arrested. There were other suspects: Bernadette, Darby's maid, whom he had seduced; Billy Jenkins, former basketball star, who played bass for Darby; and Joe Green, who was discovered to have missing cash in his room. Darby investigated aggressively with police support, using a tape recorder and a gun in the process. Height was a clue to the solution.

During *Death on the Late Show* (Zebra, 1979), Darby was a guest on a late-night performance of Gordon Garrity's talk show. She was sandwiched in between a British actor and a fish act. Garrity was killed by poisoned fish when he inserted his arm into the part of the aquarium where the non-poisonous fish were stored. Darby and Jimmy built a case against the murderer by researching their host's personal life and tapes of the show.

A Zebra with a different background.

Edwina Charles

Author: Mignon Warner

Edwina Charles had an exotic quality, perhaps arising from her Italian-Austrian heritage or her involvement in show business and clairvoyance. She was slim, slightly taller than average, with short feathering blonde hair and dark blue eyes. Her mother had been an opera star whose singer-husband decamped after Edwina's birth. A half-brother, Cyril Forbes, wandered in and out of the narratives. When Edwina ended her diminishing career in entertainment, she turned to providing psychic consultations in the village of Little Giddings. Her personal life had included three marriages by the time she was 40, all of which ended in divorce.

As *A Medium for Murder* aka *A Nice Way to Die* (McKay, 1977) opened, Edwina (stage name, Madame Adele Herrmann) had been living quietly in the village for eight years. The deaths of two women, one of whom had given her a valuable piece of jewelry, placed Edwina under suspicion until she used the jewelry and herself as bait to trap the killer.

In *The Tarot Murders* (McKay, 1978), a killer sent tarot cards to potential victims and left them on the corpses. Tarot expert Rupert Roxeth, who stabled horses in the area, had been advising the police on the case. He was not pleased when Edwina took an interest. There was a village fete scheduled at which Edwina was to read tarot cards for charity. By this time there had been three deaths connected to the cards, and Edwina believed a fourth would occur soon, perhaps during the fete. She was right, which was little comfort. Nor was the identification of the killer, a man with mental problems.

Edwina attended a magicians conference in *Death in Time* (Doubleday, 1982), the Easter Fiesta of the Mystic Circle. Nigel Playford and his sister Cynthia were to judge the skill contest. Her body was found impaled on a graveyard fence. She had been tossed off a mountain lift. It was discovered that Cynthia's past included an affair with Frank Sexton, a married man, and an abortion after another relationship. A crystal ball reading convinced Edwina that either Frank or his wife, Kath, would die, so she arranged police protection. Unfortunately, it was not enough. The resolution of Cynthia's death came from an envelope that she had left for Edwina.

In *The Girl Who Was Clairvoyant* (Doubleday, 1982), recent widow Peggy May had written Edwina for advice, but the misdirected letter arrived only after Peggy had died. Peggy May, Mary Farrow (mother of Pearl, a clairvoyant teenager), and Dorrie Kemp had grown up together. Dorrie's death was next. Edwina returned to her past and that of young Pearl Farrow, to understand the connection between Pearl and a series of murders.

Mae Holliday, the unpopular spinster postmistress of Little Giddings, in *Devil's Knell* (Doubleday, 1983) consulted Edwina about her amnesia. She revealed that she had found herself in Little Giddings at age 16 with no knowledge of her past, no identification, and 100 pounds in cash. Mae must have been a danger to someone, because she was killed and left with a stake in her heart.

In *Illusion* (Doubleday, 1984), the cast from a musical took a mini-bus to visit the country home of the show's producer-director, Danny Midas. On the way home, the bus broke down, so the group started back to Danny's but stopped at an elaborate manor. Only then did Danny reveal that this was his home, not the place they had first visited. Edwina had also been tricked into coming to the manor. Danny wanted her to discover who was trying to kill him, but it was his sister-in-law Freda Cobb who was murdered. An unexpected connection between Edwina and Danny emerged during the investigation.

A more relaxed, more personable Edwina appeared in *Speak No Evil* (Doubleday, 1985). When investigator Tony Manners died mysteriously, Edwina took an interest at the insistence of "Jimmy Valentine," a disreputable friend of one of her former husbands. Jimmy suspected that Tony's death was motivated by her participation in the Pym murder trial. Pym, an actor who had been found not guilty by reason of insanity in the death of his wife, was known to have died with his hand taped over his ear. Dr. Mac-Donald, who testified at the trial, died with his hand taped over his eyes. Justice Halahan, who tried the case, was found dead from hanging. This was an excellent mystery.

During *Exit Mr. Punch* (Breese, 1994) Edwina's reclusive half-brother Cyril offered no explanation for the inconsistencies in his alibi when young singer Judith Caldicott was murdered in his home. Cyril had discovered Judith's talent when she was singing in the church choir. The murder of Alison Cockburn just before her marriage had a definite connection and occurred while Cyril was in jail. It was followed by the suicide of Jack Graves, known to have harassed Alison. Cyril was released, but Edwina would not stop her investigation until she was satisfied the murderer had been caught. She identified him by his emotional state.

Warner's books have elaborate plots, which stress the impact of the past upon the lives of the suspects. Mrs. Charles' clairvoyance played some part in her deductions, but more often she proceeded with routine methods of investigation. Not all of the series have been reprinted in the United States.

Charlie's Angels

Author: Max Franklin, pseudonym for Richard Deming, novelization of the television series using scripts by Ivan Goff and Ben Roberts

The series featured former policewomen (three at a time) from assorted backgrounds, recruited as private investigators by a reclusive employer. They initially appeared in assorted colors: Jill Majors (ash blonde); Kelly Garrett (dark brown); and Sabrina Duncan (a divorced brunette). As actresses portraying the roles left the program, suitable substitutes were developed.

Charlie's Angels (Ballantine, 1977) revolved around the probate estate of Vincent Le Maire, whose body had never been found. Kelly posed as a bogus beneficiary, while Sabrina stood in for the real heiress, Janet Le Maire, daughter of Vincent's first marriage. Kelly used her charms on Vincent's second wife and Beau Cruel, manager of the Samarra Winery. She sought to convince him to purchase a swampy section of land that "might" have oil deposits and might contain Vincent's corpse. It didn't work out as planned, but all was tied up in time for the action ending.

In *The Killing Kind* (Ballantine, 1977), Kelly, as a fashion photographer; Jill, as a tennis pro; and Sabrina, as an attorney, investigated when Brooke Anderson, reporter friend of Charlie, was murdered. The young woman had refused to sell her material detailing problems at Moonshadows to hotel manager Paul Terranova. Sabrina hoped to acquire the manuscript from Brooke's father, but he had been kidnapped. The problem was tied in to a scheme to get reserved coastal land for a big marina development.

During *Angels on a String* (Ballantine, 1977), the trio became aware that an imposter had been substituted for Prof. Peter Wycinski, a Polish national leader. The narrative contained more than the usual amount of threatened rape and brutality. Bosley got out of the boardroom and into the action by rescuing Jill and Kelly. Sabrina saved the U.S. Assistant Secretary of State from an embarrassing situation.

Angels in Chains (Ballantine, 1977) continued to emphasize sexual aspects of the dangers to which the investigators were exposed. In order to investigate a Louisiana women's prison system, the trio allowed themselves to be arrested and sentenced to the Pine Parish Prison Farm for Women, where they were expected to entertain men who sold products to the institutions. Charlie had been tipped off to the abuses by the sister of Elizabeth Hunter, a backpacker who had been railroaded into the system.

The Angels' physical skills helped in *Angels on Ice* (Ballantine, 1978), when Kelly joined an ice show to investigate the kidnappings of skating stars Helene Robinson and Jack Ward. In their absence Kelly, an experienced skater, became a replacement. Two other substitutes were prevented from substituting real guns for fakes in a dance number in order to assassinate Arab leaders.

The pattern was that the trio went undercover until someone's true identity was revealed and she needed to be rescued by the others. The episodes did not translate well into books.

Lisa Clark

Author: Amelia Walden

Young adult Lisa Clark was an independently wealthy woman, under the guardianship of private detective Jake Jefferson. She had an excellent education, spoke a variety of mid-Eastern and European languages, owned a yacht, flew a plane, and was a skilled photographer. Lisa was provided with incredible skills and resources to pursue her chosen career. She wanted to join Jake in his international private investigation firm.

During *The Case of the Diamond Eye* (Westminster, 1969), Lisa used her father's photographic files to supplement the agency's resources, but Jake did the detecting.

In *What Happened to Candy Carmichael* (Westminster, 1970), when Jake was too busy, Lisa took on the search for missing heiress Candy Carmichael, one of twin daughters of Thornton Carmichael. Niles Erickson had broken his engagement to rebellious Candy to marry her "oh so perfect sister" Chrissie. When Candy's corpse was found, Jake took an interest. He flew all over the Caribbean seeking new friends who had become important to Candy. When he went on to Italy, he took Lisa along so he could protect her. On arriving in Paris, Jake learned that all four of the new friends had also been murdered.

As *Valerie Valentine Is Missing* (Westminster, 1971) began, Lisa was determined to prove she could handle a case on her own. Locating artist Valerie Valentine might be that opportunity. Others were looking for her, seriously enough to kill Hans Lange, a Dutch painter who had been Valerie's teacher. Her probe took Lisa on a trip through Europe, where she regularly encountered opposition, convincing her that there was a political agenda behind the search.

In *Where Was Everyone When Sabrina Screamed?* (Westminster, 1973), Lisa was contacted by actor Peter Joring, who wanted her to find his stepdaughter, Linda Demarest. Linda might be in Morocco. Jake Jefferson was already there for an international conference but in poor shape because of a beating. Gary Mitchell, a former boyfriend of Lisa, now a CIA agent, was also seeking Linda. Linda may have become Sabrina, a hippie singer. Lisa's plan for a solo case evaporated when Gary took over, trained her, and placed her in an undercover position. While Gary was out of town, Lisa saved Sabrina/Linda and discovered the man behind the drug ring that had captured her.

Lisa was in her twenties. Her series has been classified by some as young adult literature.

Constance Cobble
Author: Stanton Forbes, writing as Tobias Wells

Constance Cobble became a widow under unusual circumstances, having shot her husband, Roger, by mistake ten years before. She supported herself by writing historical novels, but had recently begun a narrative in which her friends appeared.

She and Wellesley police chief Knute Severson visited a defunct tropical resort as potential investors in *Hark, Hark, the Watchdogs Bark* (Doubleday, 1975). They wanted a tax shelter. Darby and Maria Ponsonby had just the project for them and other investors, whom they invited to La Belle Creole resort. What they found was the head of a local woman, possibly involved in the drug traffic. It was Severson who waded through the romantic entanglements of the local backers and, despite being taken prisoner, caught the killers.

Constance, now living in St. Martin, resurfaced in *The Last Will & Testament of Constance Cobble* (Doubleday, 1980), a strange and difficult book within a book, each with its own characters and plot, both including death by drowning.

Stanton Forbes had written better mysteries.

Cody
Author: David Brierley

The woman known as Cody was born in Sussex, England, and was the daughter of a doctor. Cody, who did not attend a university, was recruited by British Intelligence, then sent to CIA headquarters at Langley, Virginia, for training. She found working for the CIA oppressive and humiliating.

Rejecting government bureaucracy, Cody became an independent investigator, working out of a Paris apartment. Single at age 28, she was average height with dark curly hair and brown eyes. The lack of a first name enhanced her hard image and enigmatic character. Cody was a tough, unemotional woman, physically and mentally alert for danger.

As *Cold War* (Faber, 1979) opened, Cody visited Samuel Agate, a hospitalized man whom she had seen struck by a car while crossing the street to her apartment building. This was not an impulsive act. Agate had been on his way to meet Cody. He had a message for her, but his condition was such that she could barely understand him. It must also have been important, because he was murdered shortly thereafter. His death brought Crevecoeur, an official of Sûreté National, into Cody's life, where he remained for the rest of the series—not as a lover or friend, but as a sometime adversary, a man who used her to achieve his goals. They followed on separate tracks the disappearance of a young French scientist who had defected to the communists. Cody's CIA training came in handy when she was kidnapped and questioned during psychological torture at a facility for the criminally insane.

In *Blood Group O* (Summit, 1984), Crevecoeur sought Cody's unofficial help in the kidnapping of Simone, the nine-year-old daughter of Theo Poelsma, a diamond merchant. Although Crevecoeur had power over her through the Sûreté, Cody had evidence that he had killed a man, so a balance existed in their relationship. Cody used the Mafia, her own sexuality, and a friendly Dutch sea captain to foil efforts to assassinate the U.S. president.

Cody was hired to find Bert Borries, a pilot missing on a special assignment in Tunisia, during *Skorpion's Death* (Summit, 1986). She had been hired by Bert's wife, Ella. As usual, Crevecoeur was on the scene, but he was fighting for his own life. Cody allied herself with Antoine Nortier, a blind newspaperman. He and Cody ventured out to Borj Mechaab in the midst of an Army revolt. They were captured by Skorpion, an illegal organization that had purchased smuggled weapons from French manufacturers. Action from then on: escape, a trek across the desert, cooperation with Crevecoeur.

Snowline (Coronet, 1987) took Cody to Central America to deliver funds to what she believed to be a rural medical clinic. Her departure from France was hastened by the murder of the man who hired her to deliver the funds and the knowledge that Crevecoeur was looking for her. Later events and Crevecoeur made her aware that she had carried the ransom for a downed cocaine plane and caused the capture of a Sûreté agent who would be tortured for information. Obviously, she would have to take action to remedy the situation.

In *Death & Co.* (Little, Brown, 1999), Cody was hired by powerful businessman Andre Ledru after an incident in which his wife had been killed and their newly adopted daughter kidnapped. She was shocked to realize that what Ledru wanted was revenge for his wife's death, because it was an insult to him personally. He had little interest in the child's welfare, but Cody put it at the top of her list. Cody and a friend, journalist Al Richards, worked together, but both came under the strong influence of Crevecoeur. Cody had discovered that he and other Sûreté personnel were keeping Ledru under observation. They had a strong interest in him because he was merchandizing industrial secrets to Eastern terrorists.

Cody, who despised the CIA for their ruthless tactics, had learned her lessons well. When necessary, she was a killer. Brierley's narratives had gripping opening chapters and convoluted plots.

Maggie Courtney

Author: Ann Pearson

Maggie Courtney, a financially independent college professor at a Southern college, had little respect for the ability of local police to solve a crime, even though Police Lt. Jake Travis had been a classmate. She was unmarried but had a cat (Charlie), a beau (art professor Ted Meredith), and a housemate (Asst. Prof. Harriet McGraw).

In *Murder By Degrees* (Zebra, 1979), when Dr. Ruby Murdoch, head of the English department, was killed, Maggie found the body. She immediately decided that this was a case of murder, partly because Murdoch was so unpopular. Unpopular wasn't enough for murder, so Maggie had to look more closely to find a serious motive. There were subsequent incidents (the disappearance of new chairman George Purvis) and murder (Maggie's housemate, Harriet McGraw). The color of a hydrangea tipped her off.

A Stitch in Time (Zebra, 1979) was less pretentious. "Dr." Courtney (she did like the title) was concerned about the physical deterioration of Anna Mary Hoffman, an elderly home economics dean. The Dean had an angina attack after one look at a tapestry during her retirement party. It became plain that money set aside to purchase it and other tapestries had been misused. Substitutions had been made. This time Maggie worked with Jake Travis.

During *Cat Got Your Tongue?* (Zebra, 1980) Maggie entered her very ordinary cat, Charlie, in a cat show. Pushkin, a valuable feline owned by Phil Aronson, was kidnapped. The ransom note, unaccountably, was sent to Maggie. Although no ransom was ever paid, the cat was returned; however, Phil Aronson was murdered. Additional deaths and attacks followed, which were later attributed to the victims' knowledge of the killer's identity. A significant discovery in cat breeding motivated the killers. Maggie received a proposal from her art professor beau, and then faded from the scene.

Light reading at the Zebra level. Each book planted clues on the cover portrait.

Mrs. Elma Craggs

Author: H. R. F. Keating

Mrs. Elma Craggs, an English widow who supported herself by doing domestic chores, took great pride in her work.

During *Death of a Fat God* (Dutton, 1966) Emma (as she was known then) enjoyed cleaning the opera house. She not only knew her operas, but was familiar with the performers. She was aware of their peccadilloes: the showboating, the petty cruelties, and the pressures even on seasoned singers. Mary Arthur, an exceptional newcomer to the cast, was killed on the stage when a prop vehicle malfunctioned. Superintendent Pryde of Scotland Yard took charge, informing the media that the target for the accident had been egotistical Jean-Artaban Pivoine, the male lead. He made a quick arrest of Clarissa Glass, whom Pivione had humiliated. Mrs. Craggs had to set him straight.

Mrs. Craggs, now Elma, reappeared in *Mrs. Craggs: Crimes Cleaned Up* (St. Martin, 1986), a collection of short stories. Elma was placed in a variety of settings (the House of Lords, the opera, and an antique house). Her awareness of surroundings clued her in to solutions. She was a delightful woman, no older than in her prior book, published 20 years earlier, reminiscent of Paul Gallico's Mrs. 'Arris.

Thea Crawford

Author: Jessica Mann

Thea Crawford, an archaeologist with a photographic memory, was described as small, slim, with dark hair and blue eyes. She shared an unconventional marriage with journalist Sylvester Crawford, who had roving feet and hands. Thea accepted Sylvester's womanizing and foreign travel in exchange for acceptance of her career and an occasional infidelity of her own.

In *Troublecross* aka *The Only Security* (McKay, 1973), Thea, along with son Clovis, moved to Buriton University to fill the newly funded Chair in Archaeology. Her appointment had been a disappointment to Roger Thurston, who had hoped to be promoted. An archaeological find unearthed by Clovis at Thurston's digging became a bone of contention with local landholders. To whom did it belong? The question would hinge upon the mental stability of a prior owner at the time the property was sold. Thea exposed fraud and murder, but only after the killer disposed of others who might have implicated him.

Sylvester was the "captive" in *Captive Audience* (McKay, 1975). Injuries received in the Orient encased him in a plaster cast. Buriton was experiencing town-gown problems, exacerbated by a new administrator, which led to a serious fire. Bored and restless, Sylvester relaxed only with Jenny, a student leader. Then, able to maneuver with crutches, he attended the trial of Ian Macardle, the young student accused of arson, but his involvement with Jenny and his anger with the administrator caused him to lose control, with dire consequences.

Thea appeared in the Tamara Hoyland series as a friend and mentor of the younger woman. Mann's books produced that agreeable tension between a sense of urgency to read quickly, enjoyment of the action, and an awareness that close attention must be paid to the details in her writing.

Tessa Crichton
Author: Anne Morice, pseudonym for Felicity Shaw

Tessa Crichton was a charming actress with access to official circles through her police officer husband, Robin Price.

The couple met in *Death in the Grand Manor* (Macmillan, 1970), when Tessa, then a novice actress, visited her cousin, playwright Toby Crichton, and his second wife, Matilda. Toby wanted Tessa to keep his 11-year-old daughter, Ellen, company for a few weeks. The neighborhood was in an uproar. Douglas Cornford attempted to place a barbwire fence around the Common. The Cornford plan was designed to influence the neighbors to sell out. Douglas was notably abusive to his wife, Bronwen. When she was found dead, Robin was assigned to investigate her death. They became close, but she ignored his advice to stay out of the case. The solution was uncomfortably close to home.

Murder in Married Life (Macmillan, 1971) opened after Robin had been transferred to London and he and Tessa had married. A casual encounter with Julian Brown led to his request that she read the draft of his memoirs, of which she had a copy typed up. There was incriminating and/or embarrassing information in the memoirs, the possible source of the blackmail that Robin was investigating. They were dealing with murder now: Julian's, then a second murder. Cousin Toby rescued Tessa, who had prudently left a note with the police but given the wrong address.

Robin and Tessa combined mystery with vacation in the countryside in *Death of a Gay Dog* (Macmillan, 1971). He had suggested that they visit the Burleigh area, where there had been a series of house burglaries. Artworks, which had been part of the thefts, had been returned to the insurance companies for rewards. Tessa spent part of her time having her portrait painted by her friend Christabel Blake. When art expert Sir Maddox Brand was poisoned in their presence, Robin's vacation was over, and Tessa's investigation had just begun.

Robin and Tessa took her 16-year-old cousin Ellen to Paris in *Murder on French Leave* (Macmillan, 1972). Soon they found themselves surrounded by friends, some attracted by Tessa's fame. Ellen's interest in Sven Carlsen, who worked for International Division for Engineering & Science, made Tessa uncomfortable. Leila Baker, one of the new friends, was murdered, then Ellen was kidnapped. She proved to be very competent and escaped to help Tessa trap a spy.

Robin, now at Scotland Yard, was assigned to a Storhampton area murder in *Death and the Dutiful Daughter* (St. Martin, 1974). He was too busy with his case to help Tessa in the murder of aged diva Maud Stirling. Evidence built up that Bitsy, Maud's daughter, was the intended victim in Maud's death, in a subsequent death, and finally in her own. Fortunately, Robin finished his case and joined in the investigation. His police information, combined with insight from a dream, alerted Tessa to prevent another murder.

Tessa visited the home of Sir Magnus Benson-Jones, currently standing for Parliament, in *Death of a Heavenly Twin* (St. Martin, 1974). Benson-Jones had twin daughters: Sarah, currently engaged to actor "Kit" Cosby, and Julie, who had been disabled since she had polio as a child. Tessa was invited to give a speech at a local fete, at which Sarah was to be the fortune teller. She had the bad fortune to be killed in the tent. Suspicion was pointed first at Henry Ngali Mbwala, a black servant whom Sarah had ridiculed. That became less likely when Martin Graham, a ceramic potter subsidized by Sir Magnus, was injured by a hit-and-run driver and his wife, Babs, was killed with a golf club. Tessa was caught going through the killer's room but was rescued by a servant. Robin's official status was less important in Tessa's subsequent cases.

Killing With Kindness (St. Martin, 1975) was a disorganized account of Tessa's investigation of the death of Michael Parsons, who had been a friend, as had his wife, Brenda. In probing his associates, Tessa saw a different side of Michael: a seemingly generous man, but one who created havoc in the lives he affected. A second death followed, that of Johnny Masters, who had been convinced by Mike to have optional surgery that left him severely handicapped. Tessa settled for dual killers.

Serena Hargrove, Tessa's godmother, called on her to mediate family feuds in *Nursery Tea and Poison* (St. Martin, 1975). It concerned twins again, Pelham and Rupert Hargrave, who had very different lives. Rupert had inherited a fortune, gone into business, married, but died shortly after leaving his wife, Serena, pregnant. Pelham had traveled to Canada after dropping out of school, then on to California. He had not until recently returned to England, even though he inherited Rupert's fortune. Pelham had allowed Serena and her daughter, Primrose, the use of a small house on the estate in exchange for managing the property. Jake Farrer, a Hollywood director, had rented the manor house. Now Pelham returned with an American wife, Lindy. Not everyone welcomed them. Tessa arrived too late. Nannie, the servant who had raised the twins and Primrose, died from Warfarin. Lindy also became ill, eventually disappeared, and was found dead. Tessa had failed to share clues, including Nannie's dying words, with Robin. Too late to stop the killer from escaping.

Cousin Ellen's marriage to Jeremy Roxburgh in *Death of a Wedding Guest* (St. Martin, 1976) was marred by the death of Irene, Ellen's mother. Both Ellen and Jeremy were on the rebound from prior relationships. Irene, who had arrived late because of a hit-and-run accident she had witnessed, had keeled over after drinking the bridal toast. Was the glass meant for her? Or Desmond, Ellen's former beau, who was discovered dead in bed later? Weaker plotting than most of the series.

Tessa toured America in *Murder in Mimicry* (St. Martin, 1977) in a play written by Toby, but suffering from the dissension among staff and performers. Gilbert Mann, the male lead, was a backstabber, a manipulator, and no admirer of Toby's work. There were accidents, false messages, breaking and entering. Then Hugo Dunstan, a clever comedian and mimic in the cast, was found stabbed in his bed. A major breakthrough came when they learned that photos had been stolen, photos that might have been used for blackmail.

Tessa accepted work where she could find it. In *Scared to Death* (St. Martin, 1978), she appeared in one of Toby's plays produced as part of a local arts festival in Storhampton. Edna Mortimer controlled the estate of Benjamin, the older man she had married late in life. She had complained lately of seeing "doppelgangers," which may have contributed to her death, attributed to a stroke. After bequests to Edna's sister, Alice, and a former governess, Tilly Prettyman, the estate was left to Camilla, Benjamin's daughter, and her intended, Bernard Plowman. Tessa developed a chart tracing the appearances of the doppelgangers with the alibis for the time of their appearances and proved that someone caused the stroke through terror. That person continued a reign of terror with another murder.

In *Murder by Proxy* (St. Martin, 1978), cousin Toby was suspicious of the Purveyance ménage, his neighbors. Annie, who had gone to school with Tessa, lived with Harry Purveyance, had borne him a child, and was pregnant. She thought someone was trying to kill her. Cath, Harry's legal wife, and their daughter Mary shared the accommodations. Tessa thought Annie might be right, because if she gave birth to a male child, it could change everything. Jane Ewart had left her husband and had her eye on Harry. Annie, Mary, and Jane all died in short order. This was far too confusing. However, none of it seemed to bother Harry, an overweight and overspending man with some special appeal to women.

In her youth, Tessa had studied art and ballet at Waterside School. She returned there in *Murder in Outline* (St. Martin, 1979) to judge a drama contest. Headmistress Connie Bland was still in charge, and her husband, Billy, was still blatantly unfaithful. There were rumors of spies and a definite murder.

The manipulations of a theatrical "angel" ended in death during *Death in the Round* (St. Martin, 1980). Tessa was out in the provinces, sharing a house with a fellow actress while on tour. Elfreida Henshaw, a wealthy sponsor, was imposing her wishes on the cast by insisting that Melanie, an 18-year-old former juvenile delinquent, be given a part in the show. Elfreida's death may have solved a casting problem, but it led to Melanie's disappearance. Eventually she too was found dead. Tessa discerned a motive that would probably not sound valid other than in theatrical circles.

In *The Men in Her Death* (St. Martin, 1981), Tessa was asked to trace a young American woman in London. Lorraine, a longtime friend of Tessa, had told her about Sandy Thurloe. Sandy was an aspiring actress who had shared an apartment with Jocelyn Hunt, a male actor who sponged on her generosity. The story interested Tessa sufficiently that she interviewed Jocelyn and his sister, Jackie, plus the landlady of the apartment building. Jackie maintained that although she didn't know where Sandy was, she had left voluntarily. At that point there was a ransom demand of $2,000,000 for Sandy's return. A moot demand, as the unknown corpse in one of Robin's cases was Sandy.

Tessa withheld information from the authorities, including Robin, in *Hollow Vengeance* (St. Martin, 1982). She was invited to the countryside by her friend Elsa Carrington and made aware of the chaos created by a new neighbor, Mrs. Trelawney. She had evicted a shiftless tenant whose daughter was engaged to Elsa's son. She had cut down great old trees on her property. A neighbor's dog was injured in a trap placed on her land. Even her grandson David disassociated himself from her depredations. So who died? Sweet old Geoffrey Dearing, who had organized a group to save the trees. Tessa called on Mrs. Trelawney, whom she recognized as a woman she had met in Canada under another name. She was told to mind her own business. But Mrs. Trelawney was murdered, and murder was Tessa's business.

Dolly, the wife of aging actor Phillip Mickleton, was strangled in *Sleep of Death* (St. Martin, 1983). Before her death, Phillip had received threatening letters. Because of financial straits, the producers shut down the play in which Tessa and Phillip had been appearing. Realizing how depressed all this had made her, Robin suggested that Tessa write her recollections to find Dolly's killer.

An unsolved murder case, the death of Pauline Oakes, a real estate agency employee, bothered Robin several years later in *Getting Away with Murder* (St. Martin, 1985) when he and Tessa vacationed at Mattingly Grange. Robin might need a vacation, but Tessa wanted a murder to solve. Louisa and Jake, owners of Mattingly Grange, had lived near Chissingfield, where the unsolved murder occurred, but that was two years ago. Now there were burglaries, arson, and a fresh murder. Verity, the Mattingly Grange desk clerk with whom Jake was enjoying an affair, was found strangled.

Whenever cousin Toby had problems with his neighbors, he summoned Tessa, as in *Murder Post-Dated* (St. Martin, 1984). At a formal dinner, Tessa learned (1) that Mrs. Laycock believed that someone was trying to poison her family—this may not have been true, but two nights later she was burned to death—and (2) that everyone had worried about Rosamund, the wealthy wife of James McGrath, who had disappeared, until a letter from her was received by Louise Marsden. According to James, he had returned late one night to find her missing, a bloody knife, and stained bed sheets. He did not report this initially because he knew he would be the logical suspect. When her body was found, he was arrested. Tessa tied the two cases together

Myrtle Spragge, realizing that events described in her mystery novels were occurring to her friends, believed herself to be a witch in *Dead on Cue* (St. Martin, 1985). She had shared this problem with Tessa and revealed that the only copy of her latest book was missing. A television play script offered to Tessa sounded remarkably like Myrtle's book. Concerned about plagiarism, Tessa tried to reach Myrtle, but she had died of a heart attack. Soon afterwards Gwen, the suspected plagiarist, was also dead. So there was still the question of who was the plagiarist and who the killer.

The later Morice mysteries declined in structure and analysis.

In *Publish and Be Killed* (St. Martin, 1987), Tessa explored the relationships of playwright Sheridan Seymour with his three legitimate (Baba, a marchioness; Angie; and Dodo) and three illegitimate (Pam Tilling, Tom, and Rita) children, and their assorted progeny. Seymour had left his fortune to Tom, whose mother had been the deceased Kitty Lampeter. The others, particularly the legitimate children, were furious, even more so when Tom blew the money financing his own plays. Arson to a home supposedly occupied by a "Dodie Watson" had someone else's dead body in it. By this time the whole family was aware that Tessa was meddling. One was aware enough to slit his wrists.

During *Treble Exposure* (St. Martin, 1988) Tessa invited her friend Lorraine Thurloe (who appeared before in *The Men in Her Death*) and her friend Beverly Finkelstein to Toby's for lunch. After they ate, Beverly, who had recently recovered from a mental illness, took a walk from which she returned greatly agitated. Later the body of Barbara Landauer, an American journalist, was found nearby. Lorraine and Beverly were on a tour of mystery sites. Beverly's problems were such that she and Lorraine were forced to travel separately and meet the group at the sites. The tour group seemed to be the focus of the inquiry. Landauer was known to have done exposés of such tours. Beverly knew who had killed Barbara, and, later, another member of the group, but she withheld the information too long. Very unsatisfactory conclusion.

The 80th birthday of Evadne, the widow of deceased actor Hartley Deverell, brought family members from as far as Australia to England in *Fatal Charm* (St. Martin, 1989). Tessa was included among the guests. She and Robin learned the next morning that Eliza, the youngest of the Deverell daughters, had been murdered. Evadne had nothing good to say about Conrad, Eliza's husband and the father of the child she carried. Eliza, they learned, had come to England earlier with a script that Rodney Blakemore was seriously considering. It disappeared while in Tessa's possession. Sex, not drama, was responsible for the murder. The killer committed suicide. This was below Morice's standards. Although subordinate characters were well described, Tessa was never developed.

The narratives were low keyed, set within the upper middle class and theatrical circles that were mined for so long by Christie, Marsh, and Allingham. Morice's narratives lacked the inventive plots of the earlier writers.

Lee Crosley

Author: Robert Tralins

Lee Crosley, a shapely green-eyed blonde employed as a travel writer, was more conspicuous for her physical appearance than her intellectual qualities.

In *The Chic Chic Spy* (Belmont, 1966), she was presumed to be a widow because her husband, an agent with the Universal Intelligence Agency, disappeared in Asia shortly after their honeymoon. Confused by his absence, Lee learned that her friend Maggie O'Malley, ostensibly head of a travel agency, was the leader (MOM) of S.I.S. (Society for International Security), an organization of 200 plus exceptional women. When Maggie recruited Lee, she provided her with training in flying, demolition, and marksmanship.

In the succeeding books, *The Miss from S.I.S.* (Belmont, 1966) and *The Ring-a-Ding U.F.O.s* (Belmont, 1967), Lee worked with fellow agent and suitor David Dudley. They had access to obscure weapons (shoe dart gun, explosive in false eyelashes), escaped from brutal thugs, and killed and maimed the opposition. Only the president of the United States was aware of S.I.S.'s purposes. Their opponents were usually an extra-legal cabal or a rogue government, supplemented by disloyal American bureaucrats and wild-eyed scientists. The books blended espionage, science fiction, and sexual teasing, but the narratives were not as titillating as the titles or the covers.

A third-rate clone of Modesty Blaise.

Amanda Curzon

Author: Frank Usher aka Charles Franklin

Amanda Curzon, a young Cockney, traveled Europe as an entertainer with wrestler Oscar Sallis. She had no pretensions to a career, was sexually promiscuous, and entangled herself and Oscar in international espionage. There was little physical description of Amanda, but the dust jackets portrayed her with dark hair and eyes. Although more intelligent than Oscar, she was dominated by him. Her only control was her ability to ration his sexual access.

Amanda and her beefy partner were introduced in *The Man from Moscow* (Hale, 1965). While in East Germany, they became acquainted with Stanislov, a Russian agent who had spied for the United States. When his cover was blown, American officials made no effort to rescue Stanislov, but British Intelligence was willing to provide him with a refuge. Stanislov, a very attractive man, convinced Amanda and Oscar to smuggle him across the border to West Germany, a risky business which entailed the murder of an East German agent, for which Oscar was held responsible.

No Flowers in Brazlov (Hale, 1968) made it clear that Amanda and Oscar were already known to the police because of their prior arrest for espionage. Still, Amanda agreed to smuggle a Kruschchev document through customs and deliver it in Munich for a man she knew as Joseph Sternberg. She and Oscar were arrested and charged with criminal espionage. They were released when their questioners accepted that they were gullible fools. Sternberg and British Intelligence agents posing as Soviets were waiting for them in West Berlin. The narrative went on and on with kidnappings and escapes.

Oscar's sexual peccadilloes in *The Boston Crab* (Hale, 1970) caused him to be kidnapped and framed for the attempted murder of Sally Woodward. He had a fling with Tanya, her daughter, because he knew Amanda was unfaithful. A simplistic solution would have been the custody battle between Tanya's parents (Sally, dying founder of a cosmetics business, and Maxwell, a former SS man, now working for the Arabs). Sally lived long enough to identify the man who tried to kill her. Amanda and Oscar were reunited. Who else would want either one of them?

The series was not likely to interest a discriminating reader of either sex.

April Dancer

Authors: Michael Avallone, Peter Leslie, and Simon Latter, novelizations of the television program "The Girl from U.N.C.L.E."

To capitalize on the popularity of "The Man from U.N.C.L.E.," NBC developed a spin-off, featuring April Dancer. April was what actress Stephanie Powers showed her to be, 5' 5" and 108 pounds, with brown eyes and long dark hair. Shortly after her father, an Army colonel, had been killed in Vietnam, her mother died. April had been educated at Radcliffe and at an U.N.C.L.E. training academy, and spoke 12 languages. U.N.C.L.E. (United Network Command of Law Enforcement), a multinational agency, was pitted against T.O.R.C.H. and T.H.R.U.S.H. April never achieved the popularity of Napoleon Solo or Ilya Kuriakin of the earlier series. Mark Slade, an ex-R.A.F. pilot, was her partner; Mr. Alexander Waverly, their boss.

In *The Birds of a Feather Affair* (Avallone, Signet, 1966), April and co-worker Mark Slade were kidnapped to set up an exchange for Alek

Zorki, a T.H.R.U.S.H. agent held by U.N.C.L.E. After April and Mark were separated, she was left in a building, primed to explode, but escaped. Mr. Waverly explained that Zorki was more than a spy. He had developed the secret of everlasting life, a formula he committed to his memory. Waverly was trying to get him to defect. However, there was a traitor at U.N.C.L.E. headquarters, and the double they planned to use for Zorki was really his twin brother. April defeated the plan to blow up headquarters, but was unable to tell whether or not Zorki survived.

The Blazing Affair (Avallone, Signet, 1966) sent April and Mark to Budapest (where six black widow spiders convinced them to move on), then to South Africa. Posing as a married couple, they approached Simon Ashley, director of the Ashley Diamond Mines. Unfortunately, he was also a member of a neo-Nazi group, headed by a man called "Der Fuehrer," and saw through their pretences immediately. Ashley set them up for assassination. They escaped this danger, only to be pursued by Mau Mau warriors, and further attempts on their lives by the neo-Nazis. Another capture, another escape, another success.

The Global Globules Affair (Latter, Souvenir, 1967) pitted April (in London, not in Paris) against T.H.R.U.S.H., now planning to take over the world by undermining the banking and currency systems. While waiting to meet Mark, April saw her former mentor, Dr. Carl Karadin, under strange circumstances. Waverly listened to her story and had April and Mark check out Karadin and his daughter, Suzanne, who seemed to be involved in the development of a deadly gas. Another trap, another capture, another escape. The anti-climax came when April, Mark, and Waverly returned to the United States. They learned of a second lab in the Arizona deserts. What happened there? Another capture, another rescue.

Mr. Waverly was aware that some nefarious T.H.R.U.S.H. activity was taking place in the islands of Palaga and Taradata during *The Golden Boats of Taradata Affair* (Latter, Souvenir, 1967). A half-dozen or more agents headed by April and Mark were dispersed to the area to search, find, and destroy the T.H.R.U.S.H. activity. They had backups on a two-man submarine and a luxury cruiser when they boarded the inter-island transport, Island Traveler. Among the passengers and crew were an international bacteriologist, a married pair of T.H.R.U.S.H. agents, and a canny former World War II hero posing as purser for the ship. On shore, they found support from the local leadership deposed by the T.H.R.U.S.H. representatives.

The Cornish Pixie Affair by (Leslie, Four Square, 1967) was not located in time to be reviewed. The April Dancer paperbacks read like television scripts, cutting back and forth in the action to sustain the violent and sometimes sadistic tension. There was a *Girl From U.N.C.L.E.* magazine published during 1966-67.

Maxine Dangerfield

Author: Frank Usher, writing as Charles Franklin

Maxine Dangerfield was a widow in her late twenties, whose husband, an intelligence agent, had been killed by a terrorist. Slim, about 5' 6" tall, with fair hair and blue eyes, she was familiar with judo and karate, dressed in slacks, had an encyclopedic memory, and drank absinthe. If she kept drinking absinthe, she might have problems with that fabulous memory. Someone had a memory problem, because details about Maxine's early life changed from book to book, and it was unclear at times whether she was working as a private investigator or for British Intelligence.

Private investigator Larry Venning was hired to find Brian Tilbury, a missing young man, by his titled father, Sir James, in *The Dangerous Ones* (Hale, 1964). Brian, the heir, had been estranged from his father. In the course of his investigation, Venning met Maxine, who shared his suspicion that Brian's disappearance was connected to the Quorum Club. The place was supposed to be a social and literary resource, but in fact was used by a neo-Nazi political group. Brian had been taken to Swineshead, a country estate. While Venning checked out the Club, Maxine worked on Lola, Brian's girlfriend, who was a hostess there. It was too late for Brian. Maxine more or less admitted that she worked for MI5.

Former convict Robert Church maintained he was innocent of the murder of his business partner, John Galton, in *On the Day of the Shooting* (Hale, 1965). Church had served his sentence; then he disappeared. Maxine, then an undercover agent in a criminal conspiracy investigation, helped Church's nephew, Roger Peerless, prove his uncle's innocence. During Church's disappearance he became the suspect in another death. Working together, Roger and Maxine foiled a plot to assassinate a new Russian leader.

In *Death in the East* (Hale, 1967), John Baron disappeared during a party. Young Edward Hadley, who left the group to check on Baron's car, was murdered. It was learned that Baron had been told to leave England, but never made it to Russia. When he was found dead in Munich, it was assumed that British Intelligence was responsible. Maxine, who had been on Baron's trail, returned to England, where she checked out Robin Kingsland, who had been the host at the party. Maxine soon realized that

Ho-Chen of the United Comrades of Lenin was involved, as he had been in *On the Day of the Shooting*. She became enmeshed in the struggle between the Chinese and Russian communists.

As *The Escape* (Hale, 1968) began, diplomat Gregory Karsdale had been imprisoned by the British for espionage, but escaped. He eluded his Russian rescuers and surrendered to British custody. Maxine served as his interrogator. Jud Hudson, the radical daughter of the Prime Minister, who had helped Karsdale, was also there in custody. Maxine and the other interrogators were investigating British communists, particularly those in the Foreign Office. There was nothing innovative about their capture and escape or the success of their mission.

Charmian Daniels
Author: Jennie Melville, pseudonym for Gwendoline Butler

Charmian Daniels was a Scot of lower class origin, somewhat taller than average (5' 7"), redheaded, clumsy, but determined to improve. A graduate of Glasgow University, she was sensitive to those she interviewed, had an excellent memory, and worked painstakingly to solve her cases. When stationed in suburban Deerham, she bought her own home, cultivated a circle of local informants, and maintained files of criminal activities.

During *Come Home and Be Killed* (London House, 1964), Charmian, then a sergeant, appeared only briefly to trap a young killer.

Burning Is a Substitute for Loving (London House, 1964) involved Charmian with the problems of teenaged Harry Elder, living with his grandfather, his Aunt Jess, and her husband. He had a vague recollection of some other woman in his life, but never discussed it with the family. He shared it only with Charmian, who investigated an arson case in which Harry might be a suspect. She was also keeping her eye on Mr. Cobb, Harry's eccentric grandfather, who had been found unconscious in the park after the arson incident. She gained the impression that Mr. Cobb's other daughter (Harry's mother) might have been one of the women who died in the fire. Charmian saved the boy from serious illness and possible death.

In *Murderers' Houses* (Joseph, 1964), when young widow Velia Ryman, whom Charmian had visited professionally, was found dead, there were rumors that the two women shared a lesbian relationship. The Deerham Hills Police had been warned that an undescribed male who preyed on women was headed their way. This connected with the case of an unidentified drowned woman who was finally identified as a Mrs. Chandler, one of his victims. Charmian probed Velia's past even after the accusations against her resulted in a suspension, but was deeply hurt by a more personal betrayal.

During *There Lies Your Love* (Joseph, 1965), parallel cases involving young women caught Charmian's attention. Nan King's death from an overdose was tabled in order to concentrate on the disappearance of Arlette Grey, a young college student. In the diary that Arlette left behind, she alluded to a yellow-haired woman who had a strong influence over her. Con, wife of Prof. Tom Gilroy, had found items of clothing in the family basement, which she brought to the police. They connected her and Tom to Arlette. The police were seeking both Arlette and the yellow-haired woman, believed to be Mary Lou Pallas. Only after Con and Tom were dead did they find them both. Inspector Rupert Ascham, who was also assigned to the case, brought with him bad memories for Charmian, but, as they worked together, they became very close.

In *A Different Kind of Summer* (Hodder, 1967), Charmian traced the killer of a headless corpse sent to the local hospital. The arrival of the body came during a period of time when five local girls from the lower income section of Deerham Hills had gone missing. Charmian's investigation was both helped and impeded by the efforts of Ralph Smith and Brigitta Brunner, both of whom were looking for missing sisters. The discovery of two buried heads led Charmian and her new assistant, Christine Quinn, to the killer. Charmian's marriage to Ascham, who was off in the United States during this case, seemed shadowy.

After Ascham's death, Charmian focused even more strongly on her career, which changed in character in *A New Kind of Killer* (McKay, 1971). She attended Midport University while working full time as a detective, testing a theory about young violent criminals. She had become a more attractive, self-confident person. Although she felt guilt for the death of a young policewoman and had an unhappy relationship with a student revolutionary, she outwitted an old kind of killer.

When Charmian returned to Deerham Hills as an inspector in *Murder Has a Pretty Face* (St. Martin, 1981), she had also earned a degree in history from a Scotttish university and increased confidence in herself. She needed it when her superior officer was injured and she had to take over his cases. To investigate a series of home robberies in the area, Charmian posed as a bad cop to gain entry to a ring of female thieves. A parallel investigation connected Rupert to the death of a man, ex-convict Terry Jarvis, found drowned in cement boots. The real emphasis was on the dynamics of the four female thieves and their involvement with Charmian. Although

Charmian took a leave of absence, she found the connection between Jarvis and the women. A side story involved Tom, Rupert's son, who had been missing. He was seriously injured in a car accident, then returned unaware that his father had died.

By *Windsor Red* (St. Martin, 1988), Charmian had been granted a sabbatical to study the female criminal, starting with the premise that women were in crime because of a male influence. She associated with a group of female ex-convicts, but later wondered if one of them might be responsible for headless bodies found in the area. Charmian stayed with an old friend, Annie Cooper, whose daughter was suspected of the death of her disreputable boyfriend.

Charmian remained in Windsor during *A Cure for Dying* (Macmillan, London, 1989) but commuted to a London office. She had a motley foursome living next door to her. Her suitor, Humphrey Kent, encouraged Charmian to attend polo matches. These factors came together in a series of horrifying murders, first equine mares, then human females. Charmian and her friend and colleague Dr. Ulrika Seeley went deep into the feminine mystique for a motive for murder.

During *Making Good Blood* (St. Martin, 1990), Charmian specialized in women who act violently or who invite violence in others. She consulted with psychiatrist Ulrika Seeley. Joanna Gaynor, a teenager, was suspected in the disemboweling of her own horse, but that didn't seem logical. Even less so when the body of Irene Coleman was discovered similarly mutilated, followed by the discovery of another body in the Gaynor yard. A trail of blood led Charmian to the killer. Humphrey Kent, a suave police official, still sought her company.

During *Witching Murder* (St. Martin, 1991), Charmian became interested in a witches' coven when there were deaths within the group. Sgt. Dolly Barstow had been in touch with the witches previously and recognized the body of an unidentified female victim as Vivien Charles, one of the group. Symbolic items found near the corpse also implied witchcraft was involved. Charmian, currently on medical leave, attended a meeting of the coven with Dolly. An undercover agent, Josh Fox, was subsequently killed, so official police action was taken. Sexual misconduct, not witchcraft, was the motive.

In *Footsteps in the Blood* (Macmillan, London, 1990), Nella Fisher, a young woman with criminal connections, was murdered after she had told both Charmian's goddaughter, Kate Cooper, and Sgt. Dolly Barstow that she had valuable information. She had overheard two men at a bar talking about a man who was obsessed with a woman. Kate? Dolly? Charmian? Although she had every reason to keep Nella alive, evidence pointed to Kate as the killer. Charmian, who had just returned from the United States, made the case her priority because Kate was like a daughter to her. The trail of Nella's killer took Charmian into police corruption at a time when she needed to be able to trust other detectives. She had problems of her own, medical and romantic.

During *Dead Set* (Macmillan, 1992) Charmian, bored with her work as head of a technical unit, concerned herself with the murder of teenager Louise Farmer. Ted Gray, an historical researcher who disappeared after the body was found, was sought by Louisa's father and another man, whose son had been killed in a hit and run. These were people who lived in the posh Chapel Close area. The discovery of Ted's corpse led to several possible scenarios. Uncertain about her feelings for Humphrey, Charmian dallied with a man who might be less reliable.

Restless in *Whoever Has the Heart* (Macmillan, 1993), Charmian purchased a home in a nearby village, seeking distance from Humphrey Kent, but the building had unhappy vibrations for Charmian. The discovery of blood in the cellar of the house made it likely that Chloe Devon, who had worked for the local real estate agency, had either been murdered there or her body stored there. Charmian re-examined the death of Bea Armitage, the prior occupant; the motivations of her new neighbors, who presented themselves as stepfather and stepson; and her growing attraction for a local police inspector, Clive Barney.

Charmian's concern turned towards her pregnant goddaughter Kate in *Death in the Family* aka *Baby Drop* (St. Martin, 1995). She also took a personal interest in the disappearance of young Sarah Loomis. Was there some reason why nobody wanted Sarah back? In the search for Sarah two bodies were located; one was "Joe," a foster child, the other an infant. Lady Emily, Sarah's grandmother, and her father, Peter Loomis, visited Charmian. Lady Emily insisted that the girl had run off before. Medical information not only led to the reasons why both Sarah and her deceased mother had been disposable, but solved a problem between Charmian and Humphrey.

Charmian and Humphrey Kent were married as *The Morbid Kitchen* (St. Martin, 1996) began, but their relationship seemed as passionless as that with Ascham. Her grief for Kate's death was diminished when she became immersed in the case of a skeleton and headless corpse found in a building formerly occupied by an exclusive private school. Many of the potential suspects were dead, but vicious child abusers remained, ready to kill again.

In *The Woman Who Was Not There* (Macmillan, 1996), Humphrey was busy with conferences and meetings. He and Charmian led parallel lives. She was busy with two seemingly unrelated matters: (1) the disappearance of Alicia Ellendale, a London hooker who had arrived in Windsor by bus, ostensibly to visit Frank Felyx, a retired police officer, and (2) a bequest to her friend Fanny Fanfairly of a dwelling occupied solely by life-sized puppets. Fanny believed that the puppets, which had a sexual aspect, moved. The more pragmatic Charmian looked for the human evil behind the figures.

Although the motivation for the killer in *Revengeful Death* (Macmillan, 1997) was plausible, the method taken to wreak the revenge— the murder of two innocent persons—was not. Only when two suspects took part in an improvised dramatization of the crimes did real proof of the killer emerge. Charmian was slow on this one, skeptical of a suspect who intuited danger.

The opening of a crime bookstore by white witches Birdie Peacock and Winifred Eagle in *Stone Dead* (Macmillan, 1998) included the discovery of two bodies in a stone casket. The lower body was ancient. The second added to the list of women who had disappeared and subsequently been found dead. Top officials from several jurisdictions, including Charmian, pooled their efforts, but were thwarted by internal treachery. Charmian's long acquaintance with Birdie and Winifred motivated her to find other suspects for the deaths. Again, the motivation was weak. It had become too easy to attribute all evil to madmen or women.

In *Dead Again* (Macmillan, 2000), the final publication in the Charmian Daniels series, she was unaccountably assigned to watch over the welfare of recently released child killer, Joan Dingham. This was a total change from her administrative work as head of the Southern Register Documentation and Crime Unit. There was an element of pleasure at being reunited with Dolly Barstow, now an inspector, and George Rewley. Women with criminal records who had been associated with Joan and her partner, Rhos Campbell, met together before her release. Among those present was Diane King, whose death had been prematurely reported. Diane and two younger women were murdered close to the time of Joan's release in the same modus operandi as Joan's former killings. A strange hermit, a wandering dog, and the intuition of Winifred Eagle and Birdie Peacock, the witches who had appeared in prior narratives, added to the complications.

Charmian may not always be exciting, but she was dependable, and Melville provided interesting supporting characters. Charmian's character was less developed. She'd fall in love, marry, or have affairs, but never really connected with the men in her life. Her work was the top priority.

Kiss Darling

Author: James Yardley

Kiss Darling was an Englishwoman who lacked parental guidance. Her mother died when she was two, and her father was a British soldier of fortune. While her contemporaries were collecting Beatles records, Kiss collected degrees: Sorbonne (at age 16) and Oxford, accumulating a B.A., M.A., Ph.D. by age 20. Her other distinction for a detective: her virginity was maintained through heroic efforts. As an insurance investigator, she traveled considerably. Like Kiss, the paperback covers on the narratives promised a great deal, but provided only titillation.

In *Kiss the Boys and Make Them Die* (Signet, 1970) she was assigned by her supervisor, Angus Fane, to recover Pharaonic jewelry stolen from a Cairo museum, not realizing that she resembled an Egyptian goddess. She connected with two brothers, Tarek and Hussein Gazal, and was present at a party they hosted when Tarek's fiancée, Lucie, was murdered. It didn't help that Kiss was abducted (aren't all female sleuths abducted?) and that she fell in love with Hussein. Unfortunately he had clay feet.

A Kiss a Day Keeps the Corpses Away (Signet, 1971) reunited Kiss with supervisor Angus Fane as they journeyed to meet a representative of the Jessop Trust, only to have the man's plane crash. The mysterious "Erickson," who survived, had in his possession enough botillenum to wipe out Great Britain. Off to Africa to investigate the impact of the virus, Kiss and Fane shared experiences of capture and escape from exotic villains, similar to those of Modesty Blaise and Willy Garvin.

Arlette Van Der Valk Davidson

Author: Nicolas Freeling

Freeling's hero, Inspector Piet Van der Valk of the Dutch police, was killed in *Aupres de ma Blonde* (Harper, 1972). His French wife, Arlette, had made minor appearances in earlier books, adjusting reluctantly to Dutch society, raising their two sons, and adopting 10-year-old Ruth when her mother was killed during *Tsing Boum* (Random House, 1969).

In *Double Barrel* (Harper, 1965), she was necessarily part of the undercover operation, which sent Piet to Zwinderen, a remote community in North Holland, dominated by the Calvinistic religion and hostile to outsiders. Arlette's strong political opinions caused Piet embarrassment and may have hampered his professional advancement. In turn she tolerated the moody Piet, in spite of his rare infidelities (*Over the High Side* aka *The Lovely Ladies*), because essentially she was an optimistic woman whose personality complemented his.

In *Aupres,* Arlette overcame the shock of Piet's death to question the competence and commitment of the Dutch police in investigating his murder. During the years when he had worked as an inspector, she feared that he would be killed. Now that he was in a desk job, she had relaxed. What both she and his co-workers did not know was that Piet had an adventure as a private investigator. Richard Oddinga had come to his office with a strange story about the goings on at the jewelry store where he had recently been hired. Although he had promised Richard to keep the matters "off the records," Piet checked into the management of the shop. His attention had been noticed. After the funeral, Arlette, who had been given the notebooks in which Piet made rather cryptic references to the matter, returned to Amsterdam to find his killer and her own kind of justice.

By *The Widow* (Pantheon, 1979), Arlette had married Arthur Davidson, a British sociologist attached to a Strasbourg university. Her children were grown and out of the home. She spent time in her former profession as a physiotherapist, but, restless for an outlet for her skills, was encouraged by Arthur to set up an "advice bureau," using advertisements to solicit clients. In her investigations, Arlette combined the skills of a private investigator and a social worker. The narrative contained vignettes of individual cases.

Arlette (Pantheon, 1981) included investigations that frequently pitted Arlette against the bureaucracy. She dealt with the mother of a son who was killed while trespassing; the parents of a runaway; a man whose wife left him when he lost his job. Rene Casabianca, Strasbourg police official, wanted to use Arlette as bait. Like Piet, she questioned her ability to work within the police system at a level acceptable to her standards. Police Sergeant Subleyras, now retired because he too was uncomfortable with his job, became Arlette's ally. Ruth, the child whom Piet and Arlette had adopted, was now a medical student.

There were two later Freeling books in which Arlette had a role. *Sand Castles* (Mysterious Press, 1990), a collection of vignettes that took place while Piet was alive, revealed more about the young Arlette, a green-eyed, long-legged, rebellious student when she met Piet.

In *Lady Macbeth* (Deutch, 1988) Arlette worked with another Freeling hero, Henri Castang. Elena, a waitress at the Russian tea room that Castang frequented, was a serious suspect when her unfaithful husband, Joseph, disappeared. That segment of the book was followed by a narration by Arlette, who described her shy architect neighbor, Guy Lefebvre, whose wife, Sibille, had promoted his career. She disappeared while the couple was on a trip. It seemed unlikely to Arlette that such a woman would simply abandon her husband. When Guy was arrested, Castang came up with enough evidence to get him released, but not cleared. The suspicions of Sibille's death were premature, but her impact on Guy destroyed them both. The motif of females who kill or mastermind killings à la Lady Macbeth reappeared throughout the book.

Freeling was a master of deception unfettered by literary conventions. He changed focus frequently and without warning, used a variety of narrators and viewpoints, and questioned more often than he answered.

Felicia Dawlish

Author: Gordon Ashe, pseudonym for John Creasey

Felicia Dawlish was another of the bright young wives who made occasional appearances in series dominated by their husbands. She was a tall, fair-haired, "handsome" woman, married to Patrick Dawlish, Assistant Commissioner at Scotland Yard.

She entertained for her husband, as in *A Clutch of Coppers* (Holt, Rinehart and Winston, 1969) when Patrick was the chairman of the "Crime Hater" conference in London. The police were made aware that some of the guests at the conference were vulnerable to attack. One, Señor Jose Ruiz, had a new method of crime fighting; the other, Randy Patton, a New York police officer, had a photographic memory. Ruiz was killed. Felicia assisted Patrick in learning what Patton knew and comforting his wife, Helen, when he disappeared. A very surprising conclusion.

Her strong role was in *A Life for a Death* (Holt, Rinehart and Winston, 1973), when Patrick was injured by a Mafia-type gunman while in Rome. He was hidden in the Vatican to recuperate while presumed dead. Felicia worked with Neil Commyns, a Chicago policeman; Gordon Scott of Crime Haters, and Patrick's subordinates to unmask a criminal family. Although Patrick appeared in other books, Felicia had no other significant roles.

Cherry Delight

Author: Glen Chase, possibly a house name. At least two authors, Leonard Jordan and Rochelle Larkin, have been identified with individual books in this series.

Cherry Delight (real name Dellissio) offered few surprises. The name of her organization, N.Y.M.P.H.O. (New York Mafia Prosecution and Harassment Organization), and the titles of the books made it clear that these were books to challenge a liberal female's commitment to freedom of the press. She was an espionage agent with the usual skills needed for the job. Leisure published no less than 23 Cherry Delight books, including *Busted, Devil to Pay,* and *Mexican Stand Off;* therefore, a market existed.

Donna Bella

Author: R. T. Larkin, believed to be Rochelle Larkin

Donna Bella appeared first in *The Godmother* (Lancer, 1971) as a fiftyish widow. She and her husband, the recently deceased Godfather, had three sons and heirs. However, rather than allow authority to descend to Rico, Rocco, or Paco, the Donna took it upon herself. Devoid of scruples, she terrorized the other capos. She hired Jane Plane as her assistant and Luigi Linguini as her publicist. La Donna's exploits did not go unnoticed. Her experience as a witness before the Senate Investigating Committee motivated her to run for political office. She was elected governor of New Jersey.

In *Honor Thy Godmother* (Lancer, 1972), after consolidating her political position and expanding her criminal network, the Godmother looked for another challenge. The current U.S. President was happy to offer her one, as Ambassador to Italy. This opportunity accommodated her plan to find suitable Sicilian wives for her sons. Again her abilities were recognized. After capture by Sicilian brigands, she was granted leadership in the Sicilian community, and her three sons were married in an ostentatious ceremony.

For Godmother and Country (Lancer, 1972) found the U.S. government in chaos because the Chief Justice of the Supreme Court had decamped with the Treasurer and the keys to the Treasury. La Donna had her own problems with insurgents in the Organization, the primary culprit being her 17-year-old cousin, Antony. She sought the Chief Justice position for herself, and was appointed without the usual scrutiny afforded such candidates. Too long a widow, La Donna's personal life focused on attorney F.

Lee Bialy. Only after the wedding did F. Lee disclose that he was really Melvin Belpoese, the capo of capos, and intended to take control of her organization.

Admittedly there was humor here, but the series was junk food for mystery fans.

Catherine Alexander Douglas

Author: Sidney Sheldon

The series was set in the 1940's. Catherine Alexander, the ambitious, intelligent, and attractive daughter of an ineffectual father, had made a career for herself as a public relations expert and established a relationship with a man who loved her. Yet she felt unsatisfied until she met Larry Douglas, a dashing World War II pilot. Her marriage to a man with no potential for monogamy set her up for disaster.

Catherine was a survivor, not a sleuth in *The Other Side of Midnight* (Morrow, 1974), during which her life was intertwined with that of Noelle Page, actress and mistress of Greek tycoon Constantin Demiris. When Demiris learned that Noelle had resumed an affair with Larry, now employed as his personal pilot, he sought revenge. Noelle and Larry, who had tired of his wife, decided to kill her. Their attempt failed, but Demiris concealed Catherine's amnesiac existence and manipulated the Greek legal system to destroy them.

Catherine's return to her identity in *Memories of Midnight* (Morrow, 1990) was gradual and fragmented. Her "benefactor" Demiris found Catherine employment in his London office. Although she had been presented as a competent woman, she made no effort to go beyond his explanation that Larry and Noelle had been executed for attempted murder. Demiris wanted Catherine dead, but his plans were thwarted by her enterprise. Another victim, his wife, Melina, having tired of his infidelity and abuse, killed herself, leaving evidence that implicated Demiris.

Although these were easy reading, the plots had holes big enough to drive a Greek tanker through.

Eve Drum

Author: Rod Gray

Eve Drum's adventures were among the cruder, more demeaning of the espionage series designed to deliver soft pornography during the Sixties and Seventies. She was an American blonde whose other physical attributes were frequently mentioned, an employee of L.U.S.T. (League of Underground Spies and Terrorists), a "bastard child of the CIA and State Department," assuming tasks which more traditional agencies would decline.

Eve possessed the standard skills of the female spy: expert with guns, knives, and judo, an excellent swimmer, and able to open almost any lock. To indicate that she had a cerebral or artistic side, Eve occasionally painted for relaxation. The classic enemy of L.U.S.T. was H.A.T.E. (Humanitarian Alliance for Total Espionage). They seemed to have a great deal in common.

At least eight books were included in the series, begun in the mid-1960's by Tower. A second series, the *New Lady from Lust,* was introduced by Belmont Tower in 1975, including *Lay Me Odds* (1967) and *Go for Broke* (1975).

The titles of the books tended to be provocative. Not likely to interest anyone on the basis of mystery or literary value.

Charlotte Eliot

Author: Macartney Filgate

As *Runway to Death* (Walker, 1980) began, Charlotte Eliot had inherited an airplane from her deceased employer. A brunette with academic qualifications in archaeology and proficient in Italian, she flew off to a small Greek island hoping to sell the aircraft to Bart Somervel. She was prevailed upon to deliver a packet to Somervel by a man she met at the airfield. What she did not realize was that she and the plane were intended to break a criminal out of prison, that the proposed escapee was Bart's half-brother Ro, and that there were professionals who made a career out of rescuing men from prison on the island.

Bart Somervel had become Charlotte's lover by *Delta November* (Muller, 1979), but he deceived her as to his intentions when she landed their plane in an obscure French valley. He had led her to believe this was a stopover en route to England. Instead, Bart was considering a contract to help a German financial expert, possibly a Nazi, escape to a new life. Charlotte was caught in the rivalry between Bart and his rapacious brother Ro to gain access to gold bars.

Charlotte Ellison

Author: Anne Perry

See: Charlotte Ellison Pitt, Section 5, page 372.

Amelia Peabody Emerson

Author: Elizabeth Peters, pseudonym for Barbara Mertz

Amelia Peabody, a Victorian explorer, transcended her period in history by her courage, her spirit, and her interest in archaeology. She was described as tall at one point, short at another, but consistently had a sallow complexion, jet-black hair, and gray eyes. The youngest child and only daughter in a family of six, her widowed father, an antiquarian and scholar, had educated Amelia privately. The early death of her mother might account for Amelia's lack of interest in her appearance. She devised a traveling wardrobe, that included divided skirts and Turkish trousers comfortable for her archaeological expeditions. Archaeology was the second great passion of Amelia's life. After her father died, bequeathing Amelia a substantial amount of money, she pursued her interest in Egyptology.

Crocodile on the Sandbank (Dodd, 1975) brought Amelia to Egypt and to Radcliffe Emerson, her primary passion. Amelia was then a 32-year-old budding spinster traveling with runaway heiress Evelyn Barton-Forbes, whom Amelia had rescued from the clutches of a handsome cad. Although the initial encounters between Emerson and Amelia were adversarial, they fell in love as they worked together to rescue Evelyn's fortune. What a joy Radcliffe was to Amelia! He was her intellectual equal, recognized her beauty, and was a passionate lover. The couple referred to one another by their last names. Walter, Radcliffe's brother, married Evelyn.

By *The Curse of the Pharaohs* (Dodd, 1981) the couple had married and produced a son, Walter Peabody Emerson, better known as "Ramses." When Amelia and Radcliffe returned to Egypt, this precocious infant was left behind in the care of family. The original leader of an expedition to open a tomb in the Valley of the Kings had died mysteriously. The Emersons were to complete the project but were hampered by accidents and the deaths of their watchman Hassan and of Alan Armandale, the archaeologist who had been second in charge of the original workforce.

In *The Mummy Case* (Congdon, 1985), the Emersons, now accompanied by Ramses, accepted the inferior site they were assigned at Mazehunah. They were aware of an illegal antiquities ring, which Amelia believed to be headed by a master criminal. Their resource Abd el Atti was murdered, but not before he had parted with a scrap of papyrus, which turned out to be valuable. The Emersons stayed on, caught in a clash between Protestant missionaries and the native Coptics, between scientific exploration and religious orthodoxy.

Lion in the Valley (Atheneum, 1986) returned the Emersons, with Ramses, now eight years old, to the Giza Pyramids. Radcliffe was disdainful of Amelia's theory that there was a master criminal behind the nefarious schemes they had encountered and whose plans they had disrupted. Amelia was concerned about young Miss Debenham, who had come to Cairo alone and become attached to Prince Kalenischeff. Before they left Cairo, Kalenischeff was found stabbed to death, and Miss Debenham was not to be found anywhere. She turned up later in an exhausted condition, stating her name to be Enid Marshall. Amelia was not fooled. Not only did they learn a name for the master criminal, Sethos, but he declared his undying admiration for Amelia.

It was back to London for *The Deeds of the Disturber* (Atheneum, 1988), where Kevin O'Connell, a newspaper reporter, entangled the Emersons in a controversy concerning a cursed mummy. Family intruded into their life when James, Amelia's brother, asked for help in his problems. Emerson agreed to take in James' children while he looked to improve his fortune and his wife recovered her health. In a shocking development, Emerson showed an interest in another woman. Discarding her skirts, Amelia, wearing male attire, joined Emerson to seek out clues in opium dens.

During *The Last Camel Died at Noon* (Warner, 1991), the Emersons and Ramses entered the Sudan in search of missing explorer Willy Forth and his wife. When they were spirited to a hidden civilization in turmoil over its leadership, Amelia's medical knowledge, Emerson's physical strength, and Ramses' language skills were all tested. They came home with an addition to their family, Nefret, the Forth daughter. She would continue to play an important role in the Emerson family.

The Snake, the Crocodile, and the Dog (Warner, 1992) included young Nefret in the Emerson family. She and Ramses were left behind with Walter and Evelyn while Amelia and her husband embarked on what they had planned as a second honeymoon, hoping to rekindle the excitement of their early relationship. Vengeful enemies in Europe provided the excitement, kidnapping Emerson and destroying his recent memory. Amelia wooed him again (as in *Random Harvest* by James Hilton) during an incredible tale.

The Hippopotamus Pool (Warner, 1996) returned Amelia, Emerson, Ramses, Nefret, Walter, and Evelyn to Egypt, seeking an undiscovered royal tomb. Two lots of criminals, headed by old antagonists, vied with one another in murder, kidnapping, and assorted misbehaviors in an effort to wrest the treasures of ancient Egypt from the Emersons. Amelia's own recklessness ill prepared her for the role of mother and protector to three teenagers: her son, Ramses; her adopted daughter, Nefret; and their dear friend David Todros, who had become a member of Walter Emerson's household.

The entire family returned to Egypt in *Seeing a Large Cat* (Warner, 1997), where Emerson planned to excavate a lesser-known tomb. The agenda was disturbed by mysterious warnings about an unknown Tomb Twenty A; the pleas of old friend Enid Debenham, now married to the rehabilitated Donald Fraser; and a too recent mummy. Colonel Bellingham and his daughter, Dolly, sought to become part of the Emerson ménage, but were not accepted. Good thing, because the too recent mummy contained the body of the fourth Mrs. Bellingham. Amelia could not resist involving herself, but neither could the three youngsters (David, Nefret, and Ramses), now not so young, as Ramses had a mustache.

Amelia had involved herself in suffragette activities in England as *The Ape Who Guards the Balance* (Avon, 1998) began. She became aware that Sethos, the master criminal who loved her, was still active. He had participated in the theft of Egyptian antiquities from the home of an English politician. Soon, the Emerson family, including assorted connections, was off to Egypt, hampered in their goals by Emerson's importunate remarks to the authorities. Nevertheless, they were not to be denied when new discoveries were made in the vicinity of their camp. The youthful trio of Nefret, Ramses, and David carried on their own investigation, but their romantic inclinations threatened their extended friendships. Amelia had to cope with a vengeful rival from her past, learning that feminism among the criminal element was not necessarily to her advantage.

Focus continued to be on the new generation in *The Falcon at the Portal* (Avon, 1999). Ramses' undeclared love for Nefret suffered a serious setback. The marriage between David Todros and Lia, Emerson's niece, was disrupted by charges that young Todros was selling Egyptian antiquities that had been collected by his deceased grandfather Abdullah, the faithful servant of the family. Naturally Amelia took a strong role in the narrative, but her efforts at solutions did not culminate in a satisfactory conclusion.

An ever-expanding cast of characters and 500 plus pages of narrative in *He Shall Thunder in the Sky* (Morrow, 2000) will not deter Amelia's devoted fans, but may discourage first-time readers of the series. World War I was already taking place in Europe. Egypt guarded the Suez Canal, vital to British interests. Ramses paraded his pacifism, earning the disapproval of the expatriate community. His parents were absorbed in new archaeological discoveries. Inevitably all members of the supporting cast became involved in the struggle between England and Germany and their allies. As always, Amelia's first-person narrative was heavily supplemented by letters and historical documents.

By *Lord of the Silent* (Morrow, 2001) Ramses and Nefret had attained equal status with his parents. Emerson and Amelia were more humorous figures, while the young couple shared romance and adventures. All the regulars were there when the foursome and their retinue returned to Egypt. Ramses, in recovery from his undercover activities, had little opportunity to rest, as he was the target of the new master of thieves. Sethos, not dead but debilitated, switched his attentions to intrepid reporter Margaret Minton. Add in the Vandergelts and their son, Bertie, nefarious grave robbers, and treacherous spies in search of a fabulous treasure.

The expanded Emerson family had problems at their Luxor site and in Gaza during *The Golden One* (Morrow, 2002). Jamil, a member of Abdullah's family, had gone rogue, a disgrace to Abdullah, who had headed the Emerson workforce for decades and was dear to Amelia. She had dream visits in which Abdullah counseled and sometimes scolded her. Jamil knew of an unexplored tomb but was consumed with hatred for the Emersons. An avaricious American trio sought stolen antiquities for their collections. On the most personal level, Sethos (now known to be Emerson's illegitimate half-brother) was caught behind the Turkish lines. Some believed him to be a traitor to England; others, that he was on an espionage mission for the Allies. Either way, the double Emerson duos set out to rescue him.

The entire Emerson family and its friends had a role in *Children of the Storm* (Harper, 2003). Included were the old villains and some new ones; the old allies and a valuable recruit. Together the Emersons battled insidious enemies who wanted revenge and treasure. Cyrus Vendergelt had the treasure, antiquities from newly discovered vaults. The revenge motive sprang from past conflicts with the Emerson family, which now included Sethos.

The plea to return to the Lost Oasis in *Guardian of the Horizon* (Morrow, 2004) could not be ignored by the Emerson family. When they were told that their friend Tarek needed help, they prepared to leave. The purpose and destination of their trip had to be kept a secret, but rumors abounded, causing villains to follow their trail. The Lost Oasis had changed. Tarek was in danger, but not in the manner they had supposed. Nefret, who had been venerated at the Oasis, was even more vulnerable. Ramses suffered not only physical danger but confusion as to where his heart lay.

In *The Serpent on the Crown* (Morrow, 2005) Peters did it again. Amelia, Emerson, Ramses, and Nefret, together with an ever-increasing ensemble, successfully juggled a series of mysteries. The precipitating event was a visit from Magda von Ormond, Gothic author and widow of antiquarian collector Pringle Petherick. She turned a valuable golden statue over to Emerson because she said it carried a curse that had taken her husband's life and would take hers. Emerson insisted that he would only take tentative custody until the legitimate owner was determined. Magda's disappearance, which initially was treated as more of her melodramatics, ended in murder. Her stepson Adrian, who suffered from shell-shock, and his over-protective sister, Harriet, were investigated by the Luxor Police Department as suspects. The Petherick problem expanded into seduction, physical attacks, an explosion, and disappearances. Great fun for Peters' fans. Newcomers should read earlier books first.

The early books were fanciful adventures that verged on camp. Do not discount them. The later narratives became dependent upon their predecessors for understanding, taking on the tone of daytime serials with recurrent characters, unsolved personal problems, and plot lines that continued from one book to another. During 2003, Morrow published *Amelia Peabody's Egypt*, a collection of essays and historical material relating to Egypt and the Emersons.

Rosa Epton
Author: Michael Underwood, pseudonym for John Michael Evelyn

Rosa Epton, an English solicitor described as "elfin," was the only daughter of a Church of England rector in an English village. Her mother died when she was 18 and her much older brother lived in the United States.

Her first appearance was as Robin Snaith's law clerk in *A Pinch of Snuff* (St. Martin, 1974), during which she interviewed Brian Tanner, a gullible young wine steward who helped steal a collection of snuffboxes from his employer. He had been set up as the killer of Harry Green, another member of the gang. To what purpose?

In *Crime Upon Crime* (St. Martin, 1981), Rosa defended Arthur Kedby, a blackmailer accused of murder. He had been fool enough to blackmail a judge who then committed suicide. Therefore, he could expect little mercy in the courtroom. Actually he got none. He was killed when a bomb exploded there. That did not close the case for Rosa.

During *Double Jeopardy* (St. Martin, 1981), Toby Nash, a fellow guest at a New Year's Eve party, contacted Rosa when he was accused of date rape. Rosa had every reason to believe him innocent, because they spent that night together. Tricia Langley, whom he had brought to the party, considered dropping the charges. While Toby was out on bail, Tricia was murdered. Again Rosa was his alibi. Something of a conflict of interest.

Rosa had become the junior partner in Snaith and Epton by *Goddess of Death* (St. Martin, 1982). She became entangled in the family problems of Philip Arne, whose brother Francis was in trouble with the law. Out of friendship she agreed to represent Francis. After Philip was killed, Rosa got Francis off on the original charge against him, but wondered if he had been involved in his brother's murder.

Classmate Caroline Allard sought out Rosa in *A Party to Murder* (St. Martin, 1984), when Tom Hunsey, a troublesome co-worker, was killed at an annual Christmas party. In spite of other possible suspects, Chief Superintendent Bernard Tarr arrested Caroline prematurely. As a solicitor, Rosa was not eligible to defend Caroline in court, but she provided the counsel with evidence that made it possible for him to do a "Perry Mason" in court.

As *Death in Camera* (St. Martin, 1984) opened, unpopular judge Edmund Ambrose was murdered. Rosa cleared her client by proving that the judge was not the intended target. She was currently representing Bernard Blaker on a drug-running charge, a trial over which Ambrose would have presided. She was approached by Nigel Ambrose, nephew of the judge, who revealed that he had been given a camera to shoot pictures of his uncle. He was not the only one taking pictures, but he was the one who was arrested. Rosa had to resolve an ethical question of confidentiality before she could share information with the authorities.

When Sarah Atkins was prosecuted for vehicular homicide, her only witness was her husband, Peter. As Rosa learned in *The Hidden Man* (St. Martin, 1985), he could not be depended upon. Sarah had testified that she had no more than two or three drinks during the evening, blamed the mist, and contended that the victim, actor Jonathan Cool, was in a parked car with the lights out. Peter changed his story. He had been asleep at the time of the accident and therefore could not testify on her behalf. Rosa wondered if there might be some reason that Peter would be unwilling to appear publicly.

In *Death at Deepwood Grange* (St. Martin, 1986), Rosa renewed her acquaintance with her godmother, Margaret Lakington, and met her neighbors: David Anderson, who disappeared one night, and authoress Alison Tremlett, whom Margaret found outside unconscious. When Alison recovered, she accused Margaret of the attack. The next day Timothy Maxon, agent for the management of the Grange, was discovered dead. All these incidents blended into a diamond smuggling case that Rosa remembered from the past. Peter Chen, a handsome young Chinese-British attorney, worked with Rosa on a physically active investigation, becoming the significant male in Rosa's life.

Another jurist, Judge Celia Kilby, was murdered in *The Injudicious Judge* (St. Martin, 1988). Underwood used Rosa's defense of barrister Peter Duxbury to illustrate the distinction between the attorney-client privilege of confidentiality and the obligation to prevent a client from committing perjury. Points of law and ethics frequently figured into the narratives.

Although Snaith and Epton specialized in criminal practice, Rosa drew a will for elderly client Vernon Gray in *The Uninvited Corpse* (St. Martin, 1987). She also performed little errands and helped him look for a replacement for his housekeeper, Janet Berry. Gray's disappearance, the unidentified male corpse in his apartment, and the discovery of Gray's corpse on the seashore sent Peter Chen and Rosa into the past for Gray's real name and the ruin he had made of a business.

Three events came together in *Dual Enigma* (St. Martin, 1988): (1) the newspaper article Rosa read about the death of Jason Cutler, a schoolboy who went out late one night and was killed in a hit-and-run accident, (2) the disappearance of Trina Forbes, a young girl whose agitation upon listening to a tape called her to Rosa's attention when they were fellow passengers on a train, and (3) Rosa's success in getting her client, Philip Atherly a reduced sentence for smoking marijuana. When Atherly was murdered, Charlotte, his girlfriend (or one of them), brought Rosa £2,000 he had left to hire Rosa. He had expected to be killed. Rosa and Peter tied the three incidents together.

Underwood selected another ethical conundrum for Rosa in *A Compelling Case* (St. Martin, 1989): the responsibility of an attorney who believes her client to be innocent after he has been found guilty and sent to prison. Stephen Lumley, Rosa's client, had maintained that he went to his Uncle Bernard's jewelry store to end an estrangement and just happened to be there when two men entered, robbed the store, and wounded Bernard Hammond. Unfortunately, he had run off, only to be tackled by a spectator. Rosa persisted, examining both Bernard and his wife, Carol, for possible motives.

One problem Rosa faced in *Rosa's Dilemma* (St. Martin, 1990) was Peter Chen's marriage proposal, contingent on relocation in Hong Kong. Rosa, at 32, was not sure that she wanted to make geographic or matrimonial concessions. Her decision became more complex when she found herself attracted to Tom Berry, who was involved in her current legal case. She had agreed to defend Jeremy Scott-Pearce, one of two defendants

302 Mystery Women: An Encyclopedia of Leading Women Characters in Mystery Fiction

accused of tossing a firework in the mailbox of an important local bigwig. Malcolm Palfrey, who convinced Rosa to take on the case while he defended his goddaughter Amanda Ritchie, did not share the fact that Amanda intended to blame the incident on Jeremy. Someone shot Palfrey, leaving evidence that incriminated Jeremy. Then things really went wrong.

When Rosa vacationed in Amsterdam during *A Dangerous Business* (St. Martin, 1991), she saw Eddie Ruling, a cat-burglar client recently sentenced to five years in prison. Ruling's defense had been that he robbed the house of Miles Bilak for MI5. On her return, Rosa contacted the authorities as to Eddie's whereabouts. When his body was discovered later outside the Wandsworth Prison walls, Rosa learned that he had not even been a prisoner at that facility.

The Seeds of Murder (St. Martin, 1991) sent Rosa back into the past of client Adrian Pickard, first accused of breaking and entering a school and then suspected of murder. Although she was uncomfortable with Adrian, he was married to a dear friend. Only under pressure did Pickard reveal his connection with a disappearance that occurred decades before. Rosa was convinced that the most recent death was a cover-up for earlier crimes.

In *Guilty Conscience* (St. Martin, 1993), Evelyn Henshaw had an unusual favor to ask of Rosa: to investigate her disappearance when, and if, it occurred. She had implied that it was her husband, Ralph, whom she feared. There was a question as to the death of Ralph's first wife. Ralph appeared at Rose's office sometime later, concerned because Evelyn had disappeared. Yet it was not Evelyn's body that was fished out of the lake, but that of a young man, Stefan Michalowski, who had lived on the estate and worked part-time in a local pub. When Ralph was arrested, Rose agreed to represent him, aware that this might be a conflict of interest. Was Evelyn alive or dead?

Rosa differed from the female attorneys in American detective fiction. This distinction may be partly attributed to Michael Underwood's understated narrative style and partly to the differences between the American and British legal systems.

Kate Fansler

Author: Amanda Cross, pseudonym for Carolyn Heilbrun

Kate Fansler, an only daughter, was born when her mother was 40. Partly because of the age differential and the spirit of the Sixties, she rejected the standards of her parents and considered her brothers to be money-grubbing snobs. Although Kate never had children, she took a maternal interest in her nieces and nephews. She was portrayed as a WASP, disdainful of her own origins, and as a liberal with more than a touch of intellectual arrogance. She had strong opinions and little tolerance for those who did not share her moral stances. The narratives often focused on women's issues, not surprisingly because Heilbrun is an acknowledged authority in the field. Although Kate's husband, Reed Amhearst, was involved, this was not a "couple" series.

In the Last Analysis (Macmillan, 1964) introduced Kate as a young, single professor, who referred graduate student Janet Harrison to psychoanalyst Emanuel Bauer. When Janet was stabbed to death on Bauer's analysis couch, Kate made it her business to find the motive. Amhearst, the assistant District Attorney assigned to the case, became her confederate and lover.

In *The James Joyce Murder* (Macmillan, 1967), when an "unloaded" gun killed Kate's neighbor Mary Bradford, there were more than enough suspects. Kate played a significant role in narrowing them down. One factor that helped her was the possibility that some of the Joyce letters to publisher Samuel Longerwill were missing. Emmett Crawford was helping Kate to sort through Longerwill's papers. Amhearst and William Lenehan (who was tutoring Leo, Kate's nephew) devised a trap to entice the killer.

Poetic Justice (Knopf, 1970) involved Kate in a faculty battle over the granting of degrees to non-traditional students. The chairman of the English department, Professor Jeremiah Cudlipp, who opposed the program, died from an allergic reaction at Kate and Reed's engagement party. No action was taken against the faculty member who had been unaware of the severity of Cudlipp's allergy to aspirin and meant only to make him ill.

Kate, married and on sabbatical in *The Theban Mysteries* (Knopf, 1971), taught a seminar on *Antigone* at Theban, her high school alma mater. The United States' involvement in Vietnam was explored in the context of the seminar. It was more than just a theoretical question in the Fansler family. Kate's nephew Jack opposed the war; his father supported it. Guard dogs disclosed the hiding place of a draft dodger on school property, where he had been hidden by his sister, Angelica Jablon, a student in the seminar. Their mother, who was present, died of a heart attack, but the dogs may not have been to blame.

After Max Reston, a friend and colleague, had been named executor of the literary works of author Cecily Hutchins in *The Question of Max* (Knopf, 1976), he sought help from Kate. They traveled together to Maine to visit Cecily's home. The body of Gerry Marston, one of Kate's students, was found there. Kate's investigation of the death entered into the past of three valiant feminists at Oxford.

Kate, who was on campus on a semester fellowship, challenged gender discrimination in *Death in a Tenured Position* (Dutton, 1981) when Janet Mandelbaum, the first female professor in Harvard's English Department, ran the gauntlet of practical jokes. The jokes ceased to be funny when Janet's beverage was spiked and inferences were made that she had an alcohol problem. Later, Janet was found dead in a men's room on campus, not necessarily where she died, however. On the side Kate spent time with Moon Mandelbaum, Janet's former husband, who became a suspect in what might be murder.

In *Sweet Death, Kind Death* (Dutton, 1984), Kate visited Clare College ostensibly to serve on a gender study committee but also to determine whether or not Prof. Patrice Umphelby had been murdered. At first glance it seemed clear that Umphelby had walked into the lake with rocks in her pockets. Kate looked further in the area of who might benefit from the death. The need to publish was a powerful motivation. While there Kate ruminated on the continued existence of women's colleges.

Reed had left his law practice to become a Columbia professor by *No Word from Winifred* (Dutton, 1986). That led to an invitation to visit the prestigious law office where her brother Laurence practiced and where his daughter Leighton was on staff in a minor capacity. Kate helped Leighton search for Charlotte Lucas, a supervisor in the word processing department, who had vanished. That was only the first step in a literary journey, based on the journal of Winifred Ashby, the niece of a missing British historical novelist.

By *A Trap for Fools* (Dutton, 1989), Kate's special skills were well enough known that the college administration asked her help when Canfield Adams, an anti-feminist professor of Middle Eastern culture, died in a fall from an upper story of a college building. There were many suspects, and Kate could have been numbered among them, but she had a perfect alibi. The second murder, of Arabella Jordan, an African-American student activist, energized Kate to find the killer and expose embezzlement in the department.

The Players Come Again (Random, 1990) would not be considered a mystery story by many. In her biography of Gabrielle Foxx, wife of a prominent novelist, Kate examined the relationships of two extended families and the friendship shared by three women: Gabrielle, Anne Gringold, and Dorinda Goddard, each from different backgrounds. A past murder was uncovered, but it seemed irrelevant to the primary tensions in the narrative.

The personal and professional lives of Kate and Reed were in crisis when they decided to spend a semester at obscure Schuyler Law School in *An Imperfect Spy* (Ballantine, 1995). Reed's student clinic that provided appellate services to prisoners and Kate's class "Literature and the Law" ruffled the serenity of the moribund Schuyler campus but engendered support from students. Among Kate's new acquaintances were teacher Blair Whitson, who tested her fidelity, and clerical manager Harriet Furst, whose agenda included the reinvestigation of a murder conviction. Reed retrieved his sense of purpose, renewing his relationship with Kate.

When Reed was kidnapped at the beginning of *The Puzzled Heart* (Ballantine, 1998), the ransom was to be a retraction by Kate of positions she had taken on feminist issues. After she received this message, Kate contacted Harriet Furst, who left her position at Schuyler to become a private investigator. Harriet and her partner, Toni Giomatti, convinced Kate to let them follow up on the limousine that had picked Reed up as he disappeared and check out students with whom Kate had problems. Even after Reed's rescue, Kate examined her past, searching for persons she might have wronged who had never forgiven her. Banny, a St. Bernard dog, was added to their household.

Kate served as an interpreter of the academic world to private investigator "Woody" Woodhaven in *Honest Doubt* (Ballantine, 2000). Initially Woody had been hired by the children of Prof. Charles Haycock to investigate their father's murder. They hoped that their stepmother, Cynthia Burke, was involved, but an anonymous letter suggested that the killer was among Haycock's associates at Clifton College. Two affluent professors in the English department underwrote a further investigation. Kate's role as advisor was peripheral. There was considerable discussion of the nepotism, arrogance, and misogyny on faculties that did not really differ from other large organizations.

It was Kate's older brother Laurence who in a few words changed her life during *The Edge of Doom* (Ballantine, 2002). He revealed the existence of Jay Smith, who claimed to be and was proven to be Kate's father. Jay's introduction into her life caused Kate to reassess her feelings for her mother and her mother's husband. On another level it drew her into danger from a man who had reason to seek revenge against Jay.

Several of the later Amanda Cross books diverged from the traditional mystery novel. Possible murders were determined to be suicides or accidents. Even when murder occurred, some miscreants were no longer available, or the matter was never brought to the attention of the authorities. Readers will either enjoy or dislike the Fansler series. The wit and erudition may not reach readers who lack Heilbrun's literary expertise. Many of the books contained references and appraisals of distinguished authors, such as James Joyce, Henry James, Thomas Hardy, Edith Wharton, Rudyard Kipling, and the

Greek dramatists. She added a dimension to the mystery novel that enriched the genre and raised the consciousness of her readers. Fansler also appeared in a series of short stories, *The Collected Stories.*

Ann Fielding

Author: Mary Ingate

See: Ann Fielding Hales, Section 5, page 317.

Margo Franklin

Author: Jerry Jenkins

While the trend was to independent, secular heroines, the fundamentalist Christian press produced a highly ethical, religiously traditional heroine in Margo Franklin. The daughter of divorced parents, she was deeply depressed by the rift between her father, a garment industry executive, and Virginia, her mother, a Chicago judge. Philip Spence narrated the books, so Margo was seen through his eyes.

Margo (Moody Press, 1979) opened with Margo's attempt to commit suicide until rescued by Philip Spence, a confirmed Christian. Philip helped Margo with her suspicion that her mother was a murderess who had used her judicial power to conceal a crime.

Earl Haymeyer, an investigator for the U.S. Attorney who opened his own office in *Karlyn* (Moody Press, 1980), persuaded Philip to join his agency. They eventually included Margo in an administrative capacity, although she assisted with investigations. Karlyn wanted to know why and by whom she was being harassed before someone killed her.

In *Hilary* (Moody Press, 1980), Margo had qualms about the money bequeathed to her by her mother and coveted by her father. She confirmed her suspicion that her mother did not die a natural death in prison. Hilary was the young attorney probating Virginia Franklin's estate.

By *Paige* (Moody Press, 1981), Margo, now accepted as an investigator for the agency, realized that her employer, Earl Haymeyer, loved Paige, a woman with a suspicious past. When they learned that Paige had been tried and acquitted of the murder of her child, they investigated the case.

During *Allyson* (Moody Press, 1981), Philip and Margo's personal relationship deteriorated, causing him to take an interest in an attractive young client, Allyson Scheel, who was the co-owner of a boutique. She had been raised by her mother, Beatrice, and had few contacts with her father,

Curt. She wanted him investigated; there was a possibility that he was guilty of war crimes. This was Philip's case. Margo was undercover at a high school to trap a teacher who might be dealing drugs.

Erin (Moody Press, 1982) found Margo and Philip working together but without any personal plans for the future. They cooperated to help Bonnie, the agency secretary, suspected of murdering mobster Johnny Bizell. Earl Haymeyer hid Bonnie until she could be proven innocent. Margo played a stronger role, as her insistent questioning helped identify the real murderer.

During *Shannon* (Moody Press, 1982), the agency worked to identify a serial killer. The governor had sought Earl's help when the Chicago police were unable to find the common thread among the deaths of four men and two women.

These first seven books were gathered together in a single volume, *Margo Mysteries* (Moody Press, 1985).

In *Janell* (Moody Press, 1983), Philip's Christian values motivated him to postpone marriage with Margo until he was certain that her commitment matched his own. E. H. Detective Agency investigated the death of Adrian Rudolph, a major businessman for whom Janell Barnard, Philip's college sweetheart, worked. Margo played a minor role while Philip worked out his problems.

In *Lindsey* (Moody Press, 1983), Lindsey Bemis, an attractive blonde, convinced Earl, about to leave for a position in state government, to prove that her brother Timothy was not the killer of a postal clerk. Timothy, who had been captured by the Viet Cong, had been listed as MIA but recently turned himself in at Great Lakes Naval Base. He was unwilling to explain his absence.

In *Lyssa* (Moody Press, 1984), Lyssa Jack, who had no interest in religion, hired Philip to find her devout beau, Byron Huttmann. She insisted that Byron had been kidnapped or blackmailed into leaving. Philip found Byron and his real reason for disappearing.

During *Margo's Reunion* (Moody Press, 1984), the agency was hired to investigate the death of an elderly street person who left a million dollars to a friend and to help Earl investigate a leak in Internal Affairs at the Chicago Police Department.

While on their honeymoon trip in *Meaghan* (Moody Press, 1983), Philip and Margo became acquainted with stewardess Meaghan Hanekamp. They were surprised when she appeared later at their oceanside cabin near Boston. She had left her job in fear of a frequent passenger whom she recognized by his deformed fingernails even though he assumed different disguises and names. After Meaghan was accepted back on the job on probation, Philip and Margo were able to identify the regular passenger.

Finally, in *Courtney* (1983), Margo and Philip helped Courtney Robstown, a woman convicted of killing her abusive former husband, Buddy Knox. They had been hired by insurance investigator Marcus Rostow, Courtney's current husband, who believed her innocent. Courtney, when questioned in prison, revealed that Buddy had become a church member and that she had sobered up, so they had reunited before he was killed. She had awakened to find him dead in their bed. A careful examination of Buddy's insurance policy produced an answer.

These books can bring entertainment to sincere Christians who want some innocent excitement in their reading. They may be too preachy for others.

Dominique Frayne
Author: J. T. McIntosh, pseudonym for James MacGregor

McIntosh used a television play by Peter O'Donnell as the basis for his first Dominique Frayne book, *Take a Pair of Private Eyes* (Doubleday, 1968). The result was a lighter, more humorous narrative than the Modesty Blaise series for which O'Donnell was best known.

Dominique had little respect for the law, although her father had been a French diplomat. The tiny brunette left her job as a teacher to marry Ambrose Frayne, son of a professional criminal. She joined him and his father in Recovery Enterprises, which specialized in recovering (by theft) stolen art objects. A trained gymnast, Dominique was ideally suited for her new occupation, and developed unsuspected talents as a pickpocket, artist, and housebreaker. Ambrose's father, Hector, complicated their already exciting lives through his boast that he could steal a highly prized half-ton coffin.

A Coat of Blackmail (Doubleday, 1971), a solo effort by McIntosh, was less humorous. Hector's files contained confidential information on prominent figures, plus plans for assorted crimes, including murder. When the files were stolen, Dominique ("Nicky") and Ambrose had to recover them. Fun series while it lasted.

Virginia Freer

Author: E. X. Ferrars

Virginia and her estranged but never divorced husband, Felix, brought an unusual set of characteristics to their collaboration. Virginia was a restrained, even repressed, woman in her thirties swept into marriage by the exciting Felix. Their relationship foundered within three years, when she realized that he was a petty thief and congenital liar, living in a world which she was unwilling to share. Virginia never discounted Felix's positive qualities. He was intelligent, loyal to his many friends, and he loved her in his own way. Felix brought an excitement and warmth to Virginia that she valued but could not handle on a regular basis. There were interludes when Felix returned to Virginia's home and life, but they never included sexual intimacy. There was neither reconciliation nor dissolution.

After the separation, Virginia lived quietly in her family home in Allingford, England. Her investment income was insufficient, so she continued to work as a physiotherapist. Her social position and professional contacts provided her with access to the homes and personal lives of other characters. Mutual friends of Felix and Virginia could not understand their separation, partly because Virginia was discreet. Virginia's home was where Felix went to restore himself, and for reasons of tenderness or loneliness, she took him in.

The couple appeared first in *Last Will and Testament* (Doubleday, 1978). Virginia had provided therapeutic services to Mrs. Arliss, whose deceased daughter, Mary, had been a friend. At the time Virginia cared for Mrs. Arliss, she had not known that she gambled on the horses. Within a short time, Imogen Dale, Mrs. Arliss' niece and heir, was murdered, followed by the deaths of the Bodwells, the housekeeper and gardener. Not too surprising, considering the title of the book, that inheritance was the motive. Felix was instrumental in figuring it out.

Felix and Virginia were in their early forties by *Frog in the Throat* (Doubleday, 1980), when they were independently invited to visit Helen and Andrew Boscott, old friends. Felix announced that he was working for a detective agency. Carleen, a neighbor who co-authored historical romances with her sister Olivia, was found dead; then her body disappeared. Felix checked out the two men who were romancing the sisters, but also their host, Andrew.

In *Thinner Than Water* (Doubleday, 1982), Felix and Virginia participated in the second wedding of Gavin Brownlow, an old friend. Gavin and his first wife, Kay, had spent a lot of time together. The bride-to-be was young Rosie Flint. The nuptials were disturbed by the violent deaths of the Gavins' father, Edward, and subsequently his sister Hannah. As this narrative ended, both Felix and Virginia showed a romantic interest in others.

During *Death of a Minor Character* (Doubleday, 1983), Virginia and Felix attended a farewell party for a London friend, Audrey. Virginia's gift shopping made her aware of Marcus Avery, who, together with his wife, owned an antique shop. Even before Marcus was murdered, Felix had warned Virginia to be wary of him. Although Felix had inside information on several suspects, Virginia took a more active role than usual and showed herself to be a risk taker.

Felix's broken leg and a chance to help Hubert Brightwell, a retired civil servant, write his autobiography brought him back to Virginia in *I Met Murder* (Doubleday, 1986). She couldn't say no and took him in. Brightwell had been concerned about the safety of his paintings by Claude Baraud, an artist who had recently returned to favor. A kidnapping, which turned out to be a murder (or did it), required the sale of the Barauds to provide the ransom. Felix was uncertain that the murder and the kidnapping were connected.

Both Virginia and Felix were nearby when her elderly neighbor, Malcolm Creed, was killed by a hit-and-run driver in *Woman Slaughter* (Doubleday, 1990). Then, Mrs. Bulpitt, an officious neighbor who might have witnessed the accident, was murdered. Virginia was convinced that Felix knew more than he was telling about the accident. He had indeed taken the license number of the vehicle and traced the owner, who may at some time have been married to Mrs. Bulpitt. They continued to gather evidence as another death occurred. When she thought enough was enough, Virginia called the police.

During *Sleep of the Unjust* (Doubleday, 1991), Virginia and Felix attended another problematic wedding. An unexpected guest, Andrew Appleyard, returned after a ten-year absence to attend. Why not—he had once been engaged to Sonia, the bride, and was a college friend of the groom, David. Andrew's planned wedding to Sonia had been cancelled because she had miscarried a child with Down's disease. The next morning, the day of the wedding to David, Andrew was found dead, an overdose of sleeping pills. The ceremony was postponed. Margaret McNair, also a friend from college days, was found dead in her car later.

The plot in *Beware of the Dog* (Doubleday, 1993) was transparent, but the interplay between Felix and Virginia was as subtle as ever. When Nick Duffield was questioned in the death of his wealthy grandmother, the Freers were asked to take a hand. He and his cousin Kate had come to the funeral to check on their prospects for an inheritance. The family emeralds, a valuable asset, were determined to be paste. Virginia was particularly sensitive to relationships. This time she was treated as one of the suspects.

The narratives read easily but were not engrossing. Felix was a fascinating character who did most of the detection. Virginia spent more of her time covering up or preventing his illegalities.

Carol Gates

Author: Laura Colburn, pseudonym for Ian McMahan

Carol Gates, a freelance artist and daughter of a retired chief of detectives, lived in a New York City loft. Her investigations, however, usually took place while she was out of town. Her artistic sense, eye for detail, and visual memory (playing Kim's game with her father) helped in her detecting.

Carol was a guest at a Soho loft party during *Death in a Small World* (Zebra, 1979), when the corpse of the hostess' ex-boyfriend was placed on the top of the elevator. That put the hostess and her husband on the suspect list. Carol had talked to the victim earlier. He had mentioned "doppelgangers," perhaps someone from his past among the guests. Carol's questions put her in danger, but her father had the local police watching over her. Carol's boyfriend, Chuck, disapproved of her fascination with crime, attributing it to her desire to please her father.

During *Death Through the Mill* (Zebra, 1979), Carol illustrated a true crime book. The author, Henry Marston, who had returned to his boyhood home to clear his name by solving an old mystery, was killed in a freak accident. The old mystery had revolved around the death of James Howard, who had been killed by a rifle shot. Shortly afterwards Marston's father, Robert, had died from a heart attack. The enmity between James and Robert, who were related, was well known.

Carol went undercover within a semi-professional operatic group in *Death of a Prima Donna* (Zebra, 1979) because a sponsor was concerned about the tensions among the cast and crew. After the death of Cynthia Foyle, the second female lead, Carol convinced the local police department to let her set a trap for the killer. Her pull with the police department came not only from her father but also her good working relationship with Lt. Jake Rosen.

"The Girl from U.N.C.L.E."

Authors: Michael Avallone, Simon Latter, and Peter Leslie

See: April Dancer, Section 5, page 281.

Cynthia Godwin

Author: George Beare

Although Victor Stallard and Cynthia Godwin have been identified as a "couple," she never lived up to her resumé. The daughter of a powerful newspaper publisher, she was a reporter assigned to the Middle East. Her primary education came from a Maronite convent in Lebanon and upper class Roedean in England. Her degree at the University of Edinburgh was for first-class honors in Semitic Languages. Cynthia was tall and thin, with mouse-colored hair and emerald green eyes. She drank too much (preferring vodka), was sexually active, and was bored by the routine aspects of her job, but unlikely to be fired. Stallard was the major protagonist in the series.

In *The Bloody Sun at Noon* (Houghton, 1971), Cynthia covered a revolution in the sheikdom of Saffarja. She and a dubious former professor of archaeology used Stallard's dhow to make a secret landing in the sheikdom. Dressed as a native woman, she set across country carrying a message to the deposed ruler and assisting in his escape. Although Cynthia and Vic became lovers, neither had any interest in marriage or any scruples about stealing the royal jewels.

The Very Breath of Hell (Houghton, 1971) allowed Cynthia only a few pages while Vic smuggled gold from a downed airplane and entertained another rich young woman.

During *The Bee Sting Deal* (Houghton, 1972), they worked together only when their paths crossed. Cynthia was preoccupied with the search for Sigrid Hasseler, the adopted daughter of a financier, whose birth mother, referred to as Mrs. Black, a brothel keeper, also sought her child. Vic had been hired to captain the yacht of Jamil Bazarki, a major Jarman politician. Vic and Cynthia discovered the secret behind the "Bee Sting Deal," a plan to kill dignitaries by blowing up a causeway that had been constructed to connect Jarma and Iran.

The books were witty, comparable to other international espionage series of the time.

Alison B. Gordon

Author: Walter Wager

Alison B. Gordon had light brown hair and eyes and was of average height. There was little else average about her. She was a Phi Beta Kappa who spoke at least five languages, handled a car, knife, and gun with equal proficiency, and had a "superbody." Furthermore, she collected oriental art and was a good enough sculptor to sell her work. While in the CIA, Alison had served in Africa, Vietnam, and Thailand. Although she considered herself a widow, her husband was listed as missing in action. In her work as an investigator, she used her initials to attract clients who might not hire a woman.

As *Blue Leader* (Arbor, 1979) opened, attorney Paul Kaplan hired Alison to find Timothy Hessey, the missing grandson of an East Coast client, Ret. Gen. M. E. Steele. Finding the young man dead from pure heroin was just the first step. The client wanted vengeance, so Alison was hired to find the supplier. Finding the local contact for the drugs was the second step. That wasn't enough, either, so she located the supplier and found evidence to justify his arrest. One more demand, find the importer! Steele was ready to bomb the route by which the drugs were transported. Now things got difficult.

By *Blue Moon* (Arbor, 1980), Alison had ties with individual Mafiosos. Mr. Spinoza, a retired capo, recruited her when there was a threat to blow up the Las Vegas Strip. Alison brought her people in, even explosive-sniffing dogs. She pulled no punches. She shot one suspect in the leg so she could question him. By now she had realized that there were two groups menacing the Strip. Before she finished her high technology assignment, Alison had taken on the FBI, the IRS, and the extortionists.

Murder and mayhem continued in *Blue Murder* (Arbor, 1981), during which two carloads of killers descended upon an electronics factory, killing eight employees and a visitor. Alison was hired by singer/actress Lauri Adams, the sister of a victim, to investigate. There was a lot going on: a right-wing conspiracy to take over the federal government, a battle between the President and the military over the budget, and a mysterious government-operated mental institution. Alison took them all on and saved the President's life on his private plane.

Alison was one tough woman, who could hold her own. Although the lurid covers on the paperback editions might turn off female readers, she was worth a second look.

Kate Graham

Author: Joen Arliss

Kate was a tall, dark-haired attorney in New York City who specialized in corporate law. The daughter of a deceased lawyer, she was successful due to her analytical powers and commitment to her work. She had postponed marriage over the objection of her fiancé, Jeff Kane, who wanted a stay-at-home wife.

Jeff needed Kate's skills in *The Shark Bait Affair* (Zebra, 1979), when his newspaper chain was endangered by Hugh Harper, a family friend who was calling in a major loan. Jeff's quarrel with Harper on his yacht provided a motive when Harper was gaffed while fishing. As evidence piled up on Jeff, Kate searched among the crew for a hidden motive and a distinctive earlobe.

During *The Lady Killer Affair* (Zebra, 1980), Kate and Jeff were planning their wedding. While she was in Spain pondering whether or not to abandon her career, she attached herself to a group of tourists, one of whom was murdered. Kate was at risk because she had a clue to the killer's identity. Her vacation experience convinced her to give up both Jeff and corporate law.

Above average for a Zebra.

June Beattie Grant

Author: John Norman Harris

June Beattie made two appearances in mysteries. She was a Canadian in her thirties without visible means of support except an inheritance. Her father had been killed in World War II. Her mother, lacking any maternal instinct, turned June and her brother, Wes, over to their paternal grandmother, a gesture for which she was financially rewarded.

Grandmother Beattie had never approved of her daughter-in-law, but son Rupert stood to inherit considerable money. With his death, both June and Wes became the beneficiaries. Wes, who was considerably younger, had little ambition. Robbed of a normal childhood, he lived primarily in a world of his own construction. Uncle Edgar, his father's brother, found him a job at the bank. June traveled extensively. Wes was destined for trouble. He needed money, stole a woman's purse, and was convicted and sent to jail. His attempts to prove his innocence only emphasized his instability. June, described as a "madcap," took little interest in Wes.

When Uncle Edgar was murdered, as *The Weird World of Wes Beattie* (Harper, 1963) opened, Wes' habit of lying rather than telling an improbable truth left him vulnerable. Grandmother suggested a plea of not guilty by reason of insanity, but attorney Sidney Grant, aided by June, proved that truth was indeed stranger than fiction. Wes might be paranoid, but people were conspiring against him. During the process, June and Sidney Grant fell in love and married.

Another "hopeless" case in which June provided support to Sidney was in *Hair of the Dog* (Seal, 1990). The death of an elderly woman on the night when her home was robbed was charged against ex-convict Vince Lamberti. He faced the death penalty under Canadian law for committing murder in commission of a crime. Lamberti was unwilling to use an alibi, but Grant's probe of the members of the victim's household, aided by the family dog, led to the real killer.

Laurie Grant

Author: May Mackintosh

Laurie Grant, a schoolteacher in her twenties, had tired of her job. Depressed by an unhappy personal relationship, she was ready to leave her native Scotland. Her parents were dead, and she had no other close ties when she accepted a position as governess in the home of a Spanish hotel manager.

During *Appointment in Andalusia* (Delacorte, 1972), while en route to her new job, Laurie met insurance investigator Stewart Noble, who became her comrade and perennial fiancé, and realized that she might have unwittingly transported diamonds into Spain. Once there she was to serve as governess for Lola, the 10-year-old daughter of Paco Ruiz. She still had the perfume bottle that had been switched with hers, but was unsure of who made the change. Could it have been Stewart? The death of an Italian maid deepened her concerns enough that she shared them with him. Paco, whom she liked, was involved, but cared enough for Laurie to protect her.

Assignment in Andorra (Delacorte, 1973) began with a postponed wedding because Stewart had to investigate the death of a friend in Andorra, giving Laurie only a small role.

A second postponement began *The Sicilian Affair* (Dell, 1974). Laurie made the honeymoon trip alone because Stewart was called away on business. She did not travel alone, but escorted Mario, a 12-year-old boy, to his father's home in Sicily. When the father was not available, she kept Mario with her at the villa that she and Stewart planned to occupy. Along the way, Laurie and Mario were joined by Pia, a deaf and mute girl, a child for whose death Stewart's insurance company had received a claim. Without Stewart to depend upon, Laurie coped. This taste of freedom made Laurie aware that she was attractive to other men and not tied to the dilatory Stewart.

These are easy reading, without many pretenses at in-depth characterizations or intricate plotting, similar to Gothics.

Cordelia Gray

Author: P. D. James

Cordelia Gray, a small woman with light brown hair and "browny-green" eyes, was introspective about her career as a private detective. She had an unsettled childhood. After her mother died within an hour of her birth, her father, a left-wing activist, placed her first in foster homes and later in a convent. He sought her company only when she was old enough to be of some use. The nuns helped Cordelia to win a Cambridge scholarship, which she declined, preferring to travel about Europe with her father. After his death, she taught herself to be a secretary and moved up in Bernie Pryde's agency to detective status.

In *An Unsuitable Job for a Woman* (Scribner, 1973), Pryde killed himself, bequeathing the agency to Cordelia. He had trained her well, based on his experience as a police officer working for his hero, Adam Dagliesh (James' major protagonist). Her investigation of the "suicide" of college dropout Mark Callendar, son of a prominent scientist, became a personal quest during which she met and challenged the great Dagliesh.

Nine years passed before P. D. James wrote the second Cordelia Gray, *The Skull Beneath the Skin* (Scribner, 1982). A retired Army officer hired Cordelia to attend an isolated house party, ostensibly as a secretary companion, but actually to protect his wife, actress Clarissa Lisle. When Clarissa was bludgeoned to death in a "locked room," Cordelia overcame her initial sense of failure to identify the killer and did so. Although he might never be convicted, she had carried out her responsibility to a woman whom she disliked.

James' writing is of such quality that any female character she might develop would enrich the mystery genre. Hoped-for sequels never came to pass.

Emma Greaves

Author: Lionel Black, pseudonym for Dudley Barker

Emma grew up as an only child in the Union of South Africa, daughter of a liberal judge who had been pressured to resign his position because of his stance on racial integration. She attended college in South Africa, becoming fluent in at least Zulu, Italian, and German.

In *Chance to Die* (Cassell, 1965), Emma rescued Bernard Pine, a badly beaten, naive engineer who had been entrusted with secret information by a dying man. He and Emma encountered betrayal and abuse at the hands of the South African authorities before she revealed that she was working for British Intelligence.

When Daphne Collins, a fellow agent, was killed in *The Bait* (Cassell, 1966), Emma took over her assignment. She was to draw out enemy agents. She uncovered British citizens who were being blackmailed by Communists, one of whom, Julian Compton, admitted his guilt to Emma and Nick Whiffen, an agent assigned to guard her. The enemy agents' plan to steal atomic secrets from British scientist Sir Charles Papinian relied on letters written by his wife. By now Emma was aware that there was a mole among those she had considered allies.

While on vacation in Italy in *The Lady Is a Spy* (Paperback, 1969) aka *Two Ladies in Verona*, Emma was assigned to check on a British agent who was playing a small part in *Romeo and Giulietta*. She rescued stand-in actor Luigi Moretto, when he was being tortured. By now her cover may have been blown, but she was aware of those in the production who were foreign agents. When tycoon Andrea Barbaro was murdered, Emma was framed as the killer. She uncovered a plot to create discord between the U.S. and Russia on behalf of Chinese Communists.

Emma was a professional agent who took risks, seemed unaffected by the frequent deaths of those with whom she worked, and found a different lover in each book.

Ann Fielding Hales

Author: Mary Ingate

In *The Sound of the Weir* (Dodd, 1974) aka *Remembrance of Miranda*, Ann Fielding had been a teenager, impressed by her older cousin Miranda Montague. When Miranda's husband, Rowland, was murdered and the unfaithful Miranda arrested, Ann's testimony was a strong factor in the verdict that led to her execution. Only in later years did Ann realize how both she and Miranda had been manipulated.

The sequel, *This Water Laps Gently* (Macmillan, London, 1977), utilized flashbacks to illuminate Ann's marriage to Bernard Hales and the insidious influence of Lady Millicent Hanks, a purported friend of their Greek household. Bernard's illness and death left Ann seriously neurotic, reliant on alcohol and the affections of a handsome local guide.

Although murder played a significant role in both stories, they were more psychological studies than mysteries.

Angela Harpe

Author: James Lawrence

Angela Harpe, an African-American female private investigator, emerged from a New York City ghetto. Along the way, she earned a Radcliffe degree, gaining expertise and interest in classical music, Aldous Huxley, and art. Before becoming a private investigator, Angela worked as a New York City police officer, a fashion model, and a call girl, developing an arsenal of skills. Her trademark was a seal featuring a black silhouette of an angel playing a harp, reminiscent of Simon Templar or Jimmie Dale.

Four heavily patterned Harpe books, replete with sex and violence, were published by Pyramid in 1975: #1, *The Dream Girl Caper;* #2, *The Emerald Oil Caper;* #3, *The Gilded Snatch Caper,* and #4, *The Godmother Caper.*

Undistinguished. Much better African-American female protagonists came later.

Kate Harris

Author: Travis Macrae, pseudonym for Anita MacRae Feagles

Kate Harris and her husband, Jim, moved with their daughter to rural New York State to be closer to their Midwestern roots. A tall, big-boned woman with dark red hair, Kate was a freelance photographer, and Jim was a writer, so they often combined their talents.

In *Death in View* (Holt, 1960), Alice, an actress with whom Jim was reputed to have had an affair, was murdered in Kate's presence. Kate had been upset about the rumors. Jim was upset to return from four months in Australia to find her kissing wealthy Stuart Marshall. They both had some explaining to do. More seriously, Kate would have been in considerable danger had not all her friends been aware that she had poor eyesight when not wearing her glasses. Then the word got around that she had contact lenses.

The Harris marriage was solid in *Twenty Per Cent* (Holt, 1961), when they researched the Tompkins Village High School Class of 1941, only to discover that 20 percent of the group had died violently (four out of 20 in the small class). Clara Davidson, still a close friend, seemed upset when Jim shared this information with her. Kate and Jim followed the careers and subsequent deaths of the members of the Class of 1941, but not in time for Clara. She was found dead in a nearby gully as the group gathered for a pep rally.

Julie Hayes

Author: Dorothy Salisbury Davis

Julie Hayes, in her mid-twenties as the series began, was the daughter of an American mother and an Irish father, initially referred to as a diplomat. Her Catholic father ended the marriage through an annulment, leaving Julie's mother to raise her alone. While she attended top-ranking eastern schools, there was more than a hint that her mother earned the tuition the hard way. After college graduation, Julie married an older man, foreign correspondent Jeff Hayes. While Jeff was abroad, Julie lived in the apartment he had shared with his first wife. She was vulnerable, emotionally immature, and without a sense of purpose. Her efforts to find a career in acting, writing, and working for a columnist brought her friends, but no clear goal. There were no children in the marriage because Jeff did not want them.

In *A Death in the Life* (Scribner, 1976), Julie impulsively went into business as a fortune teller/consultant in a tough New York City neighborhood. Through set designer Pete Mallory, she met and tried to help Rita Morgan, a "16-year-old" prostitute. After Pete's murder, Rita disappeared, and so did some of Julie's innocence about life. She acquired a powerful friend in "Sweets" Romano, a racketeer whose patronage and friendship followed her through the series.

An effort to redecorate the apartment in *Scarlet Night* (Scribner, 1980) included a search for the right painting. What she sought was a home that was her own, not dominated by the decorating done by Jeff's first wife. He accepted the removal of his first wife's portrait, so they needed a replacement. The one she purchased, *Scarlet Night,* was an overlay, a painting done on top of a da Vinci in order to smuggle it into the United States. Sweets Romano found the deception when he framed the painting for Julie. The plan to return the da Vinci to Italy had flaws—an effort to make money for the IRA on the side.

Jeff was overseas in *Lullaby of Murder* (Scribner, 1984) while Julie worked on a gossip column. When columnist Tony Alexander, her employer, was murdered, Julie connected his death to the suicides of public relations man Jay Phillips and his wife, Ellen. The narrative explored the relationship between Alexander's wife and stepdaughter and ended with questions unanswered.

Julie was so devastated in *The Habit of Fear* (Scribner, 1987) by Jeff's decision to seek a divorce that she retreated to her 44th Street hideaway, only to be raped by young hoodlums. Although Romano avenged her injury, Julie reacted by visiting Ireland to trace her father, Thomas Francis

Mooney. Not only was Mooney missing, but Frank Kincaid, one of her rapists, was in Ireland. She returned with more questions than answers. Readers may find themselves similarly confused and without hopes of a solution, as the series ended at this point.

Millicent Hetherege

Author: Robert Bernard (Martin)

Dame Millicent Hetherege, the septuagenarian principal of St. Agatha's in Oxford, had a secret identity as Deirdre Desiree, the author of Gothic novels.

In *Deadly Meeting* (Norton, 1970), Dame Millicent's academic credentials led to a visiting professorship in the English department of Wilton, a New England college. She was filling a short-term vacancy because the department chairman, Peter Jackson, a man with Mafia ties and a predilection for blackmailing his associates, had been poisoned during the Modern Language Association convention. A second murder may have been committed by a different killer.

After her retirement in *Illegal Entry* (Norton, 1972), Millicent, her slightly ineffectual brother, Peregrine, and her dog, Iseult, moved to an English village near Stratford. Her personal loyalty caused her to conceal Mike Templeman, an illegal American visitor determined to prove that his brother was not a defector to Communism. Her strategy included the scent of Iseult in heat in a hectic but humorous conclusion.

Average.

Julia Homberg

Author: Sarah Gainham

It is something of a stretch to include Julia Homberg as a mystery character. She did indeed appear in a three-book series set in Austria during first the German Anschluss and then the Allied occupation. Julia was a renowned stage actress with a lifetime membership in the national theatre company that gave her some exemption from the attentions of the Germans who took over Austria. However, her husband, Dr. Franz Wedeker, was not only a Socialist politician but also a Jew. Julia was a tall, dark-haired woman whose father had been a civil servant of the Hapsburg monarchy. She had studied drama at the Academy, ascribing her need for excellence to her father's demands for perfection.

Night Falls on the City (Collins, London, 1967) began as the transition from independence to German control came to Austria. Only when a friendly U.S. reporter urged him to do so did Franz agree to leave the country. His attempt failed and he returned to the home in Vienna that he had wisely transferred to Julia's ownership. With the help of their servant Fina, whose Catholicism was tempered with her devotion to Franz, Julia kept Franz safely hidden for seven years. Julia did not remain faithful to Franz during this period, as his health failed. Liberal editor Georg Kerenyi, a close friend, became a regular visitor to the home. Although he did not survive the Russian takeover, Franz left behind a valuable treatise on the control of power that was sent out of Austria for distribution. If there was a mystery, it was that so many knew of Franz's whereabouts but did not disclose them.

The second book, *A Place in the Country* (Weidenfeld and Nicolson, London, 1969), was narrated by Robert Inglis, an Englishman who married Lali von Kasda, the sister of Julia's lover who died in the waning months of World War II. Robert, who had rescued Georg Kerenyi and other prisoners of the Russian army, was instrumental in identifying a Communist mole in the British diplomatic service. Julia returned to the stage, giving possession of her country estate to friends. She and Georg married at the conclusion.

Private Worlds (Weidenfeld and Nicolson, 1971) had even less justification for consideration as a mystery. The risk to Kerenyi after the return of an SS general who could do serious harm to his reputation, and by reference to Julia's career, was minimized when Kerenyi was rescued by a rightist group who helped him leave the country. The narrative focused more heavily on Julia's past and the difficulties in the marriage between a man with a need to dominate and a woman who had always placed her career first.

Helen Blye Horowitz

Author: David Delman

Helen Blye Horowitz, who was 5' 11" with short black curly hair, had a degree in nursing. Her marriage had produced a son, who was never again referred to after the first book. After her husband, the local sheriff, was murdered, Helen worked as a deputy. She investigated her husband's death, killed one of the two men responsible, and captured the other.

Although there had been two prior Jake Horowitz books, Helen appeared first in *He Who Digs a Grave* (Doubleday, 1973). Jake, an urban cop from the East, came to New Mexico to help an old buddy suspected of murder, but needed Helen's help. Helen was an independent woman, a worthy opponent or comrade for Jake. The development of their relationship during the murder investigation was endearing. After they married and moved out East, the emphasis was on Jake's professional life. Helen worked in the juvenile division of a local police department, although Jake preferred to be the sole provider.

One Man's Murder (McKay, 1975), in which Helen picked up on the significance of why keys and not money were stolen from John Fletcher, and *The Nice Murderers* (Morrow, 1977), in which she played no part, gave Helen few opportunities to show her skills. Jake did not want Helen working. This situation couldn't last.

By *Death of a Nymph* (Doubleday, 1985) Helen was employed as a sergeant in the juvenile division of the Tri-Town Police Department. She took charge when Jake was shot by an intruder after spending some time at posh Byrd School. His injuries required several weeks of recuperation. Although warned not to interfere, Helen cleared Deirdre Adams, a shy high school student, of murder. There was more than one suspicious death at Byrd. Helen took aggressive steps at her office against Lt. Kelsey, a supervisor also assigned to the murders, who sexually harassed her at work.

By *Murder in the Family* (Doubleday, 1985), Helen had been promoted to head of the Nassau County Juvenile Crime Prevention Squad. She remained behind when Victor, Jake's son from an earlier marriage, was murdered in Portugal. When Jake was kidnapped by local communists financed by Eric the Red Halliday, a Communist millionaire, Helen left her job to rescue him.

By *Dead Faces Laughing* (Doubleday, 1987), *The Liars League* (Doubleday, 1989), and *The Last Gambit* (St. Martin, 1991), Helen had left the police department to work as a private investigator. Her new employment might have led to increased participation in the narratives, but she was restricted to minor appearances, with one exception.

Helen, as private investigator, and Jake, as police detective, were at odds in *Bye-Bye Baby* (copy found in a "two in one" by HarperCollins, 1992). Both had been friends of chess-playing professor Bry Gilchrist and were aware that he had at one time been married to murdered tennis queen Baby Robin Cantrell. Helen's determination to prove Bry's innocence was countered by Jake's unsympathetic reaction. Her case was also hampered by the fact that Baby Robin had been smothered to death in Bry's apartment. Jake's boss put the heat on him to make Helen back off, but that didn't deter her either.

Betty Crighton Jones

Author: Charles Goodrum

Betty Crighton Jones, or, as she preferred to be called, "Crighton," public relations director of the Werner-Bok library in Washington, D.C., investigated mysterious deaths along with 70-year-old retired librarian Edward George, and researcher Steve Carson. Little background information was provided for Crighton, except that she had earned a degree in journalism.

The trio came together in *Dewey Decimated* (Crown, 1977), when anonymous letters claimed that rare documents held by Werner-Bok had been forged. When Murchison De Vier, the head of the vast manuscript collection, was killed in a fall, Steve and Crighton believed he had been murdered. They enlisted George to prove how and where.

In *Carnage of the Realm* (Crown, 1979), Steve and George found economist/historian Dr. Karl Vandermann dead. Although all utilized the library resources for research, each member of the ensemble worked on a separate track to connect Vandermann's death to silver robberies and the counterfeiting of antique coins. Vandermann had indicated that someone in his coin club wanted to kill him, so they started there. Their first prospect for the killer was murdered in a manner similar to Vandermann's death, so they had to move on to Plan B. Each would query a member as to lifestyles and financial resources.

By *The Best Cellar* (St. Martin, 1987), Steve, who regularly proposed to Crighton, had been awarded his Ph.D. and was working at Williamsburg. The disappearance of Crighton's house guest, Durance Steele, a doctoral candidate with a "secret," led to an ingenious historical quest involving the movement of books out of the Library of Congress when the British invaded Washington, D.C., in 1814. Had the books been burned as claimed, or were they hidden somewhere? They had been replaced by the purchase of Thomas Jefferson's library, but were they still in existence?

During *A Slip of the Tong* (St. Martin, 1992), Crighton served as executive officer at Werner-Bok while the director traveled. Her problems increased when two staff members, who earned extra money as desk attendants in the Asian Reading Room, were murdered on the streets. This could not be a coincidence. Crighton used new intern Kit Chang for access to the Chinese family associations. Even then there was much tension between Crighton and the associations. Their concern was the preservation of Chinese documents at a time when the Red Chinese were anti-intellectual. They located historic Chinese materials endangered by Red Chinese, but the killer of the young library workers had no personal political agenda.

Goodrum provided expertise in the field, intriguing plots, and an organized process of investigation, but little character development.

Cleopatra Jones

Author: Ron Goulart, novelization of screenplays by
Max Julien, Sheldon Keller, and William Tennant

Cleopatra was a tall, athletic, African-American woman who spoke several languages, and rode a motorcycle or drove a Porsche with easy skill. Single, she had an ongoing relationship with Reuben Masters, operator of a drug rehabilitation center for young African-Americans. Cleopatra challenged drug dealers, Nazi-lovers, and assorted caricatures of villains. It was all camp.

In *Cleopatra Jones* (Warner, 1973), "Mommy," a lesbian drug dealer, wanted revenge because Cleopatra was responsible for the destruction of Turkish opium fields. Cleopatra was enticed back to New York City by raids on Reuben's drug rehabilitation center. She was kidnapped, escaped, was recaptured and almost killed in a scrap metal lot, but survived to fight Mommy, one on one.

Cleopatra Jones and the Casino of Gold (Warner, 1975) brought Cleo a new adversary, the Dragoness Princess, a beautiful blonde named Bianca who had Melvin and Matthew Johnson, two of Cleopatra's associates, and half of a major drug payoff in her possession. Cleopatra headed for Kowloon, going into the slum district to find her friends, unaware that they had been moved to Macao. That was where Cleopatra headed next, to Bianca's casino in Macao. She needed allies and got them from an unexpected source when she became a prisoner.

The movies on which the books were based are occasionally shown on late-night television.

Anna Jugedinski

Author: Phyllis Swan

Anna (Anastasia) Jugedinski, a female private investigator, descended from Russian nobility, but the family had fallen upon hard times. Her parents were killed when their liquor store was robbed, leaving Anna to raise a younger brother, Nicholas. Family friend Mike Roark, the local police chief, brought Anna and Nicholas into his own home until his wife objected. As the series began, Anna and Nick lived above her office in a tough part of town. Anna, a tall, slim woman with brown hair and blue eyes, had been raped as a 13-year-old. Her frigidity discouraged the affection offered her by Chino Parini, a family friend. At no time did she seek any professional help for her emotional problems.

Caroline Swartz, wife of a local politician, wanted Anna to find and return her granddaughter in *Find Sherri!* (Leisure, 1979). Anna's mentor, Mike Roark, had recommended Anna as a discreet investigator. Although Anna had professional training, she went into danger unarmed, without any backup, menaced by the same gangster who had raped her as a young girl. Anna was shocked to learn that Roark, to whom she had been attracted, was her real father. This woman did not need more sexual hang-ups.

Wealthy nightclub owner Leopold Shasta, needing a companion for an elegant ball in *Trigger Lady* (Leisure, 1979), hired Anna, but expected her to carry a gun in the beautiful gown he provided. She disliked guns but took the assignment when Shasta offered to underwrite the cost of one year's college for Nick. She looked so attractive that Shasta made a move on her. Anna was also working another case involving a jewelry store robbery and had been offered a deal whereby she could get a lead on the robbers in exchange for double-crossing Shasta. That didn't interest her either. During the party she shot a member of a rival gang, which prompted Shasta to offer her his protection. Chino did him one better, offered to claim he fired the shot.

It didn't get any better for Anna. In *The Death Inheritance* (Leisure, 1980), still recovering from injuries and in debt for medical expenses, Anna concealed her personal claim when hired to trace her grandmother's heirs. The murder of a Russian art dealer was clearly tied to Communist efforts to kill any descendant of the Romanovs. The ending will leave readers cold, and Anna frigid.

You've Had It, Girl (Leisure, 1980) was still inaccessible in 2005.

Sarah Kelling

Author: Charlotte MacLeod aka Alisa Craig

Sarah, a small woman with plain brown hair and hazel eyes, was a double Kelling. A shy and sheltered young Bostonian when orphaned at 18, she had married her older cousin Alexander, who was still dominated by his mother, Caroline.

When introduced in *The Family Vault* (Doubleday, 1979), the Kelling family was in ferment because their burial vault was the repository of the recent corpse of Ruby Redd, a former dance hall girl of questionable virtue. By the time the burial mix-up had been settled, Sarah had lost both Alexander and Caroline.

By *The Withdrawing Room* (Doubleday, 1980) Sarah had opened her Boston home as a boarding house. Unfortunately, there seemed to be a jinx on her tenants. Boring Barnwell Quiffen was knocked into a subway train. The next occupant of the room, William Hartler, was bludgeoned to death in the Public Gardens. Art critic Max Bittersohn came on scene both as a suitor to Sarah and the primary investigator.

Max's role expanded in *The Palace Guard* (Doubleday, 1981) when he moved into the boarding house. Sarah's distant cousin Brooks, temporarily employed as a guard at the Fenway Court Art Museum, worked with Max when reproductions were substituted for valuable paintings. Sarah was relegated to a supporting role.

Sarah made a comeback in *The Bilbao Looking Glass* (Doubleday, 1983) when Max visited her summer home at Ireson's Landing. He researched a valuable looking glass placed in the entryway. Their wedding plans were delayed when Max was arrested at the wake of Alice Beaxitt, a nasty gossip. Anti-Semitism had contributed to the accusations against Max. A highly regarded local man was identified as responsible by Sarah.

By *The Convivial Codfish* (Doubleday, 1984) Max had earned sufficient respect with the Kelling clan to be their major resource when the Great Chain of the Convivial Cod disappeared from the possession of Cousin Jeremy. A subsequent accident to Jeremy, a mass poisoning, and the death of Wouter Tolbathy, a member of the Convivial Codfish, (who had been killed while he was guiding a private train with group members on board) made it clear that there was more than internal rivalry involved.

In *The Plain Old Man* (Doubleday, 1985) Sarah assisted in the family's regular Gilbert and Sullivan production, helping with the sets but also investigating art theft and the murder of Charles Daventer. Charles was a suitor of Sarah's Aunt Emma, on whose estate the festivities occurred, and was playing a part in the production. Although this might have been an opportunity to expand on Sarah's character, she was overwhelmed by the supporting cast.

Grab Bag (Avon, 1987) was a collection of short stories with little attention paid to Sarah. *The Recycled Citizen* (Mysterious Press, 1988) found Sarah relegated to the sidelines because she was pregnant with son David. Max protected the reputation of Dolph Kelling when he was accused of murder and misappropriation of funds from the Senior Citizen Center.

In *The Silver Ghost* (Mysterious Press, 1988) Max and Sarah attended the Billingsgate Renaissance Revels. Max was there to protect the Billingsgates' valuable antique car collection, but was unable to prevent the theft of a Rolls Royce. The watchman had been murdered, and elderly Aunt Bodie Kelling was missing.

It took a broken leg to sideline Max and leave Sarah in charge during *The Resurrection Man* (Mysterious Press, 1992). She muddled her way through a Gothic tale of bastards, artistic masterpieces, and ateliers with help from assorted relatives. Kellings were like chocolates. Too many deadened the palate.

The Gladstone Bag (Mysterious Press, 1990) had no meaningful participation by either Sarah or Max, even though the dust jacket referred to a "Sarah Kelling Mystery." Sarah's Aunt Emma, an elderly widow, dominated the book.

Sarah took a major role in *The Odd Job* (Mysterious Press, 1995), five years later when Max was in Argentina seeking a stolen artwork. Sarah challenged the new Chairman of the Board of Wilkins Art Museum, Elwyn Fleesom Turbot, when he remarked that the Bittersohn Detective Agency was doing a poor job of finding and returning the stolen artwork. This led to an investigation of the mysterious death of museum director and art forger Dolores Tawne, who had still been employed at Wilkins. Sarah sheltered herself and David with members of the Kelling-Bittersohn family until the killer could be apprehended.

The Balloon Man (Mysterious Press, 1998) began with a wedding at the Bittersohn home for Max's nephew and his bride-to-be. Her rather odd family was not too terribly interested in the proceedings. Strange, because there were some unusual incidents connected to the wedding: the reappearance of Kelling family jewels, missing for years, discovered among the gifts; a balloon crash on the grounds; and the death of a man known only as Joe MacBeth, a member of the ground crew. Max and three-year-old Davy were endangered by a probe into the history of Caroline, Sarah's first mother-in-law, who had given the family jewels to a young lover, and the identity of those who planned to steal them again.

Mary Morgan Kelly

Author: Jane Langton

Given the intricate plots and characterizations, it was disappointing that librarian Mary Morgan was relegated to background material for a considerable period of time after her appearance in *The Transcendental Murder*

(Harper, 1964) aka *The Minute Man Murder*. She assisted Homer Kelly of the Middlesex District Attorney's office in an investigation that combined murder, mysterious letters of historical interest, and a reenactment of the Concord incident in the Revolutionary War. After their marriage, both continued their education, becoming Harvard lecturers, but Mary played minor roles until late in the series. The dozen intervening books in which she had no meaningful participation are not reviewed here.

Finally, in *The Shortest Day: Murder at the Revels* (Viking, 1995), Mary had her chance. She witnessed the death of country singer Henry Shady, who was in Cambridge to take part in the Harvard Revels. Homer disparaged her account of what had happened. It was she, not Homer, who noticed the parallel motivations in the subsequent murders of attorney Tom Cobb and Jeff Peck. It was she who recognized the ravages of jealousy in the killer. Score one for Mary.

In *Dead As a Dodo* (Viking, 1996), Mary accompanied Homer to Oxford, where he was assigned as a visiting lecturer. Dr. Helen Farfree, working late at night at the museum, "saw a creature" on the glass roof but did not call the police. The next morning the body of guard Bobby Fenwick was found on the ground. He had apparently fallen off the roof. Missing items were connected to Charles Darwin's explorations. Then Helen's domineering husband, John, was killed in an accident while leaving the zoology building. The killer's suicide answered temporal questions, but the debate on the conflicts between science and religion continued. Langton's great illustrations were a delight.

The Face on the Wall (Viking, 1998) concerned Mary's niece, Annie Swann, who illustrated children's books. Annie's delight in the new addition to her house was marred by a "face" which emerged from the wall on which she was painting a mural. There were more serious problems: the disappearance of "Princess Pearl," a former student of Mary's; the Gasts, self-centered tenants who considered Eddy, their handicapped child, a burden; and Charlene, a talented young swimmer who had learned her parents' lessons too well.

Although Mary was not as enthusiastic as Homer about the invitation to visit Italy during the flood season in *The Thief of Venice* (Viking, 1999) she agreed to the trip. Her life (and, to a lesser degree, Homer's) intersected with those of an attractive but larcenous doctor, a dying library director, and a woman accused of murdering her husband. On a different level, the narrative explored the faith engendered by miracles and two millenniums of anti-Semitism.

Mary was leery about visiting the Charlottesville, Virginia, area in *Murder at Monticello* (Viking, 2001) because of serial killings in the area.

The murders were an added inducement for Homer. Old friend Ed Bailey had rental quarters available for the Kellys. The proximity of Monticello, where Fern Fisher, a former student of Mary's, worked, clinched the deal. Fern unfortunately had attracted the attention of a camper with a fascination for the Lewis and Clark expedition, a randy senior citizen, and the serial killer. Homer was able to distinguish among them. Mary served only as a link to a potential victim.

The prints of Dutch artist Maurits Escher as they were reflected in the interactions and characterizations in the narrative brought a metaphysical tone to *The Escher Twist* (Viking, 2002). That was not all that Langton fans will enjoy. Homer and Mary took on the cause of a new acquaintance, Leonard Sheldrake, when they met at the Peabody Museum. Sheldrake, who had identity problems of his own, sought a friendly woman with whom he had a casual encounter at an Escher exhibition. She, Frieda, needed an intervention in her life. A killer meant to extract revenge. Homer came to believe that his skills had peaked and that Mary's were increasing, "passing him by."

The fictional search by Mary for information about her great-great-grandfather, Seth Morgan, during the Civil War in *The Deserter* (St. Martin's Minotaur, 2003) took place against the depiction of the battle of Gettysburg. The valiant search of pregnant Ida Flint Morgan for her missing husband took her to the battlefield, then to hospitals in Baltimore and Washington, D.C. Mary and Homer gradually developed material to explain how Lt. Seth Morgan, an honorable man, had been designated a deserter.

Who else but Jane Langton could weave such diverse elements into the touching *Steeplechase* (Thomas Dunne/St. Martin's, 2005)? Homer, whose book *Hen and Chicks* had become a *Times* best seller, was urged by his agent to turn out another book as soon as possible. To that end, he and Mary roamed the Massachusetts countryside visiting churches for *Steeplechase* (a search for church steeples). It was Mary who uncovered evidence of a "lost church," the discovery of which would add interest to the book. The parallel story (set in 1868), segments of which were interspersed with the Kelly research, revealed the history of the missing church. A mighty chestnut tree caused a final breach between Pastor Horatio Biddle of the Nashoba First Church and his parishioner Rev. Josiah Gideon. Their clash was skillfully interwoven with the plight of an injured Civil War veteran, the fears of a child, and the unspoken love of a good man for his friend's wife. Literary allusions to Charles Dickens, Dr. Oliver Wendell Holmes, Cicero, and frightening children's classics embroidered the narrative. The book was a delight.

Helen Keremos

Author: Eve Zaremba

Helen Keremos had roots in both the United States and Canada. When her alcoholic Canadian mother died, Helen went to live with her father in California. After graduation, she worked for U.S. Naval Security and a California detective agency. As the series began she was in her forties and embodied many of the traditional characteristics of the private investigator. She barely made a living, had a marginal working relationship with the police department, and was a loner. She was also a lesbian, although that was not clear in the first book.

In *A Reason to Kill* (Paper Jacks, Ontario, 1978), Helen was hired to find a missing son whose sexuality was in question. No further information was available on this first book. What is provided came only from a reference in a later book.

Helen's gender was an asset in *Work for a Million* (Amanita, 1987) when she was hired to guard Sonia, a singer who would not accept either the police or a male private investigator. Helen entered the music world, and eventually uncovered the "friends" who had been harassing Sonia. Later she joined Sonia on a Western camping trip.

Beyond Hope (Virago, 1988) began as Helen visited San Francisco to search for "Ray" (Sara Ann Raymond), a female terrorist, at the request of Ray's dying mother. Ray's father had been a wealthy, reactionary Senator. The assignment was complicated by Mossad and Canadian agents who were looking for a Carol Shoreman, who could be Ray under another of her names. She had been gone for ten years. Helen combed the women's communes to find "Ray," then backpacked through national parks looking for her. When she found and rescued Ray, she returned to the women's commune. Old Ben, who had given Helen information, had been killed.

In *Uneasy Lies* (Second Story Press, 1990), Helen served as temporary security officer at Diamond Plaza Towers, an expensive residential apartment complex. Clare Harewood, manager of the facility and a former lover of Helen's, would be out of town for three of the six weeks of Helen's employment. Attorney Dennis Gurton, who occupied a unit with his wife, Rebecca, was murdered shortly after Helen arrived. Helen agreed to work on the murder along with her friend Sgt. Malory of the Toronto Police but not to cover up any environmental abuse involved in the project. There were some who might benefit from the rumors of contamination.

The Butterfly Effect (Second Story, 1994) took Helen to Tokyo on an assignment for Ladrone Investigations of Canada, searching for Julie, a missing courier. With some reluctance she teamed up with Wayne Tillion, a burly investigator. Together they tangled with art thieves and Asiatic criminal organizations, unaware that Ladrone was tainted. After surviving a complex adventure, spanning Japan, the United States, and Canada, Julie and Helen went off together. This was the most highly structured of Keremos' plots.

Homosexuality was a major factor in the Zaremba series, but the gay and lesbian characters were not locked in a closed society. Although Helen's sexual orientation became more prominent in later books, she had credibility as a private investigator within the larger community.

Jacqueline Kirby
Author: Elizabeth Peters, pseudonym for Barbara Mertz

Jacqueline Kirby was provided with height and the self-assurance to carry it off. She had auburn hair worn in a bun and the green eyes (even though hidden behind horn-rimmed glasses) that often symbolized the independent and spirited woman. Although middle aged with adult children, it was never clear whether Kirby's marriage(s) ended in divorce or widowhood. She was eccentric: she carried a police whistle, rain gear, and first aid kit in a humongous purse, broke into song on occasion, and maintained a running feud with the IRS about her "too liberal" tax deductions. A New Englander by birth, she considered her employment at a midwestern university as exile to a literary Siberia. Later she became a romance novelist.

Jacqueline (never Jackie) took a sabbatical in Rome as *The Seventh Sinner* (Dodd, 1972) opened. She became acquainted with seven American graduate students who had banded together, calling themselves the Seven Sinners. They included artists, archaeologists, and an art historian. "Hanger-on" Albert Gebara was found dying in the cellars of San Clemente, an ancient church. He had been seen alive earlier that day. In investigating, Jacqueline allied herself with Lt. Giovanni di Cavallo, a handsome Italian detective.

The ongoing controversy in mystery and history as to Richard III's guilt in the death of his royal nephews was re-explored in *The Murders of Richard III* (Dodd, 1974). Jacqueline observed the pattern between current violence among members of the Ricardian Society (devoted to proving Richard's innocence) and historical precedents. She clobbered an intended killer with her purse and exited with a new romantic interest.

In *Die for Love* (Congdon, 1984), archaeology and history were replaced by a humorous send-up of a historical romance writers conference. When Dubretta Duberstein, an aggressive columnist, died of poison amid rumors of plagiarism, Jacqueline felt a need to get involved. Dubretta died shortly after Jacqueline administered the pills for her seizure. Author Vivien Valentine believed the poisoned wine had been meant for her. Jacqueline gathered physical evidence: a sliver of the wine glass, and a sample of the wine. She did not, however, share Dubretta's little black book, probably containing calumny and libel, with Detective O'Brien. By the time she decided she had better do so, it had been stolen. Laurie Schellhammer, teenage Valerie Valentine fan club president, became the next victim. There were two kinds of criminals here: the literary and the killer.

When popular author Kathleen Darcy disappeared, Jacqueline was selected to write a sequel to her blockbuster novel in *Naked Once More* (Warner, 1989). Jacqueline reunited families, matched up couples, uncovered the missing writer, and identified a killer, then settled in Pine Grove to write her book.

Kirby was a chameleon protagonist, moving from one setting to another as her occupation and interests were changed.

Valerie Lambert

Author: Joan Allan

Valerie Lambert, a 31-year-old blonde, advanced from secretary in a New York City advertising agency to account executive at Harrison, Lundy, Ingram.

During *Who Killed Me?* (Zebra, 1979), when Valerie visited London to supervise commercials for a new fragrance, there was trouble on the set. Neither Hans Richmond, the director, nor actress Meri Melton could work with Nelson Bishop, marketing consultant, who considered Meri too old for the part. Valerie was rousted out of bed by the police seeking an identification when Bishop's body was found in an alley. A note on the body had said to contact Valerie. Inspector Haverstock welcomed Valerie's input. She convinced a handsome police detective to help her trap the killer.

In *Who's Next?* (Zebra, 1979), Valerie jaunted off to a haunted French chateau to develop an advertising campaign for a wine/champagne account. She and her secretary, Oscar Fryman, traveled to the Abbe-Roi vineyards. As one murder followed another in the isolated setting, Val rallied the guests to solve the crime before they were all killed. That was a possibility because the wine set out for their dinner had been tampered with.

As *Who's on First?* (Zebra, 1979) opened, Jeremy Bolton, the editor of the San Francisco *News-Telegraph*, was kidnapped. Valerie had been in town working on an ad campaign for the faltering newspaper. "Who's on First" was the slogan they had proposed. The police believed Bolton's absence was a publicity stunt, but the request for a ransom seemed to confirm that he had indeed been kidnapped. Hoax maybe, but with murder included.

Average for a Seventies Zebra.

Dr. Hannah Land

Author: Amanda McKay (Smith)

Hannah Land, a divorced academic, was a tall, lanky redhead employed in the Political Science Department of Duke University in North Carolina. A former New Yorker, she found the slower-paced Southern atmosphere relaxing.

During *Death Is Academic* (McKay, 1976) her adjustment was disturbed when friendly colleague Bradley Brown was poisoned by cyanide in his fruit cocktail at a farewell dinner for a colleague. Hannah had been unsure of her welcome at Duke, but Brown had made her feel comfortable. There were motives for Brown's murder, but it was not completely clear that Brown had been the intended victim. Lt. "Bobby Gene" Jenkins of the local police department welcomed Hannah's assistance because she provided an objective view of the disputatious members of her department.

As *Death on the Eno* (Little, 1981) opened, a canoe excursion had left Hannah with a broken leg and a firm conviction that the drowning of Luther Turnbull did not occur when he was alone. Lydia, Turnbull's niece, who admired Hannah, was an entrée into the family. The survivors might be more amenable to an offer from Mafia-connected Johnny Taranto to purchase family land. In a series of less than credible events, several other murders occurred. The solution came only with the suicide of the killer.

Time passers.

Ann Lang

Author: Daniel Estow

Librarian Ann Lang played a supporting role to private investigator Bill Schaefer of the Worldwide Detective Agency.

In their violent debut, *The Moment of Fiction* (Carlyle, 1979), Schaefer searched for Volume II of a sensational autobiography by James McCoit, purportedly in the possession of Guillermo Roth, an American attorney living in Madrid. Ann, Schaefer's live-in lover, read a photocopy of Volume I, while he headed off to Spain to interview Roth. After Schaefer learned that Roth did not have the book, Ann figured out the motive for its suppression. They worked together to find Volume II, or prove it never existed. Schaefer had been dissatisfied with his treatment at Worldwide and was ready to go out on his own. Ann, working on her Ph.D., joined Schaefer in Schaefer and Lang but never achieved equality.

In *The Moment of Silence* (Carlyle, 1980), client Calvin Barrett insisted that he wanted Schaefer, and no one else, to trace his daughter Janice. He needed Janice's shares in a battle for control of his corporation. His other two daughters and their husbands wanted him to sell. Ann could not stay on the sidelines. She rescued Schaefer, held illegally in an abandoned part of the jail. In a gratuitous incident, she posed for pornographic pictures to ingratiate herself with a dirty old man who could show her where Janice had been buried.

These were fast action narratives, portraying Ann primarily as a foil for Schaefer and a sexual tease.

Tracy Larrimore

Author: Jessyca Paull, pseudonym for Julia Perceval and Rosaylmer Burger

Tracy Larrimore was a footloose 21-year-old brunette in London, unwittingly involved in espionage. Back in New Jersey, Tracy had been a secretary. She accepted overseas employment from American businessman Danton, who promised excitement.

As *Passport to Danger* (Award, 1968) began, Tracy was shocked to learn that a woman named Tracy Larrimore had been found dead in a Paris hotel. She was aware that Danton was in France, then she realized that he had taken her passport. En route to the American embassy, Tracy was waylaid and flown back to the United States. Mike Thompson of British Intelligence came to the rescue and recruited her to help him. They flew to

Paris, where, ignoring all warnings from Mike, Tracy went sleuthing on her own. The action moved frequently. Tracy agreed finally to act as bait to trap Danton and his accomplice, Nadia. Simplistic.

By *Destination: Terror* (Award, 1968), Tracy had become engaged to Mike Thompson. While they were planning their honeymoon, Mike disappeared. The "Boss" (actually Sir Robert Blythe), Mike's superior officer lost trust in Mike and then in Tracy for not making him aware of Mike's absence. Using clues conveniently left behind by Mike, Tracy pitted her limited skills against a conspiracy to discredit the United Nations. Believe it or not, she was kidnapped and rescued by Mike. A happy ending for a weak story.

In *Rendezvous with Death* (Award, 1969), Mike's supervisor convinced him to spend their honeymoon on the island of Panyagua, where an anti-American conspiracy was brewing. Tracy went along with the plan reluctantly. While swimming, the couple discovered a cave filled with munitions. Their presence had been noted, so Mike was framed for murder, and Tracy kidnapped (third time in three books). At the end she decided to stay home. There was a hint that she might have twins.

Tracy found the danger, romance, and excitement young adult readers would enjoy, and that seemed to be the intended audience.

Pauline Lyons

Author: Elizabeth Anthony, pseudonym for Anthony and Page Traynor

Pauline Lyons was fortunate: a ballet dancer with Ballet American Company, who loved to cook and could eat without gaining weight. The long black hair that reached to her waist was worn in a bun during her performances. After her parents died in her teenage years, she became a boarding student at a ballet school. In her spare time, she detected.

In *Ballet of Fear* (Zebra, 1979), dancer Tory Hunt's conviction that she was the reincarnation of legendary ballerina Anna Pavlova created publicity, but also ill feeling in the company. Tory was the protégée of Lisette St. Cyr, an elderly teacher soon to retire from BAC. Pauline had her own mentor, 80-year-old Anna Garlina, who taught her a great deal about the role she would dance in *Swan Lake*. Pauline was selected for the Black Swan. Tory missed out for the White. Mrs. Diffenbocher, the bookkeeper for the company, died after being mugged on the street. Anna Garlina was found hanging. Pauline refused to accept these two deaths as mugging and suicide.

In *Ballet of Death* (Zebra, 1979), Pauline was teaching ballet while recovering from a leg injury. Susan Trippett, promoter for the summer production, demoted Pauline's student/protége, Colleen Barnett, in favor of a less qualified dancer. The next day Susan was found stabbed to death by a letter opener. Pauline, fearing that Colleen would be the primary suspect, ignored the current jealousies and found the solution in Susan's past.

Humdrum.

Sue Carstairs Maddox
Author: Elizabeth Linington aka Lesley Egan and Dell Shannon

Sue Carstairs, a small woman with dark hair and eyes, shared a home in Los Angeles with her mother, Margaret. She was in her late twenties when the series began. She had a Welsh Corgi, "Gor."

Her assignments as a policewoman in *Greenmask!* (Harper, 1964) were limited to juvenile cases or assisting male officers in cases where adult females were concerned. Future books in the series, with few exceptions, dwelt more on her relationship with Ivor Maddox and his cases than on giving her any significant role in investigations. On at least one she was portrayed on the cover, but inside it was all Maddox.

During *No Evil Angel* (Harper, 1964), Sue had difficulty searching for Jewel, a missing 13-year-old girl, partly because the girl's mother was so disinterested. When her search took her into a dangerous part of Los Angeles, fellow officer Ivor Maddox answered her request for support.

Date With Death (Harper, 1966) provided Sue with an opportunity to use her dramatic talents as a decoy hooker. Maddox had recommended her for the duty. Together they trapped a hotel manager/pimp and a misbehaving mailman.

In *Something Wrong* (Harper, 1967), Sue had several cases, which gave her a chance to shine. She investigated juvenile shoplifting, located a missing infant, and, with Ivor, probed the post-abortion death of a 15-year-old. Ensemble approach.

By *Policeman's Lot* (Doubleday, 1968), she was still classified as an "auxiliary" police officer, assigned to comfort bereaved parents or spouses, or investigate juvenile delinquency, but had an ongoing relationship with Ivor.

Ivor and Sue became engaged in *Practice to Deceive* (Harper, 1971). During one of several cases covered, Sue fit the target group for a rapist who began by stealing underwear and then raped women, preferring them to be small and dark haired. He got quite a surprise when Ivor and Sue set a trap for him.

Among the subplots in *Crime by Chance* (Lippincott, 1973) was the case of a missing young widow and her child victimized by a desperate woman.

Sue's inability to conceive a child after she and Ivor had married made her angry when she encountered abused and neglected children during *Perchance of Death* (Doubleday, 1977). Her career prospects had improved as she passed the detective exam. She was out of uniform, but still in a gender-segregated unit.

In *No Villain Need Be* (Doubleday, 1979), Sue and Ivor bought a larger house to provide room for Sue's aging mother. The ability to have a home came when an elderly lady whom Sue had befriended committed suicide, leaving her house to Sue.

Sue turned her attention to fixing up the house and buying an Akita puppy in *Consequence of Crime* (Doubleday, 1980). The household problems ran parallel to their professional responsibilities for sweeps of prostitutes, forged checks, teacher attacks, and the rape of a teenage girl.

Sue was pregnant in *Skeletons in the Closet* (Doubleday, 1982) but continued to work. A bulldozer exposed two skeletons while razing an older house. The narrative was one of the more professional in the series, detailing the procedures used (1) to trace the prior owners and renters of the dwelling in which the skeletons were found, and (2) to locate a rapist who assaulted a boy delivering newspapers.

In *Felony Report* (Doubleday, 1984) Sue, almost ready to deliver, was involved in only one of the cases presented, the murder of a teacher who planned to marry a pupil. *Strange Felony* (Doubleday, 1986) introduced baby John Ivor, who kept Sue out of action.

Policewoman Sue Carstairs played a supporting role in the series, receding even further into the background as she married and began a family. She reflected conservative viewpoints on abortion, feminism, and welfare. The series would not stand up against females in police departments as depicted in later decades.

Helen Marsh

Author: Charlotte MacLeod, writing as Alisa Craig

See: Helen Marsh Shandy, Section 5, page 401.

Megan Marshall

Author: Michelle Collins, pseudonym for Michael Collins

Megan, an attractive blonde in her twenties, managed a small art gallery in upper New York State. She had a longstanding relationship with Evan Townsend, who was something of a jerk.

During *Murder at Willow Run* (Zebra, 1979), Garrett Winters, an important but unpleasant art critic, visited the town to critique a show at Megan's gallery. Megan and the artists were anxious about his reviews, but there were others in town who had more personal grievances against Winters. When he was murdered in a room that no one could have entered and left, Megan offered her services to the police, but was rebuffed. Conversely she had little faith in their ability to solve the crime. It didn't help that Evan was one of those suspected by the police.

In *Premiere at Willow Run* (Zebra, 1980), Megan played Stella in *A Streetcar Named Desire*, produced by the artistic community to complement an art show. Charlotte Albright, a wealthy patron of the arts, agreed to place some of her collection on display at the request of Tom Chummles, the owner of the playhouse. Besides playing an important role in the production, Megan had to repaint the sets because local artist Tom Mowbray's work was unacceptable. When a valuable Monet was stolen, the police fixed on a suspect whom Megan believed to be innocent. Her involvement in the case was highlighted by her ability to recognize a reproduction.

Octavia "Tavy" Martin

Author: Diana Winsor

Octavia "Tavy" Martin had been raised by her grandmother after the death of her parents in a train wreck, but little other personal information was provided. She shared a small house with three other young women while working as a secretary at the Ministry of Defense.

In *Red on Wight* (Stein, 1978), Tavy was sent to Portsmouth by British Intelligence to investigate an explosion on a naval vessel. Her engagement to a naval officer was used to justify her move to a shoreline clerical position. While in Portsmouth Tavy lived above a pub, where she helped out as a waitress, getting a chance to know the locals. There continued to be explosions of shells and missiles on board British and American ships. An expert sailor, she used a sailboat to follow Commander Nick Vance on a trip to the Isle of Wight, where she gathered valuable information. She found the ties among Vance, a monk named Sebastian, and scientist Dr. Theo Keech, in a scheme to cripple the Allied navies.

During *The Death Convention* (Stein, 1978), Tavy was assigned to a peace conference held by the Lovers of Life in Amsterdam. The Ministry of Defense gave her a camera to use to photograph visitors to a house along the canal, while posing as an artist. Unhappily, she realized that the house she was expected to monitor was on the edge of the Amsterdam red light district. Tavy was also expected to gather information about important leaders at the conference. A major Russian speaker at the conference, who had family in England, asked Tavy for help in defecting.

Run of the mill.

Freya Matthews
Author: John Palmer, pseudonym of Edgar John Palmer Watts

Despite being an archaeologist and professional diver, Freya Matthews had a surprisingly prickly and emotional temperament. Although her first name has a Germanic ring to it, Freya was an Englishwoman who had graduated from Oxford. She was teamed with Guy Plant, a former British naval officer who described himself as retired but was working for British Intelligence. When she met Guy on a social occasion, he was interested in her underwater work off Cape Khoundros. The prior year, while diving from a sponge fishing boat, she had discovered what might be an ancient military vessel.

Freya accepted a casual invitation from Guy to use his yacht as a diving platform for the season in *Above and Below* (Hodder and Stoughton, 1967). She was totally unprepared for his agenda, intercepting two Israeli agents who had kidnapped Major von Messmer, a suspected Nazi war criminal. The plot expanded to include drug smugglers. Freya wrestled with her self-image as an avowed pacifist. In a struggle to control the yacht she almost clubbed a man to death. Still recovering from an unhappy affair with Alec Plant, Guy's brother, she developed an unrequited passion for von Messmer. When it was all sorted out, she remained on the yacht with Plant and his kindly assistant, Louie Cooper, who tended to her damaged psyche.

So Much for Gennaro (Hodder, 1968) took place in Spain, where Guy and Freya were sent to control Marcus Gennaro, a Marxist Member of the British Parliament. Gennaro had disappeared by the time they arrived. Freya had seen him kidnapped by three young men. She did not disclose her connection with British Intelligence to the Spanish police but posed as a private investigator representing Gennaro's wife, who suspected him of infidelity. The powerful father of Gennaro's mistress, Amalia Gutierrez, abducted Freya and questioned her. A rescue by the Spanish police and a second abduction dragged things out, but this time Freya managed her own escape. She used an ice pick, which she had hidden on her person, to stab her abductor. Her responsibility was to divert Madrid police captain Morales, who had been abducted with her, so that Guy Plant could find Gennaro. She certainly did.

Sharon McCone

Author: Marcia Muller

Sharon was a pioneer female private investigator, who fit few of the previous conventions. She was part Native American and the rest, Scotch-Irish. A member of a large blue-collar family, she was a single woman with a history of serial sexual relationships. Her long, dark hair became lightly streaked with gray. She dressed casually, lived first in an apartment and then in a small "earthquake" house, and finally shared homes with her permanent lover, Hy. Unlike so many prior investigators, family tradition or an effort to avenge a death or prove someone innocent did not influence her choice of occupation. Her college degree had been in sociology; her first jobs, store detective and detective agency employee. She investigated initially under the aegis of All Souls Legal Cooperative in San Francisco, working under Senior Associate Hank Zahn, who became a good friend. Later Sharon opened her own agency, recruiting former co-workers. There were successes and failures, both in her personal and professional life, but she was neither an adjunct to a male partner nor a slightly feminized version of a "tough guy." Her imitators are legion now, but her equals are few.

In *Edwin of the Iron Shoes* (McKay, 1977), the Salem Street Merchant's Association hired Sharon to investigate arson and vandalism. For some unknown reason, her investigation brought a lull in those problems. The murder of antique dealer Joan Albritton changed her assignment. Hank wanted her to stay in touch, inventorying Joan's stock. Joan's lover, junk dealer Charlie Cornish, was her heir. He moved out. Then the arson and vandalism began again.

Police Lieutenant Greg Marcus, who appeared first in *Edwin,* moved into Sharon's personal and professional lives in *Ask the Cards a Question* (St. Martin, 1982). When Molly Antonio, an elderly lady in Sharon's apartment building, was murdered, Linnea Carraway, a visiting friend, was suspected. Sharon pursued her own investigation, bypassing cooperation with Marcus and concealing information. Many of those whom she checked out were connected to a local center for the blind. She pinpointed a fencing operation and shot an intended killer. Sharon broke enough laws in the process that she had to make a deal with the authorities.

In *The Cheshire Cat's Eye* (St. Martin, 1983), the struggle between developers who modernized Victorian homes and area conservationists formed the background for murders. It began for Sharon when she went to meet her ex-beau, housepainter John Kaufman, and found him dead. Kaufman had been painting a series of row houses inherited by David Wintringham when his father died. The senior Wintringham had died in a fall in the same house three years earlier, after which it was noted that a Tiffany lamp, "The Cheshire Cat's Eye," had disappeared. Its reappearance set up a trail for Sharon to follow.

In *Games to Keep the Dark Away* (St. Martin, 1984) Sharon's search for unemployed social worker Jane Anthony did not end when she found the young woman's dead body. A nurse who had worked with Jane, Liz Schaff, joined with Sharon in checking out why Jane had been dismissed from Tidepool Nursing Home in Salmon Bay. Entry into Tidepool required the residents to will their property to the administration. There had been several such deaths recently. Sharon remained in Salmon Bay, not only to investigate, but also to advance a new relationship with disk jockey Don Del Boccio. Excellent conclusion.

Leave a Message for Willie (St. Martin, 1984), continued the Del Boccio romance, but his proximity made Sharon uncomfortable. He'd moved in with her temporarily, looking for a job in the area. Sharon didn't really want to work for fence Willie Whelan because she disapproved of his activities, but he was being followed. So she agreed to check and identified the stalker, Jerry Levin, a former thief of Torahs. Jerry was repentant, searching for Torahs he had stolen, some of which might have been in Willie's possession. This didn't make Willie look any better to Sharon, particularly when Jerry was murdered. There were worse villains out there than Willie, though.

Double (St. Martin, 1984), co-written with Bill Pronzini, brought together Sharon and "Wolf" (Pronzini's Nameless Detective) at a private investigators convention. Authors Marcia Muller and Bill Pronzini (husband and wife) contributed alternating chapters as their protagonists investigated an abduction, sado-masochistic orgies in the desert, and the killer of Sharon's friend, Elaine Picard.

During *There's Nothing to Be Afraid Of* (St. Martin, 1985), Sharon dealt with the Vang family, Vietnamese sponsored by the Refugee Assistance Center, but terrorized by someone who did not welcome them. The

Vangs were housed in the Globe Apartment Hotel in the Tenderloin. Checking out Otis Knox, owner of a porno theatre down the street, Sharon learned that he wanted young Dolly Vang to appear in one of his films. When Knox was murdered, Dolly's brother, Duc Vang, disappeared. Finding Duc led to an even more important discovery.

By *Eye of the Storm* (Mysterious Press, 1988), the romance with Del Boccio had ended. On the other hand, Hank Zahn and the All Soul's tax attorney, Anne-Marie Altman, were planning to marry. Sharon visited her younger sister Patsy on Appleby Island. It was not much of a vacation for Sharon. Patsy, an interior decorator, was busy transforming buildings on the island into a Boatel. Locals cited the ghost of Crazy Alf Eisler, a Native American who had been lynched on the island. Sharon's personal tour of the island ended up with her shanghaied and barely afloat in a terrible storm. Of course, there was a murder, that of Max, operator of the ferry boat, and manipulation of consortium funds. So going back home wasn't so bad.

In *There's Something in a Sunday* (Mysterious Press, 1988), at the request of manufacturer Rudy Goldring, Sharon was staking out ranch foreman Harlan Johnstone, who came to San Francisco every weekend. Goldring was dead when she went to deliver her report. The police focused on Bob Chateau, a street vagrant. Sharon carried out her own investigation and discovered the connection between Johnstone and Goldring, but not before there was another victim.

The death sentence of young parking lot attendant Bobby Foster was under appeal in *The Shape of Dread* (Mysterious Press, 1989). The body of his purported victim, Tracy Kostakos, had never been found, yet Bobby's fingerprints, her bloodstains, and an abandoned car were in evidence. More importantly, Foster had first confessed and then retracted his confession. If she were still alive, how could Tracy let him be executed? Sharon found a body that might be Tracy's, but even that was in question. In the process Sharon learned the kind of woman Tracy was. Tracy's husband, George, began a troubled relationship with Sharon that ended because his wife was mentally ill.

Nothing was happening between George Kostakos and Sharon as *Trophies and Dead Things* (Mysterious Press, 1990) began. Sharon kept herself busy helping Hank Zahn settle an estate for which he had been named executor. The deceased, Perry Hilderly, a former student protest leader and Vietnam newsman, was killed by a sniper's bullet. His will disinherited his sons and left his estate to four persons with whom he had been connected during his days as a protester. Sharon theorized that Hilderly felt he owed them. Two deaths later, Sharon worried about Hank Zahn and his pal Willie Whelan, both survivors of Vietnam.

During *Where Echoes Live* (Mysterious Press, 1991) Anne-Marie Altman was acting as counsel for the California Coalition for Environmental Preservation. She convinced Sharon to go to the Tufa Lake area, where mining interests and conservationists battled for power. The land in question had been sold by the Bureau of Land Management at what might be considered an unacceptably low price. Additional land owned privately also went at a low price, and the former owner could not be located. In the process of Sharon's investigation she met widowed political activist Hy Ripinsky. They connected, both questioning how Transpacific Corporation really intended to use the property. She needed a stable relationship, and maybe Hy was the answer. There was trouble in the parental McCone household. Sharon's mom, Katie, had tired of her unresponsive husband and left him for another man.

Pennies on a Dead Woman's Eyes (Mysterious Press, 1992) was one of the weaker Muller narratives, partly due to the amount of introspection, but also the difficulty of blending the current investigation with an "historic crime scene." Muller had done this successfully before in the Elena Olivarez series. (See *Beyond the Grave*, co-written with Bill Pronzini.) The immediate case dealt with Lis Benedict, who had spent 36 years in prison for the murder of her husband's younger mistress. Supreme Court Justice Joseph Stameroff, who supported the conviction, had raised Lis' daughter, Judy. Judy could not let it go at that. She had to know, because her testimony had assisted the prosecution.

Not only Sharon's tentative relationship with Hy but her future at All Soul's were at risk in *Wolf in the Shadows* (Mysterious Press, 1993). Hy had disappeared, leaving his plane and a damaged rental car behind. New leadership at All Soul's, headed by Mike Tobias and Gloria Escobar, rammed through a reorganization that would promote Sharon to administrative tasks, ending her fieldwork. Utilizing sick time, Sharon decamped to follow Hy's trail through Renshaw & Kessell (RKI), an international security firm with a tough reputation. RKI, Hy's firm, had been called in when the CEO of Phoenix Laboratories, Tim Mourning, was kidnapped. The primary suspects were environmental groups that protested the use of dolphin cartilage for a new HIV drug. Hy's welfare was the most important concern for Sharon.

In *Criminal Intent 1* (Dark Harvest, 1993, co-authored with Bill Pronzini and Ed Gorman), Sharon served in an advisory capacity to Rae Kelleher. The book was a collection of novellas. Rae appeared in *The Wall*, during which she was assigned to locate a missing teenager. The search drew Rae into life-threatening circumstances and moral decisions. Sharon was her mentor.

Although she still rented office space, Sharon broke off all formal ties with the All Soul's Cooperative in *Till the Butchers Cut Him Down* (Mysterious Press, 1994). Her first client, "Suits" Gordon, a former college friend who had always worked the corners of illegality, called on Sharon's loyalties when his life was threatened. There had been four unsuccessful attempts on his life. Suits was now a "turn-around man," called in to resuscitate failing businesses. He had big plans for a defunct naval shipyard. Sharon became a believer when she and Suits left his home just before it blew up, with the possibility that his wife, Anna, had died. With Suits missing, Sharon focused on other communities that had been impacted by his "turn-around" activities. Personally she was finding it difficult to deal with the unknown parts of Hy's life, the frequent unexplained absences.

Sharon's focus had changed over the years, as evidenced in *A Wild and Lonely Place* (Mysterious Press, 1995), by her affiliation with RKI, the anti-terrorist and hostage redemption agency, in which Hy was now a partner. Sharon's friend Inspector Adah Joslyn had already interested her in a series of bombings at foreign embassies and consulates. It was Sharon's identification with Habiba Hamid, the nine-year-old granddaughter of the Azadi ambassador who had been kidnapped, that sent her off to the Caribbean. The series had moved from classic mystery to espionage, the flying that Sharon and Hy shared, and their relationship.

Sharon's family, dysfunctional though they were, remained close, but she was surprised when her brother-in-law sought her help in *The Broken Promise Land* (Mysterious Press, 1996). Ricky Savage, now a popular country singer, and Sharon's sister Charlene had married as teenagers, doing the right thing because she was pregnant. Years of austerity, raising six children; then, success...but it was all falling apart. Notes that referred to an unsavory incident in his past worried Ricky. He was frightened that revenge might be taken against him, Charlene, or their children. Sharon's love for her family; her affection for Rae Kelleher, who left All Soul's to work with her; and her longing for a stable relationship with Hy complicated the investigation.

Sharon's interest in flying, fostered by Hy, played a role in *Both Ends of the Night* (Mysterious Press, 1997) when they sought the live-in lover of their friend, pilot Matty Wildress. John Seabrooke had disappeared, leaving Matty to care for his son, Zach, and warning her to take him and go into hiding. Matty, a competitive flyer, chose instead to compete in an air show, during which her plane crashed. Once Zach was safely placed with friends, Hy and Sharon dedicated themselves to learning who Seabrooke really was and why he and his family were targets for violence.

Sharon suffered from insomnia during that vulnerable time at night when her sense of guilt and awareness of shortcomings overwhelmed her, but in *While Other People Sleep* (Mysterious Press, 1998) she had justification for her anxieties. An unknown woman was determined to harass Sharon, invading her privacy, impersonating her in public, and threatening her stability. Her sense that this was a personal matter made it difficult for Sharon to involve her staff. Instead, she sought out her pursuer, and learned the young woman's identity, background, and something of her motivation.

Sharon was 40, off to combine business with pleasure on a vacation shared with Hy in *A Walk Through the Fire* (Mysterious Press, 1999). She hadn't planned on the aura of Kauai, the lure of an attractive Hawaiian pilot, and the complexity of her investigation. What had begun as a security operation around a documentary by friend Glenna Stanleigh became an emotional search into the past of two dysfunctional families.

Listen to the Silence (Mysterious Press, 2000) included a surprise not only to the readers but also to Sharon herself. Although her appearance differed from those of her siblings, only after "Pa's" death did she learn that she had been adopted. Her mother was unwilling to discuss the matter. Using her investigative skills and those of her staff, Sharon uncovered a concealed murder, but the killer was terminated by an unexpected source. At the conclusion she had located both parents but reaffirmed her sense of being a McCone. Very interesting.

Within weeks of her brother Joey's suicide, Sharon agreed to investigate the death of Internet journalist Roger Nagasawa in *Dead Midnight* (Mysterious Press, 2002). Roger's father, Daniel, planned to sue his son's employer, InSite, an online magazine, claiming work conditions had driven Roger to kill himself. Sharon came to believe that Roger had uncovered serious problems at InSite and had every intention of exposing them. When reporter J. D. Smith, who was pursuing a parallel investigation, died, it was not suicide. Sharon, a seeker of truth, used the resources of her agency to avenge Smith and to learn from Roger's death what had driven her brother to take his life.

Things were going too well to last, so in *The Dangerous Hour* (Mysterious Press, 2004), they went bad in a hurry. The arrest of trainee investigator Julia Rafael for credit card theft placed the future of McCone Investigations in jeopardy. The alleged victim, county supervisor Alex Aguilar, was a prominent Hispanic politician who brought charges against Sharon with the state-licensing agency. Violence followed, bringing Sharon to the realization that she was the primary target and that she could identify her enemies. It was good to have her future settled. There was a low-level appearance by Muller's Elena Olivarez, the director of the Mexican Museum where Aguilar served on the board. Elena was married, had a child, and had returned to her Catholic faith.

The McCone Files (Crippen and Landru, 1996) and *McCone and Friends* (Crippen and Landru, 2000) collected short stories in which Sharon had been featured over the years. Many of the stores had been previously published in mystery magazines or other collections of short stories. They provided some insights into the development of the character.

Aware that Laurel Greenwood had disappeared from her home 22 years ago, leaving behind a husband and two young daughters, Sharon still agreed to take on a search in *Vanishing Point* (Mysterious Press, 2006). As an adopted child herself, she empathized with Jennifer Aldin who had, according to her husband, Mark, become obsessed with learning what had happened to her mother. In less than five weeks Sharon and the reader learn how and why Laurel disappeared, not necessarily what her daughters had hoped to discover. Sharon, now married to Hy, was reluctant to move out of her beloved but tiny home so that he could have more room.

Although the young investigator of *Edwin of the Iron Shoes* had changed, it was inevitable over a long series. The broadening of Sharon's character through her relationships and her increased maturity enriched the narratives. She had become more pragmatic and less concerned about legality, but retained an element of her idealism. Muller is one of the best mystery writers of her generation.

Selena Mead

Author: Patricia McGerr

The daughter of a U.S. diplomat, Selena Mead had raven hair and violet eyes, and was a Vassar College graduate, proficient in languages. She owned the Georgetown home where she and her husband, Simon, lived before his death. Her cover for espionage activities was that she reported on politics for the magazine *Background*. Hugh Pierce became Selena's control at Section Q. He posed as an indolent artist and was not known to be involved in espionage.

Legacy of Danger (Luce, 1970), was a collection of progressive episodes, some of which had been printed as short stories, during which Selena met, fell in love with, and married Simon Mead. After Simon's death, Selena took his place at *Background* magazine, handling delicate investigations for Section Q of U.S. Intelligence. Her primary goal was to trap

Simon's killer. Her knowledge of diplomatic circles and acceptance into select social groups made her an asset to the agency.

By *Is There a Traitor in the House?* (Doubleday, 1964), Selena still grieved for Simon, but Hugh Pierce had become important in her life. Gilly Conroy, an attractive Southern "party girl," had jumped or been pushed off a bridge. She had been suspected of espionage leaks, so her death was of interest to the agency. Selena cultivated divorced Congressman Jeff Stone, a major suspect. She drew the line at using sexual intimacy to get information but risked her reputation. Since Gilly's death had never been confirmed, Selena took part in a trap. It failed to the extent that Stone considered Selena a slut, and she was still not sure whether or not he was a traitor. Someone was selling out to the Red Chinese. Remember, these were the 1960's: McCarthy, House Un-American Activities Committee, blacklists.

Among the Selena Mead short stories were two included in *Spies and More Spies* (edited by Robert Arthur, Random House, 1967). During "Ladies with a Past," Selena found a hidden microfilm in the Smithsonian, where almost anything could be found. In "Selena in Atlantic City," she attended the Democratic National Convention to find a Red Chinese spy. Above average for its time, when so many of the women in espionage novels, particularly those written by men, were slinky villainesses.

Gail Rogers Mitchell
Authors: Gordon and Mildred Gordon aka "The Gordons"

After her father moved out of the home, Gail Rogers' mother had worked as a grocery store clerk to support and educate the family. Gail used her diploma from a business college to become secretary to attorney "Mitch" Mitchell. They fell in love and planned to marry.

As *The Night Before the Wedding* (Doubleday, 1969) began, Gail was certain about her love for Mitch, but unhappy with the clients attracted to his practice. She was manipulated by a mysterious man, referred to as "X," to act as a "go-between," by threats against her invalid mother. She contacted the police but did not initially share with Mitch. Her responsibility was to meet Sam Bronson in an alley, where he would give her money to be delivered. The police apprehended Bronson, who under pressure led them to his boss. Joseph McNulty admitted the payoff was a response to X's threats to injure his children.

Cathy Doyle, another threatened young woman, approached Mitch for help in *The Night After the Wedding* (Doubleday, 1979), but, although Gail still worked in the office, she had no significant role in the story.

Very ordinary.

Mary Morgan

Author: Jane Langton

See: Mary Morgan Kelly, Section 5, page 327.

Hon. Constance Morrison-Burke

Author: Joyce Porter

The Honorable Constance Morrison-Burke (or Hon Con) was a heavyset Englishwoman who wore an Eton haircut and masculine clothing, smoked cigars, and used aftershave instead of perfume. Whenever Hon Con entered a community activity, her behavior drove other participants away. She terrorized the locals with her extravagant hobbies, but, as the independently wealthy daughter of an earl, could jettison activities when they bored her. She lived in Totterbridge with Miss Jones, a passive companion. In her gentle way, Miss Jones was often more adept in getting information from others than the blustering Con.

As *Rather a Common Sort of Crime* (McCall, 1970) began, Con had just been ejected from the Community Advice Bureau, so she decided to set up her own agency. Her first client was Mrs. Burberry, who could not accept the official decision that her son had committed suicide. Young Burberry, an ex-Borstal boy, was less than an admirable figure. Still, it seemed unlikely that he would lace his Scotch whisky with weed-killer. The police made his records available to Con. It was easier than opposing her. Although she solved the case, Con got 14 days for disturbing the peace.

This taste of detection increased Con's curiosity about crime, and in *A Meddler and Her Murder* (McKay, 1973), she probed the death of Teresa O'Coyne, an Irish au pair. Teresa had been written off as a "tease," but that didn't excuse murder. Police and neighbors thwarted Con, but Miss Jones gathered gossip to meet the deficiency. There were humorous passages when Con was inveigled into changing a baby and vacuuming and cleaning the home where the young woman had been employed.

Politically conservative Con joined a 14-day tour of the Soviet Union in *The Package Included Murder* (Bobbs, 1976). Fellow passenger Penelope Clough-Cooper, who insisted that she was in danger, recruited Con to protect her. She made a valiant effort, although there were three more attempts on Penelope's life. However, it was fellow tourist Ella Beamish who died. The fact that she was wearing a coat similar to Penelope's was noted. Although the police considered Hon Con an eccentric, she provided them with the information that led to the killer.

In *Who the Heck Is Sylvia?* (Weidenfeld, 1977), the Ottaway sisters asked Con to investigate a woman who claimed to be their long-lost sister, Sylvia. If alive, Sylvia, who had run away from home 40 years ago, would own a one-third share in a major business that was considering a merger. Following a trail, Con and Miss Jones visited Gritstone-on-the-Sea to investigate a woman known locally as bordello keeper Maisie Finnegan. Con and Miss Jones were kidnapped by a male hairdresser, then rescued from hardened criminals by Cub Scouts.

In *The Cart Before the Crime* (Weidenfeld, 1979), community leaders solicited Miss Jones to direct Con's attention elsewhere because a royal visit was expected in Totterbridge. When Con learned that a local manor was to be sold to outside interests, she investigated the prospective purchasers and their intended use of the property. She uncovered a dastardly plot to ruin the Royal Visit.

The mixture of humor and violent death required a deft hand, and sometimes achieved it. The locals commented upon the relationship between Con and Miss Jones.

Ms. Squad
Author: Mercedes Endfield, pseudonym for Bela William von Block

The Ms. Squad had an engaging premise: young women, thwarted in a male-dominated world, banding together to prove that females could be just as adept at "capers," maybe better. The squad included three New York City professionals:

- Jacqueline Cristal, a Ph.D. in chemistry and vice president of a cosmetics company, who supervised men with fewer credentials, but who were paid higher salaries;

- Deena Royce, an African-American night club singer from Harlem, who paid out a major portion of her income to the men who handled her career and to the Mafia, which owned 30 percent of her contract; and

■ Pammy Porter, a tiny, pony-tailed, Olympic gymnast who resented the fact that the big endorsements went to male competitors.

They met at a lecture given by a prominent feminist; bored, they left Carnegie Hall and adjourned to Jackie's apartment, where they aired their grievances.

To prove their point, the women selected famous crimes during which men had made errors, added feminine touches, and succeeded.

In *Lucky Pierre* (Bantam, 1975), the trio, posing as a Japanese princess, her African-American maid, and her tiny chauffeur, redid the Hotel Pierre robbery, confronting both the Mafia and the FBI. Each brought special talents to the caper. Jackie developed chemicals to control their victims and low-sound explosives. Deena cased the hotel while she performed in its cabaret. Pammy found a new skill, stealing a sable coat and a Rolls Royce.

Their second escapade, *On the Brink* (Bantam, 1975), was reminiscent of the Brink's hold-up. They successfully robbed the restaurant on top of the old Brink's building, fleeing in a Brink's car, but were confused when the management claimed that a much smaller amount was missing. They suspected that their loot came from the numbers racket, so they would again have to evade not only the police but also the Mafia.

Showed some promise.

Norah Mulcahaney

Author: Lillian O'Donnell

Norah Mulcahaney, a New York City policewoman, was described as tall (5' 8") and large boned, with a prominent jaw, dark brown hair, and gray-blue eyes. At 29 and detective third grade, she still lived with her widowed father.

In *The Phone Calls* (Putnam, 1972), Sgt. Joe Capretto's investigation into the mysterious deaths of two widows introduced him to Norah. Ruth Emerson, depressed by the death of her husband, Clem, in a car accident, jumped or was pushed out of a window. She had just received a phone call. A second widow, Vittoria, who was pregnant, gassed herself after a phone call. Young widow Arabella Broome, who was getting phone calls, contacted Joe. He enlisted Norah to present herself as Mrs. Fogarty, a recent widow. That plan didn't work, but the killer made contacts to Norah herself.

During *Don't Wear Your Wedding Ring* (Putnam, 1973) Capretto, the only son in an Italian family, romanced Norah while they investigated a call girl service employing "respectable" housewives. Diane Vance, who had a husband and children, spent her free time hustling under the name Joy Fuller. After her headless body was discovered in a hotel room, Joe was assigned the case. Norah was to infiltrate the group as a bent policewoman. The power behind the call girl ring was something of a surprise. Both Norah and Joe were injured in the investigation, in which she had a strong role.

O'Donnell continued to explore women's issues in *Dial 577-RAPE* (Putnam, 1974). When charged with the rape of Gabriella Constante, Earl Dana claimed that she submitted voluntarily. His exoneration was a tragedy for Gabriella. Her fiancé backed out of their marriage plans. Norah, who had handled the case, was determined to get Earl behind bars. When she traced a possible connection between Earl and a murder, he took the offensive. Norah accepted Joe's proposal.

By *The Baby Merchants* (Putnam, 1975), Norah had accepted that they would never have a child of their own and convinced Joe that they should adopt Mark, a three-year-old boy, through the Children's Institute. They realized eventually that they had been manipulated into a conflict of interest. Joe, who was working on the murders of three underworld figures, was threatened that Mark's adoption would be disallowed if Joe didn't back off on the Nerone case. There was no alternative for Norah and Joe.

In *Leisure Dying* (Putnam, 1976), Norah disclosed information that adversely affected Joe's professional status. After promotion, Joe was assigned to serve as commander of the 4th Homicide Division. Norah uncovered a series of murders involving elderly persons who had just received their social security checks. Her father had tipped her off to a number of those affected. Joe's unit had failed to note the pattern, casting doubts on its efficiency. For a while, he moved out of the home.

Joe visited Italy on family business in *No Business Being a Cop* (Putnam, 1978). The deaths of four female police officers were more than Norah could accept as a coincidence. She came to believe that the deaths were connected to police corruption in narcotics investigations. In the process, Norah was attracted to Sebastian Honn, a captain in the Narcotics Unit.

In *The Children's Zoo* (Putnam, 1981), Norah's offer to help when Joe's niece Toni was sexually abused was rebuffed by the girl's parents, Jake and Lena De Vecchi. Their desire to avoid further trouble for Toni outweighed their sense of justice. Professionally Norah was something of a pariah at the 4th Division. Whistleblowers are not popular among cops. She was working several cases, including the slaughter of zoo animals and the death of a zookeeper in Central Park; the murder of Jonathan Burrell, a paralytic elderly man; and the murders of Sylvie, a young schoolgirl, and her mother. All these crimes were eventually traced to teenagers. She was shocked by the tolerant treatment afforded juvenile delinquents by the courts after they were arrested.

Young hoodlums killed Joe when he intervened in a robbery/rape in *Cop Without a Shield* (Putnam, 1983). Unable to cope at work, Norah took a leave of absence, moving to a rural Pennsylvania community where a friend had a farm. She became aware of incompetence in the local police with regard to Mennonites and to crimes against immigrants. Even after she was drugged and shamed, Norah persisted, bypassing the local authorities and working with the Bureau of Immigration. After a crushing blow to her self-confidence, she returned to New York City and her work.

In *Ladykiller* (Putnam, 1984), Norah prepared to take the lieutenant's exam. She was a sergeant assigned to a series of cases involving the murders of young women who had recently had a new man in their lives, someone whose name they had not shared with family. When she identified the killer, she saved her own life by her fast driving. Initially she and officer Gary Reissig, who worked with her on the cases, didn't get along, but they developed a personal relationship. Further promotion changed Norah's approach to police work. There were more administrative tasks and less fieldwork. She was on display to the media as an example of how women could succeed in the city bureaucracy.

O'Donnell adapted a Sunny von Bulow theme in *Casual Affairs* (Putnam, 1985), in which Norah mentored Audrey Jordan, a young woman detective, working on the plight of an unconscious wealthy woman. Christina Isserman married Walther, but it hadn't worked out and he was unfaithful. When she went into a coma, her sister claimed that Walther had put drugs in Christina's drinks. A second attempt was made on Christina's life while she was in the hospital. After Christina returned home, both she and Walther were found dead. Although a lieutenant now, Norah took personal charge of the case. She did not accept the murder-suicide solution and trapped the killer at the risk of her own life. The relationship with Gary Reissig did not survive his need for a commitment from Norah. She wasn't ready.

The Other Side of the Door (Putnam, 1987) was inappropriately subtitled as a "Norah Mulcahaney Mystery"; Norah made only a token appearance. Det. Gary Reissig, who had a brief fling with Norah earlier, was now married and had children. When he had difficulty with a case, he called on Norah for advice, and later she spoke on his behalf when he was questioned by Internal Affairs.

Norah, now the head of Homicide, 4th Division, was more sophisticated and attractive by *A Good Night to Kill* (Putnam 1989). She took a personal interest in the killing of Frank Beech by Stefanie Altman, a young bookstore owner. Beech, who had no weapon on his body, had accosted Stefanie on the street, demanded money, and taken possession of her keys. Stefanie claimed self-defense, particularly since Beech had two friends with him. In a second case, her unit investigated the death of Gilda, the pregnant wife of Mafia kingpin Dario Valente. Both of these cases received considerable media attention, prompting Norah to appear on a television talk show hosted by Randall Tye.

In *A Private Crime* (Putnam, 1991), Tye and Norah, who were spending a lot of time together, quarreled over his views on an apparently random killing. A masked killer fired a semi-automatic rifle into a crowd at an outdoor flea market, killing Dolores Lopez, a young mother, and her child. Although she and Tye agreed that Dolores had been the intended target, Norah was angry when he publicly tied the attack to drugs. Rebuffed by Norah, Tye began his own investigation, going to places unavailable to her. His probe ended unfortunately, Norah finished the task, but was alone again.

By *Pushover* (Putnam, 1992), Norah had returned to casework, rejuvenating the series. She investigated a series of deaths wherein an attacker pushed women of a certain physical type under subway trains, same time of day, same day of the week. In another case, retired movie star Wilma Danay died protecting Todd Millard, her visiting grandson. The boy had either escaped or been kidnapped. Kidnapping seemed more likely when a ransom was demanded. She clashed on both of these cases with Kathryn Webber, an aggressive young policewoman who reminded Norah of herself at that age.

Norah still wanted a child, and in *Lockout* (Putnam, 1994) she returned to an adoption agency to register her name. Her career seemed secure when suddenly obstacles presented themselves. First, she encountered resentment in her unit when she rebuked Al Sutphin, a detective who had participated in a demonstration on paid time. Sutphin held a grudge and conspired against Norah. Then, her killing of a molester was questioned. Finally, she was pressured to solve the high-profile murder of entertainer Bo Russell, so she did.

Norah had passed the captain's examination and was listed for promotion by *Blue Death* (Putnam, 1998). She had settled into motherhood with her adopted son, Patrick, named after her father. Even her problems with childcare did not prevent Norah from taking an active role in the investigation of a series of police officer "suicides." Her attempt to manage the cases from her home, while caring for Patrick, was denounced by her supervisor, but Norah persisted until she discovered a killer and uncovered a police conspiracy.

Like the Energizer bunny, Norah just kept going.

Amanda Nightingale

Author: George Revelli, possible pseudonym

Amanda Nightingale, who began life as the daughter of a Church of England dean, lost her mother when she was very young. That was unfortunate, for, if anyone needed maternal guidance, it was Amanda. She subsequently attended Cheltenham Ladies College, where she played on the cricket team, but much of her behavior was definitely not "cricket." A tall, highbred woman with long silver-blonde hair, she had brief notoriety as the 1936 debutante of the year. Her marriage to the promiscuous heir to a brewery fortune produced children, but no happiness. Amanda became an espionage agent during the Second World War. Absorbed by her career, Amanda had no time for the children of her marriage.

During *Commander Amanda Nightingale* (Grove, 1968), after being dropped into Occupied France, Amanda encountered German agents, but her espionage activities were subordinate to her passion for her sadistic capturer.

Resort to War (Grove, 1971) followed the formerly frigid Amanda through her unbridled sexual activities at the home of an expatriate in France. She had become bisexual in her choices. Loyalty to government and country had no role in her selection of lovers. There were at least three other books. The narratives were sadistic and masochistic. Should have a very limited readership.

Jennifer Norrington

Author: Ivor Drummond,
pseudonym for Roger Longrigg, aka Frank Parrish

Jennifer Norrington was "Lady Jennifer," daughter of the Earl and Countess of Teffont. Her partners in Drummond's ensemble adventures were Count Alessandro "Sandro" de Ganzarello, a divorced Italian of independent means, and uncomfortably rich American Coleridge "Colly" Tucker III. Jennifer had the classic "English look," long blonde hair with large blue eyes. She enjoyed life on her family estate, but was drawn to excitement. Although very intelligent, she posed as a flighty blonde to disarm suspicion.

Colly and Sandro learned of Tamara, a young woman who had escaped from white slavers, in *The Man With the Tiny Head* (Harcourt, 1970), leaving her friend Nicola still a prisoner. They went back to the cave where she had been held and were almost killed when some gang members returned. Colly noted that valuable paintings were listed for sale. Was someone raising money for a ransom? Jennifer connected the incident with the disappearance of a student from her alma mater. She presented herself as a potential victim, a Miss Phyllida Pearce. Unfortunately she did not fool her captors, so Colly and Sandro had to rescue both Jennifer and Nicola.

The trio was visiting Los Angeles in *The Priests of the Abomination* (Harcourt, 1971), when they learned of "The Five," a cult that included outcasts of Eastern and Western religions. Colly went undercover to investigate, but was discovered and had to be rescued. The narrative was laced with orgies, sadism, and perverse sex. Tasteless.

In *The Frog in the Moonflower* (St. Martin, 1973), Sandro became aware of assassinations occurring during hunting episodes, and connected the deaths with SIPHEN (Société Internationale pour la Preservation de l'Heritage de la Nature), a prominent animal preservation society. Jennifer and Colly joined his East African trip to challenge a man-killer. The assassin fell prey to beasts. Jennifer suffered a personal loss.

While Jennifer was on board Princess Karobin's yacht in *The Jaws of the Watchdog* (St. Martin, 1973), jewel thieves headed by a man referred to as "Royston" made the first of several major coups. Returned to shore, the trio became involved in the efforts of the British government to protect Holman Walker, an American official who had been threatened. When Jennifer and Walker were kidnapped and transported to Holland, Colly and Sandro followed. To their dismay, they learned the real identity of the thieves and kidnappers, who were captured when they tried to fix a horserace. Disjointed.

During *The Power of the Bug* (St. Martin, 1974), which took place in the United States, Colly was enraged by the suicide of his dear friend David Cordle, who could no longer live with the demands of a blackmailer. The checks written by David led Colly to Antonio Gabetti, a small-time crook. When Colly became a target and was incapacitated, Jennifer and Sandro took on the chase. All three escaped from a cabin that had been set on fire. The trio fled to Mexico but created a situation where they could trap the man behind it all, a treacherous friend.

The Tank of Sacred Eels (St. Martin, 1976) found the trio in Morocco after drug smugglers. They intruded on a pyramid investment scheme perpetrated through Swiss banks. Jennifer was attracted to Fritz von Cernogratz, a handsome sportsman obsessed with the environment, who gave her a ride for her life. She survived.

In *The Necklace of Skulls* (St. Martin, 1977), they visited Calcutta to rescue Harry, the stepson of Colly's cousin, John Tucker, unaware that the young man was involved in crime, not a victim. In the process Kashi, a leader of the group who worshipped Kali, observed Jennifer. The moment Kashi saw Jennifer he was determined to have her for the mother of his son. Jennifer was kidnapped and hypnotized into the belief that she was one of the group who had captured her. When she regained her sense of identity, she used what she had learned about the group's religious beliefs to overcome them.

An Armenian scientist, Krikor Grotrian, while working for the USSR developed an easily grown poppy in *A Stench of Poppies* (St. Martin, 1978). Feeling underappreciated, Grotrian took the seeds to Turkey, where they were planted and harvested, bringing death to thousands and getting the notice of Sandro, Colly, and Jennifer. A banker friend of Sandro pointed them to a new depositor, Algan Bey, ostensibly in the rug business but actually a drug dealer. Initially neither Grotrian nor Bey realized that the Russians had ended his experiments because although the plants grew well on poor soil, their product was fatal. Mistaken for a killer who resembled him in size, Sandro was arrested. Colley and Jennifer changed identities, but Algan was never fooled. Only when Colly and Jennifer were prisoners and their captors tried the new drugs, were they free.

The Diamonds of Loreta (St. Martin, 1980) was the last and perhaps best of the series, which is not necessarily saying a lot. Jennifer, Colly, and Sandro attended the races in Prague. When Colly was kidnapped, the criminal demanded as ransom the jewels of Loreto, which Sandro and Jennifer were expected to steal. They complied, but as soon as Colly was released, they set about to recover the jewels before the police could arrest them all.

The books strained belief, but the action was fast and the backgrounds colorful. There was no sustained romance. Jennifer's dalliances were only book length.

Norah North

Author: Madelaine Duke

Dr. Norah North, a "Nordic beauty," shared her home and her life with geologist Patrick Snow and her younger sister Liz. Since their parents were killed while Norah was in medical school, she had taken responsibility for the younger girl. Patrick and Norah had role reversal to the extent that he cooked and worked around the house, while she concentrated on her career, unwilling to make a lifetime commitment. She frequently worked with Inspector Barrington and had allies within a street gang.

At the request of actress Anita Moreno in *Death of a Holy Murderer* (Joseph, 1975), Norah and Pat traveled to the U.S. to convince her daughter, June, and son-in-law, Jake, to return to England, bringing her grandson Danny along. Jake had a bad war, dropped out of London University, and joined a cult headquartered in the United States. He and June had married when she was 18, and Danny was born a year later. On their return, Jake died of an asthma attack, then Anita Moreno did. Norah refused to sign her death certificate, because she felt she had been manipulated into assisting in a crime. The conclusion was a poor end to a good narrative.

In *Death at the Wedding* (Joseph, 1976), Norah, a guest, was called upon to deal with the death of the bride's Aunt Theresa. Dr. Leon Camp, the stepfather of bride Joanna Petrie, signed the death certificate but expected Norah to sign the cremation order. Camp had spent a considerable amount of money building a laboratory attached to the family home. Fraser, Joanna's brother, who came from Australia to England for the wedding, became so ill that Dr. Camp had him admitted to a nursing home. Elsa, Norah's receptionist, was also suffering the effects of a wound and in the same facility. Norah abducted them both and did a thorough workup. She juggled her concern about the health of members of the bridal party with her concern that there was a pattern of abuse in patients on her caseload. At the end they came together.

During *Death of a Dandie Dinmont* (Joseph, 1978), Nora's professional and personal life changed. She signed on as police surgeon, then took off on an African honeymoon with Patrick. At the wedding, Nora agreed to take her friend Dr. Hamilton K. Hamilton's Dandie Dinmont if anything happened to her. That situation never occurred, because someone broke the dog's neck. While in South Africa, Nora and Patrick met with George Chester, a right-wing British politician, and Colin Morgan, son of John Morgan, who had married Dr. Hamilton after the death of his first wife. Nora was not sympathetic to the movement to turn control of African countries over to the black majority. After she returned to England, Chester was murdered. Her investigation led her into questions of political opposition to civil rights, but also a review of the death of the first Mrs. Morgan.

Norah was portrayed as liberated, yet politically conservative. Duke overloaded on plots and then had difficulty coordinating their conclusions.

Natasha O'Brien

Authors: Ivan and Nan Lyons

Someone Is Killing the Great Chefs of Europe (Harcourt, 1976) was replete with puns, double entendres, and witty repartee. The primary ingredients were the engaging Natasha O'Brien, always at odds with former husband Max Ogden, and the wacky chefs with whom she worked. Max, a food chain executive, was in London testing fast food outlets while Natasha prepared dessert for the Queen. As Natasha subsequently traveled Europe visiting friendly (very friendly) chefs, her hosts were killed in methods reminiscent of their culinary skills. Early on, the manic killer was disclosed to the reader, but the plot continued to be interesting because of its elaborate machinations.

For a second course came *Someone Is Killing the Great Chefs of America* (Little, 1993). The flavor was familiar; Natasha and Max were currently separated. Natasha hired a former friend, publisher Achille van Gulik, who was so slim as to be unrecognizable. The murders began again, ending only when the abysmal hunger of a killer broke down the barriers of psychological training. Not as good as the first, but interesting.

Deirdre O'Connor

Author: Hugh McLeave

Deirdre O'Connor, a redheaded nurse, met Dr. Gregor Maclean when he was undergoing treatment for alcoholism. When he was released, she joined him at his clinic and occupied a bedroom in his apartment, although she was consistently referred to as a moralistic, even rigid Irish Catholic.

A Question of Negligence (Harcourt, 1970) used Deirdre sparingly, screening Maclean's office patients. The real action took place at the hospital where Dr. Murdo Cameron might be losing his surgical skills.

In *No Face in the Mirror* (Walker, 1980), Maclean intervened when Dr. Evan Sutherland's radical treatment for schizophrenics led to multiple suicides. Deirdre checked the backgrounds of patients and staff members while Gregor investigated Sutherland. The narrative may tell readers more than they want to know about schizophrenia.

In *Second Time Around* (Walker, 1981), Gregor probed prostitution, international espionage, and a question of professional ethics, but Deirdre had no role.

Gregor could not investigate charges of malpractice against anesthetist Philip Rothwell, a friend and former patient, in *Death Masque* (Walker

1986). Deirdre did. Miguel Contreras Heredia died when Rothwell administered the wrong cylinder of anesthetic. This was the second such incident in six weeks and could not be ignored. Carolina, Heredia's wife, had no intention of letting that happen, but she was killed before she could contact the police. Gregor and Deirdre arranged sanctuary for Maria, Carolina's daughter, and Philip Rothwell. The final solution came after Maria revealed information about her father and his business associates. This was Deirdre's opportunity to be really involved.

Somewhat better than a medical Della Street.

Stevie O'Dowda

Author: Matthew Finch, pseudonym for Morton Fink

Stevie O'Dowda was a private investigator who specialized in industrial espionage; even her own background was confidential.

In *Eye With Mascara* (Dobson, 1968), Alex Baldwin, senior engineer at International Motor Corporation, was astounded to learn that the detective he had hired to recover a new prototype engine was a female. The sample engine was radioactive and dangerous to those who handled it inappropriately. Baldwin did not want to work on this with the police department. Stevie had the engineering and investigative skills needed to return the engine before someone suffered from its radioactivity. Those responsible for the theft were determined to baulk her investigation. Stevie's ability to create an explosive out of household products enabled her and Alex to escape and save the day.

During *Eye Spy* (Dobson, 1975) Stevie disliked client William Browne, who hired her to follow his mistress, Helen Troy, as she traveled to Norway. Since Browne refused to provide his own address and paid in cash, Stevie had every reason to be suspicious. Too late, Stevie realized that Helen was not Browne's mistress, but served as a decoy in an effort to smuggle a Jewish refugee to freedom in Israel. Dated humor.

Christie Opara

Author: Dorothy Uhnak

Christie Opara, a New York City policewoman, was described as a slim, long-legged woman with blonde hair. The only daughter of a widowed Greek construction crew chief, she grew up as a tomboy with three brothers. After a teenage drug addict killed her husband, Michael, a police officer, her mother-in-law, Nora, cared for five-year-old Mickey so that Christie could continue to work.

Christie was the only female in the District Attorney's Special Investigation squad in *The Bait* (Simon, 1968). Her arrest of Murray Rogoff, a retarded man who exposed himself on the subway, made her the target of phone calls. Her contact with Murray was incidental, as she was working on a drug case. However, his continued phone calls fit into the pattern of a current serial killer/rapist, so Christie was assigned as "bait." ADA Casey Reardon showed considerable interest in Christie, but he was a married man.

Reardon, who had a troubled marriage, was concerned about his daughter, Barbara, during *The Witness* (Simon, 1969). While her twin sister, Ellen, focused on fashion and trying to get her dad's attention, Barbara became involved in the civil rights movement. Reardon assigned Christie to protect Barbara during a mass demonstration that ended in the death of the demonstration's peaceful leader, Billy Everett, a young black law student. Witnesses including Barbara Reardon agreed that the shot had been fired by police officer Nick Linelli. Christie not only disagreed but tested the witnesses' accuracy. It became apparent that there was an aggressive group within the Civil Rights movement seeking to get control.

When Elena Vargas, the mistress of a drug dealer, was put under police protection in *The Ledger* (Simon, 1970), Christie was assigned to guard and interrogate Ellen. Christie began her assignment prejudiced against Ellen because her husband, Michael, had been killed by junkies. Closer contact made her aware that Ellen was also a victim. Once Christie discovered the leverage the dealers had on Elena, she could turn her into a valuable asset.

Uhnak's empathy for the powerless extended not only to her heroine working in a male-dominated occupation, but also to women characters generally, including both victims and criminals. She wrote several excellent single books. Her 14 years of experience as a New York City Transit police officer added credibility to the narratives. Read more about her personally in *Police Woman* (Simon & Schuster, 1964).

Molly Owens

Author: Stephen Overholser

Molly Owens, a private detective working out West, was employed by Fenton Investigations Agency of New York. She was tough and uneducated. Her parents had died in a railroad accident when she and her brother Chick were children. As an adult, her only home was a Denver boarding house where she spent time between assignments. Molly was a slim and athletic blonde, an excellent rider, proficient with a variety of weapons, and skilled in a form of jujitsu. She was rebellious and unconventional, particularly so for a heroine of the late 19 century. At a time when casual sex often led to unwanted pregnancy, Molly was sexually active, with multiple partners over the series.

In *Molly and the Confidence Man* (Doubleday, 1975), she was escorting confidence man Charley Castle to Topeka when she learned that her brother Chick had been killed. She reviewed letters Chick had sent detailing his boss' struggle against an encroaching landowner. With the help of Charley and Clarence Hoffman, an alcoholic Fenton employee, Molly snared a lawman killer.

Before *Molly and the Gold Baron* (Bantam, 1981) began, Molly had been jailed for helping Castle to escape. Once released, she was sent to help mining millionaire Winfield Shaw, who was facing a paternity charge. Molly moved into a brothel (on inactive status) to meet Candy Smith, the alleged mother, who was murdered soon afterwards. Molly's attention was diverted to the plight of miners who had been denied an increase in wages when their hours were increased. Shaw was interested in negotiations with the miners' union, but there were others among the mine owners and union members who preferred to resort to violence.

During *Molly on the Outlaw Trail* (Bantam, 1982), she helped Butch, a 14-year-old boy who had run away from an orphans home. Butch had rescued Molly from a grizzly bear, so she had a sense of obligation. The father whom Butch sought was attractive outlaw Cole Estes. Even when Molly and Butch located Cole, he seemed disinterested. Soon Cole was on the run again, pursued by Union Pacific detective Will Parlow and his men. Molly was suspicious of Parlow's motivation and his brutal tactics.

In *Molly and the Indian Agent* (Bantam, 1982), General Zachary Monroe Holcomb hired Molly to find the killer of Isaiah, his rancher brother. The townspeople in Crowheart had already blamed the death on local Indians. Molly entered the community as a relative of Nell, Isaiah's invalid widow. Within days, she had beaten up an army deserter; defended Morning Star, a young Native American woman who worked at the hotel; and challenged Joe Pardee, the foreman at the Holcomb ranch. Before she left she had convinced the locals to look elsewhere for Isaiah's killer.

Molly and the Railroad Tycoon (Bantam, 1983) involved Molly in the traditional battle between farmers and ranchers. The Fenton Agency had assigned her to the case, which displeased railroad magnate Preston Brooks.

He wanted peace in the area to promote the transportation of cattle and farm products to Eastern markets and thought a woman would be ineffective. Brooks became a strong supporter of Molly, who presented herself as a woman seeking a missing husband. When Brooks was killed, Molly was determined to find his murderer.

In *Molly and the Gambler* (Bantam, 1984), honest gambler Dave Hughes hired Molly to find his runaway daughter Sharon. She was discovered working as a "21" dealer at the Orleans Club in boomtown Creede, Colorado. Molly carried out David's instructions and provided Sharon with adequate money to return home, but she had plans to buy a share in the club from owner Lou Drago. Hughes came to town to get to know Sharon better, but suffered rough treatment by Drago's men. With the help of Calamity Jane, an unusual ally, and U.S. Marshall Saul Phillips, Molly persisted.

Molly was an unusual Western heroine because of her work and her assertive behavior. Western heroines were expected to be spunky but dependent, and, except for prostitutes, not usually involved in casual sex. She lamented her inability to find the right man, but was drawn to men with a wild streak, uninterested in a wife.

Hildy Pace

Author: Ron Goulart

Hildy and Jake Pace were a cross between the cartoon Jetsons and Craig Rice's Justuses set in the 21st century. Hildy, in her early thirties, was tall with Titian hair, and married to the slightly older Jake. They were equal partners in a private investigation agency called Odd Jobs, Inc., that specialized in impossible crimes. At that time there were two political parties in the United States: the Republican-Democrats and the Democrat-Republicans. The Paces worked together as a case began, but usually followed different leads. Routinely either Hildy or Jake was captured by evil forces and had to be rescued by the other.

In *Calling Dr. Patchwork* (DAW, 1978), the Paces were alerted to seven crimes using the modus operandi of criminals known to be dead...or were they? Gunther Stool, U.S. Secretary of Show Biz, feared that this was related to a plot by the Amateur Mafia, headed by Bobby Thatcher, a WASP group trying to take over Show Biz. The Paces were pitted against Dr. Bascom Wolverton, who had found the true secrets of the genetic code. Their investigation included Hildy appearing in a nudist soap opera, then being stashed away in a mental institution.

It was the High Tech Mafia who opposed Jake and Hildy in *Hail Hibbler* (DAW, 1980). As the sleuths pursued their separate ways, Goulart spoofed amusement parks, real estate dealers, and religion. Among the villains who appeared were cryogenically restored Nazi Dr. Adolph Hibbler and his allies Ralph Emerson Tenn and Sheikh Sahl al-Haml.

In *Big Bang* (DAW, 1982), Patsy Hatchbaker was discovered dead in a bed shared with the amnesiac Jake. He was charged with murder. Jake had no recollection of the entire day, but was able to get it restored by Skullpopper, a mind cleanser. This diversion slowed down Jake and Hildy's primary assignment, to find out who was blowing holes in the world. Hildy learned that the holes had repercussions on Wall Street, greatly increasing the values of stocks held by Newoyl, which was owned by Novem. But who was behind Novem?

When Attorney John J. Pilgrim (a clone of Craig Rice's John J. Malone) joined forces with Hildy and Jake in *Brainz, Inc.* (DAW, 1985), the Paces began to look more and more like Helene and Jake Justus. A "Sim"/android containing the contents of Sylvie Kirkyard's brain hired the Paces to solve her murder. Sylvie was a deceased electronics heiress. A "Sim" with a Brainz chip could at that time legally hold stock and continue to operate a business. Primary suspect was Dr. Vincent Death, who may have created a mind control system that he used on important personages.

Odd Job No. 101 (Scribner, 1975) contained one short story in which the Paces were assigned to verify the mental state of U.S. President Amberson. To this end Jake pretended to be catatonic to get into the Svengali Institute in Topeka, where Amberson had been treated.

Interesting science fiction/mystery/humor combination.

Emma Peel

Authors: David Rogers, novelization of television episodes of "The Avengers," plus novels based on the characters by John Garforth and Keith Laumer

Although British Intelligence agent John Steed had several female partners during the "The Avengers" television series, Emma Peel was the best known. The daughter of wealthy industrialist Sir John Knight, she was an attractive, highly skilled "widow" whose husband had disappeared while testing an experimental plane. Described as tall and slim with auburn hair, her image remains tied to that of actress Diana Rigg.

In *The Floating Game* (Garforth, Berkley, 1967), Steed ran for the parliamentary seat formerly held by a cabinet member who had committed suicide. Because Sir Arthur's death was connected with attractive Russian scientist Tamara Petrova and with gambling losses, Emma took employment as a croupier on a gambling ship anchored off the English coast. Tamara was believed to be working on mind-altering drugs. The success of their mission was limited by the efforts of MI5 to cover up the scandal. Steed, moreover, did not win the election.

The Laugh Was on Lazarus (Garforth, Berkley, 1967) began when the body of Frank Hammond, a man dead and buried four months before, was discovered in a primate laboratory cage. After his coffin was exhumed and found empty, Peel and Steed battled zombies—creatures raised from the dead. Message Morrison, a Church of England priest who was chaplain in Steed's WW2 unit, announced that his parishioner Jacob Burns had risen from the dead. Unfortunately for Mr. Burns, he died again soon. The connection seemed to be with the Department of Scientific Research, where Hammond had been employed. Steed learned that the preserved brain of Professor Feuer directed the secret organization behind the zombies. Latest caper, to bomb the Pentagon, was prevented by Emma.

In *The Passing of Gloria Mundy* (Garforth, Berkley, 1967), Gloria, a hitchhiking singer, was terrified that "they" were going to kill her. Steed failed to take her seriously, until she was murdered. Then he enlisted Emma to find her killer, having her pose as a pop star to gain access to the music business. Sinister forces were putting subliminal messages on Gloria's records to ensure the election of their candidates for political office.

During *Heil Harris* (Garforth, Berkley, 1967) Steed's memoirs exposed connections among the death of Hitler, the death of fascist sympathizer Ernst Karsten in a motorcycle accident in 1934, and a similar recent accident to Sgt. Alf Wilkes. Emma was sent undercover to learn how seriously a neo-Fascist group should be taken. Her assignment began with attendance at a weekend party at Throgmorton, which included a masked ball. During the evening David Simmons, a Jewish guest, was attacked and abused. Further activities unmasked a plan for the neo-Fascists to take over the government. A group called the Werewolves required new initiates to commit sensational attacks on minority group members. Steed, who had been totally engrossed in his memoirs, surfaced long enough to seek out buried Nazi treasure and follow its trail back to England.

In *The Afrit Affair: The Avengers #5* (Laumer, Berkley, 1968), Emma and Steed were enticed into a chase across London, following clues hidden in Chinese food and a tube of toothpaste by AFRIT, an Arabian spirit. Steed had been assigned to watch over diplomats in London for a conference on Afro-Asian affairs. An American ally of Steed's named Blenkiron might be left over from a Richard Hannay adventure by John Buchan. Emma defused a bomb with a hairpin after Steed had been unable to deal with it. Not even a jolt of LSD could prevent Steed and Emma from completing their assignment. Disabled by the LSD they had absorbed, Steed and Emma found it difficult to warn the authorities that a British bomber was en route to bomb Berlin.

In *The Avengers: Too Many Targets* (by Rogers and John Peel, St. Martin, 1990), Steed recruited Emma and two other former partners (anthropologist Catherine Gale and the wealthy farmer's daughter Tara King) because he suspected that "Mother," the master intelligence official, was a double agent. That was entirely possible because Mother ordered Tara to kill Steed. Emma had withdrawn from espionage, returned to her husband, Peter, but had been available since his death. Somewhat rusty from their semi-retirement, Steed and Emma recognized the handiwork of an old enemy in a plot to spread plague in an African country.

Several of the original novels, earlier ascribed to Peter Leslie in the 1960's, were re-issued in the 1990's by Titan/London as written by Patrick Macnee.

The Avengers: Deadline was based on grievous misrepresentations of speeches by British Foreign Secretary Sir George Carew, appearing in Continental newspapers. The motivation for the misquotations was traced to a right-wing group stirring up nativist activity. Steed had met with the publisher of the *Courier*, one of the three papers who misquoted government speakers, because the edited copy had originated from the *Courier* building. Arrangements were made for Emma to go on staff as assistant to the beauty editor. Together they traced the methodology of the replacement items, where they were printed, and how transported. Big ending as usual. This time Steed rescued Emma.

In *The Avengers: The Dead Duck*, Emma and Steed were present when a fellow diner died after eating the renowned pressed duck. They took an interest because they too had ordered that entree. This was the fourth in a series of mysterious deaths caused by noxious poisons. They learned that the deaths were tests of substances designed eventually to kill millions. The poisons would be transported by migrating birds. This time Emma rescued Steed; then he rescued her. The plot gimmicks were ingenious, but the writing banal.

A similar series, featuring Steed with Tara King, included the following books: *The Magnetic Man* and *Moon Express* by Norman Daniels and *The Drowned Queen* and *The Gold Bomb* by Keith Laumer.

The books were disappointing, badly written, lacking tension and credibility. The television series had elements of fantasy but held viewer's attention through the witty dialogue and the interplay among the characters.

For those who enjoyed the series, a movie version with Uma Thurman in the Peel role and Ralph Fiennes as Steed was highly touted. Subsequent reviews of the film indicated it was a failed attempt. Neither Thurman nor Fiennes recaptured the essence of their characters.

Lexey Jane Pelazoni

Author: Lee Head

Lexey Jane Pelazoni, at 67, even though arthritic and occasionally confined to a wheelchair, charmed others by her wit, her wisdom, and her wealth. After her husband, Augustus, sold his prosperous chemical works to Du Pont, he died. Their daughter Anne had been murdered while living in Europe. A weaker woman might have retreated into fantasy or bitterness. Lexey chose to go on living.

In *The Terrarium* (Putnam, 1976), Lexey booked into the Terrarium, a pricey weight reduction facility with her own agenda. Both daughter Anne's sizable stock portfolio and her German husband, Otto Milhoff, had disappeared after her death. Lexey made the acquaintance of other guests, including Shirley, the wife of U.S. Senator Paul Kiker, and deeply depressed movie actress Deana Bradford, who had an alcohol problem. Lexey's attorney, Julien Strauss, called to inform her that some of Anne's stock had been traced to Senator Kiker. Lexey, after learning that the rooms were bugged, made remarks that would spring a trap.

In *The Crystal Clear Case* (Putnam, 1977), either Lexey or her long time friend Peaches Mueller owned counterfeit stock certificates, as shown by the identical identification numbers on the certificates. Before Lexey could learn who sold the stock, Peaches was killed. Lexey checked out Peaches' heir: her niece Annie Mueller Kerwin. Annie and her live-in lover were into pyramids and crystals. They may also have had a connection to forgery of wine labels...and of stock certificates? Lexey took considerable risks in following up on this connection. Unfortunately, the narrative and its conclusion became disjointed.

An interesting but short series.

Anna Peters

Author: Janice Law (Trecker)

Anna Peters began her career as a blackmailing secretary. Admittedly, she had a tough start in life: married to an abusive husband at 18, divorced at 19. Fortunately, her stenographic training enabled her to leave town and find a job. Anna's character changed considerably over the series, usually for the better.

When *The Big Payoff* (Houghton, 1976) opened, Anna, then in her thirties, was a research assistant for New World Oil. She had parlayed information gained in her work to blackmail her supervisors, improving her position until she owned a duplex and a Swiss bank account. Her plan to resign was delayed when she suspected that New World Oil was involved in a series of deaths. By clever manipulations she managed to be kept on at New World in a better job.

Aware of her talent for subterfuge, CEO Gilson of New World Oil sent Anna to Paris in *Gemini Trip* (Houghton, 1977) to trace degenerate twin stockholders. They had led unorthodox lives and would soon, through their ownership of oil stock, have huge fortunes to use or misuse. Anna and her lover, Harry Radford, became acquainted with the twins: Crystal, very much under the influence of her lover, Gabriel Celestin, a Marxist student, and Edward, a heavy drinker. The plan to induce the Blythes to return home conflicted with police and army initiatives in arresting Marxist gun smugglers.

Anna's next assignment was to evaluate a promising formula by Wilhelm Jaeger, an East German scientist, in *Under Orion* (Houghton, 1978). While Harry was preoccupied with his workshop for independent artists, Anna traveled to Europe with Philip McKenzie, a New World scientist, to check Jaeger out. After the trip she also checked McKenzie out. He was not to be trusted, but the two of them returned to Europe with a briefcase filled with cash. Anna contended with international intrigue and personal duplicity, leaving her embittered and ready to quit. As a result she established her own investigative agency (Executive Security) within the Helios Workshop run by Harry in Washington, D.C.

Old friend Henry Brammin hired Anna to check on his free-spending nephew, Red, in *The Shadow of the Palms* (Houghton, 1980). She and newspaperman John Hillery exposed antique smuggling. They could not protect Red, who was involved by his own greed.

Death Under Par (Houghton, 1981) lightened the mood as Anna and Harry married. He was hired to sketch scenes at the St. Andrew's Open in

Scotland for *Sports Illustrated*. James Sutherland, a member of the Royal and Ancient Club, recruited Anna to investigate vandalism on the course. Murder followed, but the killer could not be arrested until the last hole in the tournament was completed.

In *Time Lapse* (Walker, 1992), Anna went undercover on a film set to probe the death of heavily insured actor Henry Brook. The film *Lazarus Gambit* depicted a scheme to use blowfish secretions to preserve Adolph Hitler for the future. There had been trouble on the lot, and it was questionable whether the film could be saved after Brook's death. She discovered medical information that relieved Independence Mutual Insurance Company of its liability on Brooks, but stayed on to find a killer. Independence had to pay off on Brook's personal policy, but was relieved of a greater burden.

During *A Safe Place to Die* (St. Martin, 1993), Harry's graphics were exhibited in a Connecticut community, which boasted Ranch Hill Estates, an enclave of expensive, well-guarded homes, and a murderer. After the death of 14-year-old Angela Browning, the daughter of Anna and Harry's hostess, the locals preferred the theory that an outsider was involved. Anna forced them to recognize that the dangers they feared were not all on the other side of the estate walls.

In *Backfire* (St. Martin, 1994), Maria Rivas, a registered nurse from Guatemala, needed help after she was charged with setting the fire that caused the death of her patient, Helena Shane. An anonymous donor paid Executive Security to gather information in Maria's defense. Anna investigated Helena's family and their employees, including Joseph, her unfaithful husband; Tony, their son, who had been attracted to Maria and probably was the anonymous donor; Natalie, Joe's mistress; and chauffeur John Delano, who may have laundered money. Eventually Maria, out on bail; Tony; and Anna were all targeted.

Anna had been in the business a long time by *Cross-Check* (St. Martin, 1997), and the wear and tear were showing. Harry had opportunities at several colleges as an artist in residence, but he would not take them without Anna. Her venture into the world of professional hockey helped her make a decision. "T-Rex" Parkes had never been formally accused of the death of his Orlando Showmen teammate Alf Rene, but the inference was an extra burden for his son, Richie, fighting leukemia. He wanted Anna to prove his innocence without knowing why he and Rene had quarreled.

Anna's initial toughness was valuable when she was threatened, kidnapped, drugged, and blown up, but later adventures displayed a more sympathetic heroine.

Miss Melinda Pink

Author: Gwen Moffat

Melinda Pink's background and appearance did not fit the pattern of a risk-taker, but she was. An only child whose father died when she was young, she was bespectacled and aging, but never elderly. A well-muscled body and a keen mind belied her gray hair. She had, at various times, served as a justice of the peace and the acting director of an adventure center, but in later books was identified as an author.

In *Lady with a Cool Eye* (Gollancz, 1973), Melinda returned to her native Wales to serve as the interim director at Plas Mawr Adventure School. The school had serious personnel problems related to alcoholism, infidelity, and political agendas. The nearby abandoned mines had been used to store explosives owned by Global Minerals, some of which may have been stolen. The body of Betts, the younger wife of Charles Martin, whose place Melinda had taken, was found, still in her car, but underwater. Together with retired attorney Ted Roberts, Melinda went beyond murder to a Fascist plot.

During *Miss Pink at the Edge of the World* (Scribner, 1975), Melinda visited Ultima Thule, an isolated area of Northern Scotland, on a holiday. Trevor Stark, a courageous but vicious mountain climber, and Pincher, his companion, were killed in an "accident." Melinda was instrumental in explaining the technicalities that proved they had been murdered.

Melinda visited Sandale in the English Lake District to investigate sheep rustling in *A Short Time to Live* (Gollancz, 1976). The body of Peta Mossop, wife of the innkeeper, was found in a ditch. The assumption that it had been a hit-and-run accident, similar to one that had occurred some months earlier, was discarded when it was shown that she had been killed elsewhere and her body moved. Aware of local hostility to outsiders, Melinda moved carefully, ostensibly focusing on the anonymous letters and phone calls to Peta and Lucy Fell, an attractive widow. Then Caroline, daughter of wealthy George Harper, was kidnapped. Melinda agreed to deliver the ransom, but Caroline was never returned.

After the body of Terry Cooke, a young hitchhiker, was found in a climber's plastic bag at the local dump, police on Skye Island were happy to involve Melinda in *Over the Sea to Death* (Scribner, 1976). Among the guests at the lodge were a variety of persons, couples and singles, with sexual and romantic interests that created tension, but why young Terry? Later, Madge Fraser, a top-rate guide climber, was found dead near her tent. When Melinda discovered the sexually frustrated killer, she chose to let him die.

Roderick Bowen had successfully fought off efforts to locate a nuclear facility in his Welsh community in *Persons Unknown* (Gollancz, 1978). Melinda, on hand for Roderick's 78th birthday celebration, met his family: son, Rupert, and wife, Doreen; granddaughter, Rachel, who shared Roderick's love of the climb, and her older husband, Norman Kemp. Two murders outside of the family occurred: Sandra, author of a forthcoming political exposé, and Jokey, a 14-year-old emotionally disturbed boy, but the seeds of the killing were within Roderick's household. There was a hint at the end that prehistoric ancestors had disposed of the killer. Not one of Moffat's better offerings.

In *Die Like a Dog* (Gollancz, 1982), the frictions among Maggie Seale, a wealthy itinerant climber; Joss Lloyd, a naturalist at a Welsh nature preserve; and landowner Richard Judson, a swaggering bully, were obvious. When Judson and his overseer, Handel Evans, were murdered, Melinda and her friend Ted Roberts investigated, but it took Maggie to uncover the killer in an unlikely ending. Maggie Seale and Ted Roberts appeared in other books in the series.

Miss Pink's arthritis sent her to the western American deserts in *Last Chance Country* (Gollancz, 1983), where she visited Jack Nielsen, who had isolated himself from the outside world. He could afford to do so, and kept his land as a nature preserve. Melinda encountered a pair of vicious killers on a rampage while climbing down the mountain. The two men were apprehended only when Melinda and her friend Emma Chadwick used themselves as bait for an ambush. The narrative contained a higher level of violence than prior books.

During *Grizzly Trail* (Gollancz, 1984), Melinda visited Maggie Seale in the Rockies at a time when there was a search for four persons lost in the snowy passes. One of those missing, Irving Tye, was an investigative reporter who had stirred up local resentment by claiming that ranchers killed and buried grizzly bears. One by one the missing persons were located. Tye had been murdered or killed by a grizzly. A second body, that of poacher Jed Trotter, was found in similar condition. The most memorable scene found Melinda talking her way out of an encounter with a grizzly.

Snare (St. Martin, 1987) located Melinda in an isolated Scottish village while working on a mystery novel. She was well received by the locals, who were horrified when she warned them about the potential for violence in their community. The deaths of Ivar Campbell, who held himself out to be a spy or contract killer, and young Hamish Knox, son of the local policeman, proved her point.

The Stone Hawk (St. Martin, 1989) took place in a small Utah settlement, where violence and evil endangered children. Two were murdered.

The first was young Birdie Estwick, a part Native American child adopted by a local family, whose body initially but falsely gave the impression that she had been raped. The next victim was 10-year-old Shawn Holman, a notorious liar, who had claimed he knew who killed Birdie. Melinda, as in other instances, felt no need to share her discovery with the authorities. Moffat's later books frequently dwelt upon the twisted personalities to be found in isolated settings.

Timothy Argent, a travel writer following a pioneer trail across the West, disappeared during *Rage* (St. Martin, 1990). After Melinda was hired by his publishers to find him, she retraced his route to Gabriel, California, where she found his abandoned jeep. She learned that Argent had been accompanied by an Algerian-English woman, Joanne Emmett. Emmett, according to local police, had been seen covered with "deer" blood, and had moved on. Unfriendly Brett Vogel's body was discovered hung on barbed wire, a punishment used in Texas for informers. He managed the place that controlled entry to Dogtown. Melinda located Joanne in Los Angeles, gaining information that helped her identify the killer.

Melinda stopped off in Oregon in *The Raptor Zone* (Macmillan, London, 1990), hoping to see the elusive spotted owl. She financed her travels through the sales of her popular gothic novels. The reader was made privy to the problems in the marriage of Lois and Andy Keller. He flaunted his infidelities with Gayleen at a birthday party for Lois, then left with Gayleen in Lois' car. The car was discovered later with Gayleen's corpse in the trunk. Melinda found Andy's body while climbing. The easy solution was murder-suicide, but that did not satisfy Melinda. The ending may not satisfy the reader.

In *Veronica's Sisters* (Macmillan, London, 1992), Melinda, while exploring a New Mexico canyon, found a rifle and suspicious bones. When she reported her find to the local police, she withheld information about Kristen Scott, a teenager she had seen riding in the vicinity. The only person known to have left the area was Gregorio Ramirez, who had disappeared shortly after developmentally disabled and pregnant Veronica Scott killed herself. Much of the remainder of the narrative was devoted to a search for 12-year-old Tammy Markow, during which the body of Clayton Scott, father of Kristen and Veronica, was found. Again Melinda declined to share her information with the authorities.

By *The Lost Girls* (Constable, 1998), Melinda had lost a step but could still outpace the local inspector in Northern England as she tramped the hills to point out a buried skeleton. She presented herself as a "dotty older woman" when it served her purpose, but her sense of evil enabled her to uncover years of deceit, guilt, and blackmail, and to identify a current killer for whom it had become a solution.

As a guest of her American friend Sophie Hamilton in *Private Sins* (Constable, 1999), Melinda found herself in an unenviable position. The domineering Charlie Gunn, married to Sophie's sister, was a cruel and conniving father and grandparent. His convenient death might well have been an accident. If it were a crime, Melinda had to decide whether or not it was best left unpunished.

Melinda might have been too old and too busy to assist the Mountain Rescue teams when Phoebe Metcalf disappeared in *Retribution* (Constable, 2002), but her brain was as nimble as ever; her curiosity as strong. Nor had author Moffat lost her ability to create interesting characters; the passive husband, the unfaithful wife who became too dangerous to live, a lusty teenager who defended her brother, and best of all, a loyal wife whose husband had overestimated his tolerance for betrayal. Although she may not have shared everything she learned, Melinda got to the bottom of the mysteries.

The Pink stories transported the reader up the slopes in different localities, into the forests and deserts of the United States, and to a special world of risk taking. Moffat's characters were often those who felt compelled to go a little higher, to push a little harder, and to test themselves more rigorously than their fellow citizens.

Charlotte Ellison Pitt

Author: Anne Perry

Author Anne Perry explored the wealth and the poverty, the surface mores and the hypocrisy of the Victorian era through Inspector Thomas Pitt of the London Police Force and his upper-middle class wife, Charlotte. A spirited young woman with mahogany hair and gray eyes, Charlotte's marriage to a man of lower class origins and limited prospects had been a mixed blessing to her parents. She had always been a difficult daughter, rejecting the mold of young women of her class in society, and so outspoken that she might never have found an acceptable husband of her own class. Social position in the Victorian era depended upon the husband's status, which, at marriage, was assumed by the wife, whatever her prior position.

The young couple met in *The Cater Street Hangman* (St. Martin, 1979), when he investigated the garroting of young women, including Lily, a servant in the Ellison household. Charlotte, distressed by her sister Sarah's subsequent murder, turned to the kind and understanding Pitt. Their relationship and marriage followed, an unplanned side-effect being the help she provided when Pitt investigated crimes in upper class neighborhoods.

In *Callander Square* (St. Martin, 1980), when two infant corpses were unearthed in a park, Pitt was denied entry into the surrounding homes. Charlotte accepted a secretarial position in the household of suspect General Brandon Balantyne, while her married sister Emily used social connections to investigate neighboring families. They led Thomas to another household where tragedy had driven a husband and wife to murders. Charlotte was pregnant. General Balantyne had become an ally.

In *Resurrection Row* (St. Martin, 1981), although corpses were shuffled around to confuse the authorities, Thomas exposed pornography, blackmail, and the ownership of slum brothels by prestigious citizens. No role for Charlotte.

Now the proud mother of Jemima, Charlotte took a personal interest in *Paragon Walk* (St. Martin, 1981), when the rape and murder of Fanny Nash occurred in the fashionable neighborhood of Lord George Ashworth and his wife, Emily, Charlotte's sister. George became a suspect. His Aunt Vespasia, Lady Cumming-Gould, and Emily helped Charlotte probe witchcraft, rape, and murder.

As *Rutland Place* (St. Martin, 1983) opened, Charlotte, pregnant again, was aware of the tensions between her parents, Caroline and Edward. When Pitt investigated the poisoning of Mrs. Mina Spenser-Brown, a gossipy young woman, Charlotte, again working with Emily, solved the mysterious death before neighborhood secrets became public knowledge.

The poverty of the lower classes in London was given attention in *Bluegate Fields* (St. Martin, 1984). Arthur Wayburne, a 16-year-old boy of good family, was discovered drowned with evidence of homosexual abuse and syphilis. Pitt encountered resistance when he researched the young man's background and was pressured to back off on his investigation. Charlotte reminded him that other young boys would be in danger, stiffening his back. Moreover, she used her social contacts to get information about the Wayburne family. A young married tutor for the Wayburne boys, Maurice Jerome, was a convenient scapegoat, although he had never been infected with syphilis. Thomas was not satisfied with Jerome's conviction and sentence, but was warned by his superior officer, Athelstan, to back off or he would ruin him. Charlotte rallied a covey of important women on Jerome's behalf.

Death in the Devil's Acre (St. Martin, 1985) opened with the castration/murder of Dr. Hubert Pinchin in a slaughterhouse. This was not the first incidence of emasculation. There were hints that "high born women" were among the prostitutes in brothels. Another fine gentleman, Sir Bertie Ashby, was found dead outside a brothel. Pitt had warned Charlotte to stay out of this mess as she had no social position that would help. However, she and Emily made a condolence call on May Woolmer (Ashby's fiancée). General Balantyne's friendship was of assistance when, after Pitt was seriously injured, Charlotte and Emily investigated in his stead. This experience exposed them to the bitterness and frustration of women forced into prostitution by their poverty.

Emily became a murder suspect in *Cardington Crescent* (St. Martin, 1987) when her husband, Sir George Ashworth, was poisoned with digitalis. She had retaliated for George's infidelity with her cousin Sybilla March by a flirtation with handsome but penniless Jack Radley. George insisted that he and Sybilla had quarreled and that their affair had ended. George's Aunt Vespasia recruited Charlotte to confront Emily and learn the truth.

In *Silence in Hanover Close* (St. Martin, 1988), Thomas was investigating a three-year-old murder case in which the Foreign Office had an interest. Robert York had been murdered in his home, an incident that was treated as a burglary gone wrong. Now his widow, Veronica, planned to marry Julian Danver, also a Foreign Office employee. Thomas' task was to prove that neither Veronica nor Julian was involved in York's death. Charlotte, intrigued by what Thomas told her about the case, induced Jack Radley to introduce her to the Yorks and Danvers as his country cousin. Emily, undercover as a lady's maid, experienced the "downstairs" life. Thomas was getting too close to the truth, so was framed for murder and sent to prison, an existence to which he had sent others. Charlotte set a trap, using herself as bait. She discovered a facet of Robert's life that led to his death.

During *Bethlehem Road* (St. Martin, 1990), Aunt Vespasia enlisted Charlotte's help when suffragettes Florence Ivory and young Zenobia Gunne were suspected in the murders of three Members of Parliament. Florence had lost custody of her daughter when her husband claimed she was unfit due to her suffragette activities. She had written an angry letter to Vyvyan Etheridge when he supported her husband's claim. The circle of British women's rights activists helped in the investigation. The weak position of a mother in seeking custody of her child and the control of a husband over his wife's religious activities both figured in the narrative. With Charlotte's support, Thomas rejected a more lucrative position to continue his work in criminal investigation. Emily was off on her honeymoon with Jack Radley.

Highgate Rise (Fawcett Columbine, 1991) took place when Jack the Ripper had just begun his period of terror. Thomas had been detached from

London to investigate the death of wealthy Clemency Shaw in Highgate. She had died in a fire in the home she shared with her husband, Dr. Stephen Shaw. One possibility considered was that Dr. Shaw had been the intended target due to malpractice on his part; another, that he had set the fire to gain Clemency's fortune. Persistent "courtesy calls" by Charlotte; her mother, Caroline; Emily (now Mrs. Jack Radley); and Aunt Vespasia revealed tensions within the bereaved household.

Charlotte replaced the pregnant Emily as Jack Radley's hostess when he campaigned for Parliament in *Belgrave Square* (Fawcett Columbine, 1992). Although she was therefore privy to much of what went on, this too was Thomas' book. When the murder of blackmailer William Weems cast suspicion on Lord Sholto Byam, a prominent member of Her Majesty's government, the Inner Circle made its first appearance in the series, by hampering Thomas' discreet investigation.

In *Farrier's Lane* (Fawcett Columbine, 1993), Justice Samuel Stafford, a prominent jurist, collapsed at the theatre shortly after he consented to review a murder trial, which had elements of anti-Semitism. Thomas and Charlotte were in the audience. She was called upon to assist Stafford's younger wife, Juniper. Examination of Stafford's flask showed the presence of opium. Actress Tamar Macauley had entreated Stafford to reopen the investigation of the crucifixion death of Kingsley Blaine. Her brother Aaron had been convicted of the crime and been executed. The establishment and the judicial system stonewalled against a further investigation, but Thomas and Charlotte solved the past and current crimes. This serious cooperation between Charlotte and Thomas in one of his cases rarely occurred in future narratives.

Thomas' promotion to a supervisory position in *The Hyde Park Headsman* (Fawcett Columbine, 1994) made a more comfortable home life possible, but created stress. When men of substance were found beheaded in parks, Thomas balked at a premature arrest, while Charlotte kept busy with family matters.

Traitor's Gate (Fawcett Columbine, 1995) focused again on the Inner Circle and its stranglehold on English justice. Thomas responded to a plea from Matthew Desmond, a boyhood friend, who refused to accept the official verdict that his father had died by accident or suicide. The death of Susannah Chancellor, the socially active wife of the Secretary of State for Colonial Affairs, made the investigation even more sensitive. Thomas received more help from Aunt Vespasia than from Charlotte in this narrative overloaded with conspiracy.

Perry moved on for a short time from her preoccupation with the Inner Circle in *Pentecost Alley* (Fawcett Columbine, 1996), but provided Charlotte with little action until the final quarter of an overlong narrative. Her sister, Emily, motivated by friendship for Tallulah FitzJames, a young society woman, impinged on Thomas' sensitive investigation of the death of prostitute Ada McKinley. Charlotte made a significant difference when she tied recent deaths, which had terrified London with the fear that a maniac was at large and that the authorities had hung an innocent man, to an obscure murder.

Similar issues dominated a conference held at the country estate of Emily Radley, Charlotte's sister, during *Ashworth Hall* (Fawcett Columbine, 1997). Thomas and Charlotte were included among the guests so that he could safeguard Ainsley Greville, the moderator of the negotiations. Sexual tensions vied with national aspirations as possible motives when Greville was murdered in his bathtub. Charlotte, the Pitt housemaid Gracie Phipps, and disgruntled detective Tellman assisted Thomas in finding the killers.

Charlotte's primary connection during *Brunswick Gardens* (Fawcett Columbine, 1998) was her interest in Dominic Corde, once married to Sarah, Charlotte's murdered sister. (See *The Cater Street Hangman.*) Corde was a resident curate in the home of Rev. Ramsay Parmenter when the elderly clergyman became the primary suspect in the death of Unity Bellwood, a contentious researcher who had championed the Darwinian theory of evolution. Thomas was assigned to the case because of its delicacy, and his investigation formed the basis for the narrative. Nevertheless, it was Charlotte's insights in the final resolution that identified a real murderer.

Bedford Square (Ballantine, 1999) contained all of the intrigue, historical background, and skillful characterizations of the series. Thomas, Charlotte, Aunt Vespasia, Sgt. Tellman, and Gracie, the Pitt maid, played significant roles in identifying a cruel blackmailer who sought to protect his own misdeeds from disclosure. The failure of the police department to identify the connection among the victims and the abrupt and less than credible conclusion were unexpected flaws.

Charlotte's role diminished regularly as Perry focused on political issues, and particularly on the Inner Circle. Her sister, Emily Radley, and Lady Vespasia, had the status and the free time to get involved. Charlotte was being mother.

Charlotte was not even in England when *Half Moon Street* (Ballantine, 2000) took place. The narrative treated both the significance of freedom of expression and the potential evils that its excesses can produce. Thomas officially investigated the murder of a society photographer who expanded his income through pornography. It was Caroline, Charlotte's mother, and her difficult former mother-in-law who personally explored the limited responses of Victorian wives to sexual abuses by their husbands, complicated by a legal system that allowed only males to seek a divorce.

England was in disarray in 1892 as *The Whitechapel Conspiracy* (Ballantine, 2001) opened. Against that background Thomas was in trouble. His testimony in the trial of honored soldier John Adenit for the murder of antiquarian Martin Fetters had earned Thomas the enmity of the Inner Circle. In retribution he was discharged as Superintendent at Bow Street, and seconded to the Special Branch, where he was assigned to full-time undercover work. Charlotte, Lady Vespasia, Emily, and Gracie gathered information to bolster the prosecution against Adenit, which had failed to produce a motive for the murder. They succeeded in restoring Thomas to good graces, but Lady Vespasia paid a price.

In *Southhampton Row* (Ballantine, 2002), Thomas knew that he was still vulnerable. Charles Voisey, candidate for Tory Member of Parliament and head of the Inner Circle, had come out of the disclosures with added power. To protect his family, Thomas sent Charlotte and the children away from London. While Thomas worked on the murder of Maude Lamont, a medium who gathered information from her clients, Emily Radley, provided some help. Her husband, Jack Radley, was seeking re-election to Parliament.

Egypt was vital to England's trade and industries as *Seven Dials* (Ballantine, 2003) began. That was why the presence of senior cabinet member Saville Ryerson at the scene of a murder was important. There was no question that Ryerson had killed Lt. Lovat at the home of Ayesha Zakhari, but he had helped to dispose of the body. Thomas was sent to Alexandria to ferret out the connection between Lovat and Ayesha. On the home front, Charlotte and her maid Gracie searched for a missing servant, and as a result gained important information as to what motivated a man to endanger peace with Egypt. A suicidal act in the courtroom ended the trial. The books were getting longer, dealing with more internal and international political issues, leaving less room for character development. It was time to move on from the Inner Circle.

The days when Charlotte and Emily could take an active role in Thomas' investigations had ended by *Long Spoon Lane* (Ballantine, 2005). Thomas was on the trail of anarchists after a recent explosion. He and his boss, Victor Narraway, were present when one of the bombers was captured, one escaped, and another (Marcus Landsborough) was murdered. Marcus was the son of Lord Sheridan, so this was not to be treated lightly, especially if Marcus had been shot unnecessarily by the police. The incident was an opportunity sought by members of the right wing to justify arming the police and weaken citizen rights against search and seizure.

Lady Vespasia had a book of her own, *A Christmas Journey* (Ballantine, 2003), which explored her character as a young woman— married, but not to the man she loved.

The Christmas motif has become an annual event. In *A Christmas Guest* (Ballantine, 2005), Mariah Ellison, Charlotte's grandmother underwent a change in attitude. She was not by nature a congenial woman. Being shunted off to spend the Christmas holidays with her former daughter-in-law Caroline and Caroline's husband, Joshua, a Jewish actor, did nothing to increase her good humor. The subsequent arrival of Maude Barrington, a cousin of Joshua, similarly palmed off by her close family, had a strange impact on Mariah. Maude responded to beauty, was enthusiastic about events, and enjoyed the company of others, even Mariah. Maude's sudden death forced Mariah to re-assess her own outlook on life. Her conviction that Maude had been killed sent her on a journey to learn who so feared or resented Maude's return to England that murder was necessary.

Perry's ability not only to recreate the hypocrisy and repression of the Victorian era but also to create interesting and complex characterizations made even a long narrative difficult to put down. The narratives illuminated the past but dealt with problems that had a contemporary aspect.

Sylvia Plotkin

Author: George Baxt

Guilt-ridden New York police detective Max Van Larsen was paired with Sylvia Plotkin, a warm, boisterous Greenwich Village high school teacher. A divorcee, constantly battling a weight problem, her loud and colorful clothes and wry humor were good medicine for widower Max's grief. Max had some justifiable guilt about his wife's suicide and his failure to meet his son's needs. Sylvia and Max were surrounded by Runyanesque characters in plots reminiscent of Mickey Spillane. Quite a mixture.

In *A Parade of Cockeyed Creatures* (Random, 1967), Sylvia had taken a special interest in "Tippy" Blaney, a 17-year-old runaway from his troubled parents, Wilma and Marcus (whose activities included drug smuggling). Max and Sylvia learned why Tippy ran away and why he was tapping his weird friends for money. Through a search that ended in tragedy, Max came to terms with his own failure as a father and found understanding from Sylvia.

In *"I!" Said the Demon* (Random, 1969), Judge Armand Kramer had disappeared 30 years before—leaving behind Lita Swenson Kramer, his opera star wife, and Nola Kemp, his mistress, who disappeared later,—and removing $240,000 in cash and bonds. Max was asked to check the matter out by a San Francisco detective/parole officer. The narrative veered off into the problems of Chloe and Ramona Grace, sisters who came back from seclusion when they were influenced by the Pied Piper, an elderly storyteller, and Gypsy Marie, who used carrier pigeons to send messages to her tribe. They were not just bystanders for local color but eventually fit into the plot.

Sylvia and Max returned after 18 years in *Satan Is a Woman* (International Polgonics, 1987) to tangle with witchcraft in England. Sylvia had taken a sabbatical from teaching to finish the task that Max had begun, finding Lisa, the 19-year-old daughter of Joseph Gordon. Lisa had been researching witchcraft among the theatrical aristocracy when she disappeared. Sylvia worked with her man-eating editor, Edna St. Thomas Shelley; Max, who was in disguise; an American gypsy with a son in drag; and an aging director of Shakespearean drama.

Weird, really weird.

Mrs. Emily Pollifax

Author: Dorothy Gilman

Emily Pollifax, a New Jersey widow who felt that her children no longer needed her, cast off depression when she volunteered to serve as a secret agent, and traded bridge for karate, gossip for confidential information.

In *The Unexpected Mrs. Pollifax* (Doubleday, 1966), Emily traveled to Langley, Virginia, to make the CIA (Central Intelligence Agency) aware that she was available. After an initial brushoff, she was inadvertently assigned to contact Señor De Gamez, an American agent in Mexico City. "Just deliver the message." Nothing else was expected of her, but Emily improvised when de Gamez, who had secretly passed the information to her, was killed. John Sebastian Farrell, a CIA agent with whom she would share many of her adventures, was introduced in this narrative.

Emily's success justified her recall in *The Amazing Mrs. Pollifax* (Doubleday, 1970). Carstairs and Bishop of the CIA assigned her to contact Magda Ferenci-Sabo, a double agent on the run in Turkey. Magda was ready to retire and wanted to take her grandson Dmitri with her. Once connected, Emily's job had just begun. Utilizing help from gypsies and Turkish students, she brought them out of Turkey, but had to fly the helicopter herself.

There were few women like Emily in Bulgaria, but that was where the CIA sent her in *The Elusive Mrs. Pollifax* (Doubleday, 1971), carrying passports for members of the underground, but unaware that she was also transporting counterfeit money for other agents. She became involved in the effort to free Phillip Trenda, who was held by the police to exact ransom from his rich father. He was housed in the impregnable Panchevsky Institute.

In *A Palm for Mrs. Pollifax* (Doubleday, 1973), Emily was sent to a Swiss sanitarium armed with a scintillation counter to detect the presence of plutonium. She turned cat burglar Robin Burke-Jones into an ally in her efforts to free young Hafez and his drugged grandmother, family members of a Zabayan general, who were held prisoner in the sanitarium. Emily so distinguished herself with a combination of guile (switching peaches for plutonium) and physical dexterity (knocking a gun out of a killer's hand) that she was awarded the Zabya decoration, the Palm of Isa.

When Carstairs learned that an assassin would be on safari in Zambia, Africa, he deployed Emily to photograph the group in *Mrs. Pollifax on Safari* (Doubleday, 1977). One of the group was believed to be Aristotle, a professional assassin. Emily used a newspaper ad to contact Farrell, now living in Zambia. That came in handy when Emily and retired judge Cyrus Reed were captured by white supremacists. Insurgents led by Farrell rescued them. Later Emily identified Aristotle in time to prevent a political assassination. Romance bloomed between Emily and Cyrus Reed.

The focus of the series moved from Africa to Asia in *Mrs. Pollifax on the China Station* (Doubleday, 1983). Cyrus had returned to Africa when Carstairs sent Emily to smuggle fortifications engineer Wang Shen, a Chinese dissident, out of a prison camp. Wang Shen's need to urinate had given him an opportunity to escape into the hands of Peter, another CIA agent, who hid him in a cave. Emily's solo adventure in getting Wang Shen out of the country, which including killing a KGB agent, convinced her she wanted to marry Cyrus.

However, in *Mrs. Pollifax and the Hong Kong Buddha* (Doubleday, 1985), Cyrus was on a ten-day bird-watching trip, when Emily was the only person whom Sheng Ti, an agent in Hong Kong, would recognize. Once informed of her assignment, Cyrus flew to Hong Kong and helped rescue a badly beaten Emily from a liberation terrorist group.

In *Mrs. Pollifax and the Golden Triangle* (Doubleday, 1988), Cyrus and Emily were supposed to be on vacation in Thailand. Bishop of the CIA couldn't let the opportunity pass, so he requested that Emily pick up information from Ruamsak, a Thai-Chinese informant. The series had become patterned. Emily's extra-curricular activity led to Cyrus' kidnapping, but Ruamsak was available to help in the rescue.

Mrs. Pollifax and the Whirling Dervish (Doubleday, 1990) was more innovative. Emily was restless and alone. A year had passed since the agency had called on her. She was eager for an assignment when Carstairs and Bishop contacted her. They suspected a false agent in the CIA Moroccan network. Emily was provided pictures of seven agents and sent to find the mole.

Cyrus was busy again in *Mrs. Pollifax and the Second Thief* (Doubleday, 1993), when retired CIA agent John Sebastian Farrell sent an SOS for Emily's help. Farrell, now an art dealer, had gone to Sicily to authentic a document which wealthy art collector Ambrose Vica might buy. As a result of his unorthodox enquiry and Vica's misinformation, Farrell had been wounded and had to take refuge. Emily's involvement was important because their old enemy, Aristotle, was the villain.

Kadi Hopkirk, who had hidden in a closet in Emily's home, sent her on a wild chase in *Mrs. Pollifax Pursued* (Fawcett Columbine, 1995). Kadi was being followed because of her connection to Sammat, a childhood friend, now poised to return to his native country, Ubangiba. To confound the pursuers, Emily and young Kadi joined a carnival with some supervision from the CIA, but they needed Kadi's prowess with a gun and Emily's judo to be safe. They needed more than that when they flew to Africa to overthrow a corrupt government.

Mrs. Pollifax and the Lion Killer (Fawcett Columbine, 1996) was a sequel to *Pursued*. Sammat, the boyhood friend of Kadi Hopkirk, was about to be crowned ruler of Ubangiba when rumors of witchcraft threatened his popularity. Kadi and Emily flew there without CIA involvement to find the traitor who sought to undermine Sammat.

Emily returned to a more traditional role in *Mrs. Pollifax, Innocent Tourist* (Fawcett Columbine, 1997) when at the request of her old companion, John Sebastian Farrell, she visited Amman, Jordan. Farrell was to meet Ibrahim, a messenger who would provide him with a manuscript by Dib Assen documenting abuses in Iraq. Emily was to provide cover, but on her flight to Amsterdam, a souvenir was placed in her overnight bag. The souvenir contained a message and a key. Emily and Farrell's capacity for making new friends enabled them to escape from Saddam's hit men and rescue not a manuscript but an author who could reconstruct one.

The formula for Emily's adventures had worn a bit thin by *Mrs. Pollifax Unveiled* (Ballantine, 2000). She and Farrell were recruited to rescue a heroic young American woman kidnapped in Syria by Muslim assassins. Escapes were carried out with little trouble. Allies abounded, and the villains were not up to the usual standard. Fun, but faltering.

The scenic view changed from the African jungle to the Great Wall of China, but that was only part of the charm. However unrealistic the narratives might be, they nurtured the fantasies of a generation of women readers, who had dreamed of joining the FBI or becoming prosecuting attorneys, but instead married, raised families, and worked at less exciting jobs. Emily displayed the undervalued and under-utilized strengths of older women.

Hilary Quayle

Author: Marvin Kaye

Hilary Quayle was presented through the viewpoint of Gene, her assistant and occasional lover, who seemed to have no last name. Her physical description was appealing: tiny, blonde with blue eyes, a book collector and enthusiastic worker, but her personality was brittle and insensitive. She concentrated ruthlessly on her career. Hilary, who operated a public relations firm, was determined to become a detective like her father. Gene, a licensed private investigator, provided her investigations with credibility.

In *A Lively Game of Death* (Saturday Review, 1972), the couple had their first case in the tense world of the toy business, where decisions made in March could mean success or disaster in December. Copycat businessman Sid Goetz's corpse was discovered by Hilary and Gene. Hilary deduced the identity of the killer through information they concealed from the police.

Hilary sent Gene to Nashville to interview the singing Boulder clan in *The Grand Ole Opry Murders* (Saturday Review, 1974). He quickly became aware that the three sisters vied for opportunities for solo performances. Their manager informed them when they reached Nashville that the group would disband because Amanda was leaving. It went further when Josh, her sister Dolly's ex-husband, announced that he and Amanda planned to marry and perform as a duo. The other members of the group could continue as a quartet, of course. First Amanda, then Pearl, who replaced her as lead singer, died of a mysteriously ingested poison. Hilary, piqued by both the mystery and Gene's obvious interest in Dolly Boulder, took over the case.

By *Bullets for Macbeth* (Saturday Review, 1976), Gene had acquired a room in Hilary's apartment-office complex, but their relationship was unsettled. They were hired to do the public relations for a new production of *Macbeth*, the unlucky play. Unlucky it was. Actress Melanie Godwin, a friend of Hilary's, had her third miscarriage. Her husband, Michael, the director who was playing Banquo, and the elderly actor Armand Mills, playing Macbeth, were both killed. Realizing that Hilary was too involved to be impartial, Gene identified the killer.

The Laurel and Hardy Murders (Dutton, 1977) focused on "The Sons of the Desert," a male-only organization for Laurel and Hardy fans. Unpopular comic Wayne Poe was killed at the Sons of the Desert banquet. Gene theorized that his death was planned by members of the Sons' board of directors. Unwelcome as a member of the group, Hilary crashed the next meeting of the New York affiliate, at which Jack Black, an elderly vaudevillian, died. She and Gene, now clearly lovers, worked together on the solution.

In *The Soap Opera Slaughters* (Doubleday, 1982), Ed Nivens, a scriptwriter on the popular *Riverday* television series, jumped, or was pushed, stark naked from the top of station WBS/TV. Gene, who had left Hilary's employment to work as a private investigator, found himself attracted alternately to Hilary and her look-alike cousin, actress Laura Wells, but resolved the problem in time to recognize a murderess.

What Kaye did best was to depict glamorous backgrounds—the toy business, daytime television—but the flip dialogue has become dated.

Lucy Ramsdale

Author: Hildegarde Dolson

The widowed Lucy Ramsdale was a successful artist, utilizing her awareness of physical surroundings, visual memory, and sensitivity to the presence or absence of detail. These were assets when she investigated murders.

She and her magazine illustrator husband, Hal, had worked out of their Wingate, Connecticut, home. After his death, she turned his studio into a rental unit, which she rented to James McDougal. Lucy was initially described as small with arthritic fingers and white hair, but was rejuvenated in later books. McDougal was a retired homicide detective whose wife, Eileen, had deserted him for another man.

When the Inspector and Lucy first met in the local butcher shop in *To Spite Her Face* (Lippincott, 1971), the chemistry was all wrong. Lucy, a volunteer at the local thrift shop, suspected that co-worker Myrtle Pickering might have information about the recent death of Marian Colter at a cocktail party. When Myrtle was killed in the back shop, the shared interest of the Inspector and Lucy in solving the crime drew them together. Eventually, she offered to rent him the studio apartment.

Local art and gardening circles were outraged when patroness Grace Dilworth returned from a cruise with Davin Lowry, a handsome young escort, and plans to remodel the grounds of the Art Center in *A Dying Fall* (Lippincott, 1973). Disgruntled gardener Mario Sandini was suspected when Davin was impaled on a piece of statuary. Lucy and McDougal did not agree as to the identity of the killer, but he changed his mind in time to save Lucy from being the next victim.

Lucy's strong feelings for First Amendment rights in *Please Omit Funeral* (Lippincott, 1975) led her to challenge the censorship of school library books. Local author Lawrence Dilman, subject to the ban, was murdered, but not because of his books.

During *Beauty Sleep* (Lippincott, 1977), Lucy worked on a brochure for a beauty spa until Madame Velanie, the owner and operator, was killed. McDougal, preoccupied with the news that Eileen had divorced her second husband and decided to rescue him from Lucy, returned to Wingate in time to help Lucy solve the mystery and solidify their relationship.

This was a charming series that did not hesitate to tackle such controversial issues as homosexuality and censorship as motivating factors for murder.

Regina

Author: Dagmar, pseudonym for Virginia Egnor,
but ghostwritten by Lou Cameron

Regina was described much like her titular author, a buxom blonde with pale blue eyes. She claimed Cherokee blood to account for her ferocity, and a medical background. Her accompanist and collaborator was appropriately named Randy Kidd.

The unlikely duo surfaced in South America in *The Spy Who Came in From the Copa* (Lancer, 1967), when booked into Dirty Dick's Discotheque at a time when the Brazilian rubber industry was threatened by a machine created by Vietnamese scientist Hu that melted rubber. British agent Rev. Quivly, who occupied the seat next to Regina's on the plane to Rio de Janeiro, died after eating the provided meal. Soon after Regina's arrival, entertainer Voddie Ville was strangled. Finally Murgatroyd Schnook, a cashiered British agent, was shot. Regina agreed to help Una Hu, the professor's daughter, get to California, but she and the machine disappeared.

In *The Spy With the Blue Kazoo* (Lippincott, 1967), set in Los Perros, Central America, Randy and Regina had substantial opposition. They tangled with (1) Chinese communist Dr. Fang, a biochemist who had developed a substance that killed all but those of Mongolian ancestry, (2) Phalliphagus of the KGB, and (3) two representatives of the CIA, as the pile of corpses mounted. The narrative was heavily sprinkled with sex and violence.

The paperback covers were lurid. The plots made a Marx Brothers movie seem profound.

Clare Reynolds
Author: Michael Underwood, pseudonym for John Michael Evelyn

See: Clare Reynolds Atwell, Section 5, page 234.

Maxine Reynolds
Author: Marjorie Groves, pseudonym for Martin Grove

Maxine Reynolds was self-centered and insensitive, which probably contributed to her success as a Hollywood newspaper gossip columnist. Although Pamela Tooth, a British import, did the actual writing, "Max" gathered the information during power lunches with agents, at poolside parties, and in movie screening sessions. A long-legged redhead from New Jersey, she had a long-term relationship with Robin Allan, a divorced public relations man.

Maxine appeared in the *You'll Die...* series:

■ During *You'll Die When You Hear This* (Zebra, 1978) a tape cassette announcing the first of a series of scheduled killings was left in Maxine's car. She was warned that if she interfered, she would be killed. So, of course, she interfered.

■ *You'll Die Laughing* (Zebra, 1978) took place in London, where Maxine had been sent to solve the murder of a British comic. She was so confused by agents, counter agents, and enemy spies that Rob hurried over from the United States to rescue her.

■ In *You'll Die Tomorrow* (Zebra, 1978) Maxine and Rob were ready for a vacation in Aruba. Her plans to interview Cory Collins, a former record producer, fell through when he was murdered. They used a hotel lockbox key that they had found and appropriated to solve the problem, but this time Maxine did the detecting.

- Paris was the next stop in *You'll Die Yesterday* (Zebra, 1979). When a poison pellet in his leg killed famous French movie producer Philippe Gustave-Grenier, Maxine traced the projectile to an umbrella gun, very topical at the time.

- *You'll Die Today* (Zebra, 1979) returned Maxine to the United States for a San Francisco movie premiere. While appearing as a substitute guest on a radio call-in show, she was told of Carson Stamp's death and where his body could be found. Maxine masterminded the appearance of murder suspects leading to the identification of the guilty party.

- In *You'll Die, Darling* (Zebra, 1979), after the disappearance of popular singer Cindy Chester, Maxine received the ransom demand. No exchange was made because when the police became involved, Cindy was killed. Maxine had no faith in the ability of the police department to solve the murder, so she took it on. Actually she needed help from both the police and some gangsters.

- *You'll Die Tonight* (Zebra, 1979) sent Max to the New York premiere of a controversial anti-nuclear film. When director Justin Hanover was beaten to death with his Oscar, Maxine used her clout as a columnist to interview the suspects, but concealed evidence.

Delia Riordan
*Author: Lesley Egan, pseudonym for Elizabeth Linington
aka Dell Shannon*

Police officer Delia Riordan was a single woman in her late twenties with dark brown hair and blue eyes. Her widowed father, who left the police department due to physical disability, was cared for by a retired sergeant. Delia shared the home, but the sergeant did the household work. Her personal life was limited: reading a lot, smoking too much, driving a silver-gray Mercedes once owned by her father. Before assignment to the Glendale, California, police department, Delia had spent three years at Los Angeles City College and five years as a uniformed officer at Los Angeles Police Department.

A Dream Apart (Doubleday, 1978) introduced Delia to her new co-workers. Although the unit had some initial misgivings, she earned respect. There were several story lines, but the dominant one involved Eileen Endicott, a murder suspect who insisted upon speaking to a female officer. Delia proved Eileen was innocent even though she had confessed to killing her tyrannical mother-in-law.

In *A Choice of Crimes* (Doubleday, 1980), elderly Mrs. Potter was concerned about the sudden death of a friend. Delia followed through on this, checking out who would benefit from the woman's death. On a personal level, Delia weighed the importance of her career against her relationship with archaeologist Dr. Neal Fordyce, questioning how much her career choice had been influenced by her father.

By *Random Death* (Doubleday, 1982) Delia was over 30, trapped in her job, but with little private life. Fordyce had moved and married. Captain Riordan had entered a nursing home. Delia spruced up her clothes and made improvements in her hair and cosmetics. Her workload included depressing cases featuring psychic experiences that aroused in her a need for religious faith. Dominated until then by her father's atheism, Delia wondered if she were missing something.

During *Crime for Christmas* (Doubleday, 1984), Delia realized that she had dedicated too much of her life to her father. The cases in this holiday-oriented procedural were frothy: a pregnant stray cat and a macaw that Delia adopted when no one else would have it.

Chain of Violence (Doubleday, 1985) moved Delia out of the family home and into a condo, where she met Sgt. Dan Fitzgerald. She wondered how her male co-workers could combine career and marriage, when it was such a problem for her. Readers will never know if she found happiness. The series ended at that point. Her caseload contained no major investigations.

Linington/Egan/Shannon, who had used female characters in subsidiary roles in other series, gave Delia more autonomy but not much of a life. Characters such as Vic Varallo and his wife, Laura, from the series written as Lesley Egan appeared in these narratives.

Sheila Roath
Author: David Craig, pseudonym for Allan James Tucker

Hero Stephen Bellecroix, "tough half-caste from Tiger Bay" (West Indies), worked with Sheila Roath and Hugh Liversidge, upper class intelligence agents. Sheila, who was promiscuous, into rape fantasies, and easily bored with her sex partners, became Stephen's lover.

In *Young Men May Die* (Stein, 1970), each of the three narrated one segment of an inept search for Knuth, an arms dealer. Sheila could not decide whether she preferred the more exciting Stephen or Hugh, a member of her social class.

Craig used only two narrators, Stephen and Sheila, in *A Walk at Night* (Stein, 1971), but it was still confusing. The trio was assigned to bring Gersh Babel, a second-rate writer, out of Russia in order to entice his married lover, an agricultural scientist, to follow him. Their clumsiness again endangered their mission.

Third rate.

Gail Rogers
Authors: Gordon and Mildred Gordon aka "The Gordons"

See: Gail Rogers Mitchell, Section 5, page 347.

Helga Rolfe
Author: James Hadley Chase, pseudonym for Rene Raymond

This series was no place for a nice young woman, but Helga Rolfe was neither young nor nice. She was a nymphomaniac, incapable of fidelity, a shrewd businesswoman who could be fooled by a handsome man, and a relentless enemy. As the only child of a brilliant international attorney, Helga had a continental education, becoming fluent in French, Italian, German, and English. Except for violet eyes and a slim figure, she was described more by male reactions than by physical attributes. At 36, Helga married Herman Rolfe, a physically disabled, impotent multi-millionaire, who expected her to control her sexual urges.

By age 43, in *An Ace Up My Sleeve* (Hale, 1971), Helga was picking up young men. Ex-lover Jack Archer used Helga's weakness to blackmail her into concealing his own embezzlement.

Herman Rolfe's suspicions of Helga in *The Joker in the Pack* (Hale, 1975) caused him to limit her travel and her authority in his financial empire. When he was paralyzed by a stroke, Helga resisted the temptation to kill him, but became a wealthy widow when he died.

Jack Archer had been on the skids since his embezzlement was discovered. In *I Hold the Four Aces* (Hale, 1977), he schemed to entice Helga into ransoming Christopher Grenville, a handsome young gigolo, but was foiled by Hinkle, Helga's loyal servant.

In 1984, Hale combined the three Helga stories into *Meet Helga Rolfe*.

Maggie Rome

Author: Lucille Kallen

The significant other for Maggie Rome was no threat to her husband. Maggie, in her forties, was happily married to consulting engineer Elliott Rome and the fond mother of their two sons, Matt and Alan. The man who dominated her workday on the local weekly newspaper (*The Sloan's Ford Reporter*) and her spare time as a sleuth was editor C. B. Greenfield. C. B., a refugee from the big city, operated in the fashion of Nero Wolfe, sending Maggie off to gather information but reserving the dénouements to himself. Personally, Maggie, who narrated, was more like Erma Bombeck than Archie Goodwin.

Introducing C. B. Greenfield (Crown, 1979) opened with the crash of a hit-and-run driver into the bicycle of the *Reporter's* delivery boy, Peter Kittell. When the obvious suspect, Julian Trager, disappeared, Peter's parents were suspected of his murder.

C. B. and Maggie, who shared a love for music, attended a weekend with the Boston Symphony Orchestra in *C. B. Greenfield: The Tanglewood Murder* (Wyndham, 1980). The orchestra was plagued initially by a series of annoying incidents and finally by the murder of violinist Noel Damaskin. Damaskin and his wife, Fran, were neighbors of Greenfield. C. B. set Maggie to work researching the personal histories of orchestra members and fellow guests at the posh Wheatleigh Inn.

Maggie's task in *C. B. Greenfield: No Lady in the House* (Wyndham, 1982) was more prosaic: to find a substitute cleaning woman for her employer. Hiring Mathilda was only a temporary solution because someone bashed her head in. On C.B.'s orders, Maggie looked first at Mathilda's other employers. One of them, high-powered businesswoman and member of the village board Dina Franklin, was found shot to death in an abandoned school building. Maggie and C. B. traveled to Florida for the final clue to identify a righteous killer. That wasn't enough for C.B. He forced several discontented housewives to accept responsibility for their own roles in the tragedy.

In *C. B. Greenfield: The Piano Bird* (Random, 1984), Maggie visited her ailing mother at Sanibel-Captiva in the Gulf of Mexico. Her reportorial instincts and some overheard conversations made her aware of the conflicts among the cast and crew of a local theatre production, and between the group and local conservationist Sarah McChesney. The murder of Thea Quinn, a beautiful showgirl, caused C. B. to join Maggie. He took her tangled clues and sorted them out to unmask an imposter and murderer.

Maggie and C. B. had new passions in *C. B. Greenfield: A Little Madness* (Random, 1986). He was in love with visiting violinist Penelope Heath-Morecomb. Maggie had joined the anti-nuclear movement, yet one of her assignments was to cover an interview by Alice Dakin, who led a counter-protest group. When Dakin was murdered, C. B. and Maggie worked together, for different reasons, to find the killer. He wanted to prove that Penelope was not the killer. He came to accept, however, that she was an outrageous flirt.

Kallen presented significant social issues with a light touch, creating a warm and engaging heroine.

Rebecca Rosenthal

Author: Ellen Godfrey

Mrs. Rosenthal, far too distinguished to be referred to casually as Rebecca, was a stately Jewish widow, whose family had lived in Canada for four generations. She was proud of her heritage and the contributions her family had made to the country. A tall, thin woman of 72, she had retired from a career as an anthropologist, but was working on a book. She kept herself in good physical condition with yoga and kept her mind alert with puzzles and books. She particularly enjoyed biographies.

In *Murder Among the Well-To-Do* (Porcepic, 1977), Max Stern, Mrs. Rosenthal's younger brother, was concerned that his second wife, Gloria, might be under the influence of a blackmailer. Having moved into the Stern home on a pretext, Mrs. Rosenthal was present when Francine Martin, who had been involved with more than one man, was murdered. Salesman Jeff Gottlieb, who may also have been blackmailed, was discovered hanged at the Stern factory office. Using insights gained from a dream, she learned who had killed Francine, but left the reason for Jeff's death undisclosed.

By her second outing, Mrs. Rosenthal boasted that she had solved 11 murders, including that of her husband. The suspects in *The Case of the Cold Murderer* (Musson, Don Mills, Canada, 1976) were intimates, even members of her family. The small group, which had nurtured Chinook Publishing Company as an outlet for aspiring prose and poetry writers, was in disarray. Victor Blaine, the publisher, had been voted out of his position. He had nurtured young writers and left the running of the business to others. Gwen Masters, who had engineered his defeat, replaced him. There were sexual tensions among the survivors. Yvon Gilmour, a protégé of Victor's, was found dead in a locked room, shot with a gun sent him by his own father. The police quite naturally assumed suicide. That seemed less likely when Gwen was killed. Mrs. Rosenthal was willing to take physical risks and unmask a friend to find the truth.

Charity Ross

Author: Jack Bickham aka John Miles

Charity Ross, a tiny auburn-haired migrant from Ohio, came to the West with her husband, David, in the 1890's.

During *The War Against Charity Ross* (Doubleday, 1967), the couple's efforts to build an Oklahoma ranch were thwarted temporarily by David's murder. Charity had difficulty keeping up because her ranch hands were intimidated and quit. Lowell Stutter coveted the Ross land to move his herd from one part of his acreage to another. Abe Steinmetz, a young New Yorker, and Dan Six, who left his job as Stutter's foreman, came to her rescue. Dan stood up against an overzealous hired gunman.

In *Target: Charity Ross* (Doubleday, 1968), Jimmy Walking Stick and his wife, Minnie, a young couple employed by Charity, were murdered. The deaths of Native Americans were of little interest to the local officials. Through her investigation, Charity and Dan Six learned that Jimmy had sold peyote as a drug, betraying his Indian religious heritage.

Low-key Western of possible interest to females.

Sarah Saber

Author: David Linzee

Sarah Saber, the daughter of an American farm implement dealer of Russian extraction, was a slim blonde. She grew up in the Midwest but relocated in New York City. After Vassar and a short stint at the Columbia Law School, Sarah interned at Inquiries Incorporated (Inkwink). Chris Rockwell, assigned as her mentor, became her lover, although they operated individually within the agency. A risk taker, Sarah tired of routine industrial assignments and requested a challenge.

In *Discretion* (Seaview, 1978), Sarah was manipulated into removing a painting from an art gallery, unaware that she was stealing a copy to defraud an insurance company. Chris was assigned to find the missing art object, not knowing Sarah was his adversary. Ingenious plot.

Belgravia (Seaview, 1979) began when Jack Wilson embezzled money to buy back industrial secrets stolen from the company he managed.

Complexity degenerated into confusion as Chris and Sarah operated independently, and both became murder suspects.

Claudine St. Cyr
Author: Ian Wallace, pseudonym for John Wallace Pritchard

Claudine St. Cyr, an intergalactic police officer, was not born but created by a genetic accident. She was small and slender, with brown hair and eyes and light mahogany skin. Her education included a Ph.D. in psychology and a minor in nuclear physics.

Deathstar Voyage (Putnam, 1969) began as Claudine was assigned to guard the King of Ligeria on a "downtime mystery cruise." Not only was the cruise vehicle disabled, but the ship's officers were dying. Claudine needed supernormal powers to identify the cause of the deaths.

In *The Purloined Prince* (McCall, 1971), Claudine suffered a loss of memory and a pervasive sense of having been involved in murder. Her trial and sentencing were interspersed with flashbacks of the events preceding her arrest.

As *The Sign of the Mute Medusa* (Popular Library, 1977) began, Claudine, a captain in the Intergalactic force was, at age 31, unmarried. She visited the polluted planet Turquoise to probe the disappearance of Har Charl, industrial leader, and Vince Ryner, major galactic industrialist, two members of the ruling quartet. When people disappeared in Turquoise, they were not merely transported geographically but in time.

Claudine's role in *Heller's Leap* (DAW, 1979) was subordinate to that of Klaus Heller, the conqueror of black holes, whose subsequent death was a mystery. Claudine repeated his journey through time, space, and dream flashes, until she understood why death was the answer Heller sought.

Wallace's series combined a sense of humor with a vivid imagination, but may leave traditional mystery fans dissatisfied.

Baroness Penelope St. John Orsini
Author: Paul Kenyon, pseudonym for Nat Freedland

One of her two deceased husbands accounted for Penelope's extended name. She had married John Stanton Marlowe, who died in an air crash, then Baron Reynaldo St. John Orsini. Although from a distinguished Philadelphia family, she preferred to be known as the "Baroness." A former model, she was a tall, slim woman in her thirties with black hair and green eyes. Penelope had been recruited by the State Department after her second husband's death, but chose to work with her own team, claiming an unofficial relationship with the National Security Council.

Kenyon wrote no less than seven books featuring Penelope, published by Pocket and Futura during the mid 1970's, heavy with sex and violence. The Baroness killed easily and was sexually indiscriminate, making Modesty Blaise look like Shirley Temple.

Minnie Santangelo

Author: Anthony Mancini

Minnie Santangelo was a widow with olive skin, hazel eyes, and thick dark hair streaked with gray and worn in a bun. She blended her Catholicism with witchcraft. Her Italian-American husband, Stefano, 14 years older, had been killed on a visit to his Sicilian birthplace. Her son Raymond, an attorney, had recently returned from a stint as a VISTA volunteer in New Mexico.

In *Minnie Santangelo's Mortal Sin* (Coward, 1975), the recent death of Jerry Tedesco had similarities (cork in the dead man's mouth) to that of Minnie's husband, Stefano. This to her suggested a Sicilian family feud, a theory that was reinforced by Professore Gaetano Conti, who presented himself as studying the traditions of Mafioso. Minnie feared the Mafia and mistrusted the police. She could only depend on herself after Conti was killed (cork left behind) and an attempt was made on her life. When betrayed by a man she considered her friend, she shot her way out of trouble.

Raymond's newborn son, Stefano, suffered ill health after his well-attended baptism in *Minnie Santangelo and the Evil Eye* (Coward, 1977). Cynthia, the baby's mothe,r may have removed an amulet from the child, taking away his protection from the evil eye and leading to his death from meningitis. Who among the baptismal guests could be a witch? Arturo Longo, the white witch who placed the amulet on young Stefano, was killed. When Raymond's health also deteriorated, Minnie allied herself with Tina Corso, one-time girlfriend of Raymond, and used her own witchcraft to save her son.

Myra Savage

Author: Mark McShane

A woman of limited formal education, Myra Savage was a psychic who convinced her unemployed, asthmatic husband, Bill, to cooperate in a deadly kidnapping during *Seance* (Doubleday, 1962) aka *Séance on a Wet Afternoon*. They hoped to collect a ransom and enhance Myra's reputation by leading authorities to the child. The plan did not cover the death of young Adriana Clayton.

When Myra, by then a widow, was released from prison for her part in the child's death in *Seance for Two* (Doubleday, 1972), she was met outside the gates by William Wilson. He was a strange mother-dominated man, drawn to her powers. Myra was unsure that she still had her special gifts, but Wilson was willing to risk his life, and others, to convince Myra that she could still prevision events.

Depressing narratives.

Effie Schlupe

Author: Lloyd Biggle, Jr.

Effie Schlupe added homespun ingredients of humor and reality to the Jan Darzak science fiction/mystery series.

In *Watchers of the Dark* (Doubleday, 1966), set in the future, private investigator Darzak could not convince his Brooklyn-born secretary, Effie, to remain at the Earth office. She wanted to accompany him into the universe to combat the Agents of the Dark, who brought insanity to one planet after another. Effie's deft hand with rhubarb beer saved the day, and the universe.

Effie was retired and bored in *This Darkening Universe* (Doubleday, 1975), when Darzak was threatened by UDF (Unidentified Death Force). The Council of Supreme sent Effie to accompany dermatologist Dr. Malina Darr and her two children to Montura, a large bartering compound in space. Effie developed a cash economy, fast food outlets, and a transportation system, and established cider as the local beverage of choice on a planet where the natives lived underground. She needed Jan when the children were accused of murder.

During *The Whirligig of Time* (Doubleday, 1979), Darzak puzzled over two seemingly unrelated incidents: the creation of a double star by an explosion, and the discovery of badly burned scientist Qwasrolk at the other end of a galaxy. Effie, wealthy from her commercial enterprises, convinced Jan to follow Qwasrolk, who, like the Cheshire cat, could propel his own matter through space. It took them both to convince the citizens of Vezpro that they could not ignore threats that their planet might be next to be forced into stardom.

Considering that the stories were projected to take place in 1995, something must have delayed scientific advancements. No great loss.

Miss Emily Seeton

Authors: Original author Heron Carvic, replaced by Hampton Charles, pseudonym for James Melville; then by Hamilton Crane, pseudonym for Sarah J. Mason

Emily Seeton, a tiny retired art teacher with psychic insights, worked with Scotland Yard and, more testily, with the local constabulary. Her sketches portrayed individuals so as to reveal personal characteristics and foretell the future. Emily, who kept fit through yoga and physical exercise, used her ever-present umbrella as a weapon, but her successes were based as much on coincidence as skill. She had resigned her position in a girls' school when she inherited a home in the village of Plummergen from her godmother.

In *Picture Miss Seeton* (Carvic, Harper, 1968), Emily was unable to orally describe her encounter with gangsters running drugs in Plummergen. Members of this group had killed young Angie Venning, a friend of Nigel, the not-to-bright son of Sir George and Lady Colveden, and tried to abduct Emily. Inspector Delphick of Scotland Yard saw the twitchy fingers and provided Emily with paper.

In *Miss Seeton Draws the Line* (Carvic, Harper, 1970), Delphick and the local police had connected the deaths of young children to post office robberies. At Delphick's request, Emily drew a sketch of Effie, a nasty, spying little girl, but the face remained blurred. The information from the sketch helped Scotland Yard to avert a robbery at the Plummergen post office. However, when Emily disappeared, she became one of their suspects. Effie's death changed that. Further information from Emily assisted in the apprehension of a child killer, solved the bank robberies, and foiled an intended burglary at Colveden's.

By *Witch Miss Seeton* (Carvic, Harper, 1971) aka *Miss Seeton, Bewitched*, Emily had become a respected ally of Inspector Delphick, his assistant Sgt. Bob Ranger, and Chief Inspector Christ Brinton of Ashford Division. They called on her when they were concerned about two religious cults operating in the area. She was to infiltrate Nuscience, which had predicted the end of the world, but convinced gullible locals that they should gather their valuables and hide out in a cave where they would be protected from the catastrophe. There were devil worshippers and exorcists. The action increased geometrically, and the reader was advised to control any need for reality.

Miss Seeton Sings (Carvic, Harper, 1973) was one of the better ones in the series, although coincidence rather than skill produced the desirable results. By happenstance Emily saw the exchange of a briefcase and then boarded the wrong plane, going to Genoa, not Geneva. The men, who were counterfeiters, assumed she was on their trail. On the side, her training and special skill enabled her to see the masterpiece behind an overlay painting. Emily, more or less unaware of what was going on, wandered around Europe, followed by the criminals and the police.

During *Odds on Miss Seeton* (Carvic, Harper, 1975), the authorities used Emily as a decoy, sending her in disguise into the notorious GoldFish. Later she foiled a kidnapping at Kenharding Manor and averted a race meeting fraud. Emily muddled along from crisis to crisis. She returned a gift package (containing a bomb) to its donor's car, so this one ended with a bang.

Carvic built a company of supporting players for the sexagenarian spinster: police officers and officials at Scotland Yard; two urban reporters who shared a bed, but not scoops; the absent-minded agnostic vicar and his sister; and the Colvedens, local gentry. Not everyone approved of Emily. Erica Nuttel and Norah Blaine, two older women who shared a home in Plummergen, considered her a dangerous criminal. The initial series ended with Carvic's death in 1980.

James Melville, writing as Hampton Charles, continued the series in three Berkley paperbacks during 1990:

- During *Advantage Miss Seeton*, Mel Forby and rival reporter Thudd Banner fell in love. The reader was aware from the start that William Parson, an ex-convict, stole money to provide an abortion for his daughter, Vicky. She died, unfortunately, as the result of incompetent care. Judge Sir Wilfred Thumper sent Parson to prison as a result. On his release, Parson sought revenge against Thumper's daughter Trish, a young tennis star. Emily's sketches helped to deter a kidnapping and tied Parson to thefts at the local church. Considering the circumstances, they prevailed on Sir Wilfred to show mercy.

- In *Miss Seeton at the Helm*, Scotland Yard subsidized a cruise on the Mediterranean for Emily so she could monitor the behavior of feuding art authorities, Ferencz Szabo and Adrian Witley. Emily's skill had taken a new approach. At this point she sketched people as if they were characters in famous paintings. Ferencz made two attempts on Adrian's life, so when he was murdered, the solution seemed obvious. Delphick and Mel Forby joined the voyage in Greece. Thanks to Emily's sketches and her yoga exercises, three criminals (the killer, a blackmailer, and an art crook) were apprehended.

■ During *Miss Seeton, by Appointment*, Emily foiled a jewel robbery at Colveden's. But by now the plots and characters were so familiar that readers would be able to figure things out early in Charles' narratives.

The final author was Sarah J. Mason, writing under the name Hamilton Crane, who produced the largest number of books.

Miss Seeton Cracks the Case (Berkley, 1991) combined (1) roadside robberies whereby motor buses were stopped by "Dick Turpins" and the passengers robbed of their possessions, and (2) the drugging of senior citizens with wine by the "Sherry Gang," who gained admittance to homes by befriending the elderly and then robbing them. Delphick had hoped that Emily, after talking to victims, might be able to make one or more of her prophetic sketches. An inordinate amount of the narrative was spent on The Nuts and other minor characters.

During *Miss Seeton Paints the Town* (Berkley, 1991), the police in Ashford and Hastings were confronted with vandals called the Ashford Chappers. Emily made a temporary return to teaching art to grade school children but found a corpse when she took them on a day trip. Lady Meg Colveden, active in local beautification efforts, asked Emily to sketch how Plummergen might look if "spruced up." There was considerable rivalry between Plummergen and neighboring Murreystone. Vandalism extended to arson and murder. Emily's sketches were complex (a 1920's costume, a mole, barn owl, and a major fire) and had to be interpreted by Delphick and the local police.

In *Hands Up, Miss Seeton* (Berkley, 1992), Emily was arrested as a member of a pickpocket gang while shopping in London. Once her innocence was established, Emily tried but could not sketch the real perpetrators until late in the narrative. The main story revolved around Mentley Collier, whom Emily sketched as crazed and probably addicted, but there were many detours before the ending, in which drug distributors who used carrier pigeons and money launderers were arrested.

Miss Seeton by Moonlight (Berkley, 1992) featured a "gentleman thief," who turned out to be a real gentleman, whose unmasking was a shock. The loot from the thefts was either held for ransom or sold to a major collector, referred to as "Croesus." What was Emily's participation? She drew copies of the missing items and noted a pattern, winter scenes. Later she came upon thieves stealing a sculpture and stowed away in the gypsy wagon in which it was carried off.

By *Miss Seeton Rocks the Cradle* (Berkley, 1992), author Crane/Mason was cranking them out at a rate of two per year, and they showed it. Emily found infant Marguerite MacSporran, the missing heiress to leadership of the MacSporran clan, in a telephone booth. Nearby was a message, "Changed our minds." As a result, she was invited to the family's castle in Scotland, where the Campbells were still feuding with the MacDonalds. What Mel Forby wanted to depict as a Jacobite plot turned into a struggle over a possible gold mine.

Miss Seeton Goes to Bat (Berkley, 1993) was, not surprisingly, concerned with the local cricket matches, but there were other problems. Counterfeit 50-pence coins were being circulated in the area. Nigel Colveden was smitten by Annabelle Leigh, a traveling artist who sketched local establishments. When Emily sketched Annabelle, she appeared as a vicious bird. Meg, Lady Colveden, was busy raising money for the soccer field. The crucial match would be between Plummergen and Murreystone, traditional rivals. Both Sgt. Bob Ranger and Admiral "Buzzard" Leighton were drafted to fill in for injured players on the Plummergen squad. With everyone's eyes on the match, except Emily's, thieves were robbing the clubhouse.

Miss Seeton Plants Suspicion (Berkley, 1993) sent Emily and female reporter Mel Forby off to probe serial crimes connected with hop-picker camps, referred to as "blondes in a bag." Young Nigel Colveden (still young after all these books) became a suspect, and Emily almost a victim, before this farce ended.

During *Starring Miss Seeton* (Berkley, 1994) the locals put on a play in which Emily acted as the scenic director. While searching for Christmas greens on the Colveden estate, she set off a WW2 bomb, which exposed a beautiful Roman temple mosaic. Sir George didn't want hordes of tourists, so he made plans to send it to a museum, but that would have to wait until spring. The delay was very upsetting to visiting professor Caernavon Carter, or someone posing as Carter. Whatever—he was murdered when Colveden Hall was burgled. Emily's fingers were itchy. Fortunately, she had her umbrella along to foil another robbery by the Shotgun Gang and, during the play, she exposed a female posing as a male. Sure, Emily was busy during this one, but it was oh so cluttered.

Miss Seeton went hardcover in *Miss Seeton Undercover* (Berkley, 1994), which revolved around specialized art thefts, possibly hand-tailored to the needs of Chrysander Bullian, a wealthy, reclusive collector. Plummergen was excited about the robberies in local households, one of which ended in a murder, reinforcing Sir George's call for a night watch to patrol the area. Other items of interest included the presence of a TV crew filming a cooking show and the search for an historic apple, the Plummergen Peculier. An attempt to bomb Emily failed. Mel Forby did most of the detecting.

Miss Seeton Rules (Berkley, 1994) contained many of the themes and characters of prior books. Princess Georgina visited the area, arousing the competitive fervor of Plummergen and Murreystone. The abductions of "Georgy Girl" and, later, Emily were not motivated by nuclear protests or political disagreement, but plain British greed.

Sold to Miss Seeton (Berkley, 1995) hung all of the familiar players on a flimsy plot based on an oaken chest that Emily purchased at an auction. After a considerable amount of blither, a blacksmith opened the chest, only to find artifacts from the 15th and 16th centuries. One of the documents could seriously affect the right to inherit titles. There was a possibility of an unknown heir to a forgotten title. Authorities were concerned about a helicopter that hovered over a nearby prison dropping Christmas cards and banners and something special for Cutter, a prison inmate. There were, of course, murders to bring in Scotland Yard. Out of this, and sketches by Emily, Delphick was able to solve several cases.

Sweet Miss Seeton (Berkley, 1996) introduced a new but equally zany character, Antony Scarlett, who was determined to buy Emily's cottage to use as a mold for his chocolate entry in an art contest. The local police sought a menacing gang who defrauded the elderly, and with the help of Emily and a rejected model, found them.

During *Bonjour, Miss Seeton* (Berkley, 1997), Miss Nuttel and Mrs. Blaine came to a parting of the ways that seemed at first to be a permanent dissolution of their companionship. Miss Seeton met a charming French Count who enjoyed her company. She failed to intercept a bomb, which ended an early attempt (1974) to build a tunnel between England and France.

Miss Seeton's Finest Hour (Berkley, 1999) served not only as the end of the series but a welcome return to an emphasis on Emily. It was set in England during World War II. Emily's sketches directed Scotland Yard to a saboteur. More sadly, the romance of her life ended, leaving her with an umbrella for remembrance, a talisman she carried throughout the series. A nice touch.

The later authors, although professionally competent, spent inordinate amounts of time on the dreary "Nuts" and the immature Nigel Colveden. The deft but kindly way in which Carvic had described the rural English village was replaced by a patronizing treatment, overpopulating Plummergen with village idiots. Nevertheless, the series maintained strong readership.

Dr. Grace Severance

Author: Margaret Scherf

Grace Severance, a retired pathologist and medical school professor, was 5' 6" tall with a sturdy build, gray hair, and blue eyes. She did not hesitate to use profanity and threats to get what she wanted. She performed autopsies and bone reconstructions to identify victims as part of her detective work.

While living with her niece in Tailings, Arizona, in *The Banker's Bones* (Doubleday, 1968), Grace was bored until she and eccentric artist Paul Ward found Marie McAllister, a California bank employee, wandering in the desert after a robbery/kidnapping. Ellis Walsh had abducted Marie and Fred Bennington when he robbed the California-Pacific Bank. Marie, when rescued, vaguely remembered hearing two separate gunshots. One was explained when Sloat, a grungy junk dealer, brought meat in to be stored. It was identified as Fred Bennington's toothless corpse. Grace insisted on reconstructing the corpse's jaw just in case the dead man was not Bennington.

Grace had moved to Montana by *The Beautiful Birthday Cake* (Doubleday, 1971), where there was considerable resentment against orchard owners who used Paramordant, a potentially dangerous insecticide. Two men who attended Grace's birthday party died within 24 hours in seemingly unrelated deaths. She tested the birthday cake and the eye drops that caused the deaths, but was almost killed in another "accident."

While in Las Vegas during *To Cache a Millionaire* (Doubleday, 1972), Grace connived to meet Arthur Acuff, a reclusive millionaire who offered her financial advice and hospitality. While at The Fountains, a hotel owned by Acuff, Grace noticed the smell of embalming fluid. She connected it to a car wreck she had witnessed on the way into town. Later, Grace smelled formaldehyde when Charles Sherman, an inveterate gambler, died in the casino. Acuff's disappearance, initially labeled a kidnapping, added to the confusion. Grace remembered a message she had promised Acuff that she would deliver. It provided the solution to multiple murders. Grace's nephew Clarence, who had driven her on the trip, found romance in Las Vegas.

The citizens of Summerfield were renovating Wooding House as a museum in *The Beaded Banana* (Doubleday, 1978). During an open house, the corpse of "Rozzie" Moss, ex-Las Vegas casino owner, was found in a wooden chest. Grace's investigation was hampered by movie actors in town for location shots and the political manipulations of gamblers to influence state legislation.

The books combined humor with murder. Grace was a no-nonsense sleuth who operated out of skill and experience unlike, many other "spinster" sleuths.

Helen Marsh Shandy
Author: Charlotte MacLeod, aka Alisa Craig

Helen Marsh was 40 years old in *Rest You Merry* (Doubleday, 1978) when she came to Balaclava Agricultural College in Massachusetts. There she met, and eventually married, college professor Peter Shandy. Peter had returned home earlier than expected from a vacation, only to discover the body of Jemima Ames, wife of his best friend, Tim Ames. Helen, who had been described to Peter as "an old maiden aunt," agreed to care for Tim's house when he visited his daughter. Her attention to the holdings of the Buggins collection of first editions was crucial to the solution. Helen, a librarian with a Ph.D. degree, faded into the exaggerated cast of characters and the fanciful plots of later stories. That happened to librarians who teamed with male sleuths.

Helen remained in the area and was entertaining on campus in *The Luck Runs Out* (Doubleday, 1979) when fellow tour members robbed the silver maker's supplies. She was temporarily abducted by them but released unharmed. This all factored into Peter's investigation of the death of Miss Flackley, a well-to-do businesswoman.

Again in *Wrack and Rune* (Doubleday, 1982), Helen's research on a ruse to parlay a rune stone into a fortune and her knowledge of antique furniture assisted Peter in solving the death of a hired man. The plot revolved around efforts by assorted relatives to plunder the holdings of elderly (105 years) Hilda Horsfall and her nephew Jenny (aged 80). By this time, Peter and Helen had married, and she had been hired as assistant librarian for the Buggins Collection.

Helen's access to the Collection in the Balaclava Library was often an asset to Peter, who considered himself an amateur detective, as in *Vane Pursuit* (Mysterious Press, 1989). Her photographs taken before the local soap factory burned down led to a group that stole antique weathervanes. She and her friend Iduna Stott were set upon by the weathervane gang, dumped into the water, and barely swam to an isolated island. Peter had his own adventure in tracking down corruption among local officials and finding the connection with the weathervane gang.

Helen's assistance in decoding a notebook left behind by a victim in *An Owl Too Many* (Mysterious Press, 1991) was merely a sop. She was kept busy making fudge, poaching eggs, and working on research. Peter did call on Helen for advice as to the possible purchase of paintings during *Something in the Water* (Mysterious Press, 1994), but this was not a significant issue in his investigation of the mysterious power of local water to produce huge lupines and increase human longevity. Mystery writer Catriona McBogle, a friend of Helen's, visited on occasion and involved herself in the narratives.

Helen's participation after the first few books was scanty.

Jemima Shore

Author: Antonia Fraser

Jemima Shore was a television personality and investigative journalist with classic English good looks: tall, slim, golden haired. Her parents had been killed in a car accident when she was 18. Although Protestant, she spent several years in a Catholic girl's boarding school before attending Oxford.

In *Quiet As a Nun* (Viking, 1977), former classmate Rosa Mary Powerstock, now Sister Miriam, decided to donate her worldly possessions to the poor. As the assets were extensive and included the land on which Blessed Eleanor's convent was located, this was a controversial decision that put her at risk. Jemima returned to her alma mater after Sr. Miriam's death to locate a more recent will, which left the convent intact and confounded those who brought evil to a religious setting.

During *The Wild Island* (Norton, 1978), Jemima decided to vacation in the Highlands. Charles Beauregard, who had a cottage available for rent, was dead when Jemima arrived. This placed control of the family estate in the hands of Charles' uncle, Colonel Henry. There was a serious question as to whether or not Charles' death was murder. Much of the tension arose from local sentiment in favor of the Scottish Nationalist movement. Jemima had a tempestuous but doomed romance and an exciting "stalk" in a misty glen.

Back in London, Jemima used friend Chloe Fontaine's new apartment in *A Splash of Red* (Norton, 1981) while Chloe was expected to be out of town doing research. She never made it. Jemima found her hostess dead in bed shortly after she moved in. Chloe had confided in Jemima that she had two new loves, and mentioned an adventure she had when locked out of her apartment. Chloe had been in serious trouble, a matter which Jemima discovered as she investigated the men in her life.

In *Cool Repentance* (Norton, 1982), Jemima was assigned to cover the Larminster Festival at a time when actress Christabel Cartwright returned to the family she had deserted years before. She had left Julian, her husband, and their two daughters to run off with another man. Christabel planned a triumphant re-entry into the local theatre, unaware of what was waiting for her. The first death was that of a young actress who resembled Christabel and was wearing her swimsuit. After two more deaths, Christabel killed herself.

Jemima Shore Investigates (Methuen, 1983) was a collection of short stories by various authors. The one featuring Jemima provided more insights into her preferences. She liked only white wine and brewed coffee but disliked smoking; had a Mercedes; and enjoyed a fireplace.

During *Oxford Blood* (Norton, 1985), Elsie Connelly belatedly admitted that she had switched babies 20 years before, creating absolute consternation as to proper parentage and inheritances. Jemima, in her role as a television investigator, joined the social circle surrounding Lord Saffron, son and heir of the Marquess of St. Ives, whose title was now in controversy. Saffron, a free spender, believed that his life was at risk. Tiggie Jones, who had become engaged to Saffron, died in what he and Jemima considered murder. Jemima identified the killer, who disposed of himself. All was covered up.

Jemima Shore's First Case (Weidenfeld, 1986) dealt with Jemima's life before she appeared in *Quiet As a Nun* and included characters who had appeared in that book. The most interesting story featured 15-year old Jemima's investigation at Blessed Eleanor's School.

Your Royal Hostage (Atheneum, 1988) took place at a difficult time in Jemima's career. New management had dropped her ongoing television show. Presented with an opportunity to co-anchor a television special on Princess Amy's wedding to Prince Ferdinand, a sophisticated older man, she grasped it. An animal rights group using intimate photos of the Prince pressured the couple into supporting their cause during Jemima's interview. Some of the more aggressive members went further, kidnapping the princess. After Jemima's coup, she was rehired.

Rather fancifully in *The Cavalier Case* (Bantam, 1991), the level-headed Jemima became obsessed with the portrait of Decimus Meredith, a 17th-century poet-soldier. That made her vulnerable to his handsome descendant, also Decimus, but referred to as Dan, now the 18th Viscount Lackland. Jemima had been commissioned to do a series on British homes, their owners, and ghosts. The portrait of the early Decimus was reputed to house his spirit. The reputed ghost was shown to be a fake when Jemima discovered a hidden costume. Dan, a womanizing tennis star, planned to turn the family estate into a posh tennis club. This was anathema to Dan's sister Zena, now writing a family history. Information gained by her research would spice up the history, but that was not what Zena intended. Jemima used a play to expose the killer.

Jemima Shore at the Sunny Grave (Bantam, 1993) was another collection of short stories, four of which involved Jemima. On a visit to the Caribbean she:

- Uncovered the murderers of Miss Isabella Archer, descendant of an historic figure in the islands;

- Provided an after-dinner speech and the solution to a murder at a Mallow College function;

- Gained personal insights as to what a rape victim might feel, when she was trapped in a hotel room with a stranger; and

- Resolved her way out of a set piece on Corfu Island where other guests came prepared for murder.

Political Death (Bantam, 1996) occurred in 1993 during a fictional Parliamentary election. Jemima had developed her own production company by this time. Elderly Lady Imogen, who threatened to disclose the truth about a 30-year-old treason case, was murdered shortly after giving an interview to Jemima. Imogen's revelations about the trial, all recounted in a series of journals, one of which she gave Jemima, could imperil the career of Burgo Smyth, now Foreign Secretary. Burgo had been the love of Imogen's life. It was an excellent return to form.

Jemima was tough minded but feminine and very interested in men. She had never married and seemed attracted to inappropriate men—too young, or married, or promiscuous. Perhaps she threatened the suitors with her height and her financial security, wit, and intelligence. She was an exceptional protagonist, but that was no surprise. Her author, Lady Antonia Fraser, was a highly literate, well-educated woman who also excelled in non-fiction.

Susan Silverman

Author: Robert B. Parker

Although they did not share a home except for a failed short-term experiment, few fictional romances have been more enduring and endearing than that between Parker's private investigator Spenser and Susan Silverman.

Spenser was different. He lived in Boston, not New York or California. He cooked, read books, and was sensitive in his relationships with women. Susan rejected his proposals because of an unhappy early marriage and dedication to her career. Spenser described her as not beautiful but having shoulder-length black hair and a dark Jewish face with black eyes, and "well built." Over the decades, she and Spenser survived infidelity, her need for privacy, and the demands of their careers. Susan shared Spenser with his best friend and frequent partner in investigations, Hawk, an African-American who rivaled his skills, and sometimes excelled them. Her roles diminished later in the series.

Susan first appeared in *God Save the Child* (Houghton, 1974), when Spenser searched for Kevin Bartlett, a high school student whom Susan had counseled. She not only provided a clue as to Kevin's location, but risked danger to help him.

Hawk, first an adversary, later as close to Spenser as Susan, appeared in *Promised Land* (Houghton, 1976). Susan made a token appearance, but only in the framework of their relationship.

Susan challenged Spenser's initial perceptions in *Looking for Rachel Wallace* (Delacorte, 1980). He had been hired to guard Rachel, a militant feminist lesbian author, who had been threatened with regard to the publication of her new book on discrimination against women and gays. She'd fired him and then was kidnapped, so he returned to the case. Susan's influence made it possible for Spenser and Rachel to reach an accommodation.

Spenser developed a "big brother" type relationship with Paul Giacomo, the 16-year-old he was hired to guard in *Early Autumn* (Delacorte, 1981). That too set up a long-term relationship, which in some way met his need to parent. Neither of Paul's parents wanted him, although his custody was at issue in their divorce. It took time away from Susan, even though Spenser and Paul were building a cottage on land Susan had received in her own divorce settlement.

For several years, Susan receded into the background. Spenser glanced sadly at her picture, reminisced, or complained that she had moved to Washington, D.C., for a doctoral internship in a hospital setting. He understood her career needs on an intellectual level, but felt incomplete without her. As she advanced from high school guidance counselor to a doctorate in psychology, her realism conflicted more frequently with Spenser's romantic idealism. After graduation from Harvard, Susan had moved to California, denying Spenser even an address. During *Valediction* (Delacorte, 1984), he diverted himself with an attractive and willing advertising executive.

In *A Catskill Eagle* (Delacorte, 1985), Susan contacted Hawk, troubled by her relationship with Rusty Costigan, an unstable man who took her on a cross-country trip. Much of the excitement in the book was in Hawk's and Spenser's pursuit of the couple. The FBI and CIA were involved because they wanted Rusty's dad, Jerry Costigan, dead or alive. Freeing Susan physically was not the problem Spenser was advised. She had to end her current relationship if she wanted him to be part of her life again.

During *Taming a Sea Horse* (Delacorte, 1986) Susan helped Spenser save April Kyle, Paul Giacomo's girlfriend. April had appeared earlier and been rescued at Susan's request in *Ceremony* (Delacorte, 1982).

Their professional responsibilities clashed in *Crimson Joy* (Delacorte, 1988). The serial killer of African-American women might be a member of her therapy group. This posed a conflict of interest within Susan herself. She wanted the bloodshed to stop, but, until she was sure, guarded the confidences of those within the group. There was another lull in Susan's participation, except for hand-holding, loving, and occasional psychological insights into the people involved.

Susan's ex-husband, Brad, provided an addition to Susan's household in *Pastime* (Putnam's, 1991) when he gave her a German Shorthair, to be named Pearl. Pearl went along with Spenser and Paul Giacomo as they searched for Paul's mother.

In an unsuccessful experiment during *Double Deuce* (Putnam, 1992), Spenser moved in with Susan. Their intention was to become closer, but the tensions that arose were more than either could handle. While Spenser and Hawk cleansed a housing development of gangs, he was unable to make one house large enough for him and Susan.

Paper Doll (Putnam, 1993) limited Susan's role to loving banter, shared meals, good sex, and helpful advice. That would please the hard-core readers just fine. Not everyone valued Susan so lightly. When the series was made into a television program, Susan's character was eliminated at one point. Public indignation forced the producers to bring her back.

During *Walking Shadow* (Putnam, 1994), Susan and Spenser made another accommodation, jointly purchasing a Connecticut weekend house. Although they could not live together full time, they weekended very well. Through Susan's position on the board of directors of a Port City theatre company, Spenser was drawn into feuds within the Chinese and Vietnamese immigrant communities. He began by assigning Hawk to provide protection for Demetrius Christopholous, the artistic director of the company. However, it was Craig Sampson, the leading actor, who was shot at the opening night. It became clearer when Sampson's relationship with a young, married Chinese woman surfaced.

Susan was reduced to scenery again in *Thin Air* (Putnam, 1995), while Spenser sought Detective Frank Belson's missing spouse, and in *Chance* (Putnam, 1996) when he implicated himself and Hawk in territorial strife among Russian, Chinese, and Italian gangsters.

Susan surprised Spenser in *Small Vices* (Putnam, 1997). Her clock was ticking. She wanted to adopt a child and have Spenser be the "father." He was extremely busy trying to free an African-American man who had been framed for murder. Spenser had other problems. There was a contract out on him, and it might include Susan. Their love for one another stood the test, and they settled for that.

Susan's past surfaced in *Sudden Mischief* (Putnam, 1998) when her former husband, Brad, was sued for sexual harassment. Spenser had little sympathy for Brad, but Susan had a history with him that made Spenser vulnerable to her plea. By the time Brad became a murder suspect, they had uncovered evidence of misuse of donations to a charity and money laundering. Susan and Spenser had never talked much about her past, but she revealed herself to him (and the reader) in this narrative. She had been the only child of older parents: a mother who was annoyed by the time needed to care for a daughter and a father who doted upon her. Her mother, resenting the attention given to Susan, became increasingly neurotic. Susan and her father had collaborated in protecting Susan's mother from her fears. Susan also confronted her attraction to men who were risk takers and her sense of personal failure in her marriage to Brad, finally releasing herself from a need to protect him from his own responsibilities.

When Susan forwarded a pro bono case to Spenser involving a promiscuous college friend in *Hush Money* (Putnam, 1999), there was room for jealousy. It did not become the dominant plot line, however. Hawk had enlisted Spenser to help a college professor who had been denied tenure because of false charges. The young man was the son of Hawk's mentor. The accuser had wronged Hawk in the past. This took priority.

Their relationship had become so important to Spenser that he felt incomplete without Susan, but that did not earn her the right to share in his investigations. They each had their own professional lives. Unlike Susan, Spenser shared his cases, seeking her psychological insights and personal impressions of people. That was her contribution in *Hugger Mugger* (Putnam, 2000), when Spenser was hired to discover who was shooting breeder Walter Clive's horses. By the time Clive was murdered, Spenser was so involved in Clive's multi-problem family (compared to a Tennessee Williams cast by both Susan and Spenser) that he could not let go. He chose other allies than Susan or Hawk to back him up when his life was in danger.

Potshot (Putnam, 2001) took Spencer out West, an area that increasingly interested author Parker. Susan had problems of her own in *Widow's Walk* (Putnam, 2002), dealing with a young gay man she counseled, who finally committed suicide. Spenser had been hired to help sexy attorney Rita Fiore prove that Mary Smith had not killed her older husband, banker Nathan Smith. Spenser's probe produced information that Nathan was involved in illegal manipulations of his position on a corporate board. Susan suggested that he might also have been a homosexual, who had married a much younger woman as a "beard," even worse, a pederast. Multiple shootings included two killings by Spenser.

Back Story (Putnam, 2003) had Spenser investigating a bank robbery that occurred 28 years before. A group called the Dredd Scott Brigade had held up Shawmut Bank in Boston. The daughter of victim Emily Gordon wanted to know who killed her mother. Spencer took the case out of friendship for Paul Giacomo, now in his thirties and a stage director who was a friend of Daryl, the daughter. Along the way, Spenser, who had become increasingly violent killed, five persons. Part of his tension arose from the fact that Susan had been threatened by those who did not want the case reopened. Pearl died, but was replaced.

The folks at Kinergy provided lots of work for private investigators in *Bad Business* (Putnam, 2004). Spenser was hired to prove that Marlene Rowley's husband, Trent, was unfaithful. Susan appeared regularly as a lover and a sounding board.

Susan was on the periphery again in *Cold Services* (Putnam, 2005). She tolerated Spenser's closeness to Hawk, who had become her friend too. She did not want Spenser to do any more killing. He was more than tempted. Hawk was seriously injured guarding bookie Luther Gillespie. Gillespie, his wife, and two of his three children were murdered. Hawk and Spenser wanted revenge and financial compensation for the surviving child.

This series had appeal for both genders, partly because of its treatment of the male-female relationship, but also because the writing flows so smoothly. Parker has other interests now. He began a series about a female investigator, Sunny Randall, and has done some standalones. Maybe Susan had become old news. The latest Spenser, *School Days* (Putnam, 2005), sent Susan off to Durham, North Carolina. In her absence Spenser took on the thankless task of proving Jared Clark innocent of participation in a multiple murder.

Parker may have ignored Susan in the Spenser novels, but he gave her some space in his later Sunny Randall series where Susan, as Dr. Silverman, provided therapy to Sunny.

Paola Smith

Author: George Sampson

After Paola Smith's father, a teacher, died, her mother became increasingly dependent upon Paola's uncle, a drug smuggler with Mafia connections. When her mother died, Paola made her home with her uncle, took a job in his business, but rebelled when he selected a young Italian to be her husband.

In *A Drug on the Market* (Hale, 1967), George Watson, a Cambridge University student, met and was attracted to young Paola. George convinced Scotland Yard to let him investigate drug smuggling. Eventually he realized that Paola was unaware that her uncle was a major drug distributor. When she became aware, she worked with George to lead the police to the smugglers.

The couple married and honeymooned in Scotland in *Playing With Fire* (Hale, 1968). In need of extra money, Paola worked as barmaid, becoming aware of local resistance to liquor taxes. When George was unwillingly recruited as a courier, Paola used her Mafia connections.

Undistinguished.

Jaime Sommers

Author: Eileen Lottman

Jaime Sommers aka "The Bionic Woman" was the heroine of the Seventies television series *The Bionic Woman*. Like *The Girl from U.N.C.L.E.*, this was an offshoot of a TV series featuring a male (*The Six Million-Dollar Man*). Steve Austin, the hero on whom so much government money had been spent, was a test pilot doomed to death after a crash without massive intervention. Damaged parts were replaced by synthetics expanding his strength, speed, and vision.

As was explained in *The Bionic Woman: Welcome Home, Jaime* (Berkley, 1977), orphaned Jaime Sommers had been raised by Steve's parents. Growing up together they were close, but a romantic relationship developed as they became adults. Steve's injury and subsequent rebuilding had not been a problem for Jaime. A tragic accident while skydiving left her close to death. Steve convinced Oscar Goldman, head of OSI, the Secret Service agency that took advantage of his new powers, to reclaim Jaime. Although her transplants were initially successful, her body eventually rejected the changes. She subsequently recovered her powers, but one thing was lost—her feeling for Steve. Charlton Harris wanted revenge against

Jaime because she and Steve had caused him problems. Jaime agreed to serve as bait, but saved herself only because Harris had raised an honest son.

The Bionic Woman: Extracurricular Activities (Berkley, 1976) combined two episodes from the series. Each dealt with Jaime in her role as teacher at an elementary school connected to an Army base. First, with the help of a lonely Native American boy, Jaime foiled a plot to steal a prototype individual flying suit. Second, Katie, a shy little girl in her class, involved Jaime with Susan Victor, who trained wild animals (with love) for television and movie productions. The animals, including Neil, a lion, were allowed considerable freedom on the Victor Ranch. When a marauding cougar attacked livestock, Neil was held responsible.

The books were adapted from episodes credited to the television script authors.

Margo Franklin Spence

Author: Jerry Jenkins

See: Margo Franklin, Section 5, page 306.

Penelope Spring

Author: Margot Arnold, pseudonym for Petronelle Cook

Penelope Spring may seem to be an updated version of Aaron Marc Stein's Elsie Mae Hunt, but there were differences, some significant. Penelope was a widowed anthropologist teamed with Sir Toby Glendower, a slightly older archaeologist. A formal biography in each book revealed that Penelope was born in Cambridge, Massachusetts, attended Radcliffe College, received her Ph.D. from Columbia, and then affiliated with Oxford University as a reader in anthropology, where Sir Toby was a full professor. She was a tiny woman in her sixties with tousled, mouse-colored hair, who tended to plumpness. Other information indicated that Penelope had a practical mother and a vague archaeologist father, whom she revered, and that her son, Alexander, was initially a third-year medical student at Johns Hopkins, but said nothing about her deceased husband. Over the series, Alexander married Sir Toby's daughter and provided Sir Toby and Penelope with twin grandchildren.

Exit Actors, Dying (Playboy, 1979) found Penelope and Toby visiting Turkish archaeological sites, where they had problems with a disappearing corpse. The Turkish police were reluctant to allow them to leave the country, so they decided to solve the murders of actress Melody Martin and cameraman Wolf Vincent. Penelope's persistence landed her in a crypt, from which she escaped with some help from Toby and Gale, an aboriginal woman.

During *The Cape Cod Caper* (Playboy, 1980) Penny received desperate pleas for help from Zebediah Grange, a man she could barely remember from her college days. He might be connected to the powerful Dimola family, headed by Rinaldo an industrialist now silenced by a cerebral hemorrhage. Penny used her anthropological skills to reconstruct and identify a partly decomposed corpse. A further murder definitely tied in the Dimolas. The victim was Wanda, Rinaldo's daughter-in-law. Toby, then in Europe, provided Penelope with information about Rinaldo's first marriage (while he was serving during World War II) in time to save the old man's life.

In *Zadok's Treasure* (Playboy, 1980), Bill Pierson, Toby's old schoolmaster, disappeared on an archaeological dig in Israel. Toby found his corpse, but got in over his head (a cistern) investigating. Penny rescued him. Only fair play, because Toby had done the same for her in an earlier adventure.

In *Lament for a Lady Laird* (Playboy, 1982), Penny answered the plea of Heather Macdonell, her college roommate, who had inherited a Scottish estate and leadership of the clan, along with a ghost and a family curse. A friend, Amy McClintock, the laird of Sheena Island, had been found dead of strangulation on a beach. Her husband, Gareth, was suspected, but Heather offered him a place to stay when he was out on bail. Toby had arrived on the scene, taking an interest in a British World War II airplane that had crashed offshore. When Heather and Penny were stranded in a whirlpool, Gareth and Toby rescued them. The motivation for the crime was in the plane.

It was off to the New Orleans Mardi Gras in *Death of a Voodoo Doll* (Playboy, 1982). John Everett, Penny's publisher and friend, was suspected of murder. After an evening that included a Mickey Finn, John had awakened with a dead Arlette Gray in his bed. Gray was known to be a white voodoo mambo. John was in town to arrange publication of a book by Jules Lefau, local dignitary and Arlette's lover, about the Comus Krewe and the Mardi Gras. Penny and Toby, with help from taxi driver Mean Gene; Elviny Brosse, a black voodoo mambo; and Mimi Gardner, an historian/librarian prevented another murder at the Comus banquet.

In *Death on the Dragon's Tongue* (Playboy, 1982), Toby oversaw the relocation of a stone henge to make room for a nuclear power plant in Brittany. There was a great deal of local opposition. When plant engineer Armand Dubois was killed and his tongue removed, Toby sent for Penny.

Her efforts to help were deflected because she spent time fending off the attentions of a great chef, François Canard, who was also a Breton nationalist.

During *The Menehune Murders* (Foul Play, 1989), Giles Shaw's theory that Menehunes (Hawaiian leprechauns) still inhabited Hawaii was challenged by scientist Helmut Freyer. When Freyer was murdered, Giles was suspected. He was the widower of Emily Vernon, a college classmate of Penny's. A new challenge arose, the possibility that the tomb of Chief Kamehameha was in the area. After Penny and Toby located the tomb, nature prevented its exploitation.

In *Toby's Folly* (Foul Play, 1990) Sir Toby, a lifelong bachelor, became convinced that Russian ballerina Sonya Danerova was his daughter. Sonya had been held in custody by Scotland Yard as a suspect in the death of Vassilev Litvov. She would speak to no one but Toby, who in a period of depression was hiding out in a cave in Wales. Only Penny could locate him, and she was prevailed upon to do so. Penny was concerned that her old friend not be defrauded, and that her son, Alexander, not fall in love with an imposter. To do that, they had to find the killer.

Sonya and Alex's honeymoon coincided with Penny and Toby's vacation trip to Rome in *The Catacomb Conspiracy* (Foul Play, 1991). Margo Demarest, resident in a villa near the one rented by Toby and Penny, heard noises in the night. This convinced Toby that there was a tunnel below that had outlets at both villas. The death of the gardener Guiseppe plus the disappearance of Margo and her maid fueled Toby's interest. A warning to back off was enforced by the kidnapping of Sonya. With cooperation from the Italian police, Sonya was rescued and a major tragedy averted.

During *The Cape Cod Conundrum* (Foul Play, 1992), the discovery of the preserved corpse of Mrs. Clara Bacon, a part-time teacher so obscure that her absence was not even noted, set Penny and Toby on the trail of a killer. Initially their opinion on the preservation of the body was sought by Chief of Police Ernie Bernie, but he was unwilling to share information with them. On their own, Penny and Toby figured out where Clara's body had been hidden, how it had been moved, and a commercial motive for the killing, only to learn that the police were not necessarily incompetent.

In *Dirge for a Dorset Druid* (Foul Play, 1994), Toby intervened in a struggle between Stephen Farwell, an archaeologist working on a possible henge in an urban site, and local businessmen who preferred a parking lot. Farwell had been a student of Toby's. The discovery of a fresh corpse, that of Col. Orchard, who had opposed the dig, focused suspicion on Farwell. Toby sent for Penny amid speculation about treasure trove left by French émigrés.

The Lefau family of *Voodoo Doll* returned in *The Midas Murders* (Foul Play, 1995), during which they were engulfed (as was the reader) in a mélange of Greek millionaires. Add in children and grandchildren of the Spring/Glendower variety and several other families in a confusing narrative revolving around murders, munitions, and impersonations.

This was not a great series, but it was entertaining and well written.

Terry Spring

Author: Josephine Kains, pseudonym for Ron Goulart

Terry Spring, an auburn-haired reporter for a Boston television station, was consulted in mysteries that contained elements of the supernatural. She was teamed with cameraman Janeiro Chavez and Jessica Berkeley, her assistant. Jess did the research for the programs.

In *The Devil Mask Mystery* (Zebra, 1978), Terry was contacted when murder occurred during an occult play, *The Witch Cult*. The presenters were descendants of townspeople who took part in the historic witch trials. Some descended from those accused of witchcraft; others, from the judges. The "devil" figure in the production stabbed Garrett Brooks with a real knife. Alan Roderick, who was supposed to play the devil role, was found unconscious in his dressing room. There was blackmail involved. Brooks had been the blackmailer; now his killer had the information.

During *The Curse of the Golden Skull* (Zebra, 1978), Terry and her crew followed clues to Claire Traynor, who, at the urging of her Aunt Lu, had returned to Traynor Castle, on a Caribbean island. There had been reports that treasure had been buried on the island, its location to be learned from a gold skull. Terry, on a Voodoo cruise, saved Claire from being knocked overboard en route. It was Martha Snell, Aunt Lu's housekeeper, who was killed. Claire, who had an unhappy childhood, needed support so she invited Terry, Janeiro, and Jessica to be her guests at the castle. With their help, Claire was able to unlock the secrets of her past.

The Green Lama Mystery (Zebra, 1979) took Terry and her crew to a haunted house occupied by three cousins. They had to live in the mansion for one year to claim an inheritance. Terry's task was to videotape their stay for a documentary. Arlen, a bit actor, fell or was pushed and broke his leg. Barry, a former medical student, was bludgeoned to death, leaving only Sara and the injured Arlen to claim the estate. If all three failed to complete the year, the residual heir would be Dr. Apollo Postgate, leader of a local cult. Postgate would seem a logical suspect, but Terry set a trap to prove otherwise.

The Whispering Cat Mystery (Zebra, 1979) found Terry and her assistants in Louisiana interviewing Willa Farrway, whose "visions" had solved local crimes. When Terry talked to Willa, she spoke of a "whispering cat." Janeiro Chavez gave Willa a ride home and was with her when she found Chip Cullen dead of strangulation in her living room. A later vision led Willa, Terry, and the others to the family crypt. Terry took a risk in confronting the killer publicly and had to be rescued by police in Mardi Gras costumes.

In *The Witch's Tower Mystery* (Zebra, 1979), Terry attended a convention on Hedge Island, Connecticut, where a famous horror writer had once lived. Prominent on the scene was a witch's tower. Among the participants in the conference were horror writers Arlen Payne and Clifford Laird, who were professional rivals and detested one another. Arlen was aggressive and showed it, but he was the one who was found dead at the base of the tower.

Jess, Terry's assistant, returned to her hometown in *The Laughing Dragon Mystery* (Zebra, 1980), only to be accused of murdering her ex-husband, Dane Folkman. There had always been a cloud of suspicion over Jess because of the mysterious death of her father, a famous television puppeteer. She had come home after Dane called, hinting that he had information for sale about her father's death. Had a least likely suspect ending.

Above average for Zebra.

Morgan Studevant

Author: Chelsea Quinn Yarbro

Morgan Studevant was a prickly but attractive and brainy new law clerk in Charlie Spotted Moon's law firm. They fell in love, married, and juggled professional complexities when Morgan became a judge. Morgan might not be peripheral to Charlie's emotional well-being, but she was to his investigations. Charlie was able to transport himself into the past and feel the trauma of the victims. He was the male sleuth. Morgan, as his wife, served in a consultive and helping role.

In *Ogilvie, Tallant, & Moon* (Putnam, 1976), Charlie, a Native American attorney, defended a woman doctor charged with malpractice. Morgan lent an occasional hand, but the breakthrough came as a result of Charlie's spiritual powers.

The professional contacts between Morgan and Charlie became romance in *Music When Sweet Voices Die* (Putnam, 1979). Powerful client Elizabeth Hendries convinced Charlie to solve the murder of unpopular Gui-Adam Feuier, which had taken place at the opera house. Morgan needed no help with Sandy Halsford's abusive husband, Bret. She revealed her fighting spirit when she tossed him out a window, and her bisexuality when Charlie proposed.

By *Poison Fruit* (Jove, 1991), the couple had married, and Morgan had become a judge. Charlie's defense of a young high school teacher accused of molesting female students was successful partly because Morgan provided him with information received in the course of her work. Morgan was the helping hand that Charlie needed to bring him back from his dangerous expeditions into the past. The spiritual solutions were interesting, but bypassed the deductive process.

Preoccupied by a moral and ethical dilemma posed by a client who might be a savage serial killer in *Cat's Claw* (Jove, 1992), Charlie made time to protect Morgan. She was conducting a potentially precedent-setting trial involving toxic waste. Efforts were made to undermine her authority and cause a mistrial, but Charlie, without telling Morgan, had thwarted the plan. As before, Charlie relied upon his mystical power to utilize a physical article (this time his client's watch) to pull him back into the past. There he found the answer to his ethical crisis.

Julia Sullivan

Author: John Logue

Julia Sullivan was characterized as a "man's ideal woman" which, in this series, meant a female who would share a man's Scotch and his bed, receive admiration from other men and friendship from other women, be financially independent, and demand no commitment for the future. Julia was the widow of Monty Sullivan, a professional golfer who had invested his winnings in downtown Denver real estate. Monty, 20 years older than his wife, met her shortly after she enrolled in college. She never went back to class, content to follow him and his drinking buddies, one of whom was John Morris, an Associated Press sports reporter. Morris had been seriously injured, requiring him to walk with a cane, in the car accident that killed Monty. He and Julia shared their grief, and eventually, their lives. There was little physical description of Julia except for her brown hair and the fact that she attracted the interest and admiration of most male characters in the series.

Julia's role in the series, during which she followed Morris from football stadiums to golf courses, was subsidiary but showed growth over the years. She kept Morris company, listened to his theories, and held the hands of weeping widows and sobbing suspects, occasionally eliciting valuable information. The series was peppered with sports history, and real-life athletes and entertainers. Predictably in such a macho series, John Morris had almost all the action.

During *Follow the Leader* (Crown, 1979), Julia was relegated to sharing a bed and drinks with Morris. He saved an Atlanta police officer from arresting the wrong man when first golf instructor Jim Rossi and then John Whitlow and Tommy Fryer, two young contenders at the U.S. Open, were murdered.

During *Replay: Murder* (Ballantine, 1983), in a football setting, Julia donned a borrowed policewoman's uniform and an unloaded gun to interrupt Morris in a confrontation with a killer, but admitted she wouldn't know which end of the gun to shoot. The narrative relied for its tenor on the bonding among members of a team and with their coaches.

As *Flawless Execution* (Ballantine, 1986) began, Morris was writing an article about George Hoaglund, NFL television announcer, a man for whom he had little personal affection. Hoaglund's death by electrocution took place during a broadcast. Sullivan's ties to Marie, George's widow, provided an insight into their past relationships with other suspects, but made it more difficult to accept their actions. There was an interesting connection to a famous stamp collection.

The series was dormant for a while, but Dell resuscitated it in 1996 with *Murder on the Links*, set at the Master's in Augusta. Because Monty had won the Master's, Julia was an honored guest. Morris was no longer working for the Associated Press, but wrote articles and books on a freelance basis. In quick succession, three of the most obnoxious members of the host golf club were murdered. There would have been at least one more death if Julia hadn't taken action.

The Feathery Touch of Death (Dell, 1997) was set at St. Andrew's, Scotland, during the British Open, but was retrospective to 1978. Barry Vinson, an arrogant U.S. contender, raped the granddaughter of a venerable caddie. The subsequent murders of the rapist and the caddie by similar modus operandi raised the question: one killer, two killers, or more? It took both Morris and Julia to decide. Dell had by now subtitled their books as "Morris and Sullivan Mysteries."

Although published in 1998 by Dell, *A Rain of Death* was another retrospective, this time set at the Crosby Classic in Pebble Beach. Could these have been written earlier and adapted? There was lots of name-dropping, as amateurs and professionals competed for bragging rights and scores. Andrew McCall, a particularly obstreperous guest but a friend of Bing's, drank Scotch laced with cyanide. A short time later, Sidney Barker, a popular entertainment figure, died of cyanide poisoning. Then the older wife of movie producer Jacob Hyche was poisoned while drinking from the same bottle as her husband, who had no reaction. The interesting plots were expanded by long passages about the golf games, which might attract some readers and bore others. When Julia and Morris finally iced the solution, they found it painful.

The most recent setting, in *On a Par with Murder* (Dell, 1999), was at Shinnecock Hills, an historic U.S. golf course, where the Open was being held. Both Sullivan and Morris were attracted to Buddy Morrow, the latest prodigy, but he was killed in a car accident that was blamed on his widow. The local sheriff settled for an easy solution, leaving Morris in despair and Julia determined to get a killer who tried it once too often.

Lucilla Edith Cavell Teatime

Author: Colin Watson

A villainess, unlike male anti-heroes, is rarely portrayed with any humor in a mystery novel. Lucilla Teatime was a worthy exception in the series dominated by Inspector Walter Purbright and Sgt. Sidney Love. She had abandoned her London home to take up residence in Church Close in the village of Flaxborough, England. An attractive, slim woman in her fifties, she wore little makeup but looked younger than her years. Privately, she smoked thin black cheroots and drank tea laced with whiskey.

In *Lonelyheart 4122* (Putnam, 1967), Lucilla's interest was piqued by an advertisement from Handclasp House, a matrimonial bureau, so she sent in an application. Purbright was concerned about Handclasp because two earlier applicants had disappeared. Lucilla, as #347, agreed to meet #4122 while the police used her as bait.

Several Flaxborough residents received letters from a potential victim of domestic violence in *Charity Ends at Home* (Putnam, 1968). When Henrietta Palgrove, a prominent citizen, was found dead in her wishing well, her husband, Leonard, was suspected. Lucilla set Purbright on the right track.

Lucilla had a variety of interests, all designed to enrich her, including the Flaxborough and Eastern Counties Charities Alliance and the Maldham Meres Laboratories, producers of an herbal mixture called Samson's Salad. When, in *Just What the Doctor Ordered* (Putnam, 1969) aka *The Flaxborough Crab*, the Salad's reputation was damaged by rumors that it might cause satyriasis in elderly men, Lucilla delivered a murderer to Purbright.

Although Lucilla contemplated cooperation with a witch's coven in *Kissing Covens* (Putnam, 1972) aka *Broomsticks Over Flaxborough*, she decided against it when they were suspected of murder. Purbright and Lucilla uncovered local politicians active in the Satanic group.

Practical jokes between Henry Crispin and Arnold Hatch, two respectable citizens, ceased to be funny in *Six Nuns and a Shotgun* (Putnam, 1975) aka *The Naked Nuns* when Hatch was murdered. Purbright had been warned that an American hit man would be coming into his area. Could this be Lucilla's guest, Joe Tudor? Not so—he had been sent by a major crime figure to forestall action by an American killer in the interest of good relationships between the countries. When a young constable explained a coded message to Purbright, he looked elsewhere.

Grandma Tring approached Lucilla in *It Shouldn't Happen to a Dog* (Putnam, 1977) aka *One Man's Meat* after her grandson, Digger, had been killed in a fall from an amusement park ride. Digger's death became a factor in domestic squabbles and the acquisition of Nutripet Dogfood by a rival corporation. Subsequent Purbright books gave no meaningful role to Lucilla. More's the pity.

Readers, beware! The English narratives have different titles.

Kitty Telefair

Author: Florence Stevenson

Kitty Telefair, a slim 26-year-old with red hair and green eyes, was a hereditary member of a clan of occultists (magi, not witches). Her sister, Celia, and her mother, Amy, worked with Tarot cards. Father Rupert ran a magic show, while brother Eric was still at Oxford. Assorted aunts and cousins were involved in other aspects of the entertainment business or the occult world. Kitty appeared on the television program *The Witching Hour*, produced by her lover Colly Caswell III, also a member of an occult clan.

The series followed a pattern wherein Kitty's occult skills were needed:

- In *The Witching Hour* (Award, 1971), both Colly and young soprano Peggy Ozanne seemed under the spell of Gilda Gianini, a never-aging diva. Kitty's Aunt Astarte reminded her of Melody Blair, who had been a student of Gilda's 20 years ago and then disappeared.

- She accompanied Colly to Los Angeles in *Where Satan Dwells* (Award, 1971), where he was to air *The Witching Hour* for two weeks. She stayed at the home of director Howard Sutton and his wife, Sherry, but spent part of her day helping Colly audition talent for the programs. During the auditions, Kitty met talent agent Simon Deal. Despite the fact that she had promised to avoid evil forms of magic, Kitty helped actress Ruth Taylor, whose boyfriend, actor Eli MacNeil, had disappeared. She located Eli only when she visited the isolated mansion of Ailsa Ware, a Satanist who worked with Deal.

■ During *Altar of Evil* (Award, 1973), Miranda Blake, a beautiful but selfish woman, had been placed under a curse because she had stolen her cousin Joanna's boyfriend, Roger, and married him. John Weir, the witch who had placed the curse, had been discarded by Miranda. Kitty and Colly went to visit the couple when they returned from their honeymoon. Weir was dead. Roger told the story of what the curse had done to his wife and those who looked at her. Rupert gave Kitty advice as to a cure.

■ Young brides were in trouble again in *Mistress of Devil's Manor* (Award, 1973). Kitty had an eerie feeling about Gillian Bond and Adam Parry as they left on their honeymoon. They were to travel out West to investigate a deserted town, Cameron Gulch. She came to the rescue when Adam was discovered close to death and Gillian was missing. Rosaleen, a dead Spanish whore with the power to occupy the bodies of others, was the problem.

■ Kitty was a victim in *The Sorcerer of the Castle* (Award, 1974) when she visited an eccentric extended family on the West Coast. She had broken her ankle and had postponed her marriage to Colly, so he was not available immediately to help when Kitty fell under the influence of Buck, a vampire/Satanist.

■ Only two weeks remained before Kitty and Colly were to be married as *The Silent Watcher* (Award, 1975) began. They had heard of a nightclub act, Sebastian and his tiger Sheba, that they might want to showcase on Colly's program. Princess Tatyana, who accompanied Sebastian when he was not with Sheba, was frightening. Sheba, who had worked amiably with Sebastian, killed him during their act. Kitty needed to postpone the wedding until she could bring Sebastian back from the grave.

The series could also be classified under the horror or occult genres.

Kate Theobald

Author: Lionel Black, pseudonym for Dudley Barker
aka Anthony Matthews

Kate Theobald was so ambitious in her career as a London newspaper reporter that she lied, concealed evidence, broke promises, and manipulated people. Henry, her complaisant barrister husband, was the frequent victim of such tactics. Kate appeared to be in her early thirties, but no other physical details or information about her background were provided.

In *Swinging Murder* (Matthews, Walker, 1969), Kate and Henry attended a celebration by eccentric photographer Godfrey Launcefoot-Marston, who had recently inherited a title and fortune. The death of Willy Grantly, the family solicitor who had threatened the photographer's right to inherit, motivated Kate and Henry to solve not only this murder but also two others.

An invitation to visit Henry's friends Jonathan and Stella Sims for a country weekend sounded dull to Kate in *Death Has Green Fingers* (Matthews, Walker, 1971). Things perked up when they visited neighbor Nick Bell, only to find him dead. Bell had been working on developing a blue rose. There were other motives besides envy of this discovery. Bell had been an unprincipled lech. Henry railed at the police for not providing Kate with adequate protection after she had been attacked on two occasions.

Death by Hoax (Black, Avon, 1978) involved both Kate and Henry in a series of pranks. She made contact with businesses that had been harassed and met Carl Grossman, an émigré inventor. He was killed by a limpet bomb while at his desk. Carl left his family affairs in disarray. Was Helga his legal wife? Was her son George also his son? What about Stella, who had entered into a bigamous marriage with Grossman? Was Carl homosexual? In seeking the answers, Kate exposed herself to danger again.

Kate's visit to a "fat farm" in *A Healthy Way to Die* (Black, Avon, 1979) was less than enjoyable. She shared her morning grapefruit and lemon water with assorted guests, but had no opportunity to meet financier Philip Antrobus, who occupied the next room. Antrobus, who arrived by helicopter, had secluded himself. When Kate entered his room, she found him hanging from the bathroom pipes. Had he killed himself because of financial problems? Among the guests were several who would benefit from Antrobus' death.

In *The Penny Murders* (Black, Avon, 1980), Kate discovered the body of wealthy coin collector Miles Cabral. It was too late for the interview she wanted, so she decided to investigate his death, which had occurred in a locked room. Private investigator Arthur Grogan had been hired by Cabral to search out employees who had left the Royal Mint during 1954-1955. In the belief that the search and the death were connected to an unauthorized 1954 penny, Kate wrote a news story implying the existence of such a coin in the dead man's collection. She felt no need to explain her fabrication to either Henry or her editor. Her persistence led her, and finally the police, to evidence that coins were being counterfeited.

Fellow reporter Derek Andrews interested Kate in local poltergeist activity in *The Eve of the Wedding* (Black, Avon, 1981). The marriage of Angie Shoebury, a spoiled American heiress, to Philip, the grandson of the eccentric Letheridge family was to include the abduction of the bride by friends of the groom. When the groom's brother Gregory was murdered, Kate presumed upon her slight acquaintance to interview the suspects and pursue the certifiable killers.

Black plotted his stories with precision and provided interesting narratives, but an unappealing heroine.

Emmy Tibbett

Author: Patricia Moyes

The wife of a fictional Scotland Yard inspector in the Forties and Fifties had a hard lot. She was usually scenery, serving as evidence of the maturity and masculinity of her husband. Emmy Tibbett can be distinguished both in the contributions she made to husband Henry's deductions and by a single book in which she was a major character. Her involvement came about during the couple's leisure experiences or assignments where Emmy's presence was justified. Although childless, Emmy was a traditional wife. She shared an active and athletic life with Henry: snorkeling, dancing, skiing, and sailing. She was slightly plump with short black hair, and had an excellent sense of humor that enlivened the relationship.

Shared vacations that featured murder included:

- *Dead Men Don't Ski* (Holt, 1960): An Italian ski trip had a sub-agenda to monitor the hotel for drug smugglers. Emmy was privy to the interviews by the Italian police, because she was asked to take notes, but Henry did the detecting.

- *Down Among the Dead Men* aka *The Drunken Sailor* (Holt, 1961): When Peter Rawnsley, an experienced sailor, drowned, Emmy visited Priscilla Trigg-Willoughby, an alcoholic with a view of the harbor, but was attacked and dumped in a boat hold.

When she did not return, Henry organized a search. She was found, but by then Priscilla had been murdered

- During *Season of Snows and Sins* (Holt, 1971), cculptress Jane Weston, who lived in the area, was a friend of Anne-Marie and Robert Drivaz. She was aware of Robert's deterioration after he began an affair. When he was killed, Anne-Marie, then pregnant, was convicted. She agreed to have her child adopted by Robert's mother. When Emmy and Henry visited Jane, she prevailed upon him to review Anne-Marie's conviction.

- There were problems in *Angel Death* (Holt, 1981). While the Tibbetts were visiting their friends the Colvilles in the British Seaward Islands, Henry behaved strangely. He had taken an interest in the disappearance of Betsy Sprague, a retired teacher. Before she went missing, Betsy had told Henry that she had seen a woman who had supposedly been lost at sea. When Emmy realized something serious was wrong with her husband, she took over.

- During *A Six Letter Word for Death* (Holt, 1983), the Tibbetts were the guests of Sir Robert and Lady Pamela Oppenshaw at a gathering of mystery writers on the Isle of Wight. This was a puzzle mystery in that Henry received clues via a crossword puzzle as to suspicious deaths in the past. Emmy was not involved.

- The precipitating event in *Night Ferry to Death* (Holt, 1985) was that jewels were hidden in Emmy's luggage as they returned via a ferryboat from Europe. In order to flush out the thief, the Tibbetts made it known that they were journeying back to the Netherlands to return the jewels. The plotting in this one was unusually convoluted.

Family connections of Emmy's also involved the couple in crime or brought Emmy into Henry's investigations in:

- *Murder à la Mode* (Holt, 1963): Henry was assigned to the murder of Helen Pankhurst, fashion editor of *Style*, a magazine which employed Emmy's niece, Veronica Spence. This was Henry's book and reflected author Moyes' experience in the fashion world. She had worked for *Vogue* magazine.

- The involvement of Emmy's sister Jane and her husband, Bill Spence, in dogs, dog racing, and gambling in *The Curious Affair of the Third Dog* (Holt, 1973) had disastrous effects for Henry. Jane was the humane officer. Bill was concerned about a valuable greyhound which belonged to a man he had sent to prison. The dog was missing. Jane and Emmy rescued Henry when he was mugged and kidnapped in time for him to take appropriate action.

As Henry's status increased at Scotland Yard, resulting in overseas assignments and representation at official conferences, his spouse was expected to take part in social activities:

- During *Death on the Agenda* (Holt, 1962), Henry became involved with a young woman reporter while they were attending an International Narcotics Conference in Geneva. That was just a part of his problem, because he became a suspect when John Trapp, a member of the permanent staff, was stabbed to death. Henry rejected an offer of help in escaping the country. He had a life and a wife he wanted to keep.

- An African border dispute between Mambesi and Galunga in *Death and the Dutch Uncle* (Holt, 1968) sent the Tibbetts to Amsterdam, where the Permanent International Frontier Litigation organization was located. Now a C.I.D. superintendent, Henry was to investigate two murders, which were potentially connected to PIFL (a spot of humor on Moyes' part). An injured Henry rescued Emmy when she was abducted.

- An Ouija board warned Lady Crystal Balaclava in *Many Deadly Returns* aka *Who Saw Her Die?* (Holt, 1970) that her life was in danger. Henry and Emmy were sent undercover to a house party at the Balaclava estate. Henry's best efforts failed. Lady Crystal was poisoned by parathion. In order to determine the killer, it was necessary to figure out how the poison had been administered. Henry learned the answers in time to save the life of Lady Crystal's personal heir.

- *Black Widower* (Holt, 1975) took the Tibbetts to the fictional Caribbean county of Tampica. The death of the British wife of Sir Edward Ironmonger, Tampican Ambassador to the United States, had occurred in Georgetown. Once in the Caribbean, Henry investigated. Emmy snorkeled.

- Another politically sensitive case took Henry back to the British Seaward Islands in *The Coconut Killings* aka *To Kill a Coconut* (Holt, 1977). His task was to investigate the murder of United States Senator Brett Olsen, who had been killed on an exclusive golf course by a machete. Olsen was there hobnobbing with lobbyists from the cotton industry. The man under suspicion was

Sandy Robbins, handyman at the inn owned by the Colvilles, good friends of Henry and Emmy. The Colvilles expected Henry to prove Sandy's innocence. He did so with the help, not of Emmy, but of octogenarian Lucy Pontefract-Deacon.

■ Lucy appeared again in *Black Girl, White Girl* (Holt, 1989), when Henry returned to the islands to conduct a drug smuggling investigation. Henry, who presented himself as a sleazy businessman, was pressured to cooperate with the smugglers when Emmy was abducted. She returned to plead his case when the authorities charged Henry with involvement in the smuggling.

Emmy's major appearance was in *Johnny Under Ground* (Holt, 1966), when she researched the biography of a heroic pilot, believed to have committed suicide. Emmy, who served in the Women's Auxiliary Air Force in World War II, had been in love with "Beau" Guest. When she attended a reunion at the base, she agreed to research exactly what had happened to Beau. The death of her collaborator brought Henry on the scene. He was warned that Emmy, who was the last to see Beau alive, was a suspect. Emmy had done the detective work until Henry arrived, then he took over.

Emmy suffered the fate of most spouses, a place on the sidelines in *Falling Star* (Holt, 1964), *Murder Fantastical* (Holt, 1967), *Who Is Simon Warwick?* (Holt, 1979), and *Twice in a Blue Moon* (Holt, 1993). Some of the books were identified as a Henry Tibbett mystery, others as Henry and Emily Tibbett mysteries.

Over the series, Moyes combined a humorous touch, memorable characters, and in-depth knowledge of her locations. There were some weaknesses of plotting in the later books, but they are all above-average reading.

Katy Touchfeather

Author: Jimmy Sangster

Regardless of the name, Katy was not a Native American, but a redheaded, widowed espionage agent, another of the promiscuous female spies who appeared during the Sixties. Katy (Katherine) had been an English airline hostess, when her pilot husband died. Tom had acted as a courier for a little-known government agency that then recruited Katy to take his place. Although she had no college education, she spoke French, German, Spanish, and Italian. Katy regularly carried a weapon, and was capable of shooting a man with whom she had shared affection and sex.

In *Touchfeather* (Norton, 1968), Katy was assigned to monitor science professor Bill Portman, suspected of passing information to the Russians. Katy became very close to Portman, and eventually both were kidnapped.

In *Touchfeather, Too* (Norton, 1970), Blaser, Katy's supervisor, was troubled by the unexplained increase of gold in the international economy. Katy was to seduce Antonio, a young Spanish bullfighter, searching his luggage while both were passengers on a yacht. Although he was killed and her cover (what little she had) was blown, she obtained a sample of the gold.

Charity Tucker
Author: Patrick Buchanan, pseudonym for Edwin Corley and Jack Murphy

Charity Tucker needed help. A tall, athletic blonde, she had been frigid since a rape attempt. Ben Shock, her private investigator partner, had rescued her. Ben, a self-righteous tough and initially a police officer, had romantic feelings for Charity, which went unfulfilled. Charity, an intelligent former television reporter, was described by Shock as having "more gray matter inside that lovely head than females are supposed to possess."

In *A Murder of Crows* (Stein, 1970), the couple visited Subrinea Brown, a college friend of Charity, now living in Kentucky, but was welcomed with rifle shots. Subsequently both Subrinea and her father, Adger Brown, who was building a racetrack, were killed in bizarre accidents. The land Brown planned to use for the race track was sought by other interests, and there were sinister elements hanging about the woods.

A Parliament of Owls (Stein, 1971) returned to an earlier period, when Charity invited Ben to meet her family. As Ben and Charity approached the harbor, they saw her father's yacht struck by a bazooka rocket. They killed to get their happy ending, causing his resignation from the police department and their decision to join forces as private investigators.

In *A Requiem of Sharks* (Dodd, 1973), the couple appeared in Singing River, Mississippi, too late to rescue Millie Wiggins, the sister of a client, from a shark in the swimming pool. Lisa Dantzler had hired Shock and Tucker to guard her from harassment by those who opposed her oil drilling operations. Their new assignment was to find the killer.

Ben and Charity visited London for *A Sounder of Swine* (Dodd, 1974), investigating kidnappings that featured mutilations and murder. Although Ben took the lead, Charity investigated on her own. She was sexually attacked again, recovering to rescue Ben with the aid of pigs and ugly Americans. Depressed with the prospects of a more personal relationship, Ben left Charity. He'd already lost hope.

Both Ben and Charity could have benefited from counseling.

Paola Smith Watson

Author: George Sampson

See: Paola Smith, Section 5, page 409.

Kate Weatherly

Author: Maisie Birmingham

Kate Weatherly was an English social worker who served as deputy director of a foundation that ran a settlement house and advice bureau in London. Although born in Ghana, she had lived in England for many years. Married at one time, she had been separated from her husband and lost touch with him.

In *You Can Help Me* (Collins, 1974), Kate was working late in the office when she was struck on the head and the key to the residence stolen. She received attention at the hospital. When she returned, the keys were in her bedroom and Rose Salter's body was in her bed. Rose was staying at the shelter while looking for a missing sister. Although a suspect herself, Kate sifted among the clues to identify the staff member responsible for the killing.

Kate returned to Ghana in *The Heat of the Sun* (Collins, 1976) to visit her brother Jim, his family, and his fellow teachers at a local school. Kate had received an anonymous warning that she might be involved in a pseudo suicide. That made her suspicious when teacher Quentin Jackson died shortly after he had announced his engagement. Kate correctly identified the killer but was spared the need to prove guilt. The descriptions of Ghana were lovely.

Sleep in a Ditch (Scribner, 1979) began when a dead body, resembling her husband, Ralph, was placed on Kate's office doorway. Under British law, Ralph's death in less than a ten-year separation would leave Kate as heiress to a major trust fund. They had been separated for nine and a half years, and she hadn't seen him in more than six years. Kate searched and found the living, but very ill, Ralph, but barely escaped from a fire meant to kill her.

Low-key narratives.

Bea Wentworth

Author: Richard Forrest

The pairing of Bea Wentworth and her husband, Lyon, constituted a role reversal in that Bea had a prominent political career while combat veteran Lyon wrote mystical books for children. An honors graduate in history and a former high school teacher, politics and government had been Bea's life. Lyon, working with his wartime buddy, Chief of Police Rocco Herbert, did more than his share of the detecting. The Wentworths occupied a remodeled riverside home near Murphysville, Connecticut. Their only child had been killed in a tragic accident while riding her bicycle. Bea was a tall, slim woman with a high energy level; Lyon spent much of his time either in a world populated by the Wobblies, the fictional characters who made his books famous, or aloft in his balloon.

In *A Child's Garden of Death* (Bobbs, 1975), the Wentworths were intrigued when a bulldozer uncovered the skeletons of a man, woman, and child. The presence of a car and trailer in the nearby lake eventually identified the family as that of Moshe Mayerson, a Jewish refugee en route to California. Lyon, aware that the little girl was the age of his daughter, became obsessed with their deaths. Bea, then a Connecticut state senator, was in and out, but it was Lyon's book.

Bea's political activities took the spotlight in *The Wizard of Death* (Bobbs, 1977). The candidate she supported for governor, Randolph Llewyn, was assassinated. The shot just missed Bea. Lyon and Bea found the hired killer, dead. They had to keep looking for his employer, because an attempt was made on Bea's life. This was a taut narrative, which dealt with both political corruption and sexual aberrations.

Bea was enraged in *Death Through the Looking Glass* (Bobbs, 1978) when Lyon experienced a mid-life crisis involving 18-year-old Robin Thornburton, who had a crush on him. He was even more absorbed in the mysterious plane crash of prep school friend Tom Giles. Lyon had been up in a new balloon basket when Tom's plane crashed into the ocean. Before Tom's body was recovered, Lyon had received a phone call from him asking for help. Before Lyon was through, he and his friend Rocco Herbert needed help badly.

Bea had a larger part in *Death in the Willows* (Holt, 1979), doing some detecting on her own. She, currently Secretary of State for Connecticut, was busy running for Congress. Lyon used a gun to kill Willie Shep, who hijacked a bus on which he was traveling. Lyon, who had been handed the gun by a bearded fellow passenger, took this hard. His war experience had made him abhor violence. The bus had incinerated, and Lyon was one of only two survivors. They trailed a Mafia deserter to find the computer spook who had been docketing illegal Mafia activities.

Bea had no political job when *The Death at Yew Corner* (Holt, 1980) opened, so was available to investigate the mysterious death of Dr. Fabian Bunting, her former mentor, in a nursing home. Lyon and Rocco took over the action in an escalating narrative, featuring a locked room, a man dying in a sealed coffin, and a killer who tried to kidnap the Wentworths.

In *Death Under the Lilacs* (St. Martin, 1985), Bea had an admirer who abducted her from a darkened supermarket parking lot. The kidnapper called Lyon with a request for a ransom, but there was more than money involved here. The call included a taped message from Bea, containing a clue to her location, a reference to her lilacs.

Death on the Mississippi (St. Martin, 1989) returned Bea to the State Senate as majority leader while Lyon suffered the doldrums of writer's block. When Dalton Turman, an army buddy, disappeared on a houseboat trip, Bea resented Lyon's involvement and his close attention to Pam, Dalton's wife. There were others interested in Dalton's whereabouts: the IRS, loan sharks, and Randy Dice, Dalton's partner. The first thing Lyon found was the corpse of Dalton's mistress. Lyon took off in a small runabout to track Dalton's journey down the river.

After an eight-year gap, *The Pied Piper of Death* (St. Martin, 1997) revealed more about Bea and Lyon. Her real name was Bernice, and Lyon, before turning to writing about the Wobblies, had been an English professor at Middleburg University. This became difficult to believe when he referred to male poet Joyce Kilmer, who died during World War I, as "she." Peyton Piper, head of a munitions corporation, who intended to run for U.S. Senator from Connecticut, sought Bea's influence in state politics. Lyon accompanied Bea to a party at the Piper mansion. Another guest was historian Markham Swan, who was writing a history of the Piper family. He had warned young Paula Piper, Peyton's only child, that she risked an early death. The danger to Paula was based on a tragic incident during the Civil War that had triggered five deaths in succeeding generations of the Piper family. Bea cooperated, but Lyon was the primary investigator.

Bea was given the outward trappings of success in her career and marriage, but her feelings were rarely explored in an otherwise excellent series.

Nell Willard

Author: Miriam Lynch, pseudonym for Mary Wallace

Nell Willard, a reporter for the *Independent Transcript*, constantly battled for better assignments. She accomplished this with minimal ethics.

A tall blonde with green eyes, Nell was on hand when former actress Alyce Weldon found her servant dead down the cellar steps in *Time to Kill* (Zebra, 1979). Alyce was murdered later. Even while dating the local police lieutenant, Nell withheld valuable information until she found a missing bank robber hidden in a cubbyhole.

There seemed no reason for the death of retiring math teacher Sarah Plunkett in *You'll Be the Death of Me* (Zebra, 1979). Nell speculated that the poison might have been meant for someone else at the head table.

Zebra level.

Persis Willum

Author: Clarissa Watson

A wealthy and socially prominent aunt raised Persis Willum after her parents were lost at sea. Aunt Lydia delegated responsibility to boarding schools for most of Persis' teenage years, but took a personal interest in seeing that she learned such social graces as riding sidesaddle, distinguishing among wines, and conversing with the elite. After a brief marriage to a young attorney who drank himself to death, Persis shared a long-term arrangement with adoring art critic Oliver Reynolds. Although her husband had depleted her inheritance, Persis lived comfortably in her own home with household help and a cat named Isidore Duncan. An artist, she supplemented her income by working in Gregor Olitsky's art gallery.

In *The Fourth Stage of Gainsborough Brown* (McKay, 1977), Aunt Lydia, an art collector, planned her own 65th birthday party, during which artist Gainsborough Brown was to provide the entertainment. His work had recently become very sought after. He had handled his good fortune badly. When he turned up dead in Lydia's swimming pool, Persis researched his life for the motivation for murder. Many of those who came under suspicion were important figures in Persis' life: Aunt Lydia, Oliver, and Gregor Olitsky.

As *The Bishop in the Back Seat* (Atheneum, 1980) opened, county executive H. Caldwell Ringwill had persuaded wealthy art collectors to loan paintings to the Waldheim Museum in exchange for his promise to oppose a contemplated bridge. During the theft of a priceless Rembrandt, Wink Gaylord, the new museum director, was injured and then killed in the hospital, and a young woman was taken hostage. There may have been a connection with valuable paintings commandeered by Nazis during the war. Persis' only clue was a sketch of a bishop by the injured museum director.

During *Runaway* (Atheneum, 1985), Persis, trespassing on horseback onto friendly neighbor Courtney Lassiter's land, was injured by a gunshot. Courtney, who had been assumed to be in Europe, was already dead. Through her identification of figures in a picture, Persis connected the incident to the deaths of British citizens in France. The connections became broader, to missing Czech gold and a terrorist organization determined to find the treasure to finance their activities. With Aunt Lydia's help, Persis survived kidnapping and a broken jaw. Her life was saved by one of the conspirators, who had never expected their venture to include multiple murders.

In *Last Plane from Nice* (Atheneum, 1988), Persis agreed to paint Jules Ribot, an anti-Mafia politician in Nice, only to learn that the assignment was a ruse to lure her to a house party where Nicol de Plessis was hostess. Present were members of the Society for the Preservation of Old Nice. Persis' resemblance to an undisclosed woman was the reason she had been sought out. Her sketching skills, her art history expertise, and the awareness of her own sexuality enabled her to distinguish the real from the false, the hero from the villain.

During *Somebody Killed the Messenger* (Atheneum, 1988), Persis and Gregor Olitsky planned a loan exhibit of paintings to raise money for charity. Her school friend Seraphine Braceley offered a nude painting, but the emissary who was to deliver the portrait disappeared. Persis kept the transatlantic airlines busy as she flew to and from Europe to discover a warehouse of nude paintings and Seraphine's killers.

Watson maintained readers' interest with narratives set in the exotic world of art and artists, luxury and international intrigue. Persis was an enchanting heroine.

Anna Zordan

Author: James Eastwood

Anna, another of the espionage agents spawned by the popularity of Modesty Blaise and James Bond, never achieved their level of success. She was bright, seductive, and affiliated, as they had been, with British Intelligence.

Anna had been born in Budapest of an American mother and Hungarian father who served in the diplomatic corps. Both parents had been killed by political assassins. Anna was proficient in weapons, flew a plane, and enjoyed risk taking. She indulged in fast cars, parachute jumping, and casual sexual encounters, and took pleasure in visiting graveyards. Her personal tastes were sophisticated: classical music and pot-stilled Scotch. Boasting an IQ of 137, she spoke or understood French, Italian, German, Hungarian, and Chinese. She avoided structure in her life, sleeping when tired, eating when hungry, living in a one-room apartment in London.

In *The Chinese Visitor* (Coward, 1965), British agent Sarratt, who had helped Anna leave Vienna when her parents were killed, was available when she killed their murderer. Sarratt's recruitment of Anna tested her sexual interests, her capacity to inflict pain on others, and her willingness to be a spy against the Red Chinese.

During *Seduce and Destroy* (Coward, 1967) aka *Little Dragon from Peking*, when she was assigned to cultivate members of the powerful Wilberforce family, Anna learned their acceptance hinged on her willingness to kill. In a series of fantastic adventures, she coped with a plan to bomb Europe, a lesbian encounter, and the rescue of Sarratt from danger and celibacy.

Diamonds Are Deadly (McKay, 1969) focused on crimes detailed in television scripts (written but never aired) by Sandy McTaggart. Anna's task was to seduce Sandy and learn the plot of the 13th narrative. Much action, including a submarine versus a passenger ship loaded with dignitaries who were at risk of having their food tampered with. Undistinguished.

Author/Character Index

Although some characters appear in all volumes of a shared series, only those in which a significant role is played will be listed; for example Della Street appears in all Perry Mason books written by Erle Stanley Gardner. Only those books in which her actions affect the plot are listed below. Books listed in Hubin or another reliable authority as including the identified sleuth but not available for a personal review are listed with an asterisk. All titles, publishers, and dates of publication were taken from my personal book reviews but were rechecked for accuracy with recognized authorities such as Hubin, Heising, *Twentieth Century Crime and Mystery Writers*. Any errors are my own.

   * *indicates a book unavailable for personal review.*

Dagmar – pseudonym for Virginia Egnor; ghostwritten by Lou Cameron

Darby, Ruth "Janie" Allen

Davis, Dorothy Salisbury

Davis, Lavinia

Dean, Amber

Kenyon, Paul – pseudonym for Nat Freedland
Baroness Penelope St. John Orsini 392
At least seven titles including:
     Death Is a Ruby Light*   *Diamonds Are for Dying**
     The Ecstasy Connection*   *Flicker of Doom**
     Hard Core Murder*   *Operation Doomsday**

Killough, Lee
Janna Brill 256
     The Doppelganger Gambit   *Dragon's Teeth*
     Spider Play

Kilpatrick, Florence
Elizabeth 153
     Elizabeth Finds a Body   *Elizabeth the Sleuth*
There are other non-mysteries in the series.

Knight, Kathleen Moore
Margot Blair 138
     Design in Diamonds   *Exit a Star*
     Rendezvous with the Past   *Terror by Twilight*

Knox, Ronald
Angela Bredon 34
     The Body in the Silo aka *Settled Out of Court*
     Double Cross Purposes   *The Footsteps at the Lock*
     Still Dead   *The Three Taps*

Lait, Jack
Polack Annie 82
     Gangster Girl   *Put on the Spot*

Lane, Gret
Kate Marsh 67
     The Cancelled Score Mystery*   *The Curlew Coombe Mystery*
     Death Visits the Summer-House   *Death in Mermaid Lane*
     Death Prowls the Cove   *The Guest with the Scythe*
     The Hotel Cremona Mystery   *The Lantern House Affair*
     The Unknown Enemy

Langham, James P.
Ethel Abbott 125
     A Pocketful of Clues   *Sing a Song of Homicide*

Langton, Jane
Mary Morgan Kelly 327
Although she made minor appearances in other Homer Kelly books, Mary
played her most significant roles in the following:
     Dead as a Dodo   *The Deserter: Murder at Gettysburg*
     The Escher Twist   *The Face on the Wall*
     Murder at Monticello   *The Shortest Day: Murder at the Revels*
     Steeplechase   *The Thief of Venice*
     The Transcendental Murder aka *The Minute Man Murder*

Troublecross aka *The Only Security*
Crawford made minor appearances in several Tamara Hoyland books; see Volume 2.

Rath, Virginia

Valerie Dundas. 50

The Dark Cavalier	*Death of a Lucky Lady*
Death Breaks the Ring	*A Dirge for Her*
Epitaph for Lydia	*Murder with a Theme Song*
Posted for Murder	*A Shroud for Rowena*

Reeve, Arthur R.

Constance Dunlap 12

Constance Dunlap, Woman Detective

Revell, Louisa – pseudonym for Ellen Hart Smith

Julia Tyler. 217

The Bus Station Murders	*The Kindest Use a Knife*
The Men with Three Eyes	*No Pockets in Shrouds*
A Party for the Shooting	*See Rome and Die*
A Silver Spade	

Revelli, George – possible pseudonym

Amanda Nightingale 354

Amanda in Berlin*	*Amanda in Spain**
Amanda's Castle*	*Commander Amanda Nightingale*
Resort to War	

Rice, Craig – pseudonym for Georgiana Ann Randolph

Helene Brand Justus 56

8 Faces at 3	*The Big Midget Murder*
But the Doctor Died	*The Corpse Steps Out*
The Fourth Postman	*Having a Wonderful Crime*
Knocked for a Loop	*The Lucky Stiff*
My Kingdom for a Hearse	*The Right Murder*
Trial by Fury	*The Wrong Murder*

Rice was the ghostwriter of the Gypsy Rose Lee series – see page 171.

Rinehart, Mary Roberts

Letitia "Tish" Carberry. 11

The Amazing Adventures of Letitia Carberry	
The Book of Tish	*More Tish*
Tish	*Tish Marches On*
Tish Plays the Game	

Hilda Adams 23

Episode of the Wandering Knife	*Haunted Lady*
Mary Roberts Rinehart's Crime Book	*Miss Pinkerton*

Roberts, Marion

Anne Layton 62

A Mask for Crime	*Red Greed*

Rogers, Dave

Emma Peel 363

The Avengers: Too Many Targets (with John Peel)

See John Garforth and Keith Laumer.

Character Index

Book Titles Index

Titles were taken from personal book reviews but were rechecked for accuracy with recognized authorities such as Hubin, Heising, *Twentieth Century Crime and Mystery Writers*. Any errors are my responsibility. Books marked with an asterisk (*) have been identified as part of the series, but neither read nor reviewed because they were not available, or only at a prohibitive price, or, on rare occasions, were too trashy to read. (ss) = short stories

Title of Book	Author	Character
4:50 from Paddington aka *What Mrs. McGillicuddy Saw!*	Agatha Christie	Jane Marple
8 Faces at 3	Craig Rice	Helene Justus
13 White Tulips	Frances Crane	Jean Abbott
101 Years' Entertainment	Viola Brothers Shore (ss)	Gwynn Leith Keats

A

Above and Below	John Palmer	Freya Matthews
An Ace Up My Sleeve	James Hadley Chase	Helga Rolfe
Adders on the Heath	Gladys Mitchell	Dame Beatrice Bradley
The Adjusters	Mark Cross aka Valentine	Daphne Wrayne
Advantage, Miss Seeton	Hampton Charles	Miss Emily Seeton
The Adventures of Judith Lee	Richard Marsh	Judith Lee
Advice, Ltd.	E. Phillips Oppenheim	Baroness Clara Linz
The Afrit Affair	Keith Laumer	Emma Peel
Aftershock	Lillian O'Donnell	Mici Anhalt
The Alarm of the Black Cat	D. B. Olsen	Rachel & Jennifer Murdock
The Aleutian Blue Mink aka *Fatal in Furs*	James M. Fox	Suzanne "Suzy" Willett Marshall
The Alington Inheritance	Patricia Wentworth	Miss Maud Silver
All for the Love of a Lady	Leslie Ford	Grace Latham
All Grass Isn't Green	A. A. Fair	Bertha Cool
All—or Something	Hilary Brand	Hilary Brand
All Over But the Shooting	Richard Powell	Arabella "Arab" Blake
Allyson	Jerry Jenkins	Margo Franklin Spence
The Almost Perfect Murder (ss)	Hulbert Footner	Madame Rosika Storey
Altar of Evil	Florence Stevenson	Kitty Telefair
*Amanda in Berlin**	George Revelli	Amanda Nightingale
*Amanda in Spain**	George Revelli	Amanda Nightingale
*Amanda's Castle**	George Revelli	Amanda Nightingale
The Amazing Adventures of Letitia Carberry	Mary Roberts Rinehart	Letitia "Tish" Carberry
The Amazing Mrs. Pollifax	Dorothy Gilman	Emily Pollifax
The Amber Eyes	Frances Crane	Jean Abbott
Amelia Peabody's Egypt	Elizabeth Peters	Amelia Peabody Emerson
The Amethyst Spectacles	Frances Crane	Jean Abbott
…And High Water	Aaron Marc Stein	Elsie Mae Hunt
And Hope to Die	Richard Powell	Arabella "Arab" Blake
And the Undead Sing	Carter Brown	Mavis Seidlitz

Angel Abroad	Graham Montrose	Angel Brown
Angel and the Nero	Graham Montrose	Angel Brown
Angel and the Red Admiral	Graham Montrose	Angel Brown
*Angel at Arms**	Graham Montrose	Angel Brown
Angel Death	Patricia Moyes	Emmy Tibbett
Angel in Paradise	Graham Montrose	Angel Brown
Angel of Death	Graham Montrose	Angel Brown
Angel of No Mercy	Graham Montrose	Angel Brown
Angel of Vengeance	Graham Montrose	Angel Brown
Angels in Chains	Max Franklin	Charlie's Angels
Angels on a String	Max Franklin	Charlie's Angels
Angels on Ice	Max Franklin	Charlie's Angels
Anna, Where Are You aka *Death at Deep End*	Patricia Wentworth	Miss Maud Silver
An Ordinary Day aka *Apprentice to Fear*	Henry Brinton	Sally Strang
Another Day Toward Dying	Melba Marlett	Sarah De Long O'Brien
Another Woman's Man	Norma Lee	Norma "Nicky" Lee
Answer in the Negative	Henrietta Hamilton	Sally Heldar
The Ape Who Guards the Balance	Elizabeth Peters	Amelia Peabody Emerson
The Applegreen Cat	Frances Crane	Jean Abbott
Appointment in Andalusia	May Mackintosh	Laurie Grant
Apprentice to Fear aka *An Ordinary Day*	Henry Brinton	Sally Strang
Arlette	Nicolas Freeling	Arlette Van Der Valk Davidson
Armed with a New Terror	Theodora DuBois	Anne McNeill
Artists in Crime	Ngaio Marsh	Agatha "Troy" Alleyn
As Good As Murdered	James O'Hanlon	Patricia "Pat" Cordry
Ashworth Hall	Anne Perry	Charlotte Pitt
Ask an Angel	Graham Montrose	Angel Brown
Ask Miss Mott	E. Phillips Oppenheim	Lucy Mott
Ask the Cards a Question	Marcia Muller	Sharon McCone
Assignment in Andorra	May Mackintosh	Laurie Grant
At Bertram's Hotel	Agatha Christie	Jane Marple
At Night to Die	Henrietta Hamilton	Sally Heldar
August Incident	Amber Dean	Abbie Harris
Aupres de ma Blonde	Nicolas Freeling	Arlette Van Der Valk Davidson
The Avengers: Deadline	Peter Leslie, also under Patrick Macnee	Emma Peel
The Avengers: The Dead Duck	Peter Leslie, also under Patrick Macnee	Emma Peel
The Avengers: Too Many Targets	Dave Rogers	Emma Peel

B

Baby Drop aka *A Death in the Family*	Jennie Melville	Charmian Daniels
The Baby Merchants	Lillian O'Donnell	Norah Mulcahaney
Bachelors Get Lonely	A. A. Fair	Bertha Cool
Backfire	Janice Law	Anna Peters
Background to Danger aka *Uncommon Danger*	Eric Ambler	Tamara Valeshoff
The Back of the North Wind	Nicolas Freeling	Vera Castang
Back Story	Susan Silverman	Robert B. Parker
Bad Business	Susan Silverman	Robert B. Parker
The Bad Neighbor Murder	Charlotte Murray Russell	Jane Amanda Edwards
The Bait	Dorothy Uhnak	Christie Opara

Blue Leader	Walter Wager	Alison B. Gordon
Blue Moon	Walter Wager	Alison B. Gordon
Blue Murder	Walter Wager	Alison B. Gordon
Bluegate Fields	Anne Perry	Charlotte Pitt
The Body Beneath a Mandarin Tree*	Frances Crane	Jean Abbott
The Body Goes Round and Round	Theodora DuBois	Anne McNeill
The Body in the Library	Agatha Christie	Jane Marple
The Body in the Silo aka Settled Out of Court	Ronald Knox	Angela Bredon
Bombshell	G. G. Fickling	Honey West
Bonjour, Miss Seeton	Hamilton Crane	Miss Emily Seeton
The Body on Page One	Delano Ames	Jane Hamish Brown
The Body Snatchers	Collin Brooks	Meg Garret
The Book of Tish	Mary Roberts Rinehart	Letitia "Tish" Carberry
The Borders of Barbarism	Eric Williams	Kate Starte
Borrower of the Night	Elizabeth Peters	Vicky Bliss
The Boston Crab	Frank Usher	Amanda Curzon
Both Ends of the Night	Marcia Muller	Sharon McCone
The Brading Collection	Patricia Wentworth	Miss Maud Silver
Brainz, Inc.	Ron Goulart	Hildy Pace
Brand Image*	Hank Janson	Hilary Brand
Brand T*	Hilary Brand	Hilary Brand
Brazen Tongue	Gladys Mitchell	Dame Beatrice Bradley
Breathe No More, My Lady	Hilea Bailey	Hilea Bailey
Bred in the Bone	Eden Phillpotts	Avis Bryden
Bright Serpent	James M. Fox	Suzanne "Suzy" Marshall
The Broadway Jungle	Norma Lee	Norma "Nicky" Lee
The Broken Promise Land	Marcia Muller	Sharon McCone
Broomsticks Over Flaxborough aka Kissing Covens	Colin Watson	Lucilla Edith Cavell Teatime
The Brotherhood of the Seven Kings	L.T. Meade and Robert Eustace	Madame Katherine Koluchy
Brunswick Gardens	Anne Perry	Charlotte Pitt
The Bugles Blowing	Nicolas Freeling	Vera Castang
A Bullet for Midas	Nigel Morland	Palmyra Pym
A Bullet for My Baby	Carter Brown	Mavis Seidlitz
Bullets for Macbeth	Marvin Kaye	Hilary Quayle
Bullets for the Bridegroom	David Dodge	Kitty McLeod Whitney
The Bump and Grind Murders	Carter Brown	Mavis Seidlitz
Burning Is a Substitute for Loving	Jennie Melville	Charmian Daniels
Bury the Hatchet	Manning Long	Liz Parrott
Busman's Honeymoon	Dorothy L. Sayers	Harriet Vane
The Bus Station Murders	Louisa Revell	Julia Tyler
Busted	Glen Chase	Cherry Delight
But the Doctor Died	Craig Rice	Helene Justus
The Buttercup Case	Frances Crane	Jean Abbott
The Butterfly Effect	Eve Zaremba	Helen Keremos
Button, Button	Marion Bramhall	Kit Marsden Acton
By the Pricking of My Thumbs	Agatha Christie	Prudence "Tuppence" Beresford
Bye-Bye Baby	David Delman	Helen Blye Horowitz

C

Cabbages and Crime	Anne Nash	Doris "Dodo" Trent and Nell Witter
The Cabinda Affair	Matthew Head	Dr. Mary Finney

Cats Have Tall Shadows	D. B. Olsen	Rachel and Jennifer Murdock
Cats Prowl at Night	A. A. Fair	Bertha Cool
A Catskill Eagle	Robert B. Parker	Susan Silverman
Catspaw for Murder	D. B. Olsen	Rachel and Jennifer Murdock
Cause for Alarm	Eric Ambler	Tamara Valeshoff
The Cause of the Screaming	David Elias	Nell Bartlett
The Cavalier Case	Antonia Fraser	Jemima Shore
The Cavalier's Corpse	Theodora DuBois	Anne McNeill
The Cavalier in White	Marcia Muller	Joanna Stark
C. B. Greenfield: A Little Madness	Lucille Kallen	Maggie Rome
C. B. Greenfield:	Lucille Kallen	Maggie Rome
No Lady in the House		
C. B. Greenfield: The Piano Bird	Lucille Kallen	Maggie Rome
C. B. Greenfield:	Lucille Kallen	Maggie Rome
The Tanglewood Murder		
Ceremony	Robert B. Parker	Susan Silverman
Chain of Violence	Lesley Egan	Delia Riordan
*Challenge to the Four**	Mark Cross aka Valentine	Daphne Wrayne
Chance	Robert B. Parker	Susan Silverman
Chance to Die	Lionel Black	Emma Greaves
Chanticleer's Muffled Crow	Amber Dean	Abbie Harris
Charity Ends at Home	Colin Watson	Lucilla Edith Cavell Teatime
Charlie's Angels	Max Franklin	Charlie's Angels
*Cheese from a Mousetrap**	James M. Fox	Suzy Marshall
The Cheshire Cat's Eye	Marcia Muller	Sharon McCone
The Chic Chic Spy	Robert Tralins	Lee Crosley
A Child's Garden of Death	Richard Forrest	Bea Wentworth
Children of the Storm	Elizabeth Peters	Amelia Peabody Emerson
The Children's Zoo	Lillian O'Donnell	Norah Mulcahaney
The Chinese Chop	Juanita Sheridan	Janice Cameron and Lily Wu
*The Chinese Kiss**	J. J. Montague	Shauna Bishop
The Chinese Shawl	Patricia Wentworth	Miss Maud Silver
The Chinese Visitor	James Eastwood	Anna Zordan
A Choice of Crimes	Lesley Egan	Delia Riordan
Chord in Crimson	Gale Gallagher	Gale Gallagher
Cinderella Goes to the Morgue	Nancy Spain	Miriam Birdseye and
		Natasha Nevkorina
The Cinnamon Murder	Frances Crane	Jean Abbott
The Circle of Freedom	Mark Cross aka Valentine	Daphne Wrayne
The Circular Study	Anna Katharine Green	Amelia Butterworth
Cleopatra Jones	Ron Goulart	Cleopatra Jones
Cleopatra Jones and the	Ron Goulart	Cleopatra Jones
Casino of Gold		
The Clock Strikes Twelve	Patricia Wentworth	Miss Maud Silver
The Clue in the Mirror	Nigel Morland	Palmyra Pym
The Clue of the Bricklayer's Aunt	Nigel Morland	Palmyra Pym
The Clue of the Careless Hangman		
aka *The Careless Hangman*	Nigel Morland	Palmyra Pym
The Clue of the Naked Eye	Charlotte Murray Russell	Jane Amanda Edwards
Clues to Burn	Lenore Offord	Coco Hastings
Clutch of Constables	Ngaio Marsh	Agatha "Troy" Alleyn
A Clutch of Coppers	Gordon Ashe	Felicity Dawlish
The Coast Road Murder	Margaret Turnbull	Juliet Jackson
A Coat of Blackmail	J. T. McIntosh	Dominique Frayne
Cobra Trap (ss)	Peter O'Donnell	Modesty Blaise

The Crozier Pharoahs	Gladys Mitchell	Dame Beatrice Bradley
Cruise with Death	F. Draco	Ginger Tintagel
A Cumshaw Cruise	E. Laurie Long	Lizzie Collins
The Crystal Clear Case	Lee Head	Lexey Jane Pelazoni
A Cure for Dying	Jennie Melville	Charmian Daniels
The Curious Affair of the Third Dog	Patricia Moyes	Emmy Tibbett
The Curlew Coombe Mystery	Gret Lane	Kate Marsh
The Curse of the Golden Skull	Josephine Kains	Terry Spring
The Curse of the Pharoahs	Elizabeth Peters	Amelia Peabody Emerson
Curtain for a Jester	Richard and Frances Lockridge	Pamela "Pam" North
Cut Thin to Win	A. A. Fair	Bertha Cool

D

Daffodil Blonde	Frances Crane	Jean Abbott
Dance to Your Daddy	Gladys Mitchell	Dame Beatrice Bradley
The Dancing Dead	Eugene Thomas	Mrs. Caywood "Julia" Weston
The Dancing Druids	Gladys Mitchell	Dame Beatrice Bradley
Dancing with Death	Joan Coggin	Lady Lupin Hastings
Danger Point aka	Patricia Wentworth	Miss Maud Silver
In the Balance		
A Dangerous Business	Michael Underwood	Rosa Epton
Dangerous Cargo	Hulbert Footner	Madame Rosika Storey
The Dangerous Hour	Marcia Muller	Sharon McCone
The Dangerous Islands	Ann Bridge	Julia Probyn
The Dangerous Ones	Charles Franklin	Maxine Dangerfield
The Dark Cavalier	Virginia Rath	Valerie Dundas
Dark Emerald	Joan Storm	Sarah Vanessa
Date with Death	Elizabeth Linington	Sue Carstairs Maddox
Daughter of Fu Manchu	Sax Rohmer	Fah Lo Suee
David Betterton	Judge K. C. Ruegg	Rosie Bright
Days of Misfortune	Aaron Marc Stein	Elsie Mae Hunt
Dead Again	Jennie Melville	Charmian Daniels
Dead As a Dinosaur	Richard and Frances Lockridge	Pamela "Pam" North
Dead as a Dodo	Jane Langton	Mary Morgan Kelly
Dead Faces Laughing	David Delman	Helen Blye Horowitz
Dead Man's Float	Amber Dean	Abbie Harris
Dead Man's Folly	Agatha Christie	Ariadne Oliver
Dead Man's Gift	Zelda Popkin	Mary Carner Whittaker
Dead Man's Handle	Peter O'Donnell	Modesty Blaise
Dead Men Don't Ski	Patricia Moyes	Emmy Tibbett
Dead Men's Morris	Gladys Mitchell	Dame Beatrice Bradley
Dead Midnight	Marcia Muller	Sharon McCone
Dead on Cue	Ann Morice	Tessa Crichton
Dead Right	Jennette Lee	Millicent Newberry
Dead Run	Helen Holley	Tessie Venable
Dead Set	Jennie Melville	Charmian Daniels
The Dead Thing in the Pool	Aaron Marc Stein	Elsie Mae Hunt
Deadlier Than the Male	Jim C. Conaway	Jana Blake
Deadly Climate	Richard Barth	Margaret Binton
Deadly Diamond	Joan Storm	Sarah Vanessa
Deadly Meeting	Robert Bernard	Millicent Hetherege
The Dear, Dead Girls	Nigel Morland	Palmyra Pym
Dear, Dead Mother-in-Law	Katharine Hill	Lorna Donahue
Death Among the Sands	Evalina Mack	Ann McIntosh aka "Mrs. Mac"
Death & Co.	David Brierley	Cody
Death and Taxes	David Dodge	Kitty McLeod Whitney

*Death Is a Ruby Light**	Paul Kenyon	Baroness Penelope St. John Orsini
Death Is Academic	Amanda Mackay	Dr. Hannah Land
Death Is Late to Lunch	Theodora DuBois	Anne McNeill
Death Is Waiting	Frank Usher	Daye Smith
Death Lights a Candle	Phoebe Atwood Taylor	Prudence Whitby
Death Looks Down	Amelia Reynolds Long	Katherine "Peter" Piper
Death Masque	Hugh McLeave	Deirdre O'Connor
Death Meets 400 Rabbits	Aaron Marc Stein	Elsie Mae Hunt
Death of a Burrowing Mole	Gladys Mitchell	Dame Beatrice Bradley
Death of a Call Girl	Leslie Trevor	Pepper Anderson
Death of a Dandie Dinmont	Madelaine Duke	Norah North
Death of a Delft Blue	Gladys Mitchell	Dame Beatrice Bradley
Death of a Dog	Leonora Eyles	Dr. Joan Marvin
Death of a Doll	Hilda Lawrence	Beulah Pond and Bessie Petty
Death of a Fat God	H. R. F. Keating	Mrs. Elma Craggs
Death of a Fellow Traveller aka *Nobody Wore Black*	Delano Ames	Jane Hamish Brown
Death of a Gay Dog	Ann Morice	Tessa Crichton
Death of a Heavenly Twin	Ann Morice	Tessa Crichton
Death of a Holy Murderer	Madelaine Duke	Norah North
Death of a Lucky Lady	Virginia Rath	Valerie Dundas
Death of a Minor Character	E. X. Ferrars	Virginia Freer
Death of a Nymph	David Delman	Helen Blye Horowitz
Death of a Portrait	Evalina Mack	Ann McIntosh aka "Mrs. Mac"
Death of a Prima Donna	Laura Colburn	Carol Gates
Death of a Tall Man	Richard and Frances Lockridge	Pamela "Pam" North
Death of a Voodoo Doll	Margot Arnold	Penelope Spring
Death of a Wedding Guest	Ann Morice	Tessa Crichton
Death of an Angel	Richard and Frances Lockridge	Pamela "Pam" North
Death of an Eloquent Man	Charlotte Murray Russell	Jane Amanda Edwards
Death of an Old Sinner	Dorothy Salisbury Davis	Mrs. Annie Norris
Death on the Agenda	Patricia Moyes	Emmy Tibbett
Death on the Aisle	Richard and Frances Lockridge	Pamela "Pam" North
Death on the Dragon's Tongue	Margot Arnold	Penelope Spring
Death on the Eno	Amanda Mackay	Dr. Hannah Land
Death on the Late Show	Jan Michaels	Darby Castle
Death on the Mississippi	Richard Forrest	Bea Wentworth
Death on the Slopes	Norma Schier	Kay Barth
Death Prowls the Cove	Gret Lane	Kate Marsh
Death Rides the Dragon	Eugene Thomas	Mrs. Caywood "Julia" Weston
Death Sails in a High Wind	Theodora DuBois	Anne McNeill
Death Sends a Cable	Margaret Tayler Yates	Anne "Davvie" McLean
Death Strikes Home	M. W. Glidden	Carey Brent
The Death Syndicate	Judson Philips	Carole Trevor
Death Takes a Bow	Richard and Frances Lockridge	Pamela "Pam" North
Death Takes a Paying Guest	Aaron Marc Stein	Elsie Mae Hunt
Death Tears a Comic Strip	Theodora DuBois	Anne McNeill
Death Through the Looking Glass	Richard Forrest	Bea Wentworth
Death Through the Mill	Laura Colburn	Carol Gates
Death to Windward	Henry Brinton	Sally Strang
Death Traps	Kay Cleaver Strahan	Lynn MacDonald
Death Under Par	Janice Law	Anna Peters
Death Under the Lilacs	Richard Forrest	Bea Wentworth
Death Visits the Summer-House	Gret Lane	Kate Marsh
Death Walks on Cat Feet	D. B. Olsen	Rachel and Jennifer Murdock

Double Barrel	Nicolas Freeling	Arlette Van der Valk Davidson
Double Cross Purposes	Ronald Knox	Angela Bredon
Double Deuce	Robert B. Parker	Susan Silverman
Double Jeopardy	Michael Underwood	Rosa Epton
Double or Quits	A. A. Fair	Bertha Cool
Down Among the Dead Men aka *The Drunken Sailor*	Patricia Moyes	Emmy Tibbett
Dragoman Pass	Eric Williams	Kate Starte
Dragon's Claw	Peter O'Donnell	Modesty Blaise
Dragon's Teeth	Lee Killough	Janna Brill
A Dream Apart	Lesley Egan	Delia Riordan
*The Dream Girl Caper**	James Lawrence	Angela Harpe
Dressed to Kill	Emma Lou Fetta	Susan Yates
Dressed to Kill	Nigel Morland	Palmyra Pym
A Dressing of Diamond	Nicolas Freeling	Vera Castang
Drown Her Remembrance	Susan Gilruth	Liane "Lee" Craufurd
A Drug on the Market	George Sampson	Paola Smith Watson
The Drums of Fu Manchu	Sax Rohmer	Fah Lo Suee
The Drunken Sailor Down aka *Among the Dead Men*	Patricia Moyes	Emmy Tibbett
Dual Enigma	Michael Underwood	Rosa Epton
Dudie Dunne or the Exquisite Detective	Harlan Halsey (The Old Sleuth)	Caroline "Cad" Mettie
Dulcie Bligh	Gail Clark	Dulcie Bligh
Dull Thud	Manning Long	"Liz" Parrott
A Dwarf Kingdom	Nicolas Freeling	Vera Castang
A Dying Fall	Hildegarde Dolson	Lucy Ramsdale

E

Early Autumn	Robert B. Parker	Susan Silverman
Easy to Kill	Hulbert Footner	Madame Rosika Storey
The Echoing Strangers	Gladys Mitchell	Dame Beatrice Bradley
*The Ecstasy Connection**	Paul Kenyon	Baroness Penelope St. John Orsini
The Edge of Doom	Amanda Cross	Kate Fansler
Edwin of the Iron Shoes	Marcia Muller	Sharon McCone
Elephants Can Remember	Agatha Christie	Ariadne Oliver
Elizabeth Finds a Body	Florence Kilpatrick	Elizabeth
Elizabeth the Sleuth	Florence Kilpatrick	Elizabeth
The Elusive Mrs. Pollifax	Dorothy Gilman	Emily Pollifax
*The Emerald Oil Caper**	James Lawrence	Angela Harpe
Emergency in the Pyrenees	Ann Bridge	Julia Probyn
The Episode at Toledo	Ann Bridge	Julia Probyn
Episode of the Wandering Knife	Mary Roberts Rinehart	Hilda Adams
Epitaph for Lydia	Virginia Rath	Valerie Dundas
Erin	Jerry Jenkins	Margo Franklin Spence
The Escape	Charles Franklin	Maxine Dangerfield
Escape to Danger	Peter Conway	Lucy Beck
The Escher Twist	Jane Langton	Mary Morgan Kelly
Eternity Ring	Patricia Wentworth	Miss Maud Silver
The Eve of the Wedding	Lionel Black	Kate Theobald
Evidence Unseen	Lavinia Davis	Nora Hughes Blaine
The Evil Men Do	Cortland Fitzsimmons	Ethel Thomas
Exit a Star	Kathleen Moore Knight	Margot Blair
Exit Actors Dying	Margot Arnold	Penelope Spring
Exit Mr. Punch	Mignon Warner	Edwina Charles

First to Kill	Frank Usher	Daye Smith
Fish or Cut Bait	A. A. Fair	Bertha Cool
A Flair for Affairs	Hilary Brand	Hilary Brand
Flander's Sky aka *The Pretty Howtown*	Nicolas Freeling	Vera Castang
Flawless Execution	John Logue	Julia Sullivan
The Flaxborough Crab aka *Just What the Doctor Ordered*	Colin Watson	Lucilla Edith Cavell Teatime
*Flicker of Doom**	Paul Kenyon	Baroness Penelope St. John Orsini
The Floating Game	John Garforth	Emma Peel
The Flying Red Horse	Frances Crane	Jean Abbott
Fog Off Weymouth	Henrietta Clandon	Penny Mercer
Follow the Leader	John Logue	Julia Sullivan
Fools Die on Friday	A. A. Fair	Bertha Cool
Footprints	Kay Cleaver Strahan	Lynn MacDonald
Footsteps in the Blood	Jennie Melville	Charmian Daniels
The Footsteps at the Lock	Ronald Knox	Angela Bredon
The Footsteps	Theodora DuBois	Anne McNeill
For Godmother and Country	R. T. Larkin	Donna Bella
For Old Crime's Sake aka *Lucky Jane*	Delano Ames	Jane Hamish Brown
Forever Wilt Thou Die	Barbara Ninde Byfield	Helen Bullock
Forsythia Finds Murder	Rachel Payes	Forsythia Brown
Foul Deeds Will Arise	Mark Cross aka Valentine	Daphne Wrayne
Foul Hawsers	E. Laurie Long	Lizzie Collins
*The Four at Bay**	Mark Cross aka Valentine	Daphne Wrayne
Four Feet in the Grave	Amelia Reynolds Long	Katherine "Peter" Piper
The Four Get Going	Mark Cross aka Valentine	Daphne Wrayne
Four Lost Ladies	Stuart Palmer	Miss Hildegarde Withers
The Four Make Holiday	Mark Cross aka Valentine	Daphne Wrayne
Four Square Jane	Edgar Wallace	Four Square Jane
The Four Strike Home	Mark Cross aka Valentine	Daphne Wrayne
Four Times a Widower	Adam Bliss	Alice Penny
The Fourth Postman	Craig Rice	Helene Justus
The Fourth Stage of *Gainsborough Brown*	Clarissa Watson	Persis Willum
Fowl Play	Theodora DuBois	Anne McNeill
*The French Kiss**	J. J. Montague	Shauna Bishop
The Frightened Stiff	Kelley Roos	Haila Troy
The Frightened Amazon	Aaron Marc Stein	Elsie Mae Hunt
Frog in the Throat	E. X. Ferrars	Virginia Freer
The Frog in the Moonflower	Ivor Drummond	Jennifer Norrington
From This Dark Stairway	Mignon Eberhart	Sarah Keate
Fu Manchu's Bride	Sax Rohmer	Fah Lo Suee
Fuzz	Ed McBain	Eileen Burke

G

The G-String Murders	Gypsy Rose Lee	Gypsy Rose Lee
Games to Keep the Dark Away	Marcia Muller	Sharon McCone
Gangster Girl	Jack Lait	Polack Annie
Gaudy Night	Dorothy L. Sayers	Harriet Vane
The Gazebo	Patricia Wentworth	Miss Maud Silver
Gemini Trip	Janice Law	Anna Peters
The Gentle Hangman	James M. Fox	"Suzy" Marshall
A Gentleman Called	Dorothy Salisbury Davis	Mrs. Annie Norris

J

The James Joyce Murder	Amanda Cross	Kate Fansler
Jane Carberry, Detective	Beryl Symons	Jane Carberry
Jane Carberry Investigates	Beryl Symons	Jane Carberry
Jane Carberry and the Laughing Fountain	Beryl Symons	Jane Carberry
Jane Carberry's Weekend	Beryl Symons	Jane Carberry
Janell	Jerry Jenkins	Margo Franklin Spence
A Javelin for Jonah	Gladys Mitchell	Dame Beatrice Bradley
The Jaws of the Watchdog	Ivor Drummond	Jennifer Norrington
The Jaws of Darkness	Mark Cross aka Valentine	Daphne Wrayne
Jaws Pellegrini*	Ben Sarto	Miss Mabie Otis
Jemima Shore at the Sunny Grave (ss)	Antonia Fraser	Jemima Shore
Jemima Shore's First Case (ss)	Antonia Fraser	Jemima Shore
Jemima Shore Investigates (ss)	Antonia Fraser	Jemima Shore
John Clutterbuck	Judge Ruegg, K.C.	Rosie Bright
Johnny Under Ground	Patricia Moyes	Emmy Tibbett
The Joker in the Pack	James Hadley Chase	Helga Rolfe
Journey Into Danger*	James M. Fox	Suzy Marshall
The Judas Kiss*	J. J. Montague	Shauna Bishop
The Judge Is Reversed	Richard and Frances Lockridge	Pamela "Pam" North
Judith Lee	Richard Marsh	Judith Lee
Julia in Ireland	Ann Bridge	Julia Probyn
The Juror	Michael Underwood	Clare Reynolds Atwell
Just What the Doctor Ordered aka *The Flaxborough Crab*	Colin Watson	Lucilla Edith Cavell Teatime

K

The Kahuna Killer	Juanita Sheridan	Janice Cameron and Lily Wu
Karlyn	Jerry Jenkins	Margo Franklin Spence
Kept Women Can't Quit	A. A. Fair	Bertha Cool
A Key to Death	Richard and Frances Lockridge	Pamela "Pam" North
The Key	Patricia Wentworth	Miss Maud Silver
Killing the Goose	Richard and Frances Lockridge	Pamela "Pam" North
The Killer Is Kissable*	Carter Brown	Mavis Seidlitz
Killing With Kindness	Ann Morice	Tessa Crichton
The Killing Kind	Max Franklin	Charlie's Angels
The Kindest Use a Knife	Louisa Revell	Julia Tyler
The Kingdom of Death aka *The Fear Sign*	Marjorie Allingham	Amanda Fitton Campion
Kiss for a Killer	G. G. Fickling	Honey West
A Kiss a Day Keeps the Corpses Away	James Yardley	Kiss Darling
Kiss the Boys and Make Them Die	James Yardley	Kiss Darling
Kisses of Death	Henry Kane	Marla Trent
Kissing Covens aka *Broomsticks Over Flaxborough*	Colin Watson	Lucilla Edith Cavell Teatime
A Knife for the Killer aka *Murder at Radio City*	Nigel Morland	Palmyra Pym
Knife in My Back	Sam Merwin, Jr.	Amy Brewster
Knife in the Dark	G. D. H. and Margaret Cole	Mrs. Elizabeth Warrender
Knocked for a Loop	Craig Rice	Helene Justus

L

Ladies' Bane	Patricia Wentworth	Miss Maud Silver

Lady Molly of Scotland Yard	Baroness Emmuska Orczy	Lady Molly Robertson-Kirk
Lady Macbeth	Nicolas Freeling	Arlette Van Der Valk Davidson
Lady, Get Your Gun	Paul Ernst	Shirley Leighton Harper
The Lady Had a Gun	Nigel Morland	Palmyra Pym
The Lady Is a Spy aka	Lionel Black	Emma Greaves
Two Ladies in Verona		
The Lady Regrets	James M. Fox	Suzy Marshall
The Lady Saw Red	Amelia Reynolds Long	Katherine "Peter" Piper
Lady With a Cool Eye	Gwen Moffat	Miss Melinda Pink
The Lady Killer Affair	Joen Arliss	Kate Graham
Ladykiller	Lillian O'Donnell	Norah Mulcahaney
Lament for a Lady Laird	Margot Arnold	Penelope Spring
Lament for Leto	Gladys Mitchell	Dame Beatrice Bradley
Lament for a Lousy Lover	Carter Brown	Mavis Seidlitz
Landscape With Corpse	Delano Ames	Jane Hamish Brown
The Lantern House Affair	Gret Lane	Kate Marsh
The Last Camel Died at Noon	Elizabeth Peters	Amelia Peabody Emerson
Last Chance Country	Gwen Moffat	Miss Melinda Pink
Last Day in Limbo	Peter O'Donnell	Modesty Blaise
The Last Doorbell	Joseph Harrington	Jane Boardman
The Last Gambit	David Delman	Helen Blye Horowitz
The Last Known Address	Joseph Harrington	Jane Boardman
The Last Laugh	Winifred Graham	Louisa Woolfe
Last Plane From Nice	Clarissa Watson	Persis Willum
The Last Set	Jan Ellery	Adrienne Bishop
Last Will and Testament	E. X. Ferrars	Virginia Freer
Last Will and Testament of	Tobias Wells	Constance Cobble
Constance Cobble		
The Late Lamented Lady	Marie Blizard	Eve MacWilliams
Late, Late in the Evening	Gladys Mitchell	Dame Beatrice Bradley
Latter End	Patricia Wentworth	Miss Maud Silver
The Laugh Was on Lazarus	John Garforth	Emma Peel
The Laughing Dragon Mystery	Josephine Kains	Terry Spring
The Laughing Fish aka	Selwyn Jepson	Eve Gill
The Verdict in Question		
The Laurel and Hardy Murders	Marvin Kaye	Hilary Quayle
Laurels Are Poison	Gladys Mitchell	Dame Beatrice Bradley
The Law and the Lady	Wilkie Collins	Valeria Woodville
Lay Me Odds	Rod Gray	Eve Drum
Lay That Pistol Down	Richard Powell	Arabella "Arab" Blake
Leave a Message for Willie	Marcia Muller	Sharon McCone
The Ledger	Dorothy Uhnak	Christie Opara
Legacy of Danger	Patricia McGerr	Selena Mead
Leisure Dying	Lillian O'Donnell	Norah Mulcahaney
A Lesson in Crime	G. D. H. and Margaret Cole	Mrs. Elizabeth Warrender
The Liar's League	David Delman	Helen Blye Horowitz
A Life for a Death	Gordon Ashe	Felicia Dawlish
The Light-Hearted Quest	Ann Bridge	Julia Probyn
Lightning	Ed McBain	Eileen Burke
Lindsey	Jerry Jenkins	Margo Franklin Spence
Lion in the Valley	Elizabeth Peters	Amelia Peabody Emerson
The Lion Game	James Schmitz	Telzey Amberdon
Listen to the Silence	Marcia Muller	Sharon McCone
The Listening Eye	Patricia Wentworth	Miss Maud Silver
Little Dragon From Peking aka	James Eastwood	Anna Zordan
Seduce and Destroy		

A Lively Game of Death	Marvin Kaye	Hilary Quayle
Lockout	Lillian O'Donnell	Norah Mulcahaney
The Lonely Cage	Frank Usher	Daye Smith
Lonelyheart 4122	Colin Watson	Lucilla Edith Cavell Teatime
Lonesome Road	Patricia Wentworth	Miss Maud Silver
The Long Island Murders	M. W. Glidden	Carey Brent
The Long Skeleton	Richard and Frances Lockridge	Pamela "Pam" North
Long Spoon Lane	Anne Perry	Charlotte Pitt
The Longer Bodies	Gladys Mitchell	Dame Beatrice Bradley
Look in Any Doorway	Nigel Morland	Palmyra Pym
Looking for Rachel Wallace	Robert B. Parker	Susan Silverman
The Lord of the Silent	Elizabeth Peters	Amelia Peabody Emerson
Lord Peter	Dorothy L. Sayers	Harriet Vane
The Lost Girls	Gwen Moffat	Miss Melinda Pink
Lost Man's Lane	Anna Katharine Green	Amelia Butterworth
The Lovely Ladies	Nicolas Freeling	Arlette Van der Valk Davidson
Lover—Say It With Mink	Norma Lee	Norma "Nicky" Lee
Lovers, Make Moan	Gladys Mitchell	Dame Beatrice Bradley
The Loving and the Dead	Carter Brown	Mavis Seidlitz
The Luck Runs Out	Charlotte MacLeod	Helen Shandy
Lucky Jane aka	Delano Ames	Jane Hamish Brown
For Old Crime's Sake		
Lucky Pierre	Mercedes Endfield	Ms. Squad
The Lucky Stiff	Craig Rice	Helene Justus
Lullaby of Murder	Dorothy Salisbury Davis	Julie Hayes
Lullaby	Ed McBain	Eileen Burke
Lyssa	Jerry Jenkins	Margo Franklin Spence

M

Madame Storey (ss)	Hulbert Footner	Madame Rosika Storey
Madame Aubry and the Police	Hugh Travers	Dominique Aubry
Madame Aubry Dines With Death	Hugh Travers	Dominique Aubry
Madame Judas	Margaret Turnbull	Juliet Jackson
Madame Maigret's Own Case	Georges Simenon	Madame Maigret
Madame X	J.W. McConaughy	Madame X
Made Up to Kill	Kelley Roos	Haila Troy
Madeline Payne, the	Lawrence L. Lynch	Madeline Payne
Detective's Daughter		
Magnet for Murder	Beryl Symons	Jane Carberry
Make-Up for Murder	June Wright	Mother Paul
Making Good Blood	Jennie Melville	Charmian Daniels
The Malady in Madeira	Ann Bridge	Julia Probyn
The Man From Moscow	Frank Usher	Amanda Curzon
The Man in Gray	Frances Crane	Jean Abbott
Man Missing	Mignon Eberhart	Sarah Keate
Man Running aka	Selwyn Jepson	Eve Gill
Outrun the Constable		
The Man Who Grew Tomatoes	Gladys Mitchell	Dame Beatrice Bradley
The Man With the Tiny Head	Ivor Drummond	Jennifer Norrington
The Man With a Paper Skull	Dwight Marfield	Gail McGurk
The Mano Murders	Juanita Sheridan	Janice Cameron and Lily Wu
Many Deadly Returns aka	Patricia Moyes	Emmy Tibbett
Who Saw Her Die?		
Margo	Jerry Jenkins	Margo Franklin Spence
Margo Mysteries	Jerry Jenkins	Margo Franklin Spence
Margo's Reunion	Jerry Jenkins	Margo Franklin Spence

Miss Otis Goes French*	Ben Sarto	Mabie Otis
Miss Otis Goes Up	Ben Sarto	Mabie Otis
Miss Otis Has a Daughter	Ben Sarto	Mabie Otis
Miss Otis Hits Back*	Ben Sarto	Mabie Otis
Miss Otis Makes a Date*	Ben Sarto	Mabie Otis
Miss Otis Makes Hay*	Ben Sarto	Mabie Otis
Miss Otis Moves In*	Ben Sarto	Mabie Otis
Miss Otis Plays Ball*	Ben Sarto	Mabie Otis
Miss Otis Plays Eve*	Ben Sarto	Mabie Otis
Miss Otis Relents*	Ben Sarto	Mabie Otis
Miss Otis Says Yes*	Ben Sarto	Mabie Otis
Miss Otis Takes the Rap*	Ben Sarto	Mabie Otis
Miss Otis Throws a Comeback	Ben Sarto	Mabie Otis
Miss Pink at the Edge of the World	Gwen Moffat	Miss Melinda Pink
Miss Pinkerton	Mary Roberts Rinehart	Hilda Adams
Miss Pym Disposes	Josephine Tey	Lucy Pym
Miss Seeton at the Helm	Hampton Charles	Miss Emily Seeton
Miss Seeton, Bewitched aka *Witch Miss Seeton*	Heron Carvic	Miss Emily Seeton
Miss Seeton, by Appointment	Hampton Charles	Miss Emily Seeton
Miss Seeton by Moonlight	Hamilton Crane	Miss Emily Seeton
Miss Seeton Cracks the Case	Hamilton Crane	Miss Emily Seeton
Miss Seeton Draws the Line	Heron Carvic	Miss Emily Seeton
Miss Seeton's Finest Hour	Hamilton Crane	Miss Emily Seeton
Miss Seeton Goes to Bat	Hamilton Crane	Miss Emily Seeton
Miss Seeton Paints the Town	Hamilton Crane	Miss Emily Seeton
Miss Seeton Plants Suspicion	Hamilton Crane	Miss Emily Seeton
Miss Seeton Rocks the Cradle	Hamilton Crane	Miss Emily Seeton
Miss Seeton Rules	Hamilton Crane	Miss Emily Seeton
Miss Seeton Sings	Heron Carvic	Miss Emily Seeton
Miss Seeton Undercover	Hamilton Crane	Miss Emily Seeton
Miss Silver Comes to Stay	Patricia Wentworth	Miss Maud Silver
Miss Silver Deals in Death	Patricia Wentworth	Miss Maud Silver
Miss Withers Regrets	Stuart Palmer	Miss Hildegarde Withers
Missing from His Home	Mark Cross aka Valentine	Daphne Wrayne
The Missing Link	Katharine Farrar	Clare Liddicotte Ringwood
Mister X	Collin Brooks	Meg Garret
Mistress of Devil's Manor	Florence Stevenson	Kitty Telefair
Modesty Blaise	Peter O'Donnell	Modesty Blaise
Moina, A Detective Story	Lawrence L. Lynch	Madeline Payne
Molly and the Confidence Man	Stephen Overholser	Molly Owens
Molly and the Gambler	Stephen Overholser	Molly Owens
Molly and the Gold Baron	Stephen Overholser	Molly Owens
Molly and the Indian Agent	Stephen Overholser	Molly Owens
Molly and the Railroad Tycoon	Stephen Overholser	Molly Owens
Molly on the Outlaw Trail	Stephen Overholser	Molly Owens
The Moment of Fiction	Daniel Estow	Ann Lang
The Moment of Silence	Daniel Estow	Ann Lang
Money, Murder and the McNeills aka *It's Raining Violence*	Theodora DuBois	Anne McNeill
The Moon Murders	Nigel Morland	Palmyra Pym
Moonmilk and Murder	Aaron Marc Stein	Elsie Mae Hunt
The Morbid Kitchen	Jennie Melville	Charmian Daniels
More Tish	Mary Roberts Rinehart	Letitia "Tish" Carberry
Mother Finds a Body	Gypsy Rose Lee	Gypsy Rose Lee
Motive for Revenge	Peter Conway	Lucy Beck

Murder Has Its Points	Richard and Frances Lockridge	Pamela "Pam" North
Murder in a Hurry	Richard and Frances Lockridge	Pamela "Pam" North
Murder in Any Language	Kelley Roos	Haila Troy
Murder in Black	Mark Cross aka Valentine	Daphne Wrayne
Murder in Blue Street	Frances Crane	Jean Abbott
Murder in Bright Red	Frances Crane	Jean Abbott
Murder in Five Columns	Frank Diamond	Vicky Gaines
Murder in Married Life	Ann Morice	Tessa Crichton
Murder in Maytime	Gordon Brandon	Terry Terence
Murder in Mimicry	Ann Morice	Tessa Crichton
Murder in Okefenokee	Cecile Matschat	Andrea Reid Ramsey
Murder in Outline	Ann Morice	Tessa Crichton
Murder in Style	Emma Lou Fetta	Susan Yates
Murder in the Act	Elizabeth St. Clair	Marilyn Ambers
Murder in the Air	Mark Cross aka Valentine	Daphne Wrayne
Murder in the Family	David Delman	Helen Blye Horowitz
Murder in the Mist	Zelda Popkin	Mary Carner Whittaker
Murder in the O.P.M.	Leslie Ford	Grace Latham
Murder in the Pool*	Mark Cross aka Valentine	Daphne Wrayne
Murder in Wardour Street aka *A Gun for a God*	Nigel Morland	Palmyra Pym
Murder Is a Collector's Item	Elizabeth Dean	Emma Marsh
Murder Is a Serious Business	Elizabeth Dean	Emma Marsh
Murder Is an Evil Business	Marion Bramhall	Kit Marsden Acton
A Murder Is Announced	Agatha Christie	Jane Marple
Murder Is Contagious	Marion Bramhall	Kit Marsden Acton
Murder Is Served	Richard and Frances Lockridge	Pamela "Pam" North
Murder Is So Nostalgic!	Carter Brown	Mavis Seidlitz
Murder Is Suggested	Richard and Frances Lockridge	Pamela "Pam" North
Murder, Maestro, Please	Delano Ames	Jane Hamish Brown
Murder Maritime	Claudia Cranston	Clarice Claremont
The Murder of a Fifth Columnist	Leslie Ford	Grace Latham
Murder of a Missing Man	Arthur M. Chase	Matilda Townsend
The Murder of Busy Lizzie	Gladys Mitchell	Dame Beatrice Bradley
A Murder of Crows	Patrick Buchanan	Charity Tucker
Murder on Fifth Avenue	Claudia Cranston	Clarice Claremont
Murder on French Leave	Ann Morice	Tessa Crichton
Murder on Russian Hill	Lenore Offord	Coco Hastings
Murder on the Aphrodite	Ruth Burr Sanborn	Angeline Tredennick
Murder on the Blackboard	Stuart Palmer	Miss Hildegarde Withers
Murder on the Face of It	Emma Lou Fetta	Susan Yates
Murder on the Glass Floor	Viola Brothers Shore	Gwynn Leith Keats
Murder on the Links	John Logue	Julia Sullivan
Murder on the Purple Water	Frances Crane	Jean Abbott
Murder on Wheels	Stuart Palmer	Miss Hildegarde Withers
Murder Out of Turn	Richard and Frances Lockridge	Pamela "Pam" North
Murder Post-Dated	Ann Morice	Tessa Crichton
Murder Rides a Rocket	Frank Diamond	Vicky Gaines
Murder Solves a Problem	Marion Bramhall	Kit Marsden Acton
Murder Strikes an Atomic Unit	Theodora DuBois	Anne McNeill
Murder Under Construction	Sue MacVeigh	Sue MacVeigh
Murder Upstairs	Adam Bliss	Alice Penny
Murder Wears a Mantilla	Carter Brown	Mavis Seidlitz
Murder Will Out aka *Profile in Guilt*	Jeannette Covert Nolan	Lace White
Murder Will Speak	Mark Cross aka Valentine	Daphne Wrayne

N

No Flowers in Brazlov	Frank Usher	Amanda Curzon
No Mourners Present	Frank Presnell	Anne Seymour Webb
No Mourning for the Matador	Delano Ames	Jane Hamish Brown
No Outlet	Arthur M. Chase	Matilda Townsend
No Part in Your Death	Nicolas Freeling	Vera Castang
No Pockets in Shrouds	Louisa Revell	Julia Tyler
No Time for Crime	Charlotte Murray Russell	Jane Amanda Edwards
No Traveller Returns	Amber Dean	Abbie Harris
No Villain Need Be	Elizabeth Linington	Sue Carstairs Maddox
No Winding Sheet	Gladys Mitchell	Dame Beatrice Bradley
No Word from Winifred	Amanda Cross	Kate Fansler
The Nodding Canaries	Gladys Mitchell	Dame Beatrice Bradley
None But the Lethal Heart	Carter Brown	Mavis Seidlitz
Noonday and Night	Gladys Mitchell	Dame Beatrice Bradley
The Norths Meet Murder	Richard and Frances Lockridge	Pamela "Pam" North
Not as Far as Velma	Nicolas Freeling	Vera Castang
Not Long to Live	Mark Cross aka Valentine	Daphne Wrayne
Not Wanted on Voyage	Nancy Spain	Miriam Birdseye and Natasha Nevkorina
The Notorious Sophie Lang	Frederick Irving Anderson	Sophie Lang
Nude in Mink	Sax Rohmer	Sumuru
The Numbered Account	Ann Bridge	Julia Probyn
Nursery Tea and Poison	Ann Morice	Tessa Crichton

O

October House	Kay Cleaver Strahan	Lynn MacDonald
The Odd Job	Charlotte MacLeod	Sarah Kelling
Odd Job No.101 and Other Future Crimes & Intrigues (ss)	Ron Goulart	Hildy Pace
Odds on Miss Seeton	Heron Carvic	Miss Emily Seeton
Ogilvie, Tallant, and Moon	Chelsea Quinn Yarbro	Morgan Studevant
Old Lover's Ghost	Leslie Ford	Grace Latham
Old Sinners Never Die	Dorothy Salisbury Davis	Mrs. Annie Norris
Old Man in the Corner	Baroness Emmuska Orczy	Mary J. "Polly" Burton
Olga Knaresbrook, Detective	Hazel Campbell	Olga Knaresbrook
On a Par With Murder	John Logue	Julia Sullivan
On the Night of the 14th	Mark Cross aka Valentine	Daphne Wrayne
On the Day of the Shooting	Charles Franklin	Maxine Dangerfield
On the Brink	Mercedes Endfield	Ms. Squad
Once Upon a Crime	Mark Cross aka Valentine	Daphne Wrayne
Once Too Often	Mark Cross aka Valentine	Daphne Wrayne
One Dollar Death	Richard Barth	Margaret Binton
One Down and Two to Slay	Henry Brinton	Sally Strang
One False Move	Kelley Roos	Haila Troy
One Man's Meat aka *It Shouldn't Happen to a Dog*	Colin Watson	Lucilla Edith Cavell Teatime
One Man's Murder	David Delman	Helen Blye Horowitz
One Remained Seated	John Slate	Maria Black
The Only Security aka *Troublecross*	Jessica Mann	Thea Crawford
Only the Guilty	Aaron Marc Stein	Elsie Mae Hunt
*Operation Doomsday**	Paul Kenyon	Baroness Penelope St. John Orsini
Other Than Natural Causes	Mark Cross aka Valentine	Daphne Wrayne
The Other Side of Midnight	Sidney Sheldon	Catherine Douglas
The Other Side of the Door	Lillian O'Donnell	Norah Mulcahaney

The Riddle of the Florentine Folio	E. S. Liddon	Peggy Fairfield
The Riddle of the Russian Princess	E. S. Liddon	Peggy Fairfield
The Right Murder	Craig Rice	Helene Justus
The Ring-a-Ding UFOs	Robert Tralins	Lee Crosley
The Rising of the Moon	Gladys Mitchell	Dame Beatrice Bradley
Rocket to the Morgue	H. H. Holmes	Sister Ursula
Rogues March	Margaret Turnbull	Juliet Jackson
Rope by Arrangement	Henrietta Clandon	Penny Mercer
A Rope for the Hanging	Nigel Morland	Palmyra Pym
Rosa's Dilemma	Michael Underwood	Rosa Epton
Rubies, Emeralds, and Diamonds	Bridget Chetwynd	Petunia Best
Running Scared	Hilary Brand	Hilary Brand
Run to Death	Patrick Quentin	Iris Duluth
Runaway	Clarissa Watson	Persis Willum
Runway to Death	Macartney Filgate	Charlotte Eliot
Ruth Fielding and Baby June	Alice B. Emerson	Ruth Fielding
Ruth Fielding at Briarwood Hall	Alice B. Emerson	Ruth Fielding
Ruth Fielding at Cameron Hall	Alice B. Emerson	Ruth Fielding
Ruth Fielding in Moving Pictures	Alice B. Emerson	Ruth Fielding
Rutland Place	Anne Perry	Charlotte Pitt

S

Sabina aka *Lake Isle*	Nicolas Freeling	Vera Castang
Sabre Tooth	Peter O'Donnell	Modesty Blaise
The Sad Variety	Nicholas Blake	Clare Massenger
A Safe Place to Die	Janice Law	Anna Peters
Said With Flowers	Anne Nash	Doris "Dodo" Trent and Nell Witter
Sailor, Take Warning!	Kelley Roos	Haila Troy
St. Peter's Finger	Gladys Mitchell	Dame Beatrice Bradley
Sally of Scotland Yard	Leonard Gribble and Geraldine Laws	Sally Dean
The Saltmarsh Murders	Gladys Mitchell	Dame Beatrice Bradley
Sand Castles	Nicolas Freeling	Arlette Van Der Valk Davidson
The Sandcastle Murders	Elizabeth St. Clair	Marilyn Ambers
Satan Is a Woman	George Baxt	Sylvia Plotkin
Savage Breast	Manning Long	Liz Parrott
Say It with Flowers	Gladys Mitchell	Dame Beatrice Bradley
Scared to Death	Ann Morice	Tessa Crichton
The Scarlet Macaw	G.E. Locke	Mercedes Quero
Scarlet Night	Dorothy Salisbury Davis	Julie Hayes
The Scarlet Slippers	James M. Fox	Suzy Marshall
The Seacoast of Bohemia	Nicolas Freeling	Vera Castang
Seagull Crag	Elizabeth Welles	Jannine Austin
Seance aka	Mark McShane	Myra Savage
Seance on a Wet Afternoon		
Seance for Two	Mark McShane	Myra Savage
Season of Snows and Sins	Patricia Moyes	Emmy Tibbett
The Second Burial	Aaron Marc Stein	Elsie Mae Hunt
The Second Man	Edward Grierson	Marion Kerrison
Second String*	Hank Janson	Hilary Brand
Second Time Around	Hugh McLeave	Deirdre O'Connor
The Secret Adversary	Agatha Christie	Prudence "Tuppence" Beresford
The Secret of Chimneys	Agatha Christie	Eileen "Bundle" Brent
A Secret Service Woman	Henri de Halsalle	Olga von Kopf
The Secret of the Grange	Mark Cross aka Valentine	Daphne Wrayne

Sing a Song of Homicide	James P. Langham	Ethel Abbott
Sing a Song of Murder	Jan Michaels	Darby Castle
Sinister Madonna	Sax Rohmer	Sumuru
The Sinister Widow	Raymond Armstrong	Laura Scudamore
The Sinister Widow Again	Raymond Armstrong	Laura Scudamore
The Sinister Widow at Sea	Raymond Armstrong	Laura Scudamore
The Sinister Widow Comes Back	Raymond Armstrong	Laura Scudamore
The Sinister Widow Down Under	Raymond Armstrong	Laura Scudamore
The Sinister Widow Returns	Raymond Armstrong	Laura Scudamore
Siren in the Night	Leslie Ford	Grace Latham
A Six Letter Word for Death	Patricia Moyes	Emmy Tibbett
Six Nuns and a Shotgun aka *The Naked Nuns*	Colin Watson	Lucilla Edith Cavell Teatime
Skeleton Island	Gladys Mitchell	Dame Beatrice Bradley
Skeleton Key	Lenore Offord	Georgine Wyeth McKinnon
Skeletons in the Closet	Elizabeth Linington	Sue Carstairs Maddox
Skorpion's Death	David Brierley	Cody
The Skull Beneath the Skin	P. D. James	Cordelia Gray
Sleep in a Ditch	Maisie Birmingham	Kate Weatherly
Sleep of Death	Ann Morice	Tessa Crichton
Sleep of the Unjust	E. X. Ferrars	Virginia Freer
Sleeping Murder	Agatha Christie	Jane Marple
A Slip of the Tong	Charles Goodrum	Betty Crighton Jones
The Small Rain	Madeleine L'Engle	Katherine Forrester Vigneras
Small Vices	Robert B. Parker	Susan Silverman
The Smiler With a Knife	Nicholas Blake	Georgia Cavendish Strangeways
The Smiling Corpse	Hilea Bailey	Hilea Bailey
The Smiling Tiger	Lenore Offord	Georgine Wyeth McKinnon
The Snake Is Living Yet	Susan Gilruth	Liane "Lee" Craufurd
The Snake, the Crocodile, and the Dog	Elizabeth Peters	Amelia Peabody Emerson
Snare	Gwen Moffat	Miss Melinda Pink
Snipe Hunt	Amber Dean	Abbie Harris
Snowline	David Brierley	Cody
So Quiet a Death	Nigel Morland	Palmyra Pym
The Soap Opera Slaughters	Marvin Kaye	Hilary Quayle
The Sock-It-To-'Em Murders (Mod Squad #3)	Richard Deming	Julie Barnes (Mod Squad)
The Solange Stories	F. Tennyson Jesse	Solange Fontaine
Sold to Miss Seeton	Hamilton Crane	Miss Emily Seeton
Solemn High Murder	Barbara Ninde Byfield	Helen Bullock
Some Slips Don't Show	A. A. Fair	Bertha Cool
Some Women Won't Wait	A. A. Fair	Bertha Cool
Somebody Killed the Messenger	Clarissa Watson	Persis Willum
Someone Is Killing the Great Chefs of America	Nan and Ivan Lyons	Natasha O'Brien
Someone Is Killing the Great Chefs of Europe	Nan and Ivan Lyons	Natasha O'Brien
Something in the Water	Charlotte MacLeod	Helen Shandy
Something Wrong	Elizabeth Linington	Sue Carstairs Maddox
So Much for Gennaro	John Palmer	Freya Matthews
The Sorcerer of the Castle	Florence Stevenson	Kitty Telefair
The Sorceress of the Strand	L. T. Meade and Robert Eustace	Madame Sara
Soeur Angele and the Bell Ringer's Niece	Henri Catalan	Soeur Angele

The Tarot Murders	Mignon Warner	Edwina Charles
A Taste for Death	Peter O'Donnell	Modesty Blaise
Taste of Vengeance	Lavinia Davis	Nora Hughes Blaine
The Telzey Toy and Other Stories	James Schmitz	Telzey Amberdon
The Tentacles	Dana Lyon	Hilda Trenton
The Terrarium	Lee Head	Lexey Jane Pelazoni
Terror by Twilight	Kathleen Moore Knight	Margot Blair
That Affair at Portstead Manor	G. E. Locke	Mercedes Quero
That Affair Next Door	Anna Katharine Green	Amelia Butterworth
The Theban Mysteries	Amanda Cross	Kate Fansler
There Is No Return	Anita Blackmon	Adelaide Adams
There Lies Your Love	Jennie Melville	Charmian Daniels
There Was a Crooked Man	Kelley Roos	Haila Troy
There's Nothing to Be Afraid Of	Marcia Muller	Sharon McCone
There's Something in a Sunday	Marcia Muller	Sharon McCone
They Do It With Mirrors	Jim C. Conaway	Jana Blake
They Do It With Mirrors aka *Murder with Mirrors*	Agatha Christie	Jane Marple
They Wanted Him Dead	Leonora Eyles	Dr. Joan Marvin
The Thief of Venice	Jane Langton	Mary Morgan Kelly
Thin Air	Robert B. Parker	Susan Silverman
The Thin Man	Dashiell Hammett	Nora Charles
Thinner Than Water	E. X. Ferrars	Virginia Freer
Third Girl	Agatha Christie	Ariadne Oliver
The Third Possibility	Selwyn Jepson	Eve Gill
Third Time Unlucky	Mark Cross aka Valentine	Daphne Wrayne
This Darkening Universe	Lloyd Biggle, Jr.	Effie Schlupe
This Delicate Murder	Henrietta Clandon	Penny Mercer
This Girl for Hire	G. G. Fickling	Honey West
This Water Laps Gently	Mary Ingate	Ann Fielding Hales
Those in Peril	Nicolas Freeling	Vera Castang
Three Bright Pebbles	Leslie Ford	Grace Latham
Three for the Chair (*Too Many Detectives*)	Rex Stout	Theolinda "Dol" Bonner
Three Quick and Five Dead	Gladys Mitchell	Dame Beatrice Bradley
The Three Taps	Ronald Knox	Angela Bredon
Three—with Blood	Aaron Marc Stein	Elsie Mae Hunt
Thrones, Dominations	Dorothy Sayers and Jill Paton Walsh	Harriet Vane
Through the Wall	Patricia Wentworth	Miss Maud Silver
Thy Arm Alone	John Slate	Maria Black
Tied Up in Tinsel	Ngaio Marsh	Agatha "Troy" Alleyn
Till the Butchers Cut Him Down	Marcia Muller	Sharon McCone
Time Off for Murder	Zelda Popkin	Mary Carner Whittaker
Time Lapse	Janice Law	Anna Peters
A Time to Die	Hilda Lawrence	Beulah Pond and Bessie Petty
Time to Kill	Miriam Lynch	Nell Willard
The Tiny Diamond	Charlotte Murray Russell	Jane Amanda Edwards
Tish	Mary Roberts Rinehart	Letitia "Tish" Carberry
Tish Marches On	Mary Roberts Rinehart	Letitia "Tish" Carberry
Tish Plays the Game	Mary Roberts Rinehart	Letitia "Tish" Carberry
To Cache a Millionaire	Margaret Scherf	Dr. Grace Severance
To Kill a Coconut aka *The Coconut Killings*	Patricia Moyes	Emmy Tibbett
To Spite Her Face	Hildegarde Dolson	Lucy Ramsdale
To This Favour	Susan Gilruth	Liane "Lee" Craufurd
Toby's Folly	Margot Arnold	Penelope Spring

Up for Grabs	A. A. Fair	Bertha Cool
Up to No Good	Aaron Marc Stein	Elsie Mae Hunt

V

Valediction	Robert B. Parker	Susan Silverman
Valerie Valentine Is Missing	Amelia Walden	Lisa Clark
Vane Pursuit	Charlotte MacLeod	Helen Shandy
Vanishing Point	Marcia Muller	Sharon McCone
Vanishing Point	Patricia Wentworth	Miss Maud Silver
The Velvet Hand	Hulbert Footner	Madame Rosika Storey
The Verdict in Question aka *The Laughing Fish*	Selwyn Jepson	Eve Gill
Veronica's Sisters	Gwen Moffat	Miss Melinda Pink
The Very Breath of Hell	George Beare	Cynthia Godwin
Vicious Circle	Manning Long	Liz Parrott
Voyage Into Violence	Richard and Frances Lockridge	Pamela "Pam" North

W

The Waikiki Widow	Juanita Sheridan	Janice Cameron and Lily Wu
A Walk at Night	David Craig	Sheila Roath
Walking Shadow	Lenore Offord	Georgine Wyeth McKinnon
Walking Shadow	Robert B. Parker	Susan Silverman
A Walk Through the Fire	Marcia Muller	Sharon McCone
Wanted for Questioning	Mark Cross aka Valentine	Daphne Wrayne
The War Against Charity Ross	Jack Bickham	Charity Ross
Washington Whispers Murder	Leslie Ford	Grace Latham
Watchers of the Dark	Lloyd Biggle, Jr.	Effie Schlupe
The Waters of Centaurus	Rosel George Brown	Sibyl Sue Blue
The Watersplash	Patricia Wentworth	Miss Maud Silver
Waterview Manor	Elizabeth Welles	Jannine Austin
Watson's Choice	Gladys Mitchell	Dame Beatrice Bradley
The Way of the Four	Mark Cross aka Valentine	Daphne Wrayne
The Weird World of Wes Beattie	John Norman Harris	June Beattie Grant
Welcome Home, Jaime	Eileen Lottman	Jaime Sommers aka The Bionic Woman
We Saw Him Die	Aaron Marc Stein	Elsie Mae Hunt
What Happened to Candy Carmichael	Amelia Walden	Lisa Clark
What Mrs. McGillicuddy Saw! aka *4:50 from Paddington*	Agatha Christie	Jane Marple
What Night Will Bring	Hilea Bailey	Hilea Bailey
What's Wrong at Pyford?	Douglas Fisher	Martha "Ma" Tellford
When Danger Threatens	Mark Cross aka Valentine	Daphne Wrayne
When Last I Died	Gladys Mitchell	Dame Beatrice Bradley
When Thieves Fall Out	Mark Cross aka Valentine	Daphne Wrayne
*Where Angel Treads**	Graham Montrose	Angel Brown
Where Echoes Live	Marcia Muller	Sharon McCone
Where Is Jenny Now?	Frances Shelley Wees	Elizabeth Doane
Where Satan Dwells	Florence Stevenson	Kitty Telefair
Where Secrecy Begins	Jeannette Covert Nolan	Lace White
Where Was Everyone When Sabrina Screamed?	Amelia Walden	Lisa Clark
While Other People Sleep	Marcia Muller	Sharon McCone
While the Patient Slept	Mignon Eberhart	Sarah Keate
The Whirligig of Time	Lloyd Biggle, Jr.	Effie Schlupe
The Whisper in the Gloom	Nicholas Blake	Clare Massenger

X

Y

The Yellow Violet	Frances Crane	Jean Abbott
You Can Die Laughing	A. A. Fair	Bertha Cool
You Can Help Me	Maisie Birmingham	Kate Weatherly
You Who Know	Nicolas Freeling	Vera Castang
You'll Be the Death of Me	Miriam Lynch	Nell Willard
You'll Die, Darling	Marjorie Groves	Maxine Reynolds
You'll Die Laughing	Marjorie Groves	Maxine Reynolds
You'll Die Today	Marjorie Groves	Maxine Reynolds
You'll Die Tomorrow	Marjorie Groves	Maxine Reynolds
You'll Die Tonight	Marjorie Groves	Maxine Reynolds
You'll Die When You Hear This	Marjorie Groves	Maxine Reynolds
You'll Die Yesterday	Marjorie Groves	Maxine Reynolds
Young Beck	M. McDonnell Bodkin	Dora Myrl
Young Men May Die	David Craig	Sheila Roath
Your Royal Hostage	Antonia Fraser	Jemima Shore
*You've Had It, Girl**	Phyllis Swan	Anna Jugedinski

Z

Zadok's Treasure	Margot Arnold	Penelope Spring

Chronology

Year in which female character made first published appearance in a novel or collection of short stories. The chronological listing of female sleuths refers to first significant appearance. An asterisk (*) indicates that the character made at least three appearances. © Indicates copyright date, used when publication date was unavailable.

Volume I

1861:	Mrs. Paschal
1864:	Mrs. G.
1875:	Valeria Woodville
1884:	Madeline Payne
1894:	Loveday Brooke
1895:	Caroline "Cad" Mettie
1897:	Amelia Butterworth*; Dorcas Dene
1898:	Hagar Stanley
1899:	Lois Cayley; Madame Koluchy
1900:	Dora Myrl*; Hilda Wade
1903:	Madame Sara
1905:	Polly Burton; Henrietta Van Raffles
1906:	Frances Baird
1910:	Lady Molly Robertson-Kirk; Madame X
1911:	Letitia "Tish" Carberry
1912:	Judith Lee
1913:	Constance Dunlap ©; Ruth Fielding* (juvenile)
1914:	Madelyn Mack; Mercedes Quero*
1915:	Molly Morganthau*; Violet Strange

1917:   Millicent Newberry*; Evelyn Temple; Olga von Kopf

1922:   Prudence "Tuppence" Beresford*

1923:   Rosie Bright; Sylvia Shale

1924:   Fidelity Dove

1925:   Eileen "Bundle" Brent; Sophie Lang; Blue Jean Billy Race; Madame Rosika Storey*

1926:   Juliet Jackson*

1927:   Meg Garret *; Leslie Maughan in U.S.; Jane Ollerby

1928:   Angela Bredon; Lynn MacDonald*

1929:   Dame Adela Beatrice Bradley*; Four Square Jane; Sarah Keate*; Maud Silver* in U.S.

1930:   Nancy Drew* (juvenile); Ellen Gilchrist; Gwynn Leith; Gail McGurk*; Jane Marple*; Kate Marsh*; Polack Annie; Harriet Vane*; Louisa Woolfe*; Daphne Wrayne*

1931:   Fah Lo Suee*; Solange Fontaine; Prudence Whitby; Hildegarde Withers*

1932:   Hilda Adams*; Avis Bryden*; Angeline Tredennick; Mrs. Caywood "Julia" Weston

1933:   Amanda Fitton Campion; Lizzie Collins*; Olga Knaresbrook; Della Street; Mrs. Elizabeth Warrender*

1934:   Nora Charles; Clarice Claremont; Susan Dare; Peggy Fairfield; Anne Layton; Ariadne Oliver*; Alice Penny; Matilda Townsend*

1935:   Jane Amanda Edwards*; Emma Marsh*; Penny Mercer*; Matilda Perks; Palmyra Pym*

1936:   Iris Pattison Duluth*; Baroness Clara Linz in U.S.; Anne Holt McNeill*; Dr. Joan Marvin; Georgia Cavendish Strangeways; Ethel Thomas*

1937:   Adelaide Adams; Carey Brent*; Theolinda "Dol" Bonner; Patricia "Pat" Preston Cordry*; Grace Latham*; Anne "Davvie" Davenport McLean*; Daisy Jane Mott; Lucy Mott in U.S.; Tamara Valeshoff

1938:   Agatha Troy Alleyn; Mary Carner*; Kay Cornish*; Valerie Dundas; Coco Hastings; Carole Trevor; Lace White*

1939:   Hilea Bailey*; Janet "Janie" Allen Barron*; Bertha Cool*; Helene Brand Justus*; Sue MacVeigh*; Emma Marsh*; Rachel and Jennifer Murdoch*; Anne Seymour Webb; Susan Yates*

1940:   Ethel Abbott; Amanda and Lucy Beagle; Margot Blair*; Jane Carberry*; Elsie Mae Hunt*; Pamela "Pam" North*; Miss Mabie

Otis*; Katherine "Peter" Piper*; Sister Ursula; Haila Rogers Troy*; Agatha Welch

1941: Jean Abbott*; Eleanora Burke; Gypsy Rose Lee; Sarah DeLong O'Brien; Andrea Reid Ramsay; Hannah Van Doren*; Kitty McLeod Whitney*

1942: Arabella "Arab" Blake*; Louise "Liz" Boykin Parrott*; Grace Pomeroy

1943: Christine Andersen; Georgine Wyeth McKinnon; Toni Ney; Doris "Dodo" Trent; Nell Witter*

1944: Kit Marsden Acton*; Judy Ashbane; Maria Black*; Lorna Donahue; Vicky Gaines; Lady Lupin Hastings*; Abbie Harris*; Bessie Petty and Beulah Pond*

1945: Nora Hughes Blaine; Amy Brewster*; Dr. Mary Finney*; Jenny Gillette Lewis*

1946: Elizabeth; Eve MacWilliams; Maggie Slone; Tessie Venable

1947: Hortense Clinton*; Gale Gallagher; Suzanne "Suzy" Willett Marshall; Terry Terence*; Julia Tyler*; Lucy Pym

1948: Jane Hamish Brown*; Eve Gill*

1949: Miriam Birdseye*; Emily Murdoch Bryce*; Janice Cameron and Lily Wu*; Marka de Lancey*

1950: Sumuru*; Ma Tellford*; Hilda Trenton

1951: Petunia Best; Liane "Lee" Craufurd*; Shirley Leighton Harper*; Laura Scudamore, The Sinister Widow*; Ginger Tintagel; Sarah Vanessa*

1952: Ann McIntosh*; Clare Liddicotte Ringwood

1953: Nell Bartlett; Norma "Nicky" Lee*

1954: Sally Dean; Sally Strang*

1955: Miss Flora Hogg*; Mavis Seidlitz*; English translations of Soeur Angele*

1956: Eileen Burke*; Sally Merton Heldar*; Marion Kerrison; Julia Probyn*; Daye Smith*

1957: Mrs. Annie Norris*; Honey West*

1958: Mother Paul*

1959: Arabella Frant; Madame Maigret (in U.S. in her only major role); Kate Starte; Marla Trent

1960: Forsythia Brown*; Kate Harris; Emmy Tibbett* in U.S.

1962: Myra Savage in U.S.

1963:   Hilary Brand*; June Beattie

1964:   Telzey Amberdon*; Maxene Dangerfield*; Charmian Daniels* in
         U.S.; Kate Fansler*; Mary Morgan Kelly*; Sue Carstairs Maddox;
         Selena Mead

1965:   Modesty Blaise*; Jane Boardman; Amanda Curzon*; Emma
         Greaves*; Anna Zordan*

1966:   Sibyl Sue Blue; Mrs. Elma Craggs in U.S.; Lee Crosley*; April
         Dancer*; Mrs. Emily Pollifax*; Effie Schlupe*

1967:   Madame Dominique Aubry in U.S.; Felicia Dawlish; Eve Drum*;
         Julia Homberg*; Freya Matthews; Emma Peel*; Sylvia Plotkin*;
         Regina; Charity Ross; Paola Smith; Lucilla Edith Cavell Teatime*

1968:   Julie Barnes of Mod Squad*; Angel Brown*; Dominique Frayne;
         Tracy Larrimore*; Amanda Nightingale*; Stevie O'Dowda; Christie
         Opara*; Miss Emily Seeton*; Dr. Grace Severance*; Katy
         Touchfeather

1969:   Lisa Clark*; Gail Rogers Mitchell; Jennifer Norrington* in U.K.;
         Claudine St. Cyr*; Kate Theobald*

1970:   Tessa Crichton* in U.K.; Kiss Darling*; Millicent Hetherege; Hon.
         Constance Morrison-Burke*; Deirdre O'Connor; Sheila Roath;
         Charity Tucker*

1971:   Cherry Delight*; Donna Bella*; Cynthia Godwin; Lucy Ramsdale*;
         Helga Rolfe* in U.K.; Kitty Telefair*

1972:   Lucy Beck*; Arlette Van Der Valk Davidson as a primary*; Laurie
         Grant*; Cordelia Gray in U.K.; Jacqueline Kirby*; Octavia "Tavy"
         Martin in U.S.; Norah Mulcahaney*; Hilary Quayle*

1973:   Vicky Bliss*; Thea Crawford; Helen Blye Horowitz*; Cleopatra
         Jones; Baroness Penelope St. John Orsini*; Miss Melinda Pink*

1974:   Shauna Bishop*; Vera Castang; Catherine Alexander Douglas*; Rosa
         Epton* in U.S.; Ann Fielding Hales; Susan Silverman*; Kate
         Weatherly*

1975:   Pepper Anderson*; Claire Reynolds Atwell*; Helen Bullock*;
         Constance Cobble; Amelia Peabody Emerson*; Angela Harpe*; Ms.
         Squad; Dr. Nora North*; Molly Owens*; Minnie Santangelo; Bea
         Wentworth*

1976:   Jannine Austin*; Edwina Charles* in U.K.; Julie Hayes*; Dr.
         Hannah Land; Natasha O'Brien; Lexey Jane Pelazoni; Anna Peters*;
         Rebecca Rosenthal; Jaime Sommers; Morgan Studevant

1977:   Mici Anhalt*; Jana Blake; Charlie's Angels*; Betty Crighton Jones*;
         Sharon McCone*; Jemima Shore*; Persis Willum*

1978:   Marilyn Ambers*; Kay Barth*; Tory Baxter*; Margaret Binton*; Dulcie Bligh; Darby Castle; Virginia Freer*; Helen Keremos*; Hildy Pace*; Maxine Reynolds*; Delia Riordan*; Sarah Saber; Helen Marsh Shandy; Terry Spring*

1979:   Adrienne Bishop; Janna Brill*; Cody in England*; Maggie Courtney*; Charlotte Eliot; Margo Franklin*; Carol Gates*; Alison B. Gordon*; Kate Graham; Anna Jugedinski*; Sarah Kelling*; Valerie Lambert*; Ann Lang; Pauline Lyons*; Megan Marshall; Charlotte Ellison Pitt*; Maggie Rome*; Penelope Spring*; Julia Sullivan; Nell Willard

Volume II

1980:   T. T. Baldwin*; Juliet Bravo* aka Jean Darblay; Ginny Fistoulari*; Karen Kovacs*; Clarissa Lovelace*; Joan Stock*; Amy Tupper; Alicia Von Helsing; Janet Wadman (Rhys)*; Delilah West*

1981:   Cathy McVeigh Carter*; Sr. Mary Theresa "Emtee" Dempsey*; Fiona Fitzgerald*; Davina Graham* in U.S.; Lt. Sigrid Harald*; Dittany Henbit*; Viera Kolarova; Julia Larmore, Selena Jardine, and perhaps Hilary Tamar*; Anna Lee* in U.S.; Jill Smith*; Lizzie Thomas* in the U.S.; Lettie Winterbottom*

1982:   Charity Day; Sarah Deane*; Maggie Elliott*; Sgt. Carollee Fleetwood; Tamara Hoyland* in U.S.; Helen Markham; Kinsey Millhone*; Eugenia Potter*; Rebecca Schwartz*; Katherine Forrester Vigneras; Nila Wade*; V. I. Warshawski*

1983:   Mona Moore Dunbar; Norma Gold*; Jennifer Grey*; Inspector Judy Hill*; Roz Howard*; Cass Jameson*; Kyra Keaton; Elena Olivarez*; Julie Tendler Oliver; Jocelyn O'Roarke*; Bridget O'Toole*; Dolly Rawlins in U.K.; Fiona Kimber-Hutchinson Samson in U.S.; Harriet Unwin*; Rosie Vicente*; Elizabeth Lamb Worthington*

1984:   Gillian Adams*; Lauren Adler; Rev. Claire Aldington*; Sarah Cable*; Jenny Cain*; Agnes Carmichael* in U.S.; Iris Cooper*; Kate Delafield*; Vejay Haskell*; Rachel Hennings; Sgt. Hilary Lloyd in U.S.; Elizabeth MacPherson*; Dr. Tina May*; Patience "Pay" McKenna*; Mary Frances Mulrooney; Pam Nilsen*; Sr. Mary Helen O'Connor*; Amelia Trowbridge Patton in U.S.; Andrea Perkins*; Deb Ralston*; Clio Rees (Marsh)*; Eleanor Roosevelt*; Abigail "Sandy" Sanderson*; Ellie Simon (Haskell)*; Ms. Michael Tree*

1985:   Liz Archer aka Angel Eyes*; Kate Baeier* in U.S.; Susan Bright*; Liz Connors*; Serendipity "Sarah" Dahlquist; Donna Miro and Lorna Doria; Geraldine Farrar; Jessica Fletcher*; Fiora Flynn*; Paula Glenning*; Glad Gold; Ellie Gordon*; Celia Grant* in U.S.; Marian Larch*; Isabel Macintosh*; Stoner McTavish*; Michelle Merrill

(Ballard)*; Cassandra Mitchell*; Rain Morgan*; Theresa "Terri" Morrison; J. D. Mulroy; Rita Gardella O'Dea; Deirdre O'Hara* in Canada; Celia Prentisse; Maggie Ryan*; Rachel Sabin; Lucy Shannon; Gertrude Stein; Kate Trevorne; Alexandra "Alex" Winter; Matilda Worthing*

1986:   Jane Britland; Rosie Caesare; Sarah Calloway*; Doran Fairweather*; Theresa Fortunato; Cynthia Frost; Judith Hayes in U.S.; Calista Jacobs*; Gwen Jones*; Rina Lazarus (Decker); Denise Lemoyne; Claire Malloy*; Tish McWhinny*; Susan Melville*; Debbie Miles*; Kate Miskin; Ella Nidech; Molly Palmer-Jones*; Molly Rafferty*; Catherine Sayler*; Joan Spencer*; Joanna Stark*; Penny Wanawake* in U.S.

1987:   Finny Aletter; Jane Bailey*; Maggie Bennett*; Mavis Bignell* in U.S.; Dr. Marissa Blumenthal; Carlotta Carlyle*; Marlene Ciampi (Karp)*; Lisa Davis; A. J. Egan; Lindsay Gordon*; Lonia Guiu in U.S.; Meg Halloran*; Arly Hanks*; Jennifer Heath*; Nikki Holden; Bonnie Indermill*; Willa Jansson*; Charlotte Kent*; Raina Lambert*; Annie Laurance (Darling)*; Constance Leidl*; Daisy Marlow; Alvira Meehan*; Melita Pargeter* in U.S.; Amanda Pepper*; Caitlin Reese*; Countess Aline Griffith Romanones*; Quin St. James*; Sara Spooner; Dee Street* in U.K.; Dixie Flannigan Struthers*; Kate Byrd Teague; Anna Tyree*; Dee Vaughn*; Emma Victor*; Jane Winfield (Hall)*

1988:   Samantha Adams*; Inspector Carol Ashton*; Angela Benbow and Caledonia Wingate*; Kori Price Brichter*; Sydney Bryant*; Angel Cantini; Laura Di Palma*; Trixie Dolan and Evangeline Sinclair* in U.S.; Lydia Fairchild*; Kit Franklyn*; Ingrid Langley Gilliard* in U.S.; Rachel Gold*; Neil Hamel*; Barbara Havers*; Susan Henshaw*; Sara Joslyn; Meg Lacey; Loretta Lawson* in U.S.; Kate Maddox*; Daphne Matthews*; Georgia Lee Maxwell; Nina McFall*; Mom*; Karen Orr; Claire Parker* in U.S.; Marvia Plum*; Lady Margaret Priam*; Catherine Sayler*; Aline Scott*; Hana Shaner; Veronica Slate*; Sabina Swift; Tina Tamiko; Ann Tate, Dawn Markey, and Veronica Sheffield; Sally Tepper; Sheila Travis*; Jane Tregar; Claudia Valentine* in Australia; Gillian Verdean*; Evelyn Wade

1989:   Beth Austin*; Margaret Barlow*; Bertha Barstow; Martha "Moz" Brant*; Rhea Buerklin; Emma Chizzit*; Kat Colorado*; Katharine Craig; Sandrine Casette Curry*; Dr. Janet Eldine in U.S.; Nina Fischman*; Phryne Fisher* in Australia; Anne Fitzhugh; Sgt. Molly Flanagan; Sarah Fortune*; Clara Dawson Gamadge*; Peg Goodenough; Blanche Hampton*; Kate Henry in U.S.*; Lady Jane Hildreth* in U.S.; Maggie Hill and Claire Conrad; Harriet Jeffries*; Jane Jeffry*; Helena

Justina; Jennifer Terry Kaine*; Mavis Lashley*; Jane Lawless*; Darina Lisle* in U.K.; LuEllen*; Sheila Malory*; Chris Martin* in U.K.; Jennie McKay*; Rosie Monaghan in Australia; Cassie Newton; Rita Noonan; Abby Novack (McKenzie)*; Lee Ofsted*; Peggy O'Neill*; Kieran O'Shaughnessy*; Carrie Porter; Georgina Powers* in U.K.; Anabel Reed Smith*; Amanda Roberts*; Rune*; Emma Shaw in U.S.; Diane Tregarde*; Lisa Thomas in Australia; Leslie Wetzon and Xenia Smith*; Johanna Wilder; Grace Willis; Francesca Wilson* in U.S.; Miriam Winchester

Volume III

The following is a preliminary expectation of sleuths to be covered in the final volume of the series. Whether or not a character has made three or more appearances is based upon information through November 2001. Additional sleuths will undoubtedly be added to this list before Volume 3 is published. A third book may have been published subsequent to November 2001. New series are added regularly as work on Volume 3 continues.

1990: Irene Adler*; Gabrielle Amato; Connie Bartholomew; Goldy Bear (Schultz)*; Mildred Bennett*; Helen Black*; Nora Bonesteel*; Claire Breslinsky*; Paris Chandler; Edwina Crusoe*; Lark Dailey*; Abigail Danforth*; Poppy Dilworth*; Flavia Di Stefano*; Brigid Donovan*; Faith Fairchild*; Charlotte Graham*; Mary "Harry" Haristeen*; Alison Hope*; Jeri Howard*; Dewey James*; Jessica James*; Jazz Jasper*; Sister Joan*; Joanne Kilbourn*; Willow King*; Michelle "Mickey" Knight*; Skip Langdon*; Hester Latterly*; Lavinia London; Annie MacPherson*; Shirley McClintock*; Madison McGuire*; Cat Marsala*; Jayne Meadows; Alice Nestleton*; Chicago Nordejoong*; Patricia Pratt*; Gwen Ramadge*; Lucia Ramos; Cassandra Reilly*; Vonna Saucier; Kay Scarpetta*; Anna Southwood*; Aurora Teagarden*; Nicky Titus*; Nikki Trakos; Holly Winter*

1991: Jessie Arnold*; "Petey" Biggers*; Verity Birdwood*; Rev. Theodora Braithwaite*; Nell Bray*; Hollis Carpenter; Midge Cohen; Melissa Craig*; Lauren Crowder; Molly DeWitt*; Phrynne Fisher*; Jan Gallagher*; Simona Griffo*; Dr. Bernie Hebert; Barbara Holloway*; Lil Hubbert*; Kate Jasper*; Virginia Kelly*; Libby Kincaid*; Amanda Knight; Lauren Laurano*; Whitney Logan; Devon MacDonald*; Wanda Mallory*; Judith McMonigle (Flynn)*; Kathy NcNeely; Robin Miller*; Meredith Mitchell*; Lane Montana; Dr. Jean Montrose*; Kate Mulcay (one earlier book in 1958 as Kate Kincaid)*; Kit Powell; Claire Sharples*; Delta Stevens*; Blaine Stewart*; Lucy Stone*; Jane Tennison* in U.K.; Rev. Ziza Todd; Ginny Trask; Ronnie Ventana*; Liz Wareham; Fanny Zindel

1992:   Kristin Ashe; Temple Barr*; China Bayles*; Molly Bearpaw*; Becky
Belski; Christine Bennett*; Ellie Bernstein; Constable Judy Best*;
Elizabeth Blair*; Julie Blake*; Joanna Blalock*; Victoria Bowering*;
Smokey Brandon*; Harriet Bushrow*; Rosalie Cairns*; Claire
Camden*; Dr. Jessica Coran*; Karen Crist; Victoria Cross; Jane Da
Silva*; Molly De Witt*; Catherine Edison; Elizabeth Elliot*; Casey
Farrel*; Sister Frevisse*; Leslie Frost; Nell Fury*; Callahan Garrity*; Liz
Graham*; Charlie Greene*; Blanche Hampton*; Leah Hunter*; Laura
Ireland; Lucy Kingsley*; Kate Kinsella in U.S.*; Deborah Knott*;
Emma Lord*; Marti MacAlister*; Maggie MacGowan*; Caroline Masters*;
Christine McCall*; Annie McGrogan; Laura Michaels*; Kate
Millholland*; Britt Montero*; Freddie O'Neal*; Maddy Phillips*; E.J.
Pugh*; Agatha Raisin*; Regan Reilly*; Lil Ritchie; Maxene St. Clair*;
Charlotte Sams; Kate Shugak*; Diana Speed; Lee Squires*; Elena
Timafeyeva; Glynis Tryon*; Samantha Turner*; Amanda Valentine*;
Jackie Walsh*; Aunt Dimity Westwood and Lori Shepherd*; Blanche
White*; Hannah Wolfe*; Susan Donavan Wren*

1993:   Laura Ackroyd*; Angelina Amalfi*; Tory Bauer*; Angela Biwaban*;
Joanna Brady*; Barbara "Bo" Bradley*; Kate Brannigan*; Sr. Cecile
Buddenbrooke*; Caley Burke*; Maxey Burnell*; Cat Caliban*; Nora
Callum; Cliveley Sisters; Nancy Clue and Cherry Aimless*; Henrie
O'Dwyer Collins*; Nancy Cook; Mary Di Nunzio; Jessica Drake*;
Kay Engels; Laura Fleming*; Caz Flood* in U.K.; Insp. Liz Graham*;
Amanda Hazard*; Marty Hopkins*; Jo Hughes*; Kate Ivory*;
Gemma James*; Hepzipah Jeffries*; Claire Jenner (Claiborne)*; Tyler
Jones*; Alison Kaine*; Irene Kelly*; Kimmey Kruse; Barrett Lake*;
Catherine Le Vendeur*; Wyn Lewis*; Kathryn Mackay*; Kate
MacLean; Royce Madison; Casey/Kate Martinelli*; Dr. Lauren
Maxwell*; Kathleen O'Shaunessey*; Jane Perry*; Anna Pigeon*; Dr.
Amy Prescott*; Gin Prettifield; Imogen Quy; Nan Robinson*;
Laney Samms*; Phoebe Siegel*; Cecily Sinclair*; Sydney Sloane*;
Teal Stewart*; Sgt. Stone*; Catherine Swinbrooke*; Alex Tanner*;
Iris Thorne*; Betty Trenka*; Robin Vaughn*; Madame Victoire
Vernet; Lucy Wilton (Archer)*; April Woo*; Eve Wylie in U.S.*

1994:   Kathryn "Kate" Ardleigh*; Cat Austen*; Kate Austen*; Johnnie
Baker; Thea Barlow*; Nora Bonesteel*; Dr. Liz Broward; Brooke
Cassidy (Devlin)*; Molly Cates*; Olivia Chapman; Emily Charters;
Lydia Chin*; Gail Connor*; Candi and Simone Covington*; Fey
Croaker*; Daisy Dahlrymple*; Peaches Dann*; Tess Darcy*; Queenie
Davilov; Angie DaVito; Patricia Delaney*; Louise Eldridge*; Lynn
Evans; Phoebe Fairfax in Canada*; Merry Folger*; Margo Fortier;
Jill Francis*; Vicki Garcia; Angela Gennaro*; Sophie Greenway*;
Mackenzie Griffin*; Anneke Haagen*; Em Hansen*; Matilda
Haycastle*; Tamara Hayle*; Benni Harper*; Karen Hightower aka

Bast*; Samantha Holt*; Harriet Hubbley in Canada*; Robin Hudson*; Jo Hughes in the U.S.*; Sal Kilkenny* in U.K.; Michelle "Mickey" Knight*; Sgt. Kathy Kolla* in U.K.; Thea Kozak*; Robin Light*; Margaret Loftus; Dottie Loudermilk; Joanna MacKenzie*; Gianna Maglione; Sgt. Kathleen Mallory*; Saz Martin*; Angela Matelli*; Dr. Gail McCarthy*; Nuala McGrail*; Elizabeth Mendoza; Tori Miracle*; Kate Murray; Jordan Myles*; Deirdre Quinn Nightingale*; Veronica Pace*; Lorraine Page*; Daisy Perika*; Stephanie Plum*; Laura Principal*; Sarah Quillam*; Carmen Ramirez; Tammi Randall*; Mary Russell*; Desiree Shapiro*; Emily Silver; Liz Sullivan*; Jane Smith aka Stella the Stargazer*; Emily Stone*; Cassandra Swann*; Ike Tygart*; Alix Thorssen*; Penelope Warren*; Catherine Wilde*; Elizabeth Will; Jolie Wyatt*; Magdalena Yoder*; Helma Zukas*

1995:   Hannah Barlow*; Ginger Barnes*; Lilly Bennett*; Sonora Blair*; Bel Carson*; Dr. Elizabeth Chase*; Ella Clah*; Eve Dallas*; Angie Da Vito; Jane Day*; Eve Elliott*; Kay Engels; Colleen Fitzgerald; Maggie Garrett; Ariel Gold*; Natalie Gold*; Gale Grayson*; Mother Lavinia Grey*; Mackenzie Griffin*; Elizabeth Halperin; Kate Harrod*; Sharon Hays*; Helen Hewitt in U.K.; Holly-Jean Ho*; Vicky Holden*; Liz James*; Elena Jarvis*; Caroline "Fremont" Jones*; Samantha "Sam" Jones*; Carol Jordan; Sara Kingsley; Fran Kirk*; Dee Laguerre; Calista Marley*; Dorothy Martin*; Lydia Miller; Michelle "Mitch" Mitchell*; Jordan Myles*; Megan O'Malley; Phyllida Moon*; Charlie Parker*; Joanna Piercy*; the Quilliam sisters*; Garner Quinn*; Savannah Reid*; Nina Reilly*; Schuyler Ridgeway*; Sophie Rivers*; Claudia Seferius*; Jo Beth Sidden*; Margo Simon*; Marguerite Smith*; Dr. Sylvia Strange*; Judith Thornton*; Melanie Travis*; Jane Turner; Jane Whitefield*; Kate Wilkinson*; Kay Williams ©; Fran Wilson* in U.S.; (1993 in U.K.)

1996:   Rachel Alexander*; Margit Andersson; Cat Austen*; Jane Austen*; Hollis Ball* in U.K.; Lily Bard*; Vicky Bauer; Jane Bee*; Sister Agnes Bourdillon in U.S.*; Lindsay Chamberlain*; Alexandra Cooper*; Ruby Crane*; Ruby Dark; Venus Diamond*; Sister Fidelma*; Suze Figuera*; Fizz Fitzgerald*; Lucy Freers; Theresa Galloway*; Sen. Eleanor Gorzack; P. J. Gray*; Beth Hartley*; Dido Hoare*; Patricia Anne Hollowell and Mary Alice Crane*; Mrs. Emma Hudson*; Cassidy James*; Texana Jones*; Lady Aoi; Julia Lambros*; Renee LaRoche; Heaven Lee*; Lt. Tory Lennox, USCG; Molly Masters*; Cassidy McCabe*; Dr. Anne Menlo; Kali O'Brien*; Alison O'Neil; Dr. Andi Pauling*; Karen Perry-Mondori*; Josie Pigeon*; Sukey Reynolds*; Emma Rhodes*; Benny Rosato*; Nicki Scott*; Barbara Simons; Lupe Solano*; Starletta DuVall*; Bert and Nan Tatum*; Abby Timberlake*; Tory Travers*; Hannah Trevor*; Lucy Wayles*; Biggie Weatherford*; Molly West; Ruth Willmarth*

1997:   Mali Anderson*; Lady Susanna Appleton*; Kate Banning*; Miriam Bartimaeus; Ursula Blanchard*; Kathryn Bogert*; Helen Bradley; Temperance Brennan*; Dr. Clare Burtonall; Sister Rose Callahan*; Letty Campbell*; Carrie Carlin*; Kate Cavanaugh*; Rachel Crowne; Meg Darcy; Maggie Dillitz*; Delilah Doolittle*; Mandy Dyer*; Kay Farrow; Lucy Freers; P. J. Gray*; Nanette Hayes*; Brett Higgins*; Marti Hirsch*; Stevie Houston*; Casey Jones*; Loretta Kovacs*; Gloria Lamerino*; Rosie Lavine; Nell Mathews*; Haley McAlister; Lara McClintoch*; Charlotte McCrae*; Sutton McPhee*; Mavis Middleton*; Brenda Midnight*; Tess Monaghan*; Ruthie Kantor Morris; Lorelei Muldoon; Jane Nichols; Tru North*; Victory O'Shea*; Martha Patterson; Karen Pelletier*; Charlie Plato*; Rachel Porter*; Amelia Sachs; Rei Shimura*; Helen Sorby*; Dr. Michael Stone*; Evelyn Sutcliffe* (one book in a different form published earlier); Rose Trevelyan; Tessa Vance; Fran Varaday; Francesca Vierling*; Connor Westphal*; Chas Wheatley; MacLaren Yarbrough

1998:   Allie Babcock*; Madeline Bean*; Nikki Chase; Wyanet Chouinard*; Venus Diamond*; Dixie Flannigan*; Carole Ann Gibson*; Meg Gillis; Susan Given; Ann Hardaway*; Annabelle Hardy-Maratos; Sierra Lavotini*; Maggie Maguire*; Trish Maguire*; Hannah Malloy and Kiki Goldstein*; Jennifer Marsh*; Adele Monsarrat*; Kellie Montgomery*; Teddy Morelli*; Taylor Morgan*; May Morrison; Laura Owen*; Sydney Teague*; Jacobia Triptree*; Charlotte Willett*

1999:   Janet Barkin*; Betsy Devonshire*; Leigh Koslow*; Claire Rawlings*

Resources and Readings
for Volumes I and II

Although I read extensively on the political, economic, literary, and social period from 1860-1989, special credit should be given to the following books for their treatment of the subject and for the identification of authors and sleuths previously unknown to me.

Aburdene, Patricia and John Naisbitt. *Megatrends for Women*. Villard, 1992.

Allen, Frederick Lewis. *Only Yesterday, An Informal History of the 1920's*. Harper & Row, 1931.

Anderson, Bonnie S. and Judith P. Zinsser. *A History of Their Own*. Harper & Row, 1988.

Barnes, Melvyn. *Murder in Print, A Guide to Two Centuries of Crime Fiction*. Barn Owl Books, 1986.

Berkin, Carol Ruth and Mary Beth Norton. *Women of America*. Houghton Mifflin, 1979.

Billman, Carol. *The Secret of the Stratmeyer Syndicate*. Ungar, 1986.

Boardman, Fon Wyman, Jr. *America and the Jazz Age, A History of the 1920's*. Walck, 1968.

Burchill, Julie. *Girls on Film*. Pantheon, 1986.

Caprio, Betsy. *The Mystery of Nancy Drew*. Source Books, 1992.

Cawelti, John G. *Adventure, Mystery, and Romance*. University of Chicago Press, 1976.

Chafe, William H. *The American Woman, Her Changing Social, Economic, and Political Roles, 1920-1970*. Oxford University Press, 1972.

Clark, Homer H., Jr. *The Law of Domestic Relations*. West, 1968.

Cook, Michael L. *Murder by Mail*. Bowling Green State University Popular Press, 1983.

Coser, Lewis A., Charles Kadushin, and Walter W. Powell. *Books, The Culture and Commerce of Publishing*. Basic Books, 1982.

Craig, Patricia and Mary Cadogan. *The Lady Investigates, Women Detectives and Spies in Fiction*. St. Martin's Press, 1981.

Current, Richard N., T. Harry Williams, Alan Brinkley, and Frank Friedel. *American History: A Survey*, seventh edition. Knopf, 1987.

Dooley, Roger. *From Scarface to Scarlet, American Films in the 1930's*. Harcourt Brace, 1981.

East, Andy. *Cold War File*. Scarecrow Press, 1983.

Edwards, Julia. *Women of the World, The Great Foreign Correspondents*. Houghton Mifflin, 1988.

Eisenstadt v. Baird. 405 U.S. 438 (1972).

Evans, Sara M. *Born for Liberty*. The Free Press (Macmillan), 1989.

Freeman, Lucy, editor. *The Murder Mystique*. Ungar, 1982.

Freidan, Betty. *The Feminine Mystique*. W. W. Norton, 1963.

Glendon, Mary Ann. *Matrimonial Property: A Comparative Study of Law and Social Change*. 49 Tulane Law Review 21 (1974).

Gold, Annalee. *75 Years of Fashion*. Fairchild, 1975.

Gorham, Deborah. *The Victorian Girl and the Feminine Ideal*. Indiana University Press, 1982.

Grannis, Chandler B. *What Happens in Book Publishing*. Columbia University Press, 1957.

Greene, Suzanne Ellery. *Books for Pleasure, Popular Fiction, 1914-45*. Bowling Green State University Popular Press, 1974.

Greer, Germaine. *The Female Eunuch*. McGraw Hill, 1970.

Griswold v. Connecticut. 381 U.S. 479 (1965).

Grun, Bernard. *Timetables of History*, second edition, Touchstone, 1982. Third edition, 1991.

Hackett, Alice Payne and James Henry Burke. *80 Years of Best Sellers: 1895-1975*. R.R. Bowker, 1977.

Haskell, Molly. *From Reverence to Rape, The Treatment of Women in the Movies*. Holt, Rinehart and Winston, 1974.

Haycraft, Howard. *The Art of the Mystery Story*. Carroll & Graf, 1983 (first published in 1946).

Haycraft, Howard. *Murder for Pleasure*. Carroll & Graf, 1984 (first published in 1941).

Heising, Willetta. *Detecting Men*. Purple Moon Press, 1998.

Heising, Willetta. *Detecting Women*, edition 3. Purple Moon Press, 1999

Henderson, Lesley, editor. *Twentieth Century Crime & Mystery Writers*, third edition. St. James Press, 1991.

Holcombe, Lee. *Victorian Ladies at Work*. Archon Books, 1973.

Hoppenstand, Gary, editor. *The Dime Novel Detective*. Bowling Green State University Press, 1982.

Horn, Maurice, editor. *The World Encyclopedia of Comics*. Avon, 1976.

Howell, Reet, editor. *Her Story in Sport; A Historical Anthology of Women in Sports*. Leisure Press, 1982.

Hubin, Allen J. *Crime Fiction, 1749-1980: A Comprehensive Bibliography*. Garland, 1984; and its *1981-1985 Supplement*. Garland, 1988.

Hubin, Allen J. *Crime Fiction, II, A Comprehensive Bibliography, 1749-1990*. Garland, 1994.

Hubin, Allen J. *Crime Fiction III, A Comprehensive Bibliography, 1749-1995*. Locus Press on CD-ROM, 1999.

Hubin, Allen J. *Crime Fiction IV, A Comprehensive Bibliography, 1749-2000*. Locus Press on CD-ROM, 1999.

Inge, Thomas, editor. *American Popular Culture*. Greenwood Press, 1978.

Kael, Pauline. *5001 Nights at the Movies*. Holt, Rinehart, and Winston, 1982.

Kerker, Linda and Jane De Hart Matthews. *Women's America*. Oxford University Press, 1982.

Kraditor, Aileen S. *The Ideas of the Woman Suffrage Movement: 1890-1920*. Columbia University Press, 1965.

Landrum, Larry, Pat Browne, and Ray B. Browne. *Dimensions of Detective Fiction*. Popular Press, 1976.

Maida, Patricia D. *Mother of Detective Fiction*. Bowling Green Popular Press, 1989.

Maio, Kathleen. *Feminist in the Dark: Reviewing the Movies*. The Crossing Press, 1988.

Mason, Bobbie Ann. *The Girl Sleuth: A Feminist Guide to the Bobbsey Twins, Nancy Drew and Their Sisters*. Feminist Press, 1975.

Matthews, Glenna. *Just a Housewife*. Oxford University Press, 1987.

McDowell, Barbara, and Hana Unlauf, editors. *The Good Housekeeping Woman's Almanac*. Newspaper Enterprise Association, 1977.

McLaughlin, Steve D., Barbara D. Melber, John O. G. Billy, Denise M. Zimmerle, Linda D. Winges, and Terry R. Johnson. *The Changing Lives of American Women*. University of North Carolina Press, 1988.

McLeish, Kenneth and Valerie. *Bloomsbury Good Reading Guide to Murder Crime Fiction and Thrillers*. Bloomsbury, 1990.

Morello, Karen Berger. *The Invisible Bar, The Woman Lawyer in America*. Random House, 1986.

Mott, Fran Luther. *Golden Multitudes*. Macmillan, 1947.

Nichols, Victoria and Susan Thompson. *Silk Stalkings, When Women Write of Murder*. Black Lizard, 1988.

Osborne, Eric. *Victorian Detective Fiction*. Bodley Head, 1966 (a catalogue of the collection made by Dorothy Glover and Graham Greene).

Ousby, Ian. *Bloodhounds of Heaven, The Detective in English Fiction from Godwin to Doyle*. Harvard University Press, 1976.

Peterson, Audrey. *Victorian Masters of Mystery*. Ungar, 1984.

Pruett, Lorine. *Women Workers Through the Depression*. Macmillan, 1934.

Queen, Ellery. *In the Queen's Parlor, and Other Leaves from the Editor's Notebook*. Simon & Schuster, 1957.

Queen, Ellery, editor. *101 Years' Entertainment, The Great Detective Stories, 1841-1941*. Little, Brown, 1941.

Reddy, Maureen T. *Sisters in Crime: Feminism and the Crime Novel*. Continuum, 1988.

Reilly, John M., editor. *Twentieth Century Crime & Mystery Writers,* first edition. St. Martin's Press, 1980.

Reilly, John M., editor. *Twentieth Century Crime & Mystery Writers*, second editon. St. Martin's Press, 1985.

Roberts, Gary G., Gary Hoppenstand and Ray B. Browne. *Old Sleuth's Freaky Female Detectives*. Bowling Green State University Popular Press, 1990. From the dime novels.

Rodell, Marie F. *Mystery Fiction, Theory and Technique*, revised edition. Hermitage House, 1952.

Roe v. Wade. 410 U.S. 113 (1973).

Rogers, Katharine M. *The Troublesome Helpmate*. University of Washington Press, 1966.

Routley, Eric. *Puritan Pleasures of the Detective Story*. Gollancz, 1972.

Sayers, Dorothy, editor. *The Omnibus of Crime*. Harcourt Brace, 1929.

Slung, Michelle, editor. *Crime on Her Mind*. Pantheon, 1975.

Solomon, Barbara Miller. *In the Company of Educated Women*. Yale University Press, 1985.

Smuts, Robert. *Women and Work in America*. Schocken, 1971.

Steedman, Carolyn. *Policing the Victorian Community*. Routledge & Kegan Paul, 1984.

Swanson, Jean and Dean James. *By a Woman's Hand*. Berkley, 1994.

Symons, Julian. *Mortal Consequences*. Harper & Row, 1972.

Taylor, Joan Kennedy. *Reclaiming the Mainstream*. Prometheus, 1988.

Terrace, Vincent. *The Complete Encyclopedia of Television Programs 1947-79*. A. S. Barnes & Company, 1979.

Tobias, Sheila and Lisa Anderson. *What Really Happened to Rosie the Riveter? Demobilization and the Female Labor Force, 1944-47*. MSS Modular Publications. Date unavailable.

Vicinius, Martha. *Independent Women*. University of Chicago Press, 1985.

Van Dover, J. Kenneth. *Murder in the Millions*. Ungar, 1984.

Ware, Susan. *Holding Their Own, American Women in the 1930's*. Twayne, 1982.

Weiss, Daniel Evans. *The Great Divide: How Females and Males Really Differ*. Poseidon, 1991.

Winks, Robin W. *Modus Operandi*. Godine, 1982.

Wrong, E. M., editor. *Crime and Detection*. Oxford University Press, 1926.

I wish to thank Jon Breen for his corrections to my listings on Dorothy Sayers and E. M. Wong.

To receive a free catalog of other Poisoned Pen Press titles, please contact us in one of the following ways:

Phone: 1-800-421-3976
Facsimile: 1-480-949-1707
Email: info@poisonedpenpress.com
Website: www.poisonedpenpress.com

Poisoned Pen Press
6962 E. First Ave. Ste 103
Scottsdale, AZ 85251